# Sectoral Systems of Innovation

Innovation and technological change have different characteristics and follow different paths depending on the sector in which they take place. The knowledge, actors and institutions of a sector all exert a major influence on innovation. With contributions from nineteen experts in their field, this book proposes a "sectoral system of innovation" (SSI) homework to analyze the innovation process, the factors affecting innovation, the relationship between innovation and industry dynamics, the changing boundaries and the transformation of sectors, and the determinants of the innovation performance of firms and countries in different sectors. Innovation in a sector is considered to be affected by three groups of variables: knowledge and technologies; actors and networks; and institutions. In addition to providing a general framework, this book examines innovation in six major sectors in Europe: pharmaceuticals and biotechnology, telecommunications equipment and services, chemicals, software, machine tools and services.

FRANCO MALERBA is Professor of Industrial Economics and Director of CESPRI (Centro di Ricerca sui Processi di Innovazione e Internazionalizzazione – Center for Research on Innovation and Internationalization) at Università Bocconi, Milan. He is currently President of the International Schumpeter Society (2002 to 2004), and President of the European Association of Research in Industrial Economics (EARIE), (2003 to 2005). He is also the author of numerous articles and books on industrial organization and the economics of technological change.

T0339951

# Sectoral Systems of Innovation

*Concepts, issues and analyses of six
major sectors in Europe*

*edited by*

Franco Malerba

CAMBRIDGE
UNIVERSITY PRESS

CAMBRIDGE UNIVERSITY PRESS
Cambridge, New York, Melbourne, Madrid, Cape Town, Singapore, São Paulo, Delhi

Cambridge University Press
The Edinburgh Building, Cambridge CB2 8RU, UK

Published in the United States of America by Cambridge University Press, New York

www.cambridge.org
Information on this title: www.cambridge.org/9780521111386

First published 2004
This digitally printed version 2009

*A catalogue record for this publication is available from the British Library*

*Library of Congress Cataloguing in Publication data*
Sectoral systems of innovation: concepts, issues and analyses of six major sectors
in Europe / edited by Franco Malerba.
    p.   cm.
Includes bibliographical references and index.
ISBN 0 521 83321 3
1. Technological innovations – Economic aspects – Europe – Case studies.
I. Malerba, Franco, 1950–
HC240.9.T4S43   2004
338′.064′094 – dc22   2003065203

ISBN 978-0-521-83321-9 hardback
ISBN 978-0-521-11138-6 paperback

# Contents

**Part III   Sectoral systems and national systems;
international performance and public policy**

**Part IV   Conclusions**

# Figures

# Tables

# Contributors

STEVEN CASPER
Keck Graduate Institute, Claremont, California
Steven_Casper@kgi.edu

FABRIZIO CESARONI
Laboratory of Economics and Management (LEM), Scuola Superiore
    Sant'Anna, Pisa
cesaroni@sssup.it

BENJAMIN CORIAT
Centre de Recherche en Economie Industrielle Internationale (CREII),
    Université Paris XIII
Coriat@club-internet.fr

CHARLES EDQUIST
Department of Design Sciences, Lund Institute of Technology, Lund
    University, Sweden
charles.edquist@innovation.Ith.se

ALFONSO GAMBARDELLA
Scuola Superiore Sant'Anna, Pisa
GAMBARDELLA@sssup.it

WALTER GARCIA-FONTES
Department of Economics, Universitat Pompeu Fabra, Barcelona
wgarcia@upf.es

FRANCO MALERBA
Centro di Ricerca sui Processi di Innovazione e Internazionalizzazione
    (CESPRI), Università Bocconi, Milan
franco.malerba@uni-bocconi.it

MYRIAM MARIANI
Maastricht Economic Research Institute on Innovation and Technology
    (MERIT), University of Maastricht, and Università di Camerino,
    Italy
mymarian@tin.it

MAUREEN McKELVEY
Department of Industrial Dynamics, Chalmers University of
 Technology, Göteborg
mckelvey@mot.chalmers.se

J. STAN METCALFE
Centre for Research on Innovation and Competition (CRIC),
 University of Manchester
Stan.Metcalfe@man.ac.uk

FABIO MONTOBBIO
Università degli Studi dell'Insubria, Varese
fmontobbio@eco.uninsubria.it

LUIGI ORSENIGO
Università di Brescia and CESPRI, Università Bocconi, Milan
luigi.orsenigo@uni-bocconi.it

FABIO PAMMOLLI
Università di Firenze
fabio.pammolli@cce.unifi.it

PHILIP SHAPIRA
School of Public Policy, Georgia Institute of Technology, Atlanta
philip.shapira@pubpolicy.gatech.edu

DAVID SOSKICE
Duke University, Durham, North Carolina
soskice@duke.edu

W. EDWARD STEINMUELLER
Science Policy Research Unit (SPRU), University of Sussex, Brighton
W.E.Steinmueller@sussex.ac.uk

BRUCE S. TETHER
Centre for Research on Innovation and Competition (CRIC),
 University of Manchester
Bruce.Tether@man.ac.uk

OLIVIER WEINSTEIN
Centre de Recherche en Economie Industrielle Internationale (CREII),
 Université Paris XIII
weinstei@seg.univ-parisl3.fr

JÜRGEN WENGEL
Fraunhofer-Institut für Systemtechnik und Innovationsforschung
 (ISI – Institute for Systems and Innovation Research), Karlsruhe
J.Wengel@isi.fraunhofer.de

# Acknowledgements

This book draws on the main results of the project "European Sectoral Systems of Innovation (ESSY) – Innovation, Competitiveness and Growth" (a project financed within the Targeted Socio-Economic Research [TSER] programme – contract no. SOE1-CT 98–1116). ESSY was a three-year project conducted by ten leading research centers in Europe: CESPRI (Università Bocconi), SPRU (University of Sussex), WZB (Berlin), S. S. Sant'Anna (Pisa), CRIC (Manchester University), CREII (Paris XIII), TEMA (Linköping University), Universitat Pompeu Fabra (Barcelona), ISI (Karlsruhe) and IKE (Alborg University). It was supported by the European Union, with the specific aim of analyzing sectoral systems of innovation (SSIs) in Europe. I wish to thank the main participants in ESSY: R. O'Brien (the EU officer responsible for the project), B. Coriat, G. Dosi, C. Edquist, J. S. Metcalfe, D. Soskice, W. E. Steinmueller, B. Dalum, W. Garcia-Fontes, J. Wengel, F. Montobbio, S. Breschi, M. Harvey, F. Lissoni, M. McKelvey, L. Orsenigo, F. Pammolli, O. Weinstein, L. D'Adderio, G. Bottazzi, F. Cesaroni, N. Corrocher, P. Geoffron, L. Hommen, A. James, H. Kettler, M. Riccaboni, D. Rivaud-Danset and B. S. Tether. In discussing outlines and drafts the authors met for intensive and extensive workshops in various places: Milan, Manchester, Berlin, Brighton and Milan (again). Paraskevas Caracostas (European Union), David Mowery (Berkeley), Richard Nelson (Columbia University), Fabrizio Onida (Università Bocconi) and Salvatore Torrisi (University of Camerino) as well as industrialists and policy makers – Fabrizio Gianfrate (Smith Kline Foundation), Bruno Lamborghini (Olivetti), Ernesto Hoffman (IBM), Vittorio Maglia (Federchimica) and Donato Speroni (Unione Costruttori Italiani Macchine Utensili – UCIMU) – commented on the papers of these volumes during the final conference, held at Università Bocconi in Milan.

The supporting papers for the whole project, "Sectoral Systems in Europe" – the ESSY working papers, can be downloaded from the ESSY website at http://www.cespri.it/ricerca/es_wp.htm.

I am particularly grateful to Fabio Montobbio for his excellent collaboration and superb work during the whole project. I also thank Monica Cappi and Roberta Ometti for their editorial work. Mike Richardson of Cambridge University Press has been an excellent copy-editor of the book.

# Introduction

*Franco Malerba*

Innovation and technological change are highly affected by the sector in which they take place. The agents, the relationships among actors and the institutions of a sector all exert a major and profound influence on the differences in innovation across sectors. How to consider these effects on innovation? And how to take into account differences across sectors?

This book examines innovation in six major sectors in Europe and in other advanced countries: pharmaceuticals and biotechnology, telecommunications equipment and services, chemicals, software, machine tools and services (airports, medical and retailing). These sectors have been chosen because, in them, technological change is quite rapid, and innovation plays a major role in fostering growth and in affecting the competitiveness of firms and countries.

This volume proposes a novel approach to looking at innovation in sectors. It provides a *sectoral systems of innovation* framework, which uses a multidimensional, integrated and dynamic view of sectors in order to analyze innovation. Although this book focuses on innovation, the concept of sectoral systems can also be applied to *production*. The notion of SSIs departs from the traditional concept of sector used in industrial economics because it examines other agents in addition to firms, places great emphasis on knowledge, learning and sectoral boundaries, focuses on non-market as well as on market interactions, and pays much attention to institutions. In an SSI perspective, firms are active actors that shape their technological and market environments. Innovation is considered a process that involves continuous and systematic interactions among a wide variety of actors.

In this book innovation in a sector is considered to be affected by three main factors:
*a. Knowledge and technologies;*
*b. Actors and networks;*
*c. Institutions.*

*a. Knowledge and technologies.* Any sector can be characterized by a specific knowledge base, technologies and inputs. In a dynamic way, the focus on knowledge and technology places the issue of sectoral boundaries at the centre of analysis. In sectors in which innovation is quite rapid, sectoral boundaries are not fixed but change over time. Knowledge and basic technologies constitute major constraints on the full range of diversity of the behaviors and organizations of firms. Links and complementarities among artifacts and activities also play a major role in defining the real boundaries of a sectoral system. These links and complementarities can be static (as input-output links are) or dynamic. Dynamic complementarities take into account interdependencies and feedback, both at the demand and at the production levels. They are major sources of the transformation and growth of sectoral systems, and may set in motion virtuous cycles of innovation and change.

*b. Actors and networks.* A sector consists of heterogeneous agents that are organizations or individuals (e.g. consumers, entrepreneurs, scientists). Organizations may be firms (e.g. users, producers and input suppliers) or non-firm organizations (e.g. universities, financial organizations, government agencies, trade unions or technical associations), including subunits of larger organizations (e.g. research and development – R&D – or production departments) or groups of organizations (e.g. industry associations). Agents are characterized by specific learning processes, competencies, beliefs, objectives, organizational structures and behaviors. They interact through processes of communication, exchange, cooperation, competition and command. Within sectoral systems, heterogeneous agents are connected in various ways through market and non-market relationships. The types and structures of relationships and networks differ from sectoral system to sectoral system, as a consequence of the features of the knowledge base, the relevant learning processes, the basic technologies, the characteristics of demand, key links and dynamic complementarities.

Thus, in a sectoral system perspective, innovation and production are considered to be processes that involve systematic interactions among a wide variety of actors for the generation and exchange of knowledge relevant to innovation and its commercialization. Interactions include market and non-market relations that are broader than the market for technological licensing and knowledge, inter-firm alliances, and formal networks of firms. Often their outcome is not adequately captured by our existing ways of measuring economic output.

*c. Institutions.* Agents' cognition, actions and interactions are shaped by institutions, which include norms, routines, common habits, established practices, rules, laws, standards and so on. They may range from the ones that bind or impose enforcements on agents to the ones that are created by the interaction among agents (such as contracts); from more binding to less binding; and from formal to informal (such as patent laws or specific regulations versus traditions and conventions). Many institutions are national (such as the patent system), while others may be specific to sectoral systems, such as sectoral labor markets or sector-specific financial institutions.

The relationships between *national institutions* and *sectoral systems* are quite important. First, national institutions – such as the patent system, property rights or antitrust regulations – have different effects on innovation in different sectors. Second, the same institution may take on different features in different countries, and thus may affect innovation differently. Third, the characteristics of national institutions often favor specific sectors that fit them better. In some cases national institutions may constrain the development of innovations in specific sectors, with the result that mismatches between national institutions on one side and sectoral institutions and agents on the other side may take place. Fourth, the relationship between national institutions and sectoral systems may sometimes go from the sector to the national level: the institutions of a sector, extremely important for a country in terms of employment, competitiveness or strategic relevance, may end up emerging as national (thus also becoming relevant for other sectors). But, in the process of becoming national, they may change some of their original distinctive features.

*Demand* is a key part of a sectoral system. However, the focus on users and on institutions puts a different emphasis on the role of demand. Demand is made up of individual consumers, of firms and of public agencies, each characterized by knowledge, learning processes, competencies and goals, and affected by social factors and institutions. Thus, in a sectoral system, demand is not seen as an aggregate set of similar buyers, but as consisting of heterogeneous agents the interactions of which with producers are shaped by institutions. In general, the emergence and transformation of demand play a major role in the dynamics and evolution of sectoral systems.

In sum, the framework of a sectoral system may prove a useful tool in analyzing innovation, for various reasons:
- a descriptive analysis of the innovation process in sectors;
- the recognition of the factors affecting innovation;
- the analysis of the relationship between innovation and the changing boundaries of sectors;

- a full understanding of the short-term and long-term dynamics and transformation of sectors;
- the identification of the factors affecting the international performance of firms and countries in the different sectors;
- the development of new public policy indications.

This volume is unique in examining in a consistent and comparative way pharmaceuticals and biotechnology; chemicals; telecommunication equipment and services; software; machine tools; and medical, airport and retailing services along the various dimensions discussed above. It tries to answer questions such as:

- What affects the specific organization of the innovative activity of a sector? Why is this organization so different across sectors (for example, between chemicals and software, or between biotechnology and machine tools)?
- What are the main characteristics of the networks of innovators in a sector? Do these networks differ significantly among sectors, and, if so, why?
- What are the factors responsible for the changing boundaries and major transformation of sectors such as telecommunications or software?
- What is the role of institutions in affecting innovation in a sector?
- How relevant is the role of different national institutional frameworks across European countries for innovation in a sector?
- What are the factors at the base of the international competitiveness of Europe in each sector?
- Should national and European public policies pay attention to sectoral specificities and sectoral differences?

The organization of the volume is as follows. The first part of the book presents concepts and issues related to the sectoral system of innovation: chapter 1 discusses sectoral systems of innovation and production and their main building blocks, while chapter 2 introduces some basic data and contains a discussion of the link between sectoral systems and innovation systems. The second part of the book contains analyses of sectoral systems in Europe: pharmaceuticals and biotechnology (chapter 3), chemicals (chapter 4), telecommunications equipment and services (chapter 5), software (chapter 6), machine tools (chapter 7) and services (chapter 8). In the third part some major themes are addressed: the role of institutions in sectoral systems (chapter 9), the interplay between national institutional frameworks and sectoral specialization (chapter 10), the factors affecting international performance of sectoral systems (chapter 11) and the new dimensions of public policy deriving from this book (chapter 12). Finally, a summing up and concluding chapter (chapter 13) closes the book.

One note has to be advanced here. When a sectoral system is examined, different levels of aggregation and large or narrow sectoral boundaries may be chosen. This depends on the goal of the analysis. So, in this book in the chapters about specific sectoral systems of innovation, sectors have been defined broadly: pharmaceuticals, chemicals, telecommunications, software, machine tools. This broad definition allows us to emphasize interdependencies, linkages and transformations spanning a large set of products, actors and functions. However in some chapters a more disaggregated level is also used in order to show that within the broadly defined sectors different innovation systems may coexist. Also in these cases we can talk about systems of innovation, only that the level of disaggregation is much higher. In order to make this distinction clear, in this book authors have used the term "sector" for the broad aggregations mentioned above, and the terms "subsectors," "product groups" and "product segments" for more narrowly defined aggregations within broad sectors.

*Part I*

Sectoral systems: concepts and issues

# 1 Sectoral systems of innovation: basic concepts

*Franco Malerba*

## 1 Introduction

Innovation takes place in quite different sectoral environments, in terms of sources, actors and institutions. These differences are striking.

Let us take, for example, pharmaceuticals and biotechnology. Here science plays a major role, and several different types of firms are the protagonists of innovation, from large corporations to new biotechnology firms. Interaction between universities and venture capital is relevant. In this sector, regulation, intellectual property rights (IPR) and patents, national health systems and demand all play a major role in the innovation process. Quite a different set of actors, networks and institutions characterize innovation in telecommunications equipment and services, as a result of the convergence of previously separated sectors such as telecommunications, computers, the media and so on, and of the rapid growth of the Internet. In chemicals we see a different scenario: large innovators have shown great continuity in their innovativeness, and the scale of internal R&D has always been a major source of innovative advantage. In software, on the other hand, the context of application is relevant for innovation, and a vertical and horizontal division of labor among different actors has recently taken place. Finally, in machine tools incremental innovation is quite common, and R&D plays a less relevant role than in other sectors. Links with users and the on-the-job activity of skilled personnel is quite relevant. Differences in innovation across sectors also involve services, where products are closely related to processes, and knowledge embodied in equipment and in people is very important.

How to take account of and analyze these differences? The analysis of innovation in sectors developed in this book is centered around the concept of *sectoral systems of innovation*. By way of introduction, the definition that will be presented in section 3 and discussed in sections 4 and 5 is anticipated here.

A sector is a set of activities that are unified by some related product group for a given or emerging demand and that share some basic

9

knowledge. Firms in sectors have commonalities and at the same time are heterogeneous. Innovation in sectors has relevant systemic features. In this book it is proposed that a sectoral system of innovation (and production) is composed of a set of agents carrying out market and non-market interactions for the creation, production and sale of sectoral products. Sectoral systems have a knowledge base, technologies, inputs and (potential or existing) demand. The agents are individuals and organizations at various levels of aggregation, with specific learning processes, competencies, organizational structure, beliefs, objectives and behaviors. They interact through the processes of communication, exchange, cooperation, competition and command, and their interaction is shaped by institutions. A sectoral system undergoes processes of change and transformation through the coevolution of its various elements.

Thus a sectoral system has three building blocks:

- *knowledge and technology;*
- *actors and networks;*
- *institutions.*

What are the advantages of using a sectoral system perspective in the analysis of innovation? The main advantages of a sectoral system view are a better understanding of: the structure and boundaries of sectors; agents and their interaction; the learning and innovation processes specific to a sector; the types of sectoral transformations; and the factors at the base of the differential performance of firms and countries in a sector.

The theoretical and analytical approaches on which this book draws come from evolutionary theory and the system of innovation studies. It is in the evolutionary field that key concepts such as learning, knowledge and competencies and a major focus on dynamics are present. And it is in the innovation system literature that one may find relationships and networks as key elements of the innovative and production processes (Edquist, 1997). In particular, the notion of *sectoral systems of innovation* complements other concepts such as *national systems of innovation* (NSIs), which have a focus on national boundaries and on non-firm organizations and institutions (Freeman, 1987; Nelson, 1993; and Lundvall, 1992), *regional/local innovation systems*, in which the focus is on the region (Cooke, Gomez Uranga and Extebarria, 1998), and *technological systems*, in which the focus is mainly on networks of agents for the generation, diffusion and utilization of specific technologies (Carlsson and Stankiewitz, 1995; Hughes, 1984; and Callon, 1992).

This chapter is conceptual and methodological. It aims to discuss the theoretical foundations of the notion of a sectoral system of innovation, to propose a definition of a sectoral system, to identify the major dimensions and the main variables, to analyze the main factors affecting structure, agents' heterogeneity and change, and to set out the main research questions and the key challenges that lie ahead.

The chapter is organized in the following way. In section 2 the theoretical foundations of the notion of sectoral systems are presented, and in section 3 a definition and a framework is proposed. In section 4 the main building blocks of a sectoral system are examined: knowledge, learning processes, technologies and demand; the structure of interaction among heterogeneous firms and non-firm organizations and institutions. Then, in section 5, the dynamics and transformation of sectoral systems are discussed, while in section 6 the geographical boundaries are analyzed.

## 2      Antecedents and theoretical bases

In innovation studies, sectors provide a key level of analysis for economists, business scholars, technologists and economic historians. When sectors are examined, however, two different traditions are encountered.

The first is related to the industrial economics literature. The structure-conduct-performance tradition, the transaction costs approach, sunk cost models, game theoretical models of strategic interaction and cooperation, and econometric industry studies have emphasized differences across industries. Most of these approaches have considered the sectoral boundaries to be static and delimited in terms of similarity of techniques or similarity of demand. Sometimes strategic interdependence has been added as another criterion for delimiting sectors. Differences in the equilibrium structure of sectors have been identified as being determined by the underlying patterns of technology and demand, in addition to the type of sunk costs. These studies in the industrial economics tradition have examined the structure of sectors in terms of concentration, vertical integration, diversification and so on; the dynamics of sectors in terms of technical progress, entry, firms' growth and so on; and the interaction among firms in terms of strategic behavior (Bain, 1956; Scherer, 1990; Tirole, 1988; and Sutton, 1991, 1998). This tradition has obtained tremendous progress and major results in all the above-mentioned topics. In most of these studies, however, not much emphasis has been placed on the role of non-firm organizations, on the knowledge and learning processes by firms, on the wide range of relations among the agents, or on the transformation of sectors in their boundaries, actors, products and structure. These remarks could be coupled with the complementary observations by Geroski (1998), who discusses market boundaries and emphasizes the concept of the strategic market.

The second tradition dealing with sectors is much richer empirically but much more heterogeneous, eclectic and dispersed. Here one finds very rich empirical evidence on the features and working of sectors, on their technologies, production, innovation and demand, and on the type and degree of change. But most of the sector case studies focus on a single dimension (such as innovation, firms' competencies, structure of production and so on), ask different research questions, are undertaken with different methodologies and have a different level of aggregation in terms of unit of analysis. As a consequence, the possibility of having integrated and consistent analyses of sectors in their interrelated dimensions, understanding fully their working and transformation or comparing different sectors with respect to several dimensions (such as the type and role of agents, the structure and dynamics of production, the rate and direction of innovation and the effects of these variables on the performance of firms and countries) is still very limited.

In innovation studies, an intermediate level between the industrial organization tradition and the case studies approach is represented by empirical taxonomies concerning differences across sectors in innovative activities. The simplest one, widely used in international studies by the Organization for Economic Co-operation and Development (OECD), European Union and other international organizations, refers to sectors that are "high R&D-intensive" (such as electronics and drugs) and "low R&D-intensive" (such as textiles and shoes). Another distinction, coming from the Schumpeterian legacy, focuses on differences in market structure and industrial dynamics among sectors. *Schumpeter Mark I* sectors are characterized by "creative destruction," with technological ease of entry and a major role played by entrepreneurs and new firms in innovative activities. *Schumpeter Mark II* sectors are characterized by cumulative technological advancements, with the prevalence of large established firms and the presence of relevant barriers to entry for new innovators. This regime is characterized by the dominance of a stable core of a few large firms, with limited entry. A third distinction refers to sectors that are *net suppliers* of technology and sectors that are *users* of technology. On the bases of the R&D carried out by 400 American firms and of inter-sectoral flows in the American economy, Scherer (1982) identifies sectors that are net sources of R&D (such as computers and instruments) and sectors that are net users of technology (such as textiles and metallurgy). A similar analysis is done by Robson, Townsend and Pavitt (1988), who – on the basis of 4,378 innovations in the United Kingdom between 1945 and 1983 – identify "core sectors" (such as electronics, machinery, instruments and chemicals), which generate most of the innovations in the economy and are net sources of technology; secondary sectors (such as automobiles and metallurgy), which play a secondary role in terms of sources of innovation for the economy; and user sectors, such as services, which mainly absorb technology.

Finally, the taxonomy developed by Pavitt (1984) refers to the difference among sectors in the *sources of innovation* and the *appropriability mechanisms*. He proposes four types of sectoral patterns of innovative activities: supplier-dominated sectors (textiles, services), in which new technologies mainly come embodied in new components and equipment, and the diffusion of new technologies and learning takes place through learning by doing and by using; scale-intensive sectors (automobiles, steel), in which process innovation is relevant and the sources of innovation are both internal (R&D and learning by doing) and external (equipment producers) and appropriability is through secrecy and patents; specialized suppliers (such as equipment producers), in which innovation is focused on performance improvement, reliability and customization, the sources of innovation are both internal (the tacit knowledge and experience of skilled technicians) and external (user-producer interaction), and appropriability comes mainly from the localized and interactive nature of knowledge; and, finally, science-based sectors (such as pharmaceuticals, electronics and so on) which are characterized by a high rate of product and process innovations, internal R&D and scientific research done at universities and public research laboratories and appropriability means of various types, ranging from patents to lead times, learning curves and secrecy. Pavitt taxonomy has been tremendously successful in empirical research and has guided the identification of firms' and countries' advantages and the different features of the innovation process. Refinements and enrichments of the taxonomy have been proposed in the succeeding decades. A very interesting and relevant work in this direction is that of Marsili and Verspagen (2002).

In this book, a multidimensional, integrated and dynamic view of innovation in sectors – sectoral systems of innovation – is presented and used. This view is partly related to the case study tradition and to some elements of the sectoral taxonomies discussed above.

However, it is also related to other intellectual and theoretical traditions. A first group of contributions emphasized *change and transformation* in sectors. Sectors change over time. Therefore, considerable attention should be placed on their laws of motion, dynamics, emergence and transformation. This point is related both to the industry life cycle literature (Utterback, 1994; and Klepper, 1996) and to broader analyses of the long-term evolution of industries, as found in Schumpeter, Kuznets and

Clark. In particular, this long-term view was lost in the 1950s and 1960s literature on structure, conduct and performance (in which the focus was on comparative static analyses of industry structure), and in modern industrial economics, game theory and transaction cost, but it has regained considerable attention in recent years (Malerba and Orsenigo, 1996).

The second tradition is about *links and interdependencies* and, consequently, *sectoral boundaries*. It stresses that the boundaries of sectors should include interdependencies and links among related industries, and that these boundaries are not fixed but change over time. Dynamic complementarities among artifacts and activities thus provide force and trigger mechanisms of growth and innovation. The concept of *filieres* highlights the role of major vertical links among sectors in production activities. The notion of *development blocks* introduced by Dahmen (1989) stresses the idea that sequences of complementarities create dynamism in the system and generate development potential. Investments are often closely interrelated and span different technologies or activities: they may originate tensions and virtuous cycles among related products in the process of economic development.

The third tradition is the *innovation system* approach, which considers innovation as an interactive process among a wide variety of actors. It stresses the point that firms do not innovate in isolation, with the result that innovation can be seen as a collective process. In the innovative process firms interact with other firms as well as with non-firm organizations, such as universities, research centers, government agencies, financial institutions and so on. Their action is shaped by institutions (Lundvall, 1992; Carlsson, 1995; and Edquist, 1997). This approach places a great deal of emphasis on interdisciplinarity, emphasizes a historical perspective and identifies learning as a key determinant of innovation (Edquist, 1997).

Finally, *evolutionary theory* provides a broad theoretical framework for the concept of sectoral systems of innovation and production. Evolutionary theory places dynamics, process and transformation at the centre of the analysis. Learning and knowledge are key elements in the change of the economic system. "Boundedly rational" agents act, learn and search in uncertain and changing environments. Relatedly, competencies correspond to specific ways of packaging knowledge about different things and have an intrinsic organizational content. Different agents know how to do different things in different ways. Thus, learning, knowledge and behavior entail agents' heterogeneity in experience, competencies and organization, and their persistent differential performance. In addition, evolutionary theory has placed emphasis on cognitive aspects such as beliefs, objectives and expectations, in turn affected by previous learning and experience and by the environment in which agents act (Nelson, 1995; Dosi, 1997; and Metcalfe, 1998). A central place in an evolutionary approach is occupied by three economic processes driving economic change: processes of variety creation in technologies, products, firms and organizations; processes of replication (which generate inertia and continuity in the system); and processes of selection (which reduce variety in the economic system) (Nelson, 1995; and Metcalfe, 1998). Finally, in evolutionary theory, aggregate phenomena are emergent properties of interactions far from equilibrium, and have a meta-stable nature (Lane, 1993). In evolutionary theory the environment and conditions in which agents operate may differ drastically.[1] Evolutionary theory stresses major differences in opportunity conditions related to science and technologies. The same holds for the knowledge base underpinning innovative activities, as well as for the institutional context. Thus the learning, behavior and capabilities of agents are constrained and "bounded" by the technology, knowledge base and institutional context in which firms act. Heterogeneous firms facing similar technologies, searching around similar knowledge bases, undertaking similar production activities and "embedded" in the same institutional setting, share some common behavioral and organizational traits and develop a similar range of learning patterns, behavior and organizational forms. For example, a specific technological regime defines the nature of the problem that firms have to solve in their innovative activities, affects the model form of technological learning, shapes the incentives and constraints on particular behaviors and organizations, and affects the basic processes of variety generation and selection (and, therefore, the dynamics of evolution of firms) (Nelson and Winter, 1982; and Malerba and Orsenigo, 1996).

This chapter will take these broad points coming from evolutionary theory and will link them to a sectoral system perspective. The starting point will be the empirical recognition, as it has emerged from the rich literature of empirical case studies, that (i) sectors are characterized by specific knowledge bases, technologies, production processes, complementarities, demand and a population of heterogeneous firms and non-firm organizations and institutions, and that (ii) sectors differ greatly in several of these dimensions. In the following pages an attempt to spell out and link several of these dimensions and place them in a dynamic perspective is presented.

---

[1] Of course, in an evolutionary framework there is not a sharp distinction between the learning environment and the unit of learning.

## 3    Sectoral systems of innovation and production: a proposed definition and a framework

As previously mentioned, a sector is a set of activities unified by some linked product groups for a given or emerging demand and characterized by a common knowledge base. Firms in a sector have some commonalities and at the same time are heterogeneous. Thus, a sectoral system of innovation and production is composed of a set of new and established products for specific uses, and a set of agents carrying out activities and market and non-market interactions for the creation, production and sale of those products. A sectoral system has a knowledge base, technologies, inputs and (existing and potential) demand. The agents comprising the sectoral system are organizations and individuals (e.g. consumers, entrepreneurs or scientists). Organizations may be firms (e.g. users, producers and suppliers) and non-firm organizations (e.g. universities, financial institutions, government agencies, trade unions, or technical associations), including subunits of larger organizations (e.g. R&D or production departments) and groups of organizations (e.g. industry associations). Agents are characterized by specific learning processes, competencies, beliefs, objectives, organizational structures and behaviors. They interact through processes of communication, exchange, cooperation, competition and command, and their interactions are shaped by institutions (rules and regulations). Over time existing sectoral systems undergo processes of change and transformation through the coevolution of their various elements, and new sectoral systems may emerge.

This notion of the sectoral system of innovation and production highlights five key points. First, it focuses on supply as well as on demand and markets. Second, it examines other types of agents in addition to firms. Third, it places considerable emphasis on non-market as well as market interaction. Fourth, it pays attention to institutions. Fifth, it focuses on the processes of transformation of the system and does not consider sectoral boundaries as given and static.

There are several relevant consequences for the analysis of innovation and production in sectors. Emphasis is placed on a specific concept of the structure of a sector, expressed not just in terms of industrial concentration (as in traditional industrial economics) but in terms of links between agents, knowledge, products and technologies. This also implies that a sectoral system is a collective emergent outcome of the interaction and coevolution of its various elements. Finally, there is a focus on the processes of transformation of existing sectoral systems and on the emergence of new sectoral systems.

Another remark concerns the *aggregation* issue. When agents of a sectoral system are considered, agents at lower or higher levels of aggregation compared to firms can be considered. Similarly, because the notion of sectoral systems includes innovation and production with the related demand and market processes, for analytical purposes one could examine separately a sectoral *innovation* system, a sectoral *production* system and a sectoral *distribution/market* system, which in turn could be related more or less closely. The main conclusion here is that the appropriate level of analysis in terms of agents and functions depends on the specific research goal.

The same holds for the boundaries of sectoral systems. In fact, sectoral systems may be examined according to different levels of aggregation of products. Again, the level of aggregation depends on the goal of the analysis. So, in this book, in the chapters about specific sectoral systems of innovation, sectors will be defined broadly: pharmaceuticals, chemicals, telecommunications, software and machine tools. This broad definition allows emphasis to be placed on interdependencies, linkages and transformations spanning a wide range of products, actors and functions. However, in some chapters a more disaggregated level will also be used in order to show that, within the broadly defined sectors, different SIs may coexist. In these cases sectoral systems of innovation exist but their level of disaggregation is much higher. Thus, in this book, authors have used the term "sector" for the broad aggregations mentioned above, and the terms "subsectors," "product groups" and "product segments" for more narrowly defined aggregations within broad sectors.

In this book we will concentrate on *sectoral systems of innovation*. In the following pages, a more in-depth examination of their various elements will be presented.

## 4     The building blocks of a sectoral system of innovation

What are the main building blocks of a sectoral system of innovation? From the above discussion it is possible to identify them as follows:
*a. Knowledge and technologies;*
*b. Actors and networks;*
*c. Institutions.*

   *a. Knowledge and technologies.* Any sector can be characterized by a specific knowledge base, technologies and inputs. In a dynamic way, the focus on knowledge and the technological domain also places at the centre of analysis the issue of sectoral *boundaries*, which are usually not fixed but change over time.

*b. Actors and networks.* A sector is composed of heterogeneous agents, which are organizations and individuals. They interact through processes of communication, exchange, cooperation, competition and command. Within sectoral systems, heterogeneous agents are connected in various ways through market and non-market relationships. Thus, in a sectoral system perspective, innovation and production are regarded as processes that involve systematic interaction among a wide variety of actors for the generation and exchange of knowledge relevant to innovation and its commercialization. Interaction includes market and non-market relations that are broader than the market for technological licensing and knowledge, inter-firm alliances, and formal networks of firms. Often their outcome is not adequately captured by our existing systems of measuring economic output.

*c. Institutions.* Cognition, actions and interactions of agents are shaped by institutions, which include norms, routines, common habits, established practices, rules, laws, standards and so on. They may range from those that bind or impose enforcements on agents to those that are created by the interaction among agents (such as contracts); from more binding to less binding; and from formal to informal (such as patent laws or specific regulations versus traditions and conventions). Many institutions are national (such as the patent system), while others are specific to sectoral systems, such as sectoral labor markets or sector-specific financial institutions.

In the following pages, each of these building blocks will be discussed.

## 4.1    *Knowledge, learning processes and technologies*

Sectoral systems differ in terms of *technologies*. An enormous body of literature on technologies and technological change has clearly shown how much sectors differ in their basic technologies and how these technologies affect the nature, boundaries and organizations of sectors (see, for example, Rosenberg, 1976, 1982; and Granstrand, 1994). This literature has shown that often in a sectoral system more than one technology may be relevant. Thus, for each sectoral system, in principle, it could be possible to build a technology-product matrix that links the products to a range of technologies. This matrix differs from one sectoral system to another. Moreover, it has been found that, in most sectors, even firms specializing in one product often have to master several technologies: they are labelled multi-technology corporations (Granstrand, Patel and Pavitt, 1997). Within the same sectoral system, however, the profile of technological diversification among large firms is quite similar (Patel and Pavitt, 1997).

Links and complementarities among technologies, artifacts and activities play a major role in defining the real boundaries of a sectoral system. These links and complementarities are, first of all, of the static type, like input-output links. Then there are dynamic complementarities, which take into account interdependencies and feedbacks. They greatly affect a wide variety of variables in a sectoral system: firms' strategies, organization and performance, the rate and direction of technological change, the type of competition and the networks among agents. Dynamic complementarities among technologies, artifacts and activities are a major source of transformation and growth of sectoral systems and may set in motion virtuous cycles of innovation and change. They could be related to the concept of *filieres* and the notion of development blocks (Dahmen, 1989). Of course, links and complementarities change over time and differ among sectoral systems.

Knowledge is at the base of technological change and plays a central role in innovation. This point has been strongly emphasized by the evolutionary literature (Nelson, 1995; Dosi, 1997; and Metcalfe, 1998) as well as by the literature on the knowledge-based economy (Lundvall, 1992; Lundvall and Johnson, 1994; and Cowan, David and Foray, 2000). For these contributions, knowledge is highly idiosyncratic at the firm level, does not diffuse automatically and freely among firms and is absorbed by firms through their differential abilities accumulated over time.

The evolutionary literature has proposed that sectors and technologies differ greatly in terms of the knowledge base and learning processes related to innovation. Knowledge differs across sectors in terms of domains. One knowledge domain refers to the specific scientific and technological fields at the base of innovative activities in a sector (Dosi, 1988; and Nelson and Rosenberg, 1993). The second domain concerns applications, users and the demand for sectoral products. In addition, other dimensions of knowledge may be relevant for explaining innovative activities in a sector.

First, knowledge may have different degrees of *accessibility* (Malerba and Orsenigo, 2000) – i.e. opportunities for gaining knowledge that are external to firms. Knowledge that is accessible may be internal or external to the sector. In both cases the greater accessibility of knowledge decreases industrial concentration. Greater accessibility *internal* to the sector implies lower appropriability: competitors may gain knowledge about new products and processes and, if competent, imitate those new products and processes. The accessibility of knowledge that is *external* to the sector may be related to scientific and technological opportunities, in terms of level and sources. Here the external environment may affect firms through human capital with a certain level and type of knowledge, or through scientific and technological knowledge developed in non-firm organizations (such as universities or research laboratories).

The sources of technological *opportunities* differ markedly among sectors. As Freeman (1982) and Rosenberg (1982), among others, have shown, in some sectors opportunity conditions are related to major scientific breakthroughs in universities. In other sectors opportunities to innovate may often come from advancements in R&D by firms, equipment and instrumentation. In still other sectors external sources of knowledge related to suppliers or users may play a crucial role. Not all external knowledge may be easily used and transformed into new artifacts. If external knowledge is easily accessible, transformable into new artifacts and exposed to a number of actors (such as customers or suppliers), then innovative entry may take place (Winter, 1984). On the other hand, if advanced integration capabilities are necessary (Cohen and Levinthal, 1989), the industry may be concentrated and formed by large established firms.

Second, knowledge may be more or less *cumulative* – i.e. the degree to which the generation of new knowledge builds upon current knowledge. One can identify three different sources of cumulativeness. The first source is cognitive. The learning processes and past knowledge constrain current research, but also generate new questions and new knowledge. The second source is related to the firm and to its organizational capabilities. These capabilities are firm-specific and generate knowledge that is highly path-dependent. They implicitly define what a firm learns and what it can hope to achieve in the future. A third source is the feedback from the market, such as the "success breeds success" process. Innovative success yields profits that can be reinvested in R&D, thereby increasing the probability of innovating again. From this discussion, it follows that cumulativeness may be observed at various levels of analysis. One is at the technological level. Another is at the firm level: here high cumulativeness implies an implicit mechanism leading to the high appropriability of innovations. Another is at the sectoral level: this takes place in the case of low appropriability conditions and high knowledge spillovers within an industry. Finally, cumulativeness may be present at the local level. In this case high cumulativeness within specific locations is associated with low appropriability conditions and spatially localized knowledge spillovers. Cumulativeness at the technological and firm levels creates first-mover advantages and generates high concentration. Firms that have a head start develop new knowledge based on that which already exists and introduce continuous innovations of the incremental type.

Accessibility, opportunity and cumulativeness are key dimensions of knowledge and are related to the notion of *technological and learning regimes*. These regimes differ across sectors. The notion of technological regimes dates back to Nelson and Winter (1982) and provides a description of the knowledge environment in which firms operate. More generally, Malerba and Orsenigo (1996, 1997) have proposed that a technological regime is composed of opportunity and appropriability conditions; degrees of cumulativeness of technological knowledge; and characteristics of the relevant knowledge base. More specifically, *technological opportunities* reflect the likelihood of innovating for any given amount of money invested in research. High opportunities provide powerful incentives for the undertaking of innovative activities and denote an economic environment that is not functionally constrained by scarcity. In this case, potential innovators may come up with frequent and important technological innovations. The *appropriability of innovations* relates to the possibility of protecting innovations from imitation and of reaping profits from innovative activities. High appropriability means the existence of ways to protect innovation successfully from imitation, while low appropriability denotes an economic environment characterized by the widespread existence of externalities (Levin et al., 1987).[2] The *properties of the knowledge base* relate to the nature of the knowledge underpinning firms' innovative activities. Technological knowledge involves varying degrees of specificity, tacitness, complementarities and independence, and may differ greatly across sectors and technologies (Winter, 1987).

Here one could advance the following general propositions on the relationship between technological regimes and patterns of innovation in sectoral systems (Winter, 1984; and Malerba and Orsenigo, 1997). Technological regimes characterized by high levels of *opportunity* are expected to show patterns of innovation characterized by a remarkable turbulence in terms of technological entry and exit and a high instability in firms' hierarchies. High-tech opportunities allow for the continuous entry of new innovators. However, if successful, established firms may also end up gaining a substantial leap in their relative competitiveness, thus leading to the elimination from the market of less successful innovators. Conversely, conditions of low opportunity limit innovative entry and restrict the innovative growth of successful established firms. As a consequence,

---

[2] It was Pavitt who introduced the distinction between appropriability and technological barriers to entry. According to him, appropriability refers to all competitors, both within and outside the industry, while technological barriers to entry refer to the ease of innovative entry into an industry by potential entrants (Pavitt, 1984). Needless to say, this distinction is quite helpful in grouping sectors with respect to the ease of entry in an industry.

a higher stability of the major innovators may emerge. By limiting the extent of knowledge spillovers and by allowing successful innovators to maintain their innovative advantage, high degrees of *appropriability* are expected to result in a relatively high level of industrial concentration and a lower number of innovators. Conversely, by discouraging investments in innovative activities and by determining a wider diffusion of the relevant knowledge across firms, low appropriability conditions are more likely to lead to a sectoral structure characterized by the presence of a large population of innovators. Finally, high levels of *cumulativeness* at the firm level are expected to be associated with persistence in innovative activities. At the sectoral level, technological cumulativeness and persistence are expected to be associated with quite a high degree of stability in the hierarchy of innovative firms and low rates of innovative entry. In such circumstances, the selection process favors established technological leaders. Existing innovators accumulate technological knowledge and capabilities and build up innovative advantages, which greatly affect their competitiveness and act as powerful barriers to the entry of new innovators.

This difference in the organization of innovative activities at the sectoral level may be related to a fundamental distinction between *Schumpeter Mark I* and *Schumpeter Mark II* models. Schumpeter Mark I is characterized by "creative destruction," with technological ease of entry and a major role played by entrepreneurs and new firms in innovative activities. Schumpeter Mark II is characterized by "creative accumulation," with the prevalence of large established firms and the presence of relevant barriers to entry for new innovators. This pattern features the dominance of a stable core of a few large firms, with limited entry. High technological opportunities, low appropriability and low cumulativeness (at the firm level) conditions lead to a Schumpeter Mark I pattern. Conversely, high appropriability and high cumulativeness (at the firm level) conditions lead to a Schumpeter Mark II pattern.

Technological regimes and Schmpeterian patterns of innovation change over time (Klepper, 1996). According to an industry life cycle view, a Schumpeter Mark I pattern of innovative activities may turn into a Schumpeter Mark II. Early in the history of an industry (when knowledge is changing very rapidly, uncertainty is very high and barriers to entry are very low), new firms are the major innovators and the key elements in industrial dynamics. When the industry develops and eventually matures and technological change follows well-defined trajectories, economies of scale, learning curves, barriers to entry and financial resources become important in the competitive process. Thus, large firms with monopolistic power come to the forefront of the innovation process

(Utterback, 1994; Gort and Klepper, 1982; and Klepper, 1996). Conversely, in the case of major knowledge, technological and market discontinuities, a Schumpeter Mark II pattern of innovative activities may be replaced by a Schumpeter Mark I. In this case, a quite stable organization characterized by incumbents with monopolistic power is displaced by a more turbulent one, with new firms using the new technology or focusing on the new demand (Henderson and Clark, 1993; and Christensen and Rosenbloom, 1995).

The empirical evidence (Malerba and Orsenigo, 1996) suggests the existence of *differences across sectoral systems* in the patterns of innovative activities, and, for each sectoral system, of broad similarities across countries. This result provides support for the relevance of technological regimes in determining sectoral invariances across countries in innovation patterns. This is as long as appropriability, cumulativeness and opportunity conditions are quite similar across countries. Empirical analyses have shown that appropriability and cumulativeness conditions are similar across countries. On the other hand, the ability to generate and exploit opportunity conditions seems less similar across countries, because it is related to the level and range of university research, the presence and effectiveness of science-industry bridging mechanisms, vertical and horizontal links among local firms, user-producer interaction and the types and level of firms' innovative efforts (Nelson, 1993).

The specificities of technological regimes and the knowledge base provide a powerful restriction on the patterns of firms' learning, competencies, behaviors and organization of innovative and production activities in a sectoral system. Case studies in the managerial and economic history literature shed light on this aspect. Think, for example, of the differences in the types of competencies among sectors such as computers, automobiles or pharmaceuticals (Iansiti, 1998; Iansiti and Clark, 1994; and Henderson, 1994). As a first approximation, it is possible to link basic innovative behavior and strategies to some differences in the underlying knowledge and learning regimes. An exercise in this respect has been undertaken by Malerba and Orsenigo (1993), who linked the specific learning regimes in terms of opportunity, cumulativeness and appropriability of innovations to the type and range of basic innovative behavior (radical versus innovative versus imitative) in sectors such as computers, biotechnology and semiconductors. In addition, basic knowledge and complementarities, together with firms' idiosyncratic experience and competencies, also affect agents' beliefs, visions or cognitive representations of the sectoral context (basic economic processes, technology, demand, users, suppliers, competitors and so on). For interesting examples of this aspect see Fransmann (1994), and Langlois (1995) on computers.

Although rather archetypical, these analyses point in the direction of placing considerable emphasis on differences across sectors in some key factors related to knowledge and learning regimes. Much more work has to be done first to develop a finer-grained analysis of the relationship between knowledge and innovative activities at the sectoral level, and second to enlarge the scope of the analysis from sectoral innovation systems to sectoral production systems and sectoral sale and distribution systems.

Two examples may illustrate these points. In multimedia, the convergence of different types of technologies has originated a new sector with continuously expanding boundaries and with actors coming from various industries, but with new strategies more in tune with the new features of multimedia. In computers, until the 1980s, dynamic complementarities and key linkages kept hardware and software highly interdependent, and consequently affected the vertical organization and strategies of several computer firms. Later on, some of the dynamic complementarities became less strong and standard interfaces emerged, leading to the creation of strategies of specialization in computer hardware and in software.

### 4.2     *Actors and networks*

What are the major types of agents in a sectoral system? *Firms* are the key actors in a sectoral system. They are involved in the innovation, production and sale of sectoral products, and in the generation, adoption and use of new technologies. As our previous discussion of evolutionary theory stressed, they are characterized by specific beliefs, expectations, competencies and organization, and are engaged in processes of learning and knowledge accumulation. (Nelson and Winter, 1982; Dosi, Marengo and Fagiolo, 1996; Malerba, 1992; Teece and Pisano, 1994; and Metcalfe, 1998).

Firms also include *users* and *suppliers*, who have different types of relationships with the innovating, producing or selling firms. The role of *users* is extremely important in several sectors, such as agro-food or instrumentation (Lundvall, 1992; and Von Hippel, 1988). The focus on users puts a different emphasis on the role of *demand*. In a sectoral system, demand is not seen as an aggregate set of similar buyers but as comprising heterogeneous agents (with specific attributes, knowledge and competencies), who interact in various ways with producers. Similarly, *suppliers* of components and subsystems also play a major role in affecting innovation, productivity increases and the competitiveness of downstream sectors. Suppliers are characterized by specific attributes, knowledge and competencies, with more or less close relationships with firms within a sector.

The role of suppliers varies across sectors. It is enough to mention the wide range of relations between microelectronics suppliers and information technology (IT) producers, or the close links between producers of advanced machinery and downstream user industries, in the Italian industrial districts (Pavitt, 1984; and Malerba, 1993).

*Firm heterogeneity* is a key feature of sectoral systems. A higher or lower degree of agents' heterogeneity in terms of types, beliefs, competencies, behavior and organizations may stem from differences in a set of factors: the characteristics of the knowledge base; experience and learning processes; firm-specific interactions with demand; the working of dynamic complementarities; firms' histories; and differential rates and trajectories of innovation and growth. Sectoral systems differ greatly in the extent and type of agent heterogeneity.

Processes of variety generation, imitation and selection are at the base of the extent of firms' heterogeneity within sectoral systems. Processes of variety creation generate new firms as well as new strategies and behavior. They are related to several mechanisms: entry, R&D, innovation and so on. Sectoral systems differ extensively in the processes of the creation of variety in products and technologies, and of heterogeneity among agents. On the contrary, processes of imitation and selection reduce heterogeneity.

Other types of agents in a sectoral system are *non-firm organizations* such as universities, financial organizations, government agencies, local authorities and so on. In various ways they support innovation, technological diffusion and production by firms. Again, their role differs greatly among sectoral systems. Think of venture capital and universities in biotechnology, local government in machine tools, the military in the early days of semiconductors and computers, and venture capital in software, biotechnology and multimedia.

As mentioned earlier, often the most appropriate units of analysis in specific sectoral systems are not necessarily firms. They could be *individuals*, *firm subunits* (such as the R&D or the production department) or *groups of firms* (such as industry consortia). For example, in sectoral systems such as biotechnology or software, inventors, scientists and engineers are key players. In biotechnology, a key unit of analysis is also the university department and the research laboratory. In electronics, R&D consortia or alliances for standards are often a more appropriate unit of analysis for the competitive process.

Within sectoral systems, heterogeneous agents are connected in various ways through *market and non-market relationships*. In this regard, it is possible to identify different types of relations, linked to different analytical approaches. First, traditional analyses of industrial organization have examined the agents involved in the processes of exchange, competition and command (such as vertical integration). Second, in more recent analyses, processes of *formal cooperation or informal interaction* among firms or between firms and non-firm organizations have been examined in depth (as in the literature on tacit or explicit collusion, hybrid governance forms or formal R&D cooperation). This literature has analyzed firms with certain market power, suppliers and users facing opportunistic behavior or asset specificities in transactions, and firms with similar knowledge and with appropriability and indivisibility problems in the R&D process. The evolutionary approach and the innovation systems literature have also paid considerable attention to the wide range of formal and informal interaction among firms. However, according to this perspective, in uncertain and changing environments networks emerge not because agents are similar but because they are different. Thus, networks allow access to and the integration of complementarities in knowledge, capabilities and specialization (see Lundvall, 1992; Edquist, 1997; Nelson, 1995; and Teubal, Yinnon and Zuscovitch, 1991). Market and non-market relationships may involve not just firms but also non-firm organizations. For example, in innovation, universities and public research centres may be a source of innovation and change in several sectors, such as pharmaceuticals and biotechnology, information technology and telecommunications (Nelson and Rosenberg, 1993).

The types and structures of relationships and networks differ from one sectoral system to another, as a consequence of the features of the knowledge base, the relevant learning processes, the basic technologies, the characteristics of demand, the key links and the dynamic complementarities. This will be clear in the chapters below, as, for example, in the case of pharmaceuticals with the switch from old drug discovery to modern biotechnology (McKelvey, Orsenigo and Pammolli, chapter 3 in this book), and in machine tools (Wengel and Shapira, chapter 7 in this book). Other examples can be found in complex systems industries, such as flight simulation (Miller et al., 1995).[3]

---

[3] A management scholar such as Porter has clearly understood these problems and issues. In his analysis of business strategies, Porter abandoned the traditional concept of industry and market quite early. He has attempted to enlarge it in various ways. In *Competitive Strategy* (1980) he discusses firms' strategies in industries, and provides a description of industry boundaries that moves away from the similarity of technical processes or substitutability in demand by also considering suppliers and buyers, and the threat of substitutes for products or services. In *Competitive Advantage* (1985) he discusses the value chain and the collection of activities that are performed to design, produce and market a product. Later, in discussing how nations can affect the way industries compete on the international scene (in *The Competitive Advantage of Nations*, 1990), he stresses the role of factor conditions (skilled labor, infrastructure and so on), demand conditions and related

## 4.3    Institutions

Finally, sectoral systems may greatly differ with respect to their typical institutions. Institutions include norms, routines, common habits, established practices, rules, laws, standards and so on, all of which shape agent cognition and action and affect interaction among agents (Edquist and Johnson, 1997; Coriat and Dosi, 1995; and Nelson and Sampat, 2000). Institutions and related organizations differ greatly in terms of types. They may range from those that bind or impose enforcements on agents to those that are created by interaction among agents (such as contracts); from more binding to less binding; from formal to informal (such as patent laws or specific regulations versus traditions and conventions) (Edquist and Johnson, 1997; and Coriat and Weinstein, 1999). In addition, many institutions are national (such as the patent system), while others are specific to sectoral systems, such as sectoral labor markets or sector-specific financial institutions. Other examples of sectoral institutions are disclosure agreements and standards in software or regulation in pharmaceuticals. Sectoral institutions may emerge either as a result of deliberate planned decisions by firms or other organizations, or as the unpredicted consequence of agents' interaction. This requires a careful examination of each specific case of sectoral system evolution.

National institutions may have major effects on sectoral systems, as, for example, the patent system, property rights or antitrust regulations. These effects may differ from sector to sector, as a consequence of the different features of these systems (as surveys and empirical analyses have shown: see, for example, Levin et al., 1987). However, the same institution may take on different features in different national systems, and thus may affect sectors differently in different countries. The well-known difference between the first-to-invent and the first-to-file rules in the patent system in the United States and in Japan had major consequences on the behavior of firms in the two countries.

In addition, national institutions and organizations may in the long run attract the industries most compatible with them. For example, this is the case with high-tech sectors in the United States. In France, sectors related to public demand have grown considerably (Chesnais, 1993). Thus, the pattern of a country's sectoral specialization may be greatly

and supporting industries (in addition to firm strategy, structure and rivalry). Finally, in his last work ("Clusters and the new economics of competition," 1998), Porter focuses on local knowledge, trust and relationships and culture as the basis of competition (better access to employees and suppliers; access to specialized information; complementarities of various kinds; coordination with local companies; better motivation; and access to institutions and public goods such as pool of skills, reputation and technology).

affected by its institutional characteristics. Similarly, mismatches between national agents and institutions and sectoral agents and institutions may take place. The examples of the different types of interaction between national institutions and sector evolution in various advanced countries discussed in Dosi and Malerba (1996) are cases in point.

However, the relationship between national institutions and sectoral systems is not always one-way, from national to sectoral. Sometimes the direction is reversed, and the relationship goes from the sectoral to the national level. The presence of different leading sectors in different countries may help explain the institutional differences between these countries. In fact it can happen that the institutions of a sector that is extremely important for a country, in terms of employment, competitiveness or strategic relevance, end up emerging as national, thus also becoming relevant for other sectors. However, one may also mention that, in the process of becoming national, sectoral institutions may change some of their original distinctive features.

### 4.4    Demand

The focus on users, customers, public procurement and regulation puts a different emphasis on the role of demand in sectoral systems and in the innovation process. As discussed in the previous sections, demand is composed of individual consumers, firms and the public sector, each characterized by knowledge, learning processes, competencies and goals, and each affected by social factors and institutions. Thus, in a sectoral system, demand is not seen as an aggregate set of similar buyers, but as being composed of heterogeneous agents the interaction of which with producers is shaped by institutions.

In general, demand is quite important, both in affecting innovation in sectors and in the emergence and transformation of sectoral systems. Differences in demand conditions influence sectoral differences in firms' competencies, behavior and organization. Sutton's discussion of the fragmentation of demand (1998), the role of networks externalities (Arthur, 1988; David, 1985; and Katz and Shapiro, 1985) and the presence of experimental users (Malerba et al., 2003) are examples of the key role of demand. Porter's (1976) broad sectoral taxonomy of demand conditions and their effects on firms' organizations and strategies is a first attempt to generate a taxonomy of demand. And, when demand conditions are coupled with some basic features of knowledge and technology, the effect on firms' innovative behavior and organization could be significant. For example, empirical and theoretical analyses of the evolution of the computer industry show complex and relevant relationships between demand, technology, knowledge base and the boundaries of firms (Bresnahan and Malerba, 1999; and Malerba et al., 1999b).

In general, demand constitutes both a stimulus for innovation and a major constraint. Together with technologies, demand defines the nature of the problems that firms have to solve in their innovative and production activities and the types of incentives and constraints on particular behaviors and organizations. However, within these constraints, great and persistent heterogeneity in firms' innovative and productive behavior and organization is present within a sectoral system.

## 5     The dynamics and transformation of sectoral systems

### 5.1     The dynamics of sectoral systems through processes of selection and variety generation

Two key evolutionary processes – variety creation and selection (Nelson, 1995; and Metcalfe, 1998) – affect industrial dynamics and account for many of its differences across sectoral systems. *Processes of variety creation* refer to products, technologies, firms and institutions as well as to strategies and behavior. As previously mentioned, they are related to several mechanisms: entry, R&D, innovation and so on. These mechanisms interact at various levels. For example, the emergence and growth of new sectoral institutions and organizations (such as new specialized departments within universities and new scientific and educational fields) increase variety and can be associated with the emergence of new technologies and new knowledge (Nelson and Rosenberg, 1993). See, for example, the case of the chemical industry, with the emergence of new departments and engineering degrees in universities in response to new technological developments in industry (Arora, Landau and Rosenberg, 1999). Sectoral systems differ extensively in the processes of creating a variety of products and technologies and heterogeneity among agents.

The creation of *new agents* – both new firms and non-firm organizations – is particularly important for the dynamics of sectoral systems. For example, new firms bring a variety of approaches, specialization and knowledge in the innovation and production processes. They contribute to major changes in the population of agents and to the transformation of technologies and products in a sector. As examined by Audretsch (1996) and Geroski (1995), among others, the role of new firms differs drastically from sector to sector (in terms of entry rates, composition and origin), and thus has quite different effects on the features of sectoral systems and their degree of change. Sectoral differences in the level and type of entry seem to be closely related to differences in the knowledge base, the level, diffusion and distribution of competencies, the presence of non-firm organizations (such as universities and venture capital) and the working of sectoral institutions (such as regulation or labor markets) (Audretsch, 1996; Malerba and Orsenigo, 1999; and Geroski, 1995).

*Processes of selection* play the key role of reducing heterogeneity. They may refer to different environments: firms, products, activities, technologies and so on. In addition to market selection, in several sectoral systems non-market selection processes are also at work (as in the cases of the involvement of the military, the health system and so on). In general, selection affects the growth and decline of the various groups of agents and the range of viable behaviors and organizations in a sectoral system (Metcalfe, 1998). Selection may be more or less intense and frequent. It differs greatly across sectoral systems.

## 5.2    *Coevolution and the transformation of sectoral systems*

Change is a distinctive feature of sectoral systems. However, change does not simply mean a quantitative growth of the variables of a sectoral system. It also means transformation and evolution.

During the evolution of sectoral systems change may occur in the technological and learning regimes and in the patterns of innovation. As previously mentioned, over time a change in regime may transform a Schumpeter Mark I pattern of innovative activities into a Schumpeter Mark II. Or, in the presence of major knowledge, technological or market discontinuities, a Schumpeter Mark II pattern of innovative activities may be replaced by a Schumpeter Mark I. In general, the knowledge base of innovative activities may change in two different ways: an evolution toward a dominant design, or a drastic change. In the first case, a growth of concentration and the rise of large dominant firms may take place (Utterback, 1994). In the second case, new types of competencies may be required for innovation, with major industrial turbulence, the entry of new firms and turnover in industrial leadership (Jovanovič and MacDonald, 1994; Tushman and Anderson, 1986; and Henderson and Clark, 1990). Finally, changes in demand, users and applications represent another major modification in the context in which firms operate, and may favor the entry of new firms rather than the success of established ones (Christensen and Rosenbloom, 1995).

From the previous claim that the elements of a sectoral system are closely connected, it follows that their change over time results in a *coevolutionary process* of its various elements. This process involves technology, demand, knowledge base, learning processes, firms, non-firm organizations and institutions. Nelson (1994) and Metcalfe (1998) have discussed these processes at the general level by focusing on the interaction between technology, industrial structure, institutions and demand.

These processes are *sector-specific*. For example, just looking at three elements, such as technology, demand and firms, in sectors characterized by a system product and consumers with a quite homogeneous demand, coevolution leads to the emergence of a dominant design and industrial concentration (Klepper, 1996). However, in sectors with a heterogeneous demand, competing technologies with lock-ins or network externalities and standards, specialized products and a more fragmented market structure may emerge.

Often coevolution is related to path-dependent processes (Arthur, 1988; and David, 1985). Here, local learning, interaction among agents and networks may generate increasing returns and irreversibilities that may lock sectoral systems into inferior technologies. The cases of sectors with competing technologies, such as nuclear energy (Cowan, 1990), cars (and their power sources – Foreman-Peck, 1996), metallurgy (ferrous casting – Foray and Grubler, 1990) and multimedia (VCRs – Cusumano, Mylonadis and Rosenbloom, 1992), are interesting examples of path-dependent processes.

Recent work, such as by Mowery and Nelson (1999) on the long-term evolution of sectors such as semiconductors, computers, software, pharmaceuticals and biotechnology, chemicals, medical devices and machine tools, has started to shed new light on coevolutionary processes over time and across countries. In Mowery and Nelson (1999) it is shown that these coevolutionary processes clearly differ among sectors. The example is given of the computer industry, the long-term development of which cannot just be described in terms of sales growth and the introduction over time of radically new products (such as the minicomputer, the microcomputer and computer networks) with different features and demand. Rather, in this sector complementarities between changes in components and changes in computer systems have affected firms' strategies. And a coevolutionary process involving technology, demand, institutions and firm organizations and strategies has characterized the whole history of the industry (Bresnahan and Malerba, 1999).

The transformation of sectors may involve not just traditionally defined sectors, as in Mowery and Nelson (1999), but the *emergence of new clusters* that span several sectors, such as Internet/software/telecommunications, biotechnology/pharmaceuticals and new materials. Here, transformation means the integration and fusion of previously separated knowledge and technologies, as well as new relations and dynamics among different types of users and consumers, firms with different specialization and competencies, and non-firm organizations and institutions, all of them grounded in previously separated sectors.

At the modeling level, one way to proceed in order to represent some aspects of the coevolution in different sectoral systems in a stylized form is through *history-friendly models* (Malerba et al., 1999a). Models of this type have been developed for the computer sector, software, semiconductors, chemicals and pharmaceuticals and biotechnology. Let us take by way of example a history-friendly model of the computer sector. This model refers to the dynamics of technology, firms' competencies, market structure and demand in the long run. However, the model also examines the changes that major technological and demand discontinuities have on market structure and the survival of established firms. In general, the model shows that technological discontinuities have been much more successfully absorbed by industry leaders than demand discontinuities. When a technological discontinuity takes place within an existing demand, incumbents may be able to absorb the major changes in the technology through the lock-in of existing customers. On the other hand, a major change in demand is often associated with changes in the related technologies, so that firms have to pass through several shifts in terms of knowledge, with major consequences for the entry and growth of new firms. These results emphasize the need to examine the possible trade-offs and complementarities between knowledge about technologies and knowledge about demand (Malerba et al., 2003). A second history-friendly model of the computer sector examines the organization of innovative and production activities in computers in terms of vertical integration or specialization when knowledge complementarities among components and systems are present. Vertical integration and specialization become the result of the dynamic interplay of knowledge, competencies and market structure, and – more broadly – of the coevolution of the upstream and downstream sectors (Malerba et al., 1999b). A history-friendly model of pharmaceuticals and biotechnology has different features in terms of demand, technical progress and appropriability conditions. It examines the relationships between the nature of the research space, demand, the patterns of competition and sector evolution in the age of random screening and in the age of molecular biology, and shows that concentration in pharmaceuticals is shaped by market fragmentation and lack of cumulativeness in innovative activities (Malerba and Orsenigo, 2002). Different features are present in the models of the chemical (Brenner and Murmann, 2003) and semiconductor sectors (Kim and Lee, 2003). Once developed for several sectoral systems, history-friendly models may allow comparative analyses of the patterns of structural evolution and industrial dynamics, the identification of commonalities across sectors and a better understanding of the factors behind structural evolution. In addition to firms, these models focus on several elements of sectoral systems: non-firm organizations, suppliers, users, institutions and public policy. In this way they could prove quite useful in the analysis of the interaction among several elements of the sectoral systems.

## 6          The regional and national dimensions

National boundaries are not always the most appropriate ones for an examination of the structure, agents and dynamics of sectoral systems. Often the boundaries are local, with the sectoral specialization defining the specialization of the whole area. For example, machinery is concentrated in specialized regional areas, single traditional sectors define the specialization of industrial districts in Italy, and sectoral specialization and local agglomeration have overlapped in Route 128 (for minicomputers) and in Silicon Valley (for PCs, software and microelectronics) (Saxenian, 1994).

Breschi and Malerba (1997) have provided some very simple examples of the geographical boundaries of sectoral systems by considering the relevant dimensions of technological regimes. Traditional sectors made up of many innovators, geographically dispersed with no specific knowledge/spatial boundaries, are associated with technological regimes with a low level of opportunity, appropriability and cumulativeness at the firm level with a knowledge base partly embodied in equipment and materials. Machinery located in industrial districts, with many innovators, geographically concentrated with local knowledge boundaries, is associated with technological regimes of medium opportunity, low appropriability and high cumulativeness at the firm level and a tacit and specific knowledge base. Automobiles, with few innovators, geographically concentrated with local knowledge boundaries, are associated with technological regimes characterized by high cumulativeness at the firm level and a system type of knowledge (which has some tacit components). Finally, modern microelectronics, software and microcomputers with many innovators, geographically concentrated with both local and global knowledge boundaries, are associated with very high opportunity conditions and a wide variety of potential technological approaches (Breschi and Malerba, 1997).

What do we know about the *interplay between sectoral systems and national (or local) systems?* One useful starting point is to assess the similarities and differences of the features and dynamics of the same sectoral system across countries or regions. As mentioned before, empirical research on the sectoral patterns of innovative activities in terms of innovative concentration, technological entry and innovative turbulence has confirmed not only that major differences exist across sectors, but also that, for any one sector, these patterns are quite similar across countries. This similarity in the sectoral patterns has been associated with features of technological regimes, knowledge base and learning processes that are quite invariant across countries (Breschi, Malerba and Orsenigo, 2000). However, differences in national innovation systems matter, and they affect some of the features that a sectoral system may take on in a country. For example, in analyses based on patents, national innovation systems affect the absolute values of the variables related to the innovative activities of firms. For example, on average, technological entry is lower in Germany and Japan than in the United States and the United Kingdom (Malerba and Orsenigo, 1996). This theme is further developed in this book by Casper and Soskice, in chapter 10.

A different but somewhat related issue concerns the *relationship between sectoral systems and the international performance of countries (regions)*. Again, this issue may be tackled from different angles. As previously mentioned, the relationship between the features of a sectoral system and the international performance of countries (regions) in that sector is mediated by the national (regional) institutions and non-firm organizations that form a national (regional) system of innovation and production. The identification of the link between specific elements – or the structure and dynamics – of a sectoral system on the one hand, and the successful international performance of countries (regions) on the other, is still ground to be covered by empirical research. Again, the most interesting attempt in this regard is the book by Mowery and Nelson (1999). By examining six sectors in the United States, Europe and Japan, they claim that the international competitiveness of countries is closely related to the presence of competent firms, interaction among firms (for example, with users and suppliers) and advanced non-firm organizations and institutions. These are factors that may be related to sectoral systems and that differ from one sectoral system to another. Chapter 11 in this book, by Coriat, Malerba and Montobbio, is devoted to this theme.

Finally, one last remark in relation to *multinational corporations*. These firms are active in specific sectors but span different regions and countries. The analysis of how these companies are able to profit from the specificities of the sectoral systems of various countries is therefore a matter of relevant empirical enquiry, but it will not be touched upon in this volume. The work by Cantwell and associates (Cantwell, 2003) has shed much light on these aspects. For example, a multinational firm operating in a specific sectoral system may locate its research laboratories in one country, have cooperation with a top university in another, produce and have links with key suppliers in still another, and so on.

## 7      The next chapters

In this chapter the basic concepts and the methodology regarding the analysis of sectoral systems of innovation and production have been presented and discussed. Summing up, a sector is defined as a set of activities that are unified by some linked product group for a given or emerging demand and that share some basic knowledge. Firms in sectors have commonalities and at the same time are heterogeneous. Innovation in sectors has relevant systemic features. In this book it is proposed that an SSI focuses on three main dimensions of sectors: (a) knowledge, technologies and demand; (b) actors and networks; (c) institutions. It has been claimed that, over time, existing sectoral systems undergo processes involving coevolution, transformation and the emergence of novelty.

A methodological remark concerns the level of aggregation. First of all, in a sectoral system there are different levels for the analysis of actors: individuals; firms' subunits; groups of firms; and non-firm organizations. Flexibility has to be used in the choice of the unit of analysis, the variables to be examined and the fine-grained study that has to be conducted. The same holds for products and sectoral boundaries. Sometimes it is necessary to analyze very broad sectoral systems, such as for computer hardware and software; at other times it is not. Particularly with respect to the emergence of new clusters, such as software/Internet/telecommunications, new materials and pharmaceuticals/biotechnology, a high level of aggregation is important. In any case, the goals and the objectives of the analysis should dictate the appropriate level of aggregation.

In sum, sectoral systems may prove a useful tool in various respects: for a descriptive analysis of sectors; for a full understanding of their working, dynamics and transformation; for the identification of the factors affecting the performance and competitiveness of firms and countries; and, finally, for the development of new public policy indications.

One remark has to be advanced about the impossibility of identifying "optimal" structures and "optimal" working for sectoral systems. In reality, some coherence among the various elements of a sectoral system does occur, and it develops over time as a result of both conscious design and unplanned processes. And mismatches among the various parts and variables of sectoral systems can be identified and eventually eliminated.

But the actual coherence is far from being "optimal." The same is true for the working of sectoral systems. Sectoral systems may take on different features in different countries, and in different times. And in continuously changing environments, with historical processes embedded in different countries, there is no way to identify an "optimal" sectoral system.

Following the approach outlined in this chapter, the next chapter links the above discussion with the broad concept of innovation systems and presents some data and stylized facts about sectoral systems. Then six studies of sectoral systems in Europe are presented: pharmaceuticals and biotechnology (chapter 3); chemicals (chapter 4); telecommunications equipment and services (chapter 5); software (chapter 6); machine tools (chapter 7); and services (chapter 8).

REFERENCES

Arora, A., R. Landau and N. Rosenberg (1999), Dynamics of comparative advantage in the chemical industry, in D. C. Mowery and R. R. Nelson (eds.), *Sources of Industrial Leadership: Studies of Seven Industries*, Cambridge University Press, Cambridge, 217–266

Arthur, B. (1988), Competing technologies, increasing returns and lock-ins by historical events, *Economic Journal*, 99, 116–131

Audretsch, D. B. (1996), *Innovation and Industry Evolution*, MIT Press, Cambridge, MA

Bain, J. (1956), *Barriers to New Competition*, Harvard University Press, Cambridge, MA

Brenner, T., and P. Murmann (2003) *The Use of Simulations in Developing Robust Knowledge about Causal Processes: Methodological Considerations and an Application to Industrial Evolution*, working paper, Max Planck Institute, Jena

Breschi, S., and F. Malerba (1997), Sectoral systems of innovation: technological regimes, Schumpeterian dynamics and spatial boundaries, in C. Edquist (ed.), *Systems of Innovation: Technologies, Institutions and Organizations*, Frances Pinter, London, 130–155

Breschi, S., F. Malerba and L. Orsenigo (2000), Technological regimes and Schumpeterian patterns of innovation, *Economic Journal*, 110, 388–410

Bresnahan, T. F., and F. Malerba (1999), Industrial dynamics and the evolution of firms' and nations' competitive capabilities in the world computer industry, in D. C. Mowery and R. R. Nelson (eds.), *Sources of Industrial Leadership: Studies of Seven Industries*, Cambridge University Press, Cambridge, 79–132

Callon, M. (1992), The dynamics of techno-economic networks, in R. Coombs, P. Saviotti and V. Walsh (eds.), *Technical Change and Company Strategies*, Academy Press, London

Cantwell, J. (2003), Innovation and competitiveness, in J. Fagerberg, D. Mowery and R. R. Nelson (eds.), *Handbook of Innovation*, Cambridge University Press, Cambridge, forthcoming

Carlsson, B. (1995), *Technological Systems and Economic Performance: The Case of Factory Automation*, Kluwer, Dordrecht

Carlsson, B., and R. Stankiewicz (1995), On the nature, function and composition of technological systems, in B. Carlsson (ed.), *Technological Systems and Economic Performance: The Case of Factory Automation*, Kluwer, Dordrecht

Chesnais, F. (1993), The French national system of innovation, in R. R. Nelson (ed.), *National Innovation Systems: A Comparative Analysis*, Oxford University Press, Oxford

Christensen, C., and R. Rosenbloom (1995), Explaining the attacker advantage, *Research Policy*, 23, 2, 237–257

Cohen, W., and D. Levinthal (1989), Innovation and learning: the two faces of R&D, *Economic Journal*, 99, 569–596

Cooke, P., M. Gomez Uranga and G. Extebarria (1998), Regional innovation systems: institutional and organizational dimensions, *Research Policy*, 26, 4/5, 475–491

Coriat, B., and G. Dosi (1995), *Learning How to Govern and Learning How to Solve Problems*, working paper, International Institute for Applied System Analysis, Laxenburg, Austria

Coriat, B., and O. Weinstein (1999), *Organizations and Institutions in the Innovation Generation*, Centre de Recherche en Economie Industrielle Internationale, Université Paris XIII

Cowan, R. (1990), Nuclear power reactors: a study in technological lock-in, *Journal of Economic History*, 50, 3, 541–567

Cowan, R., P. David and D. Foray (2000), The explicit economics of knowledge codification and tacitness, *Industrial and Corporate Change*, 9, 2, 211–253

Cusumano, M., Y. Mylonadis and R. Rosenbloom (1992), Strategic maneuvering and mass-market dynamics: the triumph of VHS over Beta, *Business History Review*, 66, 51–94

Dahmen, E. (1989), Development blocks in industrial economics, in B. Carlsson (ed.), *Industrial Dynamics*, Kluwer, Dordrecht

David, P. (1985), Clio and the economics of QWERTY, *American Economic Review*, 75, 2, 332–337

Dosi, G. (1988), Sources, procedures and microeconomic effects of innovation, *Journal of Economic Literature*, 26, 120–171

(1997), Opportunities, incentives and the collective patterns of technological change, *Economic Journal*, 107, 1,530–1,547

Dosi, G., and F. Malerba (1996), *Organization and Strategy in the Evolution of the Enterprise*, Macmillan, London

Dosi, G., L. Marengo and G. Fagiolo (1996), *Learning in Evolutionary Environments*, International Institute for Applied System Analysis, working paper, Laxenburg, Austria

Edquist, C. (ed.) (1997), *Systems of Innovation: Technologies, Institutions and Organizations*, Frances Pinter, London

Edquist, C., and B. Johnson (1997), Institutions and organizations in systems of innovation, in C. Edquist (ed.), *Systems of Innovation: Technologies, Institutions and Organizations*, Frances Pinter, London

Foray, D., and A. Grubler (1990), Morphological analysis, diffusion and lock-out of technologies: ferrous casting in France and the FRG, *Research Policy*, 19, 5, 535–550

Foreman-Peck, J. (1996), *Technological Lock-In and the Power Source for the Motor Car*, discussion paper in economics, University of Oxford

Fransmann, M. (1994), Information, knowledge, vision and theories of the firm, *Industrial and Corporate Change*, 3, 2, 1–45

Freeman, C. (1982), *The Economics of Industrial Innovation*, Frances Pinter, London

(1987), *Technology Policy and Economic Performance: Lessons from Japan*, Frances Pinter, London

Geroski, P. (1995), What do we know about entry? *International Journal of Industrial Organization*, 4, 421–440

(1998), Thinking creatively about markets, *International Journal of Industrial Organization*, 16, 6, 677–698

Gort, M., and S. Klepper (1982), Time paths in the diffusion of product innovations, *Economic Journal*, 92, 630–653

Granstrand, O. (1994), *The Economics of Technology*, Elsevier Science, Amsterdam

Granstrand, O., P. Patel and K. Pavitt (1997), Multi-technology corporations: why they have "distributed" rather than "distinctive core" competencies, *California Management Review*, 39, 4, 8–25

Henderson, R. (1994), The evolution of integrative capabilities: innovation in cardiovascular drug discovery, *Industrial and Corporate Change*, 3, 3, 607–630

Henderson, R., and K. Clark (1990), Architectural innovation, *Administrative Science Quarterly*, 35, 9–30

Hughes, T. P. (1984), The evolution of large technological systems, in W. Bijker, T. P. Hughes and T. Pinch (eds.), *The Social Construction of Technological Systems*, MIT Press, Cambridge, MA

Iansiti, M. (1998), *Technology Integration*, Harvard Business School Press, Boston

Iansiti, M., and K. Clark (1994), Integration and dynamic capabilities: evidence from product development in automobiles and mainframe computers, *Industrial and Corporate Change*, 3, 3, 557–605

Jovanovič, B., and G. M. MacDonald (1994), The life cycle of a competitive industry, *Journal of Political Economy*, 102, 2, 322–347

Katz, M., and C. Shapiro (1985), Network externalities, competition and compatibility, *American Economic Review*, 75, 3, 424–440

Kim, C., and K. Lee (2003), Innovation technological regimes and organizational selection in industry evolution: a history-friendly model of the DRAM industry, *Industrial and Corporate Change*, 12, 6, forthcoming

Klepper, S. (1996), Entry, exit, growth and innovation over the product life cycle, *American Economic Review*, 86, 3, 562–583

Lane, D. (1993), Artificial worlds and economics, Part 1, *Journal of Evolutionary Economics*, 3, 2, 89–107

Langlois, R. (1995), Cognition and capabilities: opportunities seized and missed in the history of the computer industry, in R. Garud, Z. Nayyar and P. Shapira (eds.), *Technological Entrepreneurship: Oversights and Foresights*, Cambridge University Press, New York

Levin, R. C., A. K. Klevorick, R. R. Nelson and S. G. Winter (1987), Appropriating the returns from industrial research and development, *Brookings Papers on Economic Activity*, 3, 783–831

Lundvall, B.-Å. (1992), *National Systems of Innovation: Towards a Theory of Innovation and Interactive Learning*, Frances Pinter, London

Lundvall, B.-Å., and B. Johnson (1994), The learning economy, *Journal of Industry Studies*, 1, 2, 23–42

Malerba, F. (1992), Learning by firms and incremental technical change, *Economic Journal*, 102, 845–859

(1993) Italy, in R. Nelson (ed.), *National Innovation Systems: A Comparative Study*, Oxford University Press, Oxford

Malerba, F., R. R. Nelson, L. Orsenigo and S. G. Winter (1999a), History-friendly models of industry evolution: the case of the computer industry, *Industrial and Corporate Change*, 8, 1, 3–40

(1999b), *Vertical Integration and Specialization in the Evolution of the Computer Industry: Towards a History-Friendly Model*, mimeograph

(2003), *Demand, Innovation and the Dynamics of Market Structure: The Role of Experimental Users and Diverse Preferences*, Working Paper no. 135, Centre di Ricerca sui Processi di Innovazione e Internazionalizzazione, Università Bocconi, Milan

Malerba, F., and L. Orsenigo (1993), Technological regimes and firm behavior, *Industrial and Corporate Change*, 2, 1, 45–74

(1996), Schumpeterian patterns of innovation, *Cambridge Journal of Economics*, 19, 1, 47–65

(1997), Technological regimes and sectoral patterns of innovative activities, *Industrial and Corporate Change*, 6, 1, 83–117

(1999), Technological entry, exit and survival: an empirical analysis of patent data, *Research Policy*, 28, 6, 643–660

(2000), Knowledge, innovative activities and industrial evolution, *Industrial and Corporate Change*, 9, 2, 289–314

(2002) Innovation and market structure in the dynamics of the pharmaceutical industry and biotechnology: towards a history-friendly model, *Industrial and Corporate Change*, 11, 4, 667–703

Marsili, O., and B. Verspagen (2002), Technology and the dynamics of industrial structures: an empirical mapping of Dutch manufacturing, *Industrial and Corporate Change*, 11, 4, 791–815

Metcalfe, S. (1998), *Evolutionary Economics and Creative Destruction*, Routledge, London

Miller, R., M. Hobday, T. Leroux-Demers and X. Olleros (1995), Innovation in complex systems: the case of flight simulation, *Industrial and Corporate Change*, 4, 2, 363–400

Mowery, D. C., and R. R. Nelson (eds.) (1999), *Sources of Industrial Leadership: Studies of Seven Industries*, Cambridge University Press, Cambridge

Nelson, R. R. (ed.) (1993), *National Innovation Systems: A Comparative Analysis*, Oxford University Press, Oxford

(1994), The coevolution of technology, industrial structure and supporting institutions, *Industrial and Corporate Change*, 3, 1, 47–64

(1995), Recent evolutionary theorizing about economic change, *Journal of Economic Literature*, 33, 1, 48–90

Nelson, R. R., and N. Rosenberg (1993), Technical innovation and national systems, in R. R. Nelson (ed.), *National Innovation Systems: A Comparative Analysis*, Oxford University Press, Oxford

Nelson, R. R., and B. N. Sampat (2000), Making sense of institutions as a factor shaping economic performance, *Journal of Economic Behavior and Organization*, forthcoming

Nelson, R. R., and S. G. Winter (1982), *An Evolutionary Theory of Economic Change*, Belknapp Press of Harvard University Press, Cambridge, MA

Patel, P., and K. Pavitt (1997), Technological competencies in the world's largest firms: complex and path-dependent, but not much variety, *Research Policy*, 26, 2, 141–156

Pavitt, K. (1984), Sectoral patterns of technical change: towards a taxonomy and a theory, *Research Policy*, 13, 6, 343–373

Porter, M. (1976), *Interbrand Choice, Strategy, and Bilateral Market Power*, Harvard University Press, Cambridge, MA

(1980), *Competitive Strategy*, Free Press, New York

(1985), *Competitive Advantage*, Free Press, New York

(1990), *The Competitive Advantage of Nations*, Macmillan, London

(1998), Clusters and the new economics of competition, *Harvard Business Review*, 76, 6, 77–90

Robson, M., J. Townsend and K. Pavitt (1988), Sectoral patterns of production and use of innovations in the UK: 1945–1983, *Research Policy*, 17, 1–14

Rosenberg, N. (1976), *Perspectives on Technology*, Cambridge University Press, Cambridge

(1982), *Inside the Black Box*, Cambridge University Press, Cambridge

Saxenian, A. (1994), *Regional Advantage: Culture and Competition in Silicon Valley and Route 128*, Harvard University Press, Cambridge, MA

Scherer, F. M. (1982), Inter-industry technology flows in the United States, *Research Policy*, 11, 4, 227–245

(1990), *Industrial Market Structure and Economic Performance*, Houghton Mifflin, Boston

Sutton, J. (1991), *Sunk Costs and Market Structure*, MIT Press, Cambridge, MA

(1998), *Technology and Market Structure*, MIT Press, Cambridge, MA

Teece, D., and G. P. Pisano (1994), The dynamic capabilities of firms: an introduction, *Industrial and Corporate Change*, 3, 3, 537–556

Teubal, M., T. Yinnon and E. Zuscovitch (1991), Networks and market creation, *Research Policy*, 20, 3, 381–392

Tirole, J. (1988), *The Theory of Industrial Organization*, MIT Press, Cambridge, MA

Tushman, M., and P. Anderson (1986), Technological discontinuities and organizational environments, *Administrative Science Quarterly*, 31, 3, 439–465

Utterback, J. (1994), *Mastering the Dynamics of Innovation*, Harvard Business School Press, Boston

Von Hippel, E. (1988), *The Sources of Innovation*, Oxford University Press, New York

Winter, S. G. (1984), Schumpeterian competition in alternative technological regimes, *Journal of Economic Behaviour and Organisation*, 5, 287–320

(1987), Knowledge and competences as strategic assets, in D. Teece (ed.), *The Competitive Challenge*, Ballinger, Cambridge

# 2 Sectoral dynamics and structural change: stylized facts and "system of innovation" approaches

*Fabio Montobbio*

## 1 Introduction

The purpose of this chapter is to provide some aggregate evidence on the differences among sectors in terms of innovative activities and trends of relevant economic variables, such as value added, employment and labor productivity. It draws an aggregate picture in terms of stylized facts and open issues, with a specific focus on the sectors that are the subject of the different case studies of this book. It complements the conceptual discussion in chapter 1 and assesses the way sectoral differences have fostered structural changes in the last twenty years in industrialized countries. It points out the different innovative and economic performances of industrialized countries in each sector. Finally, it discusses the way the literature on systems of innovation can tackle these processes of sectoral transformation and provide analytical insights.

The point of departure is that – in the long run – the main source of growth is related to the ability to create, diffuse and adopt new ideas and apply them to economic activities, and that knowledge and technologies develop unevenly across both sectors and countries (Dosi, Pavitt and Soete, 1990; Nelson, 1991; Nelson and Wright, 1992; Fagerberg, Guerrieri and Versagen, 1999; and Mowery and Nelson, 1999). In particular, creation, adoption and diffusion occur at different rates across sectors, and in different periods of economic history we observe different waves of technical change characterized by specific technological traits.

An enormous amount of literature has shown in the last twenty years that sectors are different along many dimensions, as thoroughly recounted in the previous chapter on sectoral systems. The organizational rules and institutional arrangements – according to which technical change processes take place – vary with the knowledge and technological intensity of the sector because different knowledge bases require different sources of information and different problem-solving procedures (Dosi, 1997, 1988). Secondly, the likelihood of innovation and the variety of possible solutions are different according to the specific set of technological characteristics and opportunity conditions. Finally, economic agents are also influenced in their innovative choices by the structure of incentives, which, in turn, are affected by the appropriability conditions (Levin et al., 1987; and Breschi, Malerba and Orsenigo, 2000). In fact, sectors not only display differences in the technological domain but also in economic variables and in their relationships.

In parallel, we observe international differences in growth rates, labor productivity, innovative performance and export dynamics. This chapter accepts the view that the ability of countries to create and reproduce differentiated technological knowledge over time can explain a great part of these differences. These international differences are affected by the sectoral distribution of economic and technological activities at country level (Dosi, Pavitt and Soete, 1990, chapters 3 and 5; Fagerberg, 1988; and Amable and Verspagen, 1995). This, in turn, is affected by specific and cumulative national trajectories (characterized to some extent by institutional and technological irreversibilities), by the sectoral world market share dynamics and by the sectoral composition of demand, which guides the pace of structural change within countries (Dosi, Pavitt and Soete, 1990; Fagerberg, Guerrieri and Versagen, 1999; Mowery and Nelson, 1999; and Montobbio, 2003). The institutional and organizational elements driving these trajectories are more important than the relative adjustments between sectors based on relative factor prices and quantities.

This chapter is organized as follows. The first part of section 2 draws the macro-picture on sectoral differences and the patterns of structural changes in the composition of technological and economic activities in Europe, the United States and Japan. In particular, attention is focused on patenting activity, which is assessed in different technological classes. Structural change is detected; expanding and declining sectors are singled out. Moreover, the extent to which these patterns of differentiated sectoral growth can affect performances at country level is assessed. Changes in terms of world patent shares are decomposed in order to catch the sectoral and the country-specific components. This analysis sheds some light on the determinants of innovative activity at country level: whether it depends upon diffused relative improvements in all sectors; upon the type of technological specialization (which can be oriented toward classes with high or low technological opportunities); or, finally, upon the ability to adapt, change and enter in innovative sectors. The second part of the empirical analysis is more strictly related to the case studies of this book, and, accordingly, it assesses the economic and innovative relevance and the dynamics of chemicals, pharmaceuticals and biotechnology, telecommunications equipment and machine tools.

The stylized facts suggest a picture that is different from the one drawn during the second half of the 1980s, when the idea of national systems of innovation and of national technological capabilities was used to explain the process of catching up and convergence. The US economy recovered well and improved export and patent shares in many industries (in particular in high-technology sectors). Japan, conversely, is still struggling to exit a deep economic crisis. At the same time, Finland and Sweden experienced a very high rate of growth of value added, productivity, export and patent shares in the telecoms sector. Also, Italy, France, Germany and Spain had different patterns of growth in their patent and export shares across sectors. In the last section we suggest that a sectoral perspective along the dimensions of the "sectoral system" can be conducive to a better understanding of the relationship between structural changes and these different national trajectories.

## 2    Innovation, performance and structural change in European Union countries, the United States and Japan

Chapter 1 of this book discusses the dimensions along which sectors differ, and, at a conceptual level, the main processes that can explain different sectoral dynamics in innovation activities. These processes provide an interpretative key to understanding different countries' innovative performances in different sectors, and patterns of structural change (within each country). In this regard, this section provides some introductory quantitative evidence on sectoral differences in innovative and economic variables (2.1) and the impact of structural change on innovative performance at country level (2.2). While section 2 considers a large number of technological classes at a fairly high level of disaggregation, section 3 focuses on the four big manufacturing sectors examined in this book.

### 2.1    *Structural changes*

A large amount of evidence shows that sectors continuously displayed different rates of innovation activities and developed unevenly in the last decade (OECD, 2001a, 2001b; and National Science Board [NSB], 2000). Structural change has been detected for aggregate groups of sectors – such as agriculture, manufacturing and services – or for large industries (e.g. two-digit International Standard Industrial Classification [ISIC] rev. 3). In the last ten years R&D activity in telecommunications and computers and related activities grew steadily above the average trend for business R&D. The same holds for information and communication technologies (ICT) patent applications to the European Patent Office (EPO – OECD, 2001a). Wide differences across sectors are also observed in terms of (constant price) value added and labor productivity (see tables 2.3 and 2.5; and OECD, 2001a, 2001b). In the European Union, the United States and Japan, labor productivity has grown more rapidly in office machinery and equipment (which include computers) and telecommunications. Some service sectors, such as banking and finance, have also displayed above-average labor productivity growth rates.

The dynamics of the value added in the last twenty years display considerable sectoral differences. Telecommunications, computers, computer activities and services and then pharmaceuticals (all relatively high-tech sectors) are at the top of the ranking. Machinery and transport equipment exhibit a much lower contribution to national gross domestic product (GDP – table 2.3). The pattern is similar when employment dynamics are analyzed. With the exception of computer equipment, the sectors that create more value added in the industrialized countries also create more employment, with computer services and pharmaceuticals at the top (table 2.4). This translates into high productivity gains for telecommunications and computer equipment and slow growth for computer services, as we would expect from tertiary sectors (table 2.5). There is also a remarkable degree of turbulence and structural change within these broad sectors. This does not emerge in commonly used statistics, but it has, nonetheless, an important explanatory power in terms of industrial dynamics and country innovative performances (OECD, 2001a, 2001b).

These patterns are associated with differences in countries' innovative performances. So, it is worthwhile enquiring which countries are ahead in driving these structural changes, which countries seem to be able to adapt and change, and – finally – which countries seem to be penalized by being specialised in sectors with a relatively low level of technological opportunity. This chapter performs this analysis at a high level of disaggregation. We consider 135 technological classes in three industrial sectors: chemicals, electronics and machinery. In particular, we have sixty-one chemical technological classes, thirty-eight electronic technological classes and thirty-six machinery technological classes. The complete list of the technological classes and the concordance with international patent classification (IPC) can be found in Grupp and Munt (1995). Here patent data are reclassified in terms of economically meaningful technological classes (different from the IPC ones), in order to assess the patterns of structural change at a high level of disaggregation and the impact on countries' innovative performances. The data set is composed of patent applications to EPO.[1] Sixteen countries are considered: the United States, Japan and fourteen in the European Union. The period covered is from 1978 to 1998, and the values are averages on two subperiods: 1978 to 1982 and 1994 to 1998.[2]

In the structural decomposition analysis the following symbols are used:

$i$ = subscript that refers to technological classes;

$j$ = subscript that refers to countries;

$t-1$, $t$ = superscripts that refer to the initial subperiod – 1978 to 1982 – and to the final subperiod – 1994 to 1998 – of comparison respectively;

$P_{ij}$ = amount of country j's patent applications at EPO in sector i;

$p_{ij} = P_{ij}/\sum_j P_{ij}$ = share of world patents of country j in technological class i;

$p_j = \sum_i P_{ij}/\sum_i \sum_j P_{ij}$ = aggregate share of world patents of country j;

$s_i = \sum_j P_{ij}/\sum_i \sum_j P_{ij}$ = share of world patent of technological class i.

The two decades that we consider display relevant structural changes. Table 2.1 shows the values of sectoral shares at the beginning and end of the period and their rates of change.

$$ds_i = \left(s_i^t - s_i^{t-1}\right)/s_i^{t-1}$$

The results are displayed excluding fifty very small classes (representing 5 percent of the total amount of patents in the second subperiod) and selecting only the thirty significant classes with the highest and lowest values of $ds_i$. In the first group there are technological classes related to pharmaceuticals, biotechnology, telecommunications, electronics and instruments (plus detergents and cosmetics). No classes from the machinery industry are among the top fifteen. Conversely, all the traditional classes in the chemical, electronics and machinery industries record decreased shares in total patent activity. In particular, the quantitatively most important ones are in the chemical industry (insecticides and heterocyclic compounds).

Within these sectoral patterns of structural change, variation across countries, in terms of patent shares, is observed. For each technological

[1] The CESPRI/EPO data set has 1,021,266 patent applications for the period 1978 to 1998. In cases of international co-patenting activity each country has been credited with the patent. Our 135 classes cover approximately 68 percent of EPO's patents.

[2] Since technological classes in the ISI concordance (Grupp and Munt, 1995) are small, patent counts at this level of disaggregation for a single year and a single country can be subject to the volatility of the time required to file a patent application.

class the *change* in the country j share of total patents has been calculated (see table 2.1).

$$\Delta p_{ij} = p_{ij}^t - p_{ij}^{t-1}$$

Three major European Union countries (Germany, France and the United Kingdom) experienced a decline in terms of patent share in almost all the "high-growth" technological classes (with a few exceptions).[3] Conversely, the United States and, to some extent, Japan improved their patent shares in the high-opportunity technological classes. The results for the other European countries show improvements in telecommunications equipment (elek41 and elek43) in the patent shares of Finland and Sweden. In these classes (which are the biggest in the sample) there is a sharp fall for Germany and a general decline for Switzerland.

Similar country patterns – even though more nuanced – emerge for the fifteen declining classes. Germany and Italy improved their shares in the machinery sectors. Japan improved its shares considerably in almost all classes, while the United Kingdom had declining shares. The United States lost shares in important machinery classes (such as valves and metalworking) and gained shares in big chemical classes (such as insecticides and heterocyclic compounds).

In the other technological classes not included in table 2.1 there is a decline in the shares for Germany and the United States and a gain for Japan for all the biggest classes in electronics (such as diodes, transistors, microphones and speakers, recorders, typewriters and computer chips), with radio engineering devices being the most relevant exception. Germany and Italy gained shares in two big machinery classes (machines for food processing and conveyors), which have a below-average rate of growth. Finally, a decline for Switzerland in two chemical classes (in particular antibiotics and vitamins) and a gain for Sweden in electronic classes such as X-rays, control panels, circuits and transformers can be observed. Sweden also seems to be exiting some mechanical sectors, such as machines for packaging, paper production, construction and mining. Spain, which in percentage terms has recorded a fourfold increase in its country share (similar to Italy), improved in declining classes in the machinery (machines for agriculture and food processing) and electronic sectors (electric heating and insulators).

In summary, this preliminary evidence shows relevant structural change in innovative activity: the increased weight of high-tech sectors such as pharmaceuticals and biotechnology, telecommunications,

[3] The particularly bad result for Germany might also be due to institutional factors, which increased the volume of German patent applications to EPO during its early years.

Table 2.1 *Structural changes and variations in countries' share*

| Fifteen classes with the highest growth of $s_i$ | | Technological class shares and changes | | | Changes in country share ($\Delta p_i$) | | | | | |
|---|---|---|---|---|---|---|---|---|---|---|
| | | $s_i^{t-1}$ | $s_i^t$ | $ds_i$ | Germany | France | United Kingdom | Italy | Japan | United States |
| Compounds with nitrogen function | chem54 | 0.03 | 0.62 | 21.88 | -10.66 | -1.73 | 4.82 | 3.33 | -24.35 | 14.02 |
| Lasers | elek15b | 0.15 | 0.55 | 2.56 | -5.30 | 0.23 | 0.04 | -0.39 | 3.10 | 0.63 |
| Micro-organisms and vaccines | chem73 | 1.02 | 3.23 | 2.18 | -7.28 | -1.95 | -0.02 | 0.36 | -5.55 | 9.82 |
| Other pharmaceutical products | chem76 | 0.27 | 0.72 | 1.63 | -15.10 | -0.50 | -8.29 | 0.86 | 5.30 | 18.67 |
| Cosmetics (not soaps) | chem77 | 0.37 | 0.90 | 1.44 | -7.09 | 20.78 | -5.44 | 0.25 | 0.20 | -0.96 |
| Telephones (not mobile phones) | elek43 | 2.24 | 5.11 | 1.28 | -13.43 | -10.17 | -0.01 | -0.85 | 8.00 | 5.61 |
| Hormones and derivatives | chem72 | 0.26 | 0.56 | 1.16 | -21.60 | -1.98 | -4.38 | 1.39 | 3.82 | 21.78 |
| Computers and equipment | elek31 | 1.77 | 3.52 | 0.99 | -3.96 | -1.23 | -1.12 | 0.06 | 8.98 | -6.81 |
| Other special medicines | chem75 | 0.87 | 1.67 | 0.92 | -7.16 | -2.46 | -2.53 | 1.42 | -0.41 | 7.65 |
| TVs, radios, TV cameras, video cameras and antennas | elek41 | 2.25 | 4.05 | 0.80 | -13.56 | -9.91 | -1.85 | 0.70 | 13.79 | 1.57 |
| Electrical diagnostic devices (not X-rays) | elek61 | 0.87 | 1.46 | 0.67 | -10.89 | -0.84 | -0.21 | 0.25 | -10.52 | 20.06 |
| Photocopying machines and equipment | elek33 | 0.20 | 0.31 | 0.58 | -15.27 | -2.10 | 0.50 | 0.04 | 14.32 | 1.39 |

| | | | | | | | | | | |
|---|---|---|---|---|---|---|---|---|---|---|
| Proteins | chem102 | 0.40 | 0.59 | 0.46 | −7.75 | −0.62 | −3.28 | 1.09 | 1.36 | 3.51 |
| Cables (without ignition) | elek521 | 1.88 | 2.60 | 0.38 | −5.23 | −5.64 | −2.43 | 1.25 | 15.27 | −7.91 |
| Detergents | chem83 | 0.53 | 0.72 | 0.37 | 2.86 | −0.61 | −11.39 | 0.13 | 1.82 | 18.36 |
| *Fifteen classes with the lowest growth of $s_i$* | | | | | | | | | | |
| Valves | masch24b | 0.58 | 0.38 | −0.34 | 6.08 | −7.07 | −7.73 | 2.88 | 5.86 | −4.73 |
| Other machines | masch28 | 0.35 | 0.22 | −0.36 | 2.66 | −4.55 | −0.51 | 6.92 | 5.02 | −10.21 |
| Switches and fuses | elek513 | 0.88 | 0.55 | −0.37 | −3.24 | 0.41 | −3.07 | 3.58 | −2.41 | 2.93 |
| Torches and furnaces | masch19 | 0.79 | 0.49 | −0.38 | 2.59 | −2.99 | −5.35 | 3.04 | 3.60 | −1.52 |
| Metalworking rolling mills | masch17 | 0.78 | 0.48 | −0.39 | 11.38 | −3.45 | −5.14 | 4.74 | 7.89 | −5.03 |
| Nuclear power reactors | masch4 | 0.49 | 0.29 | −0.40 | −2.51 | −23.87 | −0.18 | 1.56 | 2.30 | 11.22 |
| Steam boilers | masch11 | 0.43 | 0.25 | −0.42 | 4.42 | −6.07 | −4.92 | 3.77 | 9.20 | −9.13 |
| Hydrocarbons | chem51 | 0.50 | 0.28 | −0.44 | −19.62 | 6.14 | −6.13 | 1.03 | 7.68 | 11.39 |
| Insecticides | chem92 | 5.13 | 2.80 | −0.45 | −12.13 | −0.44 | −4.12 | 1.18 | 5.03 | 9.94 |
| Additives for mineral oil etc. | chem12 | 1.05 | 0.57 | −0.46 | −8.65 | −1.06 | −4.06 | 1.07 | 8.65 | −1.29 |
| Ether and alcohol peroxide | chem58 | 0.92 | 0.49 | −0.46 | −7.87 | −0.43 | −2.03 | 1.66 | 3.11 | 9.49 |
| Other chemicals | chem13 | 0.70 | 0.37 | −0.47 | −10.59 | −0.80 | −3.58 | 2.60 | 9.67 | 0.56 |
| Heterocyclic compounds | chem56 | 3.96 | 2.10 | −0.47 | −15.61 | 0.14 | −3.08 | 1.28 | 6.71 | 11.42 |
| Carbon acid | chem53 | 0.92 | 0.39 | −0.57 | −12.54 | 0.16 | −1.55 | −1.72 | 8.48 | 8.21 |
| Synthetic organic colors and varnishes | chem61 | 0.76 | 0.28 | −0.63 | −26.17 | −0.70 | 0.30 | −0.62 | 15.53 | 9.82 |

computers and related services compared to chemicals, machinery and many technological classes related to electronics. Evidence suggests that the underlying processes encompass both innovative activities (in terms of R&D and patents) and economic variables (such as value added, employment and productivity).

This is associated with some country patterns: in Europe, Germany, France and the United Kingdom tend to have declining shares of patents, especially in high-growth classes. Finland and Sweden improve their shares in telecommunications and electronics. Italy and Spain improve their patent shares in sectors with a declining weight in world patents. Japan improves everywhere, and in particular in electronics. Finally, US patent share gains are mainly concentrated in expanding technological classes.

## 2.2    *Structural decomposition of patent share dynamics*

The "structural decomposition" methodology is now used in order to describe the different components of countries' improvements or declines in terms of world patents,[4] and to give a concise picture of the impact of structural changes on the country performances outlined above.

Accordingly, the change of country j's aggregate share of world patents can be written as

$$\Delta p_j = p_j^t - p_j^{t-1} = \mathrm{SH}_j + \mathrm{ST}_j + \mathrm{AD}_j \tag{1}$$

$\mathrm{SH}_j = \sum_i (\Delta p_{ij} s_i^{t-1})$; $\mathrm{SH}_j$ measures the *technology share effect*, which is the gain/loss of world share of country j, assuming that the world sectoral structure of patenting activities is fixed across time. This shows country j's innovative performance on the assumption that there is no structural change, and its specific position with respect to changes in technological opportunities worldwide.

$\mathrm{ST}_j = \sum_i (p_{ij}^{t-1} \Delta s_i)$; $\mathrm{ST}_j$ measures the *structural technology effect*, which indicates what the change in country j's share of world patent would be if its shares in individual sectors remained constant. $\mathrm{ST}_j$ shows whether a country increases (decreases) its share as a consequence of a "right" ("wrong") initial technological specialization. Since $p_{ij}$ is fixed, changes are guided by $\Delta s_i$, which indicates the growth in terms of technological opportunities of sector i at the world level.

---

[4] I follow the contributions of Fagerberg and Sollie (1987), which develops a new version of the methodology, and Laursen (1999), which applies it for the first time to the patenting activities of the OECD countries.

$AD_j = \sum_i(\Delta p_{ij}\Delta s_i)$; $AD_j$ measures the degree to which country j is successful in transforming the sectoral composition of its technological activities according to structural changes in world patterns of technological opportunities. Fagerberg and Sollie (1987) show that $AD_j$ is directly proportional to the correlation coefficient across i between $\Delta p_{ij}$ and $\Delta s_i$. So $AD_j$ is positive (negative) if country j's share increases in those sectors that increase (decrease) their world weight in terms of patents.

Since we are interested in understanding separately the effect of a country j increase (or decrease) in its patent share in *expanding* sectors and the same effect in *declining* sectors, we need to use a further decomposition of $AD_j$ (Laursen, 1999).

$$AD_j = GR_j + SG_j \qquad (2)$$

$GR_j = \sum_i \Delta p_{ij}(\Delta s_i + |\Delta s_i|)/2$; $GR_j$ is called *technology growth adaptation* and singles out the above-average expanding industries. The sum of $\Delta s_i$, with its absolute value $|\Delta s_i|$, is zero if $\Delta s_i$ is negative. Therefore, $GR_j$ is positive (negative) if $\Delta p_{ij}$ is positive (negative) for these sectors. This measures the ability of countries to enter sectors with increasing technological opportunities.

$SG_j = \sum_i \Delta p_{ij}(\Delta s_i - |\Delta s_i|)/2$; $SG_j$ is called *technology stagnation adaptation* and singles out industries that display a relative decline. This is because the difference between $\Delta s_i$ and its absolute value $|\Delta s_i|$ is zero if $\Delta s_i$ is positive. Therefore, $SG_j$ is positive (negative) if $\Delta p_{ij}$ is negative (positive) for these sectors. This measures the ability of countries to exit sectors with declining technological opportunities. Table 2.2 presents the results for the sixteen countries ranked for patent share change ($\Delta p_j$).

Japan and the United States have improved their shares considerably. In Europe the greatest change relates to the Italian patent share. Finland, Sweden, Spain, Denmark, the Netherlands, Norway and Belgium display positive signs of $\Delta p_j$. Note that the largest improvements in percentage terms relate to Spain and Finland; their shares of world patents have increased more than three- and fourfold respectively, due to their very low shares in the first period. Conversely, Germany, the United Kingdom, France, Switzerland, Austria and Luxembourg have declining shares. In percentage terms the worst performance is displayed by the United Kingdom and Switzerland, both of which lost around 40 percent of their initial patent share, followed by Germany and France with a decline of about 28 percent.

The share effect ($SH_j$) is the most important in every country, apart from the United States and the Netherlands. The absolute size of $SH_j$ is higher than $\Delta p_j$ for almost all EU countries, with the exception of

Table 2.2 *Structural decomposition*[a]

| | $p_j(t-1)$ | $p_j(t)$ | $\Delta p_j$ | $sh_j$ | $st_j$ | $ad_j$ | $gr_j$ | $sg_j$ |
|---|---|---|---|---|---|---|---|---|
| Japan | 7.75 | 13.40 | 5.65 | 5.17 | 0.73 | −0.24 | 0.69 | −0.93 |
| | | | | *0.91* | *0.13* | *−0.04* | *0.12* | *−0.16* |
| United States | 19.88 | 23.22 | 3.34 | 1.07 | 2.16 | 0.11 | 0.65 | −0.53 |
| | | | | *0.32* | *0.65* | *0.03* | *0.19* | *−0.16* |
| Italy | 1.37 | 2.23 | 0.86 | 1.09 | −0.06 | −0.17 | 0.07 | −0.23 |
| | | | | *1.26* | *−0.07* | *−0.19* | *0.08* | *−0.27* |
| Finland | 0.16 | 0.91 | 0.76 | 0.57 | 0.01 | 0.18 | 0.24 | −0.06 |
| | | | | *0.76* | *0.01* | *0.24* | *0.32* | *−0.08* |
| Sweden | 1.28 | 1.66 | 0.38 | 0.20 | 0.01 | 0.17 | 0.20 | −0.03 |
| | | | | *0.54* | *0.02* | *0.44* | *0.52* | *−0.08* |
| Spain | 0.08 | 0.31 | 0.23 | 0.27 | −0.01 | −0.03 | 0.03 | −0.07 |
| | | | | *1.17* | *−0.03* | *−0.14* | *0.14* | *−0.28* |
| Denmark | 0.29 | 0.50 | 0.21 | 0.24 | −0.01 | −0.02 | 0.06 | −0.08 |
| | | | | *1.15* | *−0.04* | *−0.11* | *0.29* | *−0.40* |
| Netherlands | 2.55 | 2.71 | 0.15 | −0.07 | 0.16 | 0.07 | 0.04 | 0.03 |
| | | | | *−0.47* | *1.02* | *0.45* | *0.25* | *0.19* |
| Norway | 0.11 | 0.20 | 0.09 | 0.09 | −0.02 | 0.02 | 0.03 | −0.01 |
| | | | | *1.04* | *−0.21* | *0.17* | *0.29* | *−0.12* |
| Belgium | 0.55 | 0.62 | 0.07 | 0.10 | −0.04 | 0.00 | 0.03 | −0.03 |
| | | | | *1.61* | *−0.55* | *−0.06* | *0.46* | *−0.52* |
| Luxembourg | 0.08 | 0.07 | −0.01 | 0.01 | −0.01 | 0.00 | 0.00 | 0.00 |
| | | | | *−1.13* | *1.53* | *0.60* | *0.02* | *0.58* |
| Austria | 0.64 | 0.51 | −0.13 | −0.07 | −0.07 | 0.02 | 0.01 | 0.01 |
| | | | | *0.57* | *0.56* | *−0.13* | *−0.08* | *−0.05* |
| Switzerland | 3.95 | 2.37 | −1.58 | −1.22 | −0.56 | 0.20 | −0.18 | 0.39 |
| | | | | *0.77* | *0.36* | *−0.13* | *0.11* | *−0.24* |
| France | 6.81 | 4.94 | −1.87 | −2.00 | 0.51 | −0.38 | −0.59 | 0.22 |
| | | | | *1.07* | *−0.27* | *0.20* | *0.32* | *−0.12* |
| United Kingdom | 5.91 | 3.51 | −2.40 | −2.48 | −0.22 | 0.30 | −0.22 | 0.52 |
| | | | | *1.03* | *0.09* | *−0.13* | *0.09* | *−0.22* |
| Germany | 17.97 | 12.90 | −5.08 | −4.01 | −0.74 | −0.33 | −1.37 | 1.05 |
| | | | | *0.79* | *0.15* | *0.06* | *0.27* | *−0.21* |

[a] The figures in italics represent the weight of the individual components.

Finland, Norway, the Netherlands, Austria, Switzerland and Germany. For Italy, Spain, Norway and Belgium (which have an overall growth in their patent share), improvements would be higher if sectors grew at the same rate worldwide. For France and the United Kingdom, which have a decline in their country share, the absence of structural change would further increase their decline. Conversely, without structural change, the United States would have only a third of the observed change in its patent share.

The United States and the Netherlands have increased their share as a consequence of a "right" initial technological specialization. In particular, in the Netherlands, the increase would have been even higher had shares in individual sectors remained constant. Also, in France, the initial level of technological specialization has had a positive impact, limiting the extent of its market share decrease.

Sweden and Finland have been very successful in transforming the sectoral composition of their technological activities in line with structural changes in world patterns of technological opportunities. For these two countries the technology growth adaptation effect has been particularly important. The technology growth adaptation effect has also been very important in the United States. The sign of $GR_j$ and $SG_j$ in France, Germany and the United Kingdom is related to the fact that these countries lose patent share in most of the technological classes considered. However, in the United Kingdom the technology stagnation adaptation effect is larger in absolute value. Exit from low-opportunity sectors counterbalances its share loss. In Germany and France the negative effect of exiting from expanding sectors is stronger, so the overall adaptation effect is negative.

Summing up, the United States and Japan have experienced relatively high growth in terms of technological activity, and (in particular the United States) appear to have had the "correct" sectoral distribution in the first period considered. In the European Union the picture is patchier: Italy and Spain have improved their patent shares but improvements have been hindered by technological specialization in "wrong" sectors and difficulties in adapting. Finland, Sweden and the Netherlands have grown thanks to an appropriate technological specialization and an ability to adapt and enter expanding technological fields. Large EU economies, such as the United Kingdom, France and Germany, have lost patent shares. Germany has been heavily penalized by its technological specialization and lack of adaptation. France has declined despite the correct specialization and the United Kingdom despite its exit from declining sectors.[5]

[5] Laursen (1999) performs a similar exercise for world patenting in the United States with a different sectoral disaggregation and with a different time-span. He considers the period between 1965 and 1988. Despite limited comparability, the results for Japan, Finland, Sweden, Spain, the United Kingdom and Italy form similar patterns. However, some differences in the results are striking and deserve further enquiry. In particular, his findings for the United States, France and Germany disagree with mine. There are probably two reasons for this. First, the choice of the patent office probably overemphasizes the US decline in Laursen's sample, and the German (and maybe the French) decline in my sample. Second, the United States has guided the process of structural change that has taken place in the last twenty years in relation to ICT and biotechnology (accounted for in table 2.1). This process is only partially apparent in Laursen's work.

3    **The aggregate analysis of four sectors: pharmaceuticals (and biotechnology), telecommunications, chemicals and machinery**

This book contains six sectoral studies. Four of them focus mainly on manufacturing sectors: chemicals, pharmaceuticals and biotechnology, telecommunications and machine tools. Two of them focus on software and other services. This section aims to provide some broad quantitative evidence on their dynamics in terms of innovative and economic variables, and to single out country performances within each sector. It focuses in particular on chemicals, pharmaceuticals and biotechnology, telecommunications equipment, and machinery (which includes machine tools). It intends to provide *ex ante* preliminary evidence on sectoral dynamics and country performances. Chapter 11, by Coriat, Malerba and Montobbio, in this book provides an *ex post* assessment of the determinants of the innovative and economic performances of the United States, Japan and Europe in these sectors.

In tables 2.3, 2.4, 2.5 and 2.6 the annual rate of growth of value added, employment, labor productivity and export world shares for a selected number of countries and sectors are displayed. The time-span changes according to data availability. Full details about the variables and the calculations of the indexes are given in the appendix.

Considering value added, employment and labor productivity, the hypothesis that the rates of growth have the same values across sectors cannot be accepted. Anova tables (not reported) show that sectoral means explain up to 40 percent of the total variance in all three cases. Despite limited data availability at disaggregate level, it can be shown that sectors such as telecommunications equipment, electronics and pharmaceuticals display above-average growth of value added and labor productivity (excluding pharmaceuticals, for which data are not available) in almost every country. This is the first evidence about the relevance of understanding specific sectoral dynamics and about the different ability of countries to transform and adapt.

In the following subsections we analyze the four different macro- sectors related to the case studies of this book.

*3.1    Pharmaceuticals and biotechnology*

The pharmaceutical industry is one of the most dynamic among the manufacturing sectors. In our sample the technological classes related to the pharmaceutical industry are increasing their share (proteins, vaccines and micro-organisms, reagents and diagnostics and other pharmaceutical products) (table 2.1). Biotechnology patent applications to EPO have

Table 2.3 *Annual rate of growth of 1995 constant price value added for a selected number of countries and sectors*

| Annual rate of growth of value added[a] | Finland | France | Germany | Italy | Japan | Netherlands | Spain | Sweden | United Kingdom | United States |
|---|---|---|---|---|---|---|---|---|---|---|
| Chemicals excluding pharmaceuticals | – | 2.57 (9) | – | – | – | – | – | – | 3.39 (20) | – |
| Electrical machinery and apparatus, n.e.c. | 4.66 (20) | 2.79 (9) | –1.46 (9) | – | – | – | 5.79 (4) | 2.30 (7) | – | – |
| Medical, precision and optical instruments, watches and clocks | 8.03 (20) | –1.70 (9) | –1.38 (9) | 2.77 (8) | 2.54 (19) | – | 4.75 (4) | 7.62 (7) | –0.81 (6) | –1.76 (13) |
| Office, accounting and computing machinery | 14.36 (20) | 18.00 (9) | –1.02 (9) | 0.99 (8) | – | | 2.39 (4) | –1.88 (7) | 12.90 (6) | – |
| Pharmaceuticals | – | 4.79 (9) | – | – | – | – | – | – | 5.01 (20) | – |
| Radio, television and communication equipment | 21.32 (20) | 17.14 (9) | 1.40 (9) | – | – | – | 1.50 (4) | 39.21 (7) | – | – |
| Machinery and equipment, n.e.c. | 2.42 (20) | 2.21 (9) | –1.88 (9) | 1.22 (19) | 2.75 (19) | 2.53 (20) | 5.00 (5) | 4.49 (7) | –0.45 (20) | – |
| Rubber and plastics product | 3.29 (20) | 3.51 (9) | 1.16 (9) | 2.55 (20) | 1.00 (19) | 4.37 (20) | 5.06 (5) | 5.34 (7) | 3.07 (20) | 6.34 (20) |
| Transport equipment | –0.51 (20) | 0.99 (20) | –0.94 (20) | 0.41 (20) | 1.30 (19) | 1.84 (20) | 4.96 (5) | 7.07 (7) | 2.39 (20) | 1.20 (20) |
| Total manufacturing | 3.17 (20) | 1.43 (20) | –0.71 (9) | 1.86 (20) | 2.92 (19) | 2.29 (20) | 2.37 (20) | 2.51 (20) | 1.69 (20) | 3.10 (20) |
| Computer services and related activities | 4.58 (20) | 6.12 (9) | 8.98 (9) | 5.08 (8) | – | 16.49 (5) | 8.68 (4) | 9.44 (7) | 10.01 (14) | – |

Note: For all definitions see the appendix.

[a] Figures in parentheses are the number of observations.

Table 2.4 *Annual rate of growth of employment for a selected number of countries and sectors*

| Annual rate of growth of employment[a] | Finland | France | Germany | Italy | Japan | Netherlands | Spain | Sweden | United Kingdom | United States |
|---|---|---|---|---|---|---|---|---|---|---|
| Chemicals excluding pharmaceuticals | -0.76 (19) | -1.80 (20) | -5.05 (4) | – | 0.12 (18) | – | -0.62 (20) | – | – | -0.77 (20) |
| Electrical machinery and apparatus, n.e.c. | -1.94 (20) | -0.84 (20) | -3.37 (9) | – | 1.02 (18) | – | -1.40 (20) | 1.13 (7) | – | -1.21 (20) |
| Medical, precision and optical instruments, watches and clocks | 2.94 (20) | -1.00 (20) | -3.14 (9) | 0.68 (8) | -1.59 (19) | – | 0.13 (20) | 3.46 (7) | – | -1.46 (20) |
| Office, accounting and computing machinery | -0.47 (20) | -0.14 (20) | -11.56 (9) | -1.24 (8) | 3.07 (18) | – | 2.65 (20) | -9.80 (7) | – | -3.35 (20) |
| Pharmaceuticals | 1.71 (19) | 0.94 (20) | 6.62 (4) | – | 0.79 (18) | – | 0.09 (20) | – | – | 1.73 (20) |
| Radio, television and communication equipment | 6.87 (20) | -1.67 (20) | -6.44 (9) | – | 2.34 (18) | – | -2.69 (20) | 5.06 (7) | – | 0.13 (20) |
| Machinery and equipment, n.e.c. | -1.06 (20) | -2.05 (20) | -3.98 (9) | -0.85 (20) | 0.60 (19) | 2.55 (5) | -0.09 (20) | -0.75 (20) | – | -0.09 (20) |
| Rubber and plastic products | -0.77 (20) | 0.02 (20) | -1.10 (9) | 1.71 (20) | 0.52 (19) | 0.60 (5) | 1.48 (20) | -1.08 (20) | – | 2.02 (20) |
| Transport equipment | -3.46 (20) | -2.32 (20) | -0.76 (9) | -2.50 (20) | 0.08 (19) | 0.31 (5) | -0.10 (20) | -0.85 (20) | – | -0.19 (20) |
| Total manufacturing | -2.03 (20) | -1.73 (20) | -3.01 (9) | -0.89 (20) | 0.11 (19) | 0.24 (5) | -0.48 (20) | -1.64 (20) | -1.89 (20) | -0.33 (20) |
| Computer services and related activities | 5.29 (20) | 4.51 (10) | 6.03 (9) | 2.80 (8) | – | 15.91 (5) | 8.71 (4) | 8.45 (7) | – | – |

Note: For all definitions see the appendix.

[a] Figures in parentheses are the number of observations.

Table 2.5 *Annual rate of growth of labor productivity for a selected number of countries and sectors*

| Annual rate of growth of labor productivity | Finland | France | Germany | Italy | Japan | Netherlands | Spain | Sweden | United States |
|---|---|---|---|---|---|---|---|---|---|
| Chemicals excluding pharmaceuticals | – | 4.37 | – | – | – | – | – | – | – |
| Electrical machinery and apparatus, n.e.c. | 6.60 | 3.64 | 1.90 | – | – | – | 7.18 | 1.17 | – |
| Medical, precision and optical instruments, watches and clocks | 5.08 | –0.70 | 1.76 | 2.10 | 4.13 | – | 4.61 | 4.16 | –0.30 |
| Office, accounting and computing machinery | 14.83 | 18.14 | 10.54 | 2.24 | – | – | –0.26 | 7.93 | – |
| Pharmaceuticals | – | 3.85 | – | – | – | – | – | – | – |
| Radio, television and communication equipment | 14.45 | 18.80 | 7.84 | – | – | – | 4.20 | 34.15 | – |
| Machinery and equipment, n.e.c. | 3.48 | 4.26 | 2.11 | 2.07 | 2.15 | –0.02 | 5.09 | 5.24 | – |
| Rubber and plastic products | 4.05 | 3.50 | 2.26 | 0.84 | 0.48 | 3.77 | 3.58 | 6.42 | 4.32 |
| Transport equipment | 2.95 | 3.31 | –0.19 | 2.90 | 1.22 | 1.53 | 5.06 | 7.92 | 1.39 |
| Total manufacturing | 5.21 | 3.17 | 2.29 | 2.75 | 2.82 | 2.05 | 2.86 | 4.15 | 3.43 |
| Computer and related activities | –0.71 | 1.61 | 2.94 | 2.28 | – | 0.57 | –0.03 | 0.99 | – |

Note: For all definitions see the appendix.

Table 2.6 *Annual growth rate of world export shares in selected countries and sectors: 1990–2000*

| | Austria | Belgium | Canada | Denmark | Finland | France | Germany | Italy | Japan | Mexico | Netherlands | Spain | Sweden | United Kingdom | United States |
|---|---|---|---|---|---|---|---|---|---|---|---|---|---|---|---|
| Chemicals | -0.84 | 2.29 | 1.97 | -0.36 | 0.46 | -0.77 | -1.84 | 0.75 | 1.38 | 4.24 | -2.78 | 3.20 | -0.16 | -1.02 | 1.04 |
| Pharmaceuticals | -0.37 | 3.63 | 5.50 | -1.07 | -5.33 | 0.00 | -1.84 | 2.30 | -2.22 | 9.41 | 0.35 | 0.79 | -0.02 | -1.00 | 0.73 |
| Rubber and plastic products | -2.09 | -0.79 | 5.59 | -2.68 | -0.75 | -1.39 | -1.93 | 0.55 | -1.39 | 19.72 | -3.92 | 2.97 | -0.97 | -1.63 | 3.92 |
| Machinery and equipment, n.e.c. | -1.19 | 1.99 | 5.77 | -2.02 | -0.09 | -0.73 | -2.01 | 0.15 | -0.04 | 18.27 | -2.30 | 1.73 | -0.82 | -1.04 | 2.13 |
| Office, accounting and computing machinery | -1.86 | 3.59 | 0.45 | -1.59 | 0.24 | -1.20 | -1.66 | 7.90 | -3.21 | 21.83 | 4.70 | -1.77 | -10.61 | 0.74 | 0.92 |
| Electrical machinery and apparatus, n.e.c. | -4.04 | -2.64 | 2.70 | 2.01 | 2.66 | -2.30 | -2.82 | 2.58 | -1.01 | 32.04 | -2.30 | 1.49 | -1.03 | -1.20 | 1.56 |
| Radio, television and communication equipment | -1.69 | -2.78 | 0.99 | -1.63 | 10.93 | 0.70 | -2.49 | 3.15 | -5.17 | 43.43 | 2.38 | 2.53 | 5.44 | 2.51 | 3.30 |
| Instruments | -2.58 | 2.42 | 6.18 | -1.56 | 0.70 | -2.62 | -2.31 | 2.08 | -1.06 | 30.18 | 2.96 | 2.64 | -2.74 | -1.72 | 2.03 |
| Transport equipment | 3.65 | -2.11 | 2.61 | -4.11 | -1.33 | -0.49 | -0.70 | 1.11 | -1.91 | 12.00 | -1.29 | 2.34 | -0.60 | -0.31 | 0.42 |

Note: For all definitions see the appendix.

increased their share in total EPO applications for almost all countries between 1990 and 1997. Similarly, in the last decade R&D expenditure in pharmaceuticals has grown more quickly than total business enterprise R&D in almost all OECD countries (with the exception of Italy, Norway and Finland) (OECD, 2001a).

In parallel, the pharmaceutical industry experienced an above-average rate of growth of value added and labor productivity and an increase in the ratio of imports and exports over manufactured products. Moreover, all OECD countries increased the percentage of pharmaceutical products in their export composition (OECD, 2001a; and NSB, 2000).

These changes have been led by the United States. In terms of innovative performance, the United States considerably increased its share in the patent applications to EPO in all the technological classes related to the pharmaceutical sector. Conversely, a decline has been observed in Germany, the United Kingdom and, to a lesser extent, France. The same patterns emerge from international trade data. Table 2.6 shows the annual rate of growth of export market shares between 1990 and 2000. The data display an improvement for the countries of the North American Free Trade Agreement (NAFTA) area, a market share loss in Germany, the United Kingdom and Japan, France remaining stagnant, and Spain and Italy improving their export market share. Further evidence shows that the contribution of the United States to the worldwide production of pharmaceutical products has increased between 1980 and 1997 while the German, British and Japanese share of world production declined (NSB, 2000).

Chapter 3 in this book, by McKelvey, Orsenigo and Pammolli, analyzes the pharmaceutical and biotechnology sector, focusing on the last twenty-five years and, in particular, on the molecular biology revolution. It underlines the necessity of looking at the system dynamics to understand structures and performances and shows the way this industry has become increasingly expensive, in terms of fixed costs for scientific research, and organizationally complex. This is because there are new forms of interaction and a new division of labor between big and small firms and networks with research centres and universities. A key aspect of US success, in this context, has been the ability to combine strong research competencies and a decentralized but integrated network of firms and non-firm organizations.

### 3.2    *Chemicals*

The chemical sector is undergoing a process of profound structural change. Our sample contains some technological classes that have a relatively high rate of growth in terms of world patents. However, expanding classes overlap with pharmaceuticals and life sciences (plus cosmetics and detergents). At the same time, other technological classes decline over time. The eight technological classes with the lowest rate of growth belong to chemicals, and, in particular, to the fields of hydrocarbons, carbon acid, alcohol and additives. If we exclude biochemistry, the overall weight (in terms of patents at EPO and the United States Patent and Trademark Office – PTO) of organic chemicals, materials and chemical engineering has been decreasing for at least thirty years (Laursen, 1999; and Montobbio and Rampa, 2002). The ratios between chemical R&D and value added and between chemical R&D and manufacturing R&D have both decreased in the last ten years. Economic variables seem to follow the same pattern. Value added and productivity growth have been decreasing but remaining above the manufacturing average (OECD, 2001a; see also tables 2.3 to 2.5). However, the income elasticity of demand for chemicals (excluding life sciences) is decreasing.

Chapter 4, by Cesaroni et al., on chemicals in this book shows the deep transformations in the technological knowledge base of the industry. US firms became leaders in organic chemicals, using the United States' rich oil resources and the size of the domestic market. The emergence of specialized engineering firms was an important component of US success. In the 1970s and 1980s the oil shocks and tougher competition from Europe and the developing countries began jeopardizing US leadership.

Europe is now the major actor, with one-third of world production. However, in the last decade its world share has been decreasing. European growth has been lower than in the United States, in particular in Italy and Germany (OECD, 2001a). In the last ten years, although the chemical sector is the only medium-technology sector with a growing share of manufactured exports, the volume of chemical exports has been decreasing in the United States, France, Germany and the United Kingdom. It increased in Italy, Ireland and Belgium, and in non-EU countries such as Japan and Australia. In terms of export market share dynamics we observe an improvement in the United States and Japan. In Europe, Italy, Spain and Belgium improved their market share, while Germany, the United Kingdom, the Netherlands and France declined.

## 3.3    Telecommunications

The telecommunications industry[6] is increasing its share in patent applications to EPO. In our sample, technological classes such as telephones,

---

[6] I refer mainly to telecommunications equipment. In our technological classes I consider televisions, radios, cameras and video cameras, microphones, speakers, phones, cables and circuits. For economic data I consider class 3832 ISIC rev. 2, or class 32 rev. 3. Computers and computer chips and equipment are excluded from both classifications.

televisions, radios, cameras and cables have among the highest rates of growth (table 2.1). More generally, ICT patent applications to EPO have increased their share in total EPO applications for almost all countries between 1990 and 1997 (with the exclusion of Portugal and Belgium).

Like pharmaceuticals, the telecommunications equipment industry has experienced an above-average rate of growth of value added (and labor productivity) and an increase in the ratio of imports and exports over manufactured products, especially in the second half of the 1990s (tables 2.3 to 2.5; and OECD, 2001a). Moreover, all OECD countries have increased the percentage of telecommunications products in their export composition (OECD, 2001a). The OECD (2001a) gives substantial evidence on the widespread expansion of the telecommunications sectors in all OECD countries in terms of Internet hosts or integrated services digital network (ISDN) subscribers.

In terms of innovative performance at country level, the United States and Japan have been gaining patent shares in almost all telecommunications-related classes (an exception is the United States in cables). In Europe, Germany, France and the United Kingdom show declining shares; what is relevant is the improvement of the patent shares of Finland and Sweden in these technological classes (televisions, radios, cameras and video cameras, microphones, speakers, telephones, cables and circuits – results not reported). These two countries also display the highest rates of growth in value added and labor productivity (tables 2.3 to 2.6). Again, a similar pattern emerges in the export data: the United States, Sweden, Finland (together with the United Kingdom, Spain and – to a lesser extent – France) have improved their market share, while Germany, Italy and Japan have declined, between 1990 and 2000 (table 2.6). Further evidence shows that the contribution of the United States, Japan, Germany, France and the United Kingdom to the worldwide production of telecommunications equipment has declined between 1980 and 1997. It is worthwhile to note the remarkable growth of China, Taiwan, Singapore and South Korea, which together accounted for 20 percent of world production in 1997, rising from 6 percent in 1980 (NSB, 2000).

The chapter on telecommunications by Edquist in this book focuses in particular on the Internet and fixed data communications and mobile telephones. It places emphasis on the roles of institutional transformations (in particular the standard-setting processes) and non-firm organizations (in particular government policies) as key elements to explain the success of Internet-related activities in the United States and mobile telephones in European Nordic countries. The good performances of some European countries seem to depend upon specific demand conditions and standard-setting procedures in which national telecommunications providers had a key role.

## 3.4     *Machinery and equipment*

Machinery and equipment is the second medium-technology sector considered, and, as shown in the previous section, it is decreasing in terms of world patent shares at EPO and the PTO (Laursen, 1999; and Montobbio and Rampa, 2002). Only four technological classes out of thirty-eight have increased their share. Value added and productivity growth rates have been generally below the manufacture average in the last two decades. The share of total exports has remained stagnant and, like chemicals, the percentage of exports in this sector is decreasing in the United States, France, Germany and the United Kingdom.

The world leaders in this sectors are Japan, the United States, Germany and Italy. In terms of innovative activity Germany has gained patent shares (paper production machines, pumps and filters, and engines for transports) or experienced smaller losses. Italy and Spain have had positive changes in almost all their shares in the technological classes associated with the machinery sector. The rate of growth of productivity has been particularly high in the United States between 1995 and 1998 (OECD, 2001a) and lower in Europe, with the exception of Spain and Sweden (table 2.5; and OECD, 2001a). In terms of export market share dynamics in the machinery and equipment sectors, we also observe a deteriorating European position (apart from Belgium and Spain) and an improvement for the United States over the last decade.

However, in Europe, in this declining sector, the innovative performance was good in the face of the transformation of the knowledge bases and the increased level of international competition. Chapter 7 in this book, by Wengel and Shapira, shows that a critical factor is the continuous upgrading of labor and engineering skills. In Europe firms have upgraded their human capital in terms of external formal training. Moreover, linkages with research centres, producers and users prevented strong competition from standardized, low-cost, general-purpose technologies.

In summary, we have shown that these four sectors differ in terms of innovative and economic trends and play an important role in the process of structural change. Pharmaceuticals and telecoms are expanding sectors, both in terms of innovative and economic weight. Chemicals and machinery have a lower growth, experiencing nonetheless the relevant processes of transformation. As demonstrated throughout the book, the four sectors considered are also different in terms of the composition and dynamics of the technological knowledge base and the role of university and scientific research and supporting institutions, such as intellectual property rights and standards.

At the same time, the analysis of the dynamics of export market share at sectoral level reveals a clear pattern across countries. The United States (and the NAFTA area) gained export market share during the 1990s in all sectors considered. Japan lost export shares in all sectors except chemicals. Germany declined in all sectors. Europe performed relatively well in the telecommunications equipment industry, with Finland, Sweden, the United Kingdom, the Netherlands and Spain all improving their export share.

## 4 Structural changes and national trajectories in an "innovation system perspective"

The aggregate picture drawn above underlines the fact that structural changes are deeply intertwined with changes in the relative position of countries, and that countries display different abilities to foster technological advancements and to adapt. As a general pattern, at least in the last decade, we have observed a remarkable innovative and export performance by the United States, and a relative decline for Japan, Germany, France and the United Kingdom (tables 2.1 and 2.6).

The US ability to create, over time, differentiated technological knowledge can explain a great part of this finding. The international differences in aggregate innovative and economic trends emerge together with changes in the sectoral distribution, at country level, of economic and technological activities. For example, Finland and Sweden experienced very high rates of growth of value added, productivity, export and patent shares in the telecoms sector. Also, Italy, France, Germany and Spain display different characteristics in terms of the evolution of their patent and export shares across sectors.

This picture is different in many important aspects from the one drawn during the second half of the 1980s. In this period many authors pointed to the erosion of the US lead in productivity and at the convergence processes among many industrialized countries and regions after World War II (Abramovitz, 1986; Nelson, 1991; Nelson and Wright, 1992; and Barro and Sala-i-Martin, 1992). Moreover, Japan had experienced a sustained economic and technological achievement for at least thirty years, and some European countries displayed relatively poor innovative performance.

This has important implications for the analysis of the nature and characteristics of innovation systems. The first generation of analysis on NSIs was fostered by the concern in the United States about going down the technological ladder relative to Japan and the emerging economies in East Asia. It explored the idea that technological capabilities may have an important national (or regional) dimension and that an appropriate system of institutions and organizations supporting the innovative performance of firms may be important (Freeman, 1987; Lundvall, 1992; and Nelson, 1993). This idea of NSIs was also corroborated by further empirical evidence about the persistently uneven distribution of innovation across regions and countries.[7]

This literature is built upon the idea that innovation activities depend upon knowledge and learning networks that follow in the track of common language and established communities. Moreover, the scope of these networks is molded by a wide range of institutions and organizations that have a national character. Technical training and public funds are provided, for example, on a national basis and technology policies are, in general, implemented within national borders. Emphasis has been placed on the different links and interaction among the agents (firms and organizations) involved in the innovation process.

This theoretical toolbox has to be adapted in order to explain not only the process of technological catching up and the decline of the US lead, but also the recent period of growth and technological prowess of the US economy and the differential ability of the European countries to transform and adapt. Various indicators of technology development and market competitiveness show that the United States is among the leaders in all major technology areas (NSB, 2000).

However, as shown in table 2.2, advancements in US patent share are due mainly to the "correct" technological specialization. This means that, as far as innovative activities are concerned, the United States has recovered in particular in high-growth and high-opportunity sectors. As accounted for by the NSB (2000), three of the four science-based industries that form the high-tech group (computers, pharmaceuticals and communication equipment) gained world market share in the 1990s (aerospace industry excluded). In parallel, related US service sector industries (e.g. computer software and communications services) have led the increase in R&D expenditures within the US service sector. Conversely, in Europe other countries, such as Germany, France and Italy, have experienced a weak ability to transform the sectoral composition of the economy and expand into sectors with an increased economic and innovative weight, as shown in section 2.

---

[7] Empirical evidence is provided in Amendola, Guerrieri and Padoan (1998); Archibugi and Pianta (1992); and Patel and Pavitt (1994).

This raises the issue of how national systems transform and how new sectors, technologies and the supporting institutions and organizations emerge. Institutions and organizations can no longer be considered exogenous to the agents' innovative activity but, rather, are often created to accommodate a specific trajectory of technological specialization. Innovative success in some countries and sectors can be the result not just of the appropriate institutional package but, rather, of the flexibility of the institutional environment to adapt to the new technological challenge posed by firms.

This book suggests that understanding the dynamics and interdependence between the variables at a sectoral system level is particularly important. According to the sector considered, different sets of actors and institutions have an effect on innovative and economic performance at country level. In some sectors, technological and scientific research capabilities and education have been major sources of industrial leadership (e.g. pharmaceuticals and software). In other sectors, the integration between in-house research and advancements in the relative transfer sciences have fostered US firms' competitiveness (e.g. chemical engineering, automation and robotics, computer sciences and biotechnology).

Technology and innovation policies have also affected the rate of innovative activities in different ways in different sectors. Patent policies have been particularly important in support of the activity of smaller technology-based firms, and university licensing (particularly in biotechnology and chemicals) and standardization have influenced the mobile telephone industry. The specific characteristics of demand and interaction with users have been particularly important in machine tools and chemicals, and in some segments of software and biotechnology (see chapter 11, by Coriat, Malerba and Montobbio, in this book).

Through the analysis of the dynamics of different important sectoral systems it is then possible to show why, in many sectors, industrial and innovative leadership in the long run shifted and US high-tech industries regained, during the 1990s, some of the world market share lost during the previous decade. This can be achieved through an understanding of the role of the different dimensions of sectoral systems, in particular pointing out the specific coevolution of the knowledge base, actors, networks and institutions of a sector.

## 5    Conclusions

This chapter claims that a bottom-up sectoral perspective along the dimensions of the "sectoral system" can be conducive to a better understanding of the observed sectoral differences in innovative and economic dynamics. It provides support for the idea that an analysis of the dynamics of the different components of sectoral systems (knowledge base, demand, actors, networks and institutions) can explain not only the characteristics of the processes of transformation in the sectors but also the reasons behind the innovative and industrial performance of countries – and the US recovery in many high-tech industries – during the 1990s. The "sectoral system" toolbox is intended to complement and expand the traditional notion of an NSI, which was designed to explain the process of technological catching up and the decline of the US lead observed in the 1980s.

An empirical analysis provides stylized evidence that sectors display different economic and innovative trends and that structural change occurs continuously at different levels of disaggregation in terms of innovative activities (R&D and patents) and economic variables (value added, employment and productivity). A specific focus is on the sectors that are the subject of the different case studies of this book. High-tech sectors such as pharmaceuticals and biotechnology, telecommunications, and computers and related services have increased their economic and innovative significance relative to chemicals, machinery and many technological classes related to electronics in the last twenty years.

In particular with regard to innovative activities, an analysis of patent applications to EPO shows that the technological classes related to pharmaceutical and biotechnology (proteins, vaccines and micro-organisms, reagents and diagnostics), telecommunications (televisions, phones, etc.) and instruments (lasers and diagnostic devices), together with detergents and cosmetics, display expanding patterns. Conversely, traditional classes in all chemical, electronics and mechanical sectors decrease their weight in total patent activity, the quantitatively most important declines occurring in the chemical sector.

In parallel with structural change, the innovative international position of countries has also changed: US patent share gains are mainly concentrated in expanding technological classes, where Germany, France and the United Kingdom have experienced declining shares. Japan has improved everywhere, in particular in electronics. Finland and Sweden have improved their shares in telecommunications and electronics. The variation of the overall patent share of Italy and Spain displays a positive sign. However, in these countries, improvements occurred mainly in declining sectors.

An analysis of the structural decomposition of patent share variations of countries shows that the United States benefited from having the "correct" sectoral distribution in the first period considered.

Improvements in Italy and Spain have been hindered by technological specialization in "wrong" sectors and difficulties in adapting. Germany has been heavily penalized by its technological specialization and lack of adaptation. Finland, Sweden and the Netherlands have grown thanks to an appropriate technological specialization and the ability to adapt and enter expanding technological fields.

In terms of economic variables the picture is similar. Export market share dynamics at sectoral level shows that the United States (and the NAFTA area in general) improved its relative position during the 1990s in all sectors considered. Japan lost export shares in all sectors except chemicals. Germany declined in all sectors. Europe performed relatively well in the telecommunications equipment industry, with Finland, Sweden, the United Kingdom, the Netherlands and Spain all improving their export shares.

### Appendix

In tables 2.3 to 2.5 I use the standard OECD structural analysis (STAN) database version 2002. The sectoral classification is ISIC rev. 3 and follows http://unstats.un.org/unsd./cr/registry/regcst.asp?Cl=2.

Variables used for each sector and country: value added at constant 1995 prices and total employment.

Variables are expressed in average annual rates of growth ($g_{VA}$, $g_{EMP}$). The rate of growth of labor productivity is $g_P = g_{VA} - g_{EMP}$.

g has been calculated in different ways according to the number of observations available:

- for sectors and countries with complete availability (1980 to 1999), g has been calculated as a least square growth rate. $g_{hat} = e^b - 1$; b is the ordinary least squares estimate of the logarithm of the growth equation $X_t = X_0(1 + g)^t$.
- for other sectors and countries ((a) to (h): see below), g has been calculated as a geometric growth rate. $g = \exp\{\ln(X_t/X_0)/t\} - 1$.

Different sample sizes have been referenced in tables 2.3, 2.4 and 2.5: (a) nineteen observations: 1980 to 1998; (b) fifteen observations: 1980 to 1994; (c) fifteen observations: 1985 to 1999; (d) ten observations: 1990 to 1999; (e) eight observations: 1991 to 1999; (f) eight observations: 1992 to 1999; (g) seven observations: 1993 to 1999; (h) four observations: 1995 to 1998.

The sector "computer services and related activities" includes: hardware consultancy; software consultancy and supply; data processing; database activities; maintenance and repair of office, accounting and computing machinery; and other computer-related activities.

In table 2.6 the annual growth rates of export market shares have been calculated on eleven observations from 1990 to 2000 as a geometric growth rate: $g = \exp\{\ln[(X_t + X_{t-1})/(X_0 + X_1)]/t\} - 1$. US dollar current exchange rates have been used in order to have a common currency across countries.

REFERENCES

Abramovitz, M. (1986), Catching up, forging ahead, and falling behind, *Journal of Economic History*, 46, 2, 385–406

Amable, B., and B. Verspagen (1995), The role of technology in market share dynamics, *Applied Economics*, 27, 197–204

Amendola, G., P. Guerrieri and P. C. Padoan (1998), International patterns of technological accumulation and trade, in D. Archibugi and J. Michie (eds.), *Trade, Growth and Technical Change*, Cambridge University Press, Cambridge, 141–167

Archibugi, D., and M. Pianta (1992), *The Technological Specialisation of Advanced Countries*, Kluwer, Boston

Barro, R. J., and X. Sala-i-Martin (1992), Convergence, *Journal of Political Economy*, 100, 2, 223–251

Breschi, S., F. Malerba and L. Orsenigo (2000), Technological regimes and Schumpeterian patterns of innovation, *Economic Journal*, 110, 388–410

Dosi, G. (1988), Sources, procedures and microeconomic effects of innovation, *Journal of Economic Literature*, 26, 1,120–1,171

(1997), Opportunities, incentives and the collective patterns of technological change, *Economic Journal*, 107, 1,530–1,547

Dosi, G., K. Pavitt and L. Soete (1990), *The Economics of Technical Change and International Trade*, Harvester Wheatsheaf, Hemel Hempstead

Fagerberg, J. (1988), International competitiveness, *Economic Journal*, 98, 355–374

Fagerberg, J., P. Guerrieri and B. Versagen (1999), *The Economic Challenge for Europe*, Edward Elgar Publishing, Northampton, MA

Fagerberg, J., and G. Sollie (1987), The method of constant-market-shares analysis reconsidered. *Applied Economics*, 19, 1,571–1,585

Freeman, C. (1987), *Technology Policy and Economic Performance: Lessons from Japan*, Frances Pinter, London

Grupp, G., and H. Munt (1995), *Konkordanz zwischen der internationalen Patent und Warenklassification*, Institut für Systemtechnik und Innovations forschung, Karlsruhe

Laursen, K. (1999), The impact of technological opportunity on the dynamics of trade performance, *Structural Change and Economic Dynamics*, 10, 341–357

Levin, R. C., A. K. Klevorick, R. R. Nelson and S. G. Winter (1987), Appropriating the returns from industrial research and development, *Brookings Papers on Economic Activity*, 3, 783–831

Lundvall, B.-Å. (ed.) (1992), *National Systems of Innovation: Towards a Theory of Innovation and Interactive Learning*, Frances Pinter, London

Montobbio, F. (2003), Sectoral patterns of technological activity and export market share dynamics, *Cambridge Journal of Economics*, 27, 4, 523–545

Montobbio, F., and F. Rampa (2002), *The Impact of Technology on Structural Change and Export Performance in the Developing Countries*, Working Paper no. 34, Università degli Studi dell'Insubria, Varese

Mowery, D. C., and R. R. Nelson (eds.) (1999), *Sources of Industrial Leadership: Studies of Seven Industries*, Cambridge University Press, Cambridge

National Science Board (2000), *Science and Engineering Indicators 2000*, National Science Foundations, Arlington, VA [http://www.nsf.gov/sbe/srs/seind00/]

Nelson, R. R. (1991), Diffusion of development: post-World War II convergence among advanced industrial nations, *American Economic Review*, 81, 2, 271–275

(ed.) (1993), *National Innovation Systems: A Comparative Study*, Oxford University Press, Oxford

Nelson, R. R., and G. Wright (1992), The rise and fall of American technological leadership, *Journal of Economic Literature*, 30, 1,931–1,964

Organisation for Economic Co-operation and Development (2001a), *Towards a Knowledge-Based Economy*, OECD Science, Technology and Industry Scoreboard, Organisation for Economic Co-operation and Development, Paris

(2001b), *Drivers of Growth: Information Technology, Innovation and Entrepreneurship*, Science, Technology and Industry Outlook: special edition, Organisation for Economic Co-operation and Development, Paris

Patel, P., and K. Pavitt (1994) Uneven and divergent technological accumulation among advanced countries: evidence and a framework of explanation, *Industrial and Corporate Change*, 3, 3, 759–787

*Part II*

# Six sectoral systems

# 3 Pharmaceuticals analyzed through the lens of a sectoral innovation system

*Maureen McKelvey, Luigi Orsenigo and Fabio Pammolli*[1]

## 1 Introduction

This chapter analyzes the pharmaceutical industry through the lens of a sectoral system of innovation. Intuitively, the pharmaceutical industry quite naturally lends itself to be analyzed as an SSI or as a network (see Galambos and Sewell, 1995; Chandler, 1990; Gambardella, Orsenigo and Pammolli, 2000; and McKelvey and Orsenigo, 2002). However, at the same time and precisely given the intuitive appeal of the notion of "system" and/or "network" for this industry, taking this approach forces the researcher to try to make this notion more precise and compelling and – above all – to clarify why and in what sense a "sectoral innovation system" approach is useful. This constitutes the general aim of this chapter.

Generically, the pharmaceutical industry can easily be considered as a system or a network because innovative activities involve, directly or indirectly, a large variety of actors, including: (different types of) firms; other research organizations, such as universities and other research centers; financial institutions; regulatory authorities; and consumers.

An innovation system or network is composed of actors, relationships among actors and other contextual features that affect the decisions of actors' behavior and the development of knowledge and economic competencies (Edquist and McKelvey, 2000). All the actors mentioned above are part of an SSI, and they are different in many senses. They know different things; they have different rules of action; they have different incentives and motivations, which may often conflict. All these actors are linked together through a web of different relationships: they include almost pure market transactions, command and control, competition, collaboration and cooperation and all sorts of the so-called "intermediate forms." Moreover, most of these relationships have a peculiar nature. The

[1] The authors wish to thank Massimo Riccaboni and Nicola Lacetera for their help and suggestions.

obvious example is the observation that the market for drugs is characterized by strong informational asymmetries. Consumers cannot properly
evaluate the quality of a drug; those who select a particular drug for a
specific consumer do not coincide with those who pay for the drug, etc.
Relationships and interaction among different actors are affected by contextual factors, such as the actions of regulatory authorities, e.g. patent
laws, incentives to academics to engage in commercial activities, etc. In
particular, in this industry one observes – especially in recent years – the
mix and partial overlapping of different selection principles (McKelvey,
1997a).

We would argue that the case of pharmaceuticals is a particularly
interesting example of a dynamic SSI. Pharmaceuticals are a traditional
stronghold of the European industry, which still provides by far the
largest contribution to the European trade balance in high-tech sectors.
Moreover, over the last two decades the world pharmaceutical industry has undergone profound changes in technology (biotechnology and
the molecular biology revolution), demand (cost-containment policies)
and institutions (patent legislation etc.). Taken together, these tendencies have led to a redefinition of the fundamental sources of competitive advantages in this industry, and have also led to deep organizational
changes within firms as well as to extensive network changes in relationships among companies and other actors – such as universities and public
research centers. The development of demand and the organizational and
network changes are also visible through merger and acquisition (M&A)
processes and through the emergence of new patterns in the division of
labor and collaboration. Against this background, European pharmaceuticals have been losing ground vis-à-vis the United States, and significant
changes have also been occurring within and across European countries
(Gambardella, Orsenigo and Pammolli, 2000).

We take the general definition of a sectoral system of innovation found
in this book, and we apply it to analyze the evolution of the pharmaceutical industry through this lens. Thus, the SSI perspective is in our view
particularly useful for the analysis of pharmaceuticals because it directs
us to some fundamental methodological commitments when analyzing
these processes of economic transformation. We identify four such commitments of relevance here: 1) the dynamics of the system over time; 2)
the general focus on actors, relationships and networks as explanations
for individual firm and for industry behavior; 3) changing relationships
and networks; and 4) interactions among cognitive/technological factors
and institutional/country-specific factors.

First, our analysis focuses quite naturally on the *dynamics* of the system.
Rather than trying to provide a detailed examination of the structure of

the system at a given point in time, we concentrate on trying to make some progress in understanding how the pharmaceutical system evolves over time. Specifically, although we sketch the evolution of the industry prior to the mid-1970s, we examine mainly the evolution of the pharmaceutical industry over the last twenty to twenty-five years, i.e in the age of the molecular biology revolution and of cost-containment healthcare policies.

Secondly, the SSI approach provides a focus on actors, relationships and networks *as explanations* for individual firm behavior and for industry behavior. The SSI approach illustrates vividly how the relative importance of the relevant actors – and the specific form of the linkages in sectoral and national networks – may differ across countries and over time. Thus, both sectoral and national trends, as well as global trends, can be identified over time as affecting the firm and industry.

Thirdly, and in the same vein, we focus on the changing nature of the *relationships* among selected agents, rather than on specific agents. Relationships are obviously at the heart of SSI, with the idea that no firm innovates in isolation but is instead an integral actor within collective market and knowledge processes. Even more important, changes in the *learning and selection regimes* characterizing this industry have triggered not only changes in the intensity of these relationships but also the emergence of new actors (firms and organizations), new relations and new networks. These changes are partially endogenous and partially exogenous to the learning and selection regimes.

Finally, we focus on the interaction between cognitive/technological factors (*competencies and the properties of learning processes*) and institutional/country-specific factors (*incentives and selection processes*) that shape the evolution of the pharmaceutical SI. Both factors are clearly relevant, and our contribution here is to analyze how and why these two factors meet to shape pharmaceutical competition.

Thus, this chapter describes the evolution of the SSI, in pharmaceuticals over a longer historical period, but emphasizing more recent decades. In particular, due to reasons outlined in the above four methodological commitments, the Continental European pharmaceutical SSIs differ in significant ways from the Anglo-Saxon ones. In the discussion, this chapter focuses on the larger Western European countries of Germany, France and Italy as compared to the United States and the United Kingdom. Here, we do not present directly new empirical evidence and data. Rather, we rely on secondary sources (some provided by the authors), to which readers are referred. Thus, our contribution here is to understand the pharmaceutical SSI by combining analytical perspectives with rich empirical material.

The chapter is organized as follows. In section 2 we briefly recount the main features of the development of the pharmaceutical industry until (roughly) the mid-1970s. In section 3 we move to more recent history. Here, we discuss how the changes in the knowledge base and in the technological regime induced by the advent of the molecular biology revolution on the one hand, and by the transformations in the regulatory environment and in demand on the other hand, have drastically reconfigured the SSI. First, we look at the American case. Then, against this background, we discuss the main factors that might have caused a decline in European competitiveness in this industry over time. We use the methodological and theoretical perspective outlined above to interpret causality and change over time, especially focusing on the link between changes in knowledge and in markets, as related to actors, relationships and networks. Based on this analysis, section 4 links historical evidence with more theoretically oriented analysis through conjectures. These conjectures and hypotheses are of two groups, namely those related to the general concept of an SSI, and those that are applied to the specifics of pharmaceuticals and of Europe.

## 2    Innovation and the evolution of the sectoral system of innovation in the pharmaceutical industry: an overview

The historical patterns of development in the pharmaceutical industry have been extensively analyzed by several scholars (see especially Henderson, Orsenigo and Pisano, 1999). Here, we pick up some particularly important and relevant themes for our argument, partly related to the above methodological commitments and partly related to a broad evolutionary economics approach to innovation systems.[2] In very general terms, the history of the pharmaceutical industry can be analyzed as an evolutionary process of adaptation to major technological and institutional "shocks," which have occurred both endogenously and exogenously to the sector and which allow us to divide modern history into three major epochs. The first epoch is roughly the period 1850 to 1945. The second epoch is roughly the period 1945 to the mid-1970s/early 1980s. The third epoch runs from then through the present time. Each sketch of

---

[2] This section relies especially on the work by Chandler (1990), Galambos and Sewell (1995), Galambos and Sturchio (1998), Gambardella (1995), Orsenigo (1989), Schwartzman (1976) and – above all – Henderson, Orsenigo and Pisano (1999). These references have, however, been used to give an interpretation of the history of the pharmaceutical industry in terms of our evolutionary approach to systems of innovation (McKelvey, 1997b). See also McKelvey and Orsenigo (2002).

an epoch, therefore, addresses both the dynamics within knowledge and markets as well as the changes in actors, relationships and networks.

## 2.1    The early stages of the pharmaceutical industry

The first epoch corresponds roughly to the period 1850 to 1945. This is the period when drugs were closely related to chemicals, especially with the emergence of the synthetic dye industry in Germany and Switzerland. Initially, Swiss and German chemical companies such as Ciba, Sandoz, Bayer, and Hoechst leveraged their technical competencies in organic chemistry and dyestuffs in order to begin to manufacture drugs later in the nineteenth century. Up until World War I German companies dominated the industry, producing approximately 80 percent of the world's pharmaceutical output (Henderson, Orsenigo and Pisano, 1999).

Mass production of pharmaceuticals also began in the later part of the nineteenth century in the United States and the United Kingdom. However, whereas Swiss and German pharmaceutical activities tended to emerge within larger chemical-producing enterprises, the United States and the United Kingdom witnessed the birth of specialized pharmaceutical producers, such as Wyeth (later American Home Products), Eli Lilly, Pfizer, Warner-Lambert and Burroughs Wellcome. Thus, there were early differences in organizational focus (Henderson, Orsenigo and Pisano, 1999).

In these early years the pharmaceutical industry was neither tightly linked to formal science nor characterized by extensive in-house research and development for new drugs. Until the 1930s, when sulfonamide was discovered, drug companies undertook little formal research. However, the emerging sectoral system of innovation comprised already not only firms but also – quite obviously – universities and (to a lesser extent, since regulation was not strongly developed) regulatory authorities. Universities provided the basic knowledge in chemistry and – most importantly – the inflow of trained chemists necessary to sustain innovation. Similarly, patent laws (where available) provided both the incentives and the context for innovation. Moreover, linkages among firms quickly developed due to the exchanges of licenses for the production and marketing of drugs.

Indeed, ever since its inception, the industry has been comprised of – at least – two types of firms. A first group of companies – which included the German and Swiss giants and some American companies, such as Merck and Pfizer (see Chandler, 1998) – focused more on innovation and drug discovery. A second group of firms specialized, instead, in being followers in the sense of imitating/inventing around products invented elsewhere and/or products sold over the counter. The latter group of companies included Bristol-Myers, Warner-Lambert, Plough and American Home Products, as well as most of the firms in countries such as France, Italy, Spain and Japan (Henderson, Orsenigo and Pisano, 1999).

In summary, this first epoch corresponds to the emergence of mass production within the industry, but with firms with different characteristics.

## 2.2    The "random screening" period

The second epoch runs approximately from 1945 to the early 1980s, which can be called the golden age of pharmaceuticals. This was a period of both high profits and many developments in the knowledge about pharmaceuticals and related medicine. New actors emerged, and also the network was changed quite radically by the end of this period.

This period was driven through firm R&D, which led to many new drugs in an area/space of many technological opportunities. During this period the industry became extremely R&D-intensive, both because it became clear that drug discovery and development could be a highly profitable activity and because public support for health-related research boomed to unprecedented levels after the war. Moreover, the development of the welfare state – especially of national healthcare systems – provided a rich, "organized" and regulated market for drugs. The following subsections, therefore, describe the second epoch by relating changes in knowledge and markets to changes in actors, relationships and networks.

### 2.2.1    The organization of research and development and the patterns of competition

In this second epoch R&D spending exploded, leading to an expansion of search space, to a steady flow of new drugs and to high profits. During the war the US and British governments had organized a massive research and production effort that focused on commercial production techniques and chemical structure analysis. The intense wartime efforts to develop penicillin allowed the accumulation of new technical experience and organizational capabilities by firms and national actors (particularly the Anglo-Saxon countries). In other words, many pharmaceutical companies embarked on a period of massive investment in R&D, and they built large-scale internal R&D capabilities (Henderson, Orsenigo and Pisano, 1999).

A number of structural factors supported the industry's high average level of innovation and economic performance during this second epoch. One factor was the sheer magnitude of the opportunities that research provided as well as of unmet medical needs. In every major therapeutic category, pharmaceutical companies faced an almost completely open field. While the search space could be characterized as open, the firms' methods for exploring that space and for exploiting potentially useful discoveries were less scientific than current methods – but still an advancement upon the drug discovery methods that had existed before hand (Henderson, Orsenigo and Pisano, 1999).

Lacking a detailed knowledge of the biological underpinnings of specific diseases, pharmaceutical companies invented an approach to research that is now referred to as "random screening." Under this approach, natural and chemically derived compounds were randomly screened in test tube experiments and laboratory animals for potential therapeutic activity. Thousands of compounds might be subjected to multiple screens before researchers homed in on a promising substance. Serendipity played a key role, and, since it was difficult and time-consuming to synthesize a large number of compounds, researchers tended to focus their attention on synthesizing variants of compounds that had already shown promising effects in a screen. Chemists working within this regime often had some intuitive sense of the links between any given chemical structure and its therapeutic effect. Still, little of this knowledge was codified, so that new compound "design" was driven as much by the skills of individual chemists as it was by a basis of systematic science (Henderson, Orsenigo and Pisano, 1999).

Random screening worked extremely well for many years, not least in this open search space for new knowledge and in a market situation of high demand for many therapeutic areas. Several important classes of drugs were discovered in this way and several hundred new chemical entities (NCEs) were introduced in the 1950s and 1960s. Nevertheless, the successful introduction of an NCE has to be considered quite a rare event.[3] Innovative new drugs arrived quite seldom, but those that were found experienced extremely high rates of market growth. This was backed up by the fact that firms could have temporary monopolies on NCEs through patents. In turn, patents entailed a highly skewed distribution of the returns on innovation and of product market sizes as well as of the intra-firm distribution of sales across products. So a few "blockbusters" dominated the product range of all major firms (Matraves, 1999, p. 180; and Sutton, 1998). Despite stability in the broader industrial structure, pharmaceuticals have also been characterized by a series of fragmented markets. The industry was characterized by quite low levels of concentration, both at the aggregate level (i.e. the industry as a whole) as well as in

---

[3] Estimates suggest that, out of all the new compounds that were tested, only one out of every 5,000 reached the market. The rate of introduction was on the order of a couple of dozens per year, and these were concentrated in certain fast-growing areas such as the central nervous system, cardiac therapy, anti-infectives and cytostatics.

the individual sub-markets (e.g. cardiovascular, diuretics, tranquilizers, etc.).

The success of this way of organizing the innovation process reinforced the mechanisms of appropriability for the potential profits. The pharmaceutical industry has historically been one of the few industries where patents provide solid protection against imitation for product innovations (Levin et al., 1987).[4]

Note, however, that the scope and efficacy of patent protection has varied significantly across countries.[5] The United States has provided relatively strong patent protection in pharmaceuticals. However, many other countries did not offer protection for pharmaceutical products: only process technologies could be patented. France introduced product patents in 1960, Germany in 1968, Japan in 1976, Switzerland in 1977, and Italy and Sweden in 1978. In some cases, as in Japan and Italy (and possibly France), it appears that the absence of product patent protection encouraged the firms to avoid product R&D and to concentrate instead on finding novel processes for making existing molecules. In other cases, primarily Germany and Switzerland, this negative effect on product innovations didn't happen in the same way as in the other countries.[6]

The pharmaceutical industry also provided other means of appropriating economic returns apart from simply patent regimes. The differential performance of the firms can also be related to cumulative, knowledge-related and firm-specific factors. For example, the organizational capabilities developed by the larger pharmaceutical firms may have acted as a mechanism of appropriability. Why? Random screening entailed highly disciplined processes for carrying out mass screening programs, involving firm-specific organizational capabilities and tacit skills. The firm had to have the capabilities to develop and run such complex processes and keep track of relevant information.

---

[4] Because small variants in a molecule's structure can drastically alter its pharmacological properties, potential imitators often find it hard to work around the patent.

[5] It is also worth remembering that, despite the requisition of German patents at the end of World War II, the big German giants that emerged after the split-up of IG Farben regained their leadership very quickly.

[6] More generally, these observations suggest the conjecture that strong patent laws do indeed confer an advantage to innovators, but that they are not enough to promote innovation in contexts where innovative capabilities are low or missing. Similarly, high degrees of appropriability are likely to be particularly important for sustaining innovation in highly innovative and competitive environments, rather than in situations where little innovation takes place anyhow. In other words, patents magnify the incentives to innovate, but do not create them in the absence of the competencies that make innovation possible in the first place. Thus, strong incentives can create virtuous circles when they are coupled with strong competencies, but they might be ineffective and even dangerous when the latter are insufficient. The opposite is also likely to be true: competencies without incentives are probably bound to be underutilized and wasted.

In addition, for random screening, spillovers of knowledge between firms were relatively small. Since firms essentially relied on the law of large numbers, there was relatively little to be learned from the competition, but much to be learned from large-scale screening "in house." Relatedly, the successful exploitation of the economic benefits stemming from innovation also required control over other important complementary assets, such as competencies in the management of large-scale clinical trials, in the processes of gaining regulatory approval, marketing and distribution. Thus, while patents for product innovations have been important positive (and negative) incentives, the industry also had other mechanisms that were more related to the specifics of organizations and of the types of knowledge involved (Henderson, Orsenigo and Pisano, 1999).

Still, entirely new products capture only a part of innovative activities, even in this second epoch. Firms also innovated in other ways, especially "inventing around" existing molecules, or introducing new combinations among them or new ways of delivering them, etc. These constituted a major component of firms' innovative activities, broadly defined. Thus, while market competition centered around new product introductions, firms also competed through incremental advances over time, as well as through imitation and generic competition after patent expiration. This allowed a large "fringe" of imitative firms to thrive through commodity production and development of licensed products, particularly generic competition. The preceding discussion can be seen as differential selection pressures, which are linked to the choices of individual firms.

As a consequence, the international pharmaceutical industry has been characterized by a significant heterogeneity in terms of firms' strategic orientations and innovative capabilities. The "innovative core" of the industry consisted initially of the early German and Swiss innovative entrants, and they were joined after World War II by a few American and British firms. These firms maintained an innovation-oriented strategy over time, with both radical product innovations and incremental product and process innovations. A second group of firms – either located in these countries but more frequently found in other countries, such as Continental Europe and Japan – specialized instead in imitation, minor innovations and marketing. The international industrial structure was rather stable up to the mid-1970s, with very few entrants and a relatively stable and impenetrable "core" of successful innovative firms, surrounded by a more imitative "fringe."

National contexts appear to affect specific actors and networks in the industry. However, in this period the pharmaceutical industry and the overall pharmaceutical sectoral system of innovation started to become truly international. Firms could reduce average costs by expanding into new markets, to leverage the high degree of sunk costs in R&D and marketing. Moreover, firms were often required to have a presence in foreign markets to comply with local regulation, and thereby stimulated further internationalization. Not particularly surprisingly, the largest, highly R&D-intensive German, Swiss and American companies proceeded more decisively in their international expansion. This type of firm also established global networks of relations with locally based firms through licensing and commercialization agreements.

## 2.3    Changes in the network of relations

In this second epoch the network of relations defining the pharmaceutical sectoral system of innovation underwent deep transformations. This was not really a drastic change in the structure of the network; it was more that the relationships among agents became denser and thicker. The specifics of these networks are explained in subsequent sections. Our focus here is on comparing and contrasting the broad trends found in the United States and Europe, as the pharmaceutical SSI evolved during this epoch.

### 2.3.1    Biomedical research: funding and organization

A first change in the network concerns fundamental research and industry-university relations. It was in these years that the American research system started to gain absolute leadership in scientific research. In the specific case of biomedical research, in this period linkages with universities and basic research consolidated and started to change their nature. This was partly a consequence of the increase in public spending for biomedical research and partly due to the introduction of more demanding procedures for product approval. Pharmaceutical firms needed access to systematic clinical testing, which was usually organized through the medical research system, as well as to fundamental scientific results that increased the biological understanding of diseases, drugs and cures.

Nearly every government in the developed world supports publicly funded health-related research. In the United States, public spending on health-related research took off soon after World War II, even if European public funding of biomedical research also increased dramatically. There is little question that the sheer amount of resources devoted to biomedical research in the United States in the post-war era goes a long way to explain the American leadership in life sciences.[7] As a consequence – and

---

[7] Both qualitative and quantitative evidence suggests that this spending has had a significant effect on the productivity of those large US firms that were able to take advantage of it (Ward and Dranove, 1995; Cockburn and Henderson, 1996; and Maxwell and Eckhardt, 1990).

despite the existence of centers of absolute excellence – the overall quantity and quality of scientific research lagged behind in Europe. In turn, this created a vicious circle in Europe, with a significant drain of human and financial resources from Europe to the United States. This labor mobility across countries contributed to a further strengthening of the American advantage.

In addition, the institutional structure of biomedical research evolved quite differently in Continental Europe from the United States (and, partly, from the United Kingdom). In the United States most of the funding has been administered through the National Institutes of Health (NIH), although a significant fraction goes to universities and an important fraction of the support does go toward basic or fundamental science, which is widely disseminated through publication in the refereed literature.

The American system has focused on new types of knowledge integration around specific disease classes. The NIH did not only provide an enormous financial support to basic or fundamental science in universities and public research centres. More than that, the NIH pursued a substantial integration between the production of biological knowledge on the nature and mechanisms of human diseases, clinical research and medical practice with the discovery and development of new therapeutic treatments. Moreover, the American system has been characterized by a variety of sources of funding and selection mechanisms, which complement the role of the NIH, and these mechanisms are applied – always starting from scientific excellence – according to different allocative principles. This approach introduces some form of competition between financiers, and so it allows diversity to be explored while also maintaining this emphasis on leading-edge fundamental science.

In Europe funding has been administered mainly at the national level, with strongly differentiated approaches and with broad differences across countries. This is likely to have hindered the development of a critical mass of research in key fields, especially in smaller countries. In many cases resources have either been dispersed among a large number of "small" laboratories or have been excessively concentrated in the few available centres of excellence. It is widely recognized that the absolute size and the higher degree of integration of the American research system, as opposed to the fragmented collection of national systems in Europe, constitute a fundamental difference between the two systems.

Also, the institutional structure of biomedical research itself evolved quite differently in Continental Europe from the United States (and the United Kingdom). In Europe research tended to be confined to highly specialized laboratories in universities and, especially, in public research centers, with little interaction with teaching, medical practice and, a fortiori, with industrial research. Traditionally, the medical profession in Continental Europe has had less scientific preparation than is typical in either the United Kingdom or the United States. Medical training and practice have focused less on scientific methods per se than on the ability to use the results of research (Ben-David, 1977; and Thomas, 1994). Partly as a consequence, medically oriented research within European universities has tended to have a marginal role as compared to patient care. Moreover, historically the incentives to engage in patient care at the expense of research have been very high: France and Germany have only recently implemented a full-time system designed to free clinicians from their financial ties to patient-related activities.[8]

The weakness of the research function within hospitals in Continental Europe was one of the reasons that the decision was made to concentrate biomedical research in national laboratories rather than in medical schools (as happened in the United States and the United Kingdom). However, it has often been suggested that the separation of research from daily medical practice had a negative effect on its quality, and especially on the rate at which it diffused into the medical community (Braun, 1994; and Thomas, 1994).

Jointly, these factors have interacted in Continental Europe to create an environment that not only produces less science of generally lower quality but also one in which science is far less integrated with medical practice and industrial concerns.

### 2.3.2    *Procedures for product approval*

A second fundamental change that has altered the competitive environment during this second epoch has to do with the procedures for product approval. Since the early 1960s most countries have steadily increased the stringency of their approval processes. However, it was the United States – with the Kefauver-Harris Amendment Act in 1962 – and the United Kingdom – with the Medicine Act in 1971 – that took by far the most stringent stance early on among industrialized countries. Germany and – in particular – France, Japan and Italy have historically been much

---

[8] The organizational structure of medical schools has been such as to reinforce this effect. In Continental Europe medical schools and hospitals are part of a single organizational entity, whereas in the United States and the United Kingdom they are autonomous actors, which periodically negotiate as to the character of their association. In principle, the European system should have a number of advantages with respect to research and teaching. In practice, it has tended to have negative consequences, as patient care has tended to absorb the largest fraction of time and financial resources. In these systems, resources are not usually targeted to specific activities, and, given the difficulty of quantifying their cost (even when a fraction of the subsidies provided by the government is supposed to be used for the purposes of research and teaching), patient care easily makes inroads into these supposedly "protected" resources (Braun, 1994).

less demanding in terms of regulation. Other countries fall somewhere in between the most stringent and the least demanding procedures for product approval.

In the United States the 1962 Kefauver-Harris amendments introduced a "proof of efficacy" requirement for the approval of new drugs and established regulatory controls over the clinical (human) testing of new drug candidates. As a result, after 1962 the Federal Drug Administration (FDA) shifted its role from being essentially an evaluator of evidence and research findings at the end of the R&D process to being an active participant in the process itself (Grabowski and Vernon, 1983). This shift has consequences for both building up and integrating knowledge in the network.

The effects of the amendments on innovative activities and market structure have been the subject of considerable debate (see, for instance, Chien, 1979; Peltzman, 1974; and Comanor, 1986). The regulation has certainly led to effects in terms of: 1) there have been large increases in the resources necessary to obtain the approval of a new drug application; 2) it has probably caused sharp increases in R&D costs; 3) it has probably caused sharp increases in the gestation times for NCEs; 4) there have been large declines in the annual rate of NCE introduction for the industry; as well as 5) there has been a lag in the introduction of significant new drugs therapies in the United States when compared to Germany and the United Kingdom. This thus differentiated the American context from Continental Europe.

However, the creation of a stringent drug approval process in the United States may have also helped create strong competitive pressure, favoring really innovative firm strategies. In fact, although the process of development and approval increased costs, it significantly increased the barriers to imitation, even after patents expired, thereby further penalizing the less innovative firms.[9] One hypothesis for why British firms have fared better than Continental European firms in the pharmaceutical industry in the next, third epoch is that, for a longer period, they have faced more stringent regulation, and they also been more internationally oriented (Thomas, 1994).

In the European countries, with the noticeable exception of the United Kingdom (where the institutional environment surrounding drug approval was quite similar to that in the United States), procedures for product approval of pharmaceuticals were far less stringent than in the

---

[9] Until the Waxman-Hatch Act was passed in the United States in 1984, generic versions of drugs that had gone off patent still had to undergo extensive human clinical trials before they could be sold in the US market, so that it might be years before a generic version appeared even once a key patent had expired. In 1980 generics held only 2 percent of the US drug market.

United States for a prolonged period. This regulation regime allowed the survival of smaller firms that specialized in the commercialization of minor domestic products. In short, these firms were in some sense "protected" through the less stringent regulations, but this may have led to difficulties in reacting in relation to the changing international standards of the industry (Thomas, 1994).

During much of this epoch other types of fundamental, basic scientific research seemed to play an important but less crucial role, and only a few firms surveyed systematically the developments taking place in the "new sciences." Still, the development of the increasingly demanding and sophisticated clinical trials necessary for the approval of drugs had a further effect on the pattern of industry-university relations. Rather than only linking companies to breakthroughs in science, these demand-side developments also strengthened the interaction between companies and hospitals linked to medical schools in the design and implementation of increasingly scientifically based trials. However, the main channel of interaction between pharmaceutical companies and universities continued to be teaching and the provision of skilled chemists and pharmacologists.

### 2.3.3    Demand growth, the development of healthcare systems and regulation

A final fundamental change in this second epoch was related to demand, especially the development of national healthcare systems and of medical insurance. In general, the rise and consolidation of the welfare state and the general pick-up in economic growth implied a strong increase in the demand for drugs. These developments took very different forms across countries, and thereby had differentiated effects on the profits of those firms with a significant share in domestic markets (Lacetera and Orsenigo, 2001).

The United States was the only country where a national health service was not created. Yet other factors – primarily the size of the domestic market and the high prices of drugs – supported a rapid growth in demand. In the United States the fragmented structure of healthcare markets and the consequent low bargaining power of buyers at this time further protected pharmaceutical companies' rents from competitive product innovation. Unlike most European countries (with the exception of Germany and the Netherlands) and Japan, drug prices in the United States were unregulated by government intervention, and neither did insurance companies provide a major source of pricing leverage. This pricing flexibility contributed to the high return to the firm, and hence we can argue that firm profitability was also an outcome of investments in drug R&D.

In contrast, in most European countries and in Japan the prices of drugs were subject to various forms of direct or indirect control, for different reasons. The usual justification for price regulation was generally based on social equity considerations. A related argument – but somewhat different, because it is argued in terms of efficiency rather than equity – referred (albeit not always explicitly) to some peculiar features of the market for drugs. Thus, reasons to improve the market can be said to include arguments that demand elasticity tends to be low; information tends to be asymmetric; and monopoly power tends to be exercised through patents.[10] A further set of justifications for price regulation referred to cost containment. In countries where a national health service exists or when in any case there is a third payer (typically, an insurer), demand elasticity to price tends to be lower than would otherwise have been the case. This may lead to price increases by firms enjoying market power. As a consequence of rising prices by the firms, the absence of any countervailing measure is likely to lead to an explosion of public expenditures, because neither the patients nor the physicians ultimately pay for the drug. Thus, the governments may act as monopsonist and through various instruments tend to reduce drug prices. Finally, price regulation has sometimes been used (in most cases implicitly) as an industrial policy tool, to protect and/or to promote national industries.

Both the objectives and the instruments of price controls differed widely across European countries and Japan, partly because of the role taken by the state as customer of drugs and partly because of entrenched differences in attitudes and expectations about the role of the welfare state and "policy styles" or "routines."[11]

---

[10] First, demand elasticity tends to be low, given the value that users may attribute to the product, especially in extreme cases. Second, the market for drugs is inherently characterized by information asymmetry. Producers have "more information" on the quality of the drug than consumers. In fact, it is physicians and not patients who take the decision about the use of alternative drugs, but even doctors cannot know in detail the properties of a drug, especially when a drug is new. Moreover, it was observed that much of the information available to physicians is provided by the companies themselves. Producers could then try to exploit this asymmetry by charging higher prices. Finally, it was usually stressed that producers enjoy monopoly power through patent protection. Price regulation might therefore be justified as a mechanism to countervail monopolistic pricing. In part, this attitude was reflected in the frequent accusations of excessive profits enjoyed by the industry and of aggressive and misleading marketing practices by the pharmaceutical companies. These issues, for example, figured prominently in the debates within the Kefauver Committee (see Comanor, 1986, for a survey).

[11] Germany (and also other countries, such as the Netherlands) represents an interesting case in which the presence of universal health insurance, provided by a private sickness fund (the system dates back to the Bismarck era), has not been accompanied by some form of price control.

Differences between the United Kingdom and Japan, France and Italy can be illustrative of the argument. For example, in the United Kingdom the Pharmaceutical Price Regulation Scheme was established in 1957, and defined a cap to firms' overall rate of return, regardless of the pricing policy on each single product. The profit margin was negotiated by each firm with the Department of Health. The scheme was designed to ensure that each of the firms received an appropriate return on capital investment, including research conducted in the United Kingdom – and it was set higher for export-oriented firms. In general, this scheme tended to act as a non-tariff barrier, which favored both British and foreign R&D-intensive companies that operated directly in the United Kingdom. Conversely, it tended to penalize weak, imitative firms as well as those foreign competitors (primarily the Germans) trying to enter the British market without direct innovative effort *in loco* (Burstall, 1985; and Thomas, 1994).

France, Japan and Italy, on the contrary, are examples of countries that adopted policies of direct price control in dealing with the supply side of the market. Moreover, price regulation was organized in such a way to protect the domestic industry from foreign competition, and this thus offered little incentive to firms to develop ambitious innovative strategies (Thomas, 1994; and Henderson, Orsenigo and Pisano, 1999). The strategies in these national contexts would instead be to maximize returns under conditions of fairly stable products and prices. In both France and Japan such direct price controls for pharmaceuticals have proven, according to many observers, to be rather inefficient, in that they have tended to reward incremental innovation and "me too" products. The low number of important NCEs discovered, the small average size of firms in the industry and the limited degree of internationalization are all often considered to be the effects of such a system.

In summary, in this second epoch, industrial leadership was based on the combination of strong technical and organizational capabilities in the innovative process, as well as by firm and political competencies in the processes of product approval, marketing and distribution. Moreover, the processes and the intensity of competition were largely shaped by national, contextual and institutional factors, such as patent legislation, the procedures for product approval and price regulation.

It is hard to establish any specific direction of causation – let alone a linear relation – between one particular institutional feature, the nature of competition and the degree of innovativeness. Still, it is clear that some tended to become the more innovation-oriented firms and others the marketing-oriented companies. Rather than linear causation, it appears that specific combinations of these variables conspired to produce particular competitive environments favoring the adoption of innovative strategies by firms in pharmaceuticals. Moreover, it is worth noting that many of these institutional arrangements were not devised with the explicit aim of favoring innovation or even industrial prowess. Rather, they resulted from totally different purposes – such as social policies – but ended up, after sometimes quite prolonged periods of time, bearing important consequences for the capacity and willingness to innovate of firms located nationally, partly linked to network relationships.

## 3    The advent of molecular biology and the age of cost containment

The third epoch started with the coming of the knowledge revolution to pharmaceuticals, associated with molecular biology, as well as shifts in the nature of demand. This epoch can be characterized as one with more profound changes in the actors, as well as in the structure of the networks, and with some of this change due to the increasing internationalization of the industrial sector.

### 3.1    The scientific revolution and the new learning regime

The new learning regime in the third epoch can be called "guided search." From the mid-1970s on, substantial scientific advances in physiology, pharmacology, enzymology and cell biology led to enormous progress in mankind's ability to understand the mechanisms by which some existing drugs acted, as well as the biochemical and molecular roots of many diseases. The vast majority of the advances stemmed from publicly funded research. This new knowledge, and related techniques and equipment, had a profound impact on the process of discovery of new drugs within pharmaceutical firms, leading to the "guided search" techniques.

These techniques made use of the knowledge that a particular chemical pathway was fundamental to a particular physiological mechanism (Henderson, Orsenigo and Pisano, 1999). This implied that the firm's R&D process could itself become more efficient through searching within a more precise and better defined search space (McKelvey, 1997b). Chemists were beginning to be able to "design" compounds that might have particular therapeutic effects. The techniques of "rational drug design" are the result of applying the new biological knowledge to the design of new compounds, as well as applying it to the ways in which the compounds are screened. Thus, the firm's search for pharmaceutical products could become ever more "scientific" and structured – albeit to find specific industrial targets, not general knowledge.

Knowledge advances, however, had no automatic effect on the strategies and competitiveness of any given firm. For any particular firm, the shift in the technology of drug research from "random screening" to one of "guided" discovery or "drug discovery by design" was critically dependent on the firm's ability also to take advantage of publicly generated knowledge (Gambardella, 1995; and Cockburn and Henderson, 1996) and to develop economies of scope within the firm (Henderson and Cockburn, 1996). Smaller firms, those farther from the centers of public research and those that were most successful with the older techniques of drug discovery appear to have been much slower to adopt the new techniques than their rivals (Gambardella, 1995; and Henderson and Cockburn, 1996). There was also significant geographical variation in adoption. While the larger firms in the United States, the United Kingdom and Switzerland (and, in some cases, also in Scandinavia) were amongst the pioneers of the new technology, other Continental European and Japanese firms appear to have been slow responding to the opportunities afforded by the new science (Henderson, Orsenigo and Pisano, 1999).

This transition toward new techniques of drug discovery was in mid-course when molecular genetics and recombinant DNA (rDNA) technology opened an entirely new frontier for pharmaceutical innovation. The application of these advances initially followed two relatively distinct technical trajectories. One trajectory used genetic engineering as a process technology to manufacture proteins with existing therapeutic qualities that were already quite well understood in large enough quantities to permit their development as therapeutic agents (McKelvey, 1996). The second trajectory used advances in genetics and molecular biology as tools to enhance the productivity of the discovery of conventional "small molecule" synthetic chemical drugs. As the industry has gained experience with the new technologies, these two trajectories have converged or else been superseded by the development of new knowledge, which – again – changed the rationale for actors, relationships and networks within the sectoral system of innovation (Henderson, Orsenigo and Pisano, 1999).

More recently, technologies such as genomics, gene sequencing, transgenic animal creation and molecular biology have started to supply the industry with a huge number of novel biological targets. These targets are thought to be relevant to a vast array of diseases defined at the molecular level, but need to be linked to the development of highly sensitive assays incorporating these targets. Against this background, during the 1980s and 1990s new developments in a variety of research areas have affected both the search and testing phases of pharmaceutical R&D. These advances – such as solution phase and solid phase chemistries, high-throughput screening (HTS) technologies and combinatorial chemistry – have led to the development of a set of research techniques. These research techniques to explore new areas of search space also allow the firm to achieve a higher breadth of applications, measured in terms of the number of disease areas and biological targets to which the firm may apply these techniques.[12] This move toward large numbers has been accompanied by knowledge development, which also increases the speed at which each target is tested. In summary, during the 1990s a set of generic research technologies was developed that allow researchers to screen thousands of potentially promising compounds at an unprecedented speed. Examples include polymerase chain reactions protein structure modeling, rapid computer-based drug assay and testing, recombinant chemistry techniques, drug delivery systems, and chemical separation and purification techniques.

The appearance of these new families of technologies has introduced a further distinction in the two (coexisting) search regimes, which can be used to characterize contemporary pharmaceutical R&D. The first regime is essentially based on biological hypotheses and molecules that tend to be specific to given fields of application (co-specialized technologies). The second regime is characterized by the emergence of new generic tools useful in searches based on the law of large numbers (labeled in the literature as transversal, generic or platform technologies).

In the case of co-specialized research hypotheses and molecules, the characterization of biological targets and the corresponding design/experimentation of each new drug tends to require individual analysis. Lessons learned from the design and experimentation of one biological hypothesis/molecule cannot be immediately transferred to other biological domains, in order to develop other classes of drugs. Conversely, transversal technologies are in principle applicable to multiple biological targets and diseases (Orsenigo, Pammolli and Riccaboni, 2001).

### 3.2    From the learning regime to the organization of innovative activities within and across firms

The new learning regime requires different learning and discovery procedures, implying a new structure of the search space, new definitions of the problems to be solved and the use of new heuristics and routines to solve

---

[12] Combinatorial chemistry enables the rapid and systematic assembling of a variety of molecular entities, or building blocks, in many different combinations to create tens of thousands of diverse compounds, which can be tested in drug discovery screening assays to identify potential lead compounds. Large libraries are available to be tested against both established and novel targets to yield potential lead compounds for new medicines. Such vast numbers of compounds have been introducing a substantial challenge to the drug discovery process and have created a need for faster and more efficient screening. HTS methods make it possible to screen vast populations of compounds via automated instrumentation: that is, complex workstations capable of performing several functions with the help of mechanical arms or simpler automated dilution devices.

such problems. This, in turn, has influenced the organizational structure of innovative activities, leading to a redesign of the patterns of division of labor and to different incentive structures and selection mechanisms. This transformation occurred much more quickly in the United States than, in particular, Continental Europe, where not only has there been a lag but also profoundly different forms are visible.

### 3.2.1   New biotechnology firms

The most noticeable manifestation of the transformations occurring in the pharmaceutical SSI has been the appearance of a new breed of agents, i.e. specialized new biotechnology firms (NBFs). As in many other technologies, innovation was first pursued not by incumbents but by new companies. In the United States, biotechnology was the motive force behind the first large-scale entry into the pharmaceutical industry since the early post-war period. The first new biotechnology start-up, Genentech, was founded in 1976 by Herbert Boyer (one of the scientists who developed the rDNA technique) and Robert Swanson, a venture capitalist. Genentech constituted the model for most of the new firms. They were primarily university spin-offs and they were usually formed through collaboration between scientists and professional managers, backed by venture capital. Their specific skills resided in the knowledge of the new techniques and in the research capabilities in that area, but they also quickly gained access to industrial knowledge through the hiring of employees (McKelvey, 1996). The "function" of this type of NBF has been to mobilize the fundamental knowledge created in universities and to transform it into potentially commercially useful techniques and products. However, these organizational principles (in terms of norms, incentives and practices) had to be made consistent with their commercial nature too. Thus, secrecy and the search for broad property rights became crucial features of these new firms. Moreover, financial constraints coupled with high burn rates have made "time to patent" a characteristic feature of the research style of these companies. Entry rates of NBFs soared in 1980 and have remained at a very high level thereafter, but with waves linked to both the stock market performance and to the appearance of successive new technologies. Yet it took several years before the biotechnology industry started to have an impact on the pharmaceutical market. Many of the early trajectories of research proved to be dead ends and/or much more difficult to develop than expected.[13]

---

[13] The first biotechnology product, human insulin, was approved in 1982, and between 1982 and 1992 sixteen biotechnology drugs were approved for the US market. As is the case for small molecular weight drugs, the distribution of sales of biotechnology products

While biotechnology-related products became integrated with pharmaceuticals, the large majority of these new companies never managed to become fully integrated drug producers. The growth of NBFs as pharmaceutical companies has been constrained by the need to develop competencies in different crucial areas.

First, the first generation of NBFs found it necessary to understand better the biological processes occurring in proteins and to identify the specific therapeutic effects of such proteins. In the beginning, companies turned to produce those proteins (e.g. insulin and the growth hormones) that were sufficiently well known. The subsequent progress of individual firms and of the industry as a whole was, however, predicated on the hope of being able to develop much deeper knowledge of the workings of other proteins in relation to specific diseases. Yet progress in this direction proved more difficult – and more expensive – than expected (Henderson, Orsenigo and Pisano, 1999).

Second, these companies often lacked competencies in other crucial aspects of the innovative process, in particular the knowledge and experience of clinical testing and other procedures related to product approval on the one hand and marketing on the other. Thus, with few exceptions (such as Genentech and Amgen), most of these NBFs have exploited their basic competency and acted primarily as research companies and specialized suppliers of high-technology intermediate products, performing contract research for and in collaboration with established pharmaceutical corporations. While the NBF could ideally gain such knowledge, their non-movement to become full-fledged pharmaceutical companies indicates that there are some organizational advantages or reasons for remaining specialized knowledge producers.

Third, even remaining at the level of pre-clinical R&D, most NBFs lacked crucial competencies in a rather different way. In fact, many individual NBFs were actually started on the basis of a specific hypothesis or technique, following the processes of the growth of knowledge in the field. Such processes entailed the proliferation and branching of alternative hypotheses at increasing levels of specificity (Orsenigo, Pammolli and Riccaboni, 2001). Thus, successive generations of NBFs were increasingly specialized in particular fields and techniques. The reason

is highly skewed. Three products were major commercial successes: insulin (Genentech and Eli Lilly), tissue plasminogen activator (tPA – Genentech in 1987) and erythropoietin (Amgen and Ortho in 1989). By 1991 there were over a hundred biotechnology drugs in clinical development and twenty-one biotechnology drugs with submitted applications to the FDA (Grabowski and Vernon, 1994): this was roughly one-third of all drugs in clinical trials. Sales of biotechnology-derived therapeutic drugs and vaccines had reached $2 billion, and two new biotechnology firms (Genentech and Amgen) had entered the club of the top eight major pharmaceutical innovators (Grabowski and Vernon, 1994).

this specialization worked counter to becoming a fully integrated pharmaceutical company is that the process of drug discovery (and development) still requires a broader and more "general" perspective, which integrates several. This broader perspective is necessary on many fronts, including alternative routes to the discovery of particular classes of drugs, the cognitive complementarities among different techniques and bodies of knowledge, and the realization and exploitation of economies of scope.

Later generations of NBFs (including the new "stars," such as Affymax, Incyte and Celera) were largely created on the basis of specialization into such radically different new technologies as genomics, gene therapy and combinatorial chemistry, or what are now called "platform technologies." These technologies are essentially research tools, and the companies developing them do not aim to become drug producers but providers of services to the corporations involved in drug discovery and development. As argued, for example, by Casper and Kettler (2000), these companies are characterized by radically different risk profiles, having a potentially larger market and avoiding the problems of conducting clinical trials. They may thus be able to sell specialized services to a wider range of potential buyers – which would generally be other companies rather than the end-user patients/doctors.

Collaboration with large incumbent pharmaceutical companies has allowed NBFs to survive and – in some cases – to pave the way for subsequent growth in many respects. First, clearly, collaboration with large companies provided the financial resources necessary to fund R&D. Second, it provided the access to organizational capabilities in product development and marketing. Established companies faced the opposite problem: while they needed to explore, acquire and develop the new knowledge, they had the experience and the structures necessary to control testing, production and marketing. Both types of company also wanted collaboration with the relevant basic scientific communities, in order to gain access to new sources of knowledge.

### 3.2.2    *The adoption of molecular biology by established companies*

Large established firms approached these new scientific developments mainly from a different perspective, i.e. as tools to enhance the productivity of the discovery of conventional "small molecule" synthetic chemical drugs.

For the large pharmaceutical firms, the tools of genetic engineering were initially employed as another source of "screens" with which to search for new drugs. Their use required a very substantial extension of the range of scientific skills employed by the firm. Moreover, it required a scientific workforce that was tightly connected to the larger scientific community, and an organizational structure that supported a rich and rapid exchange of scientific knowledge across the firm (Gambardella, 1995; and Henderson and Cockburn, 1996). The new techniques also increased returns to the scope of the research effort (Henderson and Cockburn, 1996). In turn, this required the recruitment of star scientists, and the adoption of organizational practices and incentive structures that attempted to replicate some of the typical characteristics of an academic environment, such as the adoption of "pro-publication" incentives (Cockburn, Henderson and Stern, 2000).

The molecular biology revolution made innovative capabilities critically dependent on publicly generated scientific research. Far from being a costless and direct process, the major changes in the knowledge base during this third epoch have implied that companies had to establish much closer and tighter linkages with the scientific community, in various forms: research contracts, long-run funding agreements to particular teams or institutions, etc. This required investment to monitor and maintain networks for potential sources of information.

However, a necessary condition for getting access to such knowledge, both from a cognitive and a sociological perspective, was that companies had to become active players in the scientific arena and not simply passive observers and users. In fact, the relation between firms and public research "is very much a bidirectional one, characterized by the rich exchange of information in both directions" (Cockburn and Henderson, 1996). In other words, companies had to build in-house competencies for at least three reasons. First, in order to develop the "absorptive capabilities" necessary to understand the scientific advances being made in academia and in the NBFs. Second, in order to get a "ticket of admission" to the scientific community. Third, because the development of new drugs required not simply the availability of specific techniques but the evaluation and testing of alternative approaches and the integration of different techniques, scientific disciplines, etc. Finally, it is important to emphasize that, for all these motives, the research capabilities built inside the firm needed to be at the leading edge.

As several authors have documented (Gambardella, 1995; Henderson and Cockburn, 1996; and Galambos and Sturchio, 1998, among others), there was enormous variation across firms in the speed with which the new techniques were adopted. In particular, Henderson has shown that the adoption of biotechnology was much less difficult for those firms – typically large ones – that had made the transition from "random" to "guided" drug discovery, as opposed to those that had chosen other search strategies. In contrast, smaller firms, and companies that were much less connected to the publicly funded research community, were much slower to follow.

### 3.2.3    The network of collaborative relations

The SSI in pharmaceuticals was transformed by the emergence of a new organizational form, namely the network of collaborative relations. Indeed, a dense web of collaborative relationships emerged, with the start-up firms positioned as upstream suppliers of technology and R&D services, and established firms positioned as downstream buyers able to provide capital as well as access to complementary assets.

One finds in the literature widely differing interpretations of the nature, motivations, structure and functions of these networks, ranging from more sociologically oriented approaches to economic explanations based on (various mixes of) alternative theoretical backgrounds – e.g. transaction costs, contract theories, game theory and competence-based accounts of firms' organization.

According to an influential interpretation, collaborations represent a new form of organization of innovative activities, which are emerging in response to the increasingly codified and abstract nature of the knowledge bases on which innovations draw (Arora and Gambardella, 1994; and Gambardella, 1995). To be sure, substantial market failures exist in the exchange of a commodity such as information. However, the abstract and codified nature of science, coupled with the establishment of property rights on such knowledge, makes it possible, in principle, to separate the innovation process into different vertical stages. Different types of institutions tend to specialize in the stage of the innovation process in which they are most efficient: universities in the first stage, small firms in the second, big established firms in the third (see also Arrow, 1983). In this view, then, a network of ties between these actors can provide the necessary coordination of the innovation process in a division of innovative labor. Collaborations are likely to be a permanent feature of the industry, with a large (and possibly continuously expanding) number of entities interacting with each other, generating an intricate network within which each subject specializes in particular stages of the innovation process, getting benefits from an increasing division of innovative labor.

According to another interpretation, collaborative relations are instead considered as a transient phenomenon, bound to decrease in scale and scope as the technology matures and as higher degrees of vertical integration are established in the industry (Pisano, 1991).[14] These arguments

---

[14] For example, empirical studies on the rates of success and failure of projects carried on entirely in-house – as compared to projects involving the acquisition of licenses from third parties – show that, indeed, licensed projects have higher probability of success (Gambardella, Orsenigo and Pammolli, 2000; and Arora et al, 2000. For conflicting evidence, see Pisano, 1997.).

depend on the relative value of knowledge exposed to others through collaborative agreements.

Finally, according to interpretations focusing on network advantages, the complex and interdisciplinary nature of relevant knowledge bases in pharmaceutical R&D tends to make technological innovations the outcome of interactions and cooperation among different types of agents commanding complementary resources and competencies (Orsenigo, 1989; Pisano, 1991; and Pammolli, 1997). In this perspective, it has also been suggested that the locus of innovation (and the proper unit of analysis) is no longer a firm but the network itself (see Powell, Koput and Smith-Doerr, 1996). In this case, the direction of causation is reversed. It is the structure of the network and the position of agents within it that fundamentally determine agents' access to relevant sources of scientific and technological knowledge and, therefore, innovative activities and performances (see also Kogut, Shan and Walker, 1992).

However, seeing NBFs simply as middlemen between universities and large firms is only part of the story. First of all, it is worth noting that collaboration does not simply involve the transfer of knowledge from a NBF lacking complementary assets to an established corporation that uses such knowledge to develop and market the drug. The innovation process involves the effective integration of a wide range of pieces of knowledge and activities (Orsenigo, 1989). The processes of drug discovery and – a fortiori – drug development require the integration of different disciplines. Substantial costs remain in transferring knowledge across different organizations, especially for the tacit and specific component of knowledge. Thus, aspects related to knowledge and networks can affect possible outcomes within the division of labor.

Moreover, access to the network of collaborations and to the market for technologies is not unrestricted. On the contrary, the network of collaborative relationships itself tends to consolidate and to become increasingly hierarchical, while also exhibiting expansion. Despite this growth, however, the network tends to consolidate around a rather stable core of companies, composed of large incumbents and early entrants into the network. This suggests the existence of first-mover advantages even in the network of collaborations, the core of which becomes increasingly difficult to enter as time goes by and can be perturbed only – and temporarily – by new and major technological discontinuities (see Orsenigo, Pammolli and Riccaboni, 2001).

As discussed in Pammolli (1997) and in Orsenigo, Pammolli and Riccaboni (2001), scientific progress did not only simplify the search space by providing more general theories. It also led to an explosion of the search space, with a continuous proliferation and branching of hypotheses and techniques at increasing levels of specificity. No single institution is able to develop internally, in the short run, all the necessary ingredients for bringing new products onto the market place.

Thus, these properties of the knowledge base and of the related learning processes induced particular patterns in the division of labor between different types of firms. In general, the results indicate that two different logics of exploration and technological advance coexisted, and that these were strongly complementary in the evolution of the network. The first trajectory generated patterns in the division of labor in which older generations of firms worked at higher levels of generality and linked with successive generations of new entrants, who typically embodied increasingly specific hypotheses and techniques. The second trajectory of more radical changes induced, instead, collaboration between all types of firms, modifying the intergenerational structure of the agreements typical of the first trajectory.

In both cases, however, incumbent firms were able over time to absorb the new knowledge and turned to the youngest entrants to get access to the newest techniques. Thus, the expansion of the network was mainly driven by the entry of new agents embodying new techniques. At the same time, the network tended to assume a distinct hierarchical structure, with different firms operating at different levels of generality, which was perturbed but not broken by transversal techniques. As Gambardella, Pammolli and Riccaboni (2000) have shown, large corporations do not seem to be characterized by any absolute disadvantage in the process of discovery: if anything, the reverse seems to be true. So, the division of labor emerges rather from the comparative advantage that big firms have in drug development as compared to NBFs and from the tumultuous rate of technical change, which continuously spurs new waves of innovations from every quarter.

### 3.2.4   *The other face of the division of labor: mergers and acquisitions*

Contextually to the processes of the division of labor and to the emergence of the network of collaborative relations, another – seemingly conflicting – phenomenon is characterizing industry evolution: namely the intensification of the processes of mergers and acquisitions since the early 1980s. Mergers and acquisitions occur at all levels: between NBFs, between large firms and NBFs (as in the case of Hoffman-La Roche and Genentech), but – above all – among the giants of the industry.

Several reasons may account for this trend. First, the rising costs of R&D and marketing imply larger markets and a rationalization of the portfolio of R&D projects and of products. Given the enormous amount of resources needed to bring a drug to the market and to sustain it afterwards, only very large organizations can engage in these efforts. Second, mergers can be justified by the need to complement the research and market portfolios, acquiring new competencies and attempting to exploit economies of scope in R&D and marketing. Third, M&As might be triggered by declining competitiveness, exhaustion of the pipeline and the expiration of patents on crucial products. Fourth, M&As can occur on rather conventional grounds for strategic purposes, e.g. to eliminate competitors. Fifth, as we discuss again later, mergers take place through vertical integration downstream, through the acquisition of distributors. Sixth, large corporations acquire producers of generics, either to preempt competition on their brand product in specific markets or to apply strategies of market segmentation, producing both the branded good at high prices and the generic version at lower prices.

The available literature provides little evidence so far on the relative role of the factors we mention above, let alone on the technological and economic outcome of M&As. If anything, casual empiricism suggests questions rather than answers. In many instances, M&As seem to respond mainly to "defensive" motivations, in that they involve "weakening" European companies (e.g. Ciba Geigy and Sandoz forming Novartis, Rhône-Poulenc and Hoechst forming Aventis, and Astra and Zeneca merging into AstraZeneca) trying to reach some ill-defined "critical mass" or to acquire a new pipeline as important patents are bound to expire (Glaxo and SmithKline Beecham). In other cases, it is successful American corporations that acquire weaker European companies. It would appear, however, at first sight, that the stronger American companies (such as Merck and Pfizer) are less involved in this type of expansion than weaker US corporations or European firms.

M&A processes are also relevant because they usually involve the relocation of research into specific geographical areas, such as the United Kingdom and Ireland and, especially, the United States. Thus, this trend is likely to be changing the geography of innovation, probably strengthening the existing leads and lags and creating stronger concentration in R&D activities.

In any event, what seems particularly interesting in this trend is that these processes of vertical and horizontal integration take place jointly with seemingly opposite processes of the division of labor in innovative activities. Despite the difficulty of accurately identifying and measuring the economies of scale and scope that are likely to motivate M&As, this observation strengthens the intuition that technological and institutional change does not simply induce unequivocal incentives toward the division of labor and the creation of markets for technology. Instead, such changes modify the very space where complementarities, and where the boundaries between markets and hierarchies, are defined.

### 3.3    *Institutional preconditions and their changes: mixing organizational and selective principles*

The transformations we have described so far in the organization of firms have been accompanied by other profound changes in the sectoral system of innovation. Such changes were particularly important in the United States, and, indeed, they are often considered as a fundamental explanation of the emerging American leadership in pharmaceuticals. Some of these changes pre-date the molecular biology revolution, and constituted a precondition for the following developments. Other changes are best understood as adaptive responses to the scientific revolution. Moreover, other transformations occurred that are largely exogenous to the R&D process but which influenced profoundly the evolution of the sectoral innovation system. This section explains how changes in the SSI affected the overall industry and its competitiveness per se in different geographical areas.

### 3.3.1    *Industry-university relations, appropriability conditions and venture capital*

The development of the biotechnology industry in the United States rested on the concomitant growth of a series of supporting organizations and institutions, which are now perceived as defining the distinct character of the "American way" to innovation, at least in high-tech industries. This system is organized around the nexus between academia, institutions governing property rights and venture capital (Mowery and Rosenberg, 2000).

The key role acquired by scientific knowledge for technological innovation in this industry manifested itself in an unprecedented intensification of both industry-university ties and in the direct involvement of academic institutions and scientists in commercial activities.

Neither phenomenon, certainly, is new in the United States. As documented by Nelson and Rosenberg (1994) and Mowery and Rosenberg (2000), among others, the very development of the US academic system was tightly linked to industry needs. Some universities have been engaged in patenting, and even in the promotion of spin-offs, ever since the beginning of the twentieth century.

However, since the mid-1970s, the drive toward an increasing commercialization of the results of research accelerated dramatically and took a variety of forms. Universities' patenting and licensing activities started to soar. The creation of spin-offs – discussed above as NBFs – became a distinct and crucial phenomenon of the American academic system. Increasingly, universities were assuming and were asked to assume the role of direct engines of (local) economic growth.

In the United States (and in the United Kingdom) departments have long been the main organizational entities, as opposed to the Continental European institutes, which are dominated by a single professor, far less interdisciplinary in nature and have feudal-like career paths. Moreover, in the United States high degrees of integration between teaching and research have been achieved through the sharp separation between undergraduate and postgraduate levels (Ben-David, 1977). The creation of research-oriented postgraduate studies entailed, in fact, a number of important consequences. In particular, postgraduate students are typically exposed and trained to the practice of scientific research within research teams composed of students and professors within departmental organizations. This arrangement not only tends to free resources for scientific research but also provides a fundamental experience in participating in and managing relatively complex organizations. In other words, it constitutes an essential source for the development of organizational capabilities. Moreover, the career of young research scientists after graduate studies has – under various perspectives – entrepreneurial characteristics. For instance, postdoctoral scientists have to raise funds for their own research in a highly competitive environment, where performance is judged on the basis of a track record and the ability to set an independent research agenda (Gittelman, 2000). Finally, graduate students joining the industrial world after the completion of their studies constitute an essential source of skilled demand for academic research.

The coupling between scientific, organizational and entrepreneurial capabilities thus constitutes an essential precondition for subsequent developments in industry-university relations. However, it is also important to note that such developments are, to some extent, to be considered as part of a much more general tendency toward the diffusion of an increasingly favorable attitude toward the establishment and enforcement of strong intellectual property rights.

The establishment of clearly defined IPR indeed played an important role in making possible the explosion of new firm foundings in the United States, because the new firms, by definition, had few complementary assets that would have enabled them to appropriate returns from the new science in the absence of strong patent rights (Teece, 1986). In the early years of "biotechnology" considerable confusion surrounded the conditions under which patents could be obtained. In the first place, research in genetic engineering was on the borderline between basic and applied science. Much of it was conducted in universities or otherwise publicly funded, and the degree to which it was appropriate to patent the results of such research became almost immediately the subject of bitter debate.[15] Similarly a growing tension emerged between publishing research results versus patenting them. Whilst the norms of the scientific community and the search for professional recognition had long stressed rapid publication, patent laws prohibited the granting of a patent to an already published discovery (Merton, 1973; and Kenney, 1986). In the second place, the law surrounding the possibility of patenting life formats and procedures relating to the modification of life forms was not defined. This issue involved a variety of problems (see OTA, 1984), but it essentially boiled down – first – to the question of whether living things could be patented at all and – second – to the scope of the claims that could be granted to such a patent (Merges and Nelson, 1994; and Mazzoleni and Nelson, 1998a).

In fact, these trends were partly spurred by a growing concern about how to exploit academic research more efficiently and by the need to introduce some order into the system that governed the conditions under which universities could obtain patents – and therefore income – on the results of publicly funded research. The Bayh-Dole Act in 1980 sanctioned these attitudes, by greatly facilitating university patenting and licensing. However, as Mowery (1998) and Mowery and Rosenberg (2000) have shown, the emergence of the "industry-university complex" (Kenney, 1986) and of the entrepreneurial university pre-dates Bayh-Dole and depends critically on the rise of the two main technological revolutions of the second half of the century, microelectronics and – especially – biotechnology.

Parallel to Bayh-Dole, a series of judicial and congressional decisions further strengthened the appropriability regime of the emerging sectoral system. In 1980 the US Supreme Court ruled in favor of granting patent protection to living things (Diamond versus Chakrabarty). In the subsequent years a number of patents were granted, establishing the right for very broad claims (Merges and Nelson, 1994). Finally, a one-year grace period was introduced for filing a patent after the publication of the invention.

---

[15] Millstein and Kohler's groundbreaking discovery – hybridoma technology – was never patented, while Stanford University filed a patent for Boyer and Cohen's process in 1974. Boyer and Cohen renounced their own rights to the patent, but, nevertheless, they were strongly criticized for having been instrumental in patenting what was considered to be a basic technology.

These developments led to the increasing relevance of courts' decisions about the fate of individual firms and of the industry in general. Litigation appears to be a distinct feature of the new biotechnology sectoral system, and IPR experts have become crucial components of firms' human resources and competencies.

Within this context, universities – and individual university scientists – began having more incentives to commercialize the results of their research. In fact, some research has even indicated that the strongest basic scientists in this sector also had the strongest patents (Zucker, Darby and Brewer, 1997). Assuming that basic scientific work also maintained autonomy, this implies that individuals and organizations have been increasingly involved in dual selection environments. On the one hand, most are still involved in pushing forward the frontiers of basic science. On the other hand, many are also involved in the search for and in the development of economically profitable ideas, either directly through patents and companies or indirectly through future wages.

The third pillar of this emerging system was, of course, venture capital. Once again, venture capital was a long-standing institution in the American financial and innovation system. It was already active – in various forms – in the 1920s (or even before), and it emerged as a vibrant industry with the electronic revolution in the 1960s. We will not review here the history and the role of venture capital, nor its embeddedness in the unique structures of the Anglo-Saxon systems of finance, corporate governance and labor markets. In the present context, it is perhaps worth just stressing how venture capital performs a crucial role of bridging and complementing different constituents and roles within the "new" system of bio-pharmaceutical innovation.

Venture capital provides, first of all, finance to prospective academic entrepreneurs. In this function, the venture capital industry is strictly dependent on – and contributes to the further strengthening of – a tight appropriability regime, since patents are the fundamental collateral – or means for extracting value – from NBFs. Second, venture capital provides not only, or simply, finance but also – and perhaps even more importantly – managerial advice and organizational capabilities. Contrary to the conventional stereotype of American financial institutions, venture capitalists are characterized by an extremely strong "hands-on" and "long-run" approach toward the companies they are financing. In this function, venture capital does not only, or simply, bridge science and markets. To perform this function, venture capitalists need not only strong specific and technical capabilities in finance but also a deep knowledge of the science and the technology in which they are investing. Thus, a significant number of Ph.D.s in biology end up working in venture capital firms, and venture capitalists have to be part of the same network of conferences, literature, scientists, etc. Thus, venture capital mixes technology, academia and finance. Once again, the overlapping of these realms is not always easy and frictionless. In some cases, financial considerations lead to accelerated initial public offerings (IPOs), which threaten the construction and consolidation of companies' technological and organizational capabilities.

## 3.4     Changes in demand and in regulation

Contextually to the changes in the technological regime, another series of important transformations was taking place at the level of the regulation and the demand side of the industry. The "regulatory revolution" interacted with the "scientific revolution" in shaping the sectoral system of innovation, once again creating or strengthening new agents, ties among agents, etc. Once again, the patterns of development of the sectoral system were quite different across countries.

### 3.4.1     Cost containment

During the 1980s the trends initiated in the previous period toward increasingly stringent controls on product approval requirements continued and, if anything, strengthened, especially in Europe.[16]

The main institutional change in this period, however, was the emergence of cost containment policies. In the OECD countries real total pharmaceutical expenditure (in constant terms) grew at an average yearly rate of 3.5 percent in the 1980s and of 4.6 percent from 1990 to 1996 (Jacobzone, 2000). This growth was determined partly by rising income. However, pharmaceutical expenditure has grown on average 1.5 percentage points more than GDP growth since the 1970s. Thus, other factors, related to the increasing prices of drugs and the aging population, also contributed to the rise of expenditures. In any case, increasing pharmaceutical expenditure also implied growing pressure on public outlays. In a period characterized by mounting concerns over budget deficits and – more generally – over the extension of public intervention in

---

[16] This section relies heavily on Lacetera and Orsenigo, 2001. In particular, the evolution toward a single market by European Union countries has involved attempts at the harmonization of national laws and approaches toward drug approval procedures. The creation in 1975 of the Committee for Proprietary Medicinal Products, an advisory body charged with the task of reviewing national procedures, and the establishment of a mutual recognition procedure in the same year represent the first concrete steps in this direction. In 1995 a parallel procedure, centralized at European Union level, came into effect, and it is now compulsory for biotech drugs. Such central application permits a manufacturer to refer directly to a single agency, the European Medicines Evaluation Agency, headquartered in London.

the economy, pharmaceutical expenditures became a primary target for expense reduction. On the other hand, healthcare is increasingly perceived as a fundamental human right, and/or in some cases as a public good. Thus, decreasing public coverage of pharmaceutical expenditure is sometimes seen as a threat to a fundamental and consolidated right and – to the extent that it hits in particular the poorer segments of the population – to a basic principle of equity. On the other hand, the inefficiencies generated by excessive public coverage of drug expenditure (e.g. excessive consumption of drugs) and by command and control measures, such as the various forms of price controls, are also stressed.

Actually, the approaches toward cost containment differ substantially across countries and over time, and reflect the specific histories and institutional settings of each country. However, a common trend is discernible toward the increasing use of policies aiming at intervening on the demand side of the market to make patients and health providers (doctors and pharmacists) more price-conscious and more price-sensitive (Mossialos, 1997), without or irrespective of direct price controls. Generic substitution also meets broad agreements, and now many countries try to promote the diffusion of non-branded drugs. Finally, price controls seem to be moving away from "cost-plus"-based systems and slowly converging toward systems of reference pricing.

Within this broad context of shifting attitudes toward regulation and, despite some deep and important changes (e.g. the United Kingdom in the Thatcher era), policy making maintains in each country strong degrees of inertia and continuity. In other words, policy making follows routines and trajectories that depend partly on the intrinsic rigidity of the constitutional and administrative systems and partly on how public agencies traditionally think and act.

Thus, in the United States, cost containment has been pursued without direct price controls. Proposals from the Clinton administration in the 1990s to control drug expenditures were harshly criticized, and only a small part of the proposed reforms has been enforced.[17] Rather, indirect measures have been adopted in the last twenty years. The 1984 Waxman-Hatch Act significantly reduced the safety control procedures for generic

---

[17] The opponents' arguments rely mainly on two lines of reasoning. The first is that higher prices allow firms to reinvest in research into new products, and price controls may hinder a country's innovative potential. According to some observers, countries in which there is some form of price control actually "free ride" on US research activity. Second, it is argued that price controls are an inefficient, ineffective and distorting instrument for the purposes of cost containment. While the argument is quite complex, it essentially relies on the observation that reductions in price go alongside an increase in demand, and that that demand is not completely inelastic (especially if there are cost-sharing measures); such demand, moreover, tends to shift toward "unnecessary" products.

drug bio-equivalents to branded products, and allowed pharmacists to sell equivalent generics instead of the branded products prescribed by doctors.[18] Today generics are estimated to account for more than 50 percent of drugs prescribed (by volume). Moreover, the rise and diffusion of the managed care organizations, such as health management organizations, preferred providers organizations, mail-order pharmaceutical organizations and pharmaceutical benefit management (PBM) companies, that now dominate the US healthcare market is considered to be the most effective device for limiting the prices of drugs, given their bargaining power and the inducement they introduce to cost-conscious behavior by prescribing doctors. Actually, managed care organizations have changed profoundly the structure of distribution and demand in the United States, and they have become crucial players in the sectoral system of innovation. The growing relevance of these actors also induced processes of vertical integration, through the acquisition of PBMs by large pharmaceutical corporations (e.g. Merck acquired Medco Containment in 1993 and SmithKline bought Diversified Pharmaceutical Services in 1994).

In Europe cost-containment policies took different routes, again because – contrary to the US case – the state is the largest customer of drugs, and partly because of much stronger resistance to measures that might be perceived as weakening a fundamental function of the welfare state. Despite profound changes in the extent and forms of price regulation, some basic features of the national systems of regulation of prices and demand continue to characterize individual European countries. For example, Italy, France, Greece, Belgium and Spain – and, to a lesser extent, Sweden – continue to implement strict price controls, while Germany and Switzerland have a much less stringent attitude. The former group of countries continues to be characterized by relatively low prices, and Germany by high prices. Yet price levels in France are now at an intermediate level, similar to the British ones. Moreover, public coverage of pharmaceutical expenditure severely decreased in Italy in the 1990s, and has actually been increasing in Norway and Ireland, and also in the United States, Canada, Switzerland, France and Greece, and – to a lesser extent – Sweden (Jacobzone, 2000).

However, assessing the impact of the various policy measures on the access to drugs by different segments of the population remains extremely difficult and controversial. In general, there seems to be some consensus on the fact that these measures did little to curb pharmaceutical expenditure, and that, at best, all they did was to prevent it from soaring.

---

[18] The same Act provided a "restoration" of patent duration to take into account delays in the approval process.

Moreover, caveats have been expressed from at least two points of view. On one side, it has been noticed that these interventions, especially the ones directed at patients, are typically regressive, as wealthier people can afford the cost of health insurance, thus covering the full drug price. Moreover, policies such as reference pricing require an adequate diffusion of information among consumers, in order to give them an effective freedom of choice. Finally, consumers' and, even more, physicians' behavior shows strong habitual components (reinforced by the advertising strategies of companies), which to date have not been adequately analyzed but which, in any event, reduce the effects of economic incentives.

On the other hand, it seems to be increasingly acknowledged that strong competition within domestic markets and exposure to international competition is conducive to a better innovative performance and higher levels of competitiveness. Despite the "invasion" of generic drugs and the more competitive environment that firms face within the domestic market, R&D resources and innovative outcome certainly do not seem to have deteriorated in the United States (which since the 1980s has consolidated its leadership in the world drug sector). Perhaps even more importantly, excessive reliance on command and control instruments appears to protect the less efficient segments of the industry (Gambardella, Orsenigo and Pammolli, 2000) rather than hindering innovation per se.

In any case, the analysis of regulation and of the evolution of demand illustrates once again the conflicts and continuing changes that characterize pharmaceuticals. The expansion of the welfare state contributed to the explosion of pharmaceutical expenses and led to cost containment policies. The objectives of equity are in a state of continuous tension with economic static and dynamic efficiency, and claims on both sides that no trade-off actually exists are, at best, difficult to prove theoretically, let alone empirically. Different goals are attributed varying importance over time, and different arguments and rationales are used to support or contradict particular policy attitudes. Thus, just as equity and information asymmetries used to be the chief motives for policy intervention, now cost containment has become the main issue. Such tensions and conflicting goals result in frequent changes in legislation, adjustments and sometimes proposals of radical reforms, never finding an equilibrium.

## 3.5    The decline of European competitiveness

There is substantive evidence that, in the age of molecular biology and cost containment, the European pharmaceutical industry has started to lose competitiveness vis-à-vis the United States. A recent report to the

European Commission (Gambardella, Orsenigo and Pammolli, 2000) documents a series of significant findings.

a) In the 1990s the European industry grew less, and was much more labor-intensive, than its US counterpart.

b) The sales of major innovative products by US multinationals increased more significantly than those of European multinationals in the 1990s. Moreover, big European corporations seem to lag behind somewhat in their ability to produce and, above all, sell new, innovative best-selling drugs. The observed differences in sales growth between the largest European and US multinationals during the 1990s derives partly, however, from the observed difference in demand growth between the two areas.

c) The 1990s witnessed an acceleration of the competitiveness of the US pharmaceutical industry as a whole, especially in the innovation-intensive segment of the industry. The leading US firms have a higher share of turnover based on recent products compared to the European firms; they also have a higher share of patents in the new biotech fields compared to "classical" pharmaceuticals, and are a preferred destination of research by the European companies as well.

d) The competitive advantage of the US companies in innovation relies both on their higher internal capabilities and on a higher reliance on collaboration, especially in the preclinical stages of research and development. More generally, the United States exhibits a more pronounced division of labor in the drug innovation process between large companies on the one hand and small biotech/specialized firms, as well as scientific institutions, on the other.

e) The US advantage and the deteriorating competitiveness in Europe have been emphasized and deepened by the advent of the molecular biology revolution. The competitiveness of the US system seems to be largely related to the extensive exploration of new technological opportunities. In fact, while the United States has become the centre of basic research in life sciences worldwide, Europe has been unable to develop and attract research and to complete the process of vertical specialization in the most innovative areas of the drug sector. In particular, Europe has not really given rise to a full-fledged industry of "innovation specialist" companies and technology suppliers like the NBFs in the United States.

f) However, the declining competitiveness of the European industry appears to be linked not only (but certainly not mainly) to the worsening performance of the largest corporations but also to the persistence of a large fringe of smaller, inefficient companies. In particular, in some European countries there seems to be too little domestic competition, which tends to nurture inefficient positions within the industry. Price-fixing mechanisms tend to protect local firms in domestic markets, allowing for the survival of infra-marginal, highly labor-intensive companies.

g) However, the decline in European competitiveness in pharmaceuticals and biotechnology is not a homogeneous phenomenon, but it actually results from largely heterogeneous performances of individual firms and countries. To a considerable extent, the European problem derives from the deterioration in the performance of the German and Italian industries. Conversely, the cases of the United Kingdom and (in the 1990s) Denmark, France, Sweden and Ireland have to be considered as success stories.

Several interacting factors might contribute to the explanation for these trends, and these factors have acted at different levels. In general, we suggest that the relative EU decline within this industry is largely determined by what happened in the transition period prior to the molecular biology/cost containment era. When it arrived, "Europe" was not able to react as quickly and efficiently as the United States, due to a combination of factors, which can be summarized as a sluggishness in designing a more complex system and in redefining complementarities and the division of labor. This means that the American path led to a much faster and more profound blurring of the roles of actors, the rise of new actors, and an increasing complexity of networks in order to develop and exploit knowledge economically. Within Europe, these trends occurred more slowly and seemed to have involved a lower number of new actors – or, rather, some of them went to the United States to access the appropriate new forms.

The interpretation of the dynamics of the SSI in pharmaceuticals during the third epoch can be analyzed in terms of four sets of variables. These variables have all been discussed previously. Further discussion is available in Gambardella, Orsenigo and Pammolli (2000). These four sets of variables combine the actors, relationships and networks in the interactions between market demand, cognitive/technological and institutional/country-specific factors. These four variables are particularly important because they are, in various ways, crucial in determining the divergent trends of the American and European industries:

a) The size and structure of the biomedical education and research systems;
b) Some basic institutions governing labor markets for skilled researchers and managers, as well as corporate governance and finance;
c) Intellectual property rights and patent law;
d) The nature and intensity of competition in the final market.

These four variables help explain the differing trajectories of American and European pharmaceutical firms over time, and are similar to the discussion in the previous section.

## 4    Conclusions: linking the empirical evidence to theory

In summary, our analysis of the pharmaceutical industry as an SSI has shown how and why trajectories and systemic developments over time can be characterized as developing spontaneously as an interdependent, integrated and self-sustaining system. This SSI in pharmaceuticals includes changing actors, relationships and networks over time. The reconfiguration of these three variables is visible in the varying and differential flows of people and knowledge between various actors, such as NBFs and pharmaceutical firms, organizations in the public and private research system, and venture capital. The actors and their relationships in a network are in turn affected by contextual factors, such as public policy, the legal system, etc. Sections 1 to 3 provide evidence about how these interactions within the SSI differ over time and country, as well as the convergence of certain features in an increasingly internationalized market.

A few features of this system are worth emphasizing because they are important both to understand the similarities and differences between European and American pharmaceuticals and to develop further the analysis of sectoral systems of innovation.

First, the system did not develop following a conscious design, but "self-organized" starting from pre-existing institutions and organizations, adaptively modifying them and creating new ones.

Second, this system is highly decentralized and fragmented, but also strongly integrated in at least two senses. In one sense, some institutions perform a critical role in orienting and integrating different strands of research and different agents. In another sense, the system is integrated because different realms and institutions are closely intertwined, are linked by a variety of ties and often perform overlapping functions. Thus, NBFs could not prosper – or even exist – without the public funding provided to academic research, nor without the contracts and the qualified demand coming from the large corporations.

Third, the system is self-sustaining, in the sense that each agent performs a complementary function, which allows other agents to exist and to act. However, the system is not completely coherent, and – above all – it is never in a state of rest. On the contrary, the system is fraught with tensions and conflicts, which continuously trigger change.[19]

---

[19] An American example discussed by Eisenberg (1996) is illuminating. The decision of the NIH not to allow the patentability of sequences of complementary DNA (c-DNA)

On the other hand, as time goes by, some types of agreements, institutions or social technologies arise, whether by conscious design or by repetitive behavior, in a population of actors. These informal patterns of behavior may become contextual features, often corresponding to a local optimi. There are often multiple outcomes of a system. Still, some system-wide consensus may be developed over time. For example, particular understandings, ways of doing things and solving conflicts – as well as techniques and discoveries – become widely accepted and are routinely used with little (if any) additional deliberation and discussion (Nelson and Sampat, 2000). Formats of the business plans or standard contracts regulating alliances between NBFs and large corporations become "institutionalized" and serve as templates for further modification whenever specific unusual circumstances arise. Such patterns of behavior may moderate the otherwise chaotic and restless nature of change.

Fourth, these trends are not simply interpretable either as a process of deepening the division of labor among agents on the basis of their comparative advantages, or as processes of vertical and horizontal integration. First of all, it is worth noting that the division of labor and processes of integration are taking place at the same time. But, more importantly, agents are changing their roles and functions, redefining their position in a new network. In other words, the space in which the division of labor was previously defined is not the same any longer, and is constantly changing. Universities are not just specializing in their "core activities" – teaching and research – but are also diversifying "downstream" into the commercial exploitation of their main product, and to this end they are creating new organizational forms (and new incentive mechanisms and selective principles). NBFs do not simply pick up knowledge acquired at universities and develop it into commercializable products for sale to large pharmaceutical corporations. They also assume the functions of integrators of different types and pieces of knowledge, embodying different roles and different incentive structures, devising once again new organizational structures to support these tasks. Large corporations internalize some basic principles of academic research into the organization of their laboratories and in the incentive structure for their researchers.

induced a scientist to start his own company selling these databases for profit. As a consequence, a large pharmaceutical corporation decided to put its own database in the public domain, on the grounds (besides other less disinterested motivations) that such knowledge was a research tool and, therefore, it should be freely shared and used by the whole research community. Later on, the "NIH spin-off" struck an agreement with a big producer of medical equipment and engaged in the ambitious project to decodify the whole human genome on the basis of the techniques originally developed to construct the c-DNA databases. Under this challenge, the efforts of the Human Genome Project teams were accelerated and a bitter discussion emerged on the priority and the completeness of the results, on how much the private team had been using publicly generated knowledge, etc.

Thus, these developments present an important challenge to economic analysis. One set of questions has to do with the conditions in which different selective mechanisms and principles can coexist and coevolve. The most prominent example is obviously given by the potential conflict, or virtuous cycle, between the selection mechanisms typical of the commercial sphere and of the academic world (Dasgupta and David, 1994; McKelvey, 1996; and Mazzoleni and Nelson, 1998b).

In a somewhat different but related perspective, one might consider that this process of "hybridization" of organizational forms and selective principles may lead on the one hand to organizational and institutional innovation, but on the other to a radical reduction in the degree of variety in the system. If universities, NBFs and large pharmaceutical corporations end up looking and acting in very much the same way, efficiency gains stemming from the division of labor and the differentiation of functions might be forgone, and – even more important – the scope for further organizational and technological progress might be reduced, to the extent that each agent acts following the same logic and the same principles. In the language of network analysis, the strength of weak ties (Granovetter, 1973) might be replaced by the weakness of strong ties. Thus, short-term efficiencies may override alternative, more long-term outcomes by reducing variety too greatly.

This summary and the empirical discussion in previous sections suggest some preliminary conceptual conclusions – or, better, conjectures – on why and how pharmaceuticals can be usefully analyzed as an SSI (see also McKelvey and Orsenigo, 2000). A first set of conjectures has a "general" nature, in that it possibly refers to the dynamics of different sectoral systems. The second set is specific to the case of pharmaceuticals.

We mentioned at the beginning that the pharmaceutical industry can be considered as a system or network because innovative activities involve, directly or indirectly, a large variety of actors, who are heterogeneous in many respects. We noted also that these actors are linked together through a web of different relationships and networks. The analysis of the evolution of pharmaceuticals found in sections 1 to 3 suggests, however, some further insights.

*First*, a crucial feature of this industry is certainly that these agents and relations are not simply coexisting but dynamically giving rise to new agents and forms of interaction. In this particular and possibly extreme case, this process of evolution has led to a striking mix and overlapping of different and hybrid forms of learning and selection principles (McKelvey, 1997a, 1997b). Learning and selection principles within a population of actors such as in an industry or in a network affect the long-term outcomes of the system.

*Second*, in no meaningful way can this set of relations be considered as completely coherent and "efficient." On the contrary, conflict, failures (think of the thalidomide case) and disequilibrium (consider the tension between "open science" and the commercial exploitation of fundamental scientific research) have always been a distinctive feature of the industry. At the same time, forms of interaction have been developed that have allowed a remarkable track record in innovativeness, economic and financial performance and (although not completely uncontroversially) welfare. Thus, the pharmaceutical industry example demonstrates both chaotic behavior in the system as well as quite positive outcomes for firms and for innovative activities, at least during certain periods.

*Third*, the nature, form and variety of these relationships may also look different when viewed from alternative levels of aggregation or scales of analysis: specific sub-markets, the drug market as a whole, individual firms and networks of firms. This implies that the cognitive/technological and the institutional/country-specific factors are particularly important for explaining the different patterns visible at different levels.

*Fourth*, the SI in pharmaceuticals should be analyzed as a simultaneous interaction among firms' specificities, sectoral actors, national contexts and international trends. In addition to the crucial importance of firms' heterogeneity, it may well be that the declines, recoveries and take-offs visible at the level of European national industries are due to the decisions of a few large corporations. Yet the sectoral dimension is fundamental. Throughout this chapter we have emphasized how the specific nature of the learning regime(s) and of the selection mechanisms shapes the patterns of competition and the forms of industry evolution. However, it is also clear that national contexts – or combinations of regional contexts – interact with sector-specific variables in defining what agents can do. These include factors such as the dominant types of university-industry interaction, the strength of basic science, the movability and availability of pooled and skilled labor forces, the availability of venture capital, and the patterns of regulation and competition. In an international world, these types of factors interact in creating various, and specific, environments from which firms may emerge – or be drawn to. At times, international convergence seems to appear as a consequence of countries trying to imitate "successful examples," as well as a consequence of the changing and international characteristics of markets and demand.

*Fifth*, quite obviously, the sectoral system changes over time. Such change results from different sources. It is spurred by the disequilibria and imbalances that permeate the system. It is driven by external shocks, both "small" ones (as would be formalized in a dynamic model by the introduction of i.i.d. disturbances) and "big" ones (such as the emergence of a new technological paradigm). The process of change is driven also, and mainly, by the interaction of endogenous learning and selection processes. This should be visible at the level of actors, relationships and networks. Agents learn how to improve their position, by developing and using new techniques, products and marketing strategies. They learn how to compete vis-à-vis their old and new competitors. They adapt and sometimes try to change to new forms of regulation and forms of market organization. Mechanisms of selection themselves change. Changes in regulation are just an obvious example. But, even more interestingly, as different selection mechanisms coexist, influence each other and sometimes mix together, the principles of selection themselves become partly endogenous. In fact, they result from the interaction of different mechanisms, from the purposive actions of agents who actively try to change the "rules of the game" and from the disequilibria that at any point in time characterize the system. For example, the thalidomide case induced tougher procedures for product approval that in turn altered the costs of R&D, industry structure, the prices of drugs, the competitiveness of firms and national industries.

In a somewhat different terminology, competencies and incentives coevolve. And it is by no means obvious at the outset what the "right" dynamic mix may be, nor whether policy agents can influence the desired outcomes through actions based on rational expectations. Again, as an example, weak patent protection induces imitative strategies, but this effect is much less important for firms and countries that have developed strong technological and scientific capabilities (as, for example, Germany until the advent of the molecular biology revolution). Conversely, the introduction of stronger patent protection may have contributed to the practical disappearance of the Italian industry, which until the mid-1970s was one of the more successful producers of generics.

*Sixth*, the evolution and adaptation of actors, organizations and networks to (internally generated and exogenous) shocks imply processes of restructuring, the division of labor and the reconfiguration of complementarities. In the language of cognitive sciences, this means the identification of new problem decompositions, within and across agents.

Thus, as we noted, the emergence of a new knowledge base (molecular biology) implied a new "problem," new ways and procedures of learning and a new technological regime. The adaptation to the new knowledge base (technological regime) implied a deep reconfiguration of the system: at the firm level, at the level of the patterns of the division of labor and relationships among firms (through the appearance of new specialized biotechnology firms, the emergence of networks of collaborative relations but also through M&As) and at the level of market structure. More generally, scientific progress certainly "simplified" the search space, eliminating certain alternatives that were proven to be wrong (Nelson, 1959; Arrow, 1962; and David, Mowery and Steinmueller, 1992). However, at the same time, scientific discoveries generated a "deformation" and an expansion of the research space, by suggesting new competing hierarchies of sub-hypotheses as well as previously inconceivable opportunities for discovery. In other words, the opportunities for the division of labor and the complementarities between different activities and pieces of knowledge were redefined in a new space, not comparable to the previous one.

*Seventh*, in this process of adaptation and change different dynamic processes lead to differential patterns of competition and performance. In other words, we suggest that it is important to look at system dynamics in order to understand the outcomes in terms of structure and performance.

*Eighth*, within the evolving system, the lack or the weakness of specific competencies, agents or relations between agents can decrease overall performance. In other words, competitiveness and performance are to some extent a function of the "completeness" and intensity of the relations and on how they are managed.

By integrating the previous section and these eight conjectures, we can make some interpretations concerning the European reaction to the molecular biology revolution and to the cost-containment problem as systemic outcomes leading to a differential trajectory from the American one. The new technological regime implied an "explosion" of the search space. "Exploration" has become more difficult, costly and important for pharmaceutical firms than in the previous epoch. Given the complexity of the space to be searched and the speed at which new hypotheses and techniques are generated, no individual firm can hope to be able to explore and to keep control of more than a small subset of such space. Competitiveness increasingly depends on strong scientific capabilities and on the ability to produce and interact with science and scientific institutions in order to explore such an immense and complex problem space.

In the United States this task was accomplished through significant transformations in the vertical structure of the industry, with the emergence of new patterns in the division of labor in the innovation process among new and established firms, and the development not just of a market for technology but also new and organizationally sophisticated forms of interaction among different types of firms and other institutions. The US system was able to evolve, building on some of its typical features, into a highly decentralized but at the same time strongly integrated structure, which appears to be rather successful in combining exploration and exploitation.

In Europe the lack of strong research competencies in the new knowledge base and the absence of, or weakness in, specific relationships among agents deeply influenced the dynamic path of evolution and the "competitiveness" of the industry. In Europe the "new problem" was reconfigured and decomposed in a different way from the US case. Europe has been lagging behind in its ability to generate, organize and sustain innovation processes that are increasingly expensive and organizationally complex.

A similar story seems to apply concerning regulation. In many European countries "invasive" regulation, with regard, for instance, to prices, has coexisted with a much softer attitude in other domains, e.g. product approval procedures. In many cases this approach has resulted in weak competitive pressures and in the survival of inefficient, marginal firms. The competitive decline of the European pharmaceutical industry appears to have its roots in insufficient degrees of organizational integration and competition within the system, still centered on individual domestic markets and fragmented research systems.

However, this analysis does not imply that the "American way" is necessarily the only or the best way. As we noted several times, the American system has its own contradictions and problems, including in the four variables of a) the education and research system, b) the labor market and governance, c) intellectual property rights, and d) competition. Nor can Europe just switch from its entrenched position to an American trajectory. Moreover, past history and inherited institutions influence the future patterns of evolution, at least up to a point. In the European case, policies aiming at promoting new biotechnology firms, the proliferation of intermediate institutions for "technology transfer" and an increasing involvement of scientific research in direct commercial activities may or may not be feasible and desirable.

Trade-offs exist at the level of the SSI in the pharmaceutical industry. These trade-offs, which exist between exploration, exploitation, efficiency and equity, are intrinsically difficult to resolve and no unambiguous, unique "best way" is likely to be definable. Thus, as in any evolutionary environment, there is always the scope for further improvement and change.

REFERENCES

Arora, A., and A. Gambardella (1994), The changing technology of technical change: general and abstract knowledge and the division of innovative labor, *Research Policy*, 23, 5, 523–532

Arora A., A. Gambardella, F. Pammolli and M. Riccaboni (2000), *Advantage Lost? On the Leveling Effect of the Market for Technology in Biopharmaceuticals*, paper prepared for the International Conference on Technology Policy and Innovation, Paris

Arrow, K. J. (1962), Economic welfare and the allocation of resources for investment, in R. R. Nelson (ed.), *The Rate and Direction of Inventive Activities: Economic and Social Factors* Princeton University Press, Princeton, NJ, 609–625

——— (1983), Innovation in large and small firms, in J. Ronen (ed.), *Entrepreneurship*, Lexington Books, Lexington, MA, 15–28

Ben-David, J. (1977), *Centers of Learning: Britain, France, Germany and the United States*, McGraw-Hill, New York

Braun, D. (1994), *Structure and Dynamics of Health Research and Public Funding: An International Institutional Comparison*, Kluwer Academic, Amsterdam

Burstall, S. (1985), *The Community Pharmaceutical Industry*, European Commission, Brussels

Casper, S., and H. E. Kettler (2000), *The Road to Sustainability in the UK and German Biotechnology Industries*, paper prepared for ESSY conference, Berlin, June 1–3

Chandler, A. D. (1990), *Scale and Scope: The Dynamics of Modern Capitalism*, Belknap Press of Harvard University Press, Cambridge, MA

Chien, R. I. (1979), *Issues in Pharmaceutical Economics*, Lexington Books, Lexington, MA

Cockburn, I., and R. Henderson (1996), Public-private interaction in pharmaceutical research, *Proceedings of the National Academy of Sciences*, 93, 23, 12,725–12,730

Cockburn, I., R. Henderson and S. Stern (2000), Untangling the origins of competitive advantage, *Strategic Management Journal*, 21, 10–11, 1,123–1, 145

Comanor, W. S. (1986), The political economy of the pharmaceutical industry, *Journal of Economic Literature*, 24, 1,178–1,217

Dasgupta, P., and P. A. David (1994), The new economics of science, *Research Policy*, 23, 5, 487–521

David, P. A., D. C. Mowery and W. E. Steinmueller (1992), Analyzing the economic payoffs from basic research, *Economics of Innovation and New Technology*, 2, 73–90

Edquist, C., and M. McKelvey (eds.) (2000*)*, *Systems of Innovation: Growth, Competitiveness and Employment*, Reference Collection (two volumes), Edward Elgar Publishing, Cheltenham

Eisenberg, R. (1996), Public research and private development: patents and technology transfer in government-sponsored research, *Virginia Law Review*, 82, 1,663–1,727

Galambos, L., and J. E. Sewell (1995), *Networks of Innovation: Vaccine Development at Merck, Sharp & Dohme, and Mulford, 1895–1995*, Cambridge University Press, New York

Galambos, L., and J. L. Sturchio (1998), Pharmaceutical firms and the transition to biotechnology: a study in strategic innovation, *Business History Review*, 72, 250–278

Gambardella, A. (1995), *Science and Innovation – The US Pharmaceutical Industry during the 1980s*, Cambridge University Press, Cambridge

Gambardella, A., L. Orsenigo and F. Pammolli (2000), *Global Competitiveness in Pharmaceuticals: A European Perspective*, report prepared for the Directorate-General Enterprise of the European Commission

Gittelman, M. (2000), *Scientists and Networks: A Comparative Study of Cooperation in the French and American Biotechnology Industry*, Ph.D. thesis, Wharton School, University of Pennsylvania

Grabowski, H. G., and J. M. Vernon (1983), *The Regulation of Pharmaceuticals*, American Enterprise Institute for Public Policy Research, Washington, DC, and London

—— (1994), Innovation and structural change in pharmaceuticals and biotechnology, *Industrial and Corporate Change*, 3, 2, 435–449

Granovetter, M. (1973), The strength of weak ties, *American Journal of Sociology*, 78, 6, 1,360–1,380

Henderson, R., and I. Cockburn (1996), Scale, scope and spillovers: the determinants of research productivity in drug discovery, *RAND Journal of Economics*, 27,1, 32–59

Henderson, R., L. Orsenigo and G. P. Pisano (1999), The pharmaceutical industry and the revolution in molecular biology: interactions among scientific, institutional and organizational change, in D. C. Mowery and R. R. Nelson (eds.), *Sources of Industrial Leadership: Studies of Seven Industries*, Cambridge University Press, Cambridge, 267–311

Jacobzone, S. (2000), *Pharmaceutical Policies in OECD Countries: Reconciling Social and Industrial Goals*, Occasional Paper no. 40, Labour Market and Social Policy Series, Organisation for Economic Co-operation and Development, Paris

Kenney, M. (1986), *Biotechnology: The Industry-University Complex*, Cornell University Press, Ithaca, NY

Kogut, B., W. Shan and G. Walker (1992), The make or cooperate decision in the context of an industry network, in N. Nohria and R. G. Eccles (eds.), *Networks and Organizations*, Harvard Business School Press, Cambridge, MA, 348–365

Lacetera, N. and L. Orsenigo (2001), *Political and Technological Regimes in the Evolution of the Pharmaceutical Industry in the USA and in Europe*, paper prepared for the Conference on Evolutionary Economics, Johns Hopkins University, Baltimore, March 30–31.

Levin, R. C., A. K. Klevorick, R. R. Nelson and S. G. Winter (1987), Appropriating the returns from industrial research and development, *Brookings Papers on Economic Activity*, 3, 783–831

McKelvey, M. (1996), *Evolutionary Innovation: The Business of Biotechnology*, Oxford University Press, Oxford

—— (1997a), Coevolution in commercial genetic engineering, *Industrial and Corporate Change*, 6, 3, 503–532

—— (1997b), Using evolutionary theory to define systems of innovation, in C. Edquist (ed.) (1997), *Systems of Innovation: Technologies, Institutions and Organisations*, Frances Pinter, London, 200–222

McKelvey, M., and L. Orsenigo (2002), European pharmaceuticals as a sectoral innovation system: performance and national selection environments, submitted for review to *Journal of Evolutionary Economics*

Matraves, C. (1999), Market structure, R&D, and advertising in the pharmaceutical industry, *Journal of Industrial Economics*, 48, 2, 169–194

Maxwell, R. A., and S. B. Eckhardt (1990), *Drug Discovery: A Casebook and Analysis*, Humana Press, Clifton, NJ

Mazzoleni, R., and R. R. Nelson (1998a), The benefits and costs of strong patent protection: a contribution to the current debate, *Research Policy*, 27, 3, 273–284

(1998b), Economic theories about the benefits and costs of patents, *Journal of Economic Issues*, 32, 1,031–1,052

Merges, R., and R. R. Nelson (1994), On limiting or encouraging rivalry in technical progress: the effect of patent scope decisions, *Journal of Economic Behavior and Organization*, 25, 1–24

Merton, D. (1973), *The Sociology of Science: Theoretical and Empirical Investigation*, University of Chicago Press, Chicago

Mossialos, E. (1997), Citizens' view on health systems in the 15 member states of the European Union, *Health Economics*, 6, 109–116

Mowery, D. C. (1998), The changing structure of the US national innovation system: implications for international conflict and cooperation in R&D policy, *Research Policy*, 27, 6, 639–654

Mowery, D. C., and N. Rosenberg (2000), *Paths of Innovation: Technological Change in 20th Century America*, Cambridge University Press, New York

Nelson, R. R. (1959), The simple economics of basic scientific research, *Journal of Political Economy*, 67, 297–306

Nelson, R. R., and N. Rosenberg (1994), American universities and technical advance in industry, *Research Policy*, 23, 3, 323–348

Nelson, R. R., and B. N. Sampat (2000), Making sense of institutions as a factor shaping economic performance, *Journal of Economic Behavior and Organization*, forthcoming

Orsenigo, L. (1989), *The Emergence of Biotechnology*, Frances Pinter, London

Orsenigo, L., F. Pammolli and M. Riccaboni (2001), Technological change and network dynamics, *Research Policy*, 30, 5, 485–508

Office of Technology Assessment (1984), *Commercial Biotechnology: An International Analysis*, US Government Printing Office, Washington, DC

Pammolli, F. (1997), *Innovation and Industry Structure: The International Pharmaceutical Industry During the Nineties*, Guerini, Milan

Peltzman, S. (1974), *Regulation of Pharmaceutical Innovation: The 1962 Amendments*, American Enterprise Institute for Public Policy Research, Washington, DC

Pisano, G. (1991), The governance of innovation: vertical integration and collaborative arrangements in the biotechnology industry, *Research Policy*, 20, 2, 237–249

(1997), *R&D Performance, Collaborative Arrangements and the Market for Knowhow: A Test of the "Lemons" Hypothesis in Biotechnology*, working paper, Harvard Business School

Powell, W. W., K. W. Doput and L. Smith-Doerr (1996), Interorganizational collaboration and the locus of innovation: networks of learning in biotechnology, *Administrative Science Quarterly*, 41, 116–145

Schwartzman, D. (1976), *Innovation in the Pharmaceutical Industry*, Johns Hopkins University Press, Baltimore

Sutton, J. (1998), *Technology and Market Structure: Theory and History*, MIT Press, Cambridge, MA

Teece, D. J. (1986), Profiting from technological innovation: implications for integration, collaboration, licensing and public policy, *Research Policy*, 15, 6, 185–219

Thomas, L. G. (1994), Implicit industrial policy: the triumph of Britain and the failure of France in global pharmaceuticals, *Industrial and Corporate Change*, 3, 2, 451–489

Ward, M., and D. Dranove (1995), The vertical chain of R&D in the pharmaceutical industry, *Economic Inquiry*, 33, 1–18

Zucker, L., M. Darby and M. Brewer (1997), *Intellectual Human Capital and the Birth of U.S. Biotechnology Enterprises*, Working Paper no. 4,653, National Bureau of Economic Research, Boston

# 4 The chemical sectoral system: firms, markets, institutions and the processes of knowledge creation and diffusion

*Fabrizio Cesaroni, Alfonso Gambardella, Walter Garcia-Fontes and Myriam Mariani*[1]

## 1 Introduction

The aim of this chapter is to analyze the chemical industry by using the theoretical framework of a sectoral system of innovation. The chapter describes the knowledge and technological base of the industry and explores the existence of complementarities among knowledge, technologies and products. It also examines the heterogeneity of the relevant agents in the industry, their learning processes and their competencies, the role of non-firm organizations and the characteristics of industry dynamics and (co)evolutionary processes (see chapter 1 in this book).

Previous studies describe the characteristics of the chemical industry and emphasize its heterogeneity (see, among others, Arora, Landau and Rosenberg, 1998). The chemical industry is composed of different subsectors, ranging from bulk chemicals to biotechnology. Each of them is characterized by specific features and is based on particular knowledge and technological bases. This heterogeneity, together with the century-long history of the industry, allows for a comprehensive study of the existence of evolutionary and coevolutionary processes in this sector.

The most relevant agents in the chemical industry are the established chemical companies, which emerged over time because of the importance of economies of scale at the level of the firm. These large companies could spread the fixed costs of plant setting and product development, and afford the big investments in production and marketing activities to reach geographically dispersed markets. Small and innovative chemical firms and public institutions interact with these large companies through cooperative and competitive relationships (Aftalion, 1999).

[1] Myriam Mariani also acknowledges the support provided by a Marie Curie Fellowship of the European Community Improving Human Potential (IHP) program, grant HPMF-CT-2000–00694.

Knowledge about chemical processes and products is key to understanding the competitive advantage of firms, regions and countries. This chapter examines the processes involved in the creation, diffusion and utilization of new knowledge. In so doing it explores research collaborations at the level of individual inventors, and compares the firm (*organizational proximity*) and the geographical cluster (*geographical proximity*) as alternative organizational modes for fostering research collaborations and for producing interdisciplinary patents. As far as the process of technology diffusion is concerned, the chemical sectoral system is characterized by a dense network among the chemical firms, specialized suppliers and engineering firms that are involved in the exchange of technological knowledge. This chapter studies the functioning of the market for process technologies, the strategies of firms with respect to licensing, and the causes and implications of the existence of the market for technology in chemicals.

The study is composed of two parts. The first (sections 2 to 4) describes the chemical industry by means of the framework of sectoral systems. Section 2 defines the boundaries of the chemical sectoral system in terms of size, traditions in innovation and R&D activities, and linkages with the downstream sectors. Section 3 explores the geographical characteristics and the international performance of the sector. Section 4 analyzes the evolution of the organization of the industry and the coevolutionary processes, with particular attention to the environmental issue.

The second part of the study empirically addresses the issue of knowledge creation and diffusion. Section 5 describes the phase of knowledge development. By means of EPO patents it compares the firm and the cluster as different organizational modes for producing innovations. Section 6 focuses on the processes of technology diffusion and licensing. It discusses the conditions for the rise of a market for technology in chemicals, and provides empirical evidence on the existence and extent of technology transactions. It then highlights the role of large firms in the development of such a market. Section 7 draws the conclusions.

## 2    The boundaries of the sector

### 2.1    *The industry structure and corporate strategies*

The heterogeneity of the chemical industry, its size, the scientific tradition, and the linkages with many other industries and products are important characteristics of the chemical sector (Cook and Sharp, 1992). They strongly influence the industry structure and firms' technology strategies.

As far as the heterogeneity is concerned, chemical products range from bulk chemicals – or basic or commodity chemicals – to specialty chemicals and biotechnology. Basic chemicals are high-quantity and low-value-added products, characterized by low differentiation. By contrast, specialty products such as dyes and paints, food additives and photographic materials are more differentiated and sophisticated products. They are also produced in low volumes and sold for high prices. This heterogeneity mirrors completely different technological, scientific and R&D strategies by subsectors and firms.

The chemical sector is also the largest manufacturing industry in the United States, and the second largest in Western Europe. It produces about 1.9 percent of US GDP and about 11.3 percent of US manufacturing value added (Arora, Landau and Rosenberg, 1998). In 1999 the European Union's chemical industry produced about 2.4 percent of total EU GDP, and contributed about 9.7 percent to total EU manufacturing production.[2] In terms of value added, the chemical industry ranked third within EU manufacturing industry. The order of magnitude of these percentages is similar for Japan. From a global perspective, in 1996 the US chemical industry had about 24 percent of the global market. Japan was second with 14 percent. The market shares of Germany and the United Kingdom were 8 percent and 4 percent respectively. The rest of the chemical production was spread across the other Western European countries and Asia. Moreover, twelve of the largest multinational chemical companies are European (Cook and Sharp, 1992).

Another important characteristic of the chemical sector is the long tradition in innovation and R&D activities. Since its origins in the second half of the nineteenth century, with the British and German dyestuff manufacturers, the chemical sector has been a science-based sector. Innovation in this industry derives from the interaction between academic institutions, individual firms, government policies and historical events. Empirical work shows the importance of the linkages between internal R&D capabilities and external sources of scientific knowledge for successful innovation (among others, see Freeman, Young and Fuller, 1963). Universities and small firms are key for carrying out basic research and developing product innovations. Firms' in-house R&D is the essential complement to exploiting external linkages. Recent studies use patent data to show the important contribution of basic research produced by universities and other public research centres to industrial innovation in emerging fields such as combinatorial chemistry (Geuna, 2001). They also show that US universities and research centres carry out research activity that positively influences the establishment of new firms in combinatorial chemistry. While European Union countries are catching up

[2] See the European Chemical Industry Council (CEFIC) web page: http://www.cefic.be/ activities/eco/ff99/01-11.htm.

in terms of university publications, the number of new firms in combinatorial synthesis is still very small. This confirms the importance of the university system and public research institutions for fostering firms' competitiveness.

Private firms are also a major source of R&D funding, and the most important means for technological applications. Today the average R&D intensity of chemical firms is about 5 percent, which is higher than in other sectors. In fields such as pharmaceuticals and biotechnology, firms' R&D intensity may exceed 20 percent. All the major technological innovations in the 1920s and 1930s – such as polystyrene, perspex, polyvinyl chloride (PVC), polyethylene, synthetic rubbers, nylon and other artificial fibers – were developed in the laboratories of large chemical companies, most of which still exist today. This is the case, for example, for Du Pont, Bayer, BASF and Dow Chemical.

The chemical industry is also an upstream sector providing intermediates for several downstream users. More than 50 percent of chemical products are intermediate goods used by a wide range of industries (Albach et al., 1996). More than 70,000 products, such as paints and coatings, fertilizers, pesticides, solvents, plastics, synthetic fibers and rubber, explosives and many others, are building blocks at every level of production and consumption in agriculture, construction, manufacturing and the service sectors. These upstream-downstream relationships are important sources of technological spillovers across sectors because they allow successful innovations in chemicals to diffuse in downstream products.

Finally, as far as innovation strategies of chemical firms are concerned, they depend strictly on the characteristics of the branch of the industry. Product heterogeneity in chemicals leads firms to follow strategies of cost leadership or specialization, depending on the products being produced (Porter, 1980). Firms adopt a cost leadership strategy in areas characterized by price competition. This is the case for basic chemicals. By using information drawn from the Community Innovation Survey, Albach et al. (1996) show that, during the previous few years, European firms in commodity chemicals focused on cost leadership strategies. In so doing they increasingly concentrated in their core areas, and engaged in strategic alliances with other companies. By contrast, firms in the specialty sectors tend to pursue specialization strategies characterized by great product differentiation and customization, and higher profit margins. In turn, the decision to follow cost leadership or specialization strategies influences firms' innovative behavior. Cost leadership leads companies to promote process innovations in order to reduce the production costs. By contrast, specialization strategies require companies to focus on product innovations in order to respond to customers' needs and to set higher prices. Albach et al. (1996) show that, in agrochemicals, paints and varnishes, more than 60 percent of firms allocate at least 75 percent of their R&D budget to product innovations. In basic chemicals, the share of companies devoting 75 percent of total R&D expenditure to product innovation falls to about 30 percent, while about 75 percent of R&D expenditure relates to process innovations. This survey also suggests that companies are increasingly entering into R&D alliances, both with other firms and with academic and research institutions. Again, however, the use of cooperative arrangements varies according to the sector. In agrochemicals, firms are very active in R&D alliances. R&D collaborations with universities, government laboratories and other research institutions are often used in basic chemicals and man-made fibers. The opposite holds for firms in soap and detergents.

## 2.2    Sectoral innovative patterns

The chemical industry has a long-standing tradition in innovation and R&D (see, for example, Arora, Landau and Rosenberg, 1998). This section describes how discoveries and innovations are developed in the chemical sectoral system, and discusses how the "upstream" features of the industry affect firms' strategies and the industry structure. Moreover, since the industry structure and firms' behavior toward innovative activities today are the result of the evolution of the industry over a century, we briefly describe this history in order to understand the characteristics of the present-day chemical sector.

The modern chemical industry started in the United Kingdom in the first half of the nineteenth century when the first inorganic chemical firms emerged. However, although the industry started by producing inorganic products – such as soda, soda ash and bleach – the engine of growth was organic chemistry, particularly dyestuffs. Due to the rapid pace of technological change in organic chemistry, firms changed their approach to innovation, which started to be based on the methodical application of scientific discoveries to chemical manufacturing.

The *synthetic dyestuff model* is a meaningful example of the new approach to innovation. Scientific knowledge was used to derive new products and processes: advances in the scientific principles governing organic chemistry provided the understanding of how carbon atoms were linked to hydrogen and to other atoms to form complex molecules. The synthetic dyestuff model was the beginning of the development of a "general-purpose technology," based on the idea that different chemical composites could be designed by using the common scientific knowledge on atoms' and bonds' properties. The direct implication of the synthetic dyestuff model was the possibility of exploiting economies of scope in knowledge: a common scientific base was used to develop a high variety of organic products. Firms that mastered this knowledge diversified into sectors that share the common scientific base, such as pharmaceuticals, explosives and photographic materials.[3] A second implication of the synthetic dyestuff model was the resurgence in the role of universities and other scientific research institutes. Since the synthetic dyestuff model was a science-based model in which the invention of new products was strictly dependent upon advances in the scientific understanding of the chemical structure of molecules, many large firms established links with academia, began to recruit researchers in the universities, fostered research collaborations and joint research centres for developing new products, and applied for joint patents (Murmann and Landau, 1998).

However, the synthetic dyestuff model was only the beginning of the science-based approach to innovation in chemicals. The continuation of the synthetic dyestuff model was *polymer chemistry*. Initiated by Herman Staudinger and other German scientists in the 1920s, polymer chemistry is based upon the idea that any material consists of long chains of molecules – i.e. polymers – linked together by chemical bonds. The scientific understanding of the existence and configuration of these long chemical macromolecules led to the principle of "materials by design" (Arora and Gambardella, 1998). According to this principle, a relationship exists between the characteristics of the macromolecular structures and the properties of materials. This scientific understanding of chemical composites is the basis for different product applications.

As in the case of the dyestuff model, the rise of polymer chemistry strongly influenced the evolution of the chemical sector in the post-war era. The reasons are twofold. *First*, polymer chemistry provided a common technological base for developing applications and product differentiation in five distinct and otherwise unconnected product markets – i.e. plastics, fibers, rubbers and elastomers, surface coatings and paintings, and adhesives. This lowered the amount of time and research needed for product innovation in the sector. But, if the use of abstract principles governing the macromolecular structures offered the solution to "how" to innovate, the question shifted to "what" to produce. In other words, while the process of producing new products was comparatively easy for any chemical firm, the discovery of the "right product" was not.

---

[3] This was the case with Hoechst, which in 1883 produced the pain-relieving Antipyrin, and Bayer, which in 1899 patented the pain-relieving, fever-reducing, anti-inflammatory aspirin. Agfa used the technological convergence of some organic intermediates and in 1887 diversified into photochemicals.

Competition among firms shifted to the correct anticipation of the users' requirements, and to the development of the most suitable applications. In order to innovate successfully, firms had to become knowledgeable about the characteristics of different market segments. Therefore, they developed extensive linkages with the downstream markets. *Second*, the new opportunities created by polymer chemistry were exploited by a large number of companies worldwide that had the required size, scope and in-house expertise to capitalize on them. As Freeman (1982) points out, the presence of a large number of firms with comparable capabilities in polymers implied that even "small" information leaks allowed very rapid imitation. Many chemical companies and some oil producers found themselves competing in very similar markets.[4] The increased competition in almost every market segment led to renewed attention to product differentiation and commercialization strategies as important sources of competitive advantage. This encouraged extensive investments in R&D to develop new product variants, and systematic linkages with the users in order to tailor products for specific applications.

The shift from coal to petroleum hydrocarbons in the years before World War II in the United States was the main reason behind a new change in the innovation strategies of chemical firms. In addition, the upsurge of chemical engineering fostered the worldwide diffusion of petrochemical technologies.

The concept of *unit operation* presented by Arthur D. Little to the Massachusetts Institute of Technology (MIT) in 1915 was key to the development of chemical engineering. The idea of the unit operation consists in the breaking down of chemical processes into a limited number of basic components or distinctive processes that are common to many product lines (Wright, 1999).[5] This abstract and general concept provided the unifying base for more contextualized and problem-solving innovations at the plant level (Rosenberg, 1998). Furthermore, it made it possible to separate product innovation from process innovation, and led to important changes in the organization of the chemical sector.

First, process technology was made into a commodity that could be traded.[6] This allowed chemical technologies to diffuse rapidly. Strong economies of specialization were achieved at the industry level, and a

---

[4] For instance, Union Carbide, Goodrich, General Electric, IG Farben and ICI were doing research into PVC and produced the polymer. Dow, IG Farben and Monsanto were involved in the polystyrene business. Du Pont, ICI, Union Carbide, Monsanto, Kodak and many other firms invested in other types of polyamides, acrylics and polyesters (Spitz, 1988; and Aftalion, 1999).

[5] See Rosenberg (1998) for the discussion of the "unit operation" and the role of MIT in the development of the chemical engineering discipline.

[6] This issue is discussed in section 6.

large number of vertical linkages developed between chemical companies and specialized engineering firms (SEFs). These vertical ties often resolved into partnering relationships of two types: between the SEFs and a number of chemical firms developing new technologies; and between the SEFs and an even larger number of firms buying these new technologies. As Freeman (1968, p. 30) points out, in the period from 1960 to 1966 "nearly three-quarters of the major new plants were 'engineered,' procured and constructed by specialist plant contractors," and the SEFs were the source for about 30 percent of all licenses for chemical processes. By supplying the necessary process technologies, the design and the engineering know-how of new plants, the SEFs facilitated the entry of new firms into the chemical industry after World War II and allowed other countries, such as Germany, to catch up quickly in petrochemicals.

A second effect of the introduction of the unit operation concept and the rise of the chemical engineering discipline was the renewed importance of university research for developing innovations. The academic research assured the orientation toward general results. The link of the university with the industry and its partial dependence upon private funding ensured the focus on industrial needs. Moreover, in order to develop processing technologies, chemical engineers needed the large-scale operations that the university alone could not supply.[7] This interaction between profit-seeking institutions and independent or semi-independent professional scientists influenced the evolution of technology in the engineering discipline. Threatened by the possibility of going to the academy as a potential employment option, firms often had to adapt their employment conditions to match those typically found at the university. They allowed a certain degree of freedom and flexibility to chemical scientists and engineers, and gave them the possibility of publishing their research achievements. In some cases this limited the appropriability of knowledge by private US firms. Germany resisted chemical engineering as an autonomous discipline until the 1960s, and drew a clear demarcation line between subjects to be studied at the university and those of more immediate usefulness of the industry. In the United Kingdom ICI showed limited interest in university-trained engineers up to World War II. Only when the United Kingdom entered the refining market did the demand for chemical engineers grow rapidly.

[7] An important example of university-industry networks in this period is that between the New Jersey Standard and MIT at the research facility in Baton Rouge, Louisiana (Landau and Rosenberg, 1992). The Ph.D. degree came to play a role in chemical engineering much earlier than in other engineering disciplines. Soon after the beginning of the discipline, the enrolment of graduate students in chemical engineering grew rapidly. At the time of the presentation of the "unit operation," the consulting company of Arthur D. Little employed a large number of MIT graduates.

The three examples of synthetic dyestuffs, polymer chemistry and unit operation allied to chemical engineering illustrate how the organization of innovative activities in chemicals has relied on the application of general scientific knowledge to the discovering of new products and processes. This approach to innovation produced major changes in firms' strategies and market structures.

## 3    The geography of the chemical sectoral system and international performance

The chemical industry has always been a "global" industry. For many years there have been considerable flows of international investment by chemical companies, together with systematic flows of engineering and process licenses.

Up to the 1980s foreign investments were confined to "first world" countries. Only during the last two decades have the developing countries become an attractive location for the large chemical companies located in industrialized countries. Developing countries are now important target markets both for foreign investment in plants and for the transfer of process technologies and engineering services. This ability to span the geographical boundaries of foreign investments as well as the possibility of complementing these investments with related technology flows through licenses or engineering services are major factors in enhancing firms' competitiveness.

The globalization of the chemical industry is shown by the rapid increase in the number of chemical plants built in foreign countries by European, American and Japanese companies (Arora, Gambardella and Garcia-Fontes, 1998). Proximity to customers in fast-growing regions, high product differentiation and customization of plants, and the need to reduce transport costs are important factors explaining the internationalization of this industry. There is empirical evidence showing that this process is more pronounced for European chemical firms than for the United States and Japan. This is because the small and fragmented European market encouraged firms to invest abroad, while facing high labor costs in Europe.

Organic chemical refining in the 1980s, and petrochemicals, plastics and rubber in the 1990s, are the main products being produced abroad. Specialty chemicals is another important example of the globalization of the chemical industry (Sharp, 2001). The specialty chemical sector was initially composed of a small number of national companies competing as oligopolists in national or regional markets (e.g. European). Then these companies expanded internationally and started competing with each other, and with companies from other countries. Moreover, the process of specialization via mergers and acquisitions – e.g. the demerger of Zeneca from ICI, and the mergers of Zeneca with Astra, Ciba Geigy with Sandoz, ICI with Unilever, and Hoechst with Rhône-Poulenc – transformed national or regional oligopolistic markets into global oligopolies. Nowadays, in each sector, the market is composed of no more than six to twelve large dominant firms. Moreover, because of the size and the strengths of the incumbents, potential entrants find it extremely hard to compete in marketing activities, and firms with good complementary assets can effectively dominate the market.

The international competitiveness of firms, countries and regions in different chemical sectors depends on the quality and quantity of the demand for chemical products, on the national scientific and technological base, on firms' research capabilities and on their capability to translate public research into commercial innovations.[8] There are examples in combinatorial chemistry, environmental technologies and agrochemicals that show the existence of differences among countries in the capability of companies to use public research results for commercial purposes. For instance, the discovery process of new agrochemicals requires the integration of various scientific disciplines. Europe shows a high number of publications in the fields related to agrochemicals. However, the numbers of patents and the numbers of agrochemical products introduced in Europe are low compared to other regions. This shows the relative weakness of Europe in bringing agrochemical research into the product market. In paints, coatings and printing inks, European firms perform much better. In new materials, where a lot of research is carried out by public research centres, large firms are the main source of incremental and cumulative innovations. They interact with the users of their products and with outside specialist firms, or specialists from academia.

National policies play a role in all this. By providing education, training and infrastructure they can contribute to fostering the competitiveness of firms, industries and regions, and attract companies from other areas to locate R&D-intensive activities within the national boundaries of specific countries (Meyer-Krahmer, 1999).

---

[8] As reported by Sharp (2001), "the presence of Hoechst, Bayer and BASF, together with the close competition from Sandoz, Ciba Geigy and Hoffman la Roche in Switzerland, was seen to provide the basis for the comparative (competitive) advantage of Germany and Switzerland in chemicals and pharmaceuticals. Britain's support for a 'cluster' of pharmaceutical firms was likewise seen to have brought the UK competitive advantage in this sector." However, "national competitiveness can be seen not so much in the performance of nationally based MNEs [multinational entities], as in the degree to which international companies are drawn to locate within national boundaries, and the quality of the jobs they bring with them and attract to them."

## 4    Evolutionary and coevolutionary processes

### 4.1    Industry dynamics: the evolution of network formation

To describe the dynamics of industry structure, this chapter now moves from an approach at the firm level to one at the network level. Linkages among firms, research institutions and users are important features of the chemical sector. Their characteristics evolved over time and influenced the evolution of the industry according to the specific historical circumstances. Although inter-firm networks, university-industry networks and user-producer networks are common to any period, each of them was particularly influential in conjunction with specific historical events. Inter-firm networks include firm-to-firm strategic agreements for R&D, production and marketing. University-industry networks are firm-to-academia linkages that, in most cases, are aimed at developing basic innovations. Finally, user-producer networks are linkages that firms develop in order to be responsive to their customers' needs, especially in more downstream specialty sectors.

During the nineteenth century, when the synthetic dyestuff model emerged, the invention of new products was strictly related to advances in the scientific understanding of the chemical structure of new molecules. Since universities and other scientific research institutes played an important role in the development of this scientific understanding, the largest and most innovative firms established many links with the scientific world. One way of interacting with academia was the recruitment of researchers by the companies. Research collaborations and joint patent applications were also frequently used.

At the same time, the dyestuff model imposed the establishment of strong interactions between firms and users. The strong interactions with the users allowed dye firms to understand better their customers' needs, and produce products better suited to a diversified demand. R&D activity benefited widely from this type of interaction, which led to a continuous stream of product innovations.

World War I brought about deep changes in the structure of the international chemical industry, and in the behavior of firms. In order to satisfy the needs of the war, government demand for explosives, drugs and fertilizers increased tremendously, and allowed chemical firms to utilize their full production capabilities. However, when the war was over and the reconstruction was completed the demand for chemical products decreased in all countries. Most chemical producers suffered during the inter-war period from overcapacity problems. This imposed a rationalization of the whole chemical industry. The increase in the number of mergers, acquisitions (e.g. IG Farben in Germany, and ICI in Britain) and cartels (e.g. the nitrogen cartel between IG Farben and ICI) was aimed at reducing production costs in all countries. Networks in this period became synonymous with collusion.

After World War II two major technological breakthroughs influenced the formation of networks and the evolution of industry structure. Section 3 explored the technological changes involved in these processes. As far as networks are concerned, polymer chemistry encouraged the formation of networks between the producers and the users of chemical products. Indeed, competition among firms shifted to the correct anticipation of users' requirements, and to the development of the most suitable applications. To innovate successfully firms had to become knowledgeable about the characteristics of different market segments. Moreover, chemical engineering encouraged the formation of university-industry linkages, and the development of vertical networks between chemical companies and specialized process design and engineering contractors (the SEFs). This process of increasing specialization and cumulative learning in process design was the basis of the SEFs' comparative advantages in developing the "market for chemical technologies." They supplied the necessary process technologies and the design and the engineering know-how for new plants, leading to an increasing division of labor at the industry level between SEFs and chemical manufacturers.

A final discontinuity in industry dynamics occurred in the 1980s. The rise of the SEFs fostered competition in the chemical sector, and led to a substantial increase in the number of chemical firms in most markets. During the 1950s and 1960s the industry could accommodate such increase because the demand for chemical products was growing rapidly. But in the 1970s and 1980s the oil shocks, the entry of competitors from the developing countries, the slower demand growth and the diminishing opportunities for product innovations made profitability decline. Firms in a large number of chemical markets, especially basic intermediates, experienced excess capacity problems. As in the period after World War I, the restructuring process also involved a large number of inter-firm networks, both in production and R&D. The formation of inter-industry associations (e.g. the Association of Petrochemicals Producers in Europe) played a role in fostering such inter-firm agreements. Furthermore, mergers, acquisitions and alliances reduced the number of businesses in which the chemical companies were active and increased the absolute size and the market share of the remaining product lines.

To sum up, during its one-hundred-year history the chemical industry faced radical discontinuities, both in technology and markets. However, it was the rise of different types of networks that allowed chemical firms to survive and remain competitive for such a long period. If the industry faced a series of major external discontinuities, chemical companies adapted to such changes. The formation of networks with academia, with other firms and with the users of chemical products helped in this process.

## 4.2    Coevolutionary processes: the case of environmental technologies

There is not a unique coevolutionary process for the chemical industry as a whole. Although the different elements of the sectoral system – demand, agents, technology, learning processes, markets and institutions – are closely connected and coevolve in this industry, different subsectors experienced different coevolutionary processes.

The flow of chemical processing technologies to developing countries is an example of the coevolution of markets, institutions and old and new agents. After World War II the demand for process technologies in developing countries was increasing constantly. This demand was mainly related to the production of new fertilizers for agriculture and to the exploitation of their large oil resources. From the supply side, chemical companies from the developed countries were interested in expanding their markets into the developing world. In addition, local governments often entered the picture by opening local barriers to foreign firms and asking them to provide processing technologies to local chemical companies. As a consequence, process technologies flowed from the developed to the developing countries, with the SEFs and the large chemical companies being the main actors in this market. The interplay between and mutual evolution of these large companies, the engineering firms, the new entrants in the emerging markets and local authorities allowed the market for chemical products and the market for process technologies to grow.

Another interesting example of coevolutionary processes in chemicals is given by environmental technologies.[9] The chemical industry has often been accused of being highly responsible for pollution. Some accidents contributed to the generation of a generalized suspicion against chemical firms and against the whole industry (e.g. Seveso and Bhopal). The interaction of two actors – consumers' demand and government regulation – led to important changes in firms' behavior concerning pollution strategies, and to the rise of a new market for environmental technologies. In particular, in many countries governments are intervening by using regulations and control measures that aim at reducing waste production and

[9] See Arduini and Cesaroni (2001) for a detailed discussion of this issue.

pollution. Legislative tools are important constraints for manufacturers. There are "command and control" measures that directly influence the environmental behavior of the social actors by determining limits, restrictions and rules related to specific products and processes. There are also more flexible means through which governments try to reduce the probability of polluting, based on economic incentives and voluntary programs such as taxes, tradable quotas, subsidies and covenants.

As a result, chemical companies are increasingly developing and adopting new production technologies (environmental technologies, or "green" processes), and new products (e.g. less polluting solvents and paints). Many firms first introduced *end-of-pipe* and *recycling* technologies. End-of-pipe technologies are purification and treatment plants that do not modify the production techniques in use. They are placed at the end of the production processes in order to transform wastes into less polluting or non-injurious compounds. Recycling technologies recover and transform wastes for future use. More recently, most chemical companies are replacing end-of-pipe technologies by *clean technologies*, the aim of which is to prevent wastes and pollution, to reduce the amount of inputs and the use of energy in the production process, and to use recycled material. They also induce increases in production efficiency and firms' productivity. The cost of adopting these technologies is the partial or radical modification of the production process.

However, there are differences across countries in the rate of adoption of environmental technologies. Germany and the United States show a higher rate in the adoption of end-of-pipe and recycling technologies compared to other countries. This might be due to public pressure and government regulations: public opinion strongly influences the adoption of environmental technologies, and both the US and German governments set extremely strict environmental standards that companies have to meet. Furthermore, patent statistics show that, while the United States has a high number of innovations in recycling technologies, Europe is much more oriented toward end-of-pipe technologies, suggesting that European companies are still set on the development of *ex post* remedies to pollution.

A consequence of the growing attention to environmental issues is the birth of an intermediate market for environmental technologies and engineering services related to environmental technologies – the so-called "green industry". The green industry started at the beginning of the 1970s in those countries that introduced environmental policies. These countries are now the most competitive ones in the green industry, with a large number of independent and small firms that specialize in the supply of environmental services and products. Similarly to the birth of the

SEFs for process technologies, new environment-related SEFs started to operate for the production of environmental technologies. The extent of this process is particularly important in the United States.

The example of environmental technologies shows that there is a process of coevolution of companies' behavior, consumers' demand and government intervention. These forces have led to the development and adoption of environmentally safe technologies. As a consequence, two new markets emerged, one for environmentally safe products and the other for green technologies. Moreover, the complexity of the technologies, together with the increasing size of the green market, led to the entry of new agents in the market that specialize in providing technological solutions and know-how in the market for environmentally safe technologies.

## 5    The knowledge base and learning processes: knowledge generation

The discussion in previous sections highlighted the fact that the process of knowledge creation and diffusion is important for determining the competitive advantage of firms and countries in the chemical industry. This section and the following one focus on the processes of knowledge generation and knowledge diffusion respectively, and report the results of some empirical analyses.

During the past decades different modes of managing innovative processes have emerged. In particular, innovation is no longer an activity conducted exclusively inside the organizational structures of large corporations. The empirical evidence suggests that innovations are increasingly the outcome of interaction between agents located within the same organization or belonging to different economic organizations or institutions. This section explores research collaborations that lead to patented innovations in the chemical industry, and addresses the issue of whether *geographical proximity* matters for establishing collaborations among inventors compared to the affiliation to the same (large) company (*organizational proximity*).[10]

Specifically, we explored some features of a population of 97,839 chemical patents granted by EPO between 1986 and 1997 that have been

---

[10] Geographical proximity is measured within and across NUTS2 and NUTS3 regions. The NUTS (Nomenclature of Territorial Units for Statistics) classification has been established by Eurostat in order to provide a single, uniform breakdown of territorial units for the production of regional statistics for the European Union. For information regarding the classification, see http://europa.eu.int/comm/eurostat/ramon/nuts/introduction_regions_en.html.

classified in one of the following five chemical sectors: biotechnology, pharmaceuticals, materials, organic chemistry or polymers.[11] As a first look at the data, consider that, while there are few patents with multiple assignees (6.8 percent), there is a great deal of collaboration among individuals (inventors). Only 18.3 percent of all chemical patents are developed by single inventors. The remaining patents (81.7 percent) are invented by two or more inventors. To a large extent, however, these networks are mostly national. Overall, 90.8 percent of the patents developed by multiple inventors are among individuals from the same country. Only 9.2 percent of patents with multiple inventors involve international linkages.

In order to analyze whether the firm or the cluster is a better coordination mode for promoting collaborations among inventors, we used a sample of 4,650 patents selected from about 10,000 chemical patents (see appendix for details). The composition of the sample is as follows: 159 are public institutions, excluding universities; 44 are universities; 133 are individual inventors (i.e. assignees who do not belong to any firm); 2,123 are large firms belonging to the *Fortune 500* list (and hence labeled as "Fortune 500" firms). The remaining 2,191 firms are not listed in *Fortune 500*, and have been labeled as "other" firms.

As the managerial literature suggests, organizational proximity is expected to be an efficient mechanism for organizing research collaborations. Indeed, the unique competencies, the internal communication systems and the routines that the firm develops over time all help reduce the cost of coordinating different parts of the organization and different individuals. Hence, patents developed by the firm are expected to have a larger number of inventors and to be more complex than the average. By contrast, geographical proximity is expected to be a feasible and efficient coordination mechanism when the inventors are located in a technology-intensive region – i.e. in a technological cluster. We then expect companies to produce more complex patents in a technological cluster than in non-cluster areas.

To describe the effectiveness of organizational proximity and geographical proximity to foster collaboration among inventors we computed the share of *de-localized* and *co-localized* patents (DL and CL respectively) over the total number of patents in the sample. We defined a patent as CL if all the inventors are located in the same region. If at least one inventor is located in a different NUTS region, then the patent is DL. In the case of DL patents, we considered the inventors to be affiliated to the same

---

[11] We thank Rossana Pammolli for developing a correspondence table between the IPC classes and the five chemical sectors used in this paper.

company.[12] The results of our analysis show that about 38 percent of total patents are DL and 62 percent are CL. The higher share of CL compared to DL patents suggests that the geographical proximity among inventors might play a role in pulling them together. Unfortunately, we cannot distinguish whether this proximity is either among inventors belonging to the same firm or among inventors located in the same small geographical area. In the case of CL patents, the effect of the firm and the cluster are blended together.

We then compared the characteristics of DL and CL patents. Specifically, we computed the mean number of inventors and the mean number of supplementary classes of CL patents, and the differences between these means and those of DL patents. The differences between these means might be related to the "quality" of the coordination played by the firm (for DL patents) and by geographical proximity (for CL patents). Indeed, the number of supplementary classes is a proxy for the *interdisciplinarity of the patent*. Each patent is classified in one main obligatory technological class according to the IPC system. However, apart from the main IPC class, the patent officers can assign other supplementary IPC classes if they believe that the patent falls into other technological classes as well. The higher the number of supplementary classes, the higher the interdisciplinarity of the patent. The number of inventors listed in the patents is a proxy for the *breadth of the network of inventors*. Intuitively, a higher coordination effort is needed when more interdisciplinary patents are developed and when more inventors are involved. Table 4.1 shows the results of this analysis.

Table 4.1 shows that, on average, the networks of inventors and the interdisciplinarity of innovations are higher for DL patents than for the whole sample (and, clearly, for CL patents). This suggests that the coordination played by the organizational proximity is more effective than the coordination played by the geographical proximity among inventors. The low share of DL patents in the sample, however, suggests that the vast majority of companies do not have internally the competencies to coordinate such collaborations across distances.

We then distinguished between the "Fortune 500" firms and the "other" firms. Table 4.2 shows that the Fortune 500 companies produce

---

[12] A CL patent can be the outcome of geographical proximity among inventors either through their belonging to the same firm, or through their belonging to different firms but located in the same region. Hence, a CL patent can be the outcome of the coordination played either by the firm or by the cluster. No distinction can be made by using the information that we have. By contrast, a DL patent is the result of collaboration among inventors located in different places. It cannot be the outcome of geographical proximity among inventors.

Table 4.1 *Characteristics of DL and CL patents*

| | Share of DL patents over the total number of patents in the sample | Number of inventors: mean and differences between means[a] | Number of supplementary classes: mean and differences between means[a] |
|---|---|---|---|
| DL patents | 1,767 (38%) | 4.1 (0.04) | 2.1 (0.05) |
| CL patents | 2,883 (62%) | −1.4 (0.05) | −0.3 (0.06) |
| Mean of the total sample | 4,650 (100%) | 3.2 (0.03) | 2.0 (0.03) |

[a] Standard errors in parentheses.
Source: Elaboration from EPO data, 1998.

Table 4.2 *Firms' characteristics versus patent characteristics*

| | DL patents: share over the total number of patents produced by the two types of companies | Number of inventors: mean and differences between means[a] | Number of supplementary classes: mean and differences between means[a] |
|---|---|---|---|
| "Fortune 500" firms | 900 (41.8%) | 3.5 (0.04) | 2.1 (0.04) |
| "Others" | 771 (30.9%) | −0.6 (0.06) | −0.3 (0.06) |
| Mean of the total sample | 1,671 (38.7%) | 3.2 (0.03) | 2.0 (0.03) |

[a] Standard errors in parentheses. These data do not include universities, governments and "individual" inventors.
Source: Elaboration from EPO data, 1998.

a higher percentage of DL patents than the other firms. The share of DL patents over the total number of patents invented by the Fortune 500 firms is 41.8 percent, compared to 30.9 percent of DL patents produced by the others. Moreover, patents assigned to these large multinational companies are produced by a larger number of inventors (3.5 inventors on average) and are more interdisciplinary (2.1 supplementary classes on average) than patents produced by the other firms.

These results confirm that, in chemicals, large companies coordinate larger networks of inventors to produce more interdisciplinary patents than the other firms. Furthermore, when patents invented by the largest corporations – i.e. the Fortune 500 companies – are DL, the networks of inventors become even larger. The average number of inventors listed in DL patents produced by Fortune 500 companies is 4.3. The number of supplementary classes is 2.2 (not shown here). This suggests that the organizational proximity in large multinational companies is more effective than in smaller firms. The former can draw on globally dispersed competencies and coordinate inventors across distances to produce interdisciplinary patents.

However, the fact that the Fortune 500 companies also develop more CL patents than DL patents seems to suggest that geographical proximity matters even for large multinational firms. They develop innovations in specific regions or subsidiaries, pulling together competencies locally, at the regional level. But the greater share of DL patents for the Fortune 500 companies compared to the other firms, and the higher average number of inventors and supplementary classes listed in their patents, suggest that these large companies can better coordinate inventors located in different places.

It remains to be seen whether the technological characteristics of the regions influence firms' innovative activity. As suggested above, the expectation is that geographical proximity in technology-intensive regions gives rise to more interdisciplinary patents and to larger networks of inventors compared to non-cluster regions. The underlining argument is that in technology-intensive regions, where innovative activities agglomerate, it is easier to find the specialized and complementary competencies needed in complex R&D projects. Moreover, since people with complementary expertise are located very close to one another, the probability of collaboration increases. We also expect this probability to be higher for smaller and less global firms. These firms might use the advantages of the technological cluster to compensate for the lack of internal scientific competencies and coordination capabilities.

To define a technological cluster, we looked at the distribution of different variables across the European regions and decided that the number of chemical laboratories – both private and public – was a good proxy for the technological intensity and infrastructure developed by a region in the chemical sector. As expected, other variables, such as the number of patents invented in each area, are correlated with the number of laboratories. Furthermore, we checked that firms in our database do not determine themselves the characteristics of the cluster. Indeed, these companies have only a small fraction of total R&D laboratories in each region (not shown here). We then defined a cluster according to the number of laboratories established in each region.[13]

---

[13] The distribution of chemical laboratories in the European regions is very skewed. The 4,650 patents in the sample have been invented in 108 European regions. The number of

Table 4.3 *Cluster versus non-cluster regions and patent characteristics*

| | CL patents: share over the total number of patents produced in the two types of regions | Number of inventors: mean and differences between means[a] | Number of supplementary classes: mean and differences between means[a] |
|---|---|---|---|
| Cluster regions | 1,816 (66.1%) | 3.3 (0.05) | 1.9 (0.05) |
| Non-cluster regions | 578 (48.3%) | −0.2 (0.06) | 0.1 (0.06) |
| Mean of the total sample | 3,944 (60.7%) | 3.2 (0.03) | 2.0 (0.03) |

[a] Standard errors in parentheses. These data do not include universities, governments and "individual" inventors. The number of observations is 3,944.
Source: Elaboration from EPO data, 1998.

Table 4.3 shows that the probability of a patent being CL in the technological clusters is higher than in non-cluster regions. The probability of CL patents goes from 49.4 percent in the non-clusters to 66.0 percent in the clusters. The share of DL patents falls correspondingly.

Table 4.3 also shows the mean number of inventors and the mean number of supplementary classes of patents invented in cluster and non-cluster regions. The results are inconclusive, however, suggesting that being in a cluster does not influence the level of interdisciplinarity of a patent and the breadth of the network of inventors. This might be due to the fact that the table does not highlight the net effect of being in a cluster over the interdisciplinarity and the breadth of the collaboration. To do so one needs to control for other factors.

However, geographical proximity in the cluster might be a better coordination mechanism for inducing research collaboration when firms do not have the organizational capabilities and the scientific competencies needed to develop complex R&D projects internally. Table 4.4 shows the percentage of patents performed in cluster and non-cluster regions by non-"Fortune 500" companies over the total number of patents performed in the two types of regions.

chemical laboratories located in these regions ranges from 0 to 647. Since the database on R&D laboratories in Europe does not provide information on the number of laboratories in Switzerland, Finland and Sweden, the regions from these countries are excluded from the analysis. We then have 91 regions, in which 4,276 patents have been invented and for which there is information on the number of laboratories that they host. Interestingly, however, 67 out of 91 regions host fewer than 100 laboratories. Only the last quartile of the European regions in our sample has between 100 and 647 chemical laboratories. We termed the regions in this quartile the technological clusters.

Table 4.4 *Technological clusters, firms' and patent characteristics*

|  | Share of patents produced by "Fortune 500" firms in the clusters and non-clusters | Share of patents produced by the "other" firms in the clusters and non-clusters | Others' number of inventors: mean and differences between means[a] | Others' number of supplementary classes: mean and differences between means[a] |
|---|---|---|---|---|
| Cluster | 1,374 (50.0%) | 1,373 (50.0%) | 3.0 (0.07) | 1.8 (0.08) |
| Non-cluster | 694 (58.0%) | 503 (42.0%) | −0.2 (0.08) | 0.1 (0.09) |

[a] Standard errors in parentheses. This is the total number of patents in cluster and non-cluster regions respectively. The data do not include universities, governments and "individual" inventors. The number of observations is 3,944.
Source: Elaboration from EPO data, 1998.

The probability of a patent being produced by the other firms increases from 42.0 percent in non-cluster areas to 50.0 percent in the clusters. Symmetrically, the probability of a patent being produced by Fortune 500 firms decreases from 58.0 percent in non-cluster areas to 50.0 percent in the clusters. These data support the idea that technological clusters are more attractive to smaller and less global firms than they are to large MNEs. This suggests that large corporations are good mechanisms to coordinate competencies and researchers located in different units and geographical areas, and that being in a technological cluster might be somewhat more beneficial for pulling together localized competencies for smaller firms than for the larger ones. Again, however, when we compute the average number of inventors and the average number of supplementary classes listed in the patents invented by other firms in the clusters, and compare them to those invented in the non-cluster regions, the results are inconclusive. The networks of inventors are slightly smaller in the non-cluster areas. The interdisciplinarity of the patents is slightly lower for patents invented in the clusters.

To sum up, compared to the geographical proximity in a technological cluster, organizational proximity in large companies enhances international networks of inventors, induces a greater number of inventors to collaborate and produces more interdisciplinary or "general" patents. Hence, large companies in chemicals seem to have a competitive advantage for producing innovations compared to smaller firms. These latter firms can compensate for their lack of competencies by clustering in technology-intensive regions.[14]

---

[14] Further analysis on this topic is needed to isolate the relative effects of these two factors. An attempt in this direction has been made by Mariani (2003).

## 6    The knowledge base and learning processes: patterns of technology diffusion

*6.1    Separability and transferability as factors fostering technology transactions*

Technology transfer and diffusion in the chemical industry mostly takes place through market-based interactions. The existence of such transactions and the functioning of markets for technology are based on two conditions:

a) the knowledge base from which innovations are developed is generic to several applications, and can be abstracted from specific contexts; and

b) self-reinforcing characteristics of the market for technology exist in chemicals.

As far as the characteristics of the knowledge base are concerned, the developments in scientific understanding in many chemical disciplines have caused chemical research to move away from "trial and error" procedures to science-based approaches to industrial research. Scientific discoveries and general principles are the bases to "design" new products and processes. As Arora and Gambardella (1994) point out, the more general and abstract a piece of knowledge is not linked to the people and organizations that develop it, the easier it is to transfer that knowledge to other people and organizations that might use it for different purposes. In turn, the possibility of transferring general and abstract knowledge allows for a division of labor in innovation, with some firms or institutions developing more general technologies and others using them for specific applications. This opens up different alternative modes for organizing the innovation process, and allows firms to pursue different strategies to get access to new technologies, from in-house development to "outsourcing."

As suggested above, starting from the period after World War II the concept of unit operation, the emergence of chemical engineering, the growing importance of petrochemicals, and the increase in the scale and complexity of chemical plants led to the rise of a new market for engineering and process design services for chemical plants. In particular, the development of chemical engineering as an academic discipline made it easier to separate the process design from the details of the compound being produced in the plants. In turn, the codification of process technologies and the rise of specialized technology suppliers led to a vertical division of labor in the chemical processing sector. Process technology was made into a "commodity" that could be traded due to the general-purpose nature of the knowledge exchanged.

This market for technological knowledge in the chemical sector was operated by a large number of small, specialized and technology-based firms, the SEFs, which was an original and persistent feature of the American chemical industry. The SEFs were good at moving down the learning curve for processes invented by the large oil and chemical companies, and acted as independent licensors on behalf of other firms' technology. They started as an American phenomenon because of the large size of the American market (Freeman, 1968).[15] Indeed, by the end of World War II the world demand for chemical products grew – especially for petrochemicals – and pushed companies to raise the scale of their production. Since the large scale increased the size and complexity of plants, chemical companies started to face a technological capability constraint and asked for external engineering specialists.

Once the market for chemical process technologies emerged, self-reinforcing mechanisms came into play. Indeed, the presence of SEFs encouraged large chemical and oil firms to license their own technologies for making profits out of them. To some extent, this was an unexpected behavior. The managerial literature (among others, see Teece, 1988) traditionally argues that companies gain rents from their R&D activity by exploiting technologies in-house. By contrast, licensing creates new competitors in the downstream product market, which reduce profits and dissipate rents. However, as described by Arora and Fosfuri (2000, 2003), the licensing activity of the SEFs creates new competitors in the final product market in any case. Hence, incumbent large chemical companies try to increase the overall returns of their R&D activity by moving into the upstream technology market and by selling their proprietary technologies.

The SEFs' licensing activity induces downstream chemical companies to become technology suppliers as well. In turn, the presence of rivals in the downstream markets licensing their technologies increases the propensity of other chemical companies to license their proprietary technologies. As a consequence, licensing strategies tend to strengthen over time (i.e. there are self-reinforcing mechanisms), and, once established, the market for process technology in chemicals persists over time. By using data on worldwide technology licensing during the 1980s, Arora and Fosfuri (2000) show that homogeneous sectors such as air separation, pulp and paper, and petrochemicals are characterized by extensive licensing. By contrast, in differentiated product groups such as organic chemicals, licensing is quite limited. They also find that in subsectors

---

[15] According to Freeman (1968), 50 percent of the total value of engineering contracts world-wide in the period 1960 to 1966 was attributable to the American SEFs.

Table 4.5 *Licensing agreements: 1980–97 (shares of total licenses by type of licensor and region)*

| Licensor | Receiving country | | | | |
|---|---|---|---|---|---|
| | Germany | United Kingdom | Japan | United States | Total |
| Top chemical firms | 1.7 | 1.4 | 2.7 | 3.7 | 9.5 |
| Other chemical firms | 0.1 | 0.2 | 0.2 | 0.3 | 0.8 |
| SEFs | 8.9 | 8.3 | 10.4 | 23.3 | 50.9 |
| Staff | 7.4 | 5.6 | 9.5 | 16.3 | 38.8 |
| Total | 18.1 | 15.5 | 22.8 | 43.6 | 100.0 |

Source: Chemintell database, 1998.

where firms without downstream assets – such as the SEFs – license more, large chemical producers themselves tend to license more.

### 6.2    *Evidence on the existence of markets for technological knowledge*

The market for process technologies and the presence of the SEFs are distinctive characteristics of the chemical industry even today. This section describes the functioning of the market for technologies by comparing different means for transferring technological knowledge in chemicals in different countries.

By using information from the Chemintell database, table 4.5 shows the country distribution of the licensors of 5,442 licensing agreements that were signed in the United States, the United Kingdom, Japan and Germany.[16] There are four potential technology suppliers:

a) *top chemical companies* – the top fifty companies in terms of number of plants owned;

b) *other chemical companies* – companies with more than five plants that do not show in the top fifty positions;

c) *SEFs*; and

d) *staff* – the companies develop their process technologies internally.

Table 4.5 shows that the SEFs are the most important source of chemical process technologies in many developed countries. They own 50.9 percent of the total market for technology. Half of their transactions are

---

[16] The Chemintell database collects information on 36,343 chemical plants built worldwide since 1980. For each plant there are data on the type of product, the production capacity, the technology used, the owner of the plant, the contractor providing the engineering services, the licensor and the year of establishment.

Table 4.6 *Licensing agreements: 1980–97 (shares of total licenses by type of licensor and licensee)*

|  | Receiving company | | | |
| Licensor | Top chemical firms | Other Chemical firms | "Non"-chemical firms[a] | Total |
|---|---|---|---|---|
| Top chemical firms | 1.6 | 6.9 | 2.7 | 11.2 |
| Other chemical firms | 0.2 | 0.9 | 0.4 | 1.5 |
| SEFs | 9.3 | 39.8 | 19.1 | 68.2 |
| Staff | 8.6 | 8.8 | 1.7 | 19.1 |
| Total | 19.7 | 56.4 | 23.9 | 100.0 |

[a] "Non"-chemical firms are companies with five or fewer plants.
Source: Chemintell database, 1998.

in the United States (23.3 percent of the total), followed by in-house technology development (16.3 percent). Conditional upon each receiving country, the shares of the SEFs and staff are very similar across countries. In all countries, roughly half the technologies are supplied by the SEFs, and two-fifths by the companies themselves. Hence, apart from using their own technology expertise, chemical companies often rely on specialized suppliers of process technologies.

Table 4.6 looks at the type of companies involved in these vertical linkages. It confirms that the SEFs are the main suppliers of technologies in the chemical sector. They cover 68.2 percent of the total market for licensing. This is true for all types of companies with at least one plant. The SEFs license almost a half of the technologies used by the top chemical firms, over two-thirds of the know-how used by the companies with at least five chemical plants, and four-fifths of the technology used by the companies with five or fewer plants. Top chemical companies have the lowest share of technology received from the SEFs, clearly because of their strong in-house technological capabilities. This is confirmed by the fact that the top chemical companies develop about a half of their technological know-how in-house and sell these technologies to other chemical companies.

As suggested above, although the SEFs started as an American phenomenon, other countries are now successfully competing with the United States, particularly in Europe and in Third World markets. This result is confirmed by table 4.7. However, while the US SEFs had a sizable share of the European market in the 1980s, the European SEFs had only a small share of the US market. Indeed, the worldwide market

Table 4.7 *Market share of SEFs – licenses: 1980–90 (shares of total number of plants by region)*

|  | Regions | | | | |
|---|---|---|---|---|---|
| Nationality of SEFs | United States | Western Europe | Japan | Rest of the world | Share of total world market |
| United States | 18.0 | 10.3 | 6.5 | 16.9 | 15.1 |
| West Germany | 3.1 | 11.3 | 1.0 | 10.2 | 8.8 |
| United Kingdom | 1.2 | 3.0 | 2.7 | 1.4 | 2.4 |
| Italy | 0.1 | 1.4 | 0.0 | 2.2 | 1.6 |
| France | 0.1 | 0.6 | 0.0 | 0.9 | 0.7 |
| Japan | 0.1 | 0.1 | 1.5 | 1.1 | 0.7 |

Source: Chemical age profile (Arora and Gambardella, 1998).

Table 4.8 *Licenses – value and number by sector: 1990–97*

|  | Estimated value per license[a] | Number of licenses | Total value per sector[a] |
|---|---|---|---|
| General chemicals | 104.2 | 248 | 25,835.4 |
| Pharmaceuticals | 117.4 | 1,394 | 163,606.7 |
| Soaps and cosmetics | 3.0 | 29 | 87.0 |
| Rubber and plastics | 3.0 | 41 | 123.0 |
| Petroleum refining | 6.2 | 33 | 203.2 |
| Average | 46.7 | 349 | |

[a] Millions of dollars.
Source: SDC database, 1998.

share of the US SEFs in licensing was about 15 percent, followed by West Germany with a share of 8.8 percent. By contrast, the share of US licenses in Europe and Japan was much higher than the size of the market for processing technologies in the United States owned by the European and Japanese SEFs.

Finally, by using information drawn from the Securities Data Company (SDC) database, we tried to estimate the "value" of the market for chemical licenses in the period 1990 to 1997.[17] Table 4.8 shows these estimates.

[17] The SDC database (1998) collects data on about 52,000 inter-firm agreements worldwide in all sectors. The database is built on Securities and Exchange Commission filings ("10-Qs"), financial journals, news wire services, proxies and quarterly reports. For

In order to calculate the values, we first considered the whole SDC database (some 52,000 transactions) and selected the licensing agreements that disclosed the unit value of the transaction. We then attributed each license to one of the five industrial sectors shown in table 4.8. For each of these five sectors we computed the average value of the licenses (first column).[18] We then calculated the number of licenses by sector and, based on the estimated mean value per license, estimated the total value of the transactions in the five sectors (third column). Pharmaceutical transactions are the most numerous, and their unit value is the highest among the five sectors. In the general chemical sector licensing agreements tend to be less numerous, but the unit value is high. The market for knowledge seems to be less developed in soaps and cosmetics, rubber and plastics and petroleum refining, where both the number and the unit value of agreements are low compared to the other sectors.

## 6.3    Licensing strategies by large companies

As shown above, large chemical corporations are relevant actors in the market for process technologies. They both buy technologies from SEFs and sell proprietary technologies to other chemical firms. Companies such as Union Carbide, Amoco, Montedison, Phillips, Exxon and British Petroleum have always been important technology suppliers. Other leading chemical producers, such as Dow Chemical, Du Pont and Monsanto, traditionally reluctant to license, have only recently started to sell their proprietary technologies. This section discusses their technology strategies.

We considered the largest corporations from Western Europe and North America, i.e. those that reported more than fifty production plants in Chemintell. Then we selected all the plants in which these companies appeared as technology suppliers. Finally, we analyzed whether these companies used their proprietary technologies in-house for production purposes, or for licensing. Table 4.9 reports the results of this exercise. The first three columns of table 4.9 show the share of technologies that they exploited in-house ("staff"), or licensed out to other firms ("licensing") or both exploited in-house and licensed out ("both"). The last three columns describe their licensing behavior. We report the

each transaction there is information on the type of agreement, the technology transfer involved, the number of partners and the sector, country and region of the transaction. Data are available from 1990 to 1997.

[18] Since in soaps and cosmetics, and rubber and plastics, there are fewer than five licenses in the SDC database, we consider the median value of the whole sample of alliances.

overall number of plants in which a process technology provided by one of our companies has been used, the number of different technologies that our companies licensed out and the ratio between these two values. This ratio represents the average number of times the same technology has been licensed to different plants.

Table 4.9 shows that large corporations license a large amount of their proprietary processing technologies. On average, 60.8 percent of internally developed technologies are sold to other firms. Companies such as Texaco, Petrofina, British Petroleum and Mobil license more than 70 percent of their proprietary technologies. At the other extreme, Bayer and Dow Chemical license out about 30 percent of their technologies. Different firms, therefore, adopt different technological strategies. Interestingly, table 4.9 also shows that many technologies (an average of 22.4 percent) are both exploited in-house and licensed out to other firms. This means that, while these companies use their technologies in order to produce chemical compounds to be sold in the downstream product markets, they license the same technologies to other firms, which might become their competitors in the same product markets.

It is worth noting that most of these companies are leading chemical producers. Their core business is not technology licensing but product selling. Hence, their main concern should be to reduce potential competition in the product markets in which they compete, in order to gain increasing market shares. In this respect, their decision to license their technologies might be the result of the presence of independent technology suppliers (i.e. the SEFs), as suggested by Arora and Fosfuri (2000, 2003).

In some cases, however, technology licensing is a deliberate strategy which companies pursue *along with* production. The last three columns of table 4.9 show that eight out of the twenty-three companies we analyzed have licensed their process technologies to more than a hundred plants, one of them to more than two hundred, and one of them to more than three hundred. This result can hardly be considered a reaction to the presence of the SEFs. Indeed, technology licensing also responds to different motivations, such as the need to impose a technology standard, the need to provide customers with secondary suppliers using the same process technology, and so on (Cesaroni, 2001). Interestingly, companies' licensing strategies also diverge in terms of the number of different technologies provided. As shown in the last two columns of table 4.9, while some companies prefer to license a wide portfolio of technologies, others concentrate their licensing activity on a narrow range of technologies. For instance, on average Monsanto has provided the same technology to

Table 4.9 *Technology strategies by large chemical corporations*

| Company | Use of proprietary technologies | | | Licensing strategies | | |
|---|---|---|---|---|---|---|
| | Staff | Licensing | Both | Number of plants licensed | Number of technologies licensed | Plants licensed/ technologies licensed |
| Petrofina | 12.50% | 75.00% | 12.50% | 29 | 7 | 4.1 |
| Texaco | 14.82% | 70.38% | 14.80% | 58 | 23 | 2.5 |
| British Petroleum | 23.25% | 53.48% | 23.27% | 150 | 30 | 5.0 |
| Mobil | 26.32% | 52.63% | 21.05% | 27 | 13 | 2.1 |
| Occidental Petroleum | 30.00% | 50.00% | 20.00% | 14 | 7 | 2.0 |
| Eni | 28.30% | 49.06% | 22.64% | 165 | 37 | 4.5 |
| Montedison | 25.72% | 48.58% | 25.70% | 97 | 24 | 4.0 |
| Phillips Petroleum | 26.67% | 43.33% | 30.00% | 97 | 19 | 5.1 |
| Atlantic Richfield | 37.84% | 43.24% | 18.92% | 56 | 22 | 2.5 |
| Hoechst | 45.16% | 40.32% | 14.52% | 114 | 34 | 3.4 |
| Monsanto | 42.86% | 37.14% | 20.00% | 221 | 20 | 11.1 |
| Rhône-Poulenc | 41.54% | 36.92% | 21.54% | 112 | 37 | 3.0 |
| Chevron | 30.00% | 36.67% | 33.33% | 32 | 21 | 1.5 |
| Imperial Chemical Industries | 34.61% | 35.89% | 29.50% | 308 | 43 | 7.2 |
| DuPont | 51.25% | 32.50% | 16.25% | 87 | 27 | 3.2 |
| Exxon | 45.28% | 30.19% | 24.53% | 50 | 29 | 1.7 |
| Norsk Hydro | 41.18% | 29.41% | 29.41% | 47 | 9 | 5.2 |
| BASF | 48.63% | 27.53% | 23.84% | 162 | 51 | 3.2 |
| Shell Transport and Trading | 47.75% | 20.72% | 31.53% | 189 | 56 | 3.4 |
| Akzo Nobel | 62.07% | 20.69% | 17.24% | 16 | 10 | 1.6 |
| Bayer | 65.22% | 17.39% | 17.39% | 79 | 16 | 4.9 |
| Dow Chemical | 68.33% | 16.67% | 15.00% | 48 | 18 | 2.7 |
| Amoco | 52.38% | 14.29% | 33.33% | 85 | 9 | 9.4 |

Source: Chemintell database, 1998.

eleven different plants. Specifically, Monsanto has licensed a technology for the production of sulfuric acid to 140 plants. On average, Amoco has provided the same technology to nine plants, but has licensed the technology for the production of sulfur to forty different plants. By contrast, BASF has licensed its technologies more evenly.

This suggests that company and sectoral characteristics have to be taken into account in order to analyze firms' strategies. Indeed, the factors that induce large chemical companies to license out their process technologies are specific to the sectoral system described in the previous sections. In particular, the characteristics of the knowledge base and the rise of the SEFs are key in this respect.

## 7 Conclusions

The objective of this study has been to assess the different dimensions of the sectoral system in chemicals. The chemical industry provides an excellent basis for analyzing this issue for a number of reasons. First, the chemical industry is a very innovative industry. Second, this is an industry with a hundred-year history that provides an opportunity to examine the evolution and coevolution processes that involved single agents – i.e. inventors, firms and research institutions – as well as the relationships among agents, and the industry as a whole. Third, as the chemical industry is a science-based industry it is possible to explore in depth the processes of technology creation and diffusion, and the role of knowledge in shaping individual companies' performances and the overall industry organization.

The history of the industry is characterized by a series of large *discontinuities*. The dyestuff model and the development of polymer chemistry (i.e. the science of chemical products) and chemical engineering (i.e. the science of chemical processes) caused major changes in the knowledge base of the industry. The shift from coal to petrochemicals in the years before World War II allowed the American chemical industry to catch up with Europe. The emergence of specialized engineering firms made it easier to outsource process technologies and allowed a division of labor at the industry level between the SEFs and the chemical companies. The decrease in world demand during the 1980s led to a process of industry restructuring.

However, the history of the chemical industry is also characterized by a major *continuity* in the presence of the major companies. BASF, Bayer, Dow Chemical, Du Pont and Agfa – i.e. some of the leading chemical companies nowadays – are more than one hundred years old and have been the top chemical producers during the whole period. Moreover, there has been a process of *coevolution* between small and large companies, markets, research institutions and other organizations, with firms playing the central role within the chemical sectoral system. This system can be summarized as follows:

- strong and frequent linkages between firms and universities;
- an important role played by networks at different levels;
- a division of labor at the industry level between chemical companies and technology suppliers;
- the importance of the linkages between the firms and the users of chemical products in order to better specify product characteristics; and
- the role of knowledge and R&D as sources of competitive advantages leading to the growth of firms, countries and regions.

This chapter has described the role of knowledge, by focusing on the mechanisms of knowledge generation and diffusion. As far as knowledge generation is concerned, we have compared the firm and the technological cluster as organizational modes for producing innovations. In this respect, the results confirm the importance of large firms for inducing a large number of inventors to collaborate, and for producing more interdisciplinary patents. Moreover, smaller companies seem to have a comparative advantage to locate in a technological cluster. This suggests that *geographical proximity* among inventors in a technology-intensive region plays a more important coordination function for companies that lack the internal scientific competencies and the organizational capabilities needed to coordinate R&D collaborations in chemicals.

Large companies also play a critical role after the innovations are produced. The traditional managerial literature considers large companies as the locus of technology development that produce innovations for internal use. In recent years, however, large chemical firms have faced a larger spectrum of strategic options, and increased their propensity to license out proprietary technologies to other firms, as the SEFs started to do during the 1960s in the United States. Why did this happen in chemicals? The answer lies in the characteristics of the knowledge base of the sector. Advances in the discipline (polymer chemistry and chemical engineering) produced a greater codifiability of chemical knowledge. Firms' behavior enhanced the transferability of chemical technologies. These factors together produced important changes in the industry structure, and influenced the competitive advantage of firms, the relationships between different institutions, and their evolution over time.

## Appendix – The networks of inventors: data description

The data used in section 5 of this study are drawn from various sources. First, from the European Patent Office we extracted a database (1998) of

201,531 chemical patents granted and applied between 1986 and 1997. From this universe of patents we selected a random sample of 10,000 chemical patents and classified them in five technological classes: biotechnology, materials, organic chemistry, pharmaceuticals or polymers. We did not make any distinction between patent applications that have been granted and those that have not yet been granted. The number of assignees, the number of inventors and the number of supplementary classes were calculated to define the breadth of the networks of assignees and inventors, and how interdisciplinary the patents were.

By using the information on the zip code contained in the addresses, we assigned each patent to a specific NUTS3 and NUTS2 region. Then we selected a sample of 4,650 patents for which at least one inventor was located in Europe, and decided whether a patent was CL or DL at the regional level. We collected information about the NUTS2 and NUTS3 regions in which the inventors were located. From the Eurostat *Regio* database (1999) we collected information about the economic characteristics of these regions, such as the GDP, the population, the size of the regions, etc. We also downloaded the names of about 9,000 chemical laboratories from the *European R&D* database (Reed Elsevier, 1996), and assigned them to their specific NUTS3 regions.

Finally, the names of the applicants of the 10,000 patents were standardized in order to merge mother and daughter firms under the same name. The *Who Owns Whom* database (1995) was used to investigate these mother-daughter relations. The *Fortune 500* table (1995) was used to select the firms, which we termed "Fortune 500."

REFERENCES

Aftalion, F. (1999), *History of the International Chemical Industry*, University of Pennsylvania Press, Philadelphia

Albach, H., D. B. Audretsch, M. Fleischer, R. Greb, E. Höfs, L. Röller and I. Schulz (1996), *Innovation in the European Chemical Industry*, Discussion Paper FS IV 96-26, Wissenschaftszentrum Berlin [also available as European Innovation Monitoring System Publication no. 38, European Commission, Luxembourg]

Arduini, R., and F. Cesaroni (2004), Development and diffusion of environmental technologies: the role of the European chemical industry, in F. Cesaroni, A. Gambardella, W. Garcia-Fontes (eds.), *The European Chemical Industry: Innovation, Performance and Competitiveness*, Kluwer Academic Publisher, Boston.

Arora, A., and A. Fosfuri (2000), The market for technology in the chemical industry: causes and consequences, *Revue d'Economie Industrielle*, 92, 317–334

(2003), Licensing the market for technology, *Journal of Economic Behavior and Organization*, forthcoming

Arora, A., and A. Gambardella (1994), The changing technology of technical change: general and abstract knowledge and the division of innovative labour, *Research Policy*, 23, 5, 523–532

(1998), Evolution of industry structure in the chemical industry, in A. Arora, R. Landau and N. Rosenberg (eds.), *Chemicals and Long-term Economic Growth: Insights from the Chemical Industry*, John Wiley, New York, 379–413

Arora, A., A. Gambardella and W. Garcia-Fontes W. (1998), *Investment Flows of Large Chemical Companies*, Universitat Pompeu Fabra, Barcelona, mimeograph

Arora, A., R. Landau and N. Rosenberg (eds.) (1998), *Chemicals and Long-term Economic Growth: Insights from the Chemical Industry*, John Wiley, New York

Cesaroni, F. (2003), Technology strategies in the knowledge economy: the licensing activity of Himont, *International Journal of Innovation Management*, 7, 2, 223–246

Cook, P. L., and M. Sharp (1992), The chemical industry, in C. Freeman, M. Sharp and W. Walker (eds.), *Technology and the Future of Europe*, Frances Pinter, London, 198–212

Freeman, C. (1968), Chemical process plant: innovation and the world market, *National Institute Economic Review*, 45, 3, 29–51

(1982), *The Economics of Industrial Innovation*, Frances Pinter, London

Freeman, C., A. Young and J. Fuller (1963), The plastics industry: a comparative study of research and innovation, *National Institute Economic Review*, 26, 22–62

Geuna, A. (2001), The evolution of specialisation: public research in the chemical and pharmaceutical industries, *Research Evaluation*, 10, 67–79

Landau, R., and N. Rosenberg (1992), Successful commercialisation in the chemical process industries, in R. Landau, D. C. Mowery and N. Rosenberg, (eds.), *Technology and the Wealth of Nations*, Stanford University Press, Stanford, CA, 73–119

Mariani, M. (2004), *What Determines Technological Hits? Geography vs. Firm Competencies*, Working Paper no. 2004/004, Maastricht Economic Research Institute on Innovation and Technology, University of Maastricht, Maastricht.

Meyer-Krahmer, F. (1999), Basic research for innovation: the case of science-based technologies, in P. Shearmur, B. Osmond and P. Pockley (eds.), *Nurturing Creativity in Research*, Institute of Advanced Studies, Canberra

Murmann, J. P., and R. Landau (1998), On the making of competitive advantage: the development of the chemical industries in Britain and Germany since 1850, in A. Arora, R. Landau and N. Rosenberg (eds.), *Chemicals and Long-term Economic Growth: Insights from the Chemical Industry*, John Wiley, New York, 27–70

Porter, M. (1980), *Competitive Strategy*, Free Press, New York

Rosenberg, N. (1998), Technological change in the chemicals: the role of university-industry relationships, in A. Arora, R. Landau and N. Rosenberg (eds.), *Chemicals and Long-term Economic Growth: Insights from the Chemical Industry*, John Wiley, New York, 193–230

Sharp, M. (2001), *Globalisation, Specialisation and Competitiveness*, Science Policy Research Unit, University of Sussex, Brighton, mimeograph

Spitz, P. H. (1988), *Petrochemicals: The Rise of an Industry*, John Wiley, New York

Teece, D. J. (1988), Technological change and the nature of the firm, in G. Dosi, C. Freeman, R. R. Nelson, G. Silverberg and L. Soete (ed.), *Technical Change and Economic Theory*, Frances Pinter, London, 256–281

Wright, G. (1999), Can a nation learn? American technology as a network phenomenon, in N. R. Lamoreaux, D. Raff and P. Temin (eds.), *Learning by Doing in Markets, Firms, and Countries*, National Bureau of Economic Research conference report, University of Chicago Press, 296–347

# 5 The fixed Internet and mobile telecommunications sectoral system of innovation: equipment production, access provision and content provision

*Charles Edquist*[1]

## 1 Introduction

This chapter focuses upon the "new" parts of the telecommunications sectoral system of innovation. This means that we concentrate on analyzing innovation in fixed data communications (including the Internet) and mobile telecommunications (including the mobile Internet). We largely disregard, for example, traditional telecommunications – i.e. equipment for fixed telecommunications systems and fixed telecommunications voice services. Rather, we concentrate on what is emerging and growing – i.e. how the SSI is currently changing and how previously independent systems are converging.[2]

We address both equipment production (material goods) and the production (provision) of intangible service products. This is because innovations in manufacturing and in services are *complementary* – in both directions: service innovations are dependent upon manufacturing innovations *and* vice versa. It is hard to imagine a mobile phone call without a mobile handset, and vice versa. And the Internet is useless without content. Such a combined approach, addressing the production of goods and services alike, is unusual.

Equipment production includes routers and other kinds of exchanges for the Internet as well as base stations, exchanges and handsets for mobile telecommunications. It might be noted that such equipment is currently constituted not only by hardware but also by software, to a very large extent. Equipment producers such as Cisco and Ericsson employ

[1] The author wishes to thank Bent Dalum, Nicoletta Corrocher, Jeffrey Funk, Leif Hommen, Per Högselius, Michael Jensen, Martin Kenney and Gert Villumsen for their very useful comments on earlier drafts of this chapter.
[2] We return later to whether it is useful to talk about *one* system or *several* systems in this field.

thousands of software engineers and might therefore be labeled giant software firms.

The provision of Internet service products is often said to be accounted for by so-called Internet service providers (ISPs). However, with this term we normally mean provision of access to the Internet – which is certainly a service product. This means that firms that are normally called Internet service providers could better be named Internet access providers (IAPs). This will increasingly include providers of access to mobile telecommunications systems. However, for the Internet to be useful and in demand there must also be a content supplied in connection with it. Other kinds of service products constitute this content and firms other than the IAPs often supply it. A proper name for these would be Internet content providers (ICPs).[3] It is for these reasons that we talk about "equipment production, access provision and content provision" in the title of this chapter.

The ESSY project was described in the introduction to this book. It included the study of the fixed Internet and mobile telecommunications SSI reported in this chapter. However, this chapter is partly a summary of a much more comprehensive study. In addition to this synthesis chapter, the study resulted in a number of reports with the following titles and authors:

- "Fixed data communications: challenges for Europe," by Bent Dalum and Gert Villumsen (Dalum and Villumsen 2003);
- "The global system for mobile telecommunications (GSM): second generation," by Leif Hommen and Esa Manninen (Hommen and Manninen 2003);
- "The universal mobile telecommunications system (UMTS): third generation," by Leif Hommen (Hommen 2003);
- "Data communication: satellite and TV subsystems," by Bent Dalum (Dalum 2003);
- "The Internet services industry: sectoral dynamics of innovation and production," by Nicoletta Corrocher (Corrocher 2003a);
- "The Internet services industry: country-specific trends in the UK, Italy and Sweden," by Nicoletta Corrocher (Corrocher 2003b); and
- "Policy implications for the future of the sectoral system," by Charles Edquist.

All these reports are included in a recently published volume (Edquist, 2003).

Section 2 of this chapter deals with the Internet and mobile telecommunications. Section 3 draws out the policy implications of the analysis and

---

[3] Hence IAPs and ICPs constitute ISPs.

discusses the future of the SSI as well as the relations between Europe, the United States and Japan within it.

## 2 The fixed Internet and mobile telecommunications sectoral system of innovation

### 2.1 Introduction

Section 2 covers the important developments in the fields of mobile telecommunications and fixed data communications (Internet) in recent decades. It provides a synthesis of the other reports produced within the ESSY study of the fixed Internet and mobile telecommunications SSI, which are mentioned in the introduction to this chapter. It is heavily based on these reports, without always explicitly referring to them. This section also tries to "fill in the gaps," in the sense of covering some important issues that are not dealt with in the reports mentioned. This implies, for example, dealing with the birth of mobile telecommunications as triggered by the Nordic Mobile Telephone (NMT) standard, i.e. part of the institutional basis for the first generation of mobile telecommunications.

Section 2 relates to some of the key questions in the ESSY project, e.g. the knowledge base of the sectoral system, its organizations and institutions and the boundaries of the (data communications and mobile telecommunications) sectoral system. Public policy, the future of the sectoral system and comparisons with the United States and Japan are addressed in section 3.

Since the main elements of all systems of innovation – including sectoral ones – are *institutions* and *organizations*, we discuss these factors – and changes in them – with regard to data communications and mobile telecommunications. The relations between different kinds of organizations and between institutions and organizations is a central focus in what follows. Institutions are often created by organizations. At the same time, existing institutions influence organizations as well as the relations between them. We try to make a clear distinction between organizations (players or actors) and institutions (the rules of the game) in order to be able to discuss the relations between them as well.

In addition there is here a certain emphasis on the *functions* in SIs.[4] It is important to address these, and not only the elements of the systems. The main function in innovation systems is – of course – the carrying out of

---

[4] The elements (institutions and organizations) and functions in SIs – national, sectoral and regional – as well as the boundaries of such systems are addressed in a more systematic, profound and theoretical manner in the introductory chapter to Edquist (2003). Similar discussions are pursued in Edquist (1997), (2001b) and (2004).

innovations. However, the functions of the SIs also include activities leading up to innovations. These secondary functions, or sub-functions, influence the ability of firms (and other organizations) to carry out innovations. Examples of important functions are knowledge creation (through R&D and in other ways), collaboration in pursuing innovation processes, the provision of relevant education, the creation of standards, etc.

Section 2 is organized in the following way. Section 2.2 briefly addresses the main functions and organizations in the sectoral system(s). In section 2.3 the focus is on institutions and institutional changes, and on their consequences for organizations and functions. Different subsections will concentrate on the fixed Internet, mobile telecommunications, satellite communications and rate structures. Section 2.4 addresses the boundaries between subsystems and convergence between them.

### 2.2     Functions and organizations in the system(s) and relations between them

*Organizations* can be defined as *formal structures with an explicit purpose, which are consciously created* (Edquist and Johnson, 1997, p. 47). They may also be called agents, actors or players. Their purpose is to perform certain *functions* in the system(s). In the fixed Internet and mobile telecommunications sectoral system(s) of innovation some of the most important functions are:

1) The development of equipment (innovation in new equipment, hardware and software);
2) R&D relevant to the further development of the system(s);
3) The provision of relevant education and training;
4) The creation of standards and other regulations of importance to the systems(s);
5) The provision of access (e.g. Internet access or mobile telecommunications subscriptions);
6) The development of new content (introduction of new services, e.g. e-commerce); and
7) The provision of consulting services related to all of this.

The functions of an SSI may refer to the development and diffusion of innovations and how smooth and efficient these processes are. In turn, this may be a result of how good the SSI is in creating new knowledge or new combinations of existing (and new) knowledge, in providing education, in creating standards, etc. Other functions could also be mentioned. They might refer to how efficient the financing of product development is, how smoothly new firms are created, how inclined firms in the system are to diversify into new product areas, or how efficiently new markets are created for the new products (goods and services). On the whole, much more research needs to be carried out on the functions in systems of innovations. It should also be noted that this is quite similar to studying the determinants of innovation.

The functions are carried out by organizations (or, in some cases, by individuals). However, there is not always – or even often – a one-to-one relation between functions and organizations. A certain organization can carry out several functions and one function may be carried out by different kinds of organizations. Below I relate the functions listed above to some important organizations that carry them out.

- The development of equipment – which is increasingly of a software kind – is carried out by telecommunications and Internet equipment producing firms, such as Siemens, Ericsson, Cisco and Motorola.
- These firms also carry out a large part of the R&D needed for developing the new systems. Some R&D is also carried out by public universities and dedicated research organizations.
- Education is of great importance to the sectoral system of innovation, and it is largely carried out by publicly controlled and funded organizations. However, firms also sponsor further education and provide training. In addition, "learning by using" and "learning by doing" take place within organizations.
- There are organizations that create the standards and regulations that are important for decreasing the degree of uncertainty for equipment producers and for coordinating their relations with various other organizations in the Internet and mobile telecommunications SSI. They have often been of a public character, although private organizations have also been intensively involved in these activities. In addition, there are various industry organizations that have a quasi-public character, but no "official mandate" from government.
- Access is provided by the Internet access providers and mobile system operators. They own (or lease) the physical infrastructure (the network) and in this way provide the backbone of the Internet and mobile telecommunications. This category includes incumbent telecommunications operators, new entrant telecommunications operators, cable TV operators, alternative network providers and "pure" IAPs.[5]
- The access providers may also – and often do – provide (some) content to be transported by the systems, but there are also pure or specialized content providers that own the content (but do not provide access to the systems). There are general content providers, such as companies running portals, and specialized content providers, such as news and financial companies. We call these Internet content providers. They include

[5] For reasons presented in the introduction to this chapter, we have chosen not to call these organizations Internet service providers, even though they certainly do provide service products.

traditional media and publishing companies as well as new firms. Often they derive their revenues from advertising but they are increasingly trying to charge a fee for the provision of content. Their ability to do so increases if their content is highly specialized and/or customized. However, consumers tend to want content to be free of charge. Electronic commerce is offered by new firms working only over the Internet, such as Amazon.com, but, increasingly, old and established firms are also using the Internet as a new marketing outlet. This includes business-to-consumer as well as business-to-business e-commerce.

• Finally, there are consultancy firms – as in all knowledge-intensive sectors – that offer various services related to the Internet and mobile telecommunications. Examples are Web design, Web hosting, the development of platforms for electronic commerce, etc.

Over the last twenty years we have seen an increased "functional differentiation" and "organizational diversity" in the telecommunications SSI (in a wide sense). For example, in the past it was common that (monopolistic) access providers were also regulators. Now separate organizations have been created to perform the regulatory functions.

Digitization, or "digitalization," has provided the technological basis on which it is possible to separate telecommunications and Internet network operation (access provision) from content provision. It was therefore possible to make this kind of separation between "infrastructure" and "access" and "content services" with the emergence of the fixed Internet – and even earlier with the digitalization of fixed telecommunications. This separation was a very real possibility when the second generation of mobile telecommunications first appeared. Nevertheless, this separation was not fully implemented with the second-generation mobile standards such as GSM, despite the best efforts of the European Commission (see section 2.3.2.2). This will change with the third generation of mobile telecommunications (see section 2.3.2.3).

In telecommunications – in a wide sense – the set-up and character of organizations has changed very much during the most recent decades. For example:

– Publicly controlled telecommunications operators have been transformed into joint-stock companies and privatized; they are no longer public sector monopolies (with regulatory power).

– The relations between the most important organizations in the system have changed considerably.

– Formerly close ties between "national champions" in equipment production and monopolistic access providers have been progressively loosened.

– Important new organizations have emerged in the system, such as IAPs and ICPs.

– Similarly, new regulatory agencies have been created, concomitant with the privatization of public telephone operators (PTOs).

## 2.3    *Institutional changes and their consequences for organizations and functions*

*Institutions* can be defined as *sets of common habits, routines, established practices, rules or laws that regulate the relations and interactions between individuals, groups and organizations* (Edquist and Johnson, 1997, p. 46). Relevant examples in this context are laws concerning deregulation and liberalization, technical standards (particularly relevant for Internet and mobile telecommunications), access tariffs, rules with regard to intellectual property rights, etc. The institutions constitute the rules of the game, which influence the players – or organizations, e.g. firms – when they are trying to achieve their purposes. However, the relations between institutions and organizations are mutual. Institutions are formed and changed by the actions of (some) organizations. We now discuss the relations between institutions, organizations and functions in various parts of the sectoral system.

### 2.3.1    *The fixed Internet*

As we see in section 2.3.2, an institution – i.e. the NMT 450 mobile telecommunications standard – provided the cradle for the development of mobile telecommunications in Europe. But what provided the cradle for fixed data communications or the Internet?

Fixed telephone lines have existed for more than a century now. As mentioned in the introduction to this chapter, we do not deal with fixed voice telecommunications here (except occasionally for reasons of comparison). Instead we start our story when fixed telephone systems started to carry significant amounts of data in their cables, in addition to voice telecommunications. At the same time – or, rather, as a precondition for this – the fixed networks became digitized. There were two technological breakthroughs that made this digitalization possible: packet-switching technologies, and the Internet Protocol (IP).

In packet-switching technology "packets" of information share the network lines (bandwidth) with other packages, optimizing the use of the existing bandwidth. In packet-switched transmission protocols any type of information (voice, data, video, etc.) is broken down into packets, which are sent from one computer to another with no chronological order. A "header" on each single packet directs the routing from the sender to the receiver; the header contains information about the destination. The packages are sent individually and reassembled into a complete message at the receiving end.

By comparison, in the traditional circuit-switched networks an end-to-end communication path is established before the communication begins, and it stays open during the whole connection. With the conventional telecommunications network, each conversation uses a fixed amount of bandwidth for the duration of the call and the available bandwidth is dedicated to the call even if no information is transmitted (e.g. during silences in a voice conversation).

In 1968 the US Defense Advanced Research Projects Agency (DARPA) granted a contract to the engineering firm Bolt, Beranek and Newman, based in Cambridge, Massachusetts, to build the first packet switch (Mowery, 2001, p. 8). Hence this was a matter of *public technology procurement*; i.e. a public agency placed a contract with a firm ordering the development of a technology or an artifact that did not exist at the time of granting the contract, but which the partners believed could be developed (Edquist, Hommen and Tsipouri, 2000). The resulting switch was called an interface message processor (IMP), and linked several computers to each other. The result was ARPANET, which was the earliest forerunner of the Internet.

In 1973 two DARPA-funded engineers, Robert Khan and Vinton Cerf, developed an improved data networking communications protocol that simplified routing, eliminated the need for the IMP and allowed physically distinct networks to interconnect with one another. The idea of an open architecture that allowed network-to-network connectivity was a key intellectual advance in their design. Kahn and Cerf called the new protocol Transmission Control Protocol (TCP) and openly published the specification in 1974. Later it was split into two pieces and renamed TCP/IP (Transmission Control Protocol/Internet Protocol – Abbate, 2001, ch. 4; and Mowery, 2001, pp. 9–10). Hence the TCP/IP protocols, which were absolutely central to the development of the Internet, were also developed with the help of military research funds.

The TCP/IP is based on a distributed architecture, within which the IP and the TCP have separated functions: the TCP handles the transmission characteristics, while the IP manages the routing and network anomalies. The TCP/IP is embedded in distributed customer hosts that are located at the network periphery, therefore reducing the need for centralized control. The software is located with the servers and the user hosts, which makes possible Internet connectivity and integrated applications.

As a matter of fact, an increasing part of voice telecommunications is currently sent over IP networks; users may be unaware that a telephone call or a portion of a call is routed over an IP network. The transmission network is today (in part) common for Internet and voice telephone networks. This convergence has also, of course, influenced the telecommunications and Internet equipment industries.

TCP/IP was rapidly adopted. There were several reasons: it was highly reliable; it was an open standard; and it arrived just as the computing research community began to standardize on a common platform.[6] The TCP/IP protocols became an integral part of this standard platform. As a result TCP/IP became the dominant protocol for most networking applications in the early 1990s, and now it is virtually synonymous with the technical definition of the Internet (Mowery, 2001, p. 10).

One reason why TCP/IP became dominant was the decision by the National Science Foundation (NSF) in the United States to adopt it as the standard on its national university network. Beginning in 1985, any university receiving NSF funding for an Internet connection was required to provide access to all "qualified users" and use TCP/IP on its network (Kenney, 2001, pp. 12–13). Again, public action was crucial – this time for the early diffusion of TCP/IP.

Other government organizations in the United States were also important for the development of the Internet. In the late 1970s the NSF and DARPA founded a set of organizations to oversee the standardization of the backbone of TCP/IP. The Internet Configuration Control Board (ICCB) was established in 1979. In 1983, when ARPANET switched over to TCP/IP, the ICCB was reorganized and renamed the Internet Activities Board (IAB). The IAB had two primary sub-groups: the Internet Engineering Task Force (IETF), which managed the Internet's architecture and standard-setting processes (including editing and publishing), and the Internet Research Task Force, which focused on longer-term research (Mowery, 2001, pp. 12–13).

The Internet is not formally standardized as the public telecommunications network. There is no standardization body like the International Telecommunications Union (ITU), where all nations participate. The IETF is the closest equivalent to a standardization body. This voluntary organization updates standards, provides information about changes and controls the use of global addresses, but it is not an organization with formal power.

As opposed to the standard organizations involved in developing the mobile telecommunications standards, the IETF is mainly a voluntary organization, without any central management.[7] To the extent that the IETF has a management, it is embodied in the working group charters. These working groups are the main drivers in the development of Internet standards. The work is voluntary and, as such, often dominated by

---

[6] This platform was the Unix operating system, originally put forward by AT&T/Bell laboratories but gradually adopted by the main computer firms, and initially driven by some of the then newcomers in "network computing" and workstations, such as Sun Microsystems and later on the dominant incumbents of Hewlett Packard, IBM and DEC.

[7] Mobile standards are addressed in section 2.3.2.

large actors (telecommunication operators and manufacturing firms). As a consequence of the origin of the Internet in the United States, the protocol has been highly influenced by US actors via the IETF. In other words, US firms have dominated the standardization process related to the Internet.

The organizations that managed the establishment of Internet technical standards were quite informal, yet responsive. They managed to develop open standards and to adapt these standards rapidly to meet new technical and economic challenges, and this contributed powerfully to the rapid diffusion of the Internet (Mowery, 2001, p. 42).

An important institutional change that made the rapid diffusion of the fixed Internet possible was also the deregulation or liberalization of the telecommunications sector. Internet penetration came earlier and was more rapid in countries where liberalization occurred early (the United Kingdom: 1984; the United States: 1985; Sweden: 1993) than where it came late (Italy: 1998).

The early deregulation in the United Kingdom had a significant impact on the market structure. It also had an impact on the rate of technical change itself, since it allowed the entry of new companies and forced the incumbents to engage in the development of innovations. The liberalization of the telecommunications sector also had the consequence of substantially reducing the charges for telephone calls (Corrocher, 2003b).

Sweden has the highest Internet penetration in Europe and also the most advanced Internet service SSI. The telecommunications market in Sweden was liberalized in 1993 and Sweden now has the most liberalized telecommunications industry in the world. This has been a major driver for the development of alternative networks to that of the former incumbent operator (Telia). However, the unbundling of the local loop has not yet been achieved in reality since Telia is still charging too high a price for interconnection to allow others to compete on an equal basis (Corrocher, 2003b).

In contrast to what happened in the United Kingdom, one of the major obstacles to the development of the Internet in Italy has been the slow process of deregulating the telecommunications sector, which, in turn, has been caused by the lack of a clear policy for the implementation of an appropriate competition policy and of an independent regulatory authority. A telecommunications authority was established in 1997 and deregulation occurred in 1998. This delay has hindered not only the development of a competitive industry but also the diffusion of new technologies and applications (Corrocher, 2003b).

In the 1970s and 1980s the data transmitted via the Internet were primarily related to research activities and to the communications of large firms with branches in different locations. However, in the 1990s, thanks to innovations made at the Conseil Européen pour la Recherche Nucléaire (CERN) in Switzerland, data traffic became increasingly demanded by final consumers. Tim Berners-Lee and Robert Cailliau at CERN released in 1991 a new document format called HyperText Markup Language (HTML) and a related document retrieval protocol called HyperText Transfer Protocol (HTTP). Together they turned the Internet into a vast cross-referenced collection of multimedia documents. Berners-Lee and Cailliau called their invention the "World Wide Web" (WWW). A US company – Netscape – that was listed on the stock exchange in 1995 commercialized these inventions. Hence, although the HTML and the HTTP were not invented in the United States, they were first commercialized – i.e. transformed into innovations – in that country.

There were prototype networks designed that constituted alternatives to the ARPANET, for example in the United Kingdom and France. "US dominance thus did not result from a first-mover advantage in the invention or even in the early development of a packet-switched network. The factor that does seem to separate ARPANET from these simultaneous projects was sizable public funding and flexibility in its deployment . . ." (Mowery, 2001, p. 9). This resulted in a network of a large (continental) scale that included different kinds of organizations: DARPA, universities, consulting firms, research institutes, etc. Its size and the inclusion of different kinds of organizations distinguished the ARPANET from its British and French counterparts (Mowery, 2001, p. 9).

Public funds were used to develop many of the early inventions that fueled the development of the Internet in the United States, and federal R&D spending played an important role in the creation of the entire complex of "new" post-war IT industries in that country. "The origins of the Internet can be traced back to these efforts" (Mowery, 2001, p. 24). Hence, public intervention was crucial.

However, the influence of public policies was not restricted to funding. Federal regulatory, antitrust and IPR policies were also important. According to Mowery, the overall effect of these policies was to encourage the rapid commercialization of Internet infrastructure, services and content by new, frequently small, firms (Mowery, 2001, p. 28). As a result there was an Internet explosion in the United States in the 1990s.

From the late 1980s onwards, US firms achieved a dominant position in the production of equipment for the Internet.[8] This occurred very much

---

[8] As we saw earlier, they also highly influenced the creation of standards in the Internet field.

because of their "head start" in serving the large – and early-developing – US domestic market, just as US-packaged computer software firms had benefited from the rapidly growing US domestic personal computer market during the 1980s. In the Internet field the firms that came to dominate were not large system vendors, such as IBM, DEC or Sun. Instead a group of smaller firms, most of which were founded in the late 1980s, became the most important ones. Examples are Cisco, Bay Networks and 3Com (Mowery, 2001, p. 16). Cisco is still a very dominant player on this market. And it is certainly not a small firm any longer.[9]

Currently there are, basically, five ways for consumers (and small business enterprises) to access the Internet (Dalum and Villumsen, 2003):
1) "Ordinary" modems (connected directly via the telephone line);
2) ISDN modems (connected directly via the telephone line);
3) xDSL, primarily Asymmetrical Digital Subscriber Line (ADSL – connected directly via the telephone line).
4) TV networks (via "cable modems" for cable TV or "set-top boxes" for satellite TV; and
5) Fixed wireless access (FWA).

The first three use the "twisted pair" of copper wires for the last mile to the consumer. They can all be installed as an integral part of an ordinary fixed-line telephone system, which in practical terms means that the incumbent telecommunications operators have a rather clear advantage in delivering these access modes. Competing companies will have to use the existing infrastructure on the last mile to reach the customers – i.e. they will have to make arrangements with the incumbent operators. This has preserved the powerful position of the latter, which appears to be a major inhibiting factor in the diffusion of high-speed Internet access in many countries.

Since a traditional subscriber line supports only analog transmission, a modem has to be used to transport data. The simple modem access (1), which converts analog to digital signals, does not require changes or enhancements in the network. The maximum speed is 56 kilobytes per second (KB/s). A first enhancement of the modem technology is ISDN (2), which runs at a higher speed (maximum 144 KB/s). In addition, ISDN makes possible parallel connections (data and voice).

As the demand for faster access methods increases, there are several digital subscriber line technologies that make possible higher speeds. Their common name is xDSL (3), where x indicates the specific variant. Since the demand for sending and downloading for most users is

---

[9] The role of venture capital for the rapid growth of these firms is strongly stressed by Kenney (2001).

asymmetrical, a technology where the bandwidth is higher for downloading is demanded. ADSL is thus currently the most common technology for high-speed "broadband" (above 2 megabytes per second – MB/s) access over a "twisted pair."

An alternative to the telecommunications cables is access via TV networks (4). This alternative has been growing very rapidly in some countries since many telecommunications operators (the previous state monopolies) have been slow to deliver high-speed access solutions. There has been an incentive problem since they have been able to charge huge amounts of revenue because the low speed simply generates high telephone bills.[10]

According to one source (*Financial Times*, 2001) – reporting data for broadband subscriber trends without specifying what exactly "broadband" is – there were over 40 million subscribers worldwide in 2001, divided into three shares of equal size: ADSL; digital set-top boxes; and cable modems (for cable TV). The US lead in the absolute amount of broadband subscribers is, however, concentrated on cable modems and set-top boxes. The TV-network-based broadband access share appeared to be around 80 percent in the United States in 2001. It has been mainly the alternatives to the incumbent telecommunications operators – i.e. the TV networks – that have been the "carriers" of broadband access in the United States.

A final access channel is FWA (5), which uses a wireless connection on the "last mile." Potentially very large amounts of data can be transmitted through the air at reasonably short distances. Several European countries have recently been through contests over FWA licenses, which have attracted much less attention than the UMTS auctions and/or "beauty contests" for mobile systems.[11]

### 2.3.2   Mobile telecommunications

**2.3.2.1 The first generation – NMT**   The first standard for modern cellular telecommunications began to be specified in January 1970 and was called NMT 450 – i.e. the Nordic Mobile Telephone standard based on the 450 megahertz (MHz) bandwidth.[12] Important characteristics were that it was an analog standard, that it was fully automatic and that it

---

[10] Rate structures and levels are discussed in more detail in section 2.3.4.

[11] An emerging – and potentially very important – access method is via wireless local area networks (WLANs), which may become a core part of what is now considered to be fourth-generation (4G) communications systems, involving a true integration of mobile communications and the fixed Internet. See further in section 2.3.2.3.

[12] NMT is not covered in the other reports within this study of the fixed Internet and mobile telecommunications SSIs carried out within ESSY.

had a roaming function within the Nordic countries.[13] The development of the standard was initiated by the Nordic PTOs, which were state-owned monopolies at the time. A working group, its members drawn from the staff of the PTOs in Finland, Norway, Denmark and Sweden, designed the technical specifications. The Swedish PTO had a leading role in this work. In 1971 the NMT group gathered around forty national and international companies that were potential suppliers of equipment for NMT 450. They received preliminary specifications. The technical specifications were further developed in discussions within the group and were finalized between 1975 and 1978 (McKelvey, Texier and Alm, 1998, pp. 16 and 25).

In 1977/78 the implementation of the project started, and the Nordic post, telegraphs and telecommunications authorities (PTTs) started to look for suppliers of the different component technologies – namely radio base stations and switches. The NMT group opened the bidding for the supply of switches to a number of companies. This means that the mechanism of *public technology procurement* was used, as in this case, as an instrument to initiate the development of equipment. The bidding was international, but the Swedish firm Ericsson won the order to deliver switches to Sweden, Norway, Denmark and Finland. Ericsson's main competitor was the Japanese NEC. However, Ericsson first offered a computer-controlled switch with electromechanical switch elements, called AKE-13. Then Televerket (the Swedish PTO) wanted an adapted version of Ericsson's fully digital switch (AXE), and made it clear to Ericsson that they would choose the digital switch from NEC if Ericsson did not offer the AXE (McKelvey, Texier and Alm, 1998, p. 26).

The NMT 450 was very specific, which meant that network operators had the possibility of buying components from different producers and putting them together themselves. NMT 450 was implemented in Sweden in October 1980 and at the beginning of 1981 in Denmark, Finland and Norway. However, the first implementation occurred in Saudi Arabia in August 1980 (McKelvey, Texier and Alm 1998: 16).[14] In other words, it took as much as ten years to specify the standard and get it functioning.

The NMT 450 was much more successful than expected. It was initially forecast to have around 50,000 subscribers by 1990, whereas by 1992 it had approximately 250,000. Since more subscribers were joining than the standard could handle, the Nordic PTTs developed and added the NMT 900 (MHz) standard in 1986. The NMT 900 system was developed as an intermediary system, between the NMT 450 and the future European

[13] "Roaming" means locating the mobile phone handset of the person called.
[14] This turned out to be an important order for equipment producer Ericsson.

digital standard (which was later agreed to be GSM – McKelvey, Texier and Alm, 1998, p. 16).

The Nordic countries had the highest rates of penetration of mobile phones even before the advent of liberalization and before GSM – i.e. during the NMT era. It was about 7 percent in Sweden in 1992, thanks to the high quality of service provision and low tariffs. In 1990 market penetration in the United Kingdom was only 2 percent, despite much more extensive liberalization of the market for mobile (and fixed) telecommunications there.[15] The rapid penetration in Sweden was largely due to the consolidation of a strong market for mobile telecommunications via concerted action by the Nordic public telephone companies in defining the first-generation NMT standard and through low prices. Sweden's fixed subscription rates were much lower than in the United Kingdom, and call charges were only about half. The rapid subscriber penetration contributed to rapid market growth, which was important for the ability of equipment suppliers to benefit from economies of scale.

NMT 450 can be considered to be an institution – in the sense of a set of rules. This set of rules decreased the degree of uncertainty and risk for the equipment suppliers. The NMT standard was conceived primarily as a regional standard, though it later verged on becoming pan-European.

The institution of NMT 450 provided the cradle for the development of pan-European mobile telecommunications. It actually spurred the development of a whole new industry – or sectoral system – of very great economic significance. Public sector organizations dominated the development of the standard. The development was actually initiated and led by a few Nordic national PTOs.

In techno-economic development there has often been an institutional lag; i.e. institutions (rules and regulations) lag behind technical change (innovation) and constitute an obstacle to such change. This was, for example, the case with the diffusion of the fixed Internet in Italy – see section 2.3.1. However, in the case of NMT 450 the contrary happened. When this institution (NMT 450) was created it pushed – or, rather, pulled – the whole development process, for example by decreasing the uncertainty for equipment producers and operators. We might call this an "institutional push" (or "pull") instead of an "institutional lag."

The development and implementation of NMT was actually an example of the importance of user-producer relations in innovation processes, which is stressed so strongly in the systems of innovation approach. The public organizations provided a technical framework for and decreased the uncertainty of private equipment producers. The Nordic equipment

---

[15] As mentioned earlier, liberalization was initiated in the United Kingdom in 1984 and in Sweden in 1993.

producers/Ericsson and Nokia greatly benefited from this, and this is a very important factor behind their leading role in mobile telecommunications equipment production today.

However, NMT was not the only standard that was developed in the proto-period of mobile telecommunications. In the 1970s R&D on cellular systems gained momentum in parallel in a few countries (with the United States, the Nordic countries and Japan as forerunners).[16] This resulted in the introduction of as many as eight cellular standards between 1979 and 1985 (Lindmark and Granstrand, 1995, p. 386).[17]

AMPS (advanced mobile phone system) was developed by Illinois Bell Telephone, Bell Laboratories and Motorola, and the first AMPS system was launched in 1983 (as opposed to 1981 for NMT), delayed by arguments over access to radio frequencies and a complicated licensing procedure. NMT 450 was also the first standard to be adopted by multiple countries, and by the end of 1993 thirty-six countries had introduced the NMT 450 system (Funk, 2002, p. 41). AMPS was quite successful; it was diffused to a larger number of countries than NMT and had a larger number of subscribers worldwide (Funk, 2002, p. 40).[18] However, NMT in the Nordic countries showed the highest penetration rates in the world, constantly outstripping forecasts (Lindmark and Granstrand, 1995, pp. 386–388). In addition, NMT was the basis for the development of GSM, which became the globally dominant standard in second-generation mobile telecommunications – as we see in the next section.

### 2.3.2.2  The second generation – GSM

*A*      *Europe*   The GSM standard – introduced in 1992 – is an institution. It was conceived from the very start as a pan-European standard, and it was intended to cover many countries. And it certainly came to do so. In 1992 commercial GSM services were initiated in fifteen countries, but by 1996 GSM operated in 103 countries. It was possible to make phone calls between countries – even between continents – thanks to the fact that the national systems could be integrated in order to trace where a certain terminal was located (roaming).

---

[16] The laboratories of Bell are usually credited with having invented the design concept of cellular mobile telecommunications (in 1947), the main idea being to overcome radio spectrum congestion by combining space division with radio spectrum division (Lindmark and Granstrand, 1995, p. 386).

[17] The standards were: NAMTS, NMT, AMPS, TACS, C-450, RC-2000, RMTS and Comvik, although some experts argue that RC-2000, RTMS and Comvik were not fully functional cellular systems

[18] This is explained not only by the size of the home market (the United States) but also by the diffusion to some large markets in the Asia-Pacific region and Canada (Lindmark and Granstrand, 1995, p. 392).

The above means that the development of the GSM standard was characterized by the involvement of a far greater number of organizations than the NMT standard(s) and by a far greater complexity in the relations among them. There were also other differences. Until the 1980s the public telecommunications companies in Europe often had monopolistic positions with regard to network operation and service provision. They also had the role of regulating the telecommunications sector. By the mid-1990s they were much more oriented toward network operation. Separate regulatory organizations had been created, and, in turn, these new organizations created new institutions.

In Sweden the National Telecommunications Council was created in 1990, followed by the National Telecommunications Agency in 1992. This ended the double role of Televerket (the former PTO) in the area of frequency management, and it also meant the creation of an independent telecommunications regulator capable of ensuring competition in the non-monopoly telecommunications sector, which now included the mobile sector. Televerket was also increasingly exposed to competition as a network operator from new entrants, domestic and foreign-based alike.

Just as in the case of NMT, public sector organizations were very important in the development of GSM; for instance, the national telecommunications firms were central in initiating and developing the new standard. However, the number of such organizations was now much larger. The development of GSM also occurred within the formal organizational framework (and not in an ad hoc consortium) provided by two European standard development organizations: the Conference on European Post and Telecommunications (CEPT) and the European Telecommunications Standards Institute (ETSI). CEPT was an association of European telecommunications organizations while ETSI – which gradually took over the role of standard creation – was a European Union organization.[19] In addition, equipment suppliers and public research organizations also participated actively in this work. This reflected the fact that the (former) public monopolies no longer had a monopoly of knowledge and expertise in the telecommunications field (Hommen and Manninen, 2003; and Glimstedt, 2001).

The Swedish former monopoly (Televerket) was very active in the GSM work, together with other Nordic operators and equipment production firms such as Ericsson and Nokia, which formed a "Nordic coalition." Televerket – which was later transformed from a public enterprise into a joint-stock, limited liability company, and in due course partly privatized

---

[19] For an account of the role of the European Commission in the development of GSM, see Glimstedt, 2001.

in the form of Telia – effectively led the Nordic alliance. This consortium was based on the historically close collaboration between Nordic PTOs and Nordic equipment producers. In competition with a "Franco-German group" the Nordic proposal was selected, supported by thirteen of CEPT's voting members. In this way, GSM may be said to have developed "out of" NMT – i.e. along the same trajectory (Hommen and Manninen, 2003). ETSI adopted GSM without German and French support, but the two countries were still forced under EU law to use GSM as the basis for the public mobile telecommunications network (Glimstedt, 2001, p. 10).

Later, Ericsson, together with Televerket/Telia, developed and tested the first prototype of a full GSM system, thus consolidating its technological leadership, although Ericsson produced equipment for all three major international standards. Nokia also benefited – even more – from the GSM decision, since in fact it produced only base stations and switches to be used within GSM. This meant that Ericsson, Nokia and other Nordic equipment manufacturers were given a great advantage in relation to others. The way GSM developed increased the leadership they already had.

However, the Nordic proposal was based upon well-established technologies, to which a number of non-Swedish firms held the intellectual property rights; Motorola held many (50 percent) of the important patents, and it licensed them selectively to the main Nordic equipment manufacturers, Nokia and Ericsson. The second largest share (16 percent) was claimed by AT&T. Bull and Phillips claimed 8 percent each. Hence, at least 82 percent of the patents for the GSM standard were of non-Nordic origin. In this light, it is quite surprising that Nordic firms attained such a dominant position as GSM equipment producers. A relevant question is why Motorola did not (successfully) push its technology in the United States. Motorola sold licenses to Ericsson and Nokia and thereby benefited directly by collecting licensing fees. However, Motorola was not in a position to produce equipment for GSM to any large extent. A possible explanation for Motorola's behavior is that it felt that it would be unable to compete with European equipment producers in Europe, and perceived GSM as a European standard that would not necessarily develop into a world standard (Hommen and Manninen, 2003).[20]

In the first generation of mobile telecommunications, telephony and radio were combined. In the second generation, digital technology was fully implemented, creating possibilities for data transmission in addition

[20] Actually, none could, at the time, know that the result of the evolutionary development was that GSM would become the dominating standard in the world.

to voice transmission. In GSM, data transmission was first introduced through short messaging services (SMS). This is actually a two-way variant of the previously existing paging system. It has become unexpectedly popular. GSM can also provide Internet access though HTML compatibility, currently developed in the form of the wireless application protocol (WAP).

Finally, a remark on the role of deregulation for GSM. GSM was developed and implemented before large-scale liberalization in Europe, and hence the deregulation process did not play a major role for GSM. The relation was rather the reverse. GSM was actually used as a "spearhead" of the EU strategy for telecommunications deregulation in the 1990s; it was used as a tool to change the telecommunications sector in Europe.

*B    The United States and Japan*    In the United States, one of the responsible standardization agencies, the Cellular Telephone Industry Association (CTIA), chose a digital standard (D-AMPS) that was compatible with the existing first-generation (analog) systems. The idea was to facilitate a gradual shift between generations.[21]

Another relevant regulatory agency, the Federal Communications Commission (FCC), also decided that there would be no national digital standard for the United States as a whole, but that operators were free to adopt any standard. On this basis another digital standard also came into use, called code division multiple access (CDMA). It emerged later, but attracted more operators.[22] These two main standards were not directly compatible with each other; they were so only through the use of analog channels. This was the so-called "backward compatibility" insisted upon by the FCC (Hommen and Manninen, 2003).

Partly because of this, both the digital standards diffused relatively slowly in the United States. The United States had a mobile phone penetration rate of 20 percent in 1997, as opposed to 40–50 percent in the Nordic countries. In addition, 60 percent of these were subscriptions to the analog standard, while it was almost completely digital in Europe. The slower diffusion of digital systems in the United States was due to the presence of several standards and a weaker migration from the first generation to the second generation due to backward compatibility. In addition, the structure of tariffs on mobile services was different in

---

[21] This is in contrast to Europe, where the standard creators did not care about backward compatibility with a first-generation standard.

[22] CDMA was technically superior to D-AMPS, but it had limited availability of terminal equipment and was implemented differently by each operator.

Europe, and roaming and caller pay issues were resolved much earlier (Hommen and Manninen, 2003).[23]

The two main US digital standards diffused to Latin America and Asia only to a limited degree, and never became a serious international competitor to GSM. Foreign standards were used to a very small extent in the United States. Instead the most important US operators transferred to GSM. It started with AT&T Wireless in late 2001, and thereafter six additional mobile operators have decided to follow the example. Among the reasons were that GSM accounted for 60 percent of the world market even before this, and that economies of scale lead to lower prices. In addition, the transfer to 3G (W-CDMA) is being facilitated. GSM has, thereby, effectively become a world standard. The transfer has also strengthened the position of Ericsson and Nokia.

The US standard regulatory organizations seem to have wanted to secure competition between standards as well as between operators in the United States. In Europe competition took place only between operators.

In Japan the digital mobile telephone standard adopted was called personal digital cellular (PDC), and it never diffused outside Japan. It was incompatible with all other standards. The Japanese market remained closed to other (foreign) standards.

### 2.3.2.3 The third generation – UMTS/WLAN    Unlike the NMT 900 and GSM standards, the development of the UMTS standard was not driven primarily by the need to accommodate unexpectedly rapid growth in the number of subscribers. Instead, improved functionality seems to have been the main driving force.

Although UMTS is a standard supported by ETSI (i.e. it is a European standard), it also has the official sanction of the ITU, an organization with truly worldwide coverage and authority. At the same time, ETSI actually chose NTT DoCoMo's W-CDMA technology in January1998 as the European third-generation standard (Funk, 2002, pp. 78–82 and 206–208).[24] The previous development within ETSI was pursued in very general terms, and when it came to an actual decision W-CDMA was chosen. ETSI chose W-CDMA because it believed that W-CDMA offered far greater capabilities than an enhanced version of GSM and because W-CDMA included the evolution of the GSM network interface (Funk, 2002, ch. 6). Hence UMTS can be seen as a further extension of GSM, and the two systems are intended to be compatible with one another.

---

[23] The tariff structure is discussed in section 2.3.4.

[24] NTT DoCoMo is the largest mobile phone operator in Japan. It is a spin-off of NTT, the former operator monopoly. NTT is still a majority equity holder in DoCoMo.

The choice of W-CDMA has been seen as a major victory for Japanese manufacturers and its two European supporters, Ericsson and Nokia. The ETSI and ITU decisions have also made W-CDMA a global standard. The "UMTS alliance" includes the European Union and some national operators, such as Japan's NTT DoCoMo. It also includes multinational telecommunications equipment manufacturing firms such as Ericsson and Nokia. The choice of W-CDMA was a blow to supporters of other standards, such as TDMS (telecommunications data management system) and cdma2000.

UMTS will be, in important respects, a significant departure from existing mobile telecommunication systems, and will constitute a "3G" system. It involves several important breaks with GSM:

1. the use of broadband, as opposed to narrow band, radio frequencies;
2. the full integration of voice and data communications;
3. the full integration of "fixed" and "mobile" telecommunications networks; and
4. the provision of "seamless" global roaming, in addition to high functionality.

However, a certain level of wireless data transmission is already possible within GSM. For example, the further development of GSM technology (and other second-generation counterparts) has proceeded for some time within a framework consistent with UMTS objectives. A case in point is the wireless application protocol, created in 1998. WAP constitutes an intermediate stage of development between existing GSM capabilities for wireless data transmission and the UMTS goal of making the "wireless Internet" a reality through an integration of fixed and mobile communications networks. WAP is HTML-compatible, since Internet material is in HTML format.[25] WAP allows a great advance in GSM wireless data transmission by enabling Internet information to be delivered on mobile devices that already support GSM-based SMS.[26] WAP was in operation by 2001 in many countries, but it had not become a success in terms of number of users by 2002.

Another "intermediate" solution – between 2G and 3G – is the general packet radio service (GPRS). It brings the IP into the GSM network and thus enables data to be sent in small packets, users to be charged for these packages as opposed to connection times, and data transmission speeds of up to 115 KB/s. GPRS also makes multimedia services possible (Funk,

---

[25] The HTML protocol is addressed in section 2.3.1.

[26] As mentioned before, SMS is data transmission of a "paging" character, but in both directions. Here there is a direct link between mobile phones and the fixed Internet; i.e. SMS can be sent to and from fixed computers as well as mobile phones.

2002, pp. 211–212). Many GSM operators introduced GPRS during 2001.

The first operator to put UMTS in operation was NTT DoCoMo in Japan, which initiated the service in October 2001.[27] DoCoMo was a natural first mover since the company has operated the i-mode mobile Internet system since February 1999. i-mode is, like WAP, somewhere in between second- and third-generation mobile telecommunications, and had 31 million subscribers by March 2002.[28] The fact that UMTS was first introduced in Japan might provide Japanese equipment manufacturers with an advantage over other manufacturers.

Reasons for the success of i-mode in Japan include the low usage of the fixed Internet and DoCoMo's effective strategy. The reasons why DoCoMo has the largest number of subscribers and content sites are its early release of compatible handsets, a packet service, a clearing house and its use of compact HTML. The packet service enables small packets of information to be sent inexpensively. In the clearing house, DoCoMo collects money for the content provider's fee-based services and takes a percentage (9 percent) of this as a handling charge. This organizational or managerial innovation is crucial since it makes it easy for content providers to earn money from their provision without actually being responsible for collecting the charges from the users themselves (Funk, 2002, ch. 6).

In Europe auctions for UMTS licenses were held in many countries during 2000 – and the operators in some cases agreed to pay enormous fees. This has created economic problems for some operators and will certainly be an obstacle to the diffusion of UMTS in Europe. Some people believe that short-sighted governments dreamt that they could finance the increasing costs of taking care of the growing numbers of old people by taxing the new economy agents, such as the mobile telecommunications operators, and that this may in turn hurt an important part of European hi-tech industry. In some countries – e.g. Sweden – the licenses were allocated by means of "beauty contests." The investments in 3G systems will be very large and started during 2002 and 2003 in Europe, although there are delays in the build-up of the infrastructure. The United States will also be a laggard with regard to UMTS, partly because other users, e.g. the military, tie up the relevant radio frequencies.

---

[27] However, the system has suffered from a number of technical problems that have made many potential subscribers hesitate. Therefore, the 3G system had fewer than 55,000 subscribers in March 2002, which was well below DoCoMo's objective.

[28] i-mode is a transitional system, based on narrow band frequencies and a development of the Japanese PDC standard. DoCoMo established i-mode also in the Netherlands, Germany and Belgium in early 2002.

Whether third-generation mobile telecommunications systems (including mobile Internet access) will diffuse rapidly or slowly will depend on:

- the quality and importance of the services provided (as evaluated by those who pay);
- the structure and rate of the tariffs; and
- the cost of accessing similar services in other ways.

If operators want to enhance the rapid diffusion of third-generation mobile telecommunications subscriptions they should ensure that the services are good and probably offer flat subscription rates of a limited size. In addition, cultural differences between countries may be important. So may the way everyday life is organized. For example, long commutes with public means of transportation – as in Tokyo – may contribute to the rapid diffusion of third-generation systems.

The European success in NMT and GSM will not necessarily be repeated in 3G mobile telecommunications because some of the conditions behind the success of the first and second generations no longer apply. In particular, liberalization has reduced the central role of monopolistic PTOs, so that the close interaction between them and equipment producers has been diminished. Consequently, producers may find that large domestic markets are more difficult to obtain from the start for new products.

There are also alternatives and supplements to the third generation. 3G systems will not provide users with the full range of broadband services available to fixed Internet users. 3G systems are based on rather low-speed data communications: 2 MB/s is at present the absolute maximum for UMTS, and speeds lower than 400 KB/s will be normal in the next couple of years at least. Much higher speeds will be provided by a complement to UMTS called WLAN. This began with the development of customer premises networks or wireless local area networks for professional users (firms). Recently WLANs also started to be installed in public areas. Public WLANs can cover only small geographical areas or "islands" – e.g. an office, an airport or an Internet café. In these "islands" a PC or a palmtop can be used to access the Internet at speeds of 10–50 MB/s.

Currently there are signs that WLAN will diffuse very rapidly in the near future. Already by April 2002 there were about 300 public locations covered by WLAN in Sweden (*Ny Teknik*, 2002). A 4G mobile telecommunications system may be considered as an integration of a 3G mobile telecommunications system and WLAN access to the "traditional" fixed Internet (and integrated with other wireless options such as GPRS, Bluetooth, etc.). The customer will be automatically connected to that network that has the highest capacity, and the same subscription is used for all of them. The standard now emerging as the winner within WLAN is the American Institute of Electrical and Electronic Engineers' 802.11a and b. The 802.11a operates in the 5 GHz band with a potential speed of 50 MB/s, while 802.11b operates with 10 MB/s in the 2.4 GHz band. The European ETSI standard HiperLAN 2 appears to be a loser in this standardization game.[29]

The frequencies used by WLAN are unlicensed – i.e. free – and they therefore encounter interference from other WLAN systems or from different applications. The 2.4 GHz band that is currently mainly used for WLANs is also used by – and can therefore get disturbed by – Bluetooth, microwave ovens and car parking sensors. The 5 GHz band, which is the frequency proposed for new WLAN systems, is free from interfering competitors and can allow many operators to coexist.

Currently the United States is probably most advanced in private and public WLAN installations. At the same time the third generation is delayed there since no radio spectrum has been allocated. For these reasons it is more probable that WLAN will become very important in relation to 3G here than in any other country (although WLAN can, of course, not cover large areas). In Europe 3G licenses have been awarded in most countries and will be installed fairly soon. However, operators that did not buy or get any 3G licenses may be pushing WLAN. The country most committed to 3G is Japan, where 3G is already operating and where there is very little discussion about WLAN (*Wireless Web*, 2002).

Within the mobile telecommunications sector the number of categories of actors as well as the number of actors in most categories will increase. Currently the dominant categories are suppliers of equipment and access providers (operators). The vendors of systems (base stations and switches) are not likely to be threatened, since economies of scale and barriers to entry are very large. For them the matter is to wait until the current crisis is over and the operators start investing again. On the handset side we are, however, likely to see additional producers, probably with niche strategies focusing on cheap mass-market phones or very advanced ones. This increased competition will mainly influence Nokia, Motorola, Siemens and Sony-Ericsson.

The number of access providers will increase in many markets in the near future. In Sweden, for example, two new large mobile operators planned to enter when the 3G networks start to operate during 2003 and

---

[29] HomeRF is yet another variant, while Bluetooth-based solutions basically operate only within 10 meters of distance and act more as substitutes for cables. See, e.g., Garber (2002); Mannings and Cosier (2001); and *Financial Times* (2002).

2004, but one of them has withdrawn. In addition those operators that own networks may start renting capacity to others – i.e. operators without networks will enter. Hence competition will increase in several ways.

A major obstacle to the breakthrough and growth of 3G is the supply of mobile Internet content. Just like the fixed Internet sector, content providers that are independent of the access providers will have to solve this problem to a large extent. We are here talking about content such as games, music, news, information, financial services, etc. Hence the division of labor between operators and independent content providers must be cleared up. How is the final customer to pay? Via the invoice from the access provider, via a bank account or via some other intermediate actor? Here there is a struggle between various interests.

An even more difficult issue to solve is how the cake should be divided between providers of access and of content. Currently the operators appropriate most of this cake, and it is probably necessary that more be handed over to content suppliers in order to create stronger incentives for the development of content for the mobile Internet! This conflict must be solved at the latest when handsets with larger displays in color (3G phones) emerge in large numbers, i.e. in 2003 and 2004. When discussing DoCoMo's i-mode it was stressed that organizational and managerial innovations are important in this field. 3G will not become successful without content that really attracts the final customers enough to make them willing to pay. And such content will not be developed if its providers cannot charge for it.

### 2.3.3   Satellite communications

Wireless access to the Internet and to telephone lines can also be achieved via satellite communications. A communications satellite is basically a microwave repeater revolving around the earth in a specified orbit. On earth the signals can either continue in cable or mobile systems or be transferred to private houses by means of small discs. The satellites are primarily used for TV and radio transmission. For example, the European EUTELSAT system was broadcasting 750 analog and digital TV channels and 450 radio channels by the end of 2000. However, in 1999 20 percent was used for a range of broadband services, including Internet "backbone" and access and corporate networks.

So called "set-top boxes" may facilitate high-speed Internet access in remote areas. They may also represent an alternative solution if incumbent telecommunications operators are too reluctant to make high-speed access available; and – finally – they make it easier for people without computer skills to reach the Internet through their TV screen. This obviously represents a convergence between TV broadcasting and Internet access. The potential importance of TV networks for data communication (other than TV and radio) – e.g. the Internet – is enormous (Dalum, 2003).

At the beginning of the 1990s four large consortia announced plans for mega-projects of satellite-based mobile telecommunications systems. Iridium, Globalstar and ICO are the best known. They were all built up, but in the first half of 1999 Iridium and ICO went bankrupt and the Globalstar plans were significantly adjusted. Operations were geographically focused on areas where there were no terrestrial mobile communications systems available, which decreased the number of customers as well as their purchasing power.

A significant underestimation of the success and vigorous growth of cellular mobile telecommunications caused the commercial failure of these enterprises to a large extent. At the beginning of the new millennium the huge ambitions of the global mobile satellite-based systems for voice and data transmission had to be drastically scaled down (Dalum, 2003).

With widespread 3G mobile communications – or WLANs – within reach in the next five to ten years, the satellite-based mobile phone systems will have the role of complementary systems in areas with weak coverage by terrestrial mobile communications networks. They will also play a role in maritime communications, and perhaps also for systems intended to be used by the airline industry.

### 2.3.4    Rate structures and levels

The structure and level of rates and tariffs may also be considered to be "rules of the game" – i.e. a form of institution. In this case, it is an institution created, to a large extent, by firms (i.e. at the micro-level), although the firms are also influenced by other institutions – e.g. regulations. The quality and value of a telecommunications or Internet service as perceived by the user influence the rate of diffusion of the service. The cost of the service also, obviously, influences the diffusion. This implies that the comparative prices of the different modes of accessing certain services are important. So are, of course, the comparative prices of the content provided over the networks.

In GSM there was agreement that calling charges were to be billed to the caller. However, when calls were placed to a mobile handset located in another country at the time of calling, the caller was charged the local rates and the cost for forwarding the call outside the home country was paid by the receiver.[30]

---

[30] This decision was taken because the caller would otherwise not know the cost of calling.

In the United States, however, the receiver has traditionally been charged. If a call is placed from a fixed telephone line to a mobile phone, only the receiver is charged (if the receiving handset is located in the vicinity). This is because there is normally no variable cost for local phone calls from fixed lines in the United States, but only a fixed subscription fee. For long-distance calls there is also a variable cost. If the receiver is located outside the local area, then both the caller and the receiver pay. If a call is placed between two mobile phones, both also pay a variable fee.

This posed an obstacle to the diffusion of mobile telecommunications in the United States as compared to Europe. It constituted a disincentive to subscribe to mobile services. It also created an incentive for users to switch off the handsets – which led to non-availability. There was also a disincentive to give out mobile numbers because of this.

The importance of the level of charges (related to the quality and value of the service provided as well as to the cost of the alternatives for getting access to the same or a similar service) can also be illustrated by the fact that mobile subscriptions diffused rapidly in Sweden  (in comparison, with the United Kingdom), due to the low tariffs already in place during the analog era (see section 2.3.2.1).

The introduction of the prepaid card was also instrumental in increasing the diffusion in those countries where it became available. In Sweden these cards were first introduced in 1997 by Comviq – one of the three operators (now called Tele 2). The prepaid cards are, for example, used by people that are not able to subscribe, such as young people and those who are not creditworthy for other reasons.

The structure and level of costs for access to the fixed Internet also vary between countries and continents. In the United States only a flat rate is normally charged, which makes possible unlimited Internet access. Local dial-up is not metered.[31] In the United Kingdom, and also in Italy, Internet access has been provided to a large extent free of charge, although this phenomenon might be gradually disappearing in the near future. In Sweden most consumer Internet access has been mediated by a modem and a variable cost has been paid (in addition to the subscription fee). However, the US pricing structure is currently becoming increasingly common in Sweden. In Japan the cost structure is similar to that in Sweden – i.e. both a fixed and a variable cost are charged.

The rate structure is probably part of the explanation of the high penetration of Internet access in the United States – and the low ratio in Japan.

---

[31] Other OECD countries with unmetered local telecommunications services are Australia, Canada and New Zealand. In all these countries, and in the United States, there is a high penetration of Internet hosts (Mowery, 2001, p. 37).

However, the rapid diffusion in Sweden certainly cannot be explained by rates. Neither is the slow Internet penetration rate in Italy a consequence of the pricing structure, but, rather, of a lack of familiarity with ICT applications, of the inertia of Italian consumers and of the limited knowledge of English.

The low diffusion of the fixed Internet in Japan – together with the low density of home PCs – may, in turn, partly explain the rapid diffusion of the i-mode mobile Internet operated by NTT DoCoMo. Further, this may be a reason why DoCoMo was the first operator to install a full-scale third-generation mobile telephone system, in October 2001 – as discussed in section 2.3.2.3.

### 2.4    *Boundaries between systems and convergence between subsystems*

What is the sectoral system of innovation in the telecommunications field? Is there one sectoral system or are there several systems?

The telecommunications sector – in a wide sense – is growing rapidly and there is convergence between various parts or subsystems. It is possible to talk about convergence in several senses and respects.

First, we saw a convergence between IT and communication technologies into ICT, which occurred in the 1980s. There was also a convergence between ICT and the broadcasting/audio-visual technologies in the 1990s. This constituted the starting point of the so-called multimedia revolution.

The transfer to digitized mobile telecommunications systems in the 1990s implied a convergence of formerly separate technologies. The technological base had broadened to include innovations from outside the traditional telecommunications sector, mainly from computer and software firms. This actually meant that telecommunications equipment producers in essence became IT and software firms, although with a specialization toward telecommunications. It also meant that traditional telecommunications firms had to confront new entrants with a competency that had originated in other sectors. In addition, standard-setting organizations became important. There has also been considerable growth of publicly funded research in telecommunications in Europe during this past decade.

In the 1990s we also experienced a convergence between traditional telecommunications and the Internet. The emergence of the Internet meant that another subsystem entered the telecommunications sector. This also implied that new functions became important, and new kinds of organizations entered the sector – e.g. new IAPs (such as telecommunications operators and cable TV operators), ICPs (such as e-commerce companies) and software and Internet specialized consulting companies.

Further, we will see a convergence between the fixed Internet and mobile telecommunications in the near future with the emergence of third-generation mobile telecommunications. This kind of convergence has already started with SMS, WAP and GPRS (and with UMTS in Japan). What WLANs will mean in terms of convergence is still unclear.

We have also seen a convergence process with regard to receiving devices or customer premises equipment. For example, third-generation cellular phones offer Internet connection and narrow band services. Similarly, desktop computers can be used to make telephone calls or to watch a video, and set-top boxes are also starting to become an alternative device for Internet access. Organizers of the "palm pilot" kind may also be used for Internet access. There are also combinations of these devices. In 1994 Nokia introduced one of the first data interface products – a "PC" card that could be inserted into a portable computer connected to a mobile handset by means of a cable.

All this has meant that the knowledge base for the telecommunications sectoral system (in a wide sense) has become increasingly complex. Convergence also means that boundaries are changing and that sectoral systems may be moving targets, becoming larger and more complex. However, boundaries may also change in the opposite direction and sectoral systems may become more specialized and more isolated from other systems and subsystems because of increasing specialization, and they may become smaller. Therefore, both convergence and divergence might occur.

There is a certain degree of arbitrariness when it comes to the specification of sectoral boundaries. Therefore, we can consider data communications to be one sectoral system, and mobile telecommunications to be another. However, we could also see both of them as belonging to one combined system (particularly if they are converging). It is partly a matter of choice and convenience. Some minimum degree of coherence is nevertheless required to make it useful to talk about a sectoral system. We would not regard paper pulp and telecommunications to be the same sectoral system of innovation.

Here, we take a very pragmatic view of whether we are talking about one SSI or about several within telecommunications in a wide sense. Sometimes it may be useful to regard the whole field as one system. At other times it might be more fruitful to consider the Internet and mobile telecommunications to be separate SSIs. It depends on the context – e.g. on the purpose of the study to be carried out. In addition, equipment production, network operation (access provision) and content provision can be regarded as separate systems or as one common system.

However, *when* an empirical study is to be carried out it is absolutely necessary to identify the boundaries of the sectoral system that is to be scrutinized. The boundaries have to be specified in a sectoral as well as in a functional sense (and in a geographical sense, if the system is not global).

The functional boundaries of SIs are identifiable with the determinants of the relevant innovation processes. If we can identify the determinants of different kinds of innovations in the fixed Internet and mobile telecommunications, then we can say that these determinants constitute the functional boundaries of the relevant SSI. However, we do not know these determinants in detail, given the present state of the art.

## 3    Policies and strategies

Specific policy implications for the Internet and mobile telecommunications are discussed in this section. They are mainly based upon the analysis in section 2.

Institutional rules may be created, redesigned or abolished. Those institutions that can be influenced by public agencies are public policy instruments. Similarly, those institutions that are influenced by firms are firm strategy instruments. Further, organizations may be phased out, redesigned or created. If policy makers do this, these changes are also policy instruments. If firm managers do it, they are firm strategy instruments.

### 3.1    The fixed Internet

Although several of the important inventions that served as bases for the development of the Internet did not emerge in the United States – e.g. HTML and HTTP – it was there that the Internet developed commercially *first and most rapidly*. The Internet was commercialized and diffused on a large scale in the United States before anywhere else.

The US *state* was extremely important in the *very early stages* of the development of fixed data communications – i.e. in the period when the SSI of fixed data communication was fragile and not well established. Government agencies were very important as financiers of research developing fixed data communications; they initiated the public technology procurement of elements of the system. Other agencies required that organizations receiving public economic support had to use a certain data communications protocol. The state also injected increased dynamism into the telecommunications sector by pursuing deregulation.

State agencies were not strong leaders, however, in the creation of standards for the Internet in the United States. This was, instead, a rather spontaneous process where private firms had a large influence. The idea of "open standards" or the "compatibility of standards" appears to have been the characteristic US strategy.

The *relations* among various organizations were crucial for the development of innovations in the SSI. These included the relations between public and private organizations – as in public research funding and in public technology procurement. Relations among different private organizations were also important, both in terms of competition and in terms of collaboration.

The fact that the early development and diffusion of the Internet took place in the United States – with government support – gave a "head start" to US Internet equipment producers. This is an important explanatory factor behind the fact that US Internet equipment producing firms, such as Cisco, are still very dominant globally. It is obviously very important for firm competitiveness in high-tech areas to be *early movers* in the sector and to be close to customers in these early stages.

### 3.2     Mobile telecommunications

*State-controlled organizations* were very important in creating the first successful mobile telecommunications *standard* in Europe. Public telecommunications monopolies in the Nordic countries created the NMT 450 mobile telecommunications standard in collaboration with firms. The PTOs pushed the technical development of the standard and pulled national equipment producers along their trajectory. They placed orders to firms and partly used the instrument of public technology procurement to create incentives for firms to develop equipment for NMT 450. NMT 450 provided the cradle for the development of mobile telecommunications in Europe. *Deregulation* of the telecommunications sector was also important in some European countries, such as Sweden and the United Kingdom. However, liberalization was not a key factor in Sweden's success with NMT and GSM. At most it aided the diffusion process that was already under way at the time of deregulation (1993).

*Relations* among organizations were obviously important in this process. So were the relations between various kinds of institutions – such as NMT 450 – and the firms and other organizations involved. The relations between the operators – the main standard creators – and equipment producers were very important for the fact that European equipment producers became leaders at the global level. For firms such as Nokia and Ericsson it was also important that mobile telecommunications got a "head start" in the Nordic countries, and that they grew rapidly.

Most second-generation standards were developed with the potential to become de facto world standards through international adoption. The

European GSM standard – which developed out of the NMT standard – more than fulfilled the expectation of wide international diffusion. Initially conceived as a pan-European standard, it became a world standard. No other second-generation standard achieved this. Deregulated operators (such as Swedish Televerket/Telia) as well as firms (such as Ericsson and Nokia) were very active in the consortium that supported the development of the GSM standard. Hence, the close relations between users and producers continued. Over the longer term, however, these close relations gradually became more and more loose. The GSM success could not be ascribed only to the strategies of a few innovative organizations but also to the *collaborations* between a variety of different organizations: PTOs, standard-setting organizations and research organizations, as well as equipment producers.

The European Commission also had a leading role in the development of GSM. The European Union was pushing *one* standard and it was developed *ex ante*. This was also a standard that was technologically advanced and operated well, and – therefore – it diffused rapidly outside Europe. In contrast, the US digital standards diffused internationally only to a limited extent, and the single Japanese standard not at all. The European Commission pushed liberalization and competition in the (mobile) telecommunications sector.[32] But it did so within one single standard and did not care about letting standards compete – as in the US standards policy. The standard pushed by the European Union was secured to serve all EU members, while the US digital standards were not completely compatible with each other. What the European Union did over (originally) thirteen European countries the United States did not manage to do over one country (albeit large).

It proved to be a major policy mistake to have several standards in the United States. This can be considered a serious policy failure for the United States as well as a great policy success for the European Union. The reasons for this are that it led to a slower diffusion of mobile telecommunications in the United States than in Europe, and that the strongest equipment producers emerged in Europe.

The US policy was conscious and consistent. The FCC was against *ex ante* standardization – which was preferred by ETSI – and advocated an open network architecture.[33] The arguments were that the open architecture was very important for the creation of the Internet and that closing it could block further innovation. The FCC was passive in relation to the

---

[32] In 1996 the Commission decided that mobile services had to be competitive, with multiple GSM licenses in each member state.
[33] The FCC preferred market- and user-driven *ex post* standards.

European invitation to participate in *ex ante* standardization in wireless services. The FCC also later blocked the route toward 3G convergence in the form of W-CDMA as a global standard (supported by ETSI). This all happened in the latter half of the 1990s. One interpretation of this is that the FCC was tied by the fact that US participants in the 3G race represented different technological alternatives, and therefore the FCC remained "neutral" in the standardization process. At the same time there is a trend that "the regulation of the new information infrastructure has gravitated toward a clearer recognition of market-driven standards. As the world of mobile telecommunications and computer communication (the Internet) collide, the clear trend is for direct regulation to withdraw from the market" (Glimstedt, 2001, p. 22).

Firms such as Ericsson and Nokia are also moving away from their original idea of a single standard for the 3G services and toward the position that the new mobile telecommunications services should be based on several different but compatible standards – a "family of standards." This is similar to the idea of open architecture in relation to the Internet. This idea is that "network architecture should be as open as possible, allowing user-led innovation and new combinations of radical technologies" (Glimstedt, 2001, p. 22). At the same time, however, we saw that the most important US mobile telecommunications access providers have, during the first years of the new millennium, transferred to GSM. If a reason for this is that the transfer to W-CDMA will be facilitated, then *ex ante* standardization seems to be winning the game anyway. This may be because market sizes and economies of scale created by *ex ante* standardization lead actors into the dominant trajectory in the evolutionary process of standard creation.[34]

The promotion of one single standard was of great importance for the European dominance in the production of equipment for the mobile telecommunications industry; for example, economies of scale could be exploited. The fact that the relations between users and producers were close also proved very important, primarily for the producers. The way GSM developed increased the leadership position of Nokia and Ericsson. This is all the more notable in the light of the lack of European success – and US/Asian dominance – in most other ICT sectors. The mobile telecommunications market was growing rapidly and was a major job creator in Europe.

Europe has emerged as a clear leader in mobile telecommunications due to its success in defining good standards in mobile communications.

---

[34] In this chapter it is argued that there has been an evolutionary process from NMT 450 through GSM to W-CDMA.

Ericsson's and Nokia's dominance among equipment producers in mobile telecommunications is often traced to the early success of the NMT standard, and GSM is similarly regarded as the means by which early Nordic success was generalized to other European Union countries in the second generation of mobile communications.

One reason for the relatively poor international performance of US-based 2G mobile standards was the "division" of the market between standards, none of which could match the subscriber base of GSM. These developments are considered to account for the subsequent loss of market share by US equipment manufacturers to European rivals during the second generation of mobile telecommunications. The slower transfer from first- to second-generation standards in the United States was due to regulatory decisions that stressed the necessity of achieving "backward compatibility" with the existing analog standards, rather than compatible digital standards. Decisions with regard to charges were another factor contributing to the low subscriber penetration rates; often the receiver has to pay for all or part of a mobile phone call.

The crisis at Ericsson during 2001–03 – as well as with much of the mobile telecommunications equipment industry – is mainly caused by a drastic decrease in demand because of the slowdown in the international business cycle (and thereby in telecommunications system investments) as well as the slow development of 3G. It serves to conceal the fact that Ericsson is still dominant in base stations and switches, while Nokia strongly dominates global handset production.

In the 1990s we experienced a convergence between traditional telecommunications, the Internet and mobile telecommunications. This was also accompanied by a wave of mergers and acquisitions (and strategic alliances), both among equipment producers and among operators. A strategic decision for the equipment producers is whether they should select voice as their main business area and thus go for the growing mobile phone markets; whether they should concentrate on the rapidly growing Internet equipment market; or whether they should go for the mobile Internet.

### 3.3    The future of the sectoral system and relations between Europe, the United States and Japan

It is clear that Europe has, so far, had the initiative in mobile voice telephony. Whether this will continue during the third-generation UMTS standard is unclear. NTT DoCoMo's i-mode had 31 million subscribers in 2002, and DoCoMo was also the first operator to enter 3G in October 2001. This means that the locus of the center of experimentation may have moved from Europe to Japan. This can spur equipment producers since user/producer interaction had proved to be important earlier. In the United States some operators have transferred to GSM, and they will be more standardized in 3G than they were in 2G. However, the United States is a slow starter in third-generation mobile telecommunications. Although Europe will probably enter 3G earlier than the United States, it is doing so at a slower pace than Japan. This might partly be because of the very high prices European operators had to pay in some countries for a 3G license – i.e. it might partly be a consequence of public policy.

Currently 3G is developing quite slowly. However, telecommunications operators' revenue was growing by 10 percent per year in 2001 and the immediately preceding years. This indicates that telecommunications operators were not subject to a structural crisis but were hit by the downturn of the business cycle during 2000 and 2001 – which is expected to take off again in 2004.

The most important obstacles to the diffusion of 3G are – in the short run – the availability of handsets and – in the longer run – the supply of attractive content suited to the mobile Internet. This points to the crucial role of demand in the emergence of new sectoral systems. As far as equipment is concerned, the demand-side policy instrument of public technology procurement was used both with regard to the Internet (the United States) and with regard to mobile telecommunications (Scandinavia). When it comes to content in the 3G mobile Internet, most of the demand has to be provided by final consumers – firms and individuals – outside the public sphere, to the largest extent. The success of i-mode in Japan seems to indicate that this will happen,[35] but access providers and content providers will have to be innovative not only with regard to access and content proper but also when it comes to charging systems and other innovations in the field of management and administration. It is also a matter of developing niche strategies adapted to the new medium: movies will never best be watched on a mobile phone!

Fixed Internet diffusion is proceeding. In 2002 about 70 percent of households had access in the United States. In other countries the degree of diffusion varies a lot. The dominance of US equipment producers, which was established early in the history of the fixed Internet, is likely to remain stable, at least in the medium term. At the same time, this sector may be entering a more mature stage of development, with slower growth and smaller profits.

If WLAN becomes a serious competitor or an alternative to third-generation mobile telecommunications – i.e. if the development jumps the 3G "step" and goes directly into 4G – this will probably benefit the United

---

[35] But the slow diffusion of WAP and GPRS in Europe and the United States points in the opposite direction.

States. The reasons for this are that 3G will not be implemented there in the near future, there are already a fair amount of WLAN installations, and because the United States is very strong in PCs and palmtops. There seems to be a possibility of leapfrogging here.

### 3.4    *The three most important policy issues*

Here follows a summary of the three most important policy issues with regard to the fixed Internet and mobile telecommunications. They are presented in abbreviated form, and in no particular order.

*The role of institutions has been crucial for policy.* Standards have played a major role in innovation and the success of European mobile telecommunications, both in terms of the diffusion of use and with regard to the success of equipment producing companies. Deregulation has also played a role in the diffusion of the Internet and mobile telecommunications. Other important institutions are the structure and level of tariffs. Some institutions are national, some are sectoral and others are firm-specific. An important firm strategy objective has been to influence institutions to the firm's benefit.

*The relations between different organizations and between institutions and organizations are crucial for the functioning and performance of (sectoral) systems of innovation.* Examples are the relations between private and public organizations in the form of research funding, standard setting or public technology procurement. Relations between different kinds of firms and other private organizations are also important – e.g. collaboration between users and producers. Organizations provoke institutional changes, and when the new institutions come into effect they may greatly influence the same or other organizations.

*It is of crucial importance that public policy intervention occurs early in the development of the sectoral system.* Public technology procurement was crucial for the very early development of the Internet in the United States and the formulation of standards was crucial for the very early development of mobile telecommunications in the Nordic countries. This proved to be very important also for equipment producers in these fields. It is in the very early stages in the development of an SSI that the uncertainty and risks are greatest, and private actors and markets therefore operate least efficiently and dynamically.[36] Therefore policy intervention in these very early stages often means the difference between success and failure.

---

[36] That public policy intervention in the field of innovation should be practiced only in situations where private firms and markets fail to achieve the wanted results spontaneously is argued in Edquist (2002, 2001a). This means that public policy action should not replace or duplicate markets and private actors.

Hence policy resources – which are always scarce – should mainly be allocated to the very early stages of the development of new SSIs or new product areas.

REFERENCES

Abbate, J. (2001), *Inventing the Internet*, MIT Press, Cambridge, MA

Corrocher, N. (2003a), The Internet services industry: sectoral dynamics of innovation and production, in C. Edquist (ed.), *Systems of Innovation: Technologies, Institutions and Organisations*, Frances Pinter London, 177–209

(2003b), The Internet services industry: country-specific trends in the UK, Italy and Sweden, in C. Edquist (ed.), *The Internet and Mobile Telecommunications System of Innovation: Developments in Equipment, Access and Content*, Edward Elgar Publishing, Cheltenham, 210–235

Dalum, B. (2003), Data communication: satellite and TV subsystems, in C. Edquist (ed.), *The Internet and Mobile Telecommunications System of Innovation: Developments in Equipment, Access and Content*, Edward Elgar Publishing, Cheltenham, 162–176

Dalum, B., and G. Villumsen (2003), Fixed data communications: challenges for Europe, in C. Edquist (ed.), *The Internet and Mobile Telecommunications System of Innovation: Developments in Equipment, Access and Content*, Edward Elgar Publishing, Cheltenham, 40–70

Edquist, C. (1997), Systems of innovation approaches – their emergence and characteristics, in C. Edquist (ed.), *Systems of Innovation: Technologies, Institutions and Organizations*, Frances Pinter, London, 1–35

(2001a), Innovation policy in the systems of innovation approach: some basic principles, in M. M. Fischer and J. Fröhlich (eds.), *Knowledge Complexity and Innovation Systems*, Springer-Verlag, Berlin

(2001b), *The Systems of Innovation Approach and Innovation Policy: An Account of the State of the Art*, paper presented at the Danish Research Unit for Industrial Dynamics conference, Aalborg, June 12–15

(2002), Innovation policy – a systemic approach, in D. Archibugi and B.-A. Lundvall (eds.), *The Globalising Learning Economy: Major Socio-Economic Trends and European Innovation Policy*, Oxford University Press, Oxford

(ed.) (2003), *The Internet and Mobile Telecommunications System of Innovation: Developments in Equipment, Access and Content*, Edward Elgar Publishing, Cheltenham

(2004), Systems of innovation – perspectives and challenges, in J. Fagerberg, D. Mowery, R. R. Nelson (eds.), *The Oxford Handbook of Innovation*, Oxford University Press, Oxford, forthcoming

Edquist, C., and B. Johnson (1997), Institutions and organisations in systems of innovation, in C. Edquist (ed.), *Systems of Innovation: Technologies, Institutions and Organizations*, Frances Pinter, London, 41–63

Edquist, C., L. Hommen and L. Tsipouri (eds.) (2000), *Public Technology Procurement: Theory, Evidence and Policy*, Kluwer Academic, Dordrecht

*Financial Times* (2001), Broadband's slow start hides its potential, December 13

(2002), Wireless world offers true laptop mobility, March 13

Funk, J. L. (2002), *Global Competition Between and Within Standards: The Case of Mobile Phones*, Palgrave, New York

Garber, L. (2002), Will 3G really be the next big wireless technology? *IEEE Computer*, 35, 1

Glimstedt, H. (2001), *The Competitive Dynamics of Technological Standards*, Stockholm School of Economics, mimeo

Hommen, L. (2003), The Universal Mobile Telecommunications System (UMTS): Third generation, in C. Edquist (ed.), *The Internet and Mobile Telecommunications System of Innovation: Developments in Equipment, Access and Content*, Edward Elgar Publishing, Cheltenham, 129–161

Hommen, L. and E. Manninen (2003), The global system for mobile telecommunications (GSM): second generation, in C. Edquist (ed.), *The Internet and Mobile Telecommunications System of Innovation: Developments in Equipment, Access and Content*, Edward Elgar Publishing, Cheltenham, 71–128

Kenney, M. (2001), The growth and development of the Internet in the United States, in B. Kogut (ed.), *The Global Internet Economy*, MIT Press, Cambridge, MA, 129–161

Lindmark, S., and O. Granstrand (1995), Technology and systems competition in mobile communications, in D. Lamberton (ed.), *Beyond Competition: The Future of Telecommunications*, Elsevier Science, Amsterdam

McKelvey, M., F. Texier and H. Alm (1998), *The Dynamics of High-Tech Industry: Swedish Firms Developing Mobile Telecommunications Systems*, Working Paper no. 187, Department of Technology and Social Change, Linköping University, Sweden

Mannings, R., and G. Cosier (2001), Wireless everything – unwiring the world, *BT Technology Journal*, 19, 4

Mowery, D. C. (2001), *Is the Internet a U.S. Invention? An Economic and Technological History of Computer Networking*, paper presented at Danish Research Unit for Industrial Dynamics conference, Aalborg, June 12–15

*Ny Teknik* (2002), 290 heta platser för surning med datorn, April 4

*Wireless Web* (2002), Battling a mindset: WLAN could threaten 3G future, http://wireless.iop.org/article/feature/3/2/5

# 6 The European software sectoral system of innovation

*W. Edward Steinmueller*[1]

## 1 Introduction

The global software industry is young, large and very dynamic (Mowery, 1996). Markets for software as a commodity independent of computer systems have been established for little more than three decades, while a vast amount of software continues to be produced by firms to meet their own specialized information processing requirements. Revenues from software sales to European companies and individuals amounted to approximately €47.9 billion in 2000 and are expected to continue to grow at double-digit percentage rates in the near future (European Information Technology Observatory [EITO], 2001). At least 2 million European workers (1.35 percent of the European Union labor force) are directly engaged in the production of software as part of their direct job responsibilities.[2]

Software is the collection of instructions that computers follow in executing the tasks of acquiring, storing and processing data and exchanging them with their human operators, as well as the guides and reference information that humans need to specify what can be, should be or is done in these processes. Like food, software can be pre-packaged, constructed from ingredients or served where it is consumed. When it is pre-packaged it is reasonable to think of it as a product, and when it is produced "to order" it may be thought of as a service. The nature of the market for software creation and exchange activities, and the technologies supporting these activities, are shaped by three fundamental issues: the nature of software as an economic commodity; the historical patterns of the division of labor involved in software creation; and distinctions in the design and use of software that define the nature of software markets.

---

[1] This chapter summarizes the key findings and policy implications of research conducted by SPRU and the WZB on the European software sectoral system of innovation. The research underlying this chapter was conducted by Luciana D'Adderio, Mark Lehrer and the author.

[2] See below for the derivation of this estimate.

These issues are introduced in the following three subsections (1.1 to 1.3) with the aim of identifying the interests that European stakeholders have in the evolution of the software industry. The remainder of the chapter is devoted to examining how these interests are being, or are likely to be, influenced by the evolution of the SSI peculiar to the software industry.

Unlike industries characterized by relatively stable configurations of actors and networks, the software SSI can best be understood in terms of interactions between the specific purposes for which software is created, the capabilities for fulfilling these purposes, and the means for commercializing the results. These elements of the software SSI are associated with specific actors. However, these actors' roles are malleable: the purposes that software innovations fulfill and the capabilities that they employ, as well as the means by which these innovations may be commercialized, have shifted dramatically in the industry's evolution and are likely to do so again in the future. This instability in the software SSI has a fundamental influence on the strategies of companies that have their principal revenues derived from the sale of software products. This instability is also the principal reason why it is particularly difficult to develop an effective technology policy for the industry, and it further explains the centrality of intellectual property rights in the policy agenda of the dominant actors.

The subsequent sections of this chapter, therefore, are organized around the purposes of software production (section 2), the development of capabilities for meeting these purposes (section 3) and the means for commercializing the results of software creation (section 4). These sections are followed by a conclusion that distills some of the key responses that European stakeholders, including the policy-making community, might choose to make to strengthen European software performance.

## 1.1    *Software as an economic commodity*

Economic production involves the output of many goods and services that never pass through a market.[3] The creation of the class of economic commodities called "software" is a relatively recent development. Until the late 1960s computer manufacturers or users, or those offering specific services employing computers (such as payroll accounting services), produced the computer instructions needed to make use of computers – i.e.

---

[3] For example, much of the production that occurs within households, such as home-cooked meals or home repairs, is recorded in national income accounts only as the consumption of the materials for delivering these services. When restaurants or building contractors produce these services for payment, the value added by the chef or carpenter is recorded as well.

software. In all of these cases the value of the software was never separately recorded, nor was it "sold" as a commodity.

Three significant events supported software becoming a traded commodity. First, the complexity and cost of software development for IBM's System 360, as well as continuing US and European government concerns about IBM's dominant position in the computer industry, led IBM to "unbundle" software from its sale and lease of computer systems in 1968.[4] This development supported the creation of the independent software vendors (ISVs) and the development of software as a commodity "product" the use of which was, for the most part, governed by licensing agreements providing users with the right to utilize the software with specific computer hardware in return for a periodic or subscription charge.[5]

The second event was the failure of time-sharing as the dominant method for providing "user-centered" computing services in the 1968–74 period. Among other things, time sharing was a means to deliver software as a service rather than as a component for the user to assemble into a system.[6] Instead of choosing a delivered service involving access to large systems, users in scientific and academic environments chose to adopt minicomputer systems for "on-line" problem-solving activities and real-time instrumentation of scientific or engineering projects. The minicomputer market grew significantly throughout the 1970s, providing further market opportunities for ISVs. The failure of time-sharing to achieve a dominant position in the computer applications market prevented the reabsorption of software production and maintenance activities by time-sharing service companies that, otherwise, would have commanded a major share of resources for software development. In recent times the time-sharing model for software and service delivery has re-emerged with Internet-based application service providers and Internet computation centres, repeating some of the features of the time-sharing era.[7]

---

[4] See Steinmueller (1996) for a more detailed history of these developments and citations to the relevant literature.

[5] It is now a difficult problem in technological history to reconstruct the forms in which early software was distributed, although a significant amount of software in this period was distributed with commented source code. At the same time, there was widespread knowledge of the holdings and configurations of the existing computer stock. This, along with the distribution of frequent maintenance revisions of software, strongly encouraged computer users to enter into a licensing arrangement for the use of software.

[6] Time-sharing also provided a means of "distributing" the acquisition and reporting of data to local terminals. While unsuccessful as a general-purpose service, time-sharing provided the platform for important new service industries, such as airline reservation systems.

[7] One of the critical problems for early time-sharing systems was servicing multiple user sessions, which produced uneven processing demands. The high costs of central processing and memory required the use of "virtual" memory in which portions of software

The third event was the emergence of the personal computer as a stand-alone information processing and multimedia platform and as the dominant user terminal for distributed computing applications. The PC provided the first mass-market "platform" for software applications – an opportunity that was exploited by the creation of the packaged software market. Compared to earlier software distribution models, the packaged software market made computer software a full-fledged "product." Although packaged software still involves licensing provisions similar to the software provided by ISVs, the principal legal mechanism for its protection from software piracy is the use of copyright – a form of IPR protection that was previously an adjunct to the "appropriability" conditions accompanying the licensing regime.[8]

Over a twenty-year period the market size for packaged software has grown at a rapid and sustained pace. Global sales of packaged software in 2000 were estimated at $175 billion by IDC, a leading market research firm (*Business Week*, 2001). It is important to emphasize, however, that the purchase of software is only one component in the delivery of information processing services. In addition to the obvious requirement to purchase hardware that can be utilized by the software, the customization and integration of software involves large additional investments. Moreover, a substantial amount of software continues to be produced internally – a subject examined in the next section (section 2). Table 6.3 in section 2 details the investment in software products by country for the European Union. The total EU market for software products amounts to €47.9 billion, or about one-quarter of world demand.

It is commonly maintained that Europe plays a larger role in the consumption than in the production of software. This contention reflects the dominant position of US producers in the packaged software market, particularly in the leading operating systems and user applications for personal computers. It is important to emphasize several features of this position from a European perspective. First, companies make investments in customizing and adapting packaged software to make workable information processing systems and "outsource" consulting, implementation, operations management and maintenance activities to other companies, often European – an issue considered in more detail in section 2.

---

code were written to hard disks or other mass storage devices, creating delays familiar to contemporary users of PCs based on Microsoft Windows who attempt multi-tasking without sufficient computer memory.

[8] Source code, which is annotated and formatted in ways meant to make its logical structure plain, is compiled into "object" code, which, although mathematically equivalent to the source code, is essentially unreadable by humans. With most packaged software, copyright is buttressed by the retention of the "source" code as a commercial secret.

Second, in most cases the use of software is not an end in itself but is an intermediate process involved in the production of added value. The availability of packaged software, sometimes referred to as commercial off-the-shelf (COTS) software, may substantially reduce the investment in software, allowing companies to devote their resources to other investments that may contribute to their commercial success and are at least as important as the production of their own software.

Third, packaged software is used in the production of "content" and business data – intangible assets with substantial value the production of which is only partially recorded in national income statistics. The value of these assets, as well as the value of the software and software-related services produced internally by companies, does not appear in national income balance sheets.

In short, the market valuation of software as a commodity is partial and complementary to other investments, and is an input to the production of products and services in which Europeans have vital interests. To understand European participation in software markets it is therefore necessary to consider, but also to go beyond, an analysis of the US dominance of packaged software markets.

Limitations in publicly available data make the determination of a European market share in the packaged software industry extremely difficult. A major reason for this is that there is little reason for international shipments of software "packages" because the local reproduction of electronic media and the printing of manuals and manufacture of packaging materials are more efficient logistical solutions than attempting to replenish local inventories with international shipments. The consequence is that European affiliates or distributors receive the revenues from the sales of packaged software products that were originally designed by US producers. There are two approaches to resolving this accounting problem. The first is to combine the revenues of software producers by their national headquarters. This approach encounters two difficulties. The first is that companies may not report revenues by geographic market.[9] The second is that publicly available lists of software companies are incomplete; differences in the size distribution of software companies between countries may lead to the under-counting of small and medium-sized firms.

A second approach to estimating international market share is to examine the international flow of licensing fees associated with software. The US Department of Commerce reports fragmentary data on these flows,

---

[9] They may not report sales publicly at all. A significant number of software companies are not organized as corporations.

which, with heroic assumptions, suggest a rough estimate of international market shares. Table 6.1 summarizes the method and estimates for 1999. The reported data are for the regional distribution of total receipts of royalties and license fees for "other" intellectual property from unaffiliated organizations.[10] A footnote to the source table provides the global receipts for the rights to use and distribute software ($3.7 billion in receipts to US companies from unaffiliated foreign companies and $0.5 billion payments by US companies to unaffiliated foreign companies),[11] and it is on this footnote that the entire estimation rests. The first heroic assumption is to distribute these software rights receipts according to the regional distribution of *all* intellectual property receipts in order to provide a regional distribution of receipts. The second heroic assumption is to attribute the same share of software royalty and license fees to the total receipts recorded for all types of royalty and license income from foreign affiliates of US companies. This is accomplished by assuming that the share of "other" in total receipts is the same for affiliated as for unaffiliated (the second column in the table) and then weighting these by the shares of total receipts in each region (which *are* reported).[12]

Although elaborate, the estimation basically reproduces the relative shares of receipts by a) US companies from European companies and b) European companies from US companies for the rights to use and distribute software (shares of 88 percent and 12 percent respectively). After attribution, the resulting levels are $6.585 billion and $1.151 billion – shares of 85 percent and 15 percent respectively. These results are limited to trade related to software rights compensation between the United States and Europe. Although global US receipts are tabulated, the receipts of European firms from other parts of the world are not. The estimate is, therefore, an underestimate of the share of European companies in global packaged software markets.

The final point to make about these estimates is that the amount accruing to US firms as a share of total sales is less than 15 percent of the total revenues from European software sales. Although some part of the remainder may be accounted for by directly repatriated profits to US companies from foreign affiliates, it is unlikely that this is a major channel, since such profits would be taxed at source in Europe. Thus, although

---

[10] The table separately accounts for royalties and license fees for industrial processes; books, records and tapes; the broadcasting and recording of live events; franchise fees; and trademarks.

[11] The receipts of US affiliates from their foreign parents and the payments of foreign parents to their US affiliates are ignored in this estimation.

[12] The "rest of the world" is computed arithmetically as a residual since not all other regions have reported totals.

Table 6.1 *Indicators of software trade: 1999 (millions of dollars)*

### Unaffiliated payments to US companies

Total "other" receipts for royalties and license fees

| World total (all types) | 10,160 |
|---|---|

| | World | Europe | Asia/Pacific | Rest of the world |
|---|---|---|---|---|
| | 4,214 | 1,743 | 1,552 | 919 |

US receipts for the rights to use and distribute software

| | World | Europe | Asia/Pacific | Rest of the world |
|---|---|---|---|---|
| World total | 3,700 | 1,530 | 1,363 | 807 |

### US foreign affiliates to US parents

Attributed total receipts for "other" royalties and license fees

| World total (all types) | 24,576 |
|---|---|

| | World | Europe | Asia/Pacific | Rest of the world |
|---|---|---|---|---|
| | 10,193 | 5,757 | 2,428 | 2,008 |

Attributed US receipts for the rights to use and distribute software

| | World | Europe | Asia/Pacific | Rest of the world |
|---|---|---|---|---|
| World total | 8,950 | 5,055 | 2,132 | 1,763 |

### Unaffiliated payments of US companies to foreign companies

Total "other" payments for royalties and license fees

| World total (all types) | 3,067 |
|---|---|

| | World | Europe | Asia/Pacific | Rest of the world |
|---|---|---|---|---|
| | 651 | 469 | 32 | 150 |

US payments for the rights to use and distribute software

| | World | Europe | Asia/Pacific | Rest of the world |
|---|---|---|---|---|
| World total | 500 | 360 | 25 | 115 |

### US foreign affiliates to foreign parents

Attributed total payments for royalties and license fees

| World total (all types) | 8,074 |
|---|---|

| | World | Europe | Asia/Pacific | Rest of the world |
|---|---|---|---|---|
| | 1,714 | 1,030 | 533 | 151 |

US payments for the rights to use and distribute software

| | World | Europe | Asia/Pacific | Rest of the world |
|---|---|---|---|---|
| World total | 1,316 | 791 | 409 | 116 |

Note: Figures in italics are calculated arithmetically to complete the world total. Figures in italics and bold are "attributed" based upon the share of US receipts for the rights to use and distribute software from unaffiliated companies in total receipts or payments.
Source: US Department of Commerce, 2000.

US packaged software producers appear to have a very high share of the market relative to European firms, up to 80 percent of their European turnover is likely to remain in Europe as payments to distributors and retailers, advertising agencies and other local companies.

Although packaged software is clearly a significant market, it is important to emphasize that the division of labor related to software production and to the use of software involves ancillary services. This is the subject of the next subsection (1.2).

### 1.2    *The division of labor in software creation*

The vast majority of software authors work for companies that have no interest in marketing software products. Instead, the software that these authors write will be used to support their employer's business operations. Torrisi (1999) reports IDC estimates that internally produced software may account for 60 percent of software expenditures in the largest European markets. Existing statistical measures do not provide a comparable Europe-wide estimate of the number of individuals whose employment involves writing software. Indeed, making such an estimate is becoming increasingly difficult because of the extent to which commonly used software, such as spreadsheet or World Wide Web content creation software, allow the user to record computer instructions as well as data.

Nonetheless, it is possible to establish a lower bound on the size of this employment by examining the employment classifications of individuals in Europe. Table 6.2 provides such an estimate. This table counts the number of individuals whose jobs are in the categories of computing professionals or computing associate professionals. Significant inter-country differences exist in the classification of individuals in these two categories, and it is appropriate in reaching an approximate total to consider the sum of both categories. Although many of the individuals accounted for by this table are engaged in producing software, there are clearly some whose responsibilities do not involve such engagement. However, other professional categories, such as engineers and engineering technicians, are ignored even though some share of the individuals in these professions is engaged in software production. It therefore seems reasonable to conclude that a *lower bound* for the number of individuals engaged in software production is 2 million. This represents approximately 1.35 percent of total European Union employment, as mentioned earlier.

Many of these individuals are engaged in the development of organization-specific software products as well as in the substantial tasks of adapting and extending packaged software products to create information and information processing resources that are useful to their organizations. Packaged software can therefore be seen as one input into a

Table 6.2 *Employees in software-related professions*

| Country | Computing professionals | Computing associate professionals |
|---|---|---|
| Austria | 12,031 | 39,073 |
| Belgium | 59,387 | 4,076 |
| Denmark | 33,735 | 20,056 |
| Finland | 38,081 | 10,893 |
| France | 234,456 | 119,692 |
| Germany | 247,702 | 220,642 |
| Greece | 4,569 | 6,474 |
| Ireland | *19,000* | *17,500* |
| Italy | 11,963 | 171,448 |
| Luxembourg | 2,084 | 1,137 |
| Netherlands | 109,926 | 101,413 |
| Portugal | *23,000* | 23,424 |
| Spain | 69,947 | 5,687 |
| Sweden | 75,881 | 24,474 |
| United Kingdom | *175,891* | *118,858* |
| Europe | 1,117,653 | 884,847 |
| Total | Approximately 2 million | |

Note: Figures in italics are crudely estimated by the author based upon relative shares of these categories in the employed labor force of France and Germany. Other estimates are from the Eurostat Community Labor Survey, as cited in Millar and Jagger (2001).

more complex process that employs a very substantial number of Europeans. One of the key issues is the potential for the level or nature of this employment to change over time as companies adopt "generic" packaged software products as a foundation for their internal information system development efforts. At present the effects of this trend, which is gathering momentum, are unknown.

The other important development in the division of labor in software production involves the outsourcing of activities related to software creation, implementation and maintenance. These activities are recorded as business services and include analysis, planning and problem-solving activities as well as software creation. Table 6.3 shows the distribution of revenues by country and type of activity along with the revenues from system and application software.[13]

[13] System software controls the computational, storage and other resources of the computer. It can be used directly by the user for certain purposes, but is most heavily used by application programs, such as Microsoft Windows. Application programs are used to create and process data resources as well as perform computations under the user's direction – e.g. word processing or spreadsheets. An additional category of software, middleware, serves to extend the operating system to provide additional capabilities, such as software for controlling local area networks or World Wide Web browsers.

Table 6.3 *European market for software products and services: 2000 (millions of euros)*

| | System software | Application software | Total software products | Consulting | Implementation | Operations management | Support services | Total IT services | Total software products and IT services |
|---|---|---|---|---|---|---|---|---|---|
| Austria | 486 | 471 | 957 | 173 | 559 | 630 | 372 | 1,734 | 2,691 |
| Belgium/ Luxembourg | 989 | 822 | 1,811 | 189 | 1,029 | 263 | 680 | 2,161 | 3,972 |
| Denmark | 439 | 423 | 862 | 253 | 911 | 579 | 454 | 2,197 | 3,059 |
| Finland | 260 | 305 | 565 | 195 | 541 | 297 | 292 | 1,325 | 1,890 |
| France | 3,338 | 3,642 | 6,980 | 2,404 | 6,560 | 8,233 | 3,983 | 21,180 | 28,160 |
| Germany | 6,164 | 8,424 | 14,588 | 1,827 | 6,383 | 4,511 | 2,777 | 15,498 | 30,086 |
| Greece | 72 | 90 | 162 | 36 | 119 | 128 | 77 | 360 | 522 |
| Ireland | 121 | 99 | 220 | 37 | 124 | 144 | 76 | 381 | 601 |
| Italy | 2,065 | 1,545 | 3,610 | 711 | 2,276 | 3,643 | 1,908 | 8,538 | 12,148 |
| Netherlands | 1,637 | 1,474 | 3,111 | 421 | 1,603 | 804 | 812 | 3,640 | 6,751 |
| Norway | 392 | 362 | 754 | 233 | 793 | 465 | 343 | 1,834 | 2,588 |
| Portugal | 127 | 96 | 223 | 44 | 133 | 167 | 98 | 442 | 665 |
| Spain | 994 | 439 | 1,433 | 361 | 1,031 | 1,241 | 847 | 3,480 | 4,913 |
| Sweden | 603 | 645 | 1,248 | 461 | 2,120 | 972 | 847 | 4,400 | 5,648 |
| United Kingdom | 5,738 | 5,614 | 11,352 | 1,901 | 6,016 | 6,305 | 3,584 | 17,806 | 29,158 |
| EU total | 23,425 | 24,451 | 47,876 | 9,246 | 30,198 | 28,382 | 17,150 | 84,976 | 132,852 |

Note: The EU totals are computed from country totals and do not exactly agree with the source summary table.
Source: EITO, 2001, pp. 459–474.

As the table shows, IT service activities are about 80 percent larger than the direct investment in software products. The relation between packaged software use and the consumption of IT-related business services is very tight. The correlation between expenditure on software and on IT-related business services is 0.95. There is no basis for assigning a "causal" relationship between software purchases and IT-related business services. However, for the purposes of illustration, the simple regression of business service revenue on software investment indicated by the values in table 6.3 yields a "multiplier" of 2.36; i.e. expenditure of one additional euro on software is associated with €2.36 of expenditure on IT-related business services.[14]

In sum, the division of labor in the production of software is complex. A substantial market for packaged software has emerged, in which US firms have a dominant share. At the same time, however, European firms benefit from the availability of this packaged software, which reduces the investment costs in creating specialized applications. In addition, software creation activities, including both custom software creation and the adaptation and extension of packaged software, account for at least 2 million European jobs. The activities associated with IT consulting, information system implementation, operations management and support services generate revenues 80 percent larger than the expenditures on software. All of these jobs and revenues are associated with software development and application. At the same time, however, software is a component in information system development and application; it is no less or more "essential" than the computers or supporting services that are necessary for the creation, adaptation, maintenance and use of information resources and services.

The final set of distinctions needed to understand the software "industry" or "sector" of the economy are related to the different types of software – the subject of the next subsection (1.3).

## 1.3   *The design and use of software*

Software is used for many different purposes. Traditionally, a distinction has been made between software that controls the operations of the computer system, and provides the "platform" upon which other functionalities can be constructed, and the software employing these functionalities.[15] This distinction serves to define operating system software and

---

[14] This regression explains 90 percent of the inter-country variance between the variables, and the statistical significance of the multiplier is very high ($t = 11$).

[15] Examples of these functionalities include the receipt of keystrokes from the keyboard, movements of pointing devices such as the "mouse" and the display of characters or cursor movements on the computer display.

application software respectively. The boundary between operating system and application software has become less distinct over time, however. For example, although the majority of PCs are based upon the WINTEL "standard" (a Microsoft Windows operating system and a microprocessor based on Intel architectural specifications), most of these contain a heterogeneous collection of "peripheral devices" – graphics, sound and communication "cards" – that enhance the resources that are controlled by extensions to the operating system. Similar complexities have long been present in the case of minicomputer and mainframe systems. They constitute a major challenge for the design of their operating systems.

For PC operating systems, what is part of the operating system and what is an "application" are design decisions. For example, at present Microsoft has chosen to define its Windows operating system to include only rather basic functionalities for creating text (WordPad) or managing calculations (Calculator). There is no technical reason why Microsoft's operating system product could not include the complete functionality of Microsoft Office (the suite of "application software" including Word, Excel, PowerPoint, Outlook and Access). The considerable controversy generated by Microsoft's incorporation of WWW "browser" technology in its Windows operating system was based upon claims of Microsoft's abuse of its dominant market position rather than any "natural" division between operating system and application software.

This observation of the mutability of the boundary between operating system and application software is the opening for two fundamental insights into the process of software design definition. The first is the dynamic between "inward" and "outward" integration of software functions. Producers of system level software have an incentive to move closer – "upward" – to the user interface in order to reach markets that would otherwise be served by distinct software products. In response to this, and in order to preserve their product differentiation, software designers who produce "application" software, or other software that is closer to the user interface, have an incentive to move closer to the definition of system resources – i.e. "downward." These countervailing pressures are depicted in figure 6.1. The processes influencing the outcomes of these tendencies are examined further in sections 2 and 3.

The other insight into the design of software is the extent to which any particular software "artifact" (packaged or custom-designed software) is systemically integrated with other software to produce a larger "software system." At the simplest level, this distinction arises from the fact that any particular software often produces outputs that become inputs into other software. For example, word-processing software allows the user to produce text that may be an input to an editor who produces

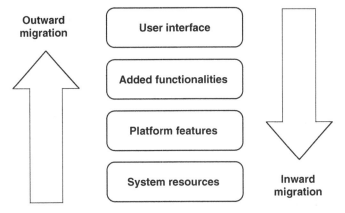

Figure 6.1  Inward and outward migration of software design

WWW pages or a dictionary. Similarly, the same word-processing package may accept inputs from other software, such as an e-mail program, for further elaboration by the user. The process of integrating individual software "modules" into software systems involves a contest between the "horizontal" integration of software functionalities and the advantages of specialization in performing a particular information-processing function. Thus, for example, users are likely to find it desirable to be able to format the output from a database program to allow it to be an input into a spreadsheet program. These systemic interdependencies between software programs can be coordinated across firm boundaries by the existence of de facto or *de jure* standards with regard to information representation.[16] Alternatively, a single firm may attempt to "bundle" together several of the possible interdependencies in a single product – e.g. a word processor that produces WWW pages and has its own dictionary.

Almost all software that involves the user in the creation of symbolic representations, such as formatted text or other forms of data, is subject to this tension between horizontal integration and specialization. However, there are at least three classes of software in which this tension is not as significant. The first is multimedia software. Multimedia software, such as games or educational software, employs the user interface and system resources to create an interactive environment for the user that either does not involve the creation of significant amounts of data or involves data creation that is not relevant to other software products. The second is embedded software. Embedded software, which is used for the real-time

---

[16] See David and Greenstein (1990) for an introduction to the economics of standards.

control of electronic or electromechanical systems, often accepts instructions from users, but is principally dedicated to its control purposes.[17] The third class of software, in which the tensions between horizontal integration and specialization are diminished, is scientific software: software that is designed for automating either the operation or recordings of scientific apparatus. In each of these three classes of software it is the relative specialization of the software that reduces the incentives to integrate the software, either horizontally or vertically, in other software packages. Each of these three areas is important for European software products. A current development of considerable interest in the European context is the possibility that embedded software may become more influenced by the pressures between vertical migration and horizontal integration in the near future – a development that is examined in section 3.2.

In short, the "vertical" tension affecting whether operating system software encompasses particular applications or application software defines system resources and functionality is an economically relevant design dynamic in the software industry. A second such design dynamic involves the "horizontal" coordination tensions governing the transfer of data between software programs. There is a trade-off, although it is difficult to predict *ex ante*, between the risk of new product introduction and the extent of its vertical migration and horizontal integration. These dynamics are particularly important for the major commercial markets involved in enterprise resource planning (ERP) software (see section 2.3) and the less commercially significant but nonetheless important market represented by open-source software (section 4.3).

The distinctions that have been introduced in this first section provide a foundation for an analysis of the processes of software design and innovation. The discussions of software as an economic commodity (1.1) and the design and use of software (1.3) are extended to provide an analysis of the purposes of software production in section 2. The development of capabilities for meeting these purposes, which draws upon the preceding discussion of the division of labor in the industry, is examined in section 3. Section 4 analyzes the means for commercializing the results of software creation commenting on the interactions between intellectual property rights, the changing software distribution system, and elements of the software SSI identified in the previous two sections. The final section summarizes and distills some of the insights that are relevant to public policy and company strategy.

---

[17] There are some cases where such real-time software is more complex. For example, in the case of laboratory instrumentation, embedded software may produce a stream of data that can serve as input into other programs or as a "feedback loop" for the operation of the instrumentation.

## 2 Creating software: for profit, out of necessity and for fun

The motives for creating software and the purposes for which it is created differ among the actors that are involved in the software industry. A useful way to analyze the interaction between the actors involved in software innovation is to view them as being bound together in a sectoral system of innovation (Malerba, chapter 1 in this book; and Edquist, 1997). The SSI approach indicates the need to identify all the actors contributing to relevant industrial knowledge development.

Like the "innovation studies" viewpoint, which preceded it and coexists with it, the SSI approach emphasizes the role of innovation performance in economic performance. The added value of the SSI is its emphasis on elaborating the role of systemic relationships in the flow of knowledge related to innovation. In particular, product innovations are likely to benefit from a strengthening of user-producer relationships, improvements in the capacities of public research institutions (including universities) to interact effectively with industry, and the emergence of effective inter-firm or "network" cooperation within an industry. Unfortunately, none of these mechanisms operates with any degree of reliability or stability in the software industry; their contribution is episodic and transient. This suggests that one of two alternative conclusions must hold: either the software industry has an incoherent SSI; or its system of innovation has a deeper structure that, once delineated, can provide a meaningful interpretation of the division of innovative labor in software creation. The contention of this chapter is that the latter is the correct conclusion.

Taking a sectoral approach to innovation highlights the difficulty of constructing stable knowledge-generation processes in industries such as software, where technological change involves the integration of many different types of knowledge from many different sources. In addition, the existence of well-defined technological trajectories is relatively rare in the software industry – a condition that serves to disperse rather than concentrate knowledge-generation activities. One outcome that addresses these problems is the creation of a monopolistic or oligopolistic industry in which larger actors can coordinate the integration process. This structure, however, raises concerns about pricing, the further extension of market control and the rate of innovation. The software industry is strongly influenced by the logic of "modularization," where innovative labor can be divided to take advantage of gains from specialization. The problem is that such a "modular" division of labor is vulnerable to non-cooperative strategies in constructing the interfaces between modules, and to the processes of vertical migration and horizontal integration introduced in the previous section (1.3). Non-cooperative strategies raise rivals' costs and may deter some types of small-scale entry, while the migration and integration processes threaten to absorb the process of variety generation and curtail the creation of new "modules" by independent actors.

These conditions of complex knowledge creation, the possibilities for the reabsorption of variety generation and generators, and the absence of the technological coordination mechanisms provided by stable technological trajectories simultaneously heighten the desirability and frustrate the emergence of a stable software SSI. This section examines the coexistent and coevolving structures supporting software innovation, one based upon the creation of global packaged software products, the other based on user-driven innovation. A conclusion of this section is that the incommensurability of these two SIS is a primary reason for the seeming incoherence of software innovation and the problems of crafting appropriate public policy supporting software innovation.

Viewing software as a "product" and, specifically, packaged software as the unit of industrial analysis emphasizes the current configuration of the international software industry, despite the apparent and dramatic differences in how this industry is organized in different countries.[18] To remedy this problem, it is appropriate to distinguish between *global* software products – generic software that can be localized through alterations in the user interface – and specialized or *situated* software, which is relevant only to a limited number of applications. By making this distinction it is possible to focus upon the user needs that define the demand for both types of software solution and to examine the alternatives available for the supply of these solutions. A possible problem with this approach is that it could obscure supplier innovations, leading to software for which users had no previous need or desire – i.e. innovation-induced demand. The historical record indicates that these innovations have been created by both large and small organizations, and in contexts of seeking a global product as well as solving situated software development problems.[19] It is, however, a relevant question whether larger organizations will, over time, become more dominant sources of fundamental innovations. This has not yet occurred. The issue is examined in more detail in the following section (2.1), where it is argued that larger organizations with a more global view may have or may develop an advantage in improving the "process" of software design.

---

[18] The studies collected in Mowery (1996) provide some indication of this diversity.

[19] For example, Xerox, a large company, developed the metaphor of windows and icons that plays an essential role in modern user interfaces in its Palo Alto research center. At the other end of the spectrum, Dan Bricklin created the idea for spreadsheet software while a student at business school and formed a new company to commercialize the innovation.

The "user-driven" approach to analyzing software creation activities refocuses attention on software as "tools" – tools that users employ to accumulate information and knowledge resources. Although the global versus situated distinction is still relevant in a user-driven approach, the principal unit of analysis is the software system as it is deployed as a resource for solutions to information-processing problems in the company. The two types of software are components in this larger system. The contention of the following subsections (2.1–2.3) is that both the global versus situated and user-driven approaches are useful for understanding the incentives governing software creation and the processes of innovation responsible for improvements in software design.

## 2.1    The global software product company

The global approach to software product design involves a search for "generic" solutions to information-processing problems: solutions that immediately meet user needs or that can be easily adapted to the specific needs of users. These software needs would otherwise have to be met through the design of customized software solutions, often produced internally to the user firm. For example, successful "generic" manufacturing accounting systems must provide capabilities for modeling specific production processes in order to assess accurately the value of the "work in process" inventory. Innovative "steps" are required to produce such generic solutions.

These innovative steps, however, are essentially ones involving design or vision. They cannot be accurately described within the framework of "technological trajectories," in which a limited set of parameters provides a focusing device for technological progress, or a "paradigm" (Dosi, 1982, 1988). Paradoxically, however, these design or vision innovations are often incremental in the sense that they build upon experience. Much of the knowledge relevant for innovation is derived from experience in attempting to address user needs and from the examination of designs produced by competitors. Ironically, much, if not all, of the knowledge needed to produce generic products arises from situated and specialized experience, while the innovative steps required involve the capacity to create conceptual generalizations from this experience.

The preceding analysis of *product* innovation in the software industry suggests that the SSI approach has a rather limited role in explaining innovative and market performance. The absence of systematic means for articulating a division of innovative labor or for achieving the lasting appropriation of new product ideas reduces the significance of systematic approaches to knowledge generation and distribution. A deeper analysis, however, reveals that applying the SSI approach to *process* innovation is very relevant to explaining innovative and market performance.

The process of software design involves the simultaneous definition of how information will be represented for the user and for the computer system and the aims that the software will fulfill in recording, processing, storing and outputting information. With these definitions, it is possible to devise either a generic software solution or one that is highly situated or idiosyncratic to a particular application need.

A remarkable feature of the computer as an information-processing device is the diversity of expression that it enables. As all programmers know, this is both a blessing and a curse. Hopefully outperforming the performance of the million monkeys typing randomly at keyboards, programmers attempt to manage the complexity of implementing the definitions they are given, or devise, by attending to every detail without lapsing into the errors of logic that lead to software bugs and crashes. The process of writing software code is subject to process improvement at several levels: programmers may use tools that make it more difficult to make errors; they may engage in a more "structured" process of planning for implementation that reduces the number of false starts and dead ends in the process; and they may devise software so that it can be tested in the process of its creation. These three levels of software improvement have been embodied in a collection of software tools and organizational routines that are broadly employed, both by commercial software companies and by professional programmers working to produce software internally within companies. The process technology for producing software is commonly available to all participants. Most of the tools for using these process technologies are either affordable or can be approximated with somewhat less productive and cheaper substitutes. Thus, it cannot be said that the deployment of software development tools, of itself, creates an advantage for larger or incumbent firms.

What distinguishes the global software product is the scale and complexity of the initial software design, which is one of the consequences of the competitive structure responsible for such packaged software products. This structure has three elements.[20] The first is that the global packaged software product needs to appeal to the largest possible number of users. Its designers therefore strive to include all of the features that a user might want. This element serves the dual purpose of attracting users and discouraging rivals. The leading firm or firms will imitate any features that rivals attempt to add and the leaders' growing revenues will support an ever larger and more complex development effort.

---

[20] Although the interpretation of these elements is different in this study, similar elements are the basis for Shapiro and Varian's (1998) analysis of "winner takes all" markets.

The second element, which emerged during the evolution of the packaged software market, is proprietary standards for information representation.[21] As noted earlier, a considerable share of software is used to produce information resources for individuals and organizations. The software is responsible for managing the input, storage and display of information that the user seeks to retain or to gather for some sort of information processing. If this information can be used only by the software used to record it, the company producing that software gains a market advantage over its rivals, who might otherwise produce competing tools for modifying or adding value to the user's data.

A third element is the accumulation of substantial numbers of individuals with skills in the use of specific software packages. This element is a consequence of the success of the preceding two elements of the competitive structure governing packaged software. Because of the complexity of software that is designed to meet the largest possible number of user needs, and the need to revise this software periodically to refresh the proprietary nature of the software's information representation, a degree of skill and expertise becomes necessary. The economies of training, instructional materials and user support favor the leading software. These skills and expertise are also validated by the labor market, which begins to include a specification of particular skills in job listings, which, in turn, encourages the accumulation of specific skills.

These three elements provide a strong "virtuous" circle supporting the dominance of the leading packaged software products. Achieving an early lead and endowed with a large domestic market, US companies have benefited from this dynamic competitive structure.

It is important to stress that these elements of the competitive structure are not necessarily the result of a specific strategy to raise rivals' costs and achieve a dominant position. They are consequences of the basic imperative of the global software product – a generic product that is meant to appeal to the largest possible number of users. Thus, for example, the creation of proprietary information representation can as easily be interpreted as a consequence of uncoordinated supply decisions as arising from strategic intent. The difficulties of achieving an industry standard for any particular type of information representation – i.e. achieving coordination – are substantial. The market outcome – proprietary information representation – creates social benefits, in the form of the rapid

---

[21] Although it is not possible to achieve a property right in "information representations," the complexity of these representations – coupled with the ability of their sponsors to revise their definition at will by creating new versions of software – serves to raise rivals' costs and discourage the creation of substitutes. This is nearly the same outcome that would obtain if they were granted intellectual property protection.

development of innovative ideas, as well as social costs in the creation of market power and incompatibilities between software products.

The implications of a global software product segment of the software industry are relatively straightforward. Innovation within this segment is organized around anticipating user needs. However, focusing on current user needs is likely to receive a lower priority than anticipating, or – better – constructing, the needs of individuals who are not currently users. Current users are to various degrees captured. While a policy of "doing no harm" to these users is appropriate, the focus of innovative efforts should be on individuals who could be converted into users. Innovative ideas for attracting new users may be created internally within companies with global software products, but these companies have no special comparative advantage in creating such ideas.[22]

The alternative sources of innovative ideas are the community of users who are producing software to meet their own needs and innovative smaller companies that are trying to establish a niche, based either on specialized competencies or on identifying and filling a "hole" in the larger system of software applications. Global software product companies, then, face a choice. Do they integrate the innovative idea in their own product or not? Many innovative software products may be too specialized to attract substantial numbers of new users and may be left to develop their market niche. With respect to innovative ideas that are believed to be attractive to substantial numbers of new users, the global software product company may either acquire the company or imitate the functionality of its products. Assimilation seems inevitable. When viewed in this light, the acquisition of these companies maintains the incentives for industrial innovation. This creates an interesting paradox for competition policy. While acquisition of innovative new entrant companies may reinforce the dominant position of the global software product company, suppression of such acquisition will provoke functional imitation by the dominant company, and this is likely to eliminate the market niche supporting the innovative entrant and the incentives for others to attempt innovation and entry.[23]

The competitive dynamics of the global software company also explain why some of the other features commonly associated with SSIs are absent

---

[22] This is obviously a strong contention, which would probably be challenged by representatives of such companies, and it is not offered here as being either self-evident or without the need for further research – such as an enumeration of the software innovations and their sources.

[23] Concerns about potential abuses of the dominant position must also be offset by the likelihood that the dominant company will be in a stronger position to develop and market the innovation.

in the case of software. There is no need for the dominant company to develop a "distributed system of innovation"; such a system already exists as the consequence of companies attempting to establish niche products with basic features that are observable and can be imitated. Similarly, public research institutions and university-based research are likely to provide interesting new ideas, but there is little need for intimate links with universities to extract and utilize these ideas. Universities are, in any case, likely to receive substantial funding from larger users who are interested in improving the productivity of software development. While these motives also apply to global software product companies, the development costs of these companies in relation to the value generated are likely to be seen as somewhat smaller than they are for companies that are crafting one-off implementations of complex software systems. In summary, and in other words, the absence of a structured sectoral innovation system in the software industry is compatible with the interests of the global software companies.

### 2.2    The alternative: out of necessity and for fun

An exclusive focus on global software product companies provides an incomplete picture of the software industry and its innovation system. The boundaries to the comparative advantage of the global software product company are set by the necessity of developing generic products. While it is true that these products may produce a revenue base supporting diversification into more specialized products and services, there may also be offsetting advantages available to individuals and companies developing non-generic software products.

While the definition of generic software products is very straightforward, devising a useful definition for non-generic or "situated" products is more complicated.[24] The aphorism "out of necessity and for fun" appears as the title of this subsection as a means of capturing the incentives governing the creation of these non-generic products. As documented earlier, many individuals are engaged in developing software for various "situated" and specialized purposes. Software is often called a "handicraft" industry because of the labor intensity of software creation. Individuals engaged in these efforts strive to improve their own and colleagues' productivity by developing tools and software subsystems. It is relatively common for these efforts to produce a potential innovation that can be commercialized with further development and marketing. Because of the

---

[24] Defining them as the residual is not very useful.

number of individuals engaged in similar activities, the potential market for such products is significant.

The main factors affecting the size of the "niches" that emerge from these activities are differences of opinion about and differences of effectiveness in what constitutes a good software solution for situated and specialized information-processing needs. Unlike generic products that attempt to provide a general-purpose solution, non-generic solutions are "situated" in the sense that alternative approaches may have compelling advantages in different contexts. When companies elect to produce their own software they are doing so because they believe (correctly or not) that the effectiveness of crafting their own solutions will be greater than the alternatives available to them. The same motives provide a basis for the existence of specialized software companies that thrive on making similar specific or situated innovations. The innovative products resulting from these processes can be thought of as arising from "necessity"; either the necessity of improving productivity or that of finding a niche not yet occupied by generic solutions.

While all the software production discussed so far has been motivated by serious business purposes, a substantial amount of software is written for scientific, educational or cultural purposes and simply for fun. All these reasons for writing software also represent potential business opportunities. For example, games software is a major business in its own right. Almost all of this software may be characterized as "stand-alone" software: its purpose is to transform the computer temporarily into a games console, interactive education appliance, etc. One may set the stage, animate the actors and organize the flow of software using standardized tools available to others. In this sense, writing software is very much like creating theatre (Laurel, 1993).

A final category of non-generic software is "embedded" software. Embedded software is written for the purposes of achieving the real-time control or programmability of consumer and producer goods that contain microprocessor-based control systems. In general, embedded software is designed in parallel with the artifact that it is meant to control, and these artifacts range from automobiles to musical greetings cards. The availability of components for extending control and providing hardware interfaces with the microprocessor has made such systems an attractive substitute for "dedicated" or "hard-wired" electronic control systems. Because embedded software is a case where the organization of software production is undergoing change, it is examined in section 3.2.

It is important not to underestimate the significance of non-generic software-creating activities. While a much greater amount of space could be devoted to enumerating these activities and describing their purposes, the structural features of these markets are quite similar. In each case the software is highly differentiated and the main problem is informing potential users of its existence and capabilities. The competitive feature of the markets for these products is that there are generally alternative products that are better suited to some users and applications, so that it is not possible to build these products into generic solutions of the type offered by global software products. Individual products such as games, accounting packages or mathematical workbenches may, nonetheless, be mass-market products, in the same way that some novels or films are broadly accepted. One of the most important dynamics shaping the future of these markets is the rise of new methods of distribution, and the Internet in particular – the subject of section 4.

### 2.3    The middle ground: middleware

Between the generic software product and the "stand-alone" generic product stands a small group of products of significant economic importance that share features of *both* the markets examined so far. These products are generic in the sense that they are designed to reach a large community of users, but they are also "situated" because their application involves a substantial amount of user specification and customization, often achieved with the aid of the vendor and external consultants. A term that encompasses most of the products offered in this group is integrated software solution (ISS). The ISS segment, in turn, contains several specific segments identified by the type of solution they offer; e.g. product data manager (PDM) and enterprise resource planning software. The revenues in this market segment are significant. For example, the worldwide PDM market grew by 27 percent to reach $1.4 billion in 1998, and has experienced double-digit percentage growth rates since it emerged in the early 1990s. This subsection (2.3) explains the competitive dynamics of the ISS segment, focusing on the PDM and ERP segments and their convergence, and examining the consequences for the major European participants in this market, such as SAP and Software AG.[25]

The ISS markets examined are exemplars of generic applications for situated problem-solving tasks and data recording and display. Both types of application (PDM and ERP) are an alternative to software systems that were commonly constructed internally by large firms. The creation of COTS products for addressing these applications has involved the design of a flexible and extensible architecture for data representation and display

---

[25] This section relies heavily on D'Adderio (2001).

as well as the capacity to integrate "modules" produced by specialized software firms. The addition of software modules to the basic architecture is necessary for addressing the industry-specific requirements of users. Leading firms in this market are engaged in assembling networks of supplier firms that are willing to provide modules that operate within the architecture sponsored by a specific individual leading firm. At present, the market is characterized by efforts to define standards that are particular to "groups" (the software architecture sponsor and its suppliers). User groups have argued that competing standards with substantial overlap should be combined, but they have not, as yet, found a way to enforce their preferences effectively.

As in the previous discussion of proprietary information representation standards (section 2.1), there are clear incentives for producers to sponsor proprietary standards in order to justify the costs of developing the coordinating architecture and negotiating with supplier firms for the co-development of industry-specific modules. A consequence of these incentives is that the market is quite concentrated, with SAP and Software AG engaged in vigorous competition with US firms such as Oracle and Microsoft.

The dynamics of competition in the ISS markets are particularly noteworthy. Unlike desktop productivity applications, such as word processing, ISS software is "middleware" (i.e. it occupies the position in the strata of software between the operating system and application packages). The use of ISS applications requires user-specific implementation, which is a complex process in which existing "legacy" databases as well as user interfaces must be integrated in the generic system offered by ISS suppliers. Because of its complexity the implementation cycle for ISS software is protracted, and the adoption of a particular ISS supplier represents a major commitment. As user firms move into the implementation cycle, the supplier is engaged in upgrading the software to attract new "commitments." Failing to upgrade the software would put the supplier at a competitive disadvantage, while upgrading the software adds substantially to the problems of support for earlier versions of the system. These frictions are a consequence of the "situated" nature of ISS products. The asynchronous timing of user adoption and implementation cycles is likely to dictate that this market continues to be concentrated, since only larger firms are likely to be able to maintain support across multiple generations of the product.

Until recently, the construction of the user interface for ISS software was a significant source of proprietary differentiation among the competing architectures and a major source of cost in the implementation process. The desire to address the needs of smaller firms as well as to provide large firms with the means to provide smaller suppliers with access to their systems has supported the development of WWW-based user interfaces for ISS software. It is too early to draw firm conclusions about the consequence of these developments. One speculation, however, is that this development will enlarge the potential market for new entrants at the architectural level to firms that offer strong Internet service capabilities, such as the application service providers.

A second issue regarding the ISS software market is the impact it is likely to have on European software service companies. Many of these companies, such as Cap Gemini Ernst Young, have built their business on facilitating the design, development and implementation of user-specific solutions using a combination of COTS and proprietary software (some of which is reused within the software service companies). The growing strength of COTS ISS solutions may threaten the continued health of these service companies, which constitute Europe's largest software firms (Torrisi, 1999). A principal determinant of the strength of competition of the ISS suppliers is the extent to which they can succeed in offering generic solutions that are able to deliver mission-critical solutions for users. This ability is likely to grow as a result of the adoption of Internet technology for the user interface, and to be constrained by the problems of adapting the generic architecture and specialist modules to specific user contexts.

The ISS market illustrates the difficulties of forming a coherent SSI in software. In principle, it would be useful to have a common standard for data objects that could serve all user needs and provide a basis for design competition among architecture suppliers. The specificity of user requirements and the incentives of the architecture integrators create major barriers to this "ideal" structure. These problems are not just "growing pains" due to the problems of engineering generic solutions but represent an effort to integrate the continuously evolving needs of heterogeneous users into a common structure that can support investment in unified development. While it is likely that the companies able to achieve this will be large because of the complexity of the task and the need to recruit a network of specialized suppliers, market position is likely to be unstable. As long as the market involves extensive growth (the addition of substantial numbers of new users), new entrants, or – more likely – new product offerings, may have the opportunity to gain a foothold. The market is still oriented toward this extensive growth in which new user recruitment is particularly important. This orientation is explained by the relatively high costs of changing suppliers during the implementation of ISS systems, which direct the attention of incumbent and new entrants alike to new users.

European firms do not appear to have specific disadvantages in the ISS market. Indeed, many of the ISS technical capabilities are similar to those that form the basis of European strength in the software services market and in constructing networks of suppliers cooperating with a larger system integrator. In this sense, the ISS market is an example of effective producer-user relationships, at least relative to other segments of the software industry. This market is, nonetheless, one in which US firms have achieved a strong position. Although the outcome of this competition remains uncertain, two issues may be influential.

First, several of the leading US firms (e.g. Microsoft and Oracle) have moved into this market as a means of exploiting their strong offerings in software packages developed for the COTS market. Developing the additional capabilities to define generic architectures and to recruit specialist suppliers has been supported by the revenues that these companies have derived from more limited COTS products. By contrast, European software service companies have continued to focus on supporting specific user needs with more highly customized software. One possible explanation for this development is that the larger European companies have been less willing to make the adaptations required for implementing "generic" ISS systems.

Second, the degree of enthusiasm of US users for extending the scope and pace of information systems has heightened their need for ISS systems. The early adoption of these systems therefore provides a first-mover advantage to the US companies that offer partial solutions to these problems. This explanation carries the ironic implication that ISS suppliers in the United States may benefit from the relatively chaotic conditions of domestic firms in the utilization of software systems. To the extent that European users have a more structured and organized approach to the implementation of ISS systems, they will delay the implementation of such systems in favor of internal development or software service companies that they have worked with for an extended period. This is a troubling situation, however, since the increasing adoption of COTS ISS by European firms does not suggest a long-term commitment to the existing structure, only a delay in moving toward COTS ISS that may be disadvantageous to European ISS suppliers.

In summary, the complex integration and implementation issues presented by ISS systems have favored the growth of large firms in which European firms are represented at both the system architecture and specialized supplier levels. Position in the ISS market is a mixture of stability and instability. Incumbents can rely upon firm commitments by users who elect to implement their systems because of the complexity and duration of the implementation process. Continuing extensive (new user) growth, however, may provide the basis for further concentration in the market, which could have the effect of enhancing the supplier networks for the leading products and supporting higher levels of development and promotion, to the disadvantage of some competitors. This complex competitive structure, which underlies the market performance of firms, is further complicated by the move toward Internet-based user interfaces, which enlarge the potential pool of competitors and may accelerate the pace of extensive growth (and its potential for instability). While European firms such as SAP and Software AG have been able to navigate these stormy seas, their future strength may depend in part upon the rate at which European users move away from software service companies and internally produced software toward COTS ISS systems or application service provider solutions.

At present, the scope of the SSI with regard to integrated software solutions is very limited. The leading integrator firms responsible for the architecture of ISS systems are large relative to other institutions that might produce knowledge in the field. Their needs are highly situated to their immediate experience and rely more heavily upon design than technical innovation. Their vitality depends upon the existence of industrial specialist firms. Only in this last area is there an opening for effective policy support in promoting the formation of new technically specialized small and medium-sized firms. More generally, the position and strategy of software service companies in Europe will have a major influence on the long-term evolution of this market and the role of European participants in it.

## 3  Innovative capabilities and organizations: configuring the software industry

The preceding section outlined the motives of many of the actors in the software sectoral system of innovation. This section dissects the process of technological change in software in order to identify the constraints and opportunities governing the behavior of these actors, as well as bringing into focus the contributions of universities and public research institutions.

### 3.1  The character of technological change in software

Technological change can be either incremental or radical – terms sometimes used to convey the potential for rapid technological advance. Both terms are, however, inadequate to encompass key features of technological change in many contemporary industries, including software, and from their respective association with "slow" and "rapid" change. The word "incremental" conveys, to most people, the idea that such technological change should be a stepwise and relatively gradual process. As Dosi (1988) indicates, however, this "common-sense" meaning is not accurate. What is meant, instead, is that incremental technological change is *cumulative*: current knowledge is an important input for further technological advance. Processes such as recombination extrapolation and metaphor play important roles in cumulative technological change, which are obscured by the term "incremental."

A second defect in conceptualization arising from the word "incremental" is the connotation that change is gradual. Except in certain narrow segments, such as numerical analysis software, it is difficult to identify clearly which changes in the software are gradual and which constitute significant "breaks" with past experience. At the same time, the apparent speed of change in software is considerable, as measured by the introduction of new products or significant new versions of existing products. For example, Microsoft introduces a new operating system about every eighteen months.[26] Moreover, there is little precision in the specification of *how* the contribution of current knowledge is relevant to further advance. Technical advance in software involves "threshold" effects, particularly when real-time processes are involved – for example in the case of embedded software (Steinmueller, 2001a).

The problems in characterizing technical change in software are well recognized in the industry. Many computer software producers, and particularly those involved in large internal software development projects, have, instead, focused on the productivity of programmers' efforts in the software creation process (Brooks, 1982). A complete examination of technical change in the software production process is outside the scope of this chapter.[27]

It is, however, useful to note the existence of research activities in this field that contribute to the goal of improving the productivity of software creation. The mission statement of the Software Engineering Institute (SEI) at Carnegie-Mellon University, an example of a university-based institute supported by industrial cooperation, illustrates this productivity improvement aim:

---

[26] While some might argue that the continuity of these operating systems has been high, there are clearly major discontinuities between the earlier MS-DOS-based Windows and the NT (New Technology) operating system.

[27] Boehm (1981) provides one starting point, albeit focusing on the problems of cost estimation and reduction rather than the technological methods of achieving the desired outcomes.

The Software Engineering Institute promotes the evolution of software engineering from an ad hoc, labor-intensive activity to a discipline that is well managed and supported by technology.[28]

Similar objectives are sought at several European research institutes, including the Gesellschaft für Mathematik und Datenverarbeitung (GMD) Forschungszentrum Informationstechnik, although European research institutions, both academic and public (and including the GMD), describe their mission as contributing to the advance of "cutting-edge" knowledge in computer software and its applications. There is a subtle, but important, difference between this mission and that of the SEI.

With the notable exception of efforts to improve the productivity of software, the sites of knowledge generation in the software industry are extremely dispersed among disciplines and organizations. As earlier noted (section 2.1), knowledge is gained through imitation and experimentation, in problem solving related to specific and situated bottlenecks or innovative ideas. It is also gained from basic research into computer science. An exclusive or even primary focus on the disciplinary research of computer science is likely to result only in sporadic contributions to the frontier of knowledge that is applied in practice. This is because the technological impetus to software innovation is closely bound to "complementarities" between different software components and between software and hardware. A predominant locus of innovation is the interface between these complementary components. At this locus, the source of knowledge advance is experiential and interactive as well as theoretical.

For example, what is known today about operating systems serves as an important input into the definition of new types of software. At the same time, the design and operation of application software make it clear that there are shortcomings in the design and implementation of current operating systems. This interaction between operating systems and application programs provides the experiential element for technological innovation. When such innovations are sought, current understandings of theory may be drawn upon for a solution, but theoretical understanding rarely provides either the impetus or a sufficient basis for making the innovation. The role of this interaction will be explored more deeply in subsection 3.3, which examines how the physical connection of networks stimulates innovation, and in subsection 3.4, which examines the role of user interfaces in innovation.

---

[28] Accessed at http://www.sei.cmu.edu/.

The interactive features of the software knowledge-generation process have generally frustrated efforts at systematization. It is, for example, very difficult to perform research in the university, or even in a large public research laboratory, on technologies that are highly interdependent and systemic in nature at a "full-scale" level. University research project cycles and publishing incentives are incompatible with research on large and highly situated systems because of the time required to develop such systems and the difficulties of deriving publishable generalizations from development experience. Public research institutions are constrained by the need to justify their existence to a number of different constituencies – a process that rarely is consistent with large-scale development efforts.

The same problems of systematization are one reason for the difficulties in internationalizing the sectoral system of innovation in software. A reflection on the Japanese experience in this context is useful (Leebaert, 1995, pp. 19–20):

A few years ago, many Americans were preoccupied with the challenge of Japan's software factories, expecting them to change the way the world's software is written just as Japan's automobile factories revolutionised manufacturing. After all, in every other industry Japan has first achieved high levels of production and then developed markedly better products. The trend toward industry-wide standards would help the Japanese push their software as series of broad-market products, rather than leaving it tied to exclusive operating systems. But the global software agenda is being defined by American companies, because they are the ones setting the standards . . .

Despite the dire predictions about the Japanese software threat, American companies remain the world's leaders as hardware prices spiral downward. In the United States there is clearly a strong trend toward software companies' setting the initiatives in the information technology industry. In brief, Japan, with its fragmented personal computer market, did not have a target to aim for in its software development. Japan had no prevailing standard, while the United States had DOS and the IBM PC. So the Japanese kept writing customised software for mainframes – a market in which a higher return on investment seemed a sure thing.

Technological change in software, even very far-reaching change, is often the consequence of local "fire-fighting" in large-scale development processes, where improvisation is necessary. For example, although it would certainly have been possible for university research on algorithmic structures to discover the advantages of RISCs (reduced instruction set computers), the initial RISC invention came about through empirical observation of the performance of existing computer systems aimed at widening bottlenecks in their performance. This is not to suggest that university research is irrelevant or that it need be a "backwater" in software innovation. It suggests only that it is very difficult to specify a useful division of labor between university and industry research – a feature that is particularly salient when examining the "embedded software" industry.

### 3.2     Embedded software: the potential for concentration in innovation activities

The preceding discussion indicates that innovation performance in the software industry is influenced by the prevalence of incremental change occurring in a complex systemic context in which there is rarely a well-specified "trajectory" of improvement. A specific case that is a major exception to this rule is embedded software. In the case of embedded software the need for quality, reliability and safety provides some "guide-posts" for the innovation process. The consequence is that the division of labor in the innovation process is observable in this segment. This division of labor, nonetheless, requires a degree of localization. In comparing the US and European SSIs in embedded software, Steinmueller (2001a) offers two findings of use in this context.[29]

First, a substantially higher level of university research effort on embedded software appears to be under way in the United States compared to Europe. Surprisingly, a higher level of activity in European government research institutions, which might compensate for the modest level of involvement by European universities, does not appear to be present.

Second, the creation of independent enterprises operating in the embedded software segment is markedly greater in the United States than in Europe. It is not possible to compare the relative levels of innovation investments of US and European producers of embedded software. What can be said, however, is that the United States has a more articulated division of labor in the embedded software segment. This is not necessarily a danger signal since, as in all software segments, there are trade-offs in coordinating software development between producers and users, as illustrated by the persistence of substantial internal software expenditure.

Steinmueller (2001a) suggests, however, that embedded software may be at the cusp of a major discontinuity that will offer further advantages to producers of generic systems for creating embedded software. This discontinuity is the result of growing needs for embedded software systems to demonstrate their reliability, which may be met only by a process of standardization – i.e. by creating a "generic" core to embedded

---

[29] Further important empirical research on the state of the European embedded software market may be found in Seppänen et al. (1996).

software.[30] If this is an accurate surmise, all but the largest of European firms may have difficulty in maintaining effective internal efforts for developing embedded software.

### 3.3    *The impetus of network computing for software innovation*

Major new "platforms" for software produce technological challenges that are met by innovative efforts. The World Wide Web revolution, like the client-server revolution that preceded and helped to enable it, serves to define such a new platform for software application. Like the client-server revolution, the WWW platform has a dual character. One set of innovations involves improvements in the hardware and software related to the server, a computer largely or totally dedicated as a communication "hub" for the distribution of information and the management of user interactivity. The other set of innovations involves the workstation or desktop from which server data and applications are accessed. This dual structure of the World Wide Web provides a new method of "distributing" information and computational resources, which has important similarities with and differences from client-server developments.

Like the client-server structure, the World Wide Web provides capacities for the central storage of data and applications, and thus for the centralized administration of data and improvement of applications in WWW servers. Unlike the client-server architecture, however, the communication paths to individual workstations are highly variable in performance due to the different methods by which such workstations are connected to the server and to congestion effects in the Internet. In effect, the World Wide Web enables a new form of time-sharing characterized by enormous disparities between the communication speeds of data inherent *within* either server or workstation client and the speed of communication of data *between* server and workstation client. This asymmetry produces a novel and important focusing device for technological innovation, which is only beginning to be exploited.[31] Examples of innovations stimulated by

---

[30] Technically speaking, this involves developing "provable" algorithmic structures that are demonstrably robust to the problems of real-time applications (such as discontinuous and out-of-specification inputs), the emergent properties of subsystem interaction and the need to manage system and subsystem failures by the "graceful" degradation of system performance. The development of generic solutions to these problems has previously been thought to be too expensive for internal development efforts. However, safety considerations and their liability implications indicate that such systems will need to be developed in the near future.

[31] Perhaps it would be exploited more rapidly if it were more broadly appreciated. Most software designers have exceptionally high-quality Internet connections, which reduce the innovative pressure of this asymmetry.

this asymmetry include search engines, streaming media (video or audio that is displayed or played as it is received and not retained on the user's computer) and distributed animation (e.g. Java or Shockwave applets – software code [mini-applications] that is downloaded and executed by the Java or Shockwave system).

These focusing or inducement effects of the World Wide Web illustrate the significance of major changes in platforms for innovation in software. They also highlight the highly distributed and uncoordinated nature of innovation and technological change in software. Many new companies have emerged to respond to these challenges. As in the case of PCs, the early lead by the United States in the diffusion of the Internet has created first-mover advantages for US firms in these markets. There is a diverse collection of business models for software products in this market. Many of the existing products involve selling products to individuals and companies that maintain servers and freely provide the "access" software to users. This was the model developed by Netscape for its WWW browser, which proved unsuccessful against Microsoft's incorporation of a WWW browser in its operating system.

The systemic nature of software and its relation with the computers that it animates and with other software also reinforce the cumulative nature of software technological advance. The evolution of software is "stratified" – a feature that can also be identified with the division of innovative labor and innovation performance in the software industry. Change comes in different levels of the system environment, with "push" and "pull" effects on all the interconnected elements. Thus, the persistent improvement in the operating performance of computers pulls software toward opportunities for exploiting this performance. Because of rapid progress in computer performance, innovation often involves new products. At the same time, however, these products must "interoperate" with other software in the computer system, and this interdependency between the elements of software creates a push for innovation. Systemic integration is not guaranteed. On the contrary, it is not unusual for severe problems of reliability or performance to arise from the partial incompatibilities among different parts of the system. The problems of technological coordination resulting from imperfect system integration suggest the need for specific institutions in the software SSI.

The principal "institutions" (defined as combinations of rules, norms and customs rather than any particular organizations) for resolving these coordination problems are those involved with technical compatibility standardization, particularly in the interfaces allowing data to be exchanged between software applications. The institutions supporting technical compatibility standards in the software industry have functioned imperfectly throughout the history of the industry. These imperfections are the consequence of novelty, strategic intent and technological complexity.

As noted in the introduction, rapid changes in the design of software have consistently generated novelty in the representation of data. At no time has there been a stable definition of what might constitute a data object, such as a "word processing" document or a "spreadsheet," except in reference to a specific application for creating these objects. Thus, technical compatibility standards have remained proprietary to the producers of applications who could use these standards strategically to raise rivals' costs or create entry barriers in specific segments of the software industry. If strategic opportunity were the only reason for proprietary standards policy actions would be appropriate, and, indeed, they have been undertaken in the allowances made for legally infringing copyright to construct interfaces (Mansell and Steinmueller, 2000, ch. 7). It is not clear that the further step of defining specific standards and mandating their use is in the interest of either users or suppliers. Whatever mechanisms were introduced for setting such standards, the delays would discourage innovation in data representation. It is an issue, nonetheless, that bears closer and more continuous scrutiny than is currently provided by the policy community or by the policy-making communities' requests for industry comment and action.

This issue is well illustrated by the recent history of HTML developments. HTML has evolved substantially since it was originally developed as a cornerstone of the World Wide Web. HTML supports the distribution of information over the Internet and its display on a wide variety of platforms through the use of a "browser." While the original design of HTML accurately anticipated the variety of representations that might be utilized for the display of "pages" of text and image, it did not specify how animated images or interactive applications should be implemented. These later applications were implemented using a variety of "plug-ins" to the browser applications.

In the race to implement new capabilities and the competitive struggle for dominance in browser technologies it has proven difficult to maintain cross-browser compatibility among HTML pages – a development that Tim Berners-Lee, one of the creators of the World Wide Web, has lamented as threatening to frustrate the entire WWW enterprise. While these problems could have been avoided if a more structured standard-setting process had been implemented, it is difficult to assess whether such a process would have produced a "chilling" effect on the pace of technological innovation. The problems of efficiency (minimum size of the data structure that must be sent to the user, combined with effective code execution) in the animated and interactive "features" of WWW pages are, in fact, technologically challenging. The result is difficulties in coordinating the operation of the browser with the plug-ins designed to operate these features. Rapid changes in market share in favor of Microsoft's Internet Explorer and at the expense of AOL/Netscape's Navigator can be attributed partially as sources of these problems.

### 3.4    The user interface as an impetus to innovation

The previous two subsections have focused on features of software innovation related to the problems of systemic integration and information representation. Addressing these problems is essential for the design of information processing systems and they therefore play a prominent role in attempts to systematize innovation efforts. An exclusive focus on these issues, however, leads to serious problems in creating systems that are perceived as useful. As Mitch Kapor, the founder of Lotus, noted in 1990 (reprinted in Winograd, 1996, pp. 2–3):

The great and rapid success of the personal computer industry over the past decade is not without its unexpected ironies. What began as a revolution of individual empowerment has ended with the personal computer industry not only joining the computer mainstream, but in fact defining it. Despite the enormous outward success of personal computers, the daily experience of using computers far too often is still fraught with difficulty, pain, and barriers for most people, which means that the revolution, measured by its original goals, has not yet succeeded.

Instead, we find ourselves in a period of retrenchment and consolidation, in which corporations seek to rationalise their computing investment by standardising on platforms, applications, and methods of connectivity, rather than striving for a fundamental simplification of the user experience. In fact, the need for extensive help in the installation, configuration, and routine maintenance of system functions continues to make the work of corporate data processing and MIS departments highly meaningful. But no one is speaking for the poor user.

There is a conspiracy of silence on this issue. It's not splashed all over the front pages of the industry trade press, but we all know it's true. Users are largely silent about this. There is no uproar, no outrage. Scratch the surface and you'll find that people are embarrassed to say they find these devices hard to use. They think the fault is their own. So users learn a bare minimum to get by. They under-use the products we work so hard to make and so don't help themselves or us as much as we would like. They're afraid to try anything else. In sum, everyone I know (including me) feels the urge to throw that infuriating machine through the window at least once a week. (And now, thanks to recent advances in miniaturisation, this is now possible.)

Winograd (1996, introduction, pp. xv–xvi) summarizes the reasons for this cogently:

Whenever objects are created for people to use, design is pervasive. Design may be done methodically or offhandedly, consciously or accidentally. But when people create software – or any other product – decisions are made and objects are constructed that carry with them an intention of what those objects will do and how they will be perceived and used.

The education of computer professionals has often concentrated on the understanding of computational mechanisms, and on engineering methods that seek to ensure that the mechanisms behave as the programer intends. The focus is on the objects being designed: the hardware and software. The primary concern is to implement a specified functionality efficiently. When software engineers or programers say that a piece of software *works*, they typically mean that it is robust, is reliable, and meets its functional specification. These concerns are indeed important. Any designer who ignores them does so at the risk of disaster.

But this inward-looking perspective, with its focus on function and construction, is one-sided. To design software that really *works*, we need to move from a constructor's-eye view, taking the system, the users, and the context all together as a starting point. When a designer says that something *works* (for example, a layout for a book cover or a design for a housing complex), the term reflects a broader meaning. Good design produces an object that works for people in a context of values and needs, to produce quality results and a satisfying experience.

Although the past decade has created a new wave of technological innovation in the use of software, and some improvements in the user-centered design, many of the concerns raised by Kapor and Winograd continue to be valid. They provide a significant impetus for innovation, particularly in software products that lie outside the domain of corporate computing referred to by Kapor. Products designed for entertainment, education and inter-user communication are beginning to incorporate design principles that make their use more intuitive and engaging.

The significance of user-centered design for European software companies and computer professionals is the scope that remains for innovation in this area. The growing use of Internet- and WWW-based software applications and the new opportunities offered by Internet and CD-ROM distribution channels (examined in section 4) open up new possibilities for entry and growth based upon improvements in the user experience. Now that several European countries have met or surpassed US levels of PC and Internet use, and several others are converging on these usage patterns, the first-mover advantages of the United States will diminish. If experience with the PC era is a guide, what is needed to harness this innovative potential is imagination and vision: qualities that are as well distributed in Europe as they are in other parts of the world.

### 3.5 Summary

The specific character of technological change influences innovation and market performance in the software industry. The ubiquity of incremental change, combined with the usual absence of well-specified technological trajectories, makes the industry one that is driven by innovation in "design" rather than the exploitation of new scientific and technological knowledge. This feature of the innovation process means that an effective division of labor extending beyond the boundaries of the firm is difficult to achieve. One of the most prominent exceptions to this general rule is the embedded software industry, where comparisons of the division of labor between European and US SSIs indicate the potential for European disadvantage. More generally, however, this feature of technical change does not provide a basis for explaining differences between the specialization of European software companies in services rather than packaged software, noted by Torrisi (1991, 1999).

The "stratified" nature of software development provides an important clue about one source of European company specialization in software. Stratification is a consequence of the requirements of systemic integration and involves the solving of coordination problems. One solution to these coordination problems is proprietary standards. Such standards reinforce first-mover advantages, and provided a specific advantage to US software firms due to their earlier and larger deployment of personal computer platforms. This advantage has been sustained by a rapid rate of technical change in the data "representations" that reinforce proprietary standards, raising the costs of entry and creating barriers.

Despite public policy actions (in both Europe and the United States) to mitigate these advantages of dominant firms by laws abridging the software copyright to allow the reverse engineering of interface standards, a small number of US software companies maintain a dominant position in packaged software.[32] Stratification influences the market organization of software companies by presenting two alternatives. Under one alternative, a company must find a way to develop a new class of data objects for which a proprietary standard of representation is desirable, and an application program that makes an attractive use of this class of data objects. Examples of past developments include spreadsheet files, word processing documents and databases. Two of the most prominent examples of European developed standards – compressed music files (the MP3 format) and HTML – were designed as "open standards" and thus have

---

[32] The European and American legislation abridging copyright for interfaces was not undertaken solely to curb market power but also to reduce the prospects that users would be "orphaned" if their supplier left the market.

not provided a basis for proprietary control. The second alternative is to develop superior capabilities for processing non-proprietary classes of data objects. For example, many of the software applications produced for reprocessing audio files, such as those that appear on music CDs, have been developed in Europe. To date, the first alternative has been more robust in supporting market performance, while it is unclear that either has a definitive advantage in innovative performance.

Finally, this section has directed attention to the remaining innovation potentials for improving the quality of the user experience in the use of software. Despite two decades of development, substantial opportunities remain for improving the quality of user interfaces and experiences in the use of computers. The first-mover advantages of the United States in implementing vision and imagination in the design of such interfaces have diminished, providing new opportunities for the entry and growth of European firms.

This section has laid a foundation for explaining the sources of specialization in the software industry and provides a first indication of the reasons for US software companies' comparative success in the packaged software segments of the industry. It has also indicated the issues surrounding continued European strength in the embedded software segment (which may be evolving in the direction of packaged software solutions), the European role in networked software and the potential for new innovations in the user interface. The following section (4) examines the distribution methods, which, together with the Internet technological discontinuity and the potential for user interface improvement that this section (3) has identified, indicate the potential for profound change in the market organization of the software industry.

## 4    Making it pay: models for software commercialization

Up to this point in the discussion, the primary focus has been on the determinants of market performance that are related to technical and organizational innovation. In the limited number of cases where technical performance plays a major role in the market performance of a particular segment, such as embedded software, there is clear relevance in the SSI approach for analyzing the situation facing European producers. If the SSI approach is extended to consider the market configuration of competing networks of suppliers, it can also be used to describe segments such as that of integrated software solutions. More generally, however, the technical and organizational innovations needed to support market performance do not seem to rely upon the features that are generally associated with the SSI approach.

A further extension of this approach, however, offers additional possibilities for analyzing one of the most dramatic and profound influences on the future of the software industry – the evolution of the software distribution system. Including the software distribution system in the SSI approach seems, at first glance, to stretch the boundaries of this method so much that it risks making the entire approach "shapeless." After all, the approach originated in an effort to understand relative innovation performance – an organizational linkage of the structure of knowledge exchange in which market exchange plays the indirect role of validating and valorizing the success (or failure) of innovation. To shift the analysis to the organization of markets seems to put the cart before the horse. However, it is possible to speak of innovations in markets as being an important organizational change and thus to provide a link to organizational innovation as a process that can be examined using the sectoral systems approach.

The case for including an analysis of mechanisms of market distribution in the software industry is that these mechanisms have substantial technical content and span firm boundaries, making them truly sectoral in nature. These mechanisms are not usually directly linked to product innovation, nor are they linked to process innovation in the limited sense that this term is usually employed. They do, however, involve substantial organizational innovation and engage the principal economic mechanism by which new knowledge generates revenue in the software industry: the process of design innovation.

### 4.1    Adoption externalities revisited

Many, if not most, software products are subject to the economies of scale associated with the difference between "first copy" and marginal reproduction cost. The greatest contribution reducing the costs of software is the reuse of code that is expensive and time-consuming to produce. When this reuse involves producing multiple copies of exactly the same software package, as in the case of multimedia, application and operating system products, the costs of producing the first copy can be shared among the users. This reduces the price that the user must pay to acquire the fruits of substantial development effort and cost. The effectiveness of the distribution system is, therefore, a principal means for extending the benefits from mass software "reuse" or, simply, mass distribution. The revenues or other rewards available from mass distribution, in turn, provide an incentive for investing in design innovation. An inefficient and thereby costly distribution system would not only serve to concentrate independent software development in those few companies that could make the promotional and other investments needed to overcome the deficiencies; it would also reduce the amount of investment in the creation of content. The health of the innovation performance of the software industry therefore depends in a fundamental way on the effectiveness of the distribution system.

In many segments of the software industry, adoption externalities serve to augment the inherent economies of mass distribution. An adoption externality arises when the value of someone adopting a software product increases others' willingness to pay for (or, more generally, invest in acquiring and installing) the software. A simple example of this is the case of MP3 players for digital music, which allow substantial compression in the storage requirements for the high-quality reproduction of music. The fact that other individuals may acquire the software to convert music to files stored in the MP3 format will influence your willingness to acquire the software to play such recordings, to the extent that they are willing to provide you with a copy of such files.[33] If this exchange is contingent on recording music in the MP3 format for exchange with others, you will have a further incentive to acquire MP3 recording software more than if you were able only to make recordings for your own use. MP3 players and recorders are available at a nominal price.

There are two principal routes to mitigating the negative effects of adoption externalities on innovation and competition.[34] The first is to extend the standardization of data structures so that different types of software can be employed to read and create such data structures. The second path to reducing adoption externalities is to improve upon the software distribution system so that an entrant who produces a competing product has a less costly means of distributing it.

Nonetheless, until relatively recently, this argument would be insufficient to provide a rationale for employing the SSI approach. The existing methods of distribution – subscription "licensing" for high-priced software and "packaged" software distribution for medium- and low-priced software – are much too straightforward to justify employing the SSI approach. As the following history makes clear, this has changed with

---

[33] Of course, the recording industry is not pleased that these exchanges are used to abridge the copyright on pre-recorded music.

[34] It is essential to note that adoption externalities provide important benefits for users. They extend the possibilities for the exchange of information and reduce the costs of training individuals in the use of software applications. These benefits are substantial and may exceed those available from a more diverse collection of software, regardless of the distribution method. Nonetheless, software producers that are not actual or potential dominant producers in a particular segment or who are participating in segments where adoption externalities are less important (e.g. stand-alone gaming software) have a strong incentive to develop the alternative distribution methods described.

the advent of the Internet and the availability of personal computers with CD-ROM drives. These changes have opened up the possibility of innovations that can only be characterized as sectoral, the coordination and promotion of which involves strong systemic elements with a potential for transforming the nature of the software industry that is profound.

### 4.2   The old and new software distribution channels

During the relatively short (forty-year) history of commercial software, there has been an active search for new models of product distribution. The original business model for software distribution was the high value "licensing" agreement in which the costs of physical distribution were subsidiary to the innovation-like costs of developing, maintaining and upgrading software products. High-value licensed software was an extension of the earlier organization of software production in the software services companies that preceded the existence of "independent software vendors." These vendors were independent of the producers of computer equipment. With the rise of the ISVs, computer companies began to withdraw from the software industry. With the notable exception of IBM, the current share of software in the output of computer companies is very low (Steinmueller, 1996).

The advent of the PC era provided an incentive to create a lower cost distribution method to exploit burgeoning market opportunities. The innovation of "shrink-wrapped" or packaged software, established early in the PC era, served this objective. The "shrink-wrapped" market dramatically changed the nature of software supply in two respects. First, it firmly established the idea that the purchase price of software was for a particular "version," which would probably become obsolete over time. Rather than paying the software producer a "license fee," which would entitle the user to upgrades as they became available within the term of the license agreement, the idea of a "discounted price" for product upgrades was introduced. Viewed from a "cost of ownership" perspective, this option provided both producers and users with greater flexibility. Producers could set the price according to their perception of demand (which might reflect the extent of improvement achieved at the time of price setting rather than in anticipation of product improvement). Users could hasten to purchase the new version, or delay, depending upon their need for new features and product improvements. This system has been subject to "strategic" (anti-competitive) misuse, such as the premature release of software products that have been inadequately tested or the prior announcement of products the actual availability of which is delayed. It has, nonetheless, proved to be a relatively robust model for software distribution during the first twenty years of the PC era.

In the middle of the 1990s two industrial developments emerged that have the potential to make a major impact on the software industry (Mansell and Steinmueller, 2000, chs. 3 and 4). The first was the widespread diffusion of the CD-ROM, a high-capacity (650 MB) storage medium with very low costs.[35] The CD-ROM is the "poor person's broadband," lacking real-time interactivity but providing access to substantial quantities of data. The delivery of CD-ROMs to the newsagent or by post provides a major channel for the distribution of software.

The second distribution development of the 1990s was the widespread utilization of the Internet as a means for the distribution of software. A basic service of the Internet, which was available well before its widespread use, is "file transfer" – the automated reproduction of files between a file server and a user's computer. The adaptation of this file transfer to the distribution of software was relatively straightforward.

Both of these media provided new opportunities for software distribution, but required a somewhat different business model from that of "shrink-wrapped" or packaged software. Instead of charging the user at the point of transfer for software, it became possible to provide the user with a limited time or functionality trial of the software. Sometimes referred to disparagingly as "crippleware," this distribution method allowed both producers and users new flexibility in resolving their "search" problems: the producers' search for potential users, and the users' search for relevant products. The very low costs of this distribution system also opened up many other types of business models. Producers could freely distribute earlier versions of their software while offering to sell the current version. They could sell the product in the same way as packaged software (i.e. payment before receipt of product) without the costs of printing manuals or packaging. Producers could also sell their software to magazine publishers as "content," the publication of which is ultimately supported by advertisements and the reader purchase of the magazine.

All these models arose out of early experiments in software distribution referred to as "freeware" and "shareware." Freeware, as the name implies, was the distribution of software without a license fee. The shareware model involved the distribution of fully working versions of the software with the request that users send a donation or subscription fee

---

[35] In quantity, a published CD-ROM is able to store data at less than a thousandth of a cent a megabyte – a media cost that makes it very competitive with all other existing information media (print, telecommunication and magnetic media). Price reductions in DVDs used for data storage are expected to lower this cost further.

to the author. The "bread on the waters" strategy of shareware was, from its origins, a partial success (Takeyama, 1994). A principal reason for shareware is the relatively high cost of establishing a payments system and conducting sales transactions.[36]

The elements of a sector-spanning innovation in the distribution of software include:

- User-recognized intermediary outlets for trial versions, shareware and freeware that serve as payment collection centres (e.g. Tucows.com).
- A common format for installing software in the Windows and Macintosh operating systems that permits relatively easy removal of the software.
- Compression tools for distributing software that conserve storage space or transmission time.
- The computer magazine and book publishing industry, which supports the distribution of CD-ROMs and provides guides, reviews and instructional manuals for software.
- Anti-viral programs to prevent or cure the effects of downloading viruses in the process of acquiring software.
- Social networks that provide further warning about specific hazards in downloading and that provide rapid warning when such hazards occur.

These elements are the basis for an alternative to the "shrink-wrapped" physical distribution of software, and they substantially lower the costs of entry to new software companies. Judging from the size of sites such as Tucows.com or the offerings of computer magazines, the result appears to be a substantial expansion in the number of product offerings and companies engaged in commercial software production.

### 4.3    The open-source software movement: combining networks for production and distribution

The open-source software movement may constitute the next step in the evolution of alternative software distribution (and creation) systems (Steinmueller, 2001b). Open-source software provides a means for many people to cooperate in the development of new software. At present, most open-source software is developed for Linux and other operating systems based on UNIX (universal Internet exchange) and involves the use of a collection of tools for writing computer code, annotating version modifications and compiling this code into executable software. Most

---

[36] The costs of establishing an account with a credit card company and designing a secure means of gathering credit card information, coupled with the reluctance of users to transmit their credit details into the ether, discourage this approach. This is particularly the case for software authors whose principal interest is sharing their work with others.

open-source software is a variant of freeware, with the important additional feature that rights are not granted to incorporate the software into proprietary software. The basic aim of the open-source software "movement" is to create a new segment of the software industry in which the new distribution methods are combined with cooperative production activities based on voluntary association (Steinmueller, 2002).

While the open-source software movement does provide a means for developing sophisticated and highly reliable software, it has not yet solved all the problems of supporting and maintaining software. In supporting the software, the principal problems arise from the rapid pace of change in PC hardware, which requires the development of appropriate "drivers" (software that links the hardware into the operating system). With respect to maintaining the software, frequent changes in open-source software require many users to familiarize themselves with relatively complex methods of integrating new software into their systems. These problems have been addressed by a new class of company, the Linux distributor, which packages Linux with the latest hardware drivers, software for integrating updated software into the system, and limited technical support for the initial installation of the system. Further market development has included efforts to create companies that would provide technical support for the continued use of open-source software, although these have not yet achieved substantial success. The basic model of "distribution" is also under experimentation, with "subscription" to daily updates of software that are automatically downloaded and integrated on the user machine.[37]

The open-source software movement has not yet demonstrated its capacities for making important contributions to the design of the user interface. The installation of Linux and related operating systems is highly technical and the maintenance and upgrading of software is relatively complex compared to contemporary standards for installing commercial packaged software. One reason for these problems is the difficulty of building a multi-platform user interface. While the Microsoft Windows and Apple computer operating systems define hardware compatibility and embed the functionality of user-controllable windows, Linux's user interface is based on the UNIX command line interpreter (CLI). A CLI accepts the typed input instruction from the user, greatly simplifying the problem of user interface from the designer's perspective, but, for most users, it makes the system cumbersome.[38] The various distributions of

---

[37] The introduction of an unstable update may cause problems, which would then be solved in the succeeding days. As yet, this model has not achieved broad user acceptance.

[38] For an alternative view see Stephenson (1999).

Linux include a "Windows-based" interface based upon the X-Windows – another feature of UNIX systems. The installation of X-Windows, however, is one of the principal reasons that even technically sophisticated users find it impossible to use Linux. Some contend that improving the user interface for Linux is a diversion from its more desirable application as an "engine" for WWW server and other "dedicated" applications. The widespread use of this operating system and the related applications developed for it will require substantial improvements in the user interface design.

Despite its shortcomings, a case may be made that the open-source movement is of particular interest to European firms and policy makers (Steinmueller, 2002). This case is primarily based upon the argument that the open-source movement reduces the possibilities of maintaining proprietary control over data structures and thus may offer a higher level of competition in the software industry. A related conclusion is that the open-source software movement provides a greater range of entry opportunities for software producers, and thereby more opportunities for the participation of European companies. As Kernighan and Plauger (1978, ch. 11), pioneers in the development of structured programming, argue:

Good programing cannot be taught by preaching generalities. The way to learn to program well is by seeing, over and over, how real programs can be improved by the application of a few principles of good practice and a little common sense. Practice in critical reading leads to skill in rewriting, which in turn leads to better writing.

New software companies come from individuals who have accumulated this experience. By broadening access to "real programs" – those that are able to attract substantial numbers of users – the number of individuals with this experience can be significantly increased.

Nonetheless, a principal problem with open-source software is the relative "thinness" of the revenue stream available to companies producing software for that segment. In addition, open-source software is not immune to the mechanisms for achieving commercial advantage described in this chapter. For example, the specific means to integrate and update new software in the Linux operating system may become controlled by one company, or a few. Even if the software continues to be "open" in the sense of not being protected from copying, the convenience and support in the software's use may provide the basis for a service business in the use of the software.

Packaged software and high-value subscription software have proven to be robust against challenges from the advent of shareware, the renovation of licensing represented by "versioned" software, the creation of "advertiser-supported" software, and open-source software. Each of these challenges to the pre-existing methods of distributing software, as well as several others of less commercial importance, has involved either the exploitation of the Internet's capabilities for file transfer or the mass distribution of CD-ROMs. While neither of these alternative distribution modalities has, as yet, provided a strong foundation for the construction of industry-leading firms, they sustain a large number of smaller firms and innovative efforts. The problem presented by the software industry, however, is that firm performance relies not only upon innovation but also upon the effectiveness of distribution and mechanisms supporting "network externalities" in the adoption of particular software.

## 5    Conclusions: public and private strategies for the future of the European software industry

This chapter has indicated a fundamental tension between two major alternative coordinating mechanisms: the role of technological standards and the role of dominant competitors in specific segments of the software industry. This competition has direct implications for European industry and technology policy. Although Europe has a number of world-leading companies that can accurately be described as "dominant" competitors in their respective markets, such as SAP and Software AG, the process of historical development has yielded fewer of these companies than in the United States. A consequence of this development is that many European software companies are highly reliant either on the coordinating efforts of foreign companies or on the emergence of "open standards," which serve as a means to achieve coordination – and hence system integration – on a global level.

The issue here is not so much the dependence of European companies on foreign companies; such interdependence is to be expected in many industries and is often reciprocal. What distinguishes the software industry is that the coordinating role of dominant foreign competitors may be accompanied by their direct competition at every level of software innovation with European firms. In addition, and even more importantly, both the dominant competitors and other foreign companies located closer geographically to the dominant competitor may derive competitive benefits from "insider" or "early" knowledge. Since many software markets are global in scope and the costs of "localizing" products in language and culture are relatively low, the consequence is a "winner takes all" type of competition that often disadvantages European firms.

This problem has no direct solution in European industrial or technological policy, but it can be mitigated by increasing the scope for open standards and for other software systems such as open-source software. In these systems, full and open information allows European firms to participate without disadvantage in producing added-value complements and subsystems. In short, because technological change in software is stratified at various levels of the hardware and software environment, it is important not to be disadvantaged by changes occurring outside the immediate stratum in which a European software company is operating.

The internal development of software continues to be a major source of employment for software professionals in Europe. Companies employ these individuals directly – in development projects – and indirectly, as consultants in the design, implementation, support and maintenance of corporate information systems. The principal problem with improving the sectoral system of innovation for this type of software is the dispersed and situated nature of the development efforts. The "middleware" companies that produce integrated software solutions are addressing some of these problems. European companies such as SAP and Software AG have had considerable success at a global level in this market. Examining this market reveals that it involves the creation of a "network" of related firms coordinated by the producer of a platform application. The experience of these companies with structured and systematic information system projects in a European context is one reason for their success. Similar experience may provide the basis for new entrants with vision and insight into the problem of improving the user interface. Supporting these companies involves the familiar policy advice to strengthen the ability to found and build small and specialized software companies. Many of these firms will find it attractive to tailor their products to the integrated software solution "platforms" or "architectures" supported by larger companies, either in Europe or the United States.

Aside from packaged software and middleware applications, there is a vast market for non-generic software solutions, ranging from scientific work packages to multimedia applications for education and entertainment. European firms are significant contributors to the authorship of such software and are likely to continue to be so in the future. The principal problems with this market are software marketing and distribution. Finding ways to bring these software products to the attention of users and arranging the logistics of delivering the software to them, historically, has been a major impediment for European firms. New systems of distribution based upon the Internet and the ubiquitous use of CD-ROMs show some promise for reducing these distribution costs. At present these new distribution channels provide relatively modest revenue prospects. They do, however, support variety generation and the formation of smaller European software firms.

In examining the special case of the market for embedded software, this chapter has demonstrated that technological discontinuities arising from the need to "prove" reliability and safety may force this market toward "generic" solutions. At present, US firms appear to be better positioned to take account of these developments, in significant measure because of the creation of a more diverse collection of university research efforts and a greater tendency to outsource the production of the tools for creating embedded system applications. This area is singled out for attention because of the importance of embedded software applications for the European automotive, consumer durable, consumer electronic and scientific instrument markets. A major initiative to raise the profile and funding of embedded software research efforts in Europe appears to be warranted.

The new distribution channels and the innovative use of the Internet to facilitate software production are responsible for the success of the open-source movement – a global development originating in Europe. Although offering substantial potential for innovation and growth, this movement remains mired in the problems of developing effective user interfaces for the mass market and developing business models consistent with the intention of providing users with free access to the software. Despite these difficulties, the open-source movement offers two important advantages that merit closer attention. The first is its role in promoting open standards for information representation – a feature shared with WWW-related developments that are not ordinarily considered part of the open-source movement. Open standards for information representation enhance the opportunities for competition in the tools for information creation, analysis and communication. Second, open-source software provides an important route for young programmers to gain experience in the development of full-scale commercial applications, and thus provides an important source of skills that will be relevant in future European software developments.

Finally, this chapter has documented the significance of both software production and use in a European context. The US dominance of the very important, but limited, packaged software market for generic application – the global software product – diverts attention from both the scale and scope of the European software industry and its SSI. By reconstituting the structure of the industry, often from fragmentary sources, this chapter has sought to establish the vital interests that Europeans have in the production as well as the effective use of software. The difficulty of this task is itself an indication of the need for more focused attention and a symptom of the lack of understanding about the role of software in the construction of the "information society."

REFERENCES

Boehm, B. W. (1981), *Software Engineering Economics*, Prentice-Hall, Englewood Cliffs, NJ

Brooks, F. (1982), *The Mythical Man-Month*, Addison-Wesley, London

*Business Week* (2001), Industry outlook 2001 – information, software, http://www.businessweek.com/

D'Adderio, L. (2001), Crafting the virtual prototype: how firms integrate knowledge and capabilities across organizational boundaries, *Research Policy*, 30, 9, 1,409–1,424

David, P. A., and S. Greenstein (1990), The economics of compatibility standards: an introduction to recent research, *Economics of Innovation and New Technology*, 1, 1, 3–41

Dosi, G. (1982), Technological paradigms and technological trajectories: a suggested interpretation of the determinants of technical change, 11, 3, 147–162

(1988), The nature of the innovative process, in G. Dosi, C. Freeman, R. R. Nelson, G. Silverberg and L. Soete (eds.), *Technical Change and Economic Theory*, Frances Pinter, London, 221–238

Edquist, C. (ed.) (1997), *Systems of Innovation: Technologies, Institutions and Organizations*, Frances Pinter, London

European Information Technology Observatory (2001), *EITO 2001*, European Information Technology Observatory, Frankfurt

Kernighan, B. W., and P. J. Plauger (1978), *The Elements of Programming Style*, McGraw-Hill, New York

Laurel, B. (1993), *Computers as Theatre*, Addison-Wesley, Reading, MA

Leebaert, D. (ed.) (1995), *The Future of Software*, MIT Press, Cambridge, MA

Mansell, R. E., and W. E. Steinmueller (2000), *Mobilizing the Information Society: Strategies for Growth and Opportunity*, Oxford University Press, Oxford

Millar, J., and N. Jagger (2001), *Women in ITEC Courses and Careers*, report prepared for the Department for Education and Skills and the Department of Trade and Industry, DFES/DTI/Cabinet Office Women's Unit, London

Mowery, D. C. (ed.) (1996), *The International Computer Software Industry: A Comparative Study of Industry Evolution and Structure*, Oxford University Press, Oxford

Seppänen, V., A.-M. Kähkönen, M. Oivo, H. Perunka, P. Isomursu and P. Pulli (1996), *Strategic Needs and Future Trends of Embedded Software*, Tekes Technology Development Centre, Helsinki

Shapiro, C., and H. Varian (1998), *Information Rules: A Strategic Guide to the Network Economy*, Harvard Business School Press, Cambridge, MA

Steinmueller, W. E. (1996), The US software industry: an analysis and interpretive history, in D. C. Mowery (ed.), *The International Computer Software Industry: A Comparative Study of Industry Evolution and Structure*, Oxford University Press, Oxford, 15–52

(2001a), *Embedded Software: European Markets and Capabilities*, ESSY working paper, Science Policy Research Unit, University of Sussex, Brighton [http://www.cespri.it/ricerca/es_wp.htm]

(2001b), *Open-Source Software and the Alternatives*, ESSY working paper, Science Policy Research Unit, University of Sussex, Brighton [http://www.cespri.it/ricerca/es_wp.htm]

(2002), Virtual communities and the new economy, in R. E. Mansell (ed.), *Inside the Communication Revolution: Evolving Patterns of Social and Technical Interaction*, Oxford University Press, Oxford, 21–54

Stephenson, N. (1999), *In the Beginning Was the Command Line*, Avon Books, New York

Takeyama, L. (1994), The shareware industry: some stylised facts and estimates of rates of returns, *Economics of Innovation and New Technology*, 3, 2, 161–172

Torrisi, S. (1991), *The Organisation of Innovation Activity in the European Software Industry: Some Provisional Findings*, Working Paper, Centre for Information and Communication Technologies, no. 14, Science Policy Research Unit, University of Sussex, Brighton

(1999), Firm specialisation and growth: a study of the European software industry, in A. Gambardella and F. Malerba (eds.), *The Organization of Economic Innovation in Europe*, Cambridge University Press, Cambridge, 239–268

Winograd, T. (ed.) (1996), *Bringing Design to Software*, Addison-Wesley, Reading, MA

# 7 Machine tools: the remaking of a traditional sectoral innovation system

*Jürgen Wengel and Philip Shapira*

## 1 Introduction

This chapter examines the remaking of innovation processes and boundaries in a traditional sector – the machine tool industry within the mechanical engineering segment of the economy. In the machine tool industry we observe both incremental and fundamental changes in recent years in the organization, scope and form of innovation. These offer useful insights into the driving factors of the development and disaggregation of sectoral systems of innovation. They also demonstrate the value of the concept of an SSI, complementing such parallel concepts as national systems of innovation and the idea of technological trajectories. At the same time, we argue that there is differentiation within and between SSIs that is context-sensitive, not only to broader national and international trends but also to the particular strategic orientations of constituent enterprises and regional technological infrastructures.

Our focus is the machine tool industry – a long-established sector in the regional industrial clusters of most advanced economies. We examine:
- The influence of the regional innovation system elements through reference to existing studies highlighting the regional aspects.
- The impact of the national innovation systems via comparison between countries for the same sector (Germany, Italy, the United States and Japan).
- Technological specificities by including an analysis of several characteristic technological developments in the sector.

We use these analyses to advance three principal hypotheses about sectoral innovation systems in machine tools.

1. The *sectoral boundaries* of the innovation system in machine tools have significantly shifted in recent years, in response to competitive and technological changes. Beyond conventional, regionally bound networks of machine tool companies and users we now find that the leading edge of the sectoral system involves national and international innovation networks embodying a wider array of enterprises

243

and research institutions with complementary skills in new technologies and system integration.

2. The *sectoral scope* of innovation in machine tools has broadened, with producers and customers focusing on a broader matrix of technological and organizational innovations rather than just machine tool product improvement.

3. The *sectoral form* of innovation in machine tools has evolved at the leading edges of the industry, from tacit systems based on regional agglomerations of individual firms to strategic partnerships of industry networks, some of which operate on national and multinational scales.

Traditionally, the machine tool sector is characterized as being comprised of firms engaged in producing one of two major elements: metal-cutting tools and metal-forming tools. Innovation typically focused on improving the technological characteristics of individual machines. Most producers were small. Although many of these firms have long had strong export orientations, typically they clustered in specific regional agglomerations. Innovation systems were thus predominantly regional in character, based on units of individual firms, a high degree of tacit information flow, and innovations defined in conjunction with learning loops to principal customers. Today, at the leading edges of the industry, this innovation system has changed noticeably. While the industry remains characterized by relatively small firms, the leading firms have increasingly entered into innovation partnerships through industry networks and alliances with major customers and research institutions. Such partnerships may be national or multinational in scale. Tacit information flows remain critical, but there has been a growth in strategic and more formalized approaches to innovation through networks and partnerships. In the machine tool sector, systems of innovation are now not only targeted at R&D-based product innovation but also to the dynamics of process and organizational innovations. Thus, in a sense, the target of innovation has refocused away from specific machines or machining cells to more efficiently offering production and service solutions. The four-field matrix in figure 7.1 illustrates this more comprehensive understanding of innovation in the sector.

In the first part of the chapter, general characteristics and developments of the sectoral innovation system of the machine tool industry are described using available quantitative data and referring to current phenomena. The second part analyzes how the scope and form of the sectoral innovation system is changing, drawing on country, company and technology cases. The final part of the chapter draws together conclusions and implications.

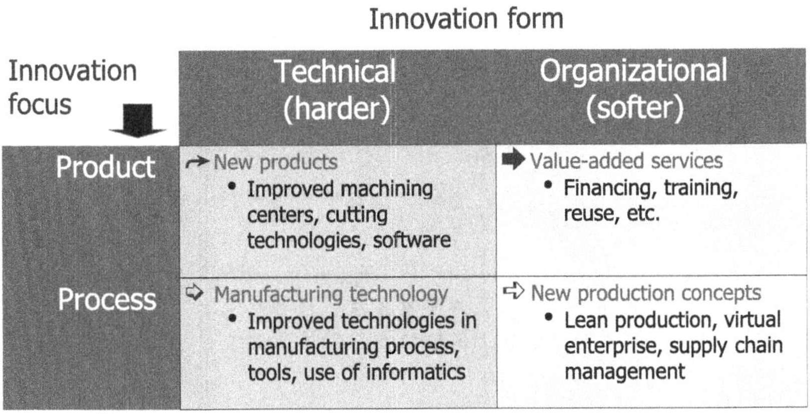

## Innovation form

| Innovation focus ⬇ | Technical (harder) | Organizational (softer) |
|---|---|---|
| **Product** | ↱ New products <br> • Improved machining centers, cutting technologies, software | ➡ Value-added services <br> • Financing, training, reuse, etc. |
| **Process** | ⇨ Manufacturing technology <br> • Improved technologies in manufacturing process, tools, use of informatics | ⇨ New production concepts <br> • Lean production, virtual enterprise, supply chain management |

Figure 7.1 The spectrum of innovations in the machine tool industry

## 2    Economic and structural trends in the sector

Japan, Germany, Italy and the United States are four of the lead-ing machine-tool-producing and -consuming countries in the world (table 7.1). However, there are major differences in the balance between production and consumption among these countries. Japan and Germany each produce just over one-fifth of the world's cutting and forming machine tools respectively (2001 figures by value of tools in dollars). Japan consumes about 9 percent of world machine tool production and is the world's leading exporter, while Germany consumes about 17 per-cent of world production and occupies the second spot among exporters. Italy has emerged as the world's third leading producer of machine tools, with about 12 percent of world production and 11 percent of consump-tion. In 2001 the United States was the world's fourth largest producer of machine tools (down from third place in 1999), producing about 8 percent of the total. The United States has traditionally been the world's largest machine tool market, but recent economic slowdowns have caused the US market consumption position to drop to second (after Germany) in 2001. The United States remains the largest importer of machine tools in the world, although it also ranks fifth among machine-tool-exporting nations.

The US machine tool industry has undergone a massive restructuring over the last two decades. In 1980 US machine tool shipments peaked at $5.6 billion (1982 dollars), but by 1983 the sector's output had col-lapsed to a little over $2 billion. The dramatic restructuring of customers, together with huge losses of orders, rapid import growth and its own competitive and technological weaknesses, hit the industry. But, most

Table 7.1 *Machine tool output, consumption and trade trends: 2001*

| | Production | | | | Consumption | | | Trade balance |
|---|---|---|---|---|---|---|---|---|
| | 2001 (estimate) (millions of dollars) | Percentage of world total | Ratio of cutting to forming | Percentage change 1998–2001 | 2001 (millions of dollars) | Per capita (dollars) | Percentage change 1998–2001 | Excess of exports over imports |
| 1. Japan | 7,900 | 22 | 84/16 | −12 | 3,044.8 | 24.06 | −15 | 4,885 |
| 2. Germany | 7,438 | 21 | 71/29 | −3 | 5,584.1 | 67.44 | 5 | 1,854 |
| 3. Italy | 4,114 | 12 | 59/41 | 11 | 3,727.5 | 67.68 | 36 | 387 |
| 4. United States | 2,945 | 8 | 74/26 | −35 | 5,367.3 | 19.48 | −32 | −2,422 |
| 5. China | 2,623 | 7 | 72/28 | 39 | 4,739.0 | 3.76 | 48 | −2116 |
| 6. Switzerland | 1,968 | 6 | 84/16 | −10 | 678.8 | 93.47 | −5 | 1,290 |
| 7. Taiwan | 1,581 | 4 | 76/24 | 3 | 1,073.1 | 6.21 | −4 | 507 |
| 8. South Korea | 1,333 | 4 | 70/30 | 175 | 1,844.8 | 38.68 | 223 | −512 |
| 9. Spain | 885 | 3 | 66/34 | −6 | 869.4 | 21.74 | 6 | 16 |
| 10. United Kingdom | 781 | 2 | 79/21 | −25 | 882.5 | 21.15 | −32 | −102 |

Source: 2002 world machine tool output and consumption survey, *Modern Machine Shop Online*.

significantly from an innovation perspective, US producers missed out on a major technological shift in the market. American firms were accustomed to producing small numbers of machine tools made to order based on customer specifications and options. Japanese firms captured much of this market, however, with highly reliable and flexible computer numerical control (CNC) tools that could be produced in larger numbers and sold at lower cost.[1]

The 1980s were a dire decade for the industry, and many well-known US tool manufacturers were downsized, bought out or closed. But the seeds of revival were also planted, in part as new non-US firms established production bases in the United States, as remaining firms restructured and new policy initiatives took hold. By the 1990s a recovery had been set in place. US machine tool output grew from about $3 billion in 1992 to about $4.5 billion in 1998, with the United States overtaking Italy as the world's third producer by value. This meant that the United States almost doubled its share of the world market from its very low nadir in the mid-1980s to about 12 percent at the end of the 1990s. However, the US industry has not escaped its boom-bust cycle, facing a slump in machine tool consumption and production of about one-third between 1998 and 2001. The United States continues to have a large negative trade balance in machine tools, and firms in the industry, while perhaps stronger now than in the 1980s, continue to be subject to financial and technological pressures.

In Germany, at the end of the 1990s, the machine tool industry employed 65,700 people. Production in 2001 reached $7.4 billion (down slightly in dollar terms from 1998, but up in terms of euros due to currency fluctuations). Some 57 percent of German machine tool production was exported in 2001, worth about $4.3 billion. This was offset by $2.4 billion of imports (see also Kokoschka, 2001). Machine tools accounted for roughly 6 percent of mechanical engineering production in Germany. As mechanical engineering and machine tool manufacturing had been a very important industrial activity in the former East Germany and most statistics do not distinguish any more, the data we present in the following reflect not only the general developments of the sector but also its restructuring in East Germany.

After a crisis around 1993 in Germany the sector has since recovered and has rebuilt employment. It showed considerable (above-average) advances in productivity: value added per employee rose 30 percent from 1995 to 1998 (euro equivalent). Capacity utilization also grew in the

---

[1] Ironically, CNC was a technology originally developed in the United States, but US producers were slow to adopt it.

1990s. Industry associations (such as the Verband Deutscher Maschinen-und Anlagenbauer – VDMA) have argued that the shortage of skilled personnel ("Facharbeiter") on the labor market is now an important limiting factor to growth (Kokoschka, 2001). Germany has a disproportionately high share of world patents in machine tools (28 percent of the world total between 1995 and 1997, according to Munich's Ifo Institute), indicating a very strong technological position. In the 1990s a recovery of production in mechanical engineering boosted demand for machine tools in Germany. However, the ratio of imports to exports grew, from 43 percent in 1995 to 59 percent in 1998. That suggests reinforced foreign competition for German machine tools even on the home market. The figures for 1999 and 2000 showed that the German machine tool industry had regained strength, aided by the weak exchange rate of the Eurozone against the dollar (Kokoschka, 2001). However, recent market conditions have again turned, with the 2003 rise of the euro against the dollar and the general post-2001 slowdown in the world economy leading to a slight decline in the value of German output (especially in dollar terms).

In Japan, the story is one of growth in the 1970s and 1980s but of restructuring in the 1990s. In this decade Japanese exporters faced restrictions in foreign markets and industrial stagnation at home. This position continued between 1998 and 2001, with production falling by 12 percent and consumption by 15 percent (in dollar terms). Japan, by far, continues to exhibit the strongest positive trade balance in machine tools of all countries, but its surplus declined by more than $1 billion from 1997 to 2001. The industry remains competitive and technologically strong, with a small group of internationally powerful medium-sized machine tool companies and many technologically sophisticated small firms.

By way of contrast, in Italy a strong growth in home demand has contributed to increased production levels. In 1998 Italy consumed $47.89 of machine tools on a per capita basis, but this had grown to $67.68 per capita in 2001 – edging out Germany, where per capita consumption grew by only about $3 over the same period. In both the United States and Japan, domestic per capita consumption declined between 1998 and 2001. Also, while Japan has been in a production and consumption slump since the early 1990s, other Asian countries have seen strong growth. China is now the world's fifth biggest producer and third largest consumer of machine tools. South Korea has seen very strong growth recently, significantly surpassing the machine tool production levels it had attained before its mid-1990s economic and currency crisis. Taiwan has also experienced steady growth in machine tool production. Among other European producers, the position is more mixed: Switzerland has

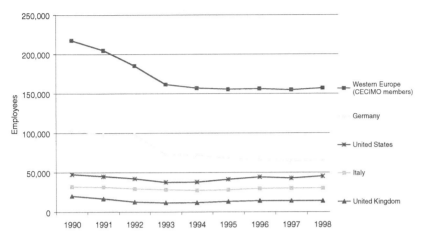

Figure 7.2 Employment developments in the machine tool industry
Source: CECIMO statistical overview, www.cecimo.be.

fallen back slightly in its machine tool production ranking, while the United Kingdom has continued its decline from eighth ranking in 1998 to tenth in 2001 (by dollar production value). Spain has now edged out the United Kingdom, and also France, in machine tool production value, although it is still behind both of these by value of consumption.

Time-series data from the Comité Européen de Coopération des Industries de la Machine-Outil (CECIMO – the European association of machine tool manufacturers) allow for comparison of the development of the machine tool market and industry between 1990 and 1998 (1997 in the case of some countries). Figure 7.2 shows that employment in the sector, particularly in Europe, was reduced in this period.

In contrast to employment, production after the recession in the mid-1990s grew such that it regained the old figures of 1990, and in the United States and Italy it had already gone beyond those levels by 1997 (figure 7.3). Only the United States' machine tool production grew steadily from 1990. Europe as a whole saw the sharpest decline, but also the steepest increase, after 1993. The German figures are strongly affected by the economic restructuring after reunification. Production – and employment, to a lesser extent – was kept up for about one or two years through public support for industrial modernization on the one hand and employment measures on the other.

The percentage changes of production, consumption and exports (figure 7.4) reflect differences in economic growth in the various countries as well as shifts in exchange rates (Kriegbaum, Uhlig and Vieweg,

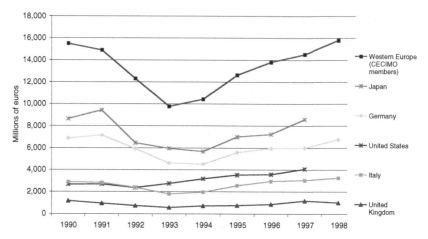

Figure 7.3  Developments in the production of machine tools
*a* Without parts and accessories; at current values.
Source: CECIMO statistical overview, www.cecimo.be.

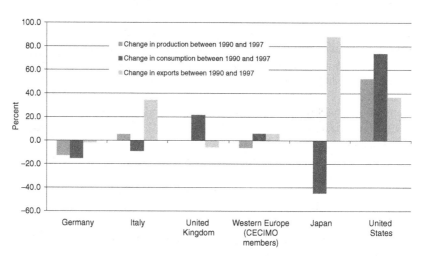

Figure 7.4  The dynamics of machine tool output, consumption and trade
Source: CECIMO statistical overview, www.cecimo.be, and own calculations.

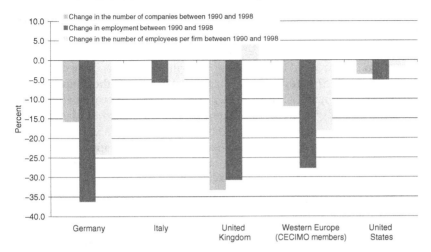

Figure 7.5 The dynamics of company structure in the machine tool industry
Source: CECIMO statistical overview, www.cecimo.be, and own calculations.

1997; and Kokoschka, 2001). Japan managed to outbalance the decline in the home market by expanding its exports. Italy even increased its production under similar circumstances, while the United States recorded positive trends in all figures.

Together with the dramatic ups and downs of the market in the 1990s, industry structures changed remarkably in some countries, although not entirely in the directions expected in a time of mergers and acquisitions. Rather than a concentration process, we see a parallel shrinkage in the number of companies and in the number of employees per company (figure 7.5). This suggests a reaction to the recession more than strategic new positioning of the companies in the sector. There are two interesting exceptions. In Italy, the number of companies decreased from 450 in 1990 to 420 in 1993/94, then increased again to 450 in 1998, leading to an even smaller average size for Italian machine tool makers and indicating that, even in an established sector, there can be considerable entries. In the United Kingdom the reduction in employment did not exceed the number of firm exits, thus leading to a slightly higher average firm size.

While developments in Europe have been relatively stable – entries apparently being the exception – the dynamics of the number of firms in the machine tool industry in the United States have been much more volatile. There were 744 manufacturers in 1990, against 717 in 1998, but in between the number had risen to 845 in 1991, then fallen to only 618 in 1997.

One of the most recent international comparisons of innovation processes and change in the machine tool industry was carried out by Lippert (1999). She studied six companies in Germany, the United States and Japan, and manufacturers of standard as well as of customer-specific machines, all of which were dominant players on the world market. She concluded, however, that there were some very general trends: time as a central factor of competitiveness; increasing standardization and modularization; the search for the trade-off between integration and specialization; and a decentralization of development processes.

The respective pressure for change and the specific national institutional settings with different scopes of action led to different national types of change in the process chains. The United States is characterized as being oriented to the process chain. Germany's change strategies refer more to the design and development area. And Japanese machine tool manufacturers aim at the building of (in-house) competencies. In addition, company specificities seem to play a role. Standard machine builders follow more integrated approaches, with simultaneous engineering and design to manufacture as a prime focus, involving representatives of manufacturing departments at an early stage, while customer-specific machine tool manufacturers keep to more sequential processes.

Lippert strongly reinforces the view that there is no "one best way," but that there is a tendency toward convergence in innovation systems in the machine tool industry. Her results can therefore be taken as supporting the contention that there are sectoral innovation patterns, which complement national and regional innovation systems.

Hirsch-Kreinsen and Seitz (1999) state that, for the machine tool industry in the past, there were few fundamental innovative transitions (e.g. electrical drive for tools and CNC) in a generally incremental innovation model. But the framework conditions for innovation have been changing since the 1980s toward less stable innovation arrangements. They see a differentiation of innovation networks in the sector. Increasingly the firms involved are far removed from the actual application environment of machine tools – namely the IT and software industries. The importance of science for new product development is growing. The need for vertical development cooperation is a consequence of outsourcing strategies. Profit centre strategies and outsourcing on the customers' side also lead to fragmentation of demand. Hirsch-Kreinsen and Seitz consider the risks inherent in innovation processes and the diversity of interests, with the number of actors growing and the stability of institutional settings diminishing.

Table 7.2 *Basic characteristics of the machine tool sector in Germany*

| Number of companies | c. 350 (1998) | |
|---|---|---|
| Number of employees | c. 65,700 (1998) | |
| Production volume | € 9.2 billion (2000) | |
| Export dependence | 54% (2000) | |
| Company size classes | Companies (percent[a]) | Employees (percent[a]) |
| up to 100 employees | 44.7 | 8.1 |
| 101 to 500 employees | 44.2 | 47.4 |
| 501 to 1,000 employees | 7.7 | 23.5 |
| more than 1,000 employees | 3.3 | 20.9 |

[a] Percentages do not sum to 100 because of rounding errors.
Source: VDW statistics and Kokoschka, 2001.

In the following sections we present case studies that assess sectoral innovation systems in the machine tool sector in different countries and from different standpoints. The first study focuses on Germany and the relationships found among machine tool builders, customers, associations and policy, as well as developments in the structure and behavior of firms vis-à-vis innovation within their walls and technological trends from the outside. The second study examines the Italian machine tool sector system, focusing on structural trends and the reasons for the astonishing performance in recent years. The third study describes innovation and strategic developments from the perspective of a Japanese machine tool company. Finally, there is a discussion of developments in the United States' machine tool sector.

## 3        Germany: digesting reunification and regaining strength

### 3.1        The structure of the German machine tool industry

The sector in Germany is characterized by small and medium-sized enterprises (see table 7.2). As figure 7.5 shows, the average number of employees per firm dropped significantly between 1990 and 1998, falling from 271 to 205, and it has risen subsequently only with the general rise of employment in the sector. Available figures for the mechanical engineering sector as a whole also indicate that there is no dramatic trend of concentration, though the number of companies in the sector is decreasing.[2] The value added ratio of 41.3 percent is above the average

---

[2] The hundred biggest of the almost 6,000 mechanical engineering firms in 1996 – the same as in 1995 – accounted for little more than one-third of the turnover.

(39 percent) in mechanical engineering. Against the common trend of outsourcing and focusing on so-called "core competencies," many machine tool manufacturers have even gone the other way and extended their depth of production. Diverse organizational strategies are used by these companies to complement their product range. For example, many machine tool manufacturers have established independent companies that offer product-related services (such as training or simulation) or combine all software activities. Others have set up units or profit centers within the company.

## 3.2    *The relationships of firms, customers, associations and policy*

### 3.2.1    *Sector organization: actors and institutions*

The strength and relevance of industrial associations in the German mechanical engineering sector (the VDMA and the Verein Deutscher Werkzeugmaschinenfabriken – VDW) has often been stressed. But rather than increasing differentiation (by new units, additional activities, etc.) as in former years, the respective organizations face decline. Important factors include decreasing income due to economic crises and a loss of members. However, the development also reflects changes in the markets, the structure of the sector, the merging of technologies, etc. One indication of this is the proposal to integrate the associations for mechanical (VDMA) and electrical engineering (Zentralverband Elektrotechnik- und Elektronikindustrie – ZVEI), although this is unlikely because of the inertia of such organizations at the moment. Joint sub-organizations are founded, for example in the area of software. The "Fachverband Software" (professional group of software firms) in the VDMA contains ninety members, including many of the biggest German software companies, such as SAP. Interestingly, big client firms (particularly from the automotive sector), on the other hand, seem to be losing interest in membership of the VDMA. What was previously organized only in the form of associations or the like (such as the Forschungskuratorium Maschinenbau) are now complemented by commercial organizational solutions (for example the VDMA-Gesellschaft für Forschung und Innovation).

The former close orientation of a number of university departments in the engineering field – namely those organized in the Wissenschaftliche Gesellschaft für Produktionstechnik (WGP – Scientific Society for Manufacturing Technology) – became looser as information technology, computer control of production, new manufacturing processes (e.g. the production of electronic boards) and organizational issues gained importance. Machine tool manufacturers are not a distinct client group any more. And this holds true for the Fraunhofer Institutes in the manufacturing cluster as well.

The company structure of the German machine tool industry is still one of medium-sized family-owned businesses. This does not mean that a standard model is to be found. There are family-owned firms with around 5,000 employees and worldwide production and R&D facilities (e.g. Trumpf), big firms under the roof of big groups (e.g. Hüller Hille of Thyssen Industrie AG), public holdings with an emphasis on machine tools (e.g. IWKA), public machine tool companies/groups stemming from mergers arising from the past crisis in German machine tools, standard ones in particular (e.g. the Gildemeister group, including Maho-Deckel, with more than 3,000 employees) and family businesses of around 200 employees with shares that have been partly put on the stock market (e.g. Hermle). Within a still-strong history of family ownership we see a diversity of business structures developing. The "professionalization" of the organization of the companies in the machine tool industry – e.g. in the form of sister companies to be directly represented in important international markets – seems to be taking place.

### 3.2.2   User-supplier relationships

Machine tool innovation has in the past – with few exceptions, such as the adoption of electrical drive or numerical control – largely been incremental. Close user-supplier relationships in which the machine tool manufacturers reacted to concrete user demand were often rewarded with a more or less exclusive supplier position. Specialist production engineers and technicians on the user's side were "natural" partners of the design engineers with the supplier. Particularly with big companies (especially from the automotive industry) they played a key role in the planning and implementation of the new manufacturing equipment. Later the suppliers were given more and more system responsibility. They now had to manage sub-suppliers and the whole implementation process, while the respective staff numbers with the users were reduced. But it was still an interaction of mutual trust and limited competition. Today we observe that the relationship develops toward "free" market structures (Hirsch-Kreinsen and Seitz, 1999). Company examples indicate that this free-market relationship may erode the system responsibility with the machine tool manufacturers, at least in the maintenance and repair business. Suppliers of complex components of machine tools develop product-related services. In the case of a small manufacturer in Baden-Württemberg, it is a twenty-four-hour repair service combined with a virtual storage of replacement parts that gives them direct access to their former indirect clients in the automotive sector.[3]

---

[3] However, a recent case in which specific features of an offer to a major German automotive firm by a (German) bidder finally appeared in the solution of a (foreign) competitor still

### 3.2.3    *Industrial and technology policy*

In the 1980s and early 1990s there was a series of programs by the German federal government directly targeted at manufacturing technologies, of which machine tools formed an important part. The first measure in 1980 largely supported cooperative R&D on flexible manufacturing systems. Later programs broadened the spectrum toward the diffusion of "other sectors' technologies" (CAD/CAM, CIM), within the manufacturing industries in order to enhance their competitiveness (Wengel, Lay and Dreher, 1995). With the quality assurance program (1992–96), other sectors were also addressed. The process continued with the "Production 2000 and Research for the Production of Tomorrow" program, although more recently there has been a call for proposals aimed specifically at machine tools. These developments are to some extent explained by the interest/request of other sectors that their manufacturing innovation problems also be taken care of with the help of public funds. But they are also a reaction to the increasing interdisciplinarity and inter-sectoral character of innovation processes taking place around mechanical engineering in general and machine tools in particular.

In general, German innovation policy seems to be moving toward a more cross-sectoral approach. In particular, so-called "Leitprojekte" (lead projects) try to integrate vertical supply chains (even including competitors) and try to achieve breakthroughs with respect to "problems" or promising technological possibilities. Technology-specific programs have already been targeted across sectors. Thus, for instance, the "Produktionsintegrierter Umweltschutz" program, aiming at manufacturing integrated solutions for environmental protection, is becoming a source for innovation funding in the machine tool sector. The same is true for information and telecommunication technology programs.

### 3.3    *Characteristics and innovation patterns in a comparative perspective*

### 3.3.1    *The Fraunhofer* Manufacturing Innovation Survey

The Fraunhofer-ISI *Manufacturing Innovation Survey* provides the opportunity to compare the characteristics and innovation patterns of different sectors in the investment goods industry (classes 29 to 35 of the Nomenclature générale des Activités économiques dans les Communautés Européennes [NACE]) using a broad scale of indicators. The survey was carried out in the autumn of 1999 for the whole of Germany

got major attention in the relevant journals. The journalist's commentary was that this should not be much of a surprise, but that it was clearly outside the "rules." What is significant is that this illustrates a weakening under today's intense market pressure of the trust relationship that had traditionally been so strong in Baden-Württemberg.

Table 7.3 *Comparison of sector distribution in Germany in the target group and the sample of the Fraunhofer-ISI Manufacturing Innovation Survey*

| Sector (NACE) | Target group[a] (percent) | Sample[b] (percent) |
|---|---|---|
| Finished metal products (28) | 33.8 | 28.2 |
| Mechanical engineering (29) | 32.5 | 38.3 |
| Computers and office machinery (30) | 1.0 | 1.0 |
| Electrical engineering (31) | 11.3 | 6.2 |
| Radio and telecommunication equipment (32) | 3.0 | 4.9 |
| Precision instruments (33) | 11.2 | 12.8 |
| Motor vehicles and parts (34) | 5.2 | 4.4 |
| Other transportation equipment (35) | 2.0 | 2.4 |
| Not classifiable | 0.0 | 1.9 |

[a] 20,660 establishments.
[b] 1,442 establishments.
Source: Statistisches Bundesamt (1999), own calculations and ISI *Manufacturing Innovation Survey* 1999.

(this was the third such survey, the previous ones having been conducted in 1995 and 1997), and covered 1,442 single establishments with twenty or more employees. Since almost ten thousand companies (establishments) had been contacted this is a response rate of about 15 percent. The structure of the sample – despite the usual under-representation of small firms – gives a good picture of the industry (see table 7.3; and Eggers, Wallmeier and Lay, 2000).

For our analysis of sector characteristics and innovation behavior, data of the mechanical engineering sector (NACE 29) and the machine tool industry (NACE 294) thereof are contrasted with data for the radio and telecommunication equipment manufacturers (NACE 32). The analysis aims to reflect a "main building block of a sectoral system of innovation" – the knowledge and learning processes (R&D expenditures, personnel, foreign activities and cooperation, and engagement in vocational training are related topics in the questionnaire).

Performance criteria covering both general competitiveness (productivity, return on sales, and growth) and innovation (share of product/market innovations and development times) in the questionnaire principally allow for an assessment of the success of different strategies but such analysis would have expanded the limits of our project. The analysis does, however, include time-series data using the previous surveys of 1995 and 1997. Though data are limited to a relatively short period of

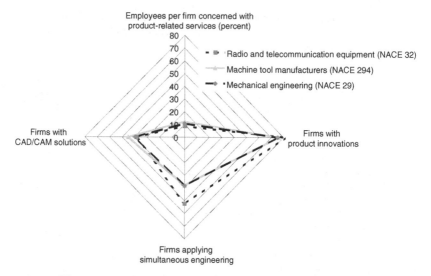

Figure 7.6 Innovation behavior in the machine tool industry in Germany compared to mechanical engineering and radio and telecommunication equipment
Source: ISI *Manufacturing Innovation Survey* 1999.

time (1995 to 1999) there are some hints on the dynamics of the above characteristics. Panel data that are available for 160 firms were used to cross-check the results of the time-series data on the basis of the respective full annual samples.

In section 1 we introduced a model of innovation in machine tool companies comprising four categories. On the basis of the 1999 ISI *Manufacturing Innovation Survey*, figure 7.6 now gives an overview of innovation behavior in the machine tool industry compared to mechanical engineering as a whole and to radio and telecommunication equipment. One indicator for each form and focus of innovation is selected. The picture suggests that machine tool companies are at the forefront in the use of new manufacturing technology and the offer of product-related services, but that other sectors may be more advanced in the use of new organizational and management methods as well as more active in product innovation.

### 3.3.2    The example of knowledge and learning processes

When we are talking about the knowledge base of a firm, internal and external sources are relevant. One very important factor is the qualification of the staff. The ISI *Manufacturing Innovation Survey* provides the share of different occupational groups in the workforce as an indicator. Table 7.4 shows that machine tool manufacturing, rather like machine building in general, is very much based on skilled personnel and applied technical qualifications as opposed to requiring academically trained staff. This qualification base is quite distinct from radio and telecommunication equipment production, where almost twice as many employees, on average, have a university degree and where a skilled shop-floor workforce plays a much smaller role. Consequently, company internal apprenticeship training in shop-floor skills according to the German dual model is an important "learning process" for the machine tool industry.

Another factor for building up the knowledge base is the effort in R&D. The predominance of incremental innovation in the machine tool industry suggests that R&D plays a relatively minor role and that innovations new to the market are the exception rather than the rule. The survey results (table 7.4) support that to some extent. Indeed, R&D expenditures are much lower than in radio and telecommunication equipment production, though higher than in mechanical engineering as a whole. The differences between mean and median figures indicate that there is a relevant group of above-average investors in R&D among the machine tool companies. The share of R&D and design personnel in the workforce was asked for as a combined figure. Though machine tool manufacturing is much more customer-specific, thus requiring specific design effort for most orders, the share of 14 percent in the machine tool industry on average is only slightly higher than in the radio and telecommunication equipment sector (13 percent). Despite lower input, the machine tool companies have a comparable output with respect to product and market innovations. The share of market innovators is even higher. However, it has to be assumed that the answer to the question whether a company had introduced any products new to the market in the past three years refers to the respective product market.

Finally, the acquisition of external knowledge via cooperation, particularly in R&D, is much discussed. The ISI survey differentiates here between clients and suppliers as partners on the one hand and the spatial dimension of such cooperation on the other. Table 7.4 shows that R&D cooperation is not a particular characteristic of the machine tool industry even though more than half of the firms do cooperate, predominantly with clients. Contrary to the common assumption of regional clusters being constitutive to the SSI of the machine tool industry, R&D cooperation mainly takes place internationally, though not to the same extent as in radio and telecommunication equipment, and also somewhat more regionally.

Table 7.4 *Knowledge base and learning processes in the machine tool industry in Germany in a sector comparison*

| | | Sector | | |
|---|---|---|---|---|
| | | | [Mechanical engineering] | |
| | | Total (NACE 29) | Machine tool manufacturers (NACE 294) | Radio and telecommunication equipment (NACE 32) |
| Share of selected occupational groups in the workforce | | | | |
| Staff with | Mean (%) | 8 | 8 | 15 |
| university | Median (%) | 5 | 5 | 8 |
| degree | Valid N | 502 | 84 | 64 |
| Technicians/ | Mean (%) | 16 | 16 | 13 |
| masters | Median (%) | 12 | 15 | 10 |
| | Valid N | 502 | 84 | 64 |
| Shop-floor | Mean (%) | 46 | 48 | 28 |
| personnel with | Median (%) | 50 | 50 | 24 |
| apprenticeships | Valid N | 502 | 84 | 64 |
| Industrial | Mean (%) | 4 | 6 | 3 |
| trainees | Median (%) | 3 | 5 | 2 |
| | Valid N | 502 | 84 | 64 |
| Business | Mean (%) | 1 | 1 | 2 |
| trainees | Median (%) | 0 | 0 | 1 |
| | Valid N | 502 | 84 | 64 |
| R&D input and output | | | | |
| R&D/design | Mean (%) | 11 | 14 | 13 |
| personnel | Median (%) | 10 | 11 | 9 |
| (percentage of workforce) | Valid N | 496 | 85 | 63 |
| R&D | Mean (%) | 5.5 | 6.7 | 8.9 |
| expenditures | Median (%) | 5.0 | 5.0 | 7.0 |
| (percentage of sales) | Valid N | 376 | 85 | 50 |
| Share of market | Mean (%) | 7 | 10 | 10 |
| innovations | Median (%) | 0 | 5 | 0 |
| in turnover | Valid N | 485 | 81 | 63 |
| Market | Percentage of | 50 | 58 | 55 |
| innovators | firms | | | |
| | Valid N | 495 | 81 | 66 |
| R&D cooperation | | | | |
| With clients in | Percentage | 48 | 52 | 68 |
| general | of firms | | | |
| | Valid N | 533 | 89 | 65 |

Table 7.4 (*cont.*)

| | | Sector | | |
| | | [Mechanical engineering] | | |
| | | Total (NACE 29) | Machine tool manufacturers (NACE 294) | Radio and telecommunication equipment (NACE 32) |
|---|---|---|---|---|
| With suppliers in general | Percentage of firms | 50 | 45 | 51 |
| | Valid N | 537 | 89 | 63 |
| With regional clients | Percentage of firms | 26 | 24 | 20 |
| | Valid N | 258 | 46 | 44 |
| With regional suppliers | Percentage of firms | 30 | 30 | 28 |
| | Valid N | 267 | 40 | 32 |
| With international clients | Percentage of firms | 45 | 46 | 55 |
| | Valid N | 258 | 46 | 44 |
| With international suppliers | Percentage of firms | 35 | 33 | 47 |
| | Valid N | 267 | 40 | 32 |

Source: ISI *Manufacturing Innovation Survey* 1999.

The general dynamics of the development of the knowledge base and learning processes are reflected to some extent in the figures of the ISI *Manufacturing Innovation Surveys* sampled since 1995 (see figure 7.7), not least because these years were a time of steady growth with hardly any outstanding shocks. Unfortunately, the data of 1995 and 1997 do not allow the machine tool industry to be separated out. The comparison has, therefore, to refer to mechanical engineering as a whole. The broader sector of mechanical engineering to which machine tools belong has many similarities, though, as we have learned.

Skilled labor on the shop floor continues to form an important part of the knowledge base in mechanical engineering. One could even argue that it is gaining in importance, though not at the cost of higher education but, rather, by driving out unskilled labor. In recent years, however, the difficulties in recruiting "Facharbeiter" have obviously come to the forefront and prevented stronger reliance on these qualified workers. As a consequence, firms have intensified their own training activities. Business and, in particular, industrial trainees pursuing apprenticeships according

Developments in the knowledge base of mechanical engineering firms

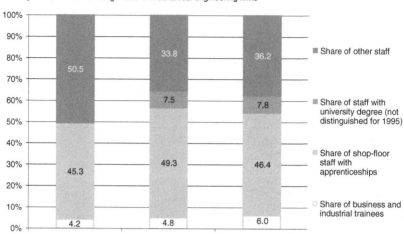

Figure 7.7  Changes in the qualification (knowledge) base in mechanical engineering in Germany between 1995 and 1999
Source: ISI *Manufacturing Innovation Surveys* 1995, 1997 and 1999.

to the German dual model account for an increasing and relevant share of the workforce.

The trend (see, for example, Kriegbaum, Uhlig and Vieweg, 1997; Hirsch-Kreinsen and Seitz, 1999; and Kalkowski, 1997) toward more science-based innovation in mechanical engineering in general, and machine tools in particular, does not seem to have impinged on the R&D effort in the sector yet. The share of R&D expenditures in turnover is relatively stable, according to the ISI survey data: 6.0 percent (1995), 6.4 percent (1997) and 5.4 percent (1999). The percentage of staff concerned with R&D and design tasks dropped slightly from 12.1 percent in 1997 to 11.3 percent in 1999. However, this could also have to do with the increasing modularization and standardization of the products. Indeed, the product range and manufacturing patterns in mechanical engineering – according to the ISI survey – show a trend toward less customer specification.

### 3.4    *Technological trends and their impact on the sectoral system: the example of mobile fuel cells*

Many automobile manufacturers are engaged at present in very intensive development of fuel cells (Marscheider-Weidemann, Mannsbart and

Schirrmeister, 2000). If they have their way, fuel cells will banish the internal combustion engine from under the car bonnet within the foreseeable future. This will generate a need for considerable technical changes throughout the sector, and this will also have far-reaching impacts on the related equipment-producing industries concerned with the motor and its subsystems. The engine and drive-train and motor account for around one-third of the value of a car; and the related manufacturing processes still depend on machine tools. Demand will tend to shift away from mechanical and machined parts, such as crankshafts, cylinders and pistons, toward fuel cells, electric motors, gas-generating equipment and other electro-technical components. There will be completely new manufacturing processes for car engines. An important question here is how the traditional innovation partnership between automotive companies and machine tool manufacturers will react to that challenge, not least as this cooperation marks the leading edge of machine tool innovation.

### 3.4.1   Technological changes and manufacturing changes

These changes in components will have significant effects on production methods and thus on current automotive equipment and parts suppliers. A study coordinated by the ISI (Wengel and Schirrmeister, 2000) examines the possible developments in the case of Baden-Württemberg and DaimlerChrysler. In particular, those production methods required for the combustion engine because of strain due to temperature and rotation (such as die casting, grinding and honing) will be necessary to a much lesser extent in fuel cell drive systems. Other technologies will grow in importance; for example, punching could be used in the production of the stacks for the fuel cell and the gas production unit.

Using the expected technological changes in the components as a base, it is possible to classify how the manufacturing methods and equipment suppliers will be affected. Capital goods suppliers may be affected negatively if they are internal or external suppliers of components that are to be omitted and if no new market for technologically comparable new components of fuel cell engines presents itself. Into this category fall, in particular, many equipment suppliers for the manufacture of components of the internal combustion engine and motor electronics. An example would be suppliers of die-stamping technology, currently used in the production of crankshafts and camshafts, and which will no longer be used in a fuel cell propulsion system.

However, this will not be the case for suppliers to the producers of vehicle electric parts, for example: although the starter and dynamo will be omitted, electric motors – for driving the compressor, cooling and metering pumps – and other controls will be required. Technologically

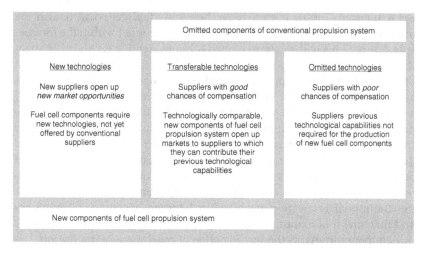

Figure 7.8  The effects of mobile fuel cell diffusion on suppliers
Source: Demuß, 2000

considered, these are similar components. This means that suppliers will not have to provide any fundamentally new manufacturing technology to the producers in order to remain part of the innovation process. Suppliers to producers of conventional components that are to be adapted need have no fear of any technological leap in innovation, since their buyers will also not be confronted with this. Quantitative adaptations may take place, however, due to the need either for extensive supply investment – for, for example, the larger cooling system – or for less extensive investments, such as is to be expected with the simpler construction of the transmission mechanism (fewer gears).

The study (Wengel and Schirrmeister, 2000) calculates the change in manufacturing volumes for three different scenarios. Depending on the "make or buy" decisions of the car companies and the necessary economies of scale, particularly in the early phase of diffusion, production will be concentrated either close to the lead market or in the country of competence. Even though the diffusion will be slow, considerable loss of markets for traditional automotive parts is on the horizon.

Consequently, the demand for machine tools will shift considerably, as the production of parts of the traditional motor and its subsystems is currently an important application field. Machine tool manufacturers seem to react to these external risks and chances rather calmly, even though their interlinkage with other SSIs (and particularly with that of their major customer) might be put on a new basis.

*3.4.2    Uncertainty and high risks: new challenges for traditional structures*
Since the production technology for the new fuel cell components is still being developed, there are opportunities for innovative businesses to develop new production technologies and acquire new markets. Even if the breakthrough is abroad, or in a scenario of technologies competing over a long period of time, new markets may appear for German suppliers, since the delivery of production tools abroad is less problematic than the delivery of components. The development of market opportunities will depend greatly on both the active role of the suppliers and on the participation of German car manufacturers in the development process, where good contacts already exist. However, it does not seem that machine tool manufacturers are intensively involved in the innovation process for the mobile fuel cell at this stage, even though there are requirements for a big cost reduction in the fuel cell system given that serial production will call for very effective production processes. It appears that automotive firms such as DaimlerChrysler have opted for an "evolutionary" approach. Rather than work with selected, traditional equipment suppliers more or less exclusively on possible manufacturing processes, the staff at DaimlerChrysler's Fuel Cell Centre, at least, seem to be trying to initiate variety. They involve other sectors in their fuel cell activities, knit networks, make publicity and invite companies to share part of their knowledge in order to acquire a critical mass and develop a pool of potential suppliers for parts – but even more so with respect to manufacturing equipment (from which they can choose when building up production facilities).

On the other hand, there are good arguments for machine tool manufacturers not to rush. For many suppliers the share of fuel cell propulsion systems plays only a small role in production figures, so long as there is no let-up in technical advances with the combustion engine, which is still expected to provide most business in the long term. These advances will be of priority in determining the demand for production equipment. In certain circumstances, the production methods used until now for the manufacture of internal combustion engines may also be used for new components.

In this connection it should also be mentioned that the competition between the internal combustion engine and the fuel cell propulsion system may also have an effect on the production technology of the combustion engine. Measures to reduce the energy consumption and emissions can bring about additional investments in the production of combustion engines. However, these investments are not expected to lead to a major alteration in the supplier structure.

The share of supplier investments varies greatly in companies, depending on their products and the stage in the manufacturing process. Even so, the share of investment costs often appears small. The effects on Baden-Württemberg (the site of the leading cluster of machine tool companies) are not to be underestimated, since there is a great concentration of suppliers there for traditional mechanical production methods of the drive-train. Over 20 percent of the turnover and employees in mechanical engineering in Baden-Württemberg are connected with the production of machine tools.

Within the supplier sector there will be a shift in emphasis due to the technological changes (new components) in the drive-train. The expected increases for suppliers in the electrical engineering and chemical sectors will probably be counterbalanced by decreases for suppliers in the vehicle manufacturing sector. In the area of automation and assembly technology, no extensive adaptation to the new production technology leading to considerable changes for suppliers is expected. In general, the supplier sector is far more independent of the share of value added within Germany than the supplier industry. Leaders in the development of new production technology may be able to acquire new markets through exports, if the value added share of the drive-train is reduced for sectors which have delivered until now.

Obviously, the situation is particularly demanding for the Baden-Württemberg cluster, which is not optimally structured to profit from the system change, with the exception of Trumpf, the laser and sheet metal technologies of which might have a big role to play. On the other hand, Baden-Württemberg has good chances of building up an appropriate regional supply structure within the next few years, since one of the present pioneers of fuel cell technology, DaimlerChrysler, is located there. Regional partnerships are already beginning to develop, but they hardly include machine tool producers yet while decisions about appropriate manufacturing processes are in the process of being made.

Therefore, the suppliers affected will need to develop a strategy corresponding to their specific conditions and competencies. This will be essential in order, at least, to be able to pursue developments systematically. Here it is not only the car industry that should be considered. Many factors suggest that the cost threshold for economically profitable applications will not be reached in automobile use but, rather, in stationary solutions.

It is clear that this innovation process is both cross-sectoral (not least as it concerns and interacts with stationary fuel cells for heating and electricity generation) and international at the same time. A machine tool manufacturer would have to bring in his competency at an international level rather than via his usual user-supplier relationship. High uncertainty about the extent and time perspective of this innovation suggests the need to look for different application areas from the very beginning, and to take account of the character of this innovation system. The sectoral boundaries of the innovation system have to be expanded.

## 4    Italy: a dynamic sector in flux

### 4.1    The structure of the Italian machine tool industry

By world rankings Italy is the fourth largest producer and third largest exporter of machine tools. There is both robust internal demand for Italian machine tools and a strong export market: in 1999 53 percent of Italy's machine tool production was sold abroad. Significantly, the international emergence of Italy's machine tool sector is relatively recent. While the first firms were founded more than one hundred years ago, the great expansion of the sector occurred in the 1960s, during the "Italian Miracle" that transformed the country into a major industrial power. During this period, Italy's growing internal manufacturing sector fueled demand for specific kinds of machine tools, allowing indigenous machine tool companies to establish themselves. Subsequently, exports took over from internal demand as a driver of growth in the 1980s. There was a crisis in the sector in the early 1990s, provoked by a contraction in Italy's internal market, but a recovery took place later in the decade. Today, orders have regained the high levels of earlier periods.

However, while Italian machine tool output has recovered, the sector is undergoing fundamental transformations. A well-noted characteristic of the Italian machine tool sector is the small size of its companies. For example, the average employment level in Italy's 450 machine tool manufacturers is seventy, compared with 200 in Germany (which has fewer firms). In 1998 about four-fifths of Italian machine tool companies produced less than $12 million of annual output and employed fewer than a hundred employees. But, over the last decade, there has been a consolidation in the sector. Now, the eighty-one firms (18 percent of the total) with more than a hundred workers account for 60 percent of production and 66 percent of exports. In particular, the biggest Italian machine tool company, Comau, produces a quarter of Italian output, with sales that are some seven times greater than those of the second largest firm (Salvagnini Italia).

Although Comau is still an exceptional case, it does illustrate how the sectoral composition of the Italian machine tool industry is changing. Italy is now developing a dualistic model, comprising a large group of small enterprises – highly specialized and geographically concentrated – and a few large companies with a high degree of diversification. Geographically, production remains concentrated in four northern Italian regions that together account for 92 percent of total output: Lombardy, Piedmont, Emilia-Romagna and Veneto. Industrial machine tool customers are also concentrated in these regions. Comau is located in Piedmont, although the biggest agglomeration of small and medium-sized enterprises (SMEs) is in Lombardy. Within the four main regions, machine tool companies cluster in small areas highly specialized in particular kinds of production. This feature has been extensively discussed in the literature on Italian industrial districts. Typically, these districts are comprised of small firms with high levels of interaction, enabling an efficient division of labor among the firms. Non-market relationships are well developed within these districts, stimulating collaboration and partnerships. Additionally, within these districts are found public and private institutions dedicated to dealing with aspects of the business that the small enterprises are not able to do by themselves in an efficient way. Examples of these activities are links with other industries, with research centres and with the public sector. Yet the characteristics of these traditional districts are changing, with the emergence of larger firms and related developments in innovation patterns, as the remainder of this section discusses.

### 4.2    *Specialization strategies and developments in innovation leadership*

The development of Italian machine tool districts has been characterized by both competition and collaboration, with these two elements balancing in different ways over time and space. Some machine tool districts have developed associations specifically designed to meet the particular needs of production that require resources that individual firms cannot employ efficiently. However, the development of new tools or the application of particular technologies is not usually undertaken by these consortia. Usually these associations provide technical and managerial expertise, and some of them interact with the local administrative and national political authorities. Typically they prepare structural studies, and they are the primary source of information for other research institutes. Most importantly, these institutions receive funding to observe the technological paths and trends of the industry worldwide, in order to gather and transfer relevant information when possible.

For Italian machine tool companies, the balance between internal development or production and external sourcing is illustrated in table 7.5. It shows that almost all firms undertake designing, mechanical assembly and testing in-house. Electronic and mechanical components

Table 7.5 *In-house development and production activities of machine tool companies in Italy*

| Percentage of companies undertaking this activity | Total | Size of company (by annual revenue) | | | | |
|---|---|---|---|---|---|---|
| | | < $2.5 million | $2.5–$5 million | $5–$10 million | $10–$15 million | > $15 million |
| Mechanical production | 45 | 43 | 53 | 59 | 33 | 36 |
| Electronic production | 26 | 33 | 10 | 33 | 28 | 23 |
| Mechanical assembling | 82 | 86 | 74 | 81 | 94 | 77 |
| Electronic assembling | 54 | 52 | 47 | 55 | 50 | 64 |
| Software | 60 | 52 | 47 | 44 | 78 | 82 |
| Mechanical testing | 88 | 81 | 89 | 96 | 88 | 82 |
| Electronic testing | 88 | 80 | 78 | 89 | 94 | 95 |
| Designing | 85 | 86 | 74 | 85 | 84 | 91 |

Source: *Technologie Meccaniche*, 2000.

are usually bought from suppliers. What is surprising is that there is no inverse relationship between revenue and the percentage of outsourcing. On the contrary, compared with SMEs the largest firms are more likely to outsource the purchase of mechanical and electronic components. But one common denominator is that the vast majority of firms, irrespective of size, conduct their own in-house designing and testing. This confirms the strong customer orientation of Italian machine tool companies, with custom design and in-house assembly and testing being core competencies. For software elements, even the majority of SMEs perform software development in-house, even if they outsource electronic components. Again, this confirms the desire to produce customer-specific interfaces, while the growing complexity of electrical and mechanical components forces producers to rely heavily on external suppliers.

The role of customization has been especially important for Italian machine tool SMEs. From the early phases of the development of the industry, machine tool producers found that local customers needed suppliers able to adapt machinery that was made abroad (from Germany, for example, or the United States). In this way, small local enterprises were able to enter the market, interfacing with larger foreign suppliers and Italian customers. This led the Italian small firm sector to specialize in phases of production where a high degree of standardization was not possible. In doing this, small Italian machine tool producers developed a particular ability in interpreting and meeting customer demands, translating imprecise requirements into accurate features of their products. This provided these companies with an important competitive advantage, which they now build upon in international markets. However, while smaller firms have specialized in adapting and customizing existing machines, the larger Italian machine tool companies are increasingly focusing on building new tools that are more technologically advanced. As a result they are investing more in innovation and in the development of new products.

Traditionally the Italian regulatory climate has encouraged small firms, for example by making it easier for them to reduce employment or report fiscal accounts. This reinforced the innate flexibility of smaller firms and the high level of customization they offered. However, with the introduction of flexible automation, larger firms can compete more flexibly in the market place and take advantage of economies of scope as well as scale. Similarly, larger firms are able to obtain finance more readily. Moreover, in the struggle to obtain scarce technical labor, larger firms have begun to develop human resource management systems, recruitment, wage levels and benefits that are attractive to workers. Larger firms have also developed links with universities and technical schools, offering new recruits a job now considered safer and with more career possibilities than the alternative offered by an SME, where the owner of the firm is usually the only manager as well.

These developments are facilitating the transformation of Italian machine tool districts from clusters of multiple small firms to networks where a few larger firms now dominate. As these leading firms grow, the network becomes increasingly dependent on these firms. However, it is possible to define two types of leadership, according to the different use of resources from inside and outside the district. First, there is a conventional leader. In this case the exchange of resources within and, especially, outside the district is driven by the needs of production, in terms of specialization or quantity elasticity. There is a dominance of market relationships, and, basically, the only peculiarities of the leader are larger size and the fact that he is usually involved in the majority of the commercial exchanges with other firms of the district (Grassi and Pagni, 1999). The second – emerging – type is an innovative leader. In this situation, the leader is not only larger but is also more dynamic in developing knowledge bases and technology. Such innovative leaders are able to observe and transfer within the district new production technologies, strategies and concepts that are developing elsewhere. In some instances, innovative leadership in a district goes beyond individual companies, with contributions being made by other types of institutions, such as universities, technical schools or associations. The association of machine tool producers, UCIMU, based in Lombardy, performs such a role. It is a powerful association that is engaged not only in lobbying but also serves as an observatory of best practices.

The pressures of globalization reinforce these changes in relationships within industrial districts. A recent study (Segre, 2000) on the multi-nationality of the Italian manufacturing sector showed that the level of foreign direct investment (FDI) outflows grew quite rapidly after 1996, while FDI inflows stayed stable at a level below the EU average. The Italian machine tool sector mirrors this trend and is expanding invest-ment abroad. Foreign firms entered the Italian market, although at a lower pace. The pattern of internationalization by Italian companies has been described as a process of globalization of the districts (Rullani, 1997), which might represent both threats and opportunities. In the future, it is possible that foreign producers will find it convenient to enter into those arenas that are now dominated by local producers. It has been suggested (Rolfo, 1998) that the competitive advantages guaranteed by the localiza-tion of the producer close to the market is becoming less and less impor-tant, and that two firms could share the same knowledge pool even if their headquarters are not located next to the market. On the other hand, there is a noticeable movement by Italian manufacturers to export their model of customer-oriented flexible production, adapting their production to the needs of local industries overseas. This could result in larger compa-nies reducing their ties to local Italian industrial districts, although the smallest companies (which do not produce internationally) will continue to use these districts for their competency and information base.

## 5    Japan: the sectoral innovation system from a firm's perspective

### 5.1    The structure of the Japanese machine tool industry

Japanese machine tool makers are now recognized as world-class leaders in innovation in this sector. The three major Japanese machine tool mak-ers are Okuma, Mori Seiki and Mazak. These firms compete in every mar-ket sector. The next group includes Hitachi Seiki, Toshiba and Toyoda (associated with Toyota). Overall, however, the industry does not con-sist of big companies. Even the largest firms employ just 2,000 to 3,000 people. Yamazaki Mazak, the largest machine tool firm in the world, is completely privately owned. It is still a comparatively small com-pany. Even companies that are associated with large industry groups are only small parts of these groups, such as the machine tool division of Mitsubishi Heavy Industries. Indeed, nearly three-quarters of the mem-ber firms of the Japan Machine Tool Builders Association have 300 or fewer employees, as table 7.6 illustrates.

Table 7.6 *Size of Japanese machine tool manufacturers: 1997*

| Employment size | Number of machine tool companies | Percentage of companies |
|---|---|---|
| Over 1,000 | 5 | 5.2 |
| 501–1,000 | 11 | 11.3 |
| 301–500 | 10 | 10.3 |
| 101–300 | 37 | 38.1 |
| 51–100 | 16 | 16.5 |
| Under 50 | 18 | 18.0 |
| Total: 29,700 employees | 97 | 100.0 |

Source: *Machine Tool Industry Japan*, 1998 Japan Machine Tool Builders' Association.

In principle, one would expect that the typically small size of Japanese machine tool companies would lead them to rely extensively on outside linkages in order to foster innovation. This is true in the sense that Japanese firms develop close contacts with major customers. Japanese firms also participate in various industry groups and collaborative projects. However, Japanese machine tool companies are characterized by their significant internal innovative capacities, and do not greatly rely on public institutions. Similarly, although there is a shift within the machine tool sector toward more software-intensive activities, this is not promoting a significant growth of independent software firms. Rather, among existing machine tool makers, there has been an increase in subsidiaries focusing on software. But the specific form differs by company: some use internal divisions, others subsidiary firms.

## 5.2    *Small but international: the case of Hitachi Seiki*

A case study of how Japanese machine tool builders are evolving sectoral innovation linkages is provided by Hitachi Seiki.[4] This company was founded in 1936 and is headquartered in Chiba prefecture, close to Tokyo Bay. Product lines of the company include machining centers, numerical control (NC) lathes, tooling and fixtures design, engineering services, servicing and leasing. The company has three major factories in Japan and two overseas factories, in Huntsville (Alabama, United States), and Krefeld (Germany). The company also has sales, distribution and training facilities in several locations in the United States and Canada, in Britain, Sweden and Germany, and in Singapore and China.

[4] Interview with Hitachi Seiki by Philip Shapira, Tokyo, February 1999.

There are about 1,300 employees. The firm is associated with the Hitachi group of companies. The company had sales of about ¥40 billion (about $350 million) in 1996. These sales were comprised as follows:

| | |
|---|---|
| Machining centers | 44% |
| NC lathes | 31% |
| Special-purpose machines | 16% |
| Other products and services | 9% |

At Hitachi Seiki, sales per employee in 1996 averaged about ¥30.8 million, or about $268,000 – roughly equal to the Japanese machine tool sector average of ¥30.7 million in shipments per employee.

Hitachi Seiki has followed the overall trends in the Japanese machine tool industry. The demand structure has changed considerably. In 1990 exports represented 34 percent of Japanese machine tool shipments. By late 1998 exports had grown to represent 60 percent of shipments. Foreign demand now exceeds domestic demand. Thus, Hitachi Seiki, like other companies, has been shifting from a domestic to an overseas emphasis. Most of the export shipments are directed toward the United States and Europe. In the past, the company used to procure parts from Japanese sources; now, however, the company is trying to develop relationships with foreign partners, including through the joint development of components and units. The company is also shifting some operations to mainland Asia and Taiwan. In Taiwan, Hitachi Seiki has taken an equity position in its partners and has helped to recruit personnel for these firms.

Domestically, because of the poor economic situation, the company has withheld the recruitment of new graduate entrants. Nonetheless, for high-end products, the company makes these mainly in Japan, where there is a known supply of good engineers; more general machines are made overseas. In the United States there are integrated facilities for making general-purpose machines, while in Germany there is only an assembly line. In general, when the company shifts production offshore it is when there is certain, established demand for the product.

In terms of innovation, Hitachi Seiki is placing increased emphasis on higher functions, software systems and services. In the manufacture of standard machines and NC machines with limited axis capabilities, South Korean and Taiwanese producers are very active and competitive. As a result, Hitachi Seiki has attempted to shift to higher-quality machines, with more functions and systems. The company is putting more emphasis on complex software systems, to add value and functionality. In an important development, Hitachi Seiki has spun off its software operations into a wholly-owned subsidiary, reflecting the company's efforts to concentrate its more able engineers.

The increased importance of software and the integration of machines is reflected in Hitachi Seiki's emphasis on electronic control systems. About 50 percent of the employment in the company and its subsidiaries is dedicated to specialized software development. Inevitably, Hitachi Seiki does use other leading software systems, such as those produced by FANUC of Fujitsu, but, generally, it uses and develops its own software. The company is therefore becoming a supplier of specialized software, and is shifting from a hardware to a software company.

Another important recent trend in the company is that there is now more emphasis on after-sales service. As Hitachi Seiki offers after-sales service through a special subsidiary, discerning what the underlying trends are here is problematic. After-sales service (including the sale of parts) now constitutes about 10 percent of total business transactions.

As the company evolves it is developing greater linkages with specialist firms. Traditionally, Hitachi Seiki has worked very closely with its automotive customers to develop machining systems. It continues to do this, but, at the same time, it now works more closely with outside specialist companies to develop and customize particular units. Another important recent trend has been the development of environment-friendly machine tools. To reduce or eliminate the wastage of oils, Hitachi Seiki has been developing machines that do not use oil ("dry processing"). There has been a similar trend in other companies. Hitachi Seiki has been working with cooperative industry groups on developing environment-friendly machines, involving other companies and university faculties. The demand for these types of machines has become relatively strong, and Hitachi Seiki expects nowadays that they will comprise around a half of its total sales.

Hitachi Seiki's smaller and more affordable machines are offered as they are, and are ordered from the catalog, but, for its more expensive machining centers, the company offers models that are customized to SMEs. These machines have simpler specifications, with fewer options and variations; they are denoted by the use of the symbol "S" – indicating a simplified version of the model. This is not really a change, however: for the complex machines, there is no such thing as a standard model. For example, Hitachi Seiki offers at least 108 variations of an NC lathe, so each machine is customized to its customer's needs. The individual cost for a machine can vary enormously, depending on the options. As a result, SMEs can customize machines to their budgets and operating needs.

A recent change in materials, which Hitachi Seiki is addressing, is the machining of ceramics. The company has a machining system, using rotary cutting edges, to machine ceramics. This system has been delivered to Kyocera. Export orders for these machines have been obtained, and a reasonable quantity have now been shipped. They are classified as "other machines" in the statistics, however, so the growth of this sector is still not well reflected in the data. Hitachi Seiki has also developed new equipment to machine the surface of semiconductors. As this represents a new generation of machines, sales are still at an early stage.

## 6     The United States: continuing sectoral change

### 6.1     The structure and development of the US machine tool industry

In the nineteenth and early twentieth centuries the US machine tool sector produced a series of innovations that led to major improvements in precision, quality and productivity. In particular, the development of mass-production systems in the United States required machine tool makers continually to improve their tools and machines. Following further massive expansion in the sector during World War II, the US machine tool sector then experienced a roller-coaster ride of upturns and downturns. There was continued growth through to the 1960s and 1970s, such that at the start of the 1980s the United States was the world's largest producer of machine tools. However, the period of the 1980s was one of substantial decline. Several hundred US machine tool firms closed in the 1980s, and by the 1990s Japan and Germany far exceeded the United States in machine tool output. There was some recovery in the mid-1990s, with output value peaking at $5.3 billion in 1998, but it then slumped again, falling to an estimated $2.9 billion in 2001. The United States continues to run a large trade deficit in machine tools.[5] Today there are about seven hundred firms in the United States in the machine tool sector, making machines that cut, form and shape metal. Mostly, these firms are small: fewer than ninety employ more than one hundred workers. A small group of bigger companies – Cincinnati Milacron, Litton Industries, Ingersoll-Rand, Monarch Machine Tool and Giddings and Lewis – account for nearly 70 percent of total industry production and sales (Forrant, 1997).

Several weaknesses in the United States' SSI and in structural relationships with customers and users help account for the change in the US position in machine tools over the last three decades. At their height, American machine tool makers were very dependent on the US defence and automotive sectors. The specialized and dedicated machines

---

[5] Net imports were $3.4 billion in 1998, although the trade deficit fell to $2.4 billion in 2001 as US domestic consumption declined.

demanded in these sectors made US makers less flexible, however, in meeting the needs of other customers and in responding rapidly to their orders. Additionally, in recent decades US firms have been unable to capitalize fully on technological innovations developed within the sector, for reasons that include poor coordination of technical standards among companies, problems in applying defense-developed technologies to commercial environments, mergers and acquisitions, and inadequately sustained R&D investment (Forrant, 1997). In the late 1970s and 1980s, nimbler and more responsive Japanese and European manufacturers entered the United States and gained significant market shares by supplying technically excellent, and in many cases superior, machines coupled with a responsiveness to customer needs.

The development and commercialization of NC and CNC tools exemplify the traditional organization of the SSI in the US machine tool sector – and the weaknesses of that system. Drawing on federal government and MIT research that began in the 1950s and continued through the 1960s, US firms were advanced in the early application of numerical and computerized control systems to machine tools (Holland, 1989). Several US firms, such as Cincinnati Milling, Bendix, General Electric and Giddings and Lewis, developed their own proprietary controllers. However, the incompatibility of these controllers, their expense and their unreliability all limited sales. US firms continued to pursue improvements, but by the 1980s Japanese producers had captured volume and technological leadership in the industry. Japanese machine tool firms developed reliable and inexpensive controllers, other innovative product technologies and process technology improvements (such as modular production) that enabled them to produce high-quality, flexible tools with a significant productivity advantage over US firms. Japanese firms, led by FANUC, have since dominated sales of CNC tools. The active role of the Japanese government, aided by collaborative R&D, supportive machine tool associations, the licensing and sharing of technological information, and the protection of the Japanese home market, contributed to the rise of the Japanese industry (Forrant, 1997). But there were also significant weaknesses in the US machine tool sector. These included: a fragmented industrial base, with few large firms able to undertake sustained R&D investment; a lack of collaboration among the sector's many small firms; difficulties in obtaining capital; and inadequate investments in workforce skills. The United States was also poor at commercializing technological research, for reasons that include weak university-industry ties, a government research focus on highly sophisticated or specialized applications with limited commercial market potential, and weak links between machine tool users and customers (Finegold et al., 1994).

In the 1990s there was some recovery in the US machine tool industry, stimulated by several factors. First, there was the strong economy, which increased demand for capital equipment in general. Second, the remaining US machine tool companies modified their practices, becoming more customer focused. Policy measures, such as the promotion of industry research collaboratives (e.g. the National Center for Manufacturing Sciences), aided the reorientation of US firms. Other programs, such as the Manufacturing Extension Partnership (MEP), increased the opportunities to disseminate new technologies and improved manufacturing practices to machinery makers. Third, foreign companies increased the number of facilities they operated in the United States, thus boosting not only production but also technology transfer.

## 6.2    *Technological and organizational innovation capability*

In the mid-1990s a RAND study argued that prospects for the US machine tool industry were beginning to brighten due to its restructuring, the strength of domestic demand and problems in Japan and Germany. It was also suggested that Japan's lead in CNC technology had been eroded and that the United States had taken a research lead in several new technologies (Finegold et al., 1994). A separate study offers some confirmation of this research finding. A Georgia Institute of Technology analysis conducted in 2001 shows (figure 7.9) that, in the research domain of ultra-precision machining (UPM), US output was comparable with that of Japan's prior to 1987. However, after 1995, US research publication grew above that of Japan. Western European output in this field also exceeded Japan's, attaining a level slightly above the United States, while there also strong research publication growth in this field in other Asian countries (led by China and South Korea). Although this analysis is limited due to the constraints of data availability (i.e. a bias toward English-language publications), it is suggestive of a trend. In typical tabulations on emerging technologies the United States leads, often followed by Japan. Usually the gap between the United States and Japan is large, reflecting the "twice as large" (very roughly) US R&D establishment. In the domain of UPM R&D, the ratio of US to Japanese publications is much closer, indicating that Japan is very strongly positioned in this field. However, the United States has enlarged its share of publications in relation to Japan in recent years, suggesting a relative improvement in the US position. The role of organized research (in addition to firm-based customization) in new technology development in today's machine tool industry is also confirmed by the affiliations of

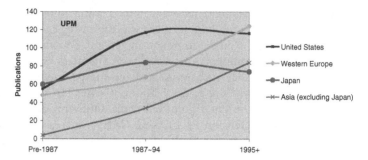

Figure 7.9  Comparative publication output – ultra-precision machining
Source: Technology Policy and Assessment Center, Georgia Institute
of Technology, 2001. Based on Technology Opportunity Analysis of
research publication domain of UPM in INSPEC and ENGI (EI Com-
pendex) publication databases.

publishers, with national laboratories, universities, research societies and
corporate R&D laboratories taking leading roles.[6]

The problem for the United States is that, although the health of its
research laboratories and universities remains strong in new technologies relevant to the future of the machine tool sector, questions remain
about other elements of the SSI. The US machine tool industry has been
affected by an ongoing wave of mergers. For example, the conglomerated
firm of UNOVA has acquired most of the machine tool operations of
Cincinnati Milacron, as well as a series of other smaller US (and some
European) machine tool makers. What may be occurring here is the short-
term purchasing of customers and expertise, rather than the longer-run
indigenous development of capability or traditional iterative linkages with
customers (Forrant, 1999). The innovation strategies in the US sector
also remain characterized by a focus on investment in machinery and IT,
rather than organizational change or personnel upgrading. This is suggested in a comparison (table 7.7) of methods to improve the competitiveness in machinery and mechanical engineering companies reported
in matched 1999 surveys in Germany and Georgia (United States).

---

[6] The leading producers of publications in UPM (cumulative rank, by affiliation of
first-named author) are: Livermore National Laboratory (United States), the Fraunhofer Institutes (Germany), Hong Kong Polytechnic University, Matsushita (Japan),
the University of Tokyo (Japan), Osaka University (Japan), the University of California
(United States), Hitachi (Japan), Nanyang Technological University (Singapore), Ibaraki
University (Japan), Philips Research (Netherlands), the Korea Advanced Institute of Science and Technology (South Korea), Oklahoma State University (United States), North
Carolina State University (United States), and Chubu University (Japan).

Table 7.7 *Comparison of strategies to improve competitiveness in German and Georgia (United States) mechanical engineering firms*

| Method to improve competitiveness | Germany[a] | Georgia[b] |
|---|---|---|
| | Percentage of firms indicating method is very important | |
| Investments in machinery and plant | 26.6 | 21.2 |
| Information technology | 25.5 | 27.3 |
| Organizational strategies | 34.1 | 18.2 |
| Personnel strategies | 32.5 | 24.2 |

[a] 552 establishments.
[b] 35 establishments.
Source: ISI *Manufacturing Innovation Survey* 1999, responses for NACE 29, and Georgia *Manufacturing Survey* 1999, responses for Standard Industrial Classification (SIC) 35.

Thus, while the United States continues to have a strong research base in the machine tool industry and has improved research-industry collaboration and consortia in recent years, the sectoral system as a whole remains unbalanced. Regional cooperative networks among tool producers, users, suppliers and technology centers are still relatively weak. Furthermore, long-term public and private investment in commercializing research and upgrading workforce skills is still limited. Finally, few US machine tool companies are able to mount a global presence in research, sales or servicing. These are significant weaknesses in an industry sector where competitive success is increasingly based on the combination of strong regional agglomerations and strategic national and international partnerships. US policy at the national level in the machine tool sector has frequently sought to defend the industry (through trade regulation) or promote narrowly targeted technologies (for defense applications), rather than actively promote development over the long term (through mechanisms to support investment, regional collaboration and workforce training). Arguably, this tilt in policy has led to continued weaknesses in the US machine tool industry's SSI, leading it to do less well in translating the results of research into commercial success, and leaving the home market open to entrants based in other countries.

## 7    Conclusions

The country, company and technological examples described in this chapter illustrate that established systems of innovation in the machine

Table 7.8 *Traditional and emerging characteristics of sectoral innovation systems in machine tools*

| Element | Traditional | Emerging |
|---|---|---|
| Form of external linkages | Bounded, stable | Open, flexible |
| Geographical scope | Regional → national | Regional → international |
| Technological basis | Mechanical | Information-intensive |
| Product development | Incremental | Incremental → systematic |
| Exchange relationships | Producers linked with users | Partnerships of producers, users and research centers |
| Knowledge base | Tacit | Tacit → codified |
| Training | Varied | Varied → internal plus external |
| Corporate form | Individual, family | Individual → corporate groups (limited multinational) |
| Work organization | Internal informal collaboration | Formalized and external cooperation |
| Entrants | Moderate technical barriers | Higher innovation barriers to entry |
| Demand | Cyclical | Cyclical |
| Policy | National sector policies | Regional, national – generic European innovation policy |

tool industry are undergoing change, while at the same time new relationships are being forged. In the past, if one wanted to characterize the old system of innovation in the machine tool industry one would probably use the following terms: closed; regional and national; mechanically based; incremental; producers linked with users; and tacit knowledge. Today the outline of the emerging SSI, as characterized by the case studies discussed in this chapter, appears as: more open; partnerships; regional to international in scope; based on new technology; information-intensive; linkages with research centers, producers and users; and increased codified knowledge. These shifts are not always complete. For example, while international linkages for innovation development have emerged, regional and national systems continue to have strength in this sector. That said, that there are shifts and changes is undeniable. These are summarized in table 7.8.

What underlies these shifts? The rise of information and science requirements and the need for R&D encourage firms to form consortia and collaborate with public research institutions to share risk, and also upgrade internal skills to develop and apply new capabilities. The added value share of IT in machine tools is steadily increasing. In some companies there are already more software than mechanical engineers. Innovation is increasingly science-based in machine tools. New materials and laser technology, as well as the developments in ICT, microelectronics and micro-systems technology, are pushing changes in manufacturing equipment. Increasingly, new technologies on the horizon (such as dry processing, high-speed cutting, cutting of hardened parts and near-netshape manufacturing) seem to depend more on scientific research and the application of material sciences, simulation and modeling, and integrated software development. These technological developments can have major impacts on market shares between different types of machine tools, which mostly have quite specialized suppliers. The need to respond rapidly to customer needs, if not to anticipate those needs, also gives rise to closer relationships between producers and users in the development of specialized tools and in after-sales service, including training and tele-service. Yet, while in the past these relationships required close physical proximity, today at least some of these linkages can be maintained at a distance.

In the German case, machine tool makers have focused their development efforts on specialized and advanced machines, using high levels of internal capability plus linkages – albeit changing – with customers and public institutions. Some traditional linkages, for example between companies and associations, seem to be eroding in Germany, while formerly tight links between specific companies and customers are being transformed into more market-like relations. At the same time, the sectoral boundaries of the machine tool sector are changing, with machine tool makers forging new links with specialist companies in new areas of technology. In Japan, machine tool makers have also focused on developing specialized and advanced machines, using their high levels of internal capability and building on linkages with customers, not public institutions. In Italy, the traditionally high number of local machine tool districts is seeing the development of a dualistic structure, with internationalized and more technology-intensive larger enterprises taking leadership positions in these districts. The United States has also seen consolidation in its production base, with the emergence of new links with public institutions, such as the MEP, to help smaller machine tool companies overcome limitations in their own internal capabilities. US firms are also reforging relationships with customers and users.

These examples highlight the fact that, within broad frameworks of change, there are important local variations. The particular form of emerging sectoral innovation system in machine tools is influenced by location and by the particular innovation strategies of firms and the cultures of innovation in different national and regional innovation systems. These examples also illustrate that, while change in innovation patterns in a traditional, mature sector such as machine tools may follow some of the directions seen in other sectors, there are also important differences. Among the differences, the machine tool sector remains characterized by its small size,[7] its limited aggregate market growth and its relatively low internal reliance on R&D. Yet, at the same time, we also see common tendencies toward internationalization, partnership and informatization. As elsewhere, there is an expansion of innovation approaches from technical to organizational, and of the innovation focus from products to processes.

These shifts in innovation systems in the machine tool sector have important implications for regions. As we have discussed, traditionally the SSI in machine tools had a strong regional clustering dimension. The regional clustering of tool builders, users and support organizations has been particularly strong in the Italian and Japanese machine tool sectors, allowing the further development of agglomeration economies of scope and scale in tacit knowledge sharing and skills development (Piore and Sabel, 1984; and Friedman, 1988). Regional clustering has also been important in Germany, for example among Baden-Württemberg's mid-sized companies (Cooke and Morgan, 1998), even in the context of well-developed organizations and technical institutions at the national level. Similarly, in the United States, the machine tool sector has historically clustered in regional locations in New England (with its strong skills and research base), the Midwest (with linkages with automotive and other engineering users) or California (with linkages to aerospace users). In the future, regional clustering is certain to remain an ongoing feature of the machine tool sector as innovative firms seek agglomeration to access skilled labor pools, be close to large users and technologically important test customers, and benefit from complementary service linkages in such areas as maintenance, finance and industrial association activities. Yet, at the leading edges of the sector, we do see new trends emerging that are making regional clusters more porous and which are likely to stimulate firms to develop innovation linkages at scales well beyond their own region. These emerging trends include: the growing role of codified knowledge and information-intensive technologies in fostering innovation in the sector; the development of new kinds of cross-sectoral, cross-regional, and international partnerships for product and system development; and the rise of larger national and – increasingly – multinational holding companies. Increasingly, we anticipate that such trends

---

[7] The sector's largest firms are typically one or two orders of magnitude smaller than the largest firms found in sectors such as automobiles, chemicals or informatics.

will add new supraregional characteristics to the innovation system in the machine tool sector, as the sector's own boundaries and technologies evolve. To the extent that this expectation is fulfilled, increasing pressure will be put on traditional, small-scale regional machine tool firms to evolve and reformulate their business, technological and networking linkages within and beyond their home regions.

What is Europe's position in this developing innovation system? In 1993, Reger and Kungl found that research-driven innovation in Europe's mechanical engineering sector remains far less important than customer-supplier relationships in generating innovation, with the innovation itself taking predominantly an incremental form. Today, an incremental, customer-focused approach remains the cornerstone of technology management in the European machine tool sector, although there remain significant differences in productivity in machinery production among European countries (Felder et al., 1997). This has proven to be an economically viable strategy over the past decade. While Europe as a whole had a negative revealed competitive advantage in the machine tool sector and somewhat fewer patents vis-à-vis Japan and the United States measured against machine tool output (Kriegbaum, Uhlig and Vieweg, 1997), some countries, namely Germany and Italy, performed very well in production output and productivity. The fears of those (e.g. Fleischer, 1997) who argued that German machine tool manufacturers were in an "inefficiency trap" as a consequence of their strategies of increased customization seem not to have been borne out. Yet the European machine tool sector still faces substantial future challenges. Among these is the maintenance and rebuilding of the knowledge base. For example, Germany (despite high joblessness overall) has been facing shortages of qualified labor, both on the shop floor and with engineers. It is feared that this will become an inhibiting factor to growth. It would appear that work in manufacturing has to be made more attractive, and training and incentive systems need to be improved. In this respect, there seems to be room for the modernization of work organization and processes in the European machine tool industry – or, in other words, the adoption of softer forms of organizational innovation.

The machine tool sector has always needed to integrate theory and practice in design and manufacturing. Traditionally, this has been done in tacit ways. However, the increasing relevance of science and informatics and the formalization of R&D and design processes away from the production area are challenging conventional approaches to innovation (Kalkowski, 1997; and Kalkowski, Mickler and Manske, 1995). This also means new challenges to the learning processes in the sector, which traditionally were internal rather than external. Although there have been periods of rapid new firm formation and entrepreneurship in the sector (such as in Japan and Germany in the 1950s), in recent decades new firm entries have not played a major role in the machine tool sector. But there are variations. Indeed, Italy and the United States have more fluid enterprise entry and exit characteristics in the machine tool sector. In the future there may be a growing role in all advanced countries for new technology-based firms in the machine tool sector that are pursuing approaches to innovation based on scientific knowledge. If so, countries such as Germany where enterprise entry and exit is more difficult may need to give additional consideration to this element as they review their innovation and regulatory frameworks.

Finally, we note that well-established and, in some respects, efficient sectoral systems may be overcome by developments elsewhere. For example, while US firms managed to invent R&D-based NC and CNC technologies, Japanese firms had a better environment and policy framework to succeed in volume commercialization. Similarly, the UK textile machine makers of the 1950s that efficiently built equipment to supply the high-volume, medium-quality UK clothing market were subsequently far surpassed in technological capabilities by Italian textile machine makers, which had to produce machines to respond to the rapidly changing, flexible and fashion-oriented thrust of the Italian clothing sector. Over time, it was the flexible Italian machines that found international market success, while the UK firms went out of business. In this light, we should pay particular attention to the rise of new producer locations, such as China, Taiwan and South Korea. These regions are adding new global complications to the mix of innovation and production capabilities in the world's machine tool sector, particularly since these emerging producers are developing stronger capabilities in research and innovation and are augmenting their human capital capabilities.

Overall, our message is that strong regional sectoral linkages and a close coupling of regional production complexes with users will probably continue to be key elements in competitive advantage in machine tools, as in the past. This is particularly true for the local recruitment and building of medium- (apprenticeship-) level competencies with workers who usually are not highly mobile. However, increased investments in system integration, innovation and emerging technologies, public-private collaboration, formal training systems, technology and market intelligence, and international partnerships and linkages are also likely to characterize the most successful elements of the sector in future years. Europe is well placed to capitalize on these emerging trends. But, with ongoing competitive pressures from established innovation locations (such as Japan, or a revitalized United States) or newly emerging innovation locations (in other parts of Asia), carefully targeted innovation support measures at regional, national and European levels will become a further important element in sectoral development in the European machine tool sector.

REFERENCES

Cooke, P., and K. Morgan (1998), *The Associational Economy: Firms, Regions, and Innovation*, Oxford University Press, Oxford

Demuß, L. (2000), Technologische Veränderungen beim Übergang vom konventionellen Antriebsstrang zur mobilen Brennstoffzelle, in J. Wengel and E. Schirrmeister (eds.), *Innovationsprozeß vom Verbrennungsmotor zur Brennstoffzelle: Chancen und Risiken für die baden-württembergische Industrie*, Fraunhofer Institut für Systemtechnik und Innovationsforschung, Karlsruhe, 111–176

Eggers, T., W. Wallmeier and G. Lay (eds.) (2000), *Innovationen in der Produktion 1999: Dokumentation der Umfrage des Fraunhofer-Instituts für Systemtechnik und Innovationsforschung*, Fraunhofer Institut für Systemtechnik und Innovationsforschung, Karlsruhe

Felder, J., G. Licht, B. Koebel and A. Spielkamp (1997), *Manufacture of Machinery and of Electrical Machinery*, European Innovation Monitoring System publication no. 49, European Commission, Brussels (EG-EIMS, 85 S, NR–EIMS Project no. 94/109)

Finegold, D., K. W. Brendley, R. Lempert, D. Henry, P. Cannon, B. Boultinghouse and M. Nelson (1994), *The Decline of the U.S. Machine Tool Industry and Prospects for Its Sustainable Recovery*, two vols., Critical Technologies Institute, Washington, DC (MR-497/1 & MR-479/2)

Fleischer, M. (1997), *The Inefficiency Trap: Strategy Failure in the German Machine Tool Industry*, Edition Sigma, Berlin

Forrant, R. (1997), *Good Jobs and the Cutting Edge: The U.S. Machine Tool Industry and Sustainable Prosperity*, Working Paper no. 199, University of Regional Economic and Social Development, and Center for Industrial Competitiveness. University of Massachusetts, Lowell

(1999), personal communication, December 21

Friedman, D. (1988), *The Misunderstood Miracle: Political Change and Industrial Development in Japan*, Cornell University Press, Ithaca, NY

Grassi, M., and R. Pagni (1999), Sistemi produttivi localizzati e imprese leader, *Economia e Politica Industriale*, 103, 241–272

Hirsch-Kreinsen, H., and B. Seitz (1999), *Innovationsprozesse im Maschinenbau*, Working Paper no. 4/1999, Lehrstuhls Technik und Gesellschaft, Dortmund

Holland, M. (1989), *When the Machine Stopped: A Cautionary Tale from Industrial America*, Harvard Business School Press, Boston

Kalkowski, P. (1997), Innovationsstrategien des deutschen Maschinenbaus, *VDI-Z Integrierte Produktion*, 139, 7/8, 26–30

Kalkowski, P., O. Mickler and F. Manske (1995), *Technologiestandort Deutschland. Produktinnovation im Maschinenbaus: traditionelle Stärken – neue Herausforderung*, Edition Sigma, Berlin

Kokoschka, H.-U. (2001), *German Machine Tool Industry in 2000*, Verband Deutscher Maschinen- und Anlagenbauer, Frankfurt

Kriegbaum, H., A. Uhlig and H.-G. Vieweg (1997), *The EU Mechanical Engineering Industry: Monitoring the Evolution in Competitiveness*, Ifo-Studien zur Industriewirtschaft no. 54, Ifo Institut für Wirtschaftsforschung, Munich

Lippert, I. (1999), *Zwischen Pfadabhängigkeit und radikalem Wandel: Neuordnung von Prozeßketten im internationalen Maschinenbau*, Edition Sigma, Berlin

Marscheider-Weidemann, F., W. Mannsbart and E. Schirrmeister (2000), Einflußfaktoren und Szenarien der Diffusion, in J. Wengel and E. Schirrmeister (eds.), *Innovationsprozeß vom Verbrennungsmotor zur Brennstoffzelle: Chancen und Risiken für die baden-württembergische Industrie*, Fraunhofer Institut für Systemtechnik und Innovationsforschung, Karlsruhe, 49–72

Piore, M., and C. Sable (1984), *The Second Industrial Divide*, Basic Books, New York

Reger, G., and H. Kungl (1993), *Research and Technology Management in Enterprises: Issues for Community Policy – Case Study on the Mechanical Engineering Sector*, Strategic Analysis in Science and Technology, European Commission, Brussels (CGNA 15428 ENC – SAST Project no. 8)

Rolfo, S. (1998), L'industria italiana della meccanica strumentale di fronte alla globalizzazione: opportunità e limiti, *L'Industria*, 19, 4, 881–894

Rullani, E. (1997), L'evoluzione dei distretti industriali: un percorso di decostruzione e internazionalizzazione, in R. Varaldo and L. Ferrucci (eds.), *Il Distretto Industriale tra Logiche di Impresa e Logiche di Sistema*, Angeli, Milan, 54–85

Segre, G. (2000), *Multinational Firms in Italy: Trends in the Manufacturing Sector*, Working Paper no. 13/2000, Istituto di Ricerca sull'Impresa e lo Sviluppo – Consiglio Nazionale delle Ricerche (Ceris-CNR), Turin

Statistisches Bundesamt (1999), *Betriebe, Beschäftigte und Umsatz des Verarbeitenden Gewarbes sowie des Bergbaus und der Gewinnung von Steinen und Erden nach Beschäftigtengrö Benklassen*, Series 4.1.2, Wiesbaden

Wengel, J., G. Lay and C. Dreher (1995), Evaluation of the indirect-specific promotion of manufacturing technology, in G. Becher and S. Kuhlmann (eds.), *Evaluation of Technology Policy Programmes in Germany*, Kluwer Academic, Dordrecht, 81–99

Wengel, J., and E. Schirrmeister (eds.) (2000), *Innovationsprozeß vom Verbrennungsmotor zur Brennstoffzelle: Chancen und Risiken für die baden-württembergische Industrie*, Fraunhofer Institut für Systemtechnik und Innovationsforschung, Karlsruhe

# 8    Services and systems of innovation

*Bruce S. Tether and J. Stan Metcalfe*

## 1    Introduction

This chapter provides an overview of findings and conceptual arguments with respect to services, and innovation in services, especially from an SI perspective. It draws especially on the work undertaken on innovation at airports, in healthcare and in retailing, but it will also be informed by wider considerations of services and their innovation activities. By "services," we mean all sectors conventionally identified as services, although telecommunications and computer software – which are especially technological – are examined more fully and separately in other chapters of this book.

This study begins, in section 2, by outlining the economic significance of services and discussing what is meant by services. Section 3 concerns the SI perspective with regard to services, and summarizes the work undertaken on services within the ESSY project. Section 4 then draws on these studies to provide summary answers to the main questions raised by the SI perspective in relation to services. Finally, section 5 provides a new perspective on SIs that has evolved out of our work within ESSY.

The main points of the chapter are the following:

- Services are not (normally) engaged in the production of tangible products but cover a huge range of diverse activities, associated with various types of transformation (i.e. physical, spatial and temporal transformations, affecting people, things and information). The great diversity of service activities is not reflected in a comparable depth in the understanding of innovation in services, which has been neglected in favor of studies on manufacturing. This said, there are certainly important connections between service innovation and artifact innovations developed by manufacturers. But more research needs to be done before we can claim a comprehensive understanding of the problems of innovation generation and diffusion in relation to services.

- The study of services brings to the fore, to a greater extent than studies of manufacturing (which tend to focus on the product produced and the process of production), the interrelationships between business models, organizational forms, technology and outputs. Studies of services also highlight the significance of knowledge forms other than, or complementary to, technological knowledge (and R&D). In particular, the significance of market knowledge and procedural knowledge is highlighted.

- Many services show high degrees of interaction and interdependency between the service provider and the service user, as well as between provider and equipment suppliers. Such interaction and interdependency is a central feature of all true systems of innovation, and, as in manufacturing, the diversity of activities within services means there is certainly no single SI. Instead, there are multiple systems, or patterns. Moreover, "sectors" or "subsectors," as these are conventionally defined (i.e. in terms of the industrial classification of activities, such as transportation, wholesaling, retailing, advertising, etc.), do not bound the SIs. This is not peculiar to services but is also true of "manufacturing sectors" and their SIs, which relate primarily to the production of tangible goods. Thus, differences with innovation systems in manufacturing are more of degree than kind (Hughes and Wood, 2000). Instead, the SIs involve a wide range of agents from many different sectors (often including both manufacturers and various service providers). An interesting feature of these systems is that the agents involved (and the interrelationships between these agents) can change over time; thus the boundaries of the system are not fixed but are dynamic and evolving.

- We consider that SIs often develop around an identifiable problem (or opportunity), or sequences of sub-problems (or opportunities), which are themselves framed by a number of contingencies (including the regulatory, cultural and technological context). In this way, the problem sequence at the heart of the SI becomes the focusing device (Rosenberg, 1976; and Hughes, 1983) around which the system is developed. As the problem (or opportunity) changes, or is redefined, so the system can change, changing the agents involved and the relations between these agents (Coombs, Harvey and Tether, 2001). One important implication of this view is that firms can take a leading role in assembling innovation systems in the pursuit of their own competitive advantage. Innovation systems at this level are, to a substantial degree, transient: they evolve as the problems of the moment evolve. Consequently, the important issues addressed in this study relate to the dynamics of the construction of innovation systems from the interaction of multiple agencies.

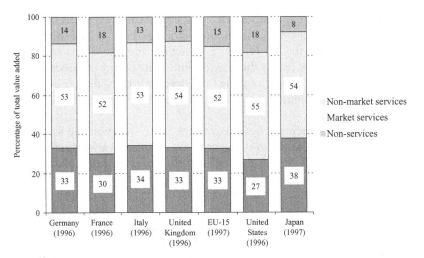

Figure 8.1  The composition of value added in the European Union, the
United States and Japan
Source: Eurostat, 1999, tables 3.1 and 3.2

## 2      Services: what are they?

That advanced economies are service economies is well known. According to official statistics, services account for roughly two-thirds of GDP
and employment in the European Union (Eurostat, 1999) – shares that
are increasing, whereas those of manufacturing are in decline. Similar
patterns exist for North America and Japan (see figure 8.1).

Statements of this kind immediately raise the problem of definition and
classification, which is bound to be arbitrary to a degree. Services are usually defined negatively (Riddle, 1986) – as the "residual" (Clark, 1940)
or "tertiary" sector (Fisher, 1939); as everything that is not agriculture
or other extractive activities (the primary sector) and not manufacturing
(the secondary sector), which is concerned with the production of tangible goods (Hill, 1977; and Miles, 1996). This "services are not" approach
has developed into a widespread prejudice, that services are non-
productive and ephemeral, whereas the "real economy" is manufacturing
(and agriculture, mining, etc.). Yet, as we have seen, the "residual" dominates employment and value added in the developed world (although the
measurement of output from services is notoriously difficult).

Even the definition of services as intangibles – as "the fruits of economic
activity that you can't drop on your foot" (Pennant-Rea and Emmott,
1983) – is negative (and contested – see Hill, 1999); it is services as
producers or providers of everything that is not tangible. Yet the absence

of outputs that are independent physical entities is an important characteristic of most services. In manufacturing there is not normally confusion between the process of production and the outcome – the product – which has led to the conventional dichotomy of process and product innovation. In services, the same term is used to denote both the process and the outcome. In short, the process is often indistinguishable from the product.[1]

Characteristics such as these encourage us to question the standard conceptualizations that are used in economics and innovation studies, but which have been developed essentially in the context of manufacturing. This brings us to the differentiated nature of services, and the multiple ways that service activities can be defined, which are central to an understanding of the complexities of innovation systems in services. One way to explore this is to enquire into the nature of the productive transformations through which services create economic value added. All productive processes relate to particular activities and transform combinations of material, energy and information into new, more highly valued combinations of these elements. The difference in economic value that follows is what the economist measures as value added: the overall measure of work done in the process. Objectively, transformations are of three kinds: of the *physical form* of materials, energy and information; of the *location in space* of those elements; and in the *temporal availability* of those elements. Thus, a first approach to defining and classifying services is to ask what is changed (or transformed) by the service and how. Agriculture and other extractive activities extract raw materials from the earth; manufacturing transforms raw materials, semi-manufactures and energy into end products (which then provide consumer or producer services). Service activities, meanwhile, can be understood in terms of a dual taxonomy of relations, first distinguishing what is transformed (i.e. a person, an object or information), and secondly distinguishing the nature of that transformation (be it physical, spatial and/or temporal) (Hill, 1977; Lovelock, 1983; and Miles, 1996). Thus there are activities that transform physical objects (e.g. physical repair and maintenance services for automobiles or computers, and transport services that move things in space) or information (e.g. banking and financial services) or people (e.g. hairdressers, hospitals and passenger transport services).

A further complication is consumers' individual and collective interpretation of the nature of the service activity, and how this (subjective) interpretation impacts upon the nature of the service provided. For

---

[1] That said, it can still be useful to make the conceptual distinction between the service process and the service outcome.

example, objectively, cosmetic surgery provides a physical transformation of the patient, but a successful (or unsuccessful) outcome is likely to have a profound (subjective) impact on the patient's mental or emotional state. Similarly, objectively, a train journey is a physical movement in space, but subjectively it may give pleasure or discomfort. Many services are bought less for their "objective" transformations than for the subjective interpretations associated with their provision. For example, a meal with others in a restaurant is rarely about nutrition alone.

Many service providers realize that they are in the business of providing more than objective physical, temporal or spatial transformations, especially when people (and their treasured possessions) are the object of the service. The subjective experience of the service is, therefore, something to be actively managed, for it can be fundamental to the value attached by the consumer to the service provided. For example, the décor and cleanliness of the carriage, the size and comfort of the seats, the number (and behavior) of other passengers, the spacing between seats, and the availability and quality of the refreshments may all impact significantly on the perceived quality of a train journey. One way to consider these issues is to ask whether the service has a recognizable core and periphery. Admittedly, for some services, there may be no discernible core or periphery – or, at least, the interpretation of core and periphery can vary between provider and consumer, or between users – but for those to which the distinction applies this can be akin to distinguishing the function and form of a product. For example, the *core function* of a transport service is the movement of people or goods from one place to another, but the *peripheral form* of the service can vary enormously, from first-class luxury to very basic travel arrangements.

It is notable also in this example that the core function of the services is normally provided without the active participation of the consumers. This is significant, because it is sometimes insisted upon that services are relational. That is: "Services involve (simultaneous) *relationships* between producers and consumer. There cannot be a producer without a consumer. A service must be provided *to* another economic unit" (Hill, 1999, p. 441; emphasis in original). This relational aspect of services relates to the non-storability of service outputs (as they lack an autonomous physical existence – Gallouj and Weinstein, 1997). It also brings to the fore the interactive aspects of services and suggests that consumers actively participate in the provision of service (i.e. service co-production). However, this is an oversimplification or overgeneralization. Although "classic services" rely on the simultaneous and conscious participation of both the service provider and the service user for the execution of the service, this is not true of all services. Services can be available whether they are used or not;

they are not always produced to order. Insurance and scheduled transport services are examples of this. Moreover, the extent to which consumers *actively* participate in the provision of the service is highly variable, but can be nil.

The nature of services and the transformations they provide also tend to have a significant bearing on their organizational form. Traditional services, which mainly undertake non-storable physical transformations, have tended to need to locate close to their consumers, and as consumers are widely distributed over space so these services have tended to be supplied by small-scale local providers. Technological and other developments have, however, reduced the power of location for many services. As consumers become more mobile through access to transport services (especially private cars) so retailers have exploited the potential economies of scale in large retail complexes. And as information technologies and networks have developed so have new forms of coordination and delivery. Where traditionally most services were provided locally, with consumers often coming to the service provider, now many services are provided at arm's length – for example over the telephone or through the Internet. Arm's-length provision typically allows the exploitation of economies of scale, which provide advantages over traditional, local provision. Developments in the banking and insurance industries are a good example of this, with a change from the provision of services through branches to the increased use of the telephone and the Internet. This encourages the development of a separation between the "front office" (which deals directly with customers) and the "back office," which carries out the service processes. This division can be real or figurative, but the nature of the service – for example in terms of the economies of scale and the divisibility of front- and back-office functions – can have a significant impact on its organization, in terms of the size of the enterprise, the number of sites and the location of functions (see figure 8.2). It is also apparent from this that many services can be seen as ongoing (technological) "systems" (i.e. as processes), which involve customers only in occasional discrete events (each of which is a "service encounter," or product).

This brings us to a further dimension, which has been used to distinguish different types of services: namely the duration of the engagement between the service provider and the service user. Some services involve long contact times between provider and client, but for others contact times are very short (Silvestrou et al, 1992; and de Jong, 1994). Up to a point, there is a relationship between contact times and the extent to which services are standardized or customized. Services that involve short contact times are typically highly standardized – or routine – and low-cost

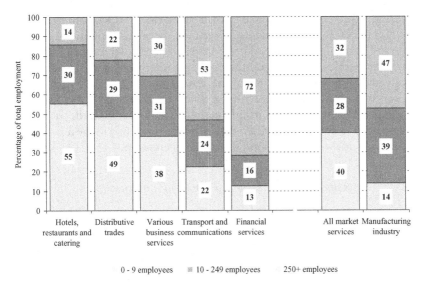

Figure 8.2  Employment by enterprise size in European union services, 1995
Source: Eurostat. 1999, table 3.9

(facilitated by a reliance on low-skilled workers), but involve few, if any, customer-specific changes. By contrast, those that involve long contact times tend to be specialized and high-cost (with a reliance on "professional," high-skilled workers); the service provided often varies considerably from customer to customer. There are, of course, many exceptions. Doctors in general practice, for example, are professionally skilled but tend to have relatively short contact times with patients. Moreover, technological, organizational, regulatory and market developments can transform these relationships, allowing new service providers opportunities to provide differentiated services – such as simplified shorter contact time services – that are substantially cheaper than those provided by the conventional service providers (e.g. the introduction of specialist conveyancing services for house buyers, which is significantly cheaper than conventional legal practices for this task). The introduction of hybrid forms of organization, such as franchises and federations, can have significant impacts on the nature of service provision.

We have surely said enough to convince the reader that classifying an activity as a particular type of service is not always straightforward. The result may be purely conventional and conditional. It is well known that the same kind of activity can be classed as manufacturing when it takes place within a firm but be classed as a service if it is bought in from an external supplier. Our purpose in discussing these issues is to highlight the highly heterogeneous nature of services. Services contain far greater diversity than manufacturing, but – other than telecommunications and computer services, which have their own peculiarities – services have also received only a small fraction of the attention that scholars and policy makers have paid to manufacturing. Because of this diversity, we cannot expect a single pattern of innovation in services; instead, there is a strong need to comprehend their diversity and relate this to the innovation processes with which each kind of service is engaged.

## 2.1    *Innovation in services: some attempts at a taxonomy*

We turn now to the implications of this discussion for the problem of innovation in services as a prelude to introducing three specific case studies of innovation systems in services. In the Pavitt taxonomy (1984), for example, services are defined as passive recipients of innovations developed by the suppliers of artifacts. In many cases this may be an adequate depiction of events: many service providers are passive, they are adopters not innovators, and many services have negligible innovation content over long periods. However, this is certainly not the whole story. As Gallouj and Weinstein (1997) assert, the analysis of innovation in services is difficult because (1) "innovation theory has been developed essentially on the basis of analysis of *technological* innovation in *manufacturing* activities" (p. 537 – emphasis in original) and because of (2) the "fuzzy" nature of service outputs, in which it can be hard to distinguish the "service product" from the background process, or organization, of provision.[2] As the quality of service outputs is often very hard to measure, it is difficult – if not impossible – to identify the improvements in efficiency that follow from innovations.

As ever with services there is a danger of oversimplifying, for there are a number of innovation trajectories in services, which are unevenly distributed across service sectors and service firms. In recent years innovation scholars have sought to develop taxonomies or typologies of services' innovation trajectories, in much the same way as Pavitt (1984) developed his famous taxonomy of technological activities essentially for manufacturers. Pavitt's taxonomy – with its emphasis on different sources of knowledge and sources of competitiveness – can be seen as one of the

---

[2] As mentioned earlier, in services the term "product" frequently denotes a process, such as a service package, a set of procedures or protocols, or an "act." This can also be associated with a close interaction between production and consumption, particularly when the service lacks an autonomous physical existence, exterior to both their producers and consumers or users. Thus, there is typically a much hazier relationship between what is produced and the process of production in services than in manufacturing.

antecedents of the SSI approach. An interesting contribution, therefore, is Miozzo and Soete's attempt to adapt the Pavitt taxonomy to services (see also Ducatel, 2000; and Coombs and Miles, 2000). In the original version, Pavitt had characterized all private services as being supplier-dominated (i.e. as being dependent on technologies developed by their [manufacturing] suppliers).

Miozzo and Soete (2001) distinguished three categories of service businesses:

1. Production-intensive, scale-intensive and network services. These services are "industrial," in that they involve considerable divisions of labor, with the simplification (and coordination) of production (and/or delivery) tasks and the substitution of (skilled) labor by machines (and lower-skilled labor). The application of this "industrial" organization logic, together with technological innovation, encourages the standardization of service outputs, or – in more sophisticated systems – the adaptation (through customization) of standard services to particular user needs. Within this group, two types of services can be distinguished:

   a. Network services, which are dependent on IT networks (e.g. banks, insurance and telecommunications). The development of IT has facilitated improvements in the complexity, precision and quality of the services offered by these providers; they have especially facilitated customization, have had an important role in setting standards in many service activities, and have had a role in redefining the spatial division of labor over which these services are conducted.

   b. Scale-intensive services. These are dependent on physical networks (e.g. transport and travel services, and wholesale trade and distribution), which are less flexible than IT in terms of facilitating customization, but do provide economies of scale and of scope. In these services there is also a heavy dependence on hardware technologies developed in the manufacturing sector.

2. Specialized technology suppliers and science-based sectors. These include such services as software and specialized business services, and laboratory and design services. Firms tend to be small in scale, and the main source of knowledge and technology is the innovative activity of the services themselves. Outputs are usually highly customized, often being designed for particular users (or groups of users).

3. Supplier-dominated sectors. This is, in effect, a residual category, of services that remain "backward" adopters of technologies developed by manufacturers. According to Soete and Miozzo, major examples include the public or collective services (education, healthcare and administration), and personal services (food and drink, repair businesses, hairdressers, etc.), together with retailing.

Evangelista (2000) makes a similar contribution, although grounded in more empirical evidence. Evangelista distinguishes between: "technology users" (which resemble Pavitt's "supplier-dominated" sectors); "science- and technology-based services" – such as R&D, engineering and computer services, which are akin to Miozzo and Soete's specialist suppliers; "interactive and IT-based services" – such as financial services and advertising, which are based on information processing and have high investments in IT systems; and "technical consultancies" – which combine the characteristics of "science- and technology-based services" with those of "interactive and IT-based services."

These contributions are useful in distinguishing types of services with regard to their technological activities and, by extension, organizational arrangements. Moreover, the identification of scale-intensive and network services brings to the fore the question of regulation, which is particularly significant in shaping the provision of some services, especially those that are considered "natural monopolies." It will be clear that the regulatory environment for services will also play an important role in shaping service innovation systems.

However, Evangelista's category of "technology users" (or "supplier-dominated services") contains a large residual of heterogeneous services, including both private and public (or collective) services, the organization of which is usually quite different, not only in scale but also in organizational logic. It is also, surely, erroneous for Miozzo and Soete to describe services such as healthcare as supplier-dominated, when what matters is the complementarities between clinical innovation in the hospitals and the penumbra of externally supplied devices and drugs that support those activities. The relationship is one of symbiosis. The worlds of manufacturing and services are not parallel and independent but mutually dependent. The same is true in retailing, amongst which large retailers often have significant influences on their suppliers. An obvious example is UK supermarket chains (see section 2.3). These retailers set quality and environmental standards, and identify new products, for their suppliers (Harvey, Quilley and Beynon, 2002). As Coombs and Miles (2000) have rightly observed, studying service activities brings to the fore neglected aspects of innovation processes that are present across the whole economy.

Another contribution that seeks to characterize a variety of innovation styles but which does not privilege technological knowledge is that by Sundbo and Gallouj (2000). These authors, who consider innovation in services to be transmitted through "loosely coupled systems," identify several patterns of innovation in services – from the classic R&D pattern (which they consider uncommon) to the service professional pattern, the organized strategic network pattern, the entrepreneurial pattern and the artisanal pattern. Sundbo and Gallouj highlight the significance of inter-action, arguing: "The innovation process in services is to a large degree an interaction process, both externally (between providers and users) and internally (within the provider)." They also argue that the service sectors are becoming more systematic in their innovation processes. Again, the wider point is that the nature of service activities, and the nature of the associated service innovation trajectories, is highly differentiated; it is problematic to speak of service innovation systems in highly generalized terms.

## 3    Services and sectoral systems of innovation

We now turn to SSIs. In chapter 1 a sectoral system of innovation and pro-duction has been defined as "a set of new and established products for spe-cific uses and the set of agents carrying out market and non-market inter-actions for the creation, production and sale of those products." These agents, which are characterized by specific learning processes, competen-cies, beliefs, objectives, structures and behaviors, include organizations[3] and individuals.[4] They interact through processes of communication, exchange, cooperation, competition and command, but – importantly – these interactions are shaped by institutions (such as rules and regula-tions). The knowledge base of the sectoral systems is of central impor-tance, as is demand, which may be existing, emerging or simply potential. Finally, sectoral systems are not static but dynamic: "Over time a sectoral system undergoes processes of change and transformation through the coevolution of its various elements."

The sectoral systems perspective is illuminating, not least because it draws attention to interactions between (knowledge-based) organizations and institutions, but also because of its emphasis on dynamics and trans-formations. However, there may be difficulties in applying the perspective to services; or, alternatively, the application of the perspective to services may highlight some problems with the perspective. One difficulty arises in defining a "sector" by its products (or outputs) and, by extension, bounding the sector by the inputs (and agents) required to generate those products. Services, as we have emphasized, are essentially *processes*, which cannot be disentangled easily from the "product outcomes" derived from

---

[3] These organizations may be firms (e.g. users, producers and input suppliers) and non-firm organizations (e.g. universities, financial institutions, government agencies, trade unions and technical associations), including subunits of larger organizations (e.g. R&D or production departments) and groups of organizations (e.g. industry associations).

[4] Such as consumers, entrepreneurs and scientists.

these processes. Thus, for example, all forms of transport move people or objects between places (the outcome is movement in space), but the processes involved in air, water and land transport can be quite different. This raises the question of how appropriate a conventional sectoral approach (defined on the basis of the standard industrial classification) is to the study of services and their SIs. Rather than study innovation within conventional "sectors," it may make more sense to map out SIs that cut across sectors, including both manufacturing and service activities, as these are conventionally defined.

Our work demonstrates that services are involved in multiple and complementary transformations that transcend any simple definition of a sector. These transformations involve both manufacturers (of tangible equipment) and providers of intangible and relational services. The corollary of this is that product-defined sectors and SSIs, focused as these are on the production (i.e. manufacturing) of goods, may provide a rather partial or blinkered understanding of the development of the sector and its products. For example, defined along conventional sectoral lines, a study of the "sectoral system" of commercial airliner production (perhaps within the wider "aerospace" or "transport equipment" sectors) is likely to highlight (and privilege) the technical challenges fundamental to the development of quieter and more fuel-efficient airliners. But, arguably, this provides a narrow viewpoint on the development of the industry. The development by Airbus Industrie of the A380 "super-jumbo" is undoubtedly the most significant innovation in the commercial airliner industry for many years, but the development of this aircraft cannot be properly understood without extending the "system" to incorporate airlines, passenger preferences, airports (including their capacity problems) and the regulatory regime (for both safety and competition). Thus, a wider understanding necessitates incorporating within the "system" activities conventionally classified in separate manufacturing and services "sectors."

We further contend that, within each conventional sector, there are commonly multiple, overlapping SIs. These shape the revealed innovative performance of different agents active within each (conventional) sector. These conclusions are drawn from our studies within the ESSY project of aspects of services innovation. The emphasis is on "aspects of" innovation because we did not attempt all-embracing studies of our sectors (i.e. airports, healthcare and retailing), each of which is large, complex and multifaceted. Furthermore, we do not claim these services (or the aspects of them that we investigated) to be representative of the wider "service sector." Instead, our research has focused on particular activities within these wider activities. In so doing, we studied three very different service activities. Within airports, air traffic control (ATC) activities are "classic services" – that is, they are co-produced by the provider and user acting together in real time. By contrast, in health services, the insertion of an intra-ocular lens (IOL) is a service provided by the producer for the passive recipient (i.e. it is akin to a repair service). Within retailing, supermarkets involve the consumers to the extent that they provide a significant part of the labor for the service (through self-selecting goods and self-delivery from shop to home). This focus on particular activities has allowed us to investigate processes of interaction and interdependency – classic properties of systems, which we would not have been able to investigate had we taken a broader approach to our research. We now highlight some of the main findings from each of these studies.

### 3.1    Airports and the creation of runway capacity[5]

For our work on airports we have focused on the central problem of runway capacity, and especially the problem of how to "squeeze out" an ever-increasing throughput of aircraft using the existing runways at Europe's busiest and most congested airports – namely Frankfurt, London Heathrow and London Gatwick. We consider that our detailed investigation has contributed to developing our understanding of several conceptually interesting matters that relate to the underlying SIs. In brief, these are:

1. The fact that runway operations are co-produced services, based on institutions and instituted practices. Consequently, even in the absence of innovation, there are interesting questions about how the "system" is coordinated.
2. The processes of innovation, both in terms of the search for capacity improvements and the actual implementation of the innovations. For both of these there is clearly a learning process, and particularly one dependent on cooperation between the service providers and the service users. Also prominent is significant procedural change, or "soft innovation," which complements innovation through the adoption of capital equipment.
3. The apparent transformation of the innovation system over time, which relates to the gradual change in the sources of knowledge used for innovation. This has changed the participants in, and thus the boundaries of, the SI.

---

[5] This section draws on Tether and Metcalfe (2003).

### 3.1.1   Co-production, institutions and the distributed process of capacity assessment

Air traffic services, including runway operations, are classic services – they are both intangible and "co-produced." This means the service cannot be stored, and is produced (or operated) jointly, consciously and in real time, by the provider (in this case ATC) and the service users (the airline pilots). "Co-production" means that efficient operations must be developed through negotiation and mutual understanding between the provider and user, particularly within the context of institutions and instituted practices.

"Slot rules" are particularly important and interesting institutions, as they influence how the "system" operates. They have been instituted because of excess demand – especially at peak times – for the use of the airports, and give the users (airlines) security in their rights of access. They also stabilize practice (i.e. scheduling) and demand. However, they and other institutions also build significant rigidities into the system. For example, airlines are reluctant to change their standard operating practices (SOPs) to suit the needs of individual airports, especially as international SOPs are followed for insurance and licensing purposes. The processes of capacity assessment and slot allocation are both instituted and distributed between agents (i.e. provider and user). This partly reflects the fact that capacity is a compromise between the traffic throughput and the average delay, and thus between service quantity and quality, but it also reflects the importance of capacity analysis and slot allocation at congested airports. Again, this situation contrasts with conventional production activities, in which the producer controls and can change – unilaterally – the extent and organization of production. Co-production thus highlights the restricted nature of the potential paths of change, as it is pointless to seek to impose change that is unacceptable to all the co-producing agents.

This sector illustrates an important theme: that institutional change can be at the very core of innovation. One "innovation" we discuss is the "bunching of aircraft" by size into a more efficient sequence than that provided on a "first come first served" (FCFS) basis. For example, if heavy, medium and small aircraft are denoted H, M and S respectively, and the original FCFS sequence of aircraft landing (or departing) is H S M H S M, it is more efficient to process these in the order S S M M H H. But essential to this resequencing (or "bunching") is abandoning the principle (or institution) of FCFS. To abandon this principle, the users had to be persuaded of the benefits but also provided with safeguards. This meant the introduction of new rules, which effect a balance between the benefits and the disruption of the resequencing procedure.

*3.1.2 Learning by cooperating and the significance of procedural change*

Secondly, we investigated the "learning" processes behind the improving efficiency of runway operations at Frankfurt, Heathrow and Gatwick – Europe's three most highly congested airports. The remarkable feature of these airports is that their runway efficiency has increased significantly over the years, despite being "full" for most of that period, and despite retaining the same basic runway infrastructure. That is, they have not responded to the need for increased capacity simply by constructing new runways (because they have not been permitted to). This increased capacity through the same infrastructure is largely due to learning processes and procedural changes that have improved the utilization of the existing infrastructure.

Because the service is co-produced, innovation is dependent on "learning by cooperating," where "cooperation" has the dual meanings of (1) operating jointly and (2) the harmonious search for mutually acceptable solutions. Thus, where "learning by doing" is an activity confined to the producer, and "learning by using" is an activity confined to the user, where each has – respectively – autonomy over how the product (a third, independent, physical entity) is produced or used, this is not the case with "learning by cooperating." Instead, changes have to be negotiated rather than merely implemented. In this, "learning by cooperating" shares commonalities with Lundvall's (1988) "learning by interacting." But, with Lundvall's learning, the producer normally refines the product to reflect user needs better, yet retains discretion over the final definition of the product. "Learning by cooperating" is, perhaps, an extreme form of "learning by interacting," in which the producer's discretion is severely curtailed. Whether a change is implemented depends on whether it is mutually acceptable to the service provider and the service users. Consequently, learning by cooperating is based on a high degree of contextual knowledge about the nature of the co-produced service and the development of a "shared mental model" (Denzau and North, 1994; and Druskat and Pescosolido, 2002) or "collective mind" (Weick and Roberts, 1993; and Weick, Sutcliffe and Obstfeld, 1999) about the activity, and the paths of possible change. As a form of learning it extends beyond (conscious) "learning by doing/using," which in effect identifies the possible changes that might be made (the possibility space), to an understanding of the needs of the other actors involved in the co-production of the service. This understanding of others' interests then reduces the number of real options for change within the possibility space.

This brings us to the second meaning of cooperating: the search for mutually acceptable solutions. Through the understanding generated by the first form of cooperating, the service provider and service users effectively narrow the options for change to those that are mutually acceptable. This does not mean that all the possible paths are identified, or their implications fully understood, but it is through this second form of learning by cooperating that the service provider and service users set out jointly to explore mutually acceptable pathways to improving the operation of the system. Importantly, at congested airports this cooperative search is conducted with the understanding that the airport is full, or very close to being full, but there is also constant pressure to expand capacity due to increasing demand. Within this context, each year a small number of opportunities to achieve small improvements to operations are found, negotiated and implemented.

This brings to the fore the significance of negotiated procedural change as a source of capacity creation (or, more generally, efficiency saving), both in its own right and as a complement to the incorporation of new equipment. This "soft side" of innovation has tended to be neglected by scholars of innovation, who have instead concentrated on hardware, yet the significance of procedural change is widely recognized in the technical literature on airports. Procedural changes are also central to the two innovations we investigated: the bunching of aircraft (which is outlined above); and the use of dual glideslopes for aircraft landing at Frankfurt airport. Admittedly, the second of these also requires advanced technologies to ensure that separations between aircraft are maintained, but in both cases the innovations were based on procedural changes, which were in turn based on negotiated agreements between the service provider (ATC) and the users (airlines). Moreover, these procedural changes are to a large extent embedded within internationally agreed SOPs.

The key point is that changes in operating procedures, which have provided efficiency and savings, are negotiated and not dictated. Many lines of change are resisted, because vested interests make them unacceptable. Thus, not only is it important to know what might be done but it is also important to know what is (likely to be) acceptable. Ultimately, a central problem in "knowing" the capacity of the runways is that this depends on how flexible the basic instituted practices are to change, which itself cannot be "known" as the flexibility of these practices can change over time.

### 3.1.3    *Changing sources of knowledge for innovation and evolving "system" Boundaries*

A third interesting feature of the study is the gradual, but apparent, transformation of the sources of knowledge used for innovation. Prior to the 1970s runway capacity was not a problem, whilst in the 1970s, 1980s and early 1990s capacity was increasingly understood and improved, albeit largely on the basis of direct operating experience and observations. Consequently, during this period, capacity-enhancing innovations were largely dependent on context-dependent operating knowledge, combined with an understanding of which changes to the existing procedures would be mutually acceptable to the service provider and service users (i.e. as outlined above). But, as the scope for "simple" procedural changes has diminished (in the 1990s), the search for continued improvements to the efficiency of operations has led to new innovation trajectories, which have involved new knowledge bases and new agents.

One such development is the further refinement of existing procedures through the use of sophisticated information technology "decision support tools." An example is the final approach separation tool (FAST), which assists air traffic controllers in maintaining minimal separations between arriving aircraft. Development of FAST began around 1990, but it was only implemented ten years later. This reflects the difficulty of developing computer tools that not only match but outperform the heuristically based methods (i.e. rules of thumb) applied by experienced air traffic controllers.

A second new innovation trajectory is the detailed assessment of the fundamental institutions underlying runway operations, and, most notably, the length of the separations required between aircraft due to aircraft wake vortices. These separations "are based more on experience than scientific research" (Civil Aviation Authority, 1993), but as demand has increased so pressure to use the minimum safe separations has grown, because if the separations are too wide then valuable runway time and hence capacity is being lost. Consequently, much more scientific research is now being undertaken into the nature of aircraft wake vortices, with the aim of reducing the necessary separations.

The broader point is that these new trajectories of innovation are involving both new types of knowledge (e.g. mathematical modeling, computer science, formal operations research and scientific knowledge of physics) and new agents (e.g. universities, specialist firms and public sector aerospace laboratories) in the SI. Thus, the distribution of knowledge in the system is changing, with an increasing component of the R&D now being conducted off-site, in public sector agencies (such as the national and pan-European aerospace laboratories and aviation authorities), universities (computer science, operational research and physics departments) and private companies. Some companies have emerged relatively recently to serve this growing industry, but others are long-standing. All are from outside the "airports sector" or "aviation sector," as conventionally defined.

Thus, there is an evolution in the state and nature of knowledge about airside operations at airports. Knowledge is increasingly codified (in complex ways, for example through the use of simulations) and is increasingly based on formal methods as well as experience. Nonetheless, it has been difficult for the "codified formal approach" to catch up and surpass the knowledge based on tacit experience that informed operations and innovation in the past. But there was nothing inevitable about this transformation (at least not with respect to its timing). If more runways were built there would be much less incentive to adopt innovation trajectories based on maximizing the efficiency of the existing facilities, and the new knowledge and agents associated with this trajectory would not have been brought into the system. Thus, the nature of the knowledge used, and the agents involved, is in part a reflection of the contingent problem – and a willingness to address the problem – of inadequate runway capacity in the face of incessantly increasing demand for more flights.

### 3.2 *Healthcare and the case of intra-ocular lenses*[6]

Like the study on airports, the study on healthcare focused on one particular "problem area"; restoring sight to patients with severe cataracts. In particular, the study concerns the emergence of an SI around the development of the IOL. This is an example of an SI in knowledge-based medical services, and, more specifically, in the field of ophthalmology.

As a distinct field of medical practice, ophthalmology has been the focus of major technological changes in the past four decades. Separate markets have been developed for the treatment of glaucoma, for the treatment of short and long sight through refractive surgery, and for the treatment of cataracts. In each case new procedures have transformed service provision, and underpinning these treatments has been a long sequence of complementary innovations – in materials, equipment and drugs and in the operative technique to perform the service. The study of the IOL provides an opportunity to follow the innovation process – and the emergence of an SI – in a way that draws attention to the interdependence between artifact and service innovations in a field of rapidly changing medical knowledge.

To summarize the main findings, we simply state that the innovation system associated with the IOL has radically transformed the conception and delivery of a major medical service – namely the removal of cataracts combined with their replacement by a functioning lens. This has brought great benefit to countless patients and has greatly increased the efficiency

---

[6] This section draws on Metcalfe and James (2002).

and effectiveness with which the clinical procedure is carried out. It has been achieved by the creativity of individual clinicians in conjunction with the development of a transnational medical-industrial complex. Over time, the innovation system has been radically transformed, from its origins in the work and craft technique of "hero surgeons" in a few hospitals to one that is a routinized procedure capable nowadays of being effected in a local medical centre by clinician nursing staff. This reflects a fundamental transformation of a service activity and its skill base.

In summary, the main findings of the study are as follows.

- Radical effects on the delivery of health services have followed from the introduction of IOLs. For the patient, an operation that formerly required months of incapacity is now recovered from in a matter of hours. For the health service, there has been an enormous increase in the capital and labor productivity associated with the increased patient throughput. Corresponding to these surface effects have been major changes in the education and training processes for nurses and clinicians and the emergence of a new division of labor between nurses and clinicians in the performance of the operation. However, not all the methods have proved successful, and, in many cases, lenses have had to be removed or, in extreme cases, eyesight has been lost. As with many medical procedures, the experimental costs are necessarily borne by the patients. Cataract surgery is a branch of human engineering; it is not based on a predictive science.

- The innovation has underpinned the development of an international medical-industrial complex, which drives the innovation process and connects together clinicians with firms in what has evolved into a science-based industry. In effect, IOL implants have evolved into a commodity provided in a market, albeit a highly regulated one that, in different countries, mixes public and private provision differently.

- The SI is sustained by and develops through the interaction between different national ophthalmic health providers (each with their own funding and other characteristics), which are connected by international networks of clinicians and the transnational health companies that develop and market their ideas.

- The innovation process around IOLs illustrates multiple facets of the innovation process, including: the importance of complementary developments in technology; the role of serendipity; an often profound hostility to new ideas by established professionals; competing and evolving lens design configurations and operative techniques; and a sequence of incremental innovations gradually improving the performance of the implants. As is so often the case, the potential of an innovation takes many years to realize, with many failures and abortive paths of development before a dominant design configuration is established. It is for this reason that a historical perspective is so helpful in establishing the processes at work in generating the innovation sequence.

- The dynamic character of the distributed innovation process for IOL-based cataract surgery. This system did not exist prior to the initial "radical" innovation, and it has coevolved with the growth of knowledge and practice. We understand a dynamic system of innovation to be one in which actors, relationships and boundaries change over time. The change may be stimulated either from the outside (for instance, by a change in regulatory regime, government policy or competitor behavior) or from within by the activity of the actors themselves. Moreover, there are important processes of institutionalization that impact on the structure of the system and the diffusion of the innovation.

- The unique role of the commercial firm to act as the locus of combinatorial capabilities, connecting together the elements of the innovation system in the search for competitive advantage. The key point is that competition leads to connection, and connection can lead to collaboration. In this process of innovation system building, problems play an important role as focal points for interaction between different actors. Moreover, the solution to one problem opens up new problems, so that the growth of knowledge is properly described as autocatalytic. Solutions to one problem raise new problems in a sequential fashion.

It is apparent that this SI is constituted by elements at multiple levels – transnational and national, sectoral and regional – but what matters for the actual course of innovation is the micro-systemic element. As with the airports' case, the innovations generated by the system did not occur "naturally" at any level; rather, they were created around cumulative sequences of problems and involved shifting patterns of interaction as new problems emerged and drew upon different kinds of specialized knowledge for their solution. To understand how these processes work we undertook a detailed investigation of the micro-innovation system and analyzed how it was constructed around connected problem sequences. Who formulates the problem sequence is thus a key issue in the evolution of these innovation systems.

National organizations – for example, in the form of healthcare systems, with their inherent differences – have certainly framed the development of IOLs, but the framing is contingent. More constraining are the established theories and practices that lie within particular branches of ophthalmic practice, and the links between surgeons and major ophthalmic companies. However, these constraints spill over national boundaries and develop over time as the innovation is diffused within different healthcare systems. Thus, while the first two decades of the innovation of the IOL are essentially a European story, the next three decades are told in the United States, where the major ophthalmic multinationals rise to dominate the industry. All these firms have a major marketing and distributive presence in Europe but the preponderance of their innovation activity remains in North America. This geographic shift marks a more subtle development in this innovation system: from one centered around hero surgeons, who publish and patent within a well-defined community of hospital and clinical practice, to one in which large firms dominate and channel the innovation process along established lines. This does not mean that the surgeons are rendered unimportant, but it does mean that their position and role in the innovation process are now very different from what they were in the early years.

### 3.3    *Retailing and the transformation of distribution*[7]

This study of retailing, which compares the UK situation with that in Sweden, takes a broadly similar approach to that used in the studies of airports and healthcare. This study focuses on a central business "problem" in the organization of supermarket retailing, but takes a broader and longer-term view of the transformation of grocery distribution from food producers to end-consumers. Like the other studies, the aim is not to provide a complete examination of the "retail sector," and nor is the study narrowly confined to "retailing" as that activity is conventionally defined. Indeed, the comparison between the United Kingdom and Sweden in the transformation of grocery distribution and retailing has been designed to reveal the dynamics of variation, in terms of the relations between the different economic agents that are conventionally understood to be active in different aspects of retailing.

This study demonstrates how changes in relations between consumers, retailers, manufacturers, logistics and primary producers brought about very different types of innovations, and innovation potentials, in the two countries. Although there are some fundamental physical, geographical and economic differences (such as the size and distribution of the population, and the level and distribution of income), which contribute to the different national patterns of transformation, the comparison of the two countries highlights the factors that underpin the process of variation in different socio-economic spaces (rather than taking these as given). Thus,

---

[7] This section draws on Harvey, Nyberg and Metcalfe (2002).

in this analysis, retailing is shown to be a node, ever more critical, in an evolving innovation complex involving actors and organizations from a variety of economic spheres.

One of the key aspects of national differences is the path-dependent and instituted nature of the trajectories of transformation. The Swedish starting point was very different from that of the United Kingdom, for, although its strong cooperative movement certainly had a parallel in the United Kingdom, it developed along substantially different lines, becoming the general pattern in Sweden, whilst in the United Kingdom cooperatives focused on working-class demand. This, in turn, underlies the central and compelling difference between the two retail configurations, which persists to this day, although both configurations share strikingly high levels of concentration.

In the United Kingdom the dominant retail supermarkets are integrated businesses. This configuration has encouraged the total and centralized integration of grocery distribution from the control of primary and secondary producers to retailing itself, and has included the bypassing of intermediates, most notably wholesalers. Consequently, the dominant retailers not only orchestrate retailing activities but also exert a significant hold on producers and distributors. This orchestration has great influence on the activities of others with different capabilities and technologies, such as logistics companies, food product manufacturers and farmers. In Sweden, by contrast, the large retailers are not single firms but federations of end-retailers. Thus, in Sweden, the locus of centralization is not – as in the United Kingdom – at the retail end but at the intermediary, wholesale, node of the complex. From this structural difference much flows in terms of innovation potentialities, patterns of collaboration and concentration, and the engagement of different knowledge bases. For example, the Swedish configuration has led to a much more decentralized pattern of local and small-scale production, fostering organics, and has blocked the innovation potential of a supply chain driven by electronic point of sale (EPOS) equipment, which is such a prominent feature of the "system" in the United Kingdom.

A major conclusion that can be drawn from this path-dependent character of transformation in different economic spaces is the intimate linkage between industrial organization – and changes in this – and innovation processes and potentialities. This brings to the fore the interlinkage between business models, organization and technologies. When comparing the "first revolution" in retailing – the emergence of the global brand manufacturers – with the "second revolution" – the dominance of large-scale supermarket enterprises – there are clear differences between the processes of innovation, the objects of innovation and the markets for innovation. Viewed as distributed processes of innovation (Coombs, Harvey and Tether, 2001), it is apparent that the nature of the distributedness changes. In the first place, the key points of articulation were between manufacturers, organic chemists (with a university base), farmers, the engineering of continuous flow production, and marketing. In the second, the retailer becomes the primary orchestrator of the different economic agents, with different capabilities stretching from biotechnology to informatics.

But not only has each of these transformations involved new patterns of distributed innovation activity, it has also led to the emergence of new classes of economic agent (e.g. logistics companies and specialist software houses) and radical transformations of existing classes of economic agent (e.g. food manufacturers, retailers, farmers and consumers). This has changed the relations between classes of economic agent; however, these changed relations are most prominent between rather than within "sectors" as these are conventionally defined. These changed relations underpin the emergence of new fields of innovation and new forms of cooperation, and the development of different knowledge bases. Thus, innovation processes within retail organizations – such as the introduction of scanning and EPOS systems at checkouts – can only be fully understood as a node of innovation within a much broader innovation complex extending beyond retailing as a distinct activity. For, despite many of the key capabilities remaining "outside" the retailer and the "retail sector," it is through their orchestrating role that – in the United Kingdom – retailers have coordinated these external capabilities and integrated them into the innovation process. It is in this context – the pursuit of individual and group competitive advantage – that retailers can be seen to assemble the innovation system by articulating the interactions between many organizations with distinctive capabilities. This division of innovative labor is not static but, rather, it is continually evolving; it is at the same time replicated and constructed.

The emergence of the retailer as a dominant player leads to another important reflection on the role of multinationals in this innovation complex. Two very different models of globalization are at play. The first model is driven by the branded manufacturers (e.g. Nestlé, Unilever, Danone, Kellogg and Campbell), which produce generic products to exploit economies of scale in manufacturing, marketing and product design. Although there are products targeted on specific national market segments, typically the target is the "global consumer." By contrast, the second model is a retailer-dominated configuration, driven by the front-end interface with the consumer. This has developed and draws upon a knowledge base that is highly focused on socio-economic profiles of consumers and differentiations in consumers within the "catchment" areas of a particular retail store. In this model the branding is that of the retailer, and it is the branding of the whole basket of products and services, rather than the branding of specific products or product categories. In the United Kingdom, supermarket own-label produce has become more and more focused on product differentiation and market segmentation. Meanwhile, and although nationally located, the supermarkets have become orchestrators of global supply chains, bringing new ranges of produce to the supermarket shelf. This creation of dedicated global supply chains tied into product and price differentiation is a very different model of "globalization" from the first model – that of the branded manufacturers (Harvey, Quilley and Beynon, 2002).

It should be emphasized that these two models of globalization coexist, although there is considerable tension and competition between them, especially at the points where their product markets intersect. Yet one does not simply replace the other. Many of the global brand manufacturers have responded to the emergence of retailer power and "own labeling" by shrinking their product portfolio to concentrate on a core of global generic products. Conversely, the retailer model of globalization is itself extending its scope, with Ahold of the Netherlands moving into Sweden, Walmart of the United States coming to the United Kingdom, and Tesco of the United Kingdom moving into Eastern Europe and South-East Asia. As yet this process of extension is only beginning (which in itself raises questions about why supermarkets did not internationalize sooner); it remains to be seen whether and how the retailer-dominated configurations will adjust to very different consumer markets from those in which they emerged. It is still very uncertain how the uneasy coexistence between the two (evolving) models of globalization will contest future economic spaces.

Finally, a striking aspect of the innovation complexes investigated in this study is that they are engaged "from seed to mouth" in a diverse range of activities, which draw upon diverse knowledge bases. There is certainly fundamental science (e.g. in genetics and biotechnology), but there is also engineering knowledge (e.g. in satellite tracking or in packaging with artificial atmospheres), operational knowledge (e.g. in logistics) and design and market knowledge. Last, but not least, there is consumer knowledge, learning and beliefs, which have been of considerable significance in recent food scares, and which have fundamentally altered the parameters of product innovation in Western Europe. Retailers have played a key role in articulating these diverse forms of knowledge as they have gained power and control over food provision. Food retailing, therefore, provides us with a rich ground for exploring the processes of variation in innovation distributed across a multiplicity of different institutions and capabilities.

## 4    Elements of systems of innovation

From the definition provided by Malerba in chapter 1 of this book, sectoral systems of innovation are characterized by a set of attributes that evolve over time and that identify system components and their mode of interaction. These attributes are: the knowledge base and learning processes; firms, non-firm organizations and networks; institutions; demand; and geographical boundaries. This is a very large agenda, even for a slow-moving and well-defined and -understood SI. Services, by contrast, are vast, diverse and often rapidly changing – but little studied. Our studies have but scratched the surface of SIs in the service sector; we cannot claim to have undertaken a complete analysis, nor one that investigated a representative set of service activities. However, as the summaries provided above demonstrate, each of the studies has yielded interesting insights into the nature of innovation systems in service-orientated activities. Below we highlight some of the main findings with respect to the various elements of innovation systems, although the strength of the "systems" perspective is in understanding phenomena in their context; much is lost when "systems" are deconstructed into their elements.

### 4.1    *Knowledge bases and learning processes*

Traditionally, services have been portrayed as mere adopters of technologies developed by manufacturers (Pavitt, 1984), but this is badly misleading. Our studies have emphasized the joint significance of technology in equipment (such as medical devices, radar at airports, and scanners and sensors in logistics) and the skills of the operatives (medical surgeons and air traffic controllers). Certainly there is an interesting interplay between embodied and disembodied knowledge, and the boundaries between these can change. Moreover, as procedures or techniques become more familiar, they can be practiced by less highly skilled people, as in the case of the IOL. The main point, however, is the significance of technique, or procedure, alongside artifacts or devices. Technique and procedure are particularly significant in services, and have been largely overlooked in innovation studies that have focused on manufacturing.

The knowledge bases of services are diverse, but an interesting characteristic of the activities we have examined is how these can also change fundamentally over time. This is true of each of our cases. In airport runway capacity there has been a gradual shift from learning through experience and cooperation to the use of formal and scientific knowledge, and specialist R&D-type departments and companies with these knowledge bases. In the case of IOLs these procedures were initially developed by highly skilled professionals (surgeons), but advances have since become the province of large, diversified medical firms. There has been a shift in the locus of knowledge/learning from the hospitals to the companies providing the devices and associated training. Thus, in these cases there is a changing dynamic in the relationship between the sources of knowledge and the boundaries of the SIs. In the retail case, integrated, computer-based methods of management and control have transformed the use of logistics information, with consequent changes for the skill base of the sector's management.

This brings us to the question of the boundaries of the SIs, which we treat as evolving and not fixed, and which do not coincide with the conventional sectoral definitions. For example, retailing is only one activity in an extended chain of activities that transform raw materials into products and which distribute and market them to consumers. As a result, the innovation system, which can to a large extent be orchestrated by retailers, extends from producers to consumers, but it also includes distribution, advertising, warehousing and many other activities. Similarly, with air traffic activities at airports, the SI involves not only ATC, the airport operator and the airlines but also aircraft manufacturers, specialist service and equipment suppliers, university researchers and others. Thus, a narrow focus on "airports" or "retailing" presents a severely curtailed picture, which fails to show the interactions and interdependencies that are a key feature of SIs.

### 4.2    Firms, non-firm organizations and networks

Although the classic mode of service provision is a vast array of fragmented, small, independent providers, often operating on a local basis, the service activities we investigated all have significant network relationships, which are also increasingly multinational. In each case, there are significant variations over time and/or space in the nature of the organizations active in the SI.

In the case of IOLs, the kinds of agencies involved and the relations between them have changed significantly over time as the innovation system has been constructed. Initially, the system involved professional clinicians working in the context of hospitals and associations of professional practitioners, but over time it has extended to include producers of ophthalmic devices, material suppliers, and managers of healthcare delivery systems. In the process, specific sets of overlapping networks have been created. Our conclusion is that competing ophthalmic supply firms have constructed their own "local" innovation systems in the pursuit of competitive advantage in international markets. These local innovation systems draw upon the resources found within networks of ophthalmic clinicians, university science networks and hospital management systems. The networks do not of themselves constitute innovation systems; rather, the systemic effect is something articulated by the ophthalmic companies and changes as the companies' perception of the innovation problem also changes.

In the case of airports and the creation of runway capacity, the "system" initially involved the airport operator, ATC, the airlines and the aviation authority, but has been expanded in recent years as the sourcing of knowledge has changed. This has drawn in specialist firms, research institutes and university departments. Also important is the changing status of the agents involved in this system. In the United Kingdom and some other countries, privatization has shifted the airlines, the airport operator and ATC from the domain of publicly owned service providers to being privately owned and governed by commercial logic. This transformation is having implications for the way in which these agents interrelate, and how they interrelate with the other contributors to the SI. For example, the United Kingdom's ATC company is now seeking to sell its expertise in international markets, whilst it is also reducing its internal research capacity and increasingly outsourcing innovation-related expertise from universities and specialist consultancy firms.

In the case of retailing, it can be seen that the contrasting nature of the firms in the United Kingdom (highly integrated businesses) and Sweden (federations and cooperatives) has resulted in rather different patterns of innovation, and rather different loci of control over the "production-distribution-retailing chains."

Non-market organizations also have a significant impact through regulation, which can impact directly and indirectly on the SIs by encouraging some forms of innovation whilst restricting others. For example, in the case of the IOL the initial regulatory frameworks were provided by clinical norms often hostile to radical innovation. As the industry has matured so regulation from the Food and Drug Administration (FDA) in the United States and its European equivalents has assumed greater significance. Moreover, legal norms have come increasingly to constrain the relationship between innovative medical practice and patients. Indeed, the inventor and innovator of the IOL retired from performing the procedure precisely because of fears of litigation at a time when the technology appeared to have hit a bottleneck.

### 4.3     Institutions

Institutions, the "rules of the game" that constrain, coordinate and enable activity, also play a central role, particularly in highly regulated services such as healthcare and air traffic operations. In the case of the IOL, for example, the operation was initially conducted if the patient's score on the so-called "Snellen test" was below 6/12. This shows the Snellen test to be an important institution in the "system," but also raises a number of questions, such as why the Snellen test is used and not any other test, and why this particular threshold value is used, and who decided upon it. Thus, not only are the institutions significant but the process of institutionalization is significant, as is potential conflict over the institutions. Moreover, as the scale with which the procedure is applied has increased, so clinicians have sought to complement an objective test with softer "lifestyle" criteria, such as the extent to which a candidate patient is socially and economically active.

In the case of airports (and retailing), "slots" are used to provide access to the runways (and for delivery to supermarkets). At airports, especially, the means of slot allocation and retention is fundamental to the operation of the system. Airport slots are allocated and retained by non-market mechanisms, and they cannot be bought or sold. But, if they were allocated by a market mechanism, such as by auction, this would have significant ramifications for airport operations. This would then impact upon the SI, quite possibly making the search for additional throughput less important; instead, the use of larger aircraft (rather than more aircraft) would be encouraged. Clearly, institutions are crucial, but to understand the system it is not adequate to list them; it is necessary to understand how they came to be instituted, and how they influence behavior. In the case of retailing, we need to develop a fuller understanding of why systems of provision developed in different ways. Why, for instance, does the Swedish system have an orientation to federations and cooperatives whilst the UK system is dominated by integrated businesses? Why, also, have these different configurations tended to be national in orientation rather than international?

### 4.4     Demand

The role of demand and how this is developed, or constructed, is very often underexplored in studies of innovation. Frequently, it is assumed that the good or service provided fulfills some basic need or want for which there is, at least, a latent demand. This demand is first stimulated by the good or service becoming available, then expanded through improvements in the quality or reductions in price. We suggest that demand side issues require urgent attention, especially in relation to how "wants" or "needs" are formed, and then expressed in terms of demand. For example, while the clinical need for the removal of cataracts is long-standing and extensive in the population aged over fifty-five, the expression of this in terms of demand for clinical services is very much influenced by the medical solutions available and the response of healthcare managers to the resource implications of enhanced demand. Thus, the link between the patient and the service is mediated by a complex of instituted relations between clinical practice and healthcare management. In the case of airports, we did not examine the level of demand – which is growing exogenously to the "airport system." However, the structure of demand – for instance, in terms of the size distribution of aircraft – has important implications for the SI. If there were only one type of aircraft the problems faced would be very much simpler.

### 4.5     The geographical boundaries and international performance comparisons

Conventionally, most services are provided locally, and can have strong cultural variations, but the services we examined were not typical in this regard. It is difficult to generalize about the boundaries of the system, for there are certainly local, national and global aspects. For example, in many ways air traffic operations are a global activity: operating practices are essentially the same the world over, and are agreed by international organizations. However, airports also tend to have their own individual problems, which require local solutions. These local solutions, meanwhile, must comply with international SOPs. As more airports in other locations confront the same problems so solutions are transferred, at least partially. In the case of the IOL, the geographic locus of innovation activity has changed over time, from a European to a North American focus, but the practice is global, albeit operating in different contexts of national healthcare provision. With retailing there is a similar story. To a large extent practices are very similar across space (for instance, the increasing use of sophisticated logistics), but there are also important and often subtle differences. Certainly, none of these systems is strictly national in character; rather, the local and the global intersect in relation to different aspects of the innovation process.

International performance comparisons of different innovation systems are also difficult to make. What is being compared, how broad should the consideration be, and over what timescale? What weight are we to give to local conditions that impinge on the innovation process? In each of our cases international differences exist, but it is difficult to relate these to innovation performance. For example, amongst airports, Paris' Charles de Gaulle has been permitted to construct new runways roughly in line with the increasing demand for flights. Because of this it performs well in terms of delays, but it has also had less need for the innovations and innovation processes that we have identified as responses to capacity constraints at London Heathrow and Frankfurt, where the airports have sought to make the most of the existing facilities.

## 5    Innovation systems as problem- or opportunity-centered and contingent

We end this paper by reconsidering SIs as problem- or opportunity-centered and contingent. A system implies not just interaction but also interdependence, and we consider that much of the existing literature on SIs fails to demonstrate the nature and function of any interdependence between the participating agents. The fundamental issue is to be clear on what interdependence involves and how it matters for the rate and direction of innovation. A "national systems" approach is particularly broad in its view of innovation, seeking as it does to explain why the pattern of innovation (and specialization) differs between countries.[8] Freeman (1987, p. 1) originally defined a national system of innovation as "the network of institutions in the public and private sectors whose activities and interactions initiate, import, modify and diffuse new technologies." Thus, within Freeman's – and Nelson's (1993) – "national systems," the systemic factors are things such as government (science and technology) policies and organizational support for technology and innovation, the extent and organization of R&D within enterprises, the training and education systems, and the financial institutions. Lundvall (1992, p. 12) also takes a broad view of national systems, including "all parts and aspects of the economic structure and the institutional set-up affecting learning as well as searching and exploring." However, arguably there is little that is systemic about these "systems" (Freeman's use of the term "network" is notable). Interaction is largely assumed rather than researched, and there is even less evidence of interdependence.

The SSI approach has built upon the "national systems" approach – arguing that technological fundamentals are at least as important as differences in national institutions. This is as true of service activities as it

---

[8] It is also primarily a policy-oriented approach. As Edquist (1997, p. 12) states: "The importance of national systems of innovation has to do with the fact that they capture the important political and policy aspects of processes of innovation."

is of any other productive activity. This meso-level approach builds on the work on technological families (Scherer, 1967) and on broad patterns of technological change – such as technological regimes, paradigms and trajectories, discussed by Dosi (1982), Nelson and Winter (1982), Pavitt (1984) and others – complementing these ideas with those from a resource- or competence-based view of the firm (Penrose, 1959; and Foss and Knudsen, 1996).[9] However, whilst the "sectoral systems" approach has tended to be more specific than the "national systems" literature (in terms of the organizations and institutions included), the sectors still tend to be defined using conventional "industries" as points of reference – e.g. chemicals, biotechnology or telecommunications.

In our work on SIs in services (Tether and Metcalfe, 2002; Metcalfe and James, 2002; and Harvey, Nyberg and Metcalfe, 2002) we have taken a different approach. We have not attempted to study entire "sectors" of service provision but have instead focused on particular problems, innovations and wider transformations arising within the production of specific services. The definition of the underlying activity is the crucial step in this approach. The implications of these case studies for the SI perspective are considerable. For such systems are, we argue, constituted by elements at multiple levels – transnational and national, sectoral and regional – but what matters for the actual course of innovation is their micro-systemic element. The systems that generate innovations do not occur "naturally" (or inevitably) at any level; rather, they are created around cumulative sequences of problems (or opportunities)[10] and involve shifting patterns of interaction as new problems (or opportunities) emerge and draw upon different kinds of specialized knowledge for their solution. To understand how these processes work we need a far more detailed understanding of micro-innovation systems and how they are constructed around connected problem (or opportunity) sequences.

In some cases the problem or opportunity is obvious – such as in the case of airports and the problem of insufficient runway capacity to meet (valuable) demand, and in the case of seeking a remedy to failing eyesight due to cataracts. In other cases the problem/opportunity is not so

---

[9] This emphasizes the creation and selection of diversity amongst firms, which is itself the result of the path-dependent accumulation of firm-specific (technological) knowledge and expertise. Thus, the creation and accumulation of specific capabilities by innovating firms reinforces the value of their participation in the relationships that constitute the "sectoral system."

[10] In English the term "problem" tends to have negative connotations, whilst the word "opportunity" has positive connotations; we would prefer a neutral term, or one that has both positive and negative (and even ambiguous) connotations.

obvious – as in the case of retailing – and in such cases the problem/opportunity is a matter of interpretation that may need to be constructed, negotiated and even institutionalized. In UK retailing, the problem/opportunity might be interpreted as being how to gain and maintain primary access to consumers (against direct and indirect competitors). Notably, this has been achieved through the centralization and control of distribution functions.

Importantly, the problem/opportunity is often contingent, not only on the technological fundamentals (and past sunk investments) but also on the regulatory and institutional constraints. For example, at airports such as Frankfurt and London Heathrow the problem of inadequate runway capacity would not exist (or, at least, would be very different) if, like Paris Charles de Gaulle, these airports were permitted to build new runways. It is because they have not that the pattern of innovation has followed a different road at these airports.

In Rosenberg's (1976) terms, the problem/opportunity is the "focusing device"[11] around which the SI is constructed, but the "system" is also framed by the contingencies – such as the regulatory framework. Thus, the SI entails a division of labor, formed around a focal problem or opportunity, framed by contingencies, and energized to confront and provide solutions to particular system elements. The problem/opportunity does not necessarily define the solutions, or the "solution pattern," but the contingencies are likely to restrict the scope of possible solutions.

Figure 8.3 attempts to represent this SI, although, as with all such diagrams, there is a danger that it appears static rather than dynamic. On the contrary, we emphasize that the "system" is likely to evolve over time in terms of its components and their interactions. The problem/opportunity is not necessarily fixed, and nor are the possible solutions. Thus the SI is a *dynamic distributed process* (Coombs, Harvey and Tether, 2001), into which new agents and new knowledge sources may be incorporated and from which unnecessary agents and exhausted knowledge sources may be discarded.

This perspective brings to the fore various questions. What energizes the SI? The answer depends upon the context, but it is, we conjecture, the organization(s) that ultimately deliver the service, for it is only these organizations that have the unique role of combining all the different innovation contributions for an explicit purpose. In the case of market-based activities, the primary stimulus is the search for business advantage – actual and potential – as perceived by the firms in the "sector." In other cases, non-market organizations play the critical role, as they do in the

---

[11] Note also Hughes' (1983) concept of the "reverse salient."

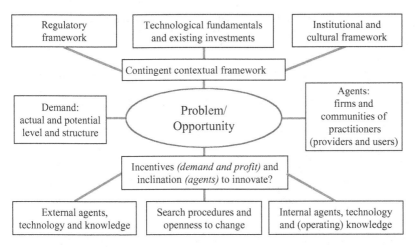

Figure 8.3 The system of innovation as contingent and problem-/ opportunity-centered

airports case study. Secondly, what is the nature and durability of the interactions and interdependencies within the system? By considering the SI to be contingent and problem-/opportunity-based we can investigate interactions and interdependencies between the agents in much greater detail than is the case with broad national or industry studies. We can also investigate the patterns of resistance to innovation, as well as the patterns of "successful" innovation and the changing sources of knowledge used. Moreover, we can examine, where appropriate, the changing balance of dependency and power within the system, and assess how that relates to the observed pattern of activities and innovation (Coombs, Harvey and Tether, 2001).

REFERENCES

Civil Aviation Authority (1993), *A Guide to Runway Capacity – For ATC, Airport and Aircraft Operators*, Civil Aviation Authority, London (CAP 627)

Clark, C. (1940), *The Conditions of Economic Progress*, Macmillan, London

Coombs, R., M. Harvey and B. S. Tether (2001), *Analysing Distributed Innovation Processes*, position paper, Centre for Research on Innovation and Competition, University of Manchester and University of Manchester Institute of Science and Technology

Coombs, R., and I. D. Miles (2000), Innovation, measurement and services: the new problematique, in J. S. Metcalfe and I. D. Miles (eds.), *Innovation Systems in the Service Economy: Measurement and Case Study Analysis*, Kluwer Academic, Boston, 85–104 de Jong, M. W. (1994), Core competencies and chain relations in service industries, in *Management of Services: a Multidisciplinary Approach*, proceedings of the Third International Research Seminar in Service Management, Institut d'Administration des Enterprises, Université d'Aix-Marseille III

Denzau, A. T., and D. C. North (1994), Shared mental models: ideologies and institutions, *Kyklos*, 47, 3–31

Dosi, G. (1982), Technological paradigms and technological trajectories: a suggested interpretation of the determinants of technical change, *Research Policy*, 11, 3, 147–162

Druskat, V. U., and A. T. Pescosolido (2002), The content of effective teamwork mental models in self-managing teams: ownership, learning and heedful interrelating, *Human Relations*, 55, 3, 283–314

Ducatel, K. (2000), Information technologies in non-knowledge services: innovations on the margin? in J. S. Metcalfe and I. D. Miles (eds.), *Innovation Systems in the Service Economy: Measurement and Case Study Analysis*, Kluwer Academic, Boston, 221–245

Edquist, C. (ed.) (1997), *Systems of Innovation: Technologies, Institutions and Organisations*, Frances Pinter, London

Eurostat (1999), *Services in Europe: 1995–1997 Data*, Eurostat, Luxembourg

Evangelista, R. (2000), Sectoral patterns of technological change in services, *Economics of Innovation and New Technology*, 9, 183–221

Fisher, A. G. B. (1939), Production, primary, secondary and tertiary, *Economic Record*, 15, 2, 24–38

Foss, N., and C. Knudsen (eds.) (1996), *Towards a Competence Theory of the Firm*, Routledge, London

Freeman, C. (1987), *Technology Policy and Economic Performance: Lessons from Japan*, Frances Pinter, London

Gallouj, F., and O. Weinstein (1997), Innovation in services, *Research Policy*, 26, 4/5, 537–556

Harvey, M., A. Nyberg and J. S. Metcalfe (2002), *Deep Transformation in the Service Economy: Innovation and Organisational Change in Food Retailing in Sweden and the UK*, ESSY working paper, Centre for Research on Innovation and Competition, University of Manchester and University of Manchester Institute of Science and Technology [http://www.cespri.it/ricerca/es_wp.htm]

Harvey, M., S. Quilley and H. Beynon (2002), *Exploring the Tomato: Transformations of Nature, Economy and Society*, Edward Elgar Publishing, Cheltenham

Hill, P. (1999), Tangibles, intangibles and services: a new taxonomy for the classification of output, *Canadian Journal of Economics*, 32, 2, 426–446

Hill, T. P. (1977), On goods and services, *Review of Income and Wealth*, 23, 4, 315–338

Hughes, A., and E. Wood (2000), Rethinking innovation comparisons between manufacturing and services: the experience of the CBR SME survey in the UK, in J. S. Metcalfe and I. D. Miles (eds.) *Innovation Systems in the Service Economy: Measurement and Case Study Analysis*, Kluwer Academic, Boston 105–124

Hughes, T. P. (1983), *Networks of Power: Electrification in Western Society, 1880–1930*, Johns Hopkins University Press, Baltimore and London

Lovelock, C. (1983), Classifying services to gain strategic marketing insights, *Journal of Marketing*, 47, 3, 9–20

Lundvall, B.-Å. (1988), Innovation as an interactive process: from user-producer interaction to the national system of innovation, in G. Dosi, C. Freeman, R. R. Nelson, G. Silverberg and L. Soete (eds.), *Technical Change and Economic Theory*, Frances Pinter, London, 349–369

   (1992), *National Systems of Innovation: Towards a Theory of Innovation and Interactive Learning*, Frances Pinter, London

Metcalfe, J. S., and A. James (2002), *Emergent Innovation Systems and the Delivery of Clinical Services: The Case of Intra-Ocular Lenses*, ESSY working paper, Centre for Research on Innovation and Competition, University of Manchester and University of Manchester Institute of Science and Technology [http://www.cespri.it/ricerca/es_wp.htm]

Miles, I. D. (1996), *Innovation in Services: Services in Innovation*, Manchester Statistical Society, Manchester

Miozzo, M., and L. Soete (2001), Internationalisation of services: a technology perspective, *Technological Forecasting and Social Change*, 67, 2/3, 159–185

Nelson, R. R. (ed.) (1993), *National Systems of Innovation: A Comparative Study*, Oxford University Press, Oxford

Nelson. R. R., and S. G. Winter (1982), *An Evolutionary Theory of Economic Change*, Harvard University Press, Cambridge, MA

Pavitt, K. (1984), Sectoral patterns of technical change: towards a taxonomy and a theory, *Research Policy*, 13, 6, 343–373

Pennant-Rea, R., and B. Emmott (1983), *Pocket Economist*, The Economist, London

Penrose, E. T. (1959), *The Theory of the Growth of the Firm*, Basil Blackwell, Oxford

Riddle, D. (1986), *Service-Led Growth*, Praeger, New York

Rosenberg, N. (1976), *Perspectives on Technology*, Cambridge University Press, Cambridge

Scherer, F. M. (1967), Market structure and the employment of scientists and engineers, *American Economic Review*, 57, 574–631

Silvestrou, R., L. Fitzgerald, R. Johnston and C. Grant (1992), Toward a classification of service processes, *International Journal of Service Industry Management*, 3, 3, 62–75

Sundbo, J., and F. Gallouj (2000), Innovation as a loosely coupled system in services, in J. S. Metcalfe and I. D. Miles (eds.), *Innovation Systems in the Service Economy: Measurement and Case Study Analysis*, Kluwer Academic, Boston

Tether, B. S., and J. S. Metcalfe (2003), Horndal at Heathrow? Capacity expansion through co-operation and system evolution, *Industrial and Corporate Change*, 12, 3, 437–476

Weick, K. E., and K. H. Roberts (1993), Collective mind in organizations – heedful interrelating on flight decks, *Administrative Science Quarterly*, 38, 3, 357–381

Weick, K. E., K. M. Sutcliffe and D. Obstfeld (1999), Organising for high reliability: processes of collective mindfulness, *Research in Organisational Behavior*, 21, 81–123

*Part III*

Sectoral systems and national systems;
international performance and public policy

# 9 National institutional frameworks, institutional complementarities and sectoral systems of innovation

*Benjamin Coriat and Olivier Weinstein*

## 1 Introduction

Long ago it was recognized that, in economic life, "institutions matter." Very influential schools of thought have been based entirely on this fundamental assumption. This is the case for the so-called "old institutionalism" promoted by Commons, Veblen and Mitchell, and this is the case too for the "new institutional economics" (NIE) school, associated with the names of Coase, Williamson and North. More recently Aoki, by defining a "comparative institutional analysis" research program, has explicitly put his name on the list. It is also the case that the French regulation approach (a research program defined in the mid-1970s) is based entirely on the idea that certain basic "structural" or "institutional" forms are the key elements underlying the dynamics of capitalist economies. In the same spirit the "varieties of capitalism" literature (see, for example, Hall and Soskice, 2001) has underscored the similarities and differences between economic and political institutions among countries, and their effects on economic behavior and performances.

In the more specific domain of the economics of innovation, the intuitions of the pioneering work by Freeman (1987) as regards the role of institutions has been completed and enlarged by Lundvall (1992), Nelson (1993) and, more recently, by Amable, Barré and Boyer (1997). All these national system of innovation or sectoral system of innovation approaches have brought the role played by institutions in the dynamics of innovation to the forefront. In the same line, Coriat and Dosi (1998a) have expounded the "institutional embeddedness dimensions of economic change," and Coriat and Weinstein (2002a) have proposed a framework to examine the respective roles of organizations and institutions in the generation of innovation.

All these studies put a strong emphasis on the ways institutions shape "national"[1] trajectories of innovation. But, in spite of the rich and varied contributions just referred to, one has to admit that the underlying notion and definition of "institution" differ from one essay to another, as do theories about "how" institutions matter and which key institutions should be considered.

The aim of this chapter is to try to clarify these points in a sectoral systems perspective. Whilst "surveying" some of the key contributions dedicated to the analysis of the economics of institutions, the study seeks to answer the three basic following questions:

1. How can we define institutions, and how do they operate?
2. As regards innovation processes, which are the relevant institutions?
3. What is the sectoral relevance of this institutional approach?

## 2    How can we define institutions? How do they operate?

### 2.1    *The double nature and dimension of institutions*[2]

To understand better what an institution is, we think it is useful to begin with a "North-like" notion of institutions, which he defines as "the rules of the game in a society or more formally . . . the humanly devised constraints that shape human interactions" (North, 1990, p. 3). Thus, institutions should be considered as the set of social constraints under which agents[3] operate and coordinate themselves.[4] According to North such "rules of the game" are required, and they are created or accepted by individual agents essentially because they reduce uncertainties and create regularities under which the economic actors can more easily and efficiently behave. This point is now well accepted, at least by most of the "institutionalist" schools, even if they may differ on other important issues.

In our view, however, to understand fully the nature of institutions one has to go a step further, and observe that the rules – or, to be more precise,

---

[1] For an emphasis on the role of institutions in firms' trajectories see Dosi, Coriat and Pavitt (2000).

[2] This section is based on previous work by the authors, namely Coriat and Weinstein (2002a).

[3] At this stage of our study, the notion of "agent" encompasses individuals or collective actors without distinction, the latter either being organized in formal interest groups (unions, associations, etc.) or not (e.g. the participants in a strike or Internet users).

[4] The acceptance of the idea that institutions frame the "rules of the game" does not imply that we accept all the categories North built around his own notion of institution. As we shall see, his concept may be used – and this seems essential to the analysis of institutions – while vesting it with contents that may implicitly or explicitly vary from North's views.

the systems of rules – shaped by institutions should not be envisaged only as "constraints." For, once established and enforced, they appear as "collective resources" to be used by the agents, which are able to use them to deploy their own strategies to achieve their goals.[5]

Moreover, some institutions give rise to entirely new fields of action. By implementing new environments, some institutions open new fields of action where individuals – and groups – will be able to develop their abilities. We can take up Searle's distinction (1995) between "regulatory rules" and "constituting rules." Rules of the first type are created to regulate existing activities, which can, nevertheless, exist without them. But other rules create new activities. These rules take the form of a system, which is at the origin of some institutional subsystems. These types of "constituting rules" create new status and positions, and new types of behavior. Many key economic institutions have to be analyzed in this perspective. To be more concrete, one may consider the case of some scientific institutions: as they become structured and institutionalized they give rise to new types of activities and create new *"patterns of behavior."* This is the case for publicly funded universities and research laboratories: the types of resources provided by these institutions (basic research, highly skilled engineers and researchers, etc.) open up new opportunities for the agents involved in the "game" of producing innovation. A crucial part of the game, for the private agents (and especially firms), is the competition to capture the benefits of the discoveries and inventions produced by these institutions.

In practice, if we wish to draw up a list of the main economic institutions, following Aoki we can establish four categories of institution, namely: (i) markets and money; (ii) the legal and political framework of the state; (iii) contracts and (private order) organizations;[6] and (iv) cultural belief and social norms (2000, p. 161).

In our economies, often defined as "market economies" (based on a very high level of specialization and division of labor), one of the various

---

[5] This approach is in accordance with some key features of Commons' view of institutions, which he conceives as "collective action in control, liberation and expansion of individual action." For Commons, collective action "is more than control of individual action – it is, by the very act of control, . . . a liberation of individual action from coercion, duress, discrimination, or unfair competition, by means of restraints placed on other individuals. [. . .] And collective action is more than restraint and liberation of individual action – it is expansion of the will of the individual far beyond what he can do by his own puny acts." (Commons, 1934, p. 73)

[6] To consider "organizations" as institutions is, of course, not a point of view shared by all scholars. On the contrary, North himself and most of the NIE theorists do differentiate "institutions" (the rules of the game) from "organizations" (the players). For their part, the authors of this paper argue elsewhere (Coriat and Weintein, 2002a) that organizations should be considered as institutions.

institutions required to enable the general exchanges of commodities may deserve special attention. This very specific institution is the market itself.

## 2.2    *The market as a central institution and the need for complementary institutional arrangements*

The market is of central importance because it is through its mechanisms (including money) that the exchanges of commodities are made possible. For this reason, the market can be regarded as one of the central operators, through which society as such is reproduced.

However, a prior basic condition is needed for markets to exist: the property rights on goods to be exchanged need to be perfectly defined, accepted and respected by the agents. As observed by Aoki, "for this institution (the market) to evolve and function, property rights to economic assets need to be clearly defined and enforced" (2000, p. 171).[7] In fact, property rights theorists insist on the fact that property rights defined as "socially enforced rights to select uses of an economic good" (Alchian, 1987) are of an institutional nature. As Alchian observes on the subject of a private property right, "its strength is measured by its probability and costs of enforcement, which depend on the government, informal social actions, and prevailing ethical norms." Thus, a series of institutional arrangements relating to the definition and enforcement of property rights are the basic ingredients of market economies.

Along with the set of property rights defined for different types of goods, a series of provisions made to guarantee the enforcement of the system are also required. This means the installation of a "third party" – "the government" in Alchian's definition of property rights, "the legal and political framework of the state" in Aoki's list. This "third party" is comprised of a set of political and administrative bodies (including, of course, the police and the judiciary) responsible for guaranteeing the permanence and effectiveness of the rules of the game.

When private property rights are not perfectly defined and enforced, there are, using neoclassical terminology, "market imperfections" and "market failures," engendering the need for "complementary institutions," the object of which is to overcome these "imperfections" and "failures."

One of the key problems comes from the fact that, in numerous domains of production, various types of "indivisibilities" and

---

[7] In certain cases the enforcement of private contracts passes by a "third party," who is the sole "player" who can guarantee the enforcement of the "rules of the game," notably when conflicts arise among agents as regards the interpretation of the rules (more on this below).

"externalities" are present, giving a character of "collective good" to products and services. In these cases a system of private property rights cannot be completely specified and enforced, or such a system can be considered as undesirable (for efficiency, but also for social and ethical reasons), and pure ("Walrasian") markets cannot be envisaged. (For the same argument in the property rights literature see Barzel, 1989.) As a consequence, a series of additional "institutional arrangements" are needed. Compared to the "first-type" institutional arrangements required to implement the markets (i.e. the system of private property rights), we can refer, for these complementary devices, to "second-type" institutional arrangements. These second-rank arrangements belong to two classes.

a) In certain cases the markets can work with just the addition of some complementary "rules of the game": this is the case, for example, with the regulations provided by agencies in telecommunications or electricity, or with patents (i.e. temporary monopolies) provided to firms involved in research activities. In the latter case, the system of intellectual property rights creates an "incentive structure" capable of encouraging firms to invest in R&D even in the presence of the indivisibilities attached to "information" as a good (Nelson, 1959; and Arrow, 1962).

b) In other cases specific non-market institutions are created in order to provide and deliver to the agents the tangible resources themselves. This is the case for resources such as basic research, for which specific institutions (universities, public research laboratories, etc.) are designed and implemented. These types of institutions are the means used to provide society with the resources required to nurture the progress of knowledge, and, in the neoclassical view, to overcome a situation of permanent under-investment in this type of basic resource (Arrow, 1962).

Thus, the existence of "market economies" is conditioned by a series of non-market mechanisms. They are implemented to make it possible for the agents to coordinate with each other even in the absence of completely defined private property rights.

## 2.3    Types and structure of institutions

To sum up what has been said above: two series of institutions should be envisaged.

1. A first series consisting in laws, regulations, contracts, etc. Their role, in a nutshell, is to provide accepted (or imposed) *rules of the game*.

It may be useful here to recall that these rules are of two kinds, as the authors argue elsewhere (Coriat and Weinstein, 2002a). i) Either they have a universal scope and are "above" all the agents. This is the case for the rights and obligations posed by the constitution and, more generally, by the system of laws (the "legal system," to paraphrase Coase). In that case they have a "national" basis and domain of application. ii) Or they are only the outcomes of contracts and/or conventions agreed between specific groups of agents that have decided to follow certain rules in their interactions. We shall call the first series of institutions *"type 1"* and the second series *"type 2"* (for more on this, see Coriat and Weinstein, 2002a).

A key issue in the analysis of institutional systems and for the evolution of institutions lies in the modes of interaction between these two types of rules. One may observe, in this respect, strong differences between different institutional systems and, more particularly, between different national systems. In some systems it is possible to consider that there is a strict hierarchy: the "emerging" rules of the game (type 2) have to be in accordance with the general and universal "constraints" posed by type 1.

This view seems well in accordance with the political and legal institutions of continental European countries, in particular France. In such cases (i) contracts and private agreements (individual or collective) have to be in strict conformity with the law, and (ii) the law is the outcome of the deliberation of political institutions.

But in other countries such as the United Kingdom or the United States, where what Commons calls the "common-law method of making law" prevails, the relations are more ambivalent: the rules of type 2, deriving from the resolution of specific local problems, can be at the origin of the transformation of the "universal" type 1 rules, through the principle of legal precedent (jurisprudence). In this case, jurisprudence plays a fundamental role in the construction of the institutional system.

We have here, in fact, two visions of the conditions for the creation and selection of institutional rules: visions that can be tied up with two different theoretical conceptions of the genesis of institutions. In the first view the institutions can be seen as the result of a conscious and deliberate collective action, personified in political institutions (a parliament that votes for laws); in the second view, which is more in line with a strict methodological individualism, the institutions are seen as "emerging properties" of the interactions between individuals and groups, and – as such – "unplanned" and "unintended" results of these interactions. But as will be argued later in this study, in both cases (the French "hierarchical" model or the more "horizontal" common-law model) the rules of the game finally enforced (i) are always social compromises between the diverging and opposite needs and demands of the agents, and (ii) are "guaranteed" by the "third party," which, from time to time, reestablishes the regularities within which the agents can behave. Thus, even in the common-law case, a change in the basic rules of the game is, in general, the responsibility of the "political" organs of the state. In the field of the economics of innovation, one may consider, for example, the voting of the Bayh-Dole Act in the United States. Such a major change (which allowed the patenting of the results of publicly funded research and the licensing of these results to private for-profit firms and organizations) would not have been achieved without the precondition of a political deliberation (for more on the "political" context of the passing of the Bayh-Dole Act, see Mowery and Rosenberg, 1993; Mowery et al., 2002; Jaffe, 2000; and Coriat and Orsi, 2002).

2. A second class of institutions aims to provide individual agents not only with "rules" but also with *"real," tangible resources* (whether of a financial or non-financial nature). What is the "raison d'être" of such institutions? The answer to this question is certainly not straightforward. Let us just mention here the standard economic explanation: for the economy to function not "too far from the optimum" (Nelson, 1959; and Arrow, 1962), some non-market entities in charge of the production of resources are required. These institutions are set up and operate, especially in situations where the goods have a structural "public" nature, where indivisibilities and externalities are at the heart of the exchange mechanisms. This is the case for basic research, education, some health services, national security, defense and so on. In most cases these institutions are of a public nature, involving the state as central agent and operator. The resources are then delivered as "public services" by specific entities. But it may happen that private for-market organizations decide to pool some of their assets to produce (and allocate between them) these types of resources according to non-market mechanisms (rules, contracts, conventions, etc. passed between them). This is the case for clubs and/or large hierarchies involving different organizations, such as "research consortia" and the like.

Finally, we shall define economic institutions in market economies as: *the set of social constructs constituted of organizations and systems of rules designed to provide agents with the intangible resources as well as some of the basic tangible resources required to coordinate their actions.*

Having examined how (and why) institutions matter, the next question is, as regards innovation activities: what are the relevant institutions to consider?

## 3      For innovation, what are the relevant "national" institutions?

As we have argued above, the key contributions here are the ones proposed by the NSI and SSI approaches. We shall use them as a basis from which to present our own views.

From the existing literature on this issue, especially that related to the NSI[8] (Amable, Barré and Boyer, 1997) or SSI approaches, as well as from previous work by these authors, three series of institutions – defined as sets of interrelated rules and non-market entities framing the "scene" in which the agents operate – are worthy of attention.

- The first series deals with the provision of the basic good used in innovation activities – namely *scientific and technological knowledge*. The system of intellectual property rights – inasmuch as it defines the conditions to capture rents from innovations – is of crucial importance here.
- The conditions of *the financing of innovation* – i.e. the set of banking and financial regulations – is the second series of institutions to consider. Here, again, the respective roles played by banks and financial markets and the body of rules governing the relations between bankers, shareholders and managers define specific trajectories of innovation.
- Finally, the *educational system, the set of national labor laws and capital/labor arrangements* (labor contracts and, more generally, the "wage relations nexus") are also a key part of the story.

Let us now be more specific about these three sets of institutional arrangements, to understand better the way they shape "national" patterns and trajectories.

### 3.1    The "knowledge base," modes of appropriability and intellectual property rights regimes

Here the NSI literature provides a series of rich and diversified tools of analysis, enabling us to distinguish neatly between very different "national" systems. In accordance with what has been stated before, we shall proceed, for purely analytical reasons, by distinguishing the "resource" dimension of institutions from their "rule of the game" dimension.

As regards the resource dimension provided by non-firm organizations, the following aspects seem of particular importance.

---

[8] Concerning the relevant institutions involved in the generation of innovation, we observe that the two series of institutions are quite at odds with what has been said in the first section of this study. The NSI approach has demonstrated at least two ways in which "institutions" influence R&D activities and performances:

1) The role of non-firm organizations (universities, publicly funded laboratories, non-profit organizations, foundations, agencies, etc.) involved in and/or concerned with research activities is made explicit. This is perfectly in accordance with what we have described as "type 1" institutions – i.e. in charge of producing resources;

2) Emphasis is also put on the role played by the system of rules, norms or conventions in the "framing" (inside a given NSI) of the "rules of the game" (to quote North's words) under which the individual agents operate and coordinate themselves.

One has first to consider the level and the distribution of the "public" effort dedicated to sustaining and nurturing the knowledge base, through R&D activities. When considered in the long term, persistent differences in the rate of investment devoted to R&D may often explain differences in the economic performances of the economies in question. More refined indicators designed to measure military versus civilian R&D investments, basic versus applied research, academic versus industrial research, etc. prove to be very useful in gaining a better understanding of the behavior and performances of the national firms.[9] Finally, the distribution analysis of public R&D funds by "domains" and/or "scientific disciplines" provides important indications about the structure of the "national knowledge bases" of different countries, some being more oriented toward "life sciences" (the US case) while others are more focused on "natural sciences" (European Union countries – see EU, 1997). In the same line of analysis it is often useful to evaluate the relative applications of funds to "new emerging" fields and disciplines (biotechnology, electronics, etc.) compared with more established and traditional ones (chemicals, physics, etc.) – an indicator that differentiates the United States from European Union countries.[10] By interlinking these different kinds of indicators and data one can finally establish something like a "mapping" of national scientific capabilities in different countries. Amable, Barré and Boyer (1997), for example, have conducted a very convincing statistical analysis, aiming at distinguishing the very different structures of "scientific endowments" built into different national systems.

For our own purposes, it is essential to observe that, in many cases, specific "agencies" are designed to operate in more and less specific subfields of the research activities, notably in that which concerns the allocation of funds and the structuring of the research activity. This is the case for explicit "sectoral" agencies (the NIH, the FDA of the Department of Defense, for instance). But these agencies may also have a much broader scope of activity aiming at coordinating vast ensembles of research: this is the case for the French Centre National de la Recherche Scientifique, or the American National Science Foundation, for example. Often equipped with their own laboratories and research entities,

---

[9] In the same way, data concerning public fund investments oriented towards (or located in) firms as compared to non-firm entities, for example, may help to differentiate different "national patterns" from each other (for example, when comparing Japan and the rest of the world, mainly the United States and the European Union, it is useful to note that in Japan 70 percent of R&D activities are located in firms, as opposed to less than 50 percent in the United States and European Union countries).

[10] The European Observatory on Scientific and Technological Indicators has made valuable contributions in comparing the European Union countries with the United States in various fields of activity with regard to the pattern of R&D funding. See Muldur (2000).

mastering and distributing large shares of total public expenditure, these agencies often play crucial roles in capturing local capabilities in "priority" programs, thus orientating resources devoted to different sub-fields of research activities. As a consequence, the "environments" created by these public policies and agencies are the loci where, to a large extent, firms are captured, and where they build their own strategies and trajectories. Thus, agencies contribute to the structuring of the characteristics of the "national" knowledge base where firms operate, creating for them a set of opportunities as well as "scarcities" and constraints.

As regards the "rule of the game" dimension of institutions, the key point lies in the way national choices made by public authorities (and/or related agencies) define the appropriability of the benefits of innovations. A basic distinction here is the opposition between domains of activity where appropriability conditions are embedded in secrecy and tacit, non-codified knowledge, and therefore not subject to disclosure by "reverse engineering" and in the great relevance of specific, collective capabilities built up by firms, and sectors and domains where reverse engineering can capture the secrets and knowledge of rival firms. Traditionally, the car industry, for example, is differentiated from pharmaceuticals, where once a new molecule has been discovered it can be reproduced at low cost.

However, the current trend in most OECD countries is toward attaching more and more importance to patent and IPR policies. In this field, the available works have emphasized that (i) the "legal principles" (i.e. the "rules") securing the innovation rents may vary greatly from one country or region to another (note in particular the "first to file/first to invent" opposition, which characterizes the difference between the Japanese and European systems on the one side and the US system on the other), and that (ii) these "national" differences (notably the ones related to the set of "obviousness," "novelty" and "utility" conditions for an invention to be patented) provide very different incentives to "local" firms. On this subject, until recently it has often been argued that the US system is designed to favor "radical" innovations, whilst the Japanese one is more suited to favoring the promotion of "gradual" or incremental innovations (Ordover, 1991).[11]

However, the changes that have taken place in the last twenty years (originating in the US system before spreading to other countries) have caused a dramatic modification in this vision. In the United States it

---

[11] Anticipating a category that will be introduced later in this study, one can here argue that the American system provides some "institutional advantage" as regards the generation of "breakthrough" innovations, whilst the Japanese system is better suited to insuring a more fluid diffusion of innovations.

is now well documented that the domain of patentability has been dramatically extended, and the criteria for patent eligibility considerably lowered.[12] Many observers have pointed out that, in the last two decades, the Courts of Justice and the PTO have extended the domain of patentability to new areas, including living organisms, computer programs and, more recently, "business models" domains that used to be explicitly excluded from patent activity (Jaffe, 2000; and Coriat and Orsi, 2001). During the same period the criteria for patentability were drastically lowered (Quillen, 1993; Hunt, 1999a, 1999b; and Krastiner, 1991), leading to a dramatic rise in the percentage of patents granted compared to the percentage of GDP expenditures dedicated to R&D activities (Hunt, 1999a; and Jaffe, 2000). We shall come back to this crucial point later on. At this point let us just observe that "national" evolutions in IPR systems may dramatically change the conditions in which firms operate. By opening up new opportunities for the commercial benefits captured from R&D activities, these changes in the IPR systems may profoundly influence the relative distribution of funds directed to different, specific R&D domains, and may even attract new actors to domains in which they have never operated. Just to illustrate the point, there is no doubt that the "Chakrabarty ruling" by the Supreme Court in 1980, granting a patent for a living organism for the first time in history (after an initial refusal by the PTO), has played a major role in attracting financial capital to new firms the central activity of which is "basic" and "fundamental" research. As we shall emphasize later, the whole biotechnology sector has emerged in the United States as a consequence of this Supreme Court decision, making patentable the scientific discoveries made in the new emerging field of genetic engineering (Orsi, 2001; Orsi and Moatti, 2001; and Coriat and Orsi, 2001).[13] This "national" evolution of the IPR system has profound "sectoral" relevance and application, since the new IPR regime installed in the United States over the last two decades has transformed the opportunities opened up to the development of some new, specific science-based sectors (see section 4).

### 3.2    Education, industrial relations systems and labor markets

Another set of institutions that play a major role in influencing firms' behavior in the deployment of their innovation policies can be found in

---

[12] On this point, see: Hunt, 1999a, 1999b; Quillen, 1993; Jaffe, 2000; and Coriat and Orsi, 2001 (more on this in section 4).

[13] To be more precise, the change was made possible only by the combined effect of the Chakrabarty ruling with the passage of the Bayh-Dole Act, which allowed publicly funded institutions (universities, public laboratories and so on) to obtain patents on the outcomes of their research activities and to license them to private for-profit firms and organizations (on this point see Mowery et al., 2001).

the analysis of educational systems. Here, again, this set of institutional structures is deeply "nationally" grounded. Educational training systems and, more generally, the set of labor regulations and industrial relations arrangements rooted in the educational systems differ greatly from one country to another. They are the outcome of very specific "social" compromises between labor and capital, embedded in very different collective bargaining agreements.

The influence of these institutions on innovation policies can be examined on at least three levels. As regards the "resource" dimension, it has often been observed that different national educational systems are unequally efficient in delivering to firms (and other individual agents involved in R&D activities) the types of skills and competencies they need, at the "right moment." This is of paramount importance with regard, in particular, to the upper segment of researchers and high-level engineers needed in the different academic disciplines in which a given research activity is engaged. As has been highlighted in a recent study on the British biotechnology sector (Casper and Kettler, 2001), in spite of the existence of an active venture capital industry the incapacity of the British university system to deliver highly skilled people trained in life sciences (partly due to the divestment policy pursued by the British government since the early 1980s in this area) may well be one of the major reasons explaining the slowness and lack of dynamism of the UK biotechnology sector.

More generally, the orientation of a given educational system toward more or less "basic" (as opposed to "vocational") training may greatly influence the R&D policies and strategies of the agents, by providing very different access to the different types of skills. The relative advantages acquired by some major German industries (including cars, machine tools and instruments) is, for example, often linked to the quality of the "vocational system" that Germany enjoys.

As regards to the "rule of the game" dimension, the key factor lies in the way the characteristics of the different national industrial relation systems structure the different sub-segments of the labor market and their functioning. Not all the economies provide active "external markets" where innovating firms can recruit the scientists and engineers they need. Japan and Germany, for example, are well known for having built their competitive strength on the creation, at the firm level, of systematic "internal markets" based on long-term employment contracts and professional careers. Such "internal markets" are generally recognized as powerful tools in enhancing a firm's competitiveness in sectors where the competitive advantage is based on high product quality, internal training and the continuous improvement of processes and products. But in other domains, on the contrary, where product life cycles are short and where innovation is generated at high speed on the basis of the most advanced scientific and technological knowledge (implying the ability to renew quickly and continuously the composition of the human resources involved in innovative activities), the lack of an active and open "external market" may constitute a considerable obstacle. We face here the "trade-off" mentioned earlier, between developing internal capacity on the one hand and the ability to absorb and integrate new "external" competencies and skills on the other.

In a similar way, if we focus on the functioning of the firm itself (looking, to paraphrase Rosenberg, into the "organizational black box"), the differences linked to the nature of labor contracts will largely condition the types of "routines" as well as the learning processes attached to or supported by them.[14] As has been argued by the authors elsewhere (Coriat and Weinstein, 2002a), the content of labor contracts may differ strongly from one country to another, opening up a set of constraints and opportunities in the use of "the relation of authority" (Simon, 1951).

### 3.3     "Banking" versus "financial market" systems: corporate governance and the financing of innovation

In what ways do corporate governance systems influence the behavior of the agents in the field of innovation and R&D activities?

Before answering this question, let us first recall that corporate governance mechanisms basically result from a double set of rules:

- on the one hand we have all the rules relating to the "*external*" *control* exerted on firms by the financial and stock market regulations implemented to ensure the protection of shareholders' interests and owners' rights. It is thus acknowledged that "good" financial regulation provides the market with a series of rules ensuring transparency and security for the firm's owners and shareholders;
- on the other hand, corporate governance mechanisms are related to the firm's "*internal*" *command modes*, via the board of directors, its composition and the distribution of prerogatives and rights given to the different members.

The combination of these two series of devices determines the way shareholders' interests, compared not only with those of managers but also those of employees or bankers (according to national regulations), are represented and protected, both inside and outside the board of directors. This is usually considered as the strategic place where the

---

[14] On this issue see Coriat and Dosi, 1998b, and Dosi, Coriat and Pavitt, 2000.

decision-making process takes place and where the key compromises are reached on the various participants' interests.

These points are of paramount importance for us, since their combination gives rise to very different "national models," with huge implications for the way innovation is financed. To distinguish between different national systems, the two following dimensions of the financing of innovations deserve attention.

1) *"Banking" versus "financial market" systems.* The existence of a "market for corporate control," as well as its extension and effectiveness, has long been one of the key features explaining the relative importance acquired by financial markets (compared to banks) in the financing of innovations. In the past it used to be convenient to contrast the Anglo-American model with the Continental European model, the first being characterized as "finance-based" and the second being more "bank-based." However, with the extension of financial deregulation all over the world during the 1980s and 1990s, this distinction became less and less relevant. The focus of the analysis was therefore transferred and the emphasis was placed on the relative power attributed to insiders or outsiders.

2) *"Insider" versus "outsider" models.* Examining the "balance" of powers as established in different national institutional settings, it is now common to contrast the British and American "outsider" models (where shareholders hold power) with the German (and Continental European) "insider" models. Even if this basic distinction has to be refined, notably by taking into account the complex role played by different types of "block-holders," whether they belong to outsider or insider alliances, it certainly highlights important differences between national systems (see Rubinstein, 2001).

Here, again, the two systems provide very different institutional advantages and disadvantages to the different countries. Whilst the insider system is considered well suited to sectors based on incremental innovation and long-term investments (Aoki, 2000), the outsider model is regarded as very conducive to "radical," breakthrough innovations. The reasoning here is that the guarantees given to the managers of institutional financial investors (pensions funds, mutual funds and the like) may moderate their reluctance to enter into the financing of risky projects. Thus, in recent years, it has been often argued that the "comeback" of many US firms in high-tech domains was largely based on some major institutional innovations related to the financing of innovation. "Venture capital," specialized stock markets dedicated to the launching of start-up firms – of which NASDAQ is the best-known – are often mentioned, in order to explain the recent "boom" of the activities related to the so-called "new economy". More particularly, the American capacity to generate radical innovation and the emergence and development of new activities (biotechnology, IT, Internet services, etc.) is thus often explained by the role played by these institutional innovations in the financing of innovative firms.[15] By comparison, Western Europe is often judged as "lagging behind" in the implementation of the type of institutional innovations required to ensure the growth of these new activities.

Once we have established the differences between different national systems as regards the three sets of institutional arrangements that play major roles in the deployment of innovation trajectories, the game is not over. We must investigate the way in which these institutional arrangements "match" with each other, and the type of institutional framework this matching creates. As we shall argue in the following section, it may happen that, in given contexts, some "institutional complementarities" (Aoki, 2000; Hall and Soskice, 2001; and Amable, 2000) link and tie together different types of institutions, giving rise to relative institutional advantages (or disadvantages) for given activities and domains of research. In this respect, this approach has strong sectoral implications and relevance.

## 4          Sectoral relevance and specificities

In this section we first emphasize the sectoral implications of the previous analyses, before focusing on some sectoral specificities linked to the nature of some particular domains and sectors.

### 4.1          "Institutional complementarities" and their role

Until now we have chosen to present the logic underlying the forces driving innovation activities by focusing on the three different sets of institutions that, according to most observers, play key roles in framing the dynamics of innovation.

However, as we have just suggested, if one considers the "real" functioning of different NSIs, the different sets of institutions defined above coexist and exert joint influences on the behavior of the agents. Since each set of institutions has been implemented and enforced under its own "time schedule" to meet specific needs and demands in evolving contexts, when envisaged as a whole (i.e. as a national system) the different sets of institutions just presented are not necessarily entirely coherent with each other. Most often, more or less open contradictions exist between

[15] For a detailed demonstration of this point in the biotechnology sector, see Orsi, 2001.

two (or more) legal devices or regulations. For the agents, this lack of coherence is not necessarily bad news. On the contrary, even if this situation complicates the life of the individual actors, it opens up a series of opportunities. Most firms' strategies, and often the smartest and most successful ones, are designed to take advantage of these contradictions.

But it may happen, too, that the different institutions coevolve in such a manner that some institutional complementarities do arise. These complementarities are most often the combined outcome of explicit "visions" and actions of the public authorities and agencies in charge of implementing the "rules of the game," and of emergent properties of complex systems where agents interact. So, in various stages of their respective evolutions, the systems of resources and constraints provided by given NSIs are unevenly favorable and conducive to the deployment of the strategies of the various types of agents engaged in innovative activities. Thus, it has been possible to argue that a given NSI may at the same time be at the origin of some specific relative institutional advantages for some sectors and activities and of some relative institutional disadvantages for others (Hall and Soskice, 2001; and Coriat and Weinstein, 2002a).

If one pushes this vision of things to the extreme, by postulating the realization of strong institutional complementarities between the three sets of institutions just described, two contrasting "models" or "ideal types" can be proposed.

### 4.2    OII versus POE: two contrasted "ideal types" and their sectoral relevance

The two "ideal type" models can be presented as follows (see figure 9.1):
In model A, complementarity is achieved between:
  i) Strong IPR and patent systems ("strong" in the sense that they are designed to guarantee firmly to the patentees the commercial benefits of their innovations, and that *even some scientific discoveries can be granted patents*);[16]
 ii) Corporate governance systems dominated by outsiders, the financing of innovations being achieved through financial markets;
iii) A fluid and efficient external labor market, providing agents with the specific skills required by innovation activities.

This "ideal type" can be named the *POE model* (for patent/outsider/external).

---

[16] We have in mind here the recent changes in the US patent system, allowing the granting of patents to some results of basic and fundamental research, especially in the field of life sciences (genes, expressed sequence tags, basic tools, etc.) and computer software (systems of mathematical equations, algorithms, etc.). More on this crucial issue below.

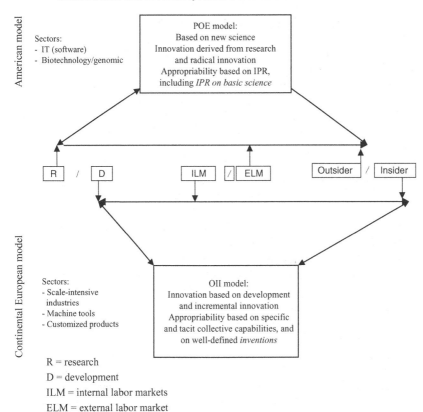

R = research
D = development
ILM = internal labor markets
ELM = external labor market

Figure 9.1 Institutional complementarities and relative institutional advantage

In model B, a completely contrary series of complementarities may link a system based on:
i)  "Open knowledge." This means that the basic knowledge – scientific and mainly technological knowledge – on which production and innovation are based is essentially public knowledge, patents being granted only for specific, well-defined inventions. This feature is linked to the fact that the appropriation of innovation, and the competitiveness of firms, is based mainly on the detention of specific capabilities rather than intellectual property rights.
ii) Corporate governance systems dominated by insiders.
iii) Efficient internal labor markets designed to generate, inside the firms, the capabilities and competencies required for innovative activities.

This opposite "ideal type" can thus be named the *OII model* (for "open knowledge"/insider/internal).

Faced with real, existing national economies, this opposition between the POE and the OII models provides useful tools of analysis for a clearer characterization of the functioning of given national systems. It is thus easy to observe that the POE model is quite at odds with the main traits of the contemporary US NSI, whilst the OII model is very close to the model prevailing in most countries of Continental Europe.

Coming now to the sectoral dimension of this approach, the question to be asked is: what is the sectoral relevance of such complementarities? To put it in other words: in what way can these categories help to understand better the sectoral differences in the relative performances of different given countries?

1) Let us first consider the *POE model*. Clearly, this type of institutional setting creates very favorable environments for sectors and activities based on the commercial exploitation of science discoveries, and more generally for activities the commercial existence of which relies on the exploration of the state of the art. In this case:

   – the existence of an IPR right regime enabling scientific discoveries to be protected through specific patents (for example, the case of "living organisms" – including human genes – or the case of "computer programs" – the granting of patents to systems of mathematical equations and algorithms: domains where the United States has completely reversed their traditional doctrine) provides firms specialized in research activities with new, specific "intangible" assets. A peculiarity of such a patent system is that rents can be built not only on innovations but on research activities. In this case, the organizations and the firms granted such property rights on scientific discoveries (say, human genes) can license them to industrial firms (say, pharmaceuticals).

   – these intangible assets, and the perspective of capturing the rents guaranteed by intellectual property rights, open the way to specific financial markets designed to speculate on these risky but potentially highly profitable firms. Of course, some specific devices in the nature of corporate governance mechanisms are required to give financial investors sufficient confidence and control on their investments; thus, the existence of an "outsider" corporate governance model is very favorable to this type of activity.

   – finally, since the activity itself (R&D in highly specialized and fast-moving fields) requires the ability to recruit quickly the right highly skilled people needed at different stages of the R&D process, the existence of fluid external labor markets and a strong and efficient university and public research system is the final condition that guarantees the success of these activities.

As we will show later, this "virtual sectoral model" is appropriate to many new "sectoral" activities in existence. This is obviously the case for biotechnology and genomics,[17] for some segments of the software industry and for the telecommunications industry – domains where new "start-up" firms built on intellectual property rights are launched on NASDAQ and recruit research staff in the external market (in fact, most often largely from universities and public laboratories[18]).

2 If we now turn to the *OII model*, analogous but contrary observations can be made. Here the institutional setting presents the following basic traits:

- an "open science" universe (Dasgupta and David, 1994) provides all the agents with the benefits of the new knowledge and the discoveries produced by basic research at low cost; precise and narrowly defined property rights on inventions structure a universe in which each new entrant ("follower") can benefit from the innovations of the "first innovator," adding his own contribution (which is, in turn, made available to his followers).[19] Such a system is all the more efficient and sustainable in that it organizes domains where appropriability conditions are based on industrial secrecy and/or on specific capabilities and internal learning developed by the firms; in such a model the innovation rents are more based on development than on research;

- strong internal labor markets are needed, as the firm's core capabilities are built mainly on organizational learning;

- finally, such a model has absolutely no need for the type of highly specialized financial markets required in the previous model. Even if the companies operating in these sectors are "publicly owned," there is no need to confer any great degree of control and power to outsiders; on the contrary, "insider" models are more convenient for monitoring and guiding the innovation policies of the firms and for managing the internal careers of the workers.

---

[17] The three basic traits of the POE model just described were first exhibited by Orsi (2001) in the field of biotechnology and genomics; this section of our study presents a tentative generalization of her work.

[18] On this point see Zucker and Darby (1996), who emphasize the role played by "star scientists" in the launching of these firms.

[19] Bessen and Maskin (2000) have elaborated a model demonstrating that, in domains where the dynamics of innovation depend on the cumulative activity of many different agents, an "open science/open technology" environment is required not only to guarantee the strength of the innovation process but also to ensure the economic health of firms.

Clearly, this OII model is more appropriate to "scale-intensive" and "specialized supplier" sectors: cars, machine tools and the like provide good illustrations of the functioning of these sectors.[20] But this model is also well suited to the first generation of science-based sectors: chemicals, pharmaceuticals and aerospace, just to mention some of the most important ones, have developed on the foundation of the series of institutional devices typical of the world of open science.

## 5    Conclusions

The aim of this chapter is to provide some analytical tools for a better understanding of how "national" institutions influence innovation practices and trajectories.

To achieve this goal we have first tried to define more clearly what should be regarded as an institution and how it operates in the shaping of the behavior of the agents. We have argued that institutions consist of both "rules of the game" and non-market organizations dedicated to providing the agents with the tangible and non-tangible resources required for their market activities.

As regards innovation activities, we have placed particular emphasis on three sets of institutions:
- the ones in charge of providing the basic scientific and technological knowledge, and the system of rules allowing firms to benefit from their involvement in innovation;
- the ones organizing the financing of innovation and the corporate governance mechanisms; and
- the ones concerned with the provision of human resources and the way they can be used according to different industrial relation systems.

To highlight the sectoral dimension of this framework, we have then turned to the analysis of institutional complementarities. We have put forward the hypothesis that some complementarities may arise between the three sets of institutions described above. On this basis, two alternative models were outlined: an "open knowledge" model contrasted with a "patent" model. The first model seems quite in accordance with the requirements of activities based on mass production and on classical science-based industries (chemicals, aerospace, etc.). The second model seems at odds with new emerging fields such as biotechnology, the Internet and new segments of the IT industries. In fact, this "patent"

---

[20] Surprisingly, however, one may observe that this model, which was dominant in the microprocessor industry and some major segments of the software industry in the 1970s, happened to be very favorable to the launching of these industries on a large scale. See, for example, Hunt, 1999a, 1999b.

model – already established in the United States – has given rise to a new type of "science-based sector," characterized elsewhere as a "science-based 2" model, to contrast it from the previous traditional "science-based" model (Coriat and Weinstein, 2002b). Note, however, that even in the United States, where innovations in the new emerging activities are largely "finance-driven," the recent bursting of the bubble on NASDAQ has raised some uncertainties about the long-term sustainability of such a model (more on this in Coriat and Orsi, 2001).

The last observation is that Europe does not seem to face special difficulties in the sectors organized around "open science" principles, but it does in the activities covered by the "science-based 2" model. In these new emerging activities, Europe has not found its way. No institutional complementarities have emerged to provide the type of institutional framework capable of favoring the large-scale launch of the new activities. This, clearly, is one of the major challenges confronting the European economies in the early years of the twenty-first century.

REFERENCES

Alchian, A. A. (1987), Property rights, in J. Eatwell, M. Milgate and P. Newman (eds.), *The New Palgrave: The Invisible Hand*, Macmillan, London, 232–238

Amable, B. (2000), Institutional complementarity and diversity of social systems of innovation and production, *Review of International Political Economy*, 7, 4, 645–687

Amable, B., R. Barré and R. Boyer (1997) *Les systèmes d'innovation à l'ère de la globalisation*, Economica, Paris

Aoki, M. (2000), *Information, Corporate Governance and Institutional Diversity*, Oxford University Press, Oxford

Arrow, K. (1962), Economic welfare and allocation of resources for inventions, in R. R. Nelson (ed.), *The Rate and Direction of Inventive Activity*, Princeton University Press, Princeton, NJ, 609–625

Barzel, Y. (1989), *Economic Analysis of Property Rights*, Cambridge University Press, Cambridge

Bessen, J., and E. Maskin (2000), *Sequential Innovation, Patents and Imitation*, Working Paper no. 00–01. Massachusetts Institute of Technology

Casper, S., and H. Kettler (2001), National institutional frameworks and the hybridization of entrepreneurial business models: the German and UK biotechnology sectors, *Industry and Innovation*, 8, 5–30

Commons, J. R. (1934), *Institutional Economics*, University of Wisconsin Press, Madison

Coriat, B., and G. Dosi (1998a), The institutional embeddedness of economic change: an appraisal of the 'evolutionary' and the 'regulationist' research programme, in K. Nielsen and B. Johnson (eds.), *Institutions and Economic Change*, Edward Elgar Publishing, Cheltenham, 3–32

(1998b), Learning how to govern and learning how to solve problems: on the coevolution of competences, conflicts and organizational routines, in A. D. Chandler, P. Hagström and Ö. Sölvell (eds.), *The Dynamic Firm*, Oxford University Press, Oxford, 103–133

Coriat, B., and F. Orsi (2002), The installation of a new regime of property rights in the United States – origins, content, problems, *Research Policy*, 31, 6, 1,491–1,507

Coriat, B., and O. Weinstein (2002a), Organizations and institutions in the generation of innovations, *Research Policy* 31, 1, 273–290

(2002b), *The Organization of R&D and the Dynamics of Innovation – A Sectoral View*, ESSY working paper [http://www.cespri.it/ricerca/es_wp.htm]

Dasgupta, P., and P. David (1994), Towards a new economics of science, *Research Policy*, 23, 5, 487–521

Dosi, G., B. Coriat and K. Pavitt (2000), *Competencies, Capabilities and Corporate Performances*, Dynacom final report, http://lem.sssup.it/Dynacom/DFR.html

European Union (1997), *Second European Report on Science and Technology Indicators*, European Commission, Brussels (EUR 17639)

Freeman, C. (1987), *Technology Policy and Economic Performance: Lessons from Japan*, Frances Pinter, London

Hall, P. A., and D. Soskice (eds.) (2001), *Varieties of Capitalism – The Institutional Foundations of Comparative Advantage*, Oxford University Press, Oxford

Hunt, R. M. (1999a), Patent reform: a mixed blessing for the US economy, *Business Review, Federal Bank of Philadelphia*, November–December, 15–29

(1999b), *Non-Obviousness and the Incentive to Innovate: An Economic Analysis on Intellectual Property Reform*, Working Paper no. 99-3, Federal Bank of Philadelphia

Jaffe, A. B. (2000), The U.S. patent system in transition: policy innovation and the innovation process, *Research Policy*, 29, 5, 531–557

Krastiner, L. G. (1991), The rival confidence in the patent system, *International Journal of Patents and Trademarks Office Society*, 73, 5–23

Lundvall, B. -Å. (1992), *National Systems of Innovation: Towards a Theory of Innovation and Interactive Learning*, Frances Pinter, London

Mowery, D. C., R. R. Nelson, B. Sampat and A. Ziedonis (2002), 'The effects of the Bayh-Dole Act on US academic research and technology transfer, *Research Policy*, 31, 1, 99–119

Mowery, D. C., and N. Rosenberg (1993), The American national system of innovations, in R. R. Nelson (ed.), *National Systems of Innovation*, Oxford University Press, Oxford

Muldur, U. (2000), L'allocation des capitaux dans le processus global d'innovation: est-elle optimale en Europe? in E. Cohen and J. H. Lorenzi (eds.), *Politiques Industrielles pour l'Europe*, Cahiers du Conseil d'Analyse Economique, Premier Ministre, La Documentation Française, Paris, 34–67

Nelson, R. R. (1959), The simple economics of basic scientific research, *Journal of Political Economy*, 67, 297–306

(ed.)(1993), *National Systems of Innovation*, Oxford University Press, Oxford

North, D. (1990), *Institutions, Institutional Change and Economic Performance*, Cambridge University Press, Cambridge

Ordover, J. (1991), A patent system for both diffusion and exclusion, *Journal of Economic Perspective*, 1, 43–60

Orsi, F. (2001), *Marchés Financiers et Droits de Propriété Intellectuelle dans les Nouvelles Relations Science/Industrie: Le Cas de la Recherche sur le Génome*, Ph.D. dissertation, Université de la Méditerranée, Aix-Marseille II

Orsi, F., and J. P. Moatti (2001), D'un droit de propriété intellectualle sur le rivant aux firmes de génomique: vers une marchandisation de la connaussance scientifique sur le génome humain, in *Economie et Prévisions*, 150/151, 123–138

Quillen, C. D. (1993), Proposal for the simplification and reform of the United States patent system, *American Intellectual Property Law Association Quarterly Journal*, 21, 3, 189–204

Rubinstein, M. (2001), Gouvernement d'entreprise et innovation, *Revue d'Economic Financière*, 63, 211–229

Searle, J. R. (1995), *The Construction of Social Reality*, Free Press, New York

Simon, H. (1951), A formal theory of the employment relationship, *Econometrica*, 19, 3, 293–305

Zucker, L. G., and M. R. Darby (1996), Star scientists and institutional transformation: patterns of invention and innovation in the formation of the biotechnology industry, *Proceedings of the National Academy of Sciences*, 93, 23, 12, 709–12, 716

# 10 Sectoral systems of innovation and varieties of capitalism: explaining the development of high-technology entrepreneurship in Europe

*Steven Casper and David Soskice*

## 1 Introduction

The national institutional framework of the United States' economy has proven favorable to the expansion of high-technology industries. Since the early 1980s the US economy has evolved to support a dramatic expansion in biotechnology, software, and a variety of other fast-moving high-tech activities with close links to basic science. In particular, the institutional framework of the United States has evolved to provide ever more venture capital to high-risk start-up companies, to develop new links between university scientists and companies, and to encourage – or, at least, not hinder – the reorganization of large companies for exploiting commercial opportunities in high technology. In Western Europe firms and policy makers are anxiously experimenting with their own institutional structures in an attempt to support science-based high-tech innovation in their own country better.

This chapter explores the influence of national institutional frameworks on the evolution (using the sectoral systems of innovation approach) of high-tech industries in Europe, focusing in particular on recent public policy and private sector initiatives to foster larger numbers of entrepreneurial technology start-up firms. Our analysis draws on extensive field research within biotechnology and software – two of the most important sectoral systems' new technologies, in which the creation of entrepreneurial start-ups is widespread. The study elaborates and then applies arguments associated with two conceptual approaches: the SSI framework, developed within this book to examine innovative dynamics within particular industries; and the "varieties of capitalism" approach (Hall and Soskice, 2001), which has explored the influence of national institutional frameworks on patterns of industrial organization within particular countries.

Our evidence supports arguments suggesting that, in recent, years, European economies have embraced important reforms that allow them systematically to foster the development of entrepreneurial start-up firms, which are widely seen as critical for long-term success in many high-tech sectors. However, our evidence also indicates that the vast majority of new technology firms in Europe's largest economy, Germany, are significantly different from their Anglo-American brethren. We also find unexpected problems within the UK biotechnology sector, which institutional explanations predict should be excelling. Finally, we find unexpected sources of technology vibrancy within Sweden – a country with a "coordinated" pattern of economic institutions long associated with more incremental innovation trajectories.

Our analysis is organized into three sections. First, we examine theoretical arguments helping to explain why national patterns of innovation should differ across European economies. Recent empirical research has highlighted important differences in patterns of industry specialization across major industrial economies, such as Germany and the United Kingdom. We suggest that these differences are caused by variations in national institutional frameworks across the two countries, and briefly discuss why they advantage different firm-level technology strategies associated with different types of SSIs. The next section then draws on this analysis to examine more carefully the challenges facing entrepreneurial technology firms in different sectoral systems in Germany, Sweden and the United Kingdom. Recent developments in each of these countries represent problem cases for national institutional explanations. Examining them in detail can help explore the relationship between institutional frameworks and firm-level technology strategies, and through doing so can highlight the strengths and limits of the "varieties of capitalism" approach. Drawing from this analysis, the final section assesses different scenarios for the continued evolution of the European innovation systems within the context of supporting new technologies, including the role of public policy.

## 2    Varieties of capitalism and patterns of innovation

In order to explore the relationship between institutional frameworks and the systematic patterns by which firms develop competencies, we need to establish that variance exists across the characteristics of industries associated with entrepreneurial technology firms. We draw upon ideas developed in this book, including research on "technology regimes" (see Malerba, chapter 1 in this book; and Malerba and Orsenigo, 1993, 1997), to illustrate how different constellations of technological and market risks facing firms within particular industry segments create differences in the organizational dilemmas facing firms. Later, when introducing institutional arguments, this leads to predictions linking the orientation of institutional frameworks to firm-level advantages in governing managerial risks associated with particular competencies.

One of the key ideas behind research on SSIs is that sectors differ in a number of technological and market dynamics. Following the discussion in chapter 1 of this book, here we discuss three such properties: the appropriability regime, levels of technological cumulativeness, and the extent to which knowledge or skill-sets are generic to most firms in an industry or firm-specific. SSI theorists have demonstrated empirically that industries differ widely in their particular constellations of these and other attributes. They also suggest that the necessary firm-level organizational capabilities needed to innovate will differ strongly across the technology regimes that characterize the various sectoral systems. To simplify analysis, we briefly explain how SSIs differ across ideal-typical, "radically innovative" sectors such as biotechnology or software, as compared to more established, "incrementally innovative" sectors such as machine tools.

Radically innovative sectors, such as the therapeutic discovery segment of biotechnology or packaged software, are associated with relatively tight appropriability regimes, meaning the intellectual property protection is strong. Furthermore, most skill-sets within such sectors are generic, or sector-wide (e.g. relatively standard laboratory methods within biotechnology, or generic programming languages within standard software). However, such firms face high levels of technology risk relating to the ability of the firm to develop the capabilities needed to pursue its chosen research and development path successfully (Woodward, 1965; and Perrow, 1985). Problems stemming from the rate of technological change, or cumulativeness, form the main technological risk for most radically innovative technology firms (see Breschi and Malerba, 1997). Low technological cumulativeness may also motivate widespread entry, creating races between several firms to be the first to innovate and capture key intellectual property in a given area. Performance incentives, such as the widespread dispersal of stocks or stock options within a firm, are commonly used to create high-powered organizational environments.

Viewed in terms of company capabilities, cumulativeness relates to the rate by which specific technological assets change during the evolution of an industry. If cumulativeness is low, this implies that Schumpeterian patterns of "competency destruction" are high within an industry. Particular technological competencies within a firm have a high probability of failing (as they are shown to be inappropriate for resolving particular research and development problems). Firms in industries where cumulativeness is low often fail or, if they have sufficient financial resources to do so, must develop a capacity to adjust their technological assets quickly.

High technological risk denotes a significant probability either of outright failure or of rapidly changing R&D trajectories that necessitate "hire and fire" personnel policies. Skilled employees may refuse to work within such firms, if doing so poses a high risk of long-term unemployment or a risk that a large percentage of the skills acquired while working within the firm are not saleable on open labor markets (see Saxenian, 1994).

Firms in more incrementally innovative sectors, such as machine tools or, as we shall discuss later, some subsectors of biotechnology and software, face higher levels of cumulativeness. However, these sectors often contain the market risks created by difficulties in capturing value from innovations. For example, "work-arounds" for patents may exist, leading to widespread entry and the assets developed from innovation acquiring a generic quality. Following Teece (1986), when appropriability regimes are relatively weak technological assets developed by the firm are generic and may be easily mimicked by competitors. In this case Teece has suggested that, to capture value from innovations, firms must develop complementary assets that are both specific to the firm and tied to the generic assets. This often involves creating co-specialized assets used to customize products for particular clients – as often occurs in the machine tool industry – or, more broadly, strategies focused on marketing and distribution.

Viewed in terms of company organization, firms developing co-specialized assets tend to create more complex organizational structures than firms innovating within tight appropriability regimes. A key attribute of a firm's competitive success can be its ability to develop an organizational culture or set of routines enabling different types of professional employees to work well in cross-functional teams. From the point of view of employees, this represents primarily firm-specific and often tacit knowledge that is difficult to sell on the open labor market. This may generate managerial dilemmas caused by employee concerns that they will be "held up" once firm-specific knowledge investments are made. Employees may worry about managers pursuing opportunistic employment policies, such as holding wages below industry norms, once extensive firm-specific knowledge investments have been made (see Miller, 1992). Unless managers can assure employees that they will not exploit firm-specific knowledge investments, employees could refuse to make long-term knowledge investments within cross-functional teams, creating patterns of suboptimal work organization that could hurt the performance of the firm.

Table 10.1 summarizes the different technology regimes surrounding these two broad SSIs. We now examine how different national institutional frameworks may help resolve the organizational dilemmas

Table 10.1 *Technology regimes for radical and incremental innovation in sectoral systems*

|  | Radically innovative sectoral systems (e.g. discovery-based biotechnology or standard software) | Incrementally innovative sectoral systems (e.g. machine tools) |
|---|---|---|
| Appropriability regime | Tight | Loose |
| Level of cumulativeness | Low | High |
| Degree of generic versus firm-specific knowledge | Generic knowledge | Firm-specific knowledge |

associated with each type of SSI. National institutional frameworks play a strong role by, among other things, influencing the relative cost of building the organizational competencies needed to pursue particular innovation strategies.

To develop this argument, we first summarize a well-known (and inevitably caricatural) analysis of patterns of economic organization across the two main systems of advanced capitalism: the Anglo-Saxon or liberal market economies (LMEs), and the Germanic/Scandinavian or (industry-) coordinated market economies (CMEs – see Hollingsworth, 1997, for related typologies). Focusing primarily on the German and UK cases, we then develop more carefully the causal linkages between national institutional environments, patterns of economic organization in the economy and innovation trajectories. We begin by providing thumbnail sketches of the institutional differences between LMEs and CMEs, and then explain how the differing patterns of employment and ownership relations that evolve in relation to these institutions favor the innovation patterns commonly associated with each country.

Within CMEs the patterns of economic organization reflect primarily to the embeddedness of large firms within networks of powerful trade and industry associations, as well as a similar, often legally mandated, organization of labor and other interest organizations within para-public institutions (for Germany, see Katzenstein, 1987, 1989). Businesses engage these associations to solve a variety of incomplete contracting dilemmas and create important non-market collective goods. To discourage individual companies from exiting the collective business system, public policy can rely on the legal system to regulate a wide variety of inter-firm and labor contracts and also to sustain neo-corporatist bargaining environments through the delegation of issue-area specific bargaining rights to

Table 10.2 *Institutional framework architectures in Germany and the United Kingdom*

|  | Germany | United Kingdom |
| --- | --- | --- |
| Labor law | Regulative (coordinated system of wage bargaining; competition clauses enforced); bias toward long-term employee careers in companies | Liberal (decentralized wage bargaining; competition clauses struck down by courts); few barriers to employee turnover |
| Company law | Stakeholder system (two-tier board system plus co-determination rights for employees) | Shareholder system (minimal legal constraints on company organization) |
| Skill Formation | Organized apprenticeship system with substantial involvement from industry; close links between industry and technical universities in designing curriculum and research | No systematized apprenticeship system for vocational skills; links between most universities and firms almost exclusively limited to R&D activities and R&D personnel |
| Financial System | Primarily bank-based with close links to stakeholder system of corporate governance; no hostile market for corporate control | Primarily capital market system, closely linked to market for corporate control and financial ownership and control of firms |

unions and other stakeholders within firms. German courts, for example, use standardized business agreements produced through neo-corporatist arrangements as the basis to apply regulatory corporate laws throughout the broader economy (see Casper, 2001).

The United Kingdom is characterized by a liberal market economy. Business organization depends primarily on market transactions and the use of a flexible, enabling, private legal system to facilitate a variety of complex contracting situations. Because courts within common-law legal systems generally refuse to adjudicate incomplete contracts (see generally Schwartz, 1992), market participants need to specify control rights in contract to as full an extent as possible or, when this is not possible, use extremely high-powered performance incentives to align interests within and across organizations (Easterbrook and Fischel, 1991).

Differing patterns of market regulation and business coordination have led to substantial differences in how institutional frameworks' structuring activity in different areas of the economy are organized. Table 10.2 presents an overview of institutional patterns that most affect the organization of companies in technology-based industries.

This table highlights the conclusion that, while most areas of economic activity within LMEs is largely deregulated with market-based patterns of business coordination, in CMEs both market regulation and non-market patterns of firm-level coordination are pervasive. Differing national institutional framework architectures allow firms in CMEs to make different types of commitments to employees and other stakeholders from those that are possible in the LMEs. Systematic differences in the organization of careers, in patterns of company organization and in relationships between firms and owners/investors exist across the two countries, which can ultimately be linked to the broader patterns of industry specialization and innovation. We will examine the German case in some detail, and then highlight the strong role that institutions play in shaping innovation patterns through a brief comparison with the United Kingdom.

First, how are *careers* for highly trained technical employees and managers typically organized within German firms? In Germany most employees spend most of their careers within one firm, often after a formal apprenticeship or, in the case of many engineers and scientists, an internship arranged in conjunction with their university degree. While there exist no formal laws stipulating long-term employment, German labor has used its power on supervisory boards as well as its formal consultative rights under co-determination law over training, work organization and hiring to obtain unlimited employment contracts (Streeck, 1984). Once the long-term employment norm for skilled workers was established, it spread to virtually all mid-level managers and technical employees. In particular, the migration of scientists and highly skilled technical employees across firms is limited, reinforced by the willingness of German courts to uphold "non-compete" clauses in employment contracts (see Keller, 1991). Thus, the active labor market for mid-career scientists and technicians is limited.

Second, long-term employment and the "stakeholder" model of corporate governance have important repercussions for patterns of *company organization* (Charkham, 1995: and Vitols, 2001). Long-term employment and limited co-determination rights for employees create incentives for management to create a broad consensus across the firm when major decisions are being made. As unilateral decision making is limited, it is difficult for German firms to create strong performance incentives for individual employees. As a result, performance rewards tend to be targeted at groups rather than individuals within German firms, and individual performance assessments and bonus schemes are limited. Until early 1998 stock options, one of the most common incentive instruments used in American firms, were illegal in Germany. Though now allowed they are still uncommon in Germany, and typically, when used below top management, they are distributed across large groups of employees to ensure that group rather than individual incentives are maintained. Finally, most career structures are well defined in German firms and based on broad education and experience within the firm rather than on short-term performance.

Third, *ownership and financial relationships* in Germany are strongly influenced by corporate governance rules. Despite the recent expansion of equity markets, Germany retains a bank-centered financial system (Vitols, 2001). Banks and other large financial actors (e.g. insurance companies) have a strong oversight role on firms through seats on supervisory boards and through continuing ownership or proxy voting ties with most large German industrial enterprises (Vitols, 2001; Edwards and Fischer, 1994). Most German firms still rely on banks or retained earnings to finance investments. Banks are generally willing to offer long-term financing for capital investments, but not for research and development. German banks usually offer financing only for investments in which collateral exists – for example, fixed investments such as property or long-term capital investments. Banks can adopt a longer-term focus in part because they know that German firms are able to offer long-term commitments to employees and other stakeholders in the firm, and can often closely monitor the status of their investments through seats on the supervisory board or other direct contacts.

These patterns of company organization are ideally suited to SSIs focused on incremental innovation. Hall and Soskice (2001), following the varieties of capitalism approach, have recently presented detailed patent analysis and an overview of numerous empirical studies linking successful German firms with incremental innovation trajectories (e.g. Katzenstein, 1989). Incremental innovation patterns generally involve the systematic exploitation of particular technologies in a wide variety of niche markets in which co-specialized assets linking product development, process engineering and customization are common. German engineering companies and, we will see below, software and biotechnology firms have successfully competed in a number of high-value-added market niches. Doing so requires a long-term dedication to particular markets and the building of firm-specific knowledge among highly trained employees. Such an approach is risky for firms in many countries, but particularly viable in Germany because of lifetime employment (see Soskice, 1997). In addition, consensus decision making ensures that, once new initiatives are agreed upon, they will not be "held up" by disgruntled units that feel their interests were not taken into account, so, while business policy formulation is not always rapid, its implementation is smooth and swift. Finally, incremental innovation patterns are well suited to Germany's bank-centered financial system. Most engineering firms have high capital equipment costs that require long-term but relatively low-risk financing, in which German banks have traditionally specialized.

On the other hand, German institutional arrangements appear less suited to higher-risk innovation strategies in many newly emerging, radically innovative technologies. High-risk, high-return "blockbuster" products are unlikely to be created from the German pattern of industrial and financial organization. It is difficult for German firms to move quickly in and out of markets characterized by rapidly evolving technologies. Since most employment contracts are unlimited, top managers of German firms must think twice before creating new competencies in high-risk areas with low technological cumulativeness, for cutting assets is difficult. Similarly, it is difficult for German firms to create the high-powered performance incentives that often characterize very high-risk technology companies. Large firms avoid creating high-powered incentives for managers, unilateral decision-making structures, and opportunities for rapid career advancement, because these organizational structures go against the logic of the established institutional framework and would risk alienating important long-term stakeholders in the firm. Sharper incentives might be created within smaller entrepreneurial firms, which, we will see below, have begun to sprout in larger numbers within Germany. However, many of the traditional institutional constraints, as well as the small labor market for mid-career scientists and technicians, continue to hamper the efforts of German high-tech start-ups. These constraints limit the ability of start-up companies to move quickly into new fields as these firms start to grow.

Similar difficulties have plagued financial markets as well. While long-term but relatively low-risk financing is available from banks, high-risk short-term financing in Germany has not generally been available. As pointed out by Tylecote and Conesa (1999), banks in "insider"-dominated corporate governance systems tend to have excellent knowledge of particular firms, but usually do not have the detailed *industry* knowledge that is necessary for investors to channel money into higher-risk technologies. Rather, financing for higher-risk activities is generally provided by venture capitalists, often in conjunction with industry "angels" that have detailed technical and market expertise within particular industries. In addition, the lack in Germany, until recently, of a viable "exit option" for initial public offerings, such as a NASDAQ-oriented stock market, has limited the development of refinancing mechanisms for venture capital funds.

To provide a brief comparison, the institutional framework in the United Kingdom encourages few, if any, of the company organizational and financial structures needed to pursue long-term incremental innovation strategies, but are ideally suited to the competitive requirements for radical innovation on a short time horizon. Particularly after the Thatcher era in the early 1980s, labor markets have been deregulated in the United Kingdom. Most firms offer limited employment contracts, poaching is widespread, and an extensive "headhunting" industry has emerged alongside most regional agglomerations of high-tech firms in Cambridge, Oxford and elsewhere. This allows firms to build or shed competencies quickly as they move in and out of different technology markets.

Compared to the "social" construction of German firms, the property rights structure of most UK firms is financial in nature (see generally Roe, 1994). No legally stipulated co-determination rights for employees or other stakeholders exist. This allows owners to create high-powered incentive structures for top management (i.e. very high salaries, often paid in company shares or share options), which is then given considerable discretion in shaping organizational structures within the firm. The top management of most UK technology firms attempts to create similarly high-powered incentive structures within the firm. These structures include large bonus systems, opportunities for star performers to advance quickly through the firm and much unilateral decision control. These organizational structures tend to facilitate quickly shifting constellations of firm competencies, which are often needed in order to innovate in rapidly changing technologies; they likewise facilitate the short-term dedication of employees to particular assignments. In contrast, the more long-term commitments and consultation rights prevalent within German firms are difficult to foster within the United States' decentralized and incentive-laden corporate environment.

Finally, a similar German-UK contrast holds concerning finance. Large capital markets in the United Kingdom fund technology firms that appear to have promising potential. This financing tends to be short-term in nature, meaning that funds will dry up if firms fail to meet development goals or if products fail to live up to expectations in the market place. However, so long as the possibilities for high, often multiple returns on investment exist, a large market of venture capitalists and, at later stages of company development, more remote portfolio investors stand ready to invest in technology firms. The national institutional structure of the United Kingdom largely explains why this is the case. First, given the deregulated nature of labor markets, high-quality managers and scientists can be found to fuel the growth of highly successful firms. Second, investors know that performance incentives can be managerially designed to "align" the risk/return preferences of investors with rewards for top management and employees of particular firms. Once more, neither of these conditions holds in Germany (Casper and Matraves, 2003).

This overview has provided a general framework for understanding why institutional frameworks in LMEs and CMEs favor different patterns of competency development within firms and, as a consequence, different commercial innovation strategies. We now apply this framework to understand recent developments in the development of entrepreneurial technology firms within Europe.

## 3   Case studies: patterns of subsector specialization in European high technology

This section applies the "varieties of capitalism" perspective to examine the development of high-tech industry in Europe, focusing on cases involving entrepreneurial technology firms. The preceding analysis predicts that, of the major European economies, the United Kingdom should perform extremely well in generating both entrepreneurial start-ups and larger technology firms within a variety of "new economy" industries. Germany, Sweden and most other "coordinated" European economies should perform poorly in sectors in which technological cumulativeness remains low. While this analysis seems correct during the 1980s and early 1990s (see Casper, Lehrer and Soskice, 1999), important changes have occurred within the European high-tech scene, many of which appear strongly contrary to the expectations of varieties of capitalism theory. We examine three such cases: German biotechnology and Internet software; Swedish Internet software; and UK biotechnology. All three cases have been selected for the challenges they pose to varieties of capitalism theory. Through examining each more carefully, the general usefulness of the varieties of capitalism approach for assessing crucial events within the European technology scene can be assessed.

A first case is the development of entrepreneurial biotechnology and Internet software firms in Germany. Varieties of capitalism theory makes strong claims regarding Germany, positing that institutional structures developed to support incremental innovation strategies directly impede the development of entrepreneurial start-ups focused on new technologies. Yet, during the late 1990s, hundreds of technology start-ups emerged in Germany. We analyze this case in detail, demonstrating that, while the German model has in some important ways accommodated itself to new models of financing technology start-ups, it has done so in a way that is strongly consistent with technology regimes underpinning incremental innovation. To support this claim we focus on patterns of *subsector specialization* within the new economy. We demonstrate that German firms have specialized in areas of biotechnology and Internet software sharing subsectoral innovation systems similar to long-established German patterns of incremental innovation.

A second challenging case for varieties of capitalism theory is the development of Swedish Internet software. The Swedish start-up boom is interesting because of its high technical intensity. The country has business institutions resembling those in Germany – i.e. favoring incremental innovation across a range of engineering-centered sectors – but in recent years it has developed a large cluster of entrepreneurial technology firms, particularly in the wireless telecommunication area. Can varieties of capitalism explain this? The Swedish case shows that large firms can sometimes develop standard-setting and human resource policies capable of tipping local institutional environments into configurations atypical for the country as a whole. To explore this argument we focus on Ericsson's activities in creating a hub of start-up firms in Stockholm around wireless technologies. We draw once more on technological regime concepts associated with the SSI approach, then use the Swedish Internet case to demonstrate that within sectors where network externalities are high, such as network communications, large standard-setting firms can – at times – develop policies that alter "normal" institutional incentives within the economy. However, the case also shows the importance of national institutional frameworks in generating the expectations of scientists, engineers and managers concerning risky knowledge investment or career moves.

The final case, UK biotechnology, is interesting for the opposite reason. The United Kingdom is in many ways an ideal-typical liberal market economy. While its large pharmaceutical firms have performed extremely well, its base of entrepreneurial biotechnology firms stagnated during the 1990s. The UK biotechnology case poses a strong challenge for varieties of capitalism theory. Why have a relatively large number of firms embedded within the "right" institutions consistently failed to innovate? To examine the problems within the UK biotechnology sector we use the varieties of capitalism perspective to understand the credible orchestration of competencies within high-risk biotechnology firms, then demonstrate that a series of small problems within UK institutions may be systematically dampening the ability of UK firms to perform well. We suggest that, while economy-wide institutional environments to support entrepreneurial firms exist within the United Kingdom, these institutions have not gelled into a sectoral support system (Mowery and Nelson, 1999) capable of systematically supporting entrepreneurial biotechnology firms.

## 3.1    Germany's engagement with the "new economy"

During the latter half of the 1990s the German economy experienced the beginning of what many commentators, particularly within the business press, see as a renaissance in the performance of its high-tech industries (*Wirtschaftswoche*, 1998). Developments in the two core "new economy" sectors – biotechnology and Internet software – strongly support this view. From virtually no dedicated biotechnology companies existing in Germany in the early 1990s, over four hundred new biotechnology start-up firms were created during the late 1990s, about a hundred and fifty of which are life sciences firms situated around German university and public research institutes (Ernst and Young, 1998). A few of Europe's most successful biotechnology firms are now based in Germany, including Qiagen, a company specializing in the manufacture of nucleic acid filtration kits, which now leads European biotechnology companies in both employment and profitability. A similar expansion of commercial activity has taken place in the software sector. The development of commercial Internet activities has spurred the creation of dozens of Internet start-ups, standing alongside numerous older software firms, which have used newly developing financial markets to arrange IPOs to fund large investments in Internet-related software areas. As of January 2001 there were sixty Internet software firms listed on a new technology-based stock market in Germany. These include several firms competing head-on with US rivals in key markets for e-commerce software tool kits.

At a more aggregate level, this turnaround is documented by shifts in the structure of Germany's venture capital market. Total venture funding rose from about DM9 billion in 1996 to DM25 billion available in 1999. Much more of this money was targeted at "new economy" industries. In 1999 roughly 35 percent of German venture capital was invested in communications and IT – the two industries strongly associated with the Internet – while strong growth also took place in biotechnology. Finally, much of this investment shifted to more risky, early-phase financing – about one-third of all German venture capital was targeted at early-stage financing in 1999, compared to about 6 percent in 1991 (German Venture Capital Association, 1999).

Germany's recent successes in high-tech industries has led to the formulation of a different analysis of the sources of commercial innovation within the economy, focusing less on national institutional determinants of innovation processes and more on sector-specific technology policies. Advocates of strong technology policies suggest that governments should search for obstacles blocking innovation processes within particular sectors and introduce new policies to transfer resources to and orchestrate the coordination of the necessary linkages within the innovation chain. The new sentiment is found in a recent report by the Ifo Institute – a respected voice on German competitiveness issues. "If there is an 'innovation crisis' in Germany, then this 'crisis' is due . . . to a high degree of inertia in shifting capital investments, human resources, and existing ingenuity talents from traditional to new high-tech areas promising higher growth rates in the future" (Büchtemann and Vogler-Ludwig, 1997, p. 36; see also Audretsch, 1985).

Following this logic, the German government has introduced a range of new technology policies designed to create clusters of entrepreneurial start-up firms. In 1996 the federal government, wary of criticisms of the lack of venture capital in Germany, decided to provide "public venture capital" in the form of "sleeping" or silent equity partnerships from federal sources (see Adelberger, 2000). A core goal of German technology policy is to channel venture capital investments into new economy sectors. As of late 1999 about 45 percent of total investments were provided to software, IT and Internet businesses, with an additional 27 percent flowing into the biotechnology sector (Technologie-Beteiligungs-Gesellschaft 2001). In addition, the German Research Ministry provided over DM150 million in grants for "pre-competitive" R&D by start-up firms within three regions selected as part of the federal "BioRegio" contest.

German public officials have crafted a dense network of support policies for university-centered spin-offs. Government intervention has focused particularly on biotechnology. As part of the federally funded BioRegio competition, which began in 1995, seventeen different German regions have created government biotechnology promotion offices. Technology offices generally aim to help scientists and local entrepreneurs organize every phase of start-up formation within the biotechnology sector. This includes: the hiring of consultants to persuade university professors or their students to commercialize their research findings and help them design viable business plans; subsidies to help defray the costs of patenting their intellectual property; and the provision of management consulting and partnering activities once new firms are founded. Most of the BioRegio programs have used public funds to create new technology parks and "incubator laboratories" to house fledgling start-ups in and around universities or public research laboratories. This model has, more recently, diffused to other areas, through an "InnoRegio" program modeled on the biotechnology policies.

Technology policy has provided an important catalyst, but cannot alone explain the recent upsurge in German high-tech entrepreneurism. At only DM400 million in 1999, federal funds form less than 5 percent of the total sum of venture capital currently available in Germany. Private sector investments in new financial markets, coupled with supportive financial regulatory reforms, have proven much more important in creating institutions for sustainable venture capital finance in Germany. The cornerstone of these initiatives was the creation in 1997 of a new technology-oriented stock exchange, the *Neuer Markt*, with substantially less burdensome listing requirements than those that exist for the main stock market. As of December 2000 about 270 firms had taken initial public offerings on the *Neuer Markt*. The vast majority of these firms are in technology-related businesses. By providing a viable "exit option" to investors in technology start-ups, the *Neuer Markt* has created a financial environment more conducive to high-risk venture capital investments. About half of all Neuer Markt firms in IT-related sectors currently have equity stakes held by venture capitalists – a strong indication that equity-leveraged financing models are increasingly viable in Germany.

These new technology policies are taking effect in an environment that has seen no major changes to the broader, economy-wide institutional frameworks emphasized by proponents of the varieties of capitalism perspective. There have been no reforms to German labor or company laws. While the success of the Neuer Markt signifies increased opportunities to raise funds through capital markets, compared to the United States or the United Kingdom Germany is still a primarily bank-centered financial system; at the end of 1996 German market capitalization was only 21 percent of GDP, compared to 151 percent in the United Kingdom and 121 percent in the United States (Deutsche Bundesbank, 1997).

When the success of recent German technology policies is taken into account in conjunction with the overall stability of German national institutional frameworks governing the economy, a strong critique of varieties of capitalism emerges. Sector-specific support structures may be able essentially to circumvent "normal" institutional incentives and constraints within the economy. Firms seeking to generate organizational structures in institutionally impoverished areas can do so through engaging specialized institutions created through sector-specific technology policies. Public policy may expand a country's range of commercial activities through designing a plurality of institutional support systems, targeted at the unique needs of firms within particular sectors.

Based on detailed research on the patterns of subsector specialization within German "new economy" biotechnology and Internet software start-ups, we present an alternate analysis, consistent with the broader varieties of capitalism framework. We argue that German firms have specialized overwhelmingly in areas of the new economy that are broadly consistent with company organizational structures, business models and patterns of human resource development within sectoral systems dominated by incremental innovation. Changes have taken place: engagement with capital markets has allowed a more rapid scale-up of firms, and the use of company-wide incentive structures such as stock options has created more intense working environments. However, essential elements of sectoral innovation systems within most German new economy start-ups have remained surprisingly consistent.

### 3.1.1    From sector to subsector systems of innovation

When considering new economy sectors such as biotechnology and Internet software, public attention has focused primarily on fashionable segments of the industries, such as therapeutics research or the creation of the technically intensive Internet protocol and navigational software (so-called "middleware") used to drive the spectacular growth of the Internet. However, in both biotechnology and Internet software a spectrum of markets exist, each of which have important differences in their subsectoral innovation systems and underlying technology regimes. We focus on two of these subsectors: platform technologies in biotechnology, and customizable enterprise software in the Internet software industry.

In the biotechnology area, platform technology firms create enabling technologies that are then sold to other research laboratories. Products include consumable kits used to rationalize common molecular biology laboratory processes, such as the purification of DNA and other important molecules. Platform technology firms have also developed a number of IT-based applications that have been used to automate many aspects of the discovery process within therapeutics. These include extremely high-throughput "combinatorial chemistry" applications to aid the screening of potential therapeutic compounds, and the development of genetic sequencing and modeling techniques to aid in the quest to decode and understand fully the human genome ("genomics").

With regard to Internet software, large markets for a range of primarily enterprise-related application software have developed to complement well-publicized navigation and middleware technologies. These include WWW-based applications for enterprise resource planning, customer relationship management (CRM), sector-specific enterprise tools, "groupware" and systems integration. In addition to these long-existing markets, the Internet has created large new markets for a variety of software tool kits to help firms develop and maintain e-commerce sites. According to estimates by Forrester Research, the e-commerce software market was worth $1.7 billion in 1999 and expected to grow to well over $10 billion by the early 2000s.

While therapeutics research and middleware Internet technologies encompass SSIs common to entrepreneurial technologies, platform technologies and enterprise software share quite different technological characteristics. The technologies in both cases are far more cumulative in nature, with shorter development cycles. In both subsectors firms typically develop libraries of core technologies, which are then further developed and customized for clients in a variety of niche markets. For example, Qiagen, a German biotechnology company that has become a world leader in the creation of disposable test kits used to simplify common laboratory procedures such as nucleic acid filtration, has over the last decade developed its core technology for over thirty different filtration markets (based on differences in yield, volume and chemical types).

Most enterprise software markets share similar characteristics. Firms develop a core library of software modules, which are then combined and customized to fit the needs of particular clients. E-commerce software firms, for example, develop a kernel of e-commerce applications (such as inventory tracking, accounting and order completion, as well as the creation of visible Web interfaces used by customers), which are then typically installed and customized by the firm in relatively expensive implementation work. What software developers call "functionality," or new features, are periodically included as technologies evolve. For example, most e-commerce toolmakers are currently incorporating next-generation scripting technologies based on extensible markup language (XML) into their front-end graphical display software.

While continual R&D is important to firms in both cases, technologies tend to be more generic, in terms of appropriability regimes, than in either the therapeutics or middleware software segments. While intellectual property protection is available for specific innovations, few blocking technologies exist, allowing innovations of the "me too" type to diffuse rapidly across competitors. This differs dramatically from either therapeutics, in which many "blockbuster" drug discoveries often remain exclusive for a number of years, or middleware software, for which standard-related network externalities create "winner takes all" markets for the inventors of major new technologies. Within platform technology and enterprise software markets dozens of firms compete in most major product segments, usually offering services based on relatively similar technologies.

Appropriability issues thus dominate the strategic calculations of most enterprise software and platform biotechnology firms. To capture value from their innovation strategies, German firms appear to be developing co-specialized asset strategies similar to those suggested by Teece (1986). In both the platform technology and enterprise software cases, firms have created large in-house capacities in a variety of sales, marketing, distribution, implementation and follow-on consulting activities. In enterprise software, firms tie in-house competencies to the development of large groups of third-party consultants trained and accredited to perform implementation work. The largest German e-commerce software developer, for example, has accredited over four thousand such consultants in addition to having a large in-house consultancy pool reserved for the larger, more lucrative contracts. Within the platform technology area, firms develop large groups of highly trained sales officers, who in many ways resemble the "detailers" long used to sell medicines to doctors and hospitals.

An additional strategy used by firms in each sector is to develop their products in such a way as to develop high switching costs for clients. This is particularly easy for enterprise software vendors, as expensive implementation work needed to customize software creates "lock-in" effects, which can be exploited through the creation of "upgrade cycles" to improve the functionality of software. Similar co-specialized asset strategies have been developed by platform technology firms in the biotechnology sector. Qiagen, for example, has attempted to lock in customers for its disposable test kits by acquiring downstream, automated, computer-assisted screening technology and then customizing its products so that they are compatible only with Qiagen test kits.

### 3.1.2 *Subsector specialization by German "new economy" firms*
German firms in biotechnology and Internet software have overwhelmingly gravitated to more technologically cumulative subsectors such as platform biotechnologies and enterprise software. We first provide empirical evidence of these patterns of specialization, then examine more carefully how German national institutional frameworks help firms resolve the core relational problems needed to innovate in these subsectors.

Germany's new biotechnology firms, with few exceptions, have specialized in platform technology areas, while very few firms have become pure therapeutics research laboratories (see Casper, 2000). For example, a recent European biotechnology survey asked over three hundred firms to identify all the market sectors in which they conduct activities. While close to 40 percent of European biotechnology firms are developing therapeutic products, less than 20 percent of German firms are in this field. Conversely, about 30 percent of German firms are developing platform technologies, compared to less than 20 percent for the European industry as a whole (Ernst and Young, 1998, 1999). This

Table 10.3 *Patterns of sub-market specialization of German* Neuer Markt *Internet software firms*

| Category | Number | Percentage |
|---|---|---|
| Enterprise software | 38 | 63 |
| Network application software | 16 | 27 |
| Packaged software | 3 | 5 |
| Middleware software | 3 | 5 |

Source: Casper (2003).

survey outcome probably exaggerates the relative German specialization in therapeutics. Many platform technology firms develop equipment that helps pharmaceutical firms identify potential therapeutic targets (both through combinatorial chemistry or genomics-based screening); little follow-on pre-clinical research or development is performed by these firms. Field research at over two dozen German firms revealed only one firm that had set up a research laboratory with biomedical research capabilities in a therapeutic class. This firm, a genomics technology specialist, had received a multimillion Deutschmark "pre-competitive" research grant from the German government to finance this laboratory. In a separate survey, when German biotechnology firms were asked to list the areas of their research activities, therapeutics came in fifth, ranked well below contract research and manufacturing, platform technologies, diagnostics and "other services" (Ernst and Young, 1998b, p. 17).

An analysis of the technological intensity of German biotechnology patents strongly supports the notion that German firms have specialized in subsectors with high cumulativeness. Casper and Kettler (2001) have examined the average number of scientific journal articles referenced in German, US, UK and Japanese patents from 1985 until 1998. This is a rough indicator of technical cumulativeness: the greater the number of basic research citations in a patent application, the "newer" or less cumulative on previous discoveries the innovation may be presumed to be. These figures show that the average number of US scientific references in 1998 (about twenty-four) is some three times as many as in Germany (about eight). This finding complements evidence that German firms have specialized in subsectors of biotechnology firms with significantly technological regimes that are generally more cumulative in nature.

A similar pattern of specialization holds for German software firms. Table 10.3 lists the patterns of sub-market specialization of all software firms based in Germany currently listed on the *Neuer Markt* that include

Internet-related activities in their core business (sixty in total). Sixty-three percent of these firms are in the enterprise software category, while there only exist three each of packaged software and middleware software firms. The enterprise software group includes seven e-commerce software, several of which are widely seen as forming the most successful group of German start-ups, designed from infancy to exploit Internet economy markets. The network application area consists of a mix of firms, including some high-intensity firms developing technologically intensive software for security-related applications (such as encryption and digital signature technology). However, most firms in this area also do a large amount of consulting-related work for clients, often implementing security or document management software purchased by middleware firms for clients.

While reliable statistics comparing the average R&D intensity of enterprise software and middleware firms do not exist, data from annual reports suggests that the R&D intensity of the German firms is quite low. Excluding the seven e-commerce software firms, the median figure for R&D as a percentage of total costs was only 8.4 percent for enterprise software firms in 1999 (Casper, 2003). The e-commerce software firms have a higher R&D intensity: 18 percent on average and 20 percent for the median firm. This is due in part to the strongly competitive nature of this segment. However, interviews at several of these companies suggest that, while firms must invest heavily to include new features, most companies in the field have developed roughly similar platforms. Complementary investments in marketing and distribution were regarded as core determinants of success (see, for example, the company presentation of Intershop, the leading German e-commerce firm, on its website: www.intershop.com). Data on licensing as a percentage of revenue are indicative of the importance of customizable software to e-commerce firms: a relatively small volume of sales comes from sales of complete software packages. Rather, about 54 percent of sales are in the form of licensing software to clients; interview evidence from visits to several of these firms suggests that consulting and implementation-related fees comprise the rest of revenue.

### 3.1.3   German institutions and the orchestration of competencies within firms

The patterns of subsector specialization in the German biotechnology and Internet sectors strongly suggest that, while changing, the German model has not converged to a "liberal market economy" system capable of fully supporting radically innovative entrepreneurial technology firms. The decision by most German firms to head for platform biotechnologies and a variety of customizable Internet software segments can be explained in two ways. A first interpretation is that German firms are in these subsectors because they *cannot* develop the competencies needed to compete within more radically innovative subsectors. While certainly true, this line of analysis carries with it the presumption that platform technologies and enterprise software have dominated German patterns of specialization because they are "easier" subsectors within the new economy to enter – seen most clearly through their more cumulative or incremental patterns of technical change.

However, this constraint-based argument ignores the fact that several of Germany's new economy firms have been extremely successful, capturing large portions of the world markets for important biotechnology platform technologies and specialized e-commerce software. This suggests an alternative view. Rather than viewing German developments as a case of failed technology policy in the face of institutional constraints, an alternative argument is that German firms have specialized in areas of the new economy with sectoral patterns of innovation broadly consistent with incremental innovation. Perhaps German firms have comparative institutional advantages in platform technologies and customizable software. A further analysis of knowledge properties within these segments leads to some support for this claim. If correct, it implies that CMEs and LMEs will develop a division of labor across the subsectors of the new economy. We now examine both views.

### 3.1.4   Constraint-based explanations

German start-up technology firms face difficulties in obtaining the necessary human resource competencies to innovate in volatile fields with frequent technological change. Labor market institutions pose obstacles to the creation of the coordination mechanisms needed to compensate for a high rate of competency destruction and firm failure. Large labor markets for experienced scientists and managers simply do not exist in Germany. Long-term employment strategies by large firms limit the development of labor markets for high-quality staff. While large German firms can sell entire subsidiaries or business units or send some lower-productivity older employees into early retirement, co-determination law makes it difficult for firms to lay off individual employees or groups of employees as part of the "normal" course of business (see Becker, Menz and Sablowski, 1999 for a discussion of Hoechst's difficulties in this area). Seen in terms of career structure, there is a high risk for senior managers and researchers in moving from an established large company or prestigious university professorship to a start-up firm.

The generally unchanging structure of German labor markets suggests that start-up firms cannot expect to be "competency-destroying" at the firm level. German technology start-ups cannot easily "hire and fire" personnel, in large part because labor markets for highly experienced technical staff and managers are limited due to the long-term employment equilibrium throughout the economy. This creates important limitations on the strategic orientation of German new economy firms, in that they cannot engage in projects in which the necessary human resource competencies can shift quickly. Rather, German firms must anticipate that most scientists and engineers hired into the firm will have a relatively long employment tenure within the firm.

Turning to the corporate governance of Germany's high-technology firms, while financing for entrepreneurial firms now exists within Germany, the governance of these investments is problematic. In addition to the "silent" venture capital guaranteed by the federal government, much venture capital in Germany has been organized through "innovation funds" administered by the banking sector, and, in particular, the public savings and investment banks (see survey in Mietsch, 1999, pp. 241–255). As discussed above, banks are unlikely to have the detailed industry knowledge that is necessary to channel venture capital into emerging industries. While there do exist several credible venture capital houses in Germany, the extensive involvement of public funds in the syndicates backing most firms creates limits on the reservoir of experience the firm can draw upon through its venture capital partners. German firms are less likely to receive the help in technological positioning that is seen as commonplace within the Silicon Valley model.

There are also constraints generated through the public subsidy model. Public officials involved in the administration of federal subsidies, as well as officials of public banks, when interviewed as part of field research conducted in early 1999 consistently stated that the "sustainability" of investments and the new markets they comprise was a core concern. Above all else, public officials want to avoid large numbers of corporate failures. In addition to risking moderate sums of public money, the political backlash created by a large number of high-tech failures could be embarrassing. Lacking the industry expertise to take an active role in the governance of these firms, it is not surprising that so many projects have been steered into lower-risk market segments.

### 3.1.5  Sources of comparative institutional advantage

Taken together, limits on the development of both human resource and corporate governance competencies within German new economy firms have impacted patterns of subsector specialization within German new economy sectors. However, these same institutions may help German biotechnology and Internet software firms in developing the patterns of skill investments among employees that are difficult to sustain by firms depending on "hire and fire" to achieve flexibility (see Casper, 2000). A contradiction exists within the incentive structures most US high-tech enterprises offer to employees, in that top management expect skilled employees to commit to the very intense working conditions needed to win innovation races with competitors, but also reserve the right to hire and fire at will. This incentive conflict is reduced through offering very high-powered short-term performance incentives to employees. To monitor performance, employees must work on projects that produce codified rather than tacit knowledge. Codified research results (patents, scholarly publications, prototypes and the like) can easily be monitored by top management, venture capitalists and other stakeholders in the firm. This strategy is less viable, however, in areas where more cumulative technological trajectories create substantial amounts of tacit knowledge and firm-specific skills among employees.

German national institutional frameworks, on the other hand, strongly encourage competency-preserving human resource development through restraints on hire and fire that facilitate long-term employment. This presents a second explanation of why so many German firms have selected areas of the Internet dominated by incremental innovation. In addition to the lower financial and competency destruction risks, it is likely that the higher degree of technological cumulativeness in these markets creates a combination of tacit, firm-specific knowledge risks. As a result, German entrepreneurial technology firms should enjoy a comparative institutional advantage in the creation of those competencies needed to support innovation in areas where long-term knowledge investments are important.

Germany's new entrepreneurial firms enjoy a comparative institutional advantage in the platform technology area over US competitors. Due to the complexity of the employee motivational problems, they require the formation of longer-term relational contracts with employees to encourage investments in firm-specific knowledge. Because German institutional frameworks strongly support the investment in firm-specific and long-term tacit knowledge within firms, it is not surprising that so many German firms have selected this area. If the long-term development of platform technology firms does create substantial amounts of long-term tacit knowledge, then there is a possibility that German institutional environments could allow more efficient governance structures to cope with these problems within the firm. Access to a superior institutional environment could lead to German firms eventually outperforming American firms in platform technologies.

### 3.2    The surprising performance of the Swedish Internet software sectoral systems

How do patterns of technological leadership influence patterns of technological specialization within an economy? Can large firms playing dominant roles in the provision of particular technologies provide spillovers within regional economies that can "override" normal institutional constraints? Under some circumstances large firms can act as de facto coordinating agents in CMEs and encourage the development of radically innovative firms in societies that otherwise would not be expected to support them. We now consider firm development in a subsectoral system of innovation: middleware software production.

Recent developments in Sweden support the argument that technological hubs created by dominant firms can dramatically change "normal" institutional incentives within economies. Sweden has long been regarded as a "coordinated market economy" with patterns of market governance similar to those in Germany. Starting in the mid-1990s, however, parts of its economy have seen a dramatic transformation (see Glimstedt and Zander, 2003). Hundreds of radically innovative software firms focusing primarily on wireless Internet technologies have developed in the area around Stockholm. Sweden's long-established telecommunications equipment manufacturer Ericsson has become a dominant provider of end-to-end wireless systems, and currently has about 40 percent of all orders for third-generation wireless equipment. Other major telecommunications equipment players such as Nokia have set up development centers in Stockholm, and Microsoft recently opened an R&D center for wireless software. Ericsson's current leadership in 3G wireless technologies has helped create a technology hub in the Stockholm area that has a technological intensity far more similar to Silicon Valley than normal patterns of industrial organization in Sweden. Surveys undertaken in the late 1990s showed that about two hundred and fifty wireless firms are active in Sweden, most in technically intensive "middleware" technologies (Casper and Glimstedt, 2001).

The SSI surrounding middleware software is more complex than that for standard software, due to the importance of technical standard coordination across firms. This depends upon the resolution of collective action dilemmas, which are difficult for numerous small firms to resolve, particularly when distributive issues hinge on the particular constellation of technical knowledge chosen (Shapiro and Varian, 1999). In addition to the human resource policy risks created by high competency destruction, middleware software firms face an additional coordination risk created by the uncertainty about which emerging standards in a firm's chosen technical field will succeed.

Though governments have at times played important roles within telecommunication standards (see Glimstedt, 2001), within much of the middleware software sector most firms are dependent upon large corporations – typically telecommunications equipment manufacturers and established companies active in network-intensive standard software products – for the provision of standards to help products become interoperable (see Casper and Glimstedt, 2001). Examples of the former include large network equipment manufacturers such as Cisco Systems, Lucent and Ericsson, while Microsoft, Sun and Oracle exemplify the latter. Each of these firms has been involved in the creation of technology platforms for emerging network communication markets. These firms hope to provide technology platforms that function as "club goods" to middleware software companies, enticing them to develop a variety of follow-on technologies aimed at eventually creating new software platforms. Large firms are self-interested when providing these standards: through controlling emerging network communication protocols, they hope to secure large markets for equipment and software using the standards.

Large firms can help stabilize technologies through attracting middleware firms to create applications for their standards. As a result, middleware software firms are most likely to exist within technology clusters dominated by large companies that can entice them to commit to a technical standard, either through a reputation of past success or through other means, such as financial incentives or technical support. By locating within regional economies dominated by such firms, middleware firms can plausibly hope to insert their software engineers into the emerging technical communities surrounding new platforms. Privileged access to such communities can provide a competitive advantage for middleware firms, through, for example, supplementing the codified technical knowledge (e.g. protocols and languages) with the tacit knowledge surrounding their efficiency.

In sum, the existence of a firm that can credibly coordinate technical standards can help lower technical coordination risks, though high levels of technical and market uncertainty may remain. By doing so, large firms may alter incentives against radical innovation strategies within CMEs. We shall use this case to examine the interplay between human resource coordination and technology coordination. The key issue here is: what constellation of policies must the large firm adopt to induce engineers, managers and financiers to make commitments to projects that are normally extremely risky within their societal contexts? Can dominant actors take actions to "tip" labor market institutions in a direction contrary to "normal" institutional incentives within an economy?

We focus here on two factors: a) the influence of technology standards in fostering a switch from firm-specific to more generic, industry-specific technical skill-sets among software engineers; and b) the initiatives taken by Ericsson to foster entrepreneurialism surrounding the technologies it is sponsoring. From the perspective of human resource coordination these factors have reduced the career risk of working in a radically innovative technology start-up, and in doing so they allow competency-destroying firm strategies to become sustainable.

Ericsson through the 1980s and early 1990s in many ways resembled Siemens, Alcatel and other European telecommunications equipment manufacturers. Operating as a quasi-monopoly equipment provider in a highly regulated domestic telecommunications market, it developed the large systems integration capabilities needed for the early digital switching technologies designed primarily for voice traffic. As the only significant telecommunications equipment manufacturer in Sweden, it could attract the country's best engineering graduates, who were then offered stable, long-term careers in Ericsson. The company developed proprietary protocols and systems integration languages. The core of Ericsson's programming staff, for example, were experts in Ericsson's in-house systems integration language, Plex – a computer language used nowhere else. While the convergence of data communication and voice-based digital communication technology has forced Ericsson to adopt new languages for its next-generation telecommunications gear, several thousand employees have been retained for their expertise in Plex, which is still used to update legacy equipment.

During the late 1990s data communication networking devices have begun to converge with traditional telecommunications switching equipment. The increased use of IP-based switching has forced firms such as Ericsson increasingly to adopt connectivity standards developed for data communication networks. An issue for such firms is how this influences internal product development. In designing switching equipment, base tower systems and the related capabilities for its Internet-compatible wireless equipment, a small group of systems engineers within Ericsson developed a new systems integration language, called Erlang. As with Plex, Ericsson's initial strategy was to make this technology proprietary. However, unlike Plex, Erlang is a systems development language based on standardized, object-oriented programming tools with the potential to help firms in a number of industries develop software to manage complex technological systems. Upset at Ericsson's move to keep Erlang proprietary, the chief developer of Erlang, along with a group of systems programmers, left Ericsson in 1999 to form an independent start-up software company (Glimstedt and Zander, 2003).

Around the same time as this personnel crisis, Ericsson faced important strategic decisions regarding its sponsorship of wireless connectivity standards. Through its strong advocacy of the GSM standard, Ericsson management learned that, in relatively open data communication network architectures, network externalities play a crucial role in determining which network standards become dominant (see Glimstedt, 2001). Ericsson was a major sponsor and developer of two important new Web-based wireless connectivity standards: WAP and Bluetooth. The firm realized that, if these standards were to succeed, dozens of other firms would have to work with them, creating unique applications software and middleware technology. By creating market places for a variety of wireless applications, demand for Ericsson's end-to-end wireless systems technology would increase. Nurturing nascent wireless technology start-ups in the Stockholm area would promote Ericsson's favored technologies.

To help promote technology spillovers into Stockholm's economy, Ericsson made two strategic moves. First, it decided to make Erlang an "open-source" development language, allowing other firms to use it as a development tool. In this case, using open-source development protocols ensured that enhancements to Erlang by third parties would flow back into Ericsson. More importantly, however, it helped to create industry-specific rather than firm-specific skills among engineers involved in large-scale systems integration. The sponsorship of emerging wireless connectivity standards such as Bluetooth and WAP or widely used mobile scripting languages such as unified modeling language (UML) produces a similar effect. The standardization of development tools, protocols and connectivity standards dramatically increases the portability of skills across local firms working in wireless technology areas.

Secondly, Ericsson has changed its personnel policy toward engineers who leave to work in start-up firms. Formerly it had strongly discouraged engineers from leaving long-term careers at Ericsson to work elsewhere by signaling that they would not be re-employed by Ericsson in the future. By creating a corporate venture capital program it now allows engineers leaving Ericsson to try their hand at technology entrepreneurialism. Given that most wireless start-ups within the Stockholm area are involved in the development of Ericsson-sponsored standards, and in many cases are using its core systems development language, local start-up ventures are working primarily to develop technologies compatible with

Ericsson's next-generation wireless technologies. If individual firms fail, their managers can now easily return to work within Ericsson, perhaps having developed new managerial skills or career perspectives through working in a start-up. If start-up firms are successful, Ericsson benefits through its sponsorship of key technologies, and it has close links with the management of the new companies.

In sum, the existence of industry- rather than firm-specific standards reduces the career risk for engineers leaving established large firms for start-ups. Industry-specific standards ensure that skill and knowledge investments made by programmers and engineers are portable. It allows managers of high-tech firms successfully to recruit highly skilled technical talent, knowing that competency destruction and the accompanying hire and fire risks are high. This, combined with a more open human resource policy at Ericsson, helps explain the rapid emergence of numerous radically innovative firms. Within the normally conservative Swedish labor markets, this employment insurance is a key catalyst for creating the extremely active labor markets necessary to sustain competency-destroying technology strategies.

The comparison with Germany is interesting. In contrast to the Swedish case, the technological intensity of the German Internet economy has suffered from a lack of important "upstream" firms in either the network or connectivity layers of Internet-based telecommunications. Siemens, in particular, has failed to play a similar role. It has not emerged as a dominant player in providing end-to-end systems for either third-generation wireless or a variety of primarily IP-based fixed network switching technologies (see Casper, 2003). Siemens has recently moved its IP-based network equipment research laboratory to New Jersey – near the location of two small IP network firms it recently acquired. Overall, Siemens has failed to match Ericsson's success in becoming a dominant player in the creation of system architectures and related standards in core emerging network or connectivity markets. The *potential* for Siemens strongly to alter the "normal" institutional incentives within Munich or other leading technology districts in Germany is low.

### 3.3 The disappointing performance of the biotechnology sectoral system in the United Kingdom

The United Kingdom has developed market institutions that closely resemble the liberal market orientation found in the United States. While we later discuss potential problems with the way firms engage these institutions in practice, this liberal market orientation should clearly support the organization of entrepreneurial business models based on the US model. Combined with strong funding for basic research and a world-class pharmaceutical industry, these institutions should provide the necessary ingredients to promote entrepreneurial biotechnology companies.

Through most of the 1990s the UK biotechnology sector dominated the European scene in virtually all performance indicators. Of the sixty-eight public biotechnology firms in Europe, fifty are of UK origin. Moreover, the UK sector started to develop rapidly in the late 1980s and early 1990s – some ten years earlier than comparable sectors in most other European countries and, especially in comparison to Germany, with relatively little in the way of subsidies or other state aid to developing firms. One result of the United Kingdom's early development is that it has many more firms edging toward maturity, which helps account for the much higher employment figures in the United Kingdom as opposed to other countries, as well as the generation of some two-thirds of all commercial revenues within the European sector. UK firms have established a pattern of specialization more in line with that seen in the United States. In particular, there is a pronounced specialization toward therapeutics research. Of the fifty public UK firms, most are involved in therapeutics research (Casper and Kettler, 2001). This pattern of specialization correlates well with expectations from varieties of capitalism theory.

During the late 1990s the situation began to change dramatically. The UK biotechnology sector underperformed. Although it has generated large numbers of firms, very few have become sustainable in terms of successfully bringing products to market. As of 2002 only one company, Chiroscience, has succeeded in developing a product that has eventually gained regulatory approval and made it to the market. Dozens of other projects are in development, but very few have made it to the advanced stages of clinical trials. Moreover, rates of project failure, particularly at very costly late stages in clinical trials, have been high within the UK industry. High-visibility clinical trials setbacks include, most notoriously, the unexpectedly poor results at British Biotech, once the United Kingdom's flagship firm, as well as poor results at Scotia Holdings and Stanford Rock (Cooke, 1999, p. 14). During the same period another prominent firm, Celltech, was rocked by the withdrawal of Bayer from its drug development efforts, while another firm, Oxford Gene Technology, became involved in a patent dispute over research on a DNA chip (Cooke, 1999, p. 14). Between 1997 and 1999 the share prices of all UK biotechnology companies were severely deflated (S G Cowen, 1999). This created a crisis in confidence in the ability of the UK venture capital and investment banking community to govern projects adequately. Finally, the scientific intensity of the UK sector, which generally tracked that of the United States throughout the 1990s, declined precipitously during 1998 and fell to the same level as the German industry (see Casper and Kettler, 2001). This was a particularly ominous sign, as the United Kingdom had an industry specialization in scientifically intensive therapeutic projects, and thus should generally have had patents with a scientific intensity similar to those in the United States.

British firms have been adopting similar patterns of subsector specialization within therapeutics to those in the United States, and enjoy an institutional infrastructure that is broadly appropriate to sustaining entrepreneurial technology firms. However, UK biotechnology firms have clearly not been able to sustain the competencies necessary to win key innovation races. To understand this failure, varieties of capitalism theory points to a series of national institutional frameworks that must gel into a vibrant sectoral support system for entrepreneurial biotechnology firms. Through its use of SSI theory, the varities of capitalism approach helps identify a series of broad organizational and corporate governance problems facing UK biotechnology firms. The apparent failure of those firms to resolve their problems points to a number of possible institutional hurdles undermining the successful orchestration of both company competencies and careers.

Success in high-risk therapeutics research endeavors requires that the orchestration of all competencies involved in innovation networks be of high quality. Each link of the competency chain must be credible before all actors will commit to working within a particular entrepreneurial project. Fledgling firms with high-profile scientific backing are the most likely to gain the attention of venture capitalists with access to the generous financing, management know-how and contacts needed to persuade high-quality managers and scientists to work with the firm. This combination of assets enhances the probability of the firm succeeding in early research races and thereby gaining access to further venture capital and, eventually, access to the investment banking community, as well as joint ventures with large pharmaceutical firms.

While such virtuous circles are common with therapeutic start-ups, they can quickly become vicious. It is important to emphasize the difficulty of therapeutics research, and point out that most projects fail. To compete in therapeutics, UK firms must enter "innovation races" with firms on a worldwide basis. For example, in an extensive mapping of research clusters working to develop therapies for Alzheimer's Disease, Penan (1996) identified some fifteen distinct research programs racing against each other. If, for institutional or other reasons, one or more links within the competency chain of an emerging therapeutics research enterprise is not credible, then it is unlikely that other participants will commit to a particular project. If the firm cannot recruit high-quality researchers or attract "star-scientists" on its scientific advisory board, then it is unlikely that venture capitalists will support the firm. Similarly, when firms fail to meet important milestones the short-term and market-driven nature of their organization facilitates their quick unraveling. Once a firm faces difficulties, venture capitalists may decline to extend further financing, often forcing firms to sell valuable intellectual property at fire-sale prices to other firms in order to stay alive. This could quickly lead to further difficulties as key researchers within the firm jump to other enterprises and star scientists affiliated with the firm turn their attention elsewhere. Such is the essence of a short-term, incentive-based contracting scheme.

In appreciating both the difficulty of successfully innovating in most therapeutics research areas of biotechnology and the easy unraveling of projects once key elements lose credibility, the difficulties currently faced by the UK industry become clearer. While generally "correct" institutional structures exist in the United Kingdom, their crystallization into an adequate sectoral support system for high-risk therapeutic firms is suspect. We briefly review the problems in finance and firm competency organization that create difficulties in sustaining projects.

*Finance.* Compared to all other European countries, the United Kingdom has developed capital-market-based financial institutions that should be able to invest successfully and "harvest" large numbers of high-risk technology firms. Despite developing a strong early position, in terms of providing both venture capital and funding through successful IPOs, the UK venture capital and investment banking markets have, in recent years, moved away from high-risk biotechnology projects. The focus of the UK venture capital industry on management buy-outs/management buy-ins (MBO/MBIs) has increased dramatically since the mid-1980s. In 1984 the structure of UK investments resembled that of the United States, with 27 percent to 30 percent in the early stage and the majority of investments in firm expansion. However, between 1991 and 1995 more than 80 percent of the increase in total UK venture capital investments went toward MBO/MBIs (Bank of England, 1996). Furthermore, little of the venture capital has gone into high-tech industries. According to McKinsey & Company (1998), 71 percent of US venture capital in 1996 was invested in high technology, compared with 16 percent in the United Kingdom.

There are a number of possible reasons why British venture capitalists remain relatively reluctant to invest in high-risk technology sectors in general and in biotechnology in particular. The risk profiles of funds' investors play a role. In the United Kingdom pension funds and insurance companies provide 61 percent of venture capital. By comparison, banks have been the primary source of venture capital funding in Germany, Spain, France and the Netherlands (Bank of England, 1996, p. 22). Though some debate exists, there is a general view that pension funds and insurance companies tend to have shorter time horizons and be more risk-averse than banks. Moreover, in the United States there are two additional categories of risk-acceptant investors in technology-based small firms that do not exist in the United Kingdom: foundations and endowment funds of universities, and individual investors (21 percent and 12 percent of funds raised by venture capital firms in 1994 respectively – Bank of England, 1996, p. 22). Finally, though little research exists in this area, dedicated UK venture capital firms might lack important technical skills needed to govern deals successfully. Biotechnology investments per deal tend to be small in scale (relative to the size of MBO/MBI deals, for example) but require specialized technology experts and close supervision and monitoring. A recent government report suggests that UK venture capital firms lack sufficient numbers of industry experts and are, perhaps, too small to afford to specialize in these high-risk sectors (Bank of England, 1996). The much larger size of the US market could create incentives for dedicated venture capital firms to develop specialized expertise in biotechnology.

In sum, the funds aimed at start-up and expansion-phase venture capital for biotechnology firms are limited, investors are relatively conservative and – in terms of industry-specific skills – the managers of UK venture capital funds may be relatively unsophisticated. The ability of the UK financial sector to discern and fund high-potential start-up firms may be limited.

*Competency orchestration within firms.* Compared to firms in the United States, British biotechnology firms tend to have a much lower scientific intensity. While funding difficulties may play a role, it is also likely that bottlenecks in the supply of high-quality scientific personnel are limiting factors. The decline in the scientific intensity of UK biotechnology patents between 1996 and 1998 is one piece of evidence supporting this claim. Additional research by Casper and Kettler (2001) suggests that the scientific intensity of UK biotechnology firms is much lower than for US firms. The aggregate R&D spending by UK biotechnology firms was, on average, only 36 percent that of the United States – adjusted for GDP – in 1999 (Casper and Kettler, 2001).

One common criticism within the UK biotechnology debate is that the basic research science base itself may be inadequate. Although the United Kingdom has developed a world-class biomedical research establishment, responsible for numerous major discoveries in biotechnology-impacted areas (Cooke, 1999; and *Science Watch*, 1992), the UK science base may not be large enough to create an adequate supply of the highly trained scientists needed to fill all the available slots in academic research, within the pharmaceutical sector and in dedicated biotechnology firms. The problems facing the UK biotechnology sector may, therefore, be ones of scale: of producing a sufficiently large and high-quality science base to generate the needed scientific *and* managerial expertise. This, again, connects to labor market shortages. Given the poor performance of UK biotechnology firms, top-class scientists may be opting for more stable careers in the United Kingdom's well-performing pharmaceutical sector. If the supply of top-quality research scientists is, in fact, limited, then the large pharmaceutical firms may be dominating this market, at the expense of smaller firms. Data by Zucker and Darby (1999, p. 120) on the activities of "star scientists" within the biotechnology sector show a small but significant emigration of such scientists from European countries, including the United Kingdom, to the United States.

The ability of managers within UK firms to create high-powered work environments is an additional problem. The widespread use of incentive plans and individual-oriented performance reviews within large UK firms creates the legitimacy and know-how for the introduction of similar schemes within smaller firms. Despite the problems discussed earlier in the financial area, the United Kingdom still has the most developed equity markets in Europe in terms of market capitalization, and remains the only market to have promoted IPOs successfully for several dozen biotechnology firms, some fifty of which remain listed on UK stock exchanges. Stock options as performance incentives are thus embedded in highly credible financial market institutions. However, they are also highly dependent on the stock price of public companies, which have been highly volatile. Low stock prices may have depressed the large differential in potential long-term performance rewards across large firms in the pharmaceutical sector and smaller dedicated biotechnology firms, creating incentives for many potentially entrepreneurially minded scientists and managers to take jobs within large, established firms. Again, the need for "success stories" is crucial in such emerging technology sectors as biotechnology.

In sum, while this analysis does not provide a complete explanation for the poor performance of UK biotechnology firms, it does suggest a series of institutional obstacles that could combine to reduce the ability of these firms to compete successfully in therapeutics innovation races. Does the United Kingdom have a large enough market of research scientists to support enough project-based firms to allow portfolio strategies by venture capitalists and follow-on investment banking markets to succeed?

Similarly, without a series of success stories to add buoyancy to IPO markets, high-powered incentives to reduce employee hold-up problems and generate extremely rigorous work regimes lack credibility. While labor markets within the United Kingdom are certainly flexible, supporting "competency-destroying" strategies, when firms fail skilled employees are likely to flock to the "winning" types of firms – be they large UK pharmaceutical firms or life sciences firms located in the United States. Again, without a history of producing successful firms, high-powered incentive chains where "exit" is relatively easy are unlikely to become credible.

Has a varieties of capitalism perspective enriched the analysis of UK biotechnology? As in the Swedish Internet software case, developments in UK biotechnology show that one cannot "read off" industrial outcomes from the structure of institutions. However, insights from the varieties of capitalism approach have helped frame the analysis at several key points. At a most basic level, the United Kingdom lacks the type of "non-market" institutions that could be harnessed to follow the German model of specializing in market segments in which firms could conceivably develop a unique comparative institutional advantage over US firms. Rather, "liberal market" institutions within the United Kingdom strongly encourage biotechnology companies to accommodate themselves to the US model of developing and governing entrepreneurial technology firms. The upside of this strategy is that UK firms can, potentially, win extremely lucrative innovative races focused on capturing "blockbuster" therapeutic markets with extremely high returns. The overwhelming success of the UK pharmaceutical industry in competing head to head with US pharmaceutical firms convincingly shows that success for UK firms is possible (Casper and Matraves, forthcoming). However, the downside is that UK firms must compete directly with the well-established and generally successful US biotechnology industry.

## 4    Conclusions and implications for policy

Policy makers across Europe and East Asia, eager to promote the formation of entrepreneurial Internet firms, have sought to implant the key institutions needed to support entrepreneurial technology firms. This has particularly been the case with venture capital. Following Germany's lead in the mid-1990s, most European economies – as well as Japan and South Korea – have created "public venture capital" programs to promote the development of high-risk finance (see Kogut, 2003). Venture capital subsidies have generally complemented initiatives to create new, high-risk stock markets modeled on NASDAQ, as well as a variety of tax and corporate governance reforms aimed at promoting equity-based financial schemes and employee remuneration.

In our view, the availability of high-risk finance, preferably associated with sophisticated technical oversight, may be a necessary precondition for the establishment of entrepreneurial technology firms, but it is not sufficient. However, the availability of venture capital does not "solve" the key competency dilemmas facing start-ups in radically innovative sectoral systems. Core problems facing such firms relate not just to venture financing but to human resource and knowledge management dilemmas. A core conclusion of our analysis is that the different subsectors of biotechnology and Internet software are associated with dramatically different technology regimes, and correspondingly different constellations of organizational risk. From a public policy perspective, this suggests that multiple pathways exist. Initiatives to mimic the "Silicon Valley model" and its associated practices will not breed success in many new technology sectors. In fact, institutions facilitating "competency-preserving" commitments between managers and skilled employees are core to the success of firms in the platform biotechnology and enterprise software segments. The German case, in particular, shows that biotechnology and Internet software firms can thrive within largely "organized" institutional environments.

Ironically, there is a risk that efforts to sponsor increased entrepreneurism within traditionally "organized" economies may produce more harm than good. Technologically intensive therapeutics and middleware software firms, while best served by liberal institutional environments, tend to develop in technology hubs, often in close conjunction with the activities of network layer firms. The deregulation of labor markets within continental European economies, to take an often discussed example, could undermine the long-term viability of firms coping with firm-specific knowledge management programs, while not necessarily spurring an increase in more technologically intense middleware activities. Furthermore, the development of Stockholm's wireless technology hubs shows that increased labor market flexibility *can* emerge within normally regulated labor markets. However, it was not state intervention that created strong technical communities of engineers and software developers working within wireless technologies, but a series of personnel and technical initiatives by Ericsson, the dominant player within Sweden's telecommunications sector.

The UK biotechnology case also poses a strong challenge for national institutional approaches. Why have a relatively large number of firms embedded within the "right" institutions consistently failed to innovate? To examine the problems within the UK biotechnology sector, we used the varieties of capitalism perspective to understand the credible orchestration of competencies within high-risk biotechnology firms and then to demonstrate that a series of small problems within UK institutions may be systematically dampening the ability of UK firms to perform well. We suggested that, although economy-wide institutional environments to support entrepreneurial firms exist within the United Kingdom, these institutions have not gelled into a sectoral innovative system capable of systematically supporting entrepreneurial biotechnology firms.

Public policy initiatives within the United Kingdom should differ from those in Germany or other "organized" economies. While German policy makers must manage the hazards of integrating new institutions supportive of "new economy" industries within the overarching context of an "organized" political economy, the UK government must develop instruments to fortify the orchestration of competencies within generally "correct" institutions. Ironically, the UK government has recently attempted to mimic some aspects of German technology policies – for example, by trying to introduce a variety of new regional venture capital subsidies. Within the United Kingdom there is little evidence of a "venture capital gap"; rather, there are difficulties in creating the mix of technical and commercial expertise needed to govern existing venture capital funds effectively. Similarly, the government has attempted to bolster the development of technology infrastructures through a variety of cluster policies, again modeled loosely on the German model (see Cooke, 1999). While less controversial, again it is not clear that, within the United Kingdom's strongly market-oriented economy, "markets" cannot do most of the job of providing incentives for patent lawyers, incubator laboratories, consultants and other support services to emerge.

In the United Kingdom, policies might aim more effectively to strengthen the development of markets for both scientists and engineers, and basic research more generally. Within the biomedical area, it is likely that issues such as the overall funding of basic research could be crucial. While funding has remained strong, UK public and private funding of biomedical research has trailed the staggering investments made in basic research by the NIH and private foundations in the United States. These investments have dramatically subsidized the US biotechnology industry by providing relatively cheap technology and helping to train vast pools of high-quality research scientists. In the United Kingdom, basic biomedical research funding has remained relatively constant. In addition to creating labor market shortages, the size of public and private sector biomedical research employment has increased, while the "pool" of technology potentially available to UK firms has not grown. Recent Wellcome Trust statistics report a massive gap between the United States and all other nations in the quality of biomedical research; the United Kingdom has performed well, but has declined relative to Germany and Japan in recent years (see Wellcome Trust, 1998). Policies to increase the size and quality of the United Kingdom's biomedical research establishment may have a far greater effect on the ability of UK biotechnology firms to succeed than cluster policies. Again, these initiatives should be viewed within the general context of the United Kingdom's liberal market economy.

Overall, while a varieties of capitalism perspective cannot provide precise explanations as to why particular firms fail, by focusing on the development of credible institutions to support firm-level competency orchestration it provides a strong investigative lens. A frequent criticism of varieties of capitalism research is that it is a static theory, incapable of explaining change. We agree that some versions of national institutional framework theory presuppose a "cookie cutter" approach (Kogut, 2003), artificially limiting the autonomy of actors within the economy to craft unique organizational solutions, even when facing massive new market opportunities such as those posed in recent years by biotechnology and the Internet. We argue that varieties of capitalism theory, by focusing more carefully on firm-centered micro-foundations, can avoid some of these pitfalls. Viewing institutions as "tool kits" available to managers, scientists and other actors, we analyze more carefully how firms engage institutional frameworks to acquire and orchestrate competencies.

REFERENCES

Adelberger, K. E. (2000), Semi-sovereign leadership? The state's role in German biotechnology and venture capital growth, *German Politics*, 9, 103–122
Audretsch, D. B. (1985), *The Innovation, Unemployment, and Competitiveness Challenge in Germany*, Discussion Paper FS IV 85–6, Wissenschaftszentrum Berlin
Bank of England (1996), *The Financing of Technology-Based Small Firms*, Bank of England, London
Becker, S., W. Menz and T. Sablowski (1999), In netz gegangen: industrielle beziehungen im netzwerk-konzern am beispiel der Hoechst AG, *Industrielle Beziehungen*, 6, 9–35
Breschi, S., and F. Malerba (1997), Sectoral systems of innovation: technological regimes, Schumpeterian dynamics and spatial boundaries, in C. Edquist (ed.), *Systems of Innovation: Technologies, Institutions and Organizations*, Frances Pinter, London, 130–155
Büchtemann, C. F., and K. Vogler-Ludwig (1997), *Das deutsche Ausbildungsmodell unter Anpassungszwang: Thesen zur Humankapitalbildung in Deutschland*, Ifo Institut für Wirtschaftsforschung, Munich

Casper, S. (2000), Institutional adaptiveness, technology policy, and the diffusion of new business models: the case of German biotechnology, *Organization Studies*, 21, 887–914

(2001), The legal framework for corporate governance: the influence of contract law on company strategies in Germany and the United States, in P. A. Hall and D. Soskice (eds.), *Varieties of Capitalism – The Institutional Foundations of Comparative Advantage*, Oxford University Press, Oxford, 387–416

(2003), The German Internet economy and the "Silicon Valley model": convergence, divergence, or something else? in B. Kogut (ed.), *The Global Internet Economy*, MIT Press, Cambridge, MA, 223–262

Casper, S., and H. Glimstedt (2001), Economic organization, innovation systems, and the Internet, *Oxford Review of Economic Policy*, 17, 265–281

Casper, S., and H. Kettler (2001), National institutional frameworks and the hybridization of entrepreneurial business models: the German and UK biotechnology sectors, *Industry and Innovation*, 8, 5–30

Casper, S., M. Lehrer and D. Soskice (1999), Can high-technology industries prosper in Germany? Institutional frameworks and the evolution of the German software and biotechnology industries, *Industry and Innovation*, 6, 6–23

Casper, S., and C. Matraves (2003), Institutional frameworks and innovation in the German and UK pharmaceutical industry, *Research Institutional Frameworks and Innovation Policy*, 32, 1,865–1,879

Charkham, J. (1995), *Keeping Good Company: A Study of Corporate Governance in Five Countries*, Oxford University Press, Oxford

Cooke, P. (1999), Biotechnology Clusters in the UK: Lessons from Localisation in the Commercialisation of Science, working paper, Centre for Advanced Studies, Cardiff University

Deutsche Bundesbank (1997), *Monthly Report*, April

Easterbrook, F., and D. Fischel (1991), *The Economic Structure of Corporate Law*, Harvard University Press, Cambridge, MA

Edwards, J., and K. Fischer (1994), *Banks, Finance and Investment in Germany*, Cambridge University Press, Cambridge

Ernst and Young (1998), *New Directions 1998 – 12th Biotechnology Industry Annual Report*, Ernst & Young LLP, Palo Alto, CA

(1999), *Biotech 99: Bridging the Gap – 13th Biotechnology Industry Annual Report*, Ernst & Young LLP, Palo Alto, CA

German Venture Capital Association (1999), *Venture Capital in Europe 1998*, special report, German Venture Capital Association, Berlin

Glimstedt, H. (2001), Competitive dynamics of technological standardization: the case of third-generation cellular communications, *Industry and Innovation*, 8, 49–78

Glimstedt, H., and U. Zander (2003), Sweden's wireless wonders: defining the Swedish Internet economy, in B. Kogut (ed.), *The Global Internet Economy*, MIT Press, Cambridge, MA, 109–152

Hall, P. A., and D. Soskice (2001), Introduction, in P. A. Hall and D. Soskice (eds.), *Varieties of Capitalism – The Institutional Foundations of Comparative Advantage*, Oxford University Press, Oxford, 1–70

Hollingsworth, R. (1997), Continuities and changes in social systems of production: the cases of Germany, Japan, and the United States, in R. Hollingsworth and R. Boyer (eds.), *Contemporary Capitalism*, Cambridge University Press, Cambridge, 265–310

Katzenstein, P. (1987), *Policy and Politics in West Germany: Towards the Growth of a Semi-Sovereign State*, Temple University Press, Philadelphia

(1989), Stability and change in the emerging third republic, in P. Katzenstein (ed.), *Industry and Politics in West Germany*, Cornell University Press, Ithaca, NY

Keller, B. (1991), *Einführung in die Arbeitspolitik*, Oldenbourg, Munich

Kogut, B. (2003), Introduction: the Internet has borders, in B. Kogut (ed.), *The Global Internet Economy*, MIT Press, Cambridge, MA, 1–39

Malerba, F., and L. Orsenigo (1993), Technological regimes and firm behavior, *Industrial and Corporate Change*, 2, 1, 45–74

(1997), Technological regimes and sectoral patterns of innovative activities, *Industrial and Corporate Change*, 6, 1, 83–117

McKinsey & Company (1998), *U.S. Venture Capital – Industry Overview and Economics*, McKinsey & Company, New York

Mietsch, A. (1999), *Bio-Technologie Das Jahr- und Adressbuch 1999*, Biocom, Berlin

Miller, G. (1992), *Managerial Dilemmas*, Cambridge University Press, Cambridge

Mowery, D. C., and R. R. Nelson (eds.) (1999), *Sources of Industrial Leadership: Studies of Seven Industries*, Cambridge University Press, Cambridge

Penan, H. (1996), R&D strategy in a techno-economic network: Alzheimer's disease therapeutic strategies, *Research Policy*, 25, 3, 337–358

Perrow, C. (1985), *Normal Accidents*, Princeton University Press, Princeton, NJ

Roe, M. (1994), *Strong Managers, Weak Owners: The Political Roots of American Corporate Finance*, Princeton University Press, Princeton, NJ

Saxenian, A. (1994), *Regional Advantage: Culture and Competition in Silicon Valley and Route 128*, Harvard University Press, Cambridge, MA

Schwartz, A. (1992), Relational contracts and the courts, *Journal of Legal Studies* 21, 780–822

*Science Watch* (1992), A ranking of university institutes by citation impact – current contents: life sciences, molecular biology/genetics subsection, Institute of Scientific Information, Philadelphia

S G Cowen (1999), Biotechnology quarterly, *S G Cowen Perspectives*, January

Shapiro, C., and H. Varian (1999), *Information Rules*, Harvard Business School Press, Cambridge, MA

Soskice, D. (1997), German technology policy, innovation, and national institutional frameworks, *Industry and Innovation*, 4, 75–96

Streeck, W. (1984), *Industrial Relations in West Germany: A Case Study of the Car Industry*, St Martin's Press, New York

Technologie-Beteiligungs-Gesellschaft (2001), *Sectoral Distribution of Public Venture Capital*, http://www.tbgbonn.de/info/index.html

Teece, D. (1986), Profiting from technological innovation: implications for integration, collaboration, licensing, and public policy, *Research Policy*, 15, 6, 285–305

Tylecote, A., and E. Conesa (1999), Corporate governance, innovation systems, and industrial policy, *Industry and Innovation*, 6, 25–50

Vitols, S. (2001), Varieties of corporate governance: comparing Germany and the UK, in P. A. Hall and D. Soskice (eds.), *Varieties of Capitalism – The Institutional Foundations of Comparative Advantage*, Oxford University Press, Oxford, 337–369

Wellcome Trust (1998), *Mapping the Landscape: National Biomedical Research Outputs, 1988–95*, Policy Report no. 9, Wellcome Trust, London

*Wistschaftswoche* (1998), Schneller Aufstieg, September 24, 134–139

Woodward, J. (1965), *Industrial Organization, Theory and Practice*, Oxford University Press, Oxford

Zucker, L., and M. Darby (1999), Star scientist linkages to firms in APEC and European countries: indicators of regional institutional differences affecting competitive advantage, *International Journal of Biotechnology*, 1, 1, 119–131

# 11 The international performance of European sectoral systems

*Benjamin Coriat, Franco Malerba and*
*Fabio Montobbio*[1]

## 1    Introduction

This chapter aims to analyze the determinants of European industrial strength in a selected number of sectors vis-à-vis the United States and Japan. We take a comparative bottom-up approach, presenting a series of results from the analysis of the six sectors (pharmaceuticals and biotechnology, chemicals, telecommunications, software, machine tools and three subsectors in services) examined in this book.

Our starting point is that differences in firms' rates of innovation and countries' economic performance are greatly affected by the features of learning, the knowledge base, the types of actors and networks involved in innovation, and the institutional setting of innovative activities.

For the six sectors we enquire, where major differences in the structure and working of sectoral systems across countries are present, whether these differences affect the international performance of countries, and whether characteristics of the sectoral systems have been major factors for industrial leadership in each sector. Section 2 provides a link between the sectoral system approach and the analysis of the determinants of industrial leadership. The sectoral system approach suggests that, in the majority of cases, differences in technological expertise and their impact on sectoral performance cannot be understood in a vacuum or simply on the basis of investment strategies at the level of the firm; rather, that they need to be analyzed with respect to many other relevant dimensions that characterize a sector and its dynamics over time. Section 3 assesses the main relationships between the characteristics of the sectoral system and economic performance in sectors. Four sectors rely heavily upon advancement in the science base and in the related transfer sciences (i.e. pharmaceuticals and biotechnology, chemicals, telecommunications and software). The other sectors (i.e. machine tools and three subsectors

[1] We thank Fabrizio Cesaroni, Nicoletta Corrocher, Luciana D'Adderio, Maureen McKelvey, Luigi Orsenigo, Edward Steinmueller and Jürgen Wengel for their useful help and suggestions.

in services), even if they typically do not belong to high-tech sectors, are highly innovative. Section 4 points out the different determinants of industrial leadership in different sectoral systems, while section 5 expands the discussion on European performance, focusing on the roles of product differentiation, industry life cycles and science.

## 2 Sectoral systems and industrial leadership

Our approach follows Mowery and Nelson (1999) and focuses on "competitiveness" and "sectoral system performance" in loose terms. We place emphasis on the ability of countries in each sector to adopt and develop better technologies that have a positive impact on the growth of firms' world market share. Like Mowery and Nelson (1999; p. 2) we adopt "the term industrial leadership to denote the focus on industries in which *being ahead of one's competitors' product or process technology, or in production and marketing*, gives firms an *advantage* in world markets. As such, we are concerned with the translation of technological expertise into commercial success." We also follow Mowery and Nelson because we have no theoretical a priori position on the specific sources of industrial leaderships and whether they are determined "by strengths firms build for themselves, or draw from their national or regional environments and support systems, as economists generally presume" (p. 2).

A considerable amount of recent empirical evidence consistently shows that non-price factors (e.g. the dynamic of technological variables or the quality and novelty of products and productive processes) significantly affect the dynamic of world market shares in the advanced countries (Fagerberg, 1988; Dosi, Pavitt and Soete, 1990; Greenhalg, 1990; Amendola, Dosi and Papagni, 1993; Magnier and Toujas-Bernate, 1994; and Amable and Verspagen, 1995). It also shows that the relationship between these factors and industrial leadership is sector-specific (Amable and Verspagen, 1995; Magnier and Toujas-Bernate, 1994; and Montobbio, 2003). We claim that industrial leadership and market share gains depend upon the reproduction over time of differentiated technological knowledge and experience (Dosi, Pavitt and Soete, 1990; and Amendola, Dosi and Papagni, 1993), which, in turn, has to be accounted for by an analysis of the wide array of variables included in the sectoral system approach. Moreover, we believe that, as the number of competing countries at the technological frontier expands and information and communication technologies diffuse, non-price factors are becoming increasingly important for success in the international arena.

Also, in the last twenty years international trade theories have moved toward a closer examination of the dynamic role of innovation and technical change within the technological gap and product cycle traditions (Posner, 1961; Vernon, 1966; and Krugman, 1979, 1994). Simplifying the argument goes as follows: if countries can be ranked by technological level (in terms of labor requirement in every industry) and goods can be ranked by technological intensity, countries that are high on the technological scale tend to specialize in the technologically intensive goods. A variety of models extend this analysis and link it to the endogenous growth framework, showing that resource allocation depends on the economic context (in particular, the endowment of skilled labor) and, especially, on the nature of knowledge spillovers (Grossman and Helpman, 1991; and Grossman, 1991).

We share with the neo-technology literature in international trade the idea that competitive advantages are built endogenously and that their evolution depends importantly upon R&D and innovation activities. Moreover, we have in common the idea that firm-level advantages (often called "competitive advantages") are built into the wider economic context. At the same time, we adopt a completely different line, similar to the approach of Mowery and Nelson (1999) and related to the concept of sectoral systems.

As we have seen in chapter 1 and in the sectoral studies, a sectoral system is the collection of economic activities organized around a common technological or knowledge base in which individual enterprises are likely to be either actual or potential competitors with one another. A sectoral system encompasses many individual markets and enterprises that are interrelated. Three broad dimensions affect the generation and adoption of new technologies and the organization of innovation and production at the sectoral level: the knowledge and technological domain; actors and networks; and institutions.

Following this analytical approach, we believe that outcomes in terms of innovative, economic and export performance are the result of specific dynamic complementarities between the three categories of variables discussed above (knowledge and technological domains, firms and other actors and networks, and institutions) and we add the following considerations.

- There is a great deal of *endogeneity* in the relation between knowledge and technological domains, firms, other actors and networks, institutions and economic performance. The probability of having competitive firms and networks depends upon the type of "institutional package," given the characteristics of the knowledge base. However, the probability of developing a specific institutional setting depends upon some of the characteristics of technological specialization. In turn, economic success at the firm level is expected – on the one hand – to be determined by the coevolution of knowledge and technological domains, actors and networks, and institutions and – on the other hand – to guide the trajectory of technological and economic development. In this respect the sectoral system methodology helps assess how binding institutional packages are – or, conversely, how binding technological paradigms are.

- This brings about the issue of *dynamics* and path-dependence. The actual outcome in terms of economic performance is the result of a specific sequence of events and causal nexus. This is in line with our emphasis on the need to generalize a methodology of enquiry and on the difficulties on reaching clear-cut conclusions or well-defined taxonomies.
- In principle, we should be able to select the main determinants of economic success in terms of the aforementioned variables. However, the greater the number of variables we bring into the picture and the more complex their features the more difficult it will be to put forward generalizations, and the more context-specific the answers will be.
- Sectoral systems and the interplay between knowledge and technological domains, actors and networks, and institutions may be conducive to patterns of technological specialization that lock in regions. Paraphrasing the famous words of Landes (1966, p. 563), prosperity and success may be their own worst enemies. A region can be displaced because a sector declines and because substitute sectors emerge and develop in other regions. Accordingly, sectors and regions should be able to create new opportunities and change. We claim, then, that there is always the necessity to evaluate a sectoral system and its impact on the economic performance of a region, not only in the specific articulation of knowledge and technological domains, actors and networks, and institutions but also within the broader dynamic of the overall technological and economic evolution.

## 3       The international performance of six European sectors

### 3.1     *Pharmaceuticals and biotechnology*

#### 3.1.1   *The knowledge and technological domain*
This industry has witnessed a major shift in the scientific knowledge base, determined by the emergence of biochemistry, enzymology, molecular biology and biotechnology, which opened up two trajectories of development: 1) processes to create proteins with well-known therapeutic properties (these advancements were brought forward mainly by US start-up

firms); and 2) the search for new drugs and therapies (this was adopted by the large and established pharmaceutical firms more evenly in the United States and Europe, in particular the United Kingdom and Switzerland) (Henderson, Orsenigo and Pisano, 1999; and McKelvey, Orsenigo and Pammolli, chapter 3 in this book).

Research on molecular biology and genetic engineering, which started in the late 1930s, mainly in the most famous US universities, has undergone unprecedented developments in the post-war years. In the 1970s these new academic disciplines appeared to be new and important sources of knowledge and discoveries, likely to revolutionize the existing therapies and treatments and to constitute, in the medium term, a source of new and original therapies. It is worthwhile noting that discoveries on molecular biology and genetic engineering are not related solely to traditional pharmaceutical products and processes but to the whole structure of life (DNA). In this respect they have an all-purpose vocation: from the treatment of human diseases to the agribusiness sector (e.g. the selective setting-up of transgenic species and plants), from cross-breeding and cloning to all the applications related to man's diseases.

### 3.1.2    *Education, scientific and technological research, university-industry relations and technological transfer*

The quality of education and research and its integration with medical applications lie at the heart of the US success and Europe's lagging behind in pharmaceuticals and biotechnology. US leadership in research is the result of the number and diversity of sources of funding and of somewhat more efficient selection mechanisms. The university system and the NIH have provided advanced basic research and trained scientists and researchers in medicinal chemistry, pharmacology, biochemistry, enzymology and molecular genetics. The economic fall-out of discoveries and research on these issues was very rapidly understood, and numerous incentives were devised to urge universities to commit themselves to such activities, fostering and to foster the research for applications within newly set up firms employing academic researchers but dedicated to commercial activities.

In Europe basic research has not been funded so much as in the United States, and has had fewer incentives and less support to change and redirect to new areas. A few areas of research at European universities were advanced and at the leading edge, but in general the competencies in advanced research were not widely diffused. Moreover, some European countries remained attached to the more academic focus of their national research institutes, with research separated from universities and confined in specialized research laboratories, and with little interaction with teaching, medical practice and industrial research (except in the cases where biomedical research was conducted in medical schools). Also, university-industry links were less developed than in the United States (McKelvey, Orsenigo and Pammolli, chapter 3 in this book).

However, in the last few years German firms seem to have benefited from a set of government-funded programs conducive to a higher level of exchange between university and industry and to a higher number of biotechnology start-ups. For example, the BioRegio program encouraged regions to establish technology transfer offices and funded pre-commercial R&D projects and other services and support. At the same time in the United Kingdom, where the institutional and organizational framework is more similar to that of the United States, universities do not seem to have been equally effective in promoting research and the commercialization of the results. The main reason, probably, is the lack of private funds required to hire highly qualified people and to invest in the development of many projects (Casper and Kettler, 2002).

### 3.1.3   Intellectual property rights protection and price and approval regulations

IPR protection and academic norms for commercial exploitation of the results, which give the right to universities to appropriate research results (even if funded by government funds), are important factors conducive to the expansion of the industry, although one could differentiate the short-term effects on the private appropriation of industrial research results from the longer-term effects of the reduced possibility of utilizing the results of basic research protected by patents (Dasgupta and David, 1994; and David, 2001). University patenting has a long history in the United States, and it was heavily influenced by the system and the amount of federal funding after World War II and by different types of financial incentives well before the Bayh-Dole Act (Mowery and Sampat, 2001).

However, the Bayh-Dole Act (which came into force in 1980), as well as other institutional or regulatory mechanisms (Jaffe, 2000; and Coriat and Weinstein, 2002), encouraged the patent registration of discoveries and/or inventions related to genetic engineering by university, licensing and firm start-ups. A decision by the Supreme Court of the United States (obtained after many years of proceedings and a very narrow 5 to 4 vote) granted a patent on a genetically modified organism. In this way the Supreme Court opened the way to a non-reversible situation, which led to a complete shift by making it possible to patent living entities. The patent granted to General Electric by the Chakrabarty ruling, allowing for an exclusive exploitation right, opened the way to the launching of specific firms dedicated to basic research as independent actors in the commercial world. The conditions were thus created for the development of independent actors and a new division of labor in the for-profit sector (see Orsi and Moatti, 2001; and Orsi, 2001).

The US government strongly supported patent protection for pharmaceuticals and provided effective regulation of the safety and efficacy of products and processes. This regulatory climate did not restrict generic experimentation. Rather, it positively affected the formation of new firms. The channel is probably the creation of a clear and unified market for technologies (McKelvey, Orsenigo and Pammolli, chapter 3 in this book).

The differences observable in the field of regulations may go a long way to account for very different firm strategies, according to the opportunities provided by the existing regulation in the pharmaceutical industry. Comparing the performances of the French and British pharmaceutical firms, Thomas (1994) emphasizes two elements of regulation framework that had major consequences for the industry in the early 1990s. First, there was the role of price fixing. Starting from the mid 1960s the French and UK authorities have taken very different paths. In France the basic principle is to fix prices on a "cost plus" basis (i.e. an evaluation of the cost of production plus a mark-up). In the United Kingdom, on the other hand, prices are designed to favor investments, especially in R&D. Thus, the profit margins (differing according to the R&D expenditures of the different firms) were fixed in order to create the incentives for firms to invest in R&D. Second, there were the regulations regarding market access for new drugs and products. In France there is a somewhat higher emphasis on safety, whilst in the United Kingdom the focus is more on efficacy, well controlled by clinical trials.

The combined effect of these two series of regulations (everything being equal) seems to have been as follows. *First,* British industry experienced a process of selection, which allowed the survival of the most dynamic firms (i.e. the ones engaged in R&D and innovative activities). In France, without specific incentives rewarding the innovative firms, a large space remained open for firms dealing with minor innovations, based largely on the use of already known molecules. *Second,* in the United Kingdom fewer but far more innovative products have been launched than in France. As a result, the UK pharmaceutical industry was able to launch more "world-class products" than its French counterpart, thus enjoying a larger share of the world market in the early 1990s (Thomas, 1994).

Moreover, evidence suggests that, as in the United Kingdom and the United States, the more stringent the regulations are in terms of the efficacy of the therapeutic contributions the more innovations will tend to be radical. Less demanding in terms of therapeutic contributions and efficacy, the French regulations left room and favored minor innovations, more directed to local markets, with few world-class products.

### 3.1.4   Firms and venture capital

Industrial leadership is linked to the behavior of the large multinational companies and, in biotechnology, also to the emergence and development of the small high-tech firm. In the United States large pharmaceutical companies and new biotechnology firms have both been major innovators. Most large pharmaceutical firms reacted slowly to the opportunities and threats posed by biotechnology, but they were faster than most European companies: these large, innovative and more experienced firms had an advantage in the exploitation of these techniques (Owen-Smith et al., 2002). Europe has fragmented and protected markets due to differences in price regulations, approval procedures and reimbursement mechanisms. These factors hindered the creation of an effective selection environment, with the result that inefficient, labor-intensive firms survived.

In biotechnology technological development is very fast and the research environment is changing continuously: as a result, companies tend to specialize in a single stage of production (research, sales or distribution), avoiding full vertical integration. Accordingly, the ability to be inserted into a network via cross-licensing and alliances is regarded as a necessary condition to meet all the technological needs (Casper and Kettler, 2000). The majority of biotechnological products are marketed by the pharmaceutical companies.

A strong science base and the size of pharmaceutical national industries were key factors for innovation. Location-specific factors affected the formation of the innovative alliances that developed mainly in the United States, where the largest critical mass of scientists and biotechnology companies existed. US and UK firms were able to tap into local advanced research and Swiss firms built strong connections with US research, suggesting that, at least in the specific product fields of biotechnology research tools, geographical proximity is not always important (Henderson, Orsenigo and Pisano, 1999). Consider also that forming alliances with big pharmaceutical companies is one of the primary sources of R&D funding for small biotechnology companies (McKelvey, Orsenigo and Pammolli, chapter 3 in this book).

The availability of venture capital considerably helped US start-ups to grow. The business model is thus founded upon the idea that the firm holds an intangible and high-level intellectual capital. Henceforth, the presence of well-known scientists (the so-called "star scientists": Zucker and Darby, 1996) within these new firms and their holding of a patent portfolio are the key elements in their setting up.

Another series of institutional prerequisites, this time relating to financial markets, was also indispensable. A new regulation was introduced on NASDAQ so as to allow for the IPO of firms with a loss (Orsi, 2001). At the same time a transformation of the "prudent man" legislation on pension funds, allowing them to penetrate high-risk firms' capital, was implemented (Gompers and Lerner, 1999; and Coriat and Weinstein, 2002). However, the lack of a diffused constellation of venture capital firms was not such a serious constraint in Europe. Many other sources of funds were available, including the big established firms and foreign venture capital. More constraining seems to be the lack of promising science-based firms.

However, in Germany a mixture of private and public venture capital, the IPOs in the *Neuer Markt* for technology companies and the support program mentioned before encouraged a great number of firm start-ups. The venture capital has focused mainly on seed capital. However, the German market is still undercapitalized and young. Expansion remains limited by uncertainty about viable exit options and by a low potential for risk diversification. The lack of European success stories in biotechnology is also a strong constraint still for the development of venture capital in the United Kingdom. There venture capital has, over the years, moved away from high-risk biotechnology projects. In addition, there appears to be a lack of highly skilled managers of UK venture funds (Casper and Kettler, 2000; and Casper and Soskice, chapter 10 in this book).

### 3.1.5    Performance

The main factors affecting industrial leadership in the pharmaceutical and biotechnology industries are a dynamic combination of many aspects: a strong science base founded upon a high-quality and efficient organization of research and education (for scientists, entrepreneurial scientists and managers); a tradition in university-industry relationships for technology transfer; and the presence of a market for technologies within clear institutional (patent legislation) and regulatory frameworks conducive to higher levels of efficacy and innovation. The size of the domestic market and its degree of competition and integration are also important in an industry with high fixed costs in R&D and, possibly, low marginal costs. Moreover, the size and the integration of the market are important because they facilitate the creation of alliances between small and big firms and an efficient division of labor.

The United States was able to become the world leader in biotechnology at the end of the 1970s and the beginning of the 1980s thanks to the excellence of its scientific base and to firm start-ups: a combination of university spin-offs, scientists, professional managers and venture capital. Geographical proximity played a major role. It is interesting to note that the United Kingdom shares these factors conducive to the expansion of biotechnology as outlined above. Nevertheless, despite being the first to develop in Europe, UK biotechnology is stagnating: only one firm has been able to launch a therapeutic product in the market. Lack of expertise at the level of scientists, managers and technology transfer offices in universities seems to be one of the main constraining factors.

However, in Europe, as Casper and Kettler (2000) and Casper and Soskice (chapter 10 in this book) show, countries may end up specializing in *subsectors* of biotechnology. German biotechnology firms have specialized in platform technologies that are then sold to other research laboratories (for example, consumable kits to rationalize common molecular biology laboratory processes). These technologies are more generic and more cumulative than the standard therapeutic products, often relate to the development of equipment for pharmaceutical firms, and have a library of core technologies that are then customized for specific market niches.

These features fit better than the standard therapeutic products with the German institutional framework (which is characterized by "insider" corporate governance, internal long-term relationships between firms and employees, and investments in firm-specific knowledge). On the other hand, firms in the United Kingdom specialized in standard therapeutic products, related to the standard products developed by the dominant American industry (Casper and Kettler, 2000; and Casper and Soskice, chapter 10 in this book).

## 3.2    Chemicals

### 3.2.1    The knowledge and technological domain

The patterns of competitiveness and leadership in the chemical sectoral system have been heavily influenced by the impact of a series of big *discontinuities* in the knowledge and technological dimension. First, the dyestuff model introduced the link with scientific research and universities. Secondly, polymer chemistry required a tighter connection with users. Finally, petrochemical technologies and, consequently, the development of chemical engineering were conducive to the emergence of specialized engineering firms, since the process design can be separated from the production of the chemical compound at the plant level. The emergence of chemical engineering as an independent research field reinforced the creation of specific markets for process technologies (see Cesaroni et al., chapter 4 in this book).

### 3.2.2    Actors, networks and institutions

In spite of these major changes in the knowledge and technological domain, continuity in companies' lives has been observed (BASF, Hoechst and Bayer in Germany, DuPont in the United States and ICI in the United Kingdom have been continuously active in the industry and innovating for between seventy and eighty years), and firms can be found among the top chemical producers that have been in existence for at least a hundred years. Thus, the sectoral system might change and the leadership at country level gradually shift, but the main actors and the related oligopoly structure remain largely unaltered. This suggests a central role for large firms in framing and guiding sectoral organization or a great ability to adapt to the transformation of the knowledge base.

The internal R&D of the major chemical firms has been complemented by external links with other firms, universities, users and the SEFs. Most of the world's large chemical firms can be categorized in three types of networks: inter-firm, university-industry and user-producer. The first type includes inter-firm partnerships for the development or production of specific products. Licenses or mergers are increasingly being used to acquire capabilities in related, or even unrelated, sectors. Large firms have also increased their propensity to license out proprietary technologies to other firms. In this respect the emergence of the SEFs was a key factor behind US competitiveness, but the benefits of the market for process technologies also became available to other countries, which were then able to reduce the technological gap (Arora, Landau and Rosenberg, 1999; and Cesaroni et al., chapter 4 in this book). University-industry relations are present in specific areas of research, while networks with users are common in downstream specialty sectors in order to specify product characteristics better (Cesaroni et al., chapter 4 in this book).

The relevance of geographical proximity also has to be noted. Inside the same territorial area small firms are able to access different and complementary competencies (mainly science and R&D). Hence, by locating in technological clusters, small firms can compensate for their lack of internal scientific competencies and coordination capabilities compared to larger firms. At the same time, regional characteristics (such as local demand and scientific and technological sophistication) guide the location of multinational corporations and determine countries' competitiveness. Indeed, national competitiveness can be seen not so much in the performance of nationally based MNEs as in the degree to which international companies are drawn to locate within national boundaries, and in the quality of the jobs that they bring with them and that are attracted to them.

In most countries, public policy directly aimed at innovation in the industry has not played a major role in innovation (except during World War II). Indirect policies through environmental regulation, strong intellectual property rights and university support has appeared to be more effective (Cesaroni et al., chapter 4 in this book). Finally, as with machine tools (see section 3.5), the majority of chemical products are intermediate goods. The size of the domestic market was an important factor for the development of the petrochemicals industry in the United States. However, as markets in many fields are increasingly global, demand seems to play an important role in guiding the location of plants of multinational corporations.

### 3.2.3   Summing-up

In parallel with the major transformation of the technological knowledge base, the leadership shifted. In particular, passing from production related to coal to production related to petrochemicals in the years before World War II, US firms caught up with Europe. They became leaders in organic chemicals, using the United States' abundant oil resources and the size of the domestic market. The emergence of SEFs was mainly a US phenomenon, linked to American strength in oil refining, because competition in this industry – having less scope for product diversification – started to be based on cost-saving processes.

German and Swiss firms remained behind, moving to pharmaceuticals, dyestuffs and synthetic fibers. Later, in the 1970s and 1980s, the oil shocks and tougher competition from Europe and the developing countries (which profited from the market for technologies promoted by the SEFs) began jeopardizing the US leadership (Arora, Landau and Rosenberg, 1999; and Cesaroni et al., chapter 4 in this book).

In summary, the factors affecting the leadership of the chemical sectoral system revolve around the following interrelated issues. The chemical industry has got increasingly oligopolistic. Large multinational firms are able to perform R&D, to build efficient networks (with universities or with specialized suppliers), to expand, and to adapt to the changing knowledge base. Accordingly, their location depends upon regional characteristics, including local demand and technological and scientific research capabilities. Finally, patent policies have been particularly important in support of the activity of smaller technology-based firms. In the United States this has created the basis for a division of labor between technology suppliers and users, and allowed the development of markets for technology. By contrast, European markets for technology are far from being developed. This requires a policy that supports their formation, first of all – but not only – in terms of a policy for intellectual property rights.

### 3.3    Telecommunications equipment and services

#### 3.3.1    The United States and Europe: different technological trajectories
The United States and Europe have followed different trajectories of development in relation to the production and adoption of ICT-related products. Many indicators (such as the number of personal computers, Internet hosts and users per inhabitant) indicate that the United States is ahead in the diffusion of ICT. In Western Europe weak adoption is particularly concentrated in the southern countries: Greece, Italy and Spain. Moreover, evidence in terms of patenting activity in the United States in the last thirty years suggests that Europe's world share of patents in ICT is lower than its world share in all technologies. This is true for all European countries with the exception of Ireland and the Netherlands, where FDI has been higher (Dalum et al., 1999).

More specifically, in telecommunications it is necessary to make a distinction between hardware and services. In telecommunications equipment, European countries have a similar market structure to American firms. Here global players dominate the scene (Dalum and Villumsen, 2002). Edquist (chapter 5 in this book) has focused on segments of telecommunications hardware and services and on Internet services that display particularly interesting features for the European case: mobile phones and services, and Internet services.

In the telecommunications hardware sector Europe is performing relatively well in communication-related areas such as telephones, mobile phones and faxes. The big European firms here are major actors, having developed around themselves the appropriate services and a network of supporting institutions and organizations (e.g. Nokia in Finland, Eriksson in Sweden and Siemens in Germany).

In Internet services national features strongly influence innovation and the rate and the direction of technological change, such that national local firms can survive and prosper despite the slow rate of adoption and diffusion in many European countries. In the various European countries the characteristics of local markets differ greatly, as the cases of the United Kingdom and Italy show (Corrocher, 2003b). Major differences also exist between Europe, the United States and Japan.

For example, recent developments in Europe (in particular the advent of free service) have seriously undermined the position of ISPs while strengthening the position of content and network providers. This phenomenon is unique to Europe, where the metered usage of the Internet (in contrast to the flat-rate structure of the US market) traditionally represented an obstacle for its diffusion. In Japan the incumbent telecommunications operator still has a significant market share for the provision of Internet services, despite the efforts by the government to promote competition. The process of standardizing the protocols for mobile communications has also played out in a quite different way in Europe from the United States, and it partly explains the leadership of the European countries in this market. This is particularly important as far as the future of the Internet is concerned, since the possibility of accessing the Web through mobile phones represents a concrete opportunity for Europe to catch up and even overtake the United States along an alternative, but not divergent, technological trajectory.

In markets with a well-developed network and with a high level of competition – not just the United States and Japan but also the United Kingdom and the Scandinavian countries – the incumbents and the new entrants compete both on traditional communications services and on more enhanced services over the Internet. In these countries, the development of new access technologies and of increasingly efficient transmission protocols stimulates the introduction of value-added services, which can be customized to the specific requirements of users. On the other hand, countries such as Italy, Spain and France have a less developed Internet market, not only in terms of the diffusion of services among potential users but also in terms of infrastructure and competition among providers. These countries generally do not have a widely installed base of cable TV infrastructure. For this reason, the introduction of broadband services could be slower, although the utilization of ADSL technology over the existing network constitutes an important step in this direction. The development of broadband infrastructure is particularly important if one considers that new Internet appliances (such as Web TV) are emerging and represent an important catalyst for the widespread diffusion of the Internet. Despite the delay in the process of increasing competition for the provision of Internet services, these countries are now catching up with the technological leaders.

### 3.3.2  *Regulations and standards*
In the telecommunications industry regulations and standards play a crucial role. Some standards are accepted *de jure* by the whole community of producers and users. They provide the "rules of the game" for all the players. Other types of standards emerge through market interaction. Many of them are sponsored. In these circumstances, specific firms'

market strategies can heavily affect the final outcome, and the existence of a large internal market (such as the US one) is often a decisive relative advantage to ensure the success of a new standard.

In terms of institutional framework, the Internet sector relies upon the regulation of the telecommunications industry, and its evolution has greatly benefited from the process of liberalization. Issues such as the degree and conditions of network unbundling and licensing, the tariff structure and rebalancing have been taken into account by regulators, and the harmonization of rules at the European Union level has allowed greater transparency in the management of the Internet. It is interesting to note that technological and market developments may anticipate, and thus constrain, regulators' decisions. This process is very much dependent upon country-specific characteristics. As we have seen, the United Kingdom and Italy have two different experiences: in the first case technological progress has anticipated the changes in the regulatory framework, while in the second case the liberalization of the market has followed the process of technological convergence, without stimulating the development of innovation.

The GSM case deserves special attention, because, by formulating an a priori standard, the European Community has been able to affect the performance of European firms, which have passed from a situation of complete dependence to a situation of world leadership. In terms of competitiveness, the European success in GSM has been the result of the interplay of several factors: the presence of large, capable and innovative firms; the increase in external cooperative links; a regionally based consortium with close collaboration among actors; and the move to a pan-European standard ratified by European standard organizations (Hommen and Manninen, 2003).[2] GSM success could not be ascribed only to the strategies of a few innovative producers but to the collaboration of a variety of quite different actors: the PTTs, standard-setting organizations such as ETSI and research organizations. It appears that the NMT system – which is the direct ancestor of GSM, thereby helping

---

[2] GSM was introduced in 1992 (and a second phase of GSM standard was introduced in 1995/96). GSM is a digital system and an open standard, with a greater variety of terminal equipment. In addition, its terminals have greater capabilities and more functions than previous systems and allow the transmission of data. Also, the functionality of the GSM handset have been greatly increased compared to the analog handset. The dual-band handset and the short messaging service are other features of GSM. GSM radio base stations are more "intelligent" than their analog counterparts, so network intelligence is concentrated in the radio base stations rather than in the switches. Switching allows an extended international roaming capability. Complementary standards were also introduced in cordless telephony (Telepoint and digital enhanced cordless technologies), cellular telephony personal communication networks (combining cellular and cordless) and paging systems.

Nordic firms' development – was the result of a concerted effort between the PTTs, public regulators and innovative firms.

One could say that past European success in GSM will not necessarily be replicated in 3G mobile telephony, because some of the conditions underlying the success of the first and second generations no longer apply. In particular, liberalization has reduced the central role of monopolistic PTTs, meaning that close interaction and large, sheltered domestic markets are more difficult to obtain for the introduction of new products.

The European success in GSM took place while in the United States rival standards were in competition with one another. They included D-AMPS, supported by the CTIA, and CDMA, which emerged later but attracted more operators. Neither of the two standards was directly compatible with the other. Contrary to the European decision on GSM, the CTIA opted for backward compatibility with 1G analog systems so that an incremental shift could take place. In addition, the FCC ruled in 1988 that there would not be a national digital standard, only compatibility among different standards.

These two decisions were to have profound effects on the competition between GSM and American standards, because they reduced the speed of transition from the first-generation to the second-generation mobile phone. Thus no single standard came to dominate the US market. CDMA was technically superior to D-AMPS in terms of capacity gains but it had limited availability of terminal equipment and was implemented differently by each operator. So the slower diffusion of digital systems in the United States was due to the presence of two standards and a weaker migration from the first generation to the second generation due to backward compatibility. In addition, in Europe the structure of tariffs on mobile services was different, and roaming and caller pay issues were resolved much earlier (Hommen and Manninen, 2003).

### 3.3.3  Summing-up

In ICT in general, and in telecommunications equipment, the European performance is weak. In other telecommunications segments, such as mobile phones and some Internet services, European firms are performing reasonably well. It is in the world of "proprietary standards" (namely in services) that the European firms are facing their most significant difficulties. The good performances by some European countries are the results of specific demand conditions and of historically contingent procedures of standard setting backed by national telecommunications providers (then public monopolies). Since a large market has been created, European firms can retain an advantage through learning effects and innovation on the production side. In order to do so they should have the appropriate level of skilled human resources.

However, as Casper and Soskice (chapter 10 in this book) have noted, recently in the telecommunications sectoral system some of the institutional features that characterize the Swedish national framework (such as long-term relationships between firms and employees) have been modified in order to take into account the new characteristics of the innovation process in mobile phones. Ericsson recognized that wireless technologies require open standards and the full exploitation of network effects. Thus, in the late 1990s Ericsson decided to make its last system integration language open rather than proprietary, and sponsored the formation of new start-ups that are spin-offs from Ericsson and which aimed to develop products compatible with Ericsson's new generation of wireless technologies.[3]

Finally, liberalization and European integration (with an active competition policy) have improved the innovative and economic performance of European firms. This may be not sufficient, however, if it is not coupled with the development of a "critical mass" in terms of networks of cooperating and competing firms at the European level.

### 3.4    Software

#### 3.4.1    The characteristics of the packaged software industry
Packaged software products are characterized by low marginal costs of reproduction, positive "network externalities" and – possibly – increasing returns. The first of these features requires that business models for software development must make a provision for recovering the cost of the "first copy" of the software. IPR systems such as software copyright licenses are one way to provide the incentives for innovation and market development. Strong IPR protection creates these incentives as well as the potential for strong monopolies where no effective substitutes exist. In the use of packaged software, positive network externalities may serve to strengthen the market position of leading firms by ensuring that, if usage is sufficiently widespread, the resulting pool of skills and knowledge reduces the incentives to develop and use alternative software products. Packaged software producers have devised a further method for reinforcing the effects of positive network externality by creating proprietary standards for recording information: the adoption of the leading software becomes necessary to realize the benefits of file exchange.

---

[3] While introducing this new policy of open standards and support for the formation of networked new firms, Ericsson maintained some of the features of the Swedish system by allowing engineers leaving Ericsson to return if their start-ups failed.

The low marginal costs of reproducing software and the potential for network externalities provide substantial incentives for investment in the creation of software that will appeal to a large user base. Although there is little evidence of substantial economies of scale in the production of software, there are considerable economies of scale in the mass promotion and distribution of packaged software products. Under these conditions, the requirements for success in packaged software markets appear to be very restrictive and can be characterized as a "winner takes all" situation.

### 3.4.2   Packaged software: US industrial leadership and European opportunities

The software industry has been characterized by a set of independent producers of tradable products since the end of the late 1960s, following the decision of IBM to "unbundle" software provision from its sale and leasing of computer equipment, and the growth of specialized application software companies serving the mainframe market. The introduction of microprocessors and the diffusion of desktop computers during the 1980s provided a major impetus for the growth of "packaged" software applications. Since then the United States has dominated most markets for packaged software. The reasons for this dominance include several interconnected elements.

The "first-mover" advantages of US producers have proven to be persistent and powerful in this part of the software market. American firms achieved first-mover advantages due to specific demand conditions: US industry was ahead in the production and adoption of computers. The origins of this first-mover advantage and its consequences for the development of system and application software pre-dated the advent of PCs, but the extent of this advantage was elevated by the rapid diffusion of PCs during the 1980s. The decision of IBM to engage Microsoft as the external supplier of the operating system software for its PC was a case in point. Microsoft's early system software was, itself, based upon prior floppy-disk-based operating system software developed for Intel's microprocessor family. US computer hardware companies internationalized their production operations at a relatively early stage and supported a liberal trade policy toward hardware imports (often imports of components and subsystems were integrated domestically), and this further accelerated the diffusion of the PC, creating a mass market for software (Mowery, 1999).

In the United States federal government investments also played an important role in stimulating research in universities, creating infrastructures and enhancing the supply of skilled personnel. The development of US software capabilities was further assisted by large-scale projects undertaken for the US military and social security systems.

Many of the factors that explain US success are also able to explain why Europe lags behind in packaged software. In Europe markets are fragmented, and languages, laws and regulations differ. Historically, "national champion" computer firms have been vertically integrated, which hindered market development of an independent software industry and thus constrained competition. For example, European mainframe and mini-computer producers were not able to decide upon a common operating system or application software standards despite their relatively small size in global markets. By choosing to remain strong in domestic markets and shelter themselves from competition these companies managed to maintain control of their markets for almost twenty years (the 1960s through much of the 1980s). By the 1990s, however, these companies had largely exited the market, taking with them the proprietary software platforms that were the basis of many business applications (Malerba and Torrisi, 1996).

During the 1970s and 1980s European government intervention largely focused upon the maintenance of the mainframe computer manufacturers – a rational policy given the scale of investment made by European companies in applications designed to run on these platforms. In Europe the PC proved, however, to be a "competency-destroying" technological innovation, disrupting the accumulation of competency that had been developed around software applications designed to operate in the mainframe environment. The PC revolution has highlighted the limited and fragmented nature of interaction in research between university and industry in the area of software and the limited role of public research laboratories (Mowery, 1999).

US advantages in the packaged software market are not unassailable, however. First-mover, network externality and scale of promotion advantages are only part of the story. The portions of the software market where these advantages do not determine competitive outcomes are significant. They include markets within the packaged software category as well as software produced according to business models other than those governing the packaged software segment. Within the packaged software category, multimedia, educational and gaming software are major markets that have both global and local features. In these markets first-mover effects are less important than innovation. With important exceptions, these packaged software markets do not have major network externality effects and are affected by localization.

Software producers from regions other than the United States have achieved considerable success in multimedia, educational and gaming packaged software markets. Of particular note is Japanese success in the games software market. Although it is sometimes argued that Japanese dominance of games software is a consequence of their strength in the games console market, there is some basis for concluding that the causation flows in both directions. The market for Japanese home electronics is one of the world's most demanding markets and a powerful "test bed" for new software. In other areas of multimedia software, European firms have achieved a strong position, including computer console games software. Educational software is also an area where European firms have retained important strengths. In no region, however, has there been a strong central government endorsement of the value of commercial educational software products for educational outcomes. Decision making about government purchases of educational software is usually decentralized, which is probably desirable. It does appear, however, that the greater centralization of European and Japanese primary and secondary school curriculum specification and development offers substantial advantages over the United States, where curricula and the textbooks and other educational materials to support them are often fragmented across the fifty individual states.

Packaged software also plays a central role in specialized applications such as SMEs and consumer tax preparation, scientific computing, and "tools" software for creating new applications or for the design of special-purpose information systems, such as WWW servers. Most of these markets involve substantial problems with regard to marketing and promotion because of the dispersed nature of their clientele. Europe has proven to be an excellent market for "shareware" distribution of packaged software. Distribution channels for shareware have been established within universities and as independent businesses within Europe. Another major distribution method for shareware is CD-ROMs accompanying major computer magazines. While these marketing channels have not yet been developed for the most specialized packaged software, such as laboratory instrumentation control, it is broadly employed for other specialized types of applications. The CD-ROM distribution of software compensates for the deficiencies in network access facing many computer users.

### 3.4.3 Exploring European specialization: integrated software solutions, multimedia software, open-source software and embedded software

It is important, however, to recognize that "packaged software" is only one method for supplying the software requirements of information systems. A considerable share of European software development involves the creation of applications that are localized and situated for specific users. While these software applications are also protected by IPR legislation (principally the rules governing trade secrets), their value in other situated contexts is limited. The economic features of this type of software favor the growth of independent companies that are able to "reuse" software code or development experience in producing value for their clients or customers. They also provide the basis for the creation of specific types of software products.

Four types of software where European firms retain a foothold have been considered in this book: integrated software solutions; multimedia software; open-source software; and embedded software. Along with the substantial resources devoted to in-house software development and the related market of software system integration and consulting, these areas represent the main areas of European economic activity in the software industry.

In terms of ISS development, most European firms have specialized in custom software where local markets and the interaction with local customers play a key role in affecting the performance of firms (Malerba and Torrisi, 1996; and D'Adderio, 2002). German firms have specialized in the specific *subsector* of enterprise-related application software, such as ERP, CRM, sector-specific enterprise tools, groupware and systems integration (D'Adderio, 2002; Lehrer, 2002; Steinmueller, 2002; and Casper and Soskice, chapter 10 in this book). One of the largest producers of such types of software – SAP – is German and a considerable amount of smaller companies are growing in Europe. In the ERP market, as well as other ISS markets (where developing an "integrating system" or "platform for customization" is a key activity), smaller firms are often involved in creating special-purpose software for specific sectoral applications.

In ISS markets the success of European players has also been the result of a strategy based on first developing a product built upon the accumulated experience about user needs and, secondly, on setting standards and becoming more open about applications developed outside. This supports the entry of specialized application suppliers. European firms are, however, not alone in developing this type of strategy. US firms such as Microsoft and Oracle have adopted similar strategies in organizing specialized suppliers. Interestingly, these are sectors where customization and interaction with users is an important feature of success (D'Adderio, 2002). The German software industry has, in particular, benefited from demanding users. Germany has also been the European country where the shortage of programmers was least constraining and the links between university and industry were most developed (Lehrer, 2002).

The European version of the open-source software activity, like similar and earlier US activities associated with GNU (Gnu Not UNIX) and public domain software distribution (such as USENET), grew out of university student efforts. Historically, university environments have provided relatively open access to computer system resources and a research "atmosphere" that tolerates experimentation and invention. Perhaps because these environments are relatively isolated from commercial incentives and motives, software development efforts in the university environment often take the form of voluntary association, with an explicit invitation to participate in the development process. Linus Torvalds achieved a major innovation by harnessing this culture to the Internet to invite anyone in the world to contribute to the construction of a high-quality version of the UNIX operating system: the invention of Linux was the result. Open-source software has important implications for the European software industry because it represents a body of emerging competency and specialization that can provide the basis for systems consulting and further software development efforts. As noted earlier, companies continue to spend considerable sums on in-house software development (often based upon standardized tools). These in-house applications are, in many cases, being implemented using Internet-related tools. An open-source product, Apache, is the leading software for implementation of WWW servers, and Apache is designed to run on Linux operating system platforms. Thus, even if the user desktop continues to be based upon Microsoft operating systems and applications, open-source software is likely to play a major role in the next generation of enterprise-specific software development. A very important policy facilitating the sustainability of these positive European developments is continuing activity in promoting open standards for the exchange of information. Without such standards, the processes favoring the mass adoption of products that store information in proprietary formats are likely to prevail.

A third area where European firms remain active is in multimedia software. The United States appears to have an advantage in this market due to the large size of its internal market, which allows larger budgets for product engineering and promotion. A share of multimedia content will, however, remain culturally specific. A critical issue in assessing European prospects in the multimedia area is whether multimedia products will prove to be more like novels or films. In the case of novels, European countries continue to support a large, vibrant and open market where domestic authors compete successfully against authors (often published in translation) from other parts of the world. In films, however, Europe has been less successful in generating the box office receipts needed to finance an increasingly expensive medium. The distinction between the two media lies largely in the effects of promotion. The added revenue available to film makers from their higher levels of promotional invest-ments substantially exceeds that available from book promotion. It is not yet clear which of these two models the multimedia market will follow.

Finally, the United States is also emerging as the leader in the develop-ment of embedded software, despite the significance of this specialized segment for European automobile, consumer durable and industrial sys-tem companies. Europe has created a much weaker infrastructure for the support of embedded software than the United States. Moreover, in Europe fewer independent companies have been able to emerge because large companies tend to be vertically integrated and to produce in-house embedded software. In addition, in Europe very few university or public research activities are visible in the area of embedded software. Perhaps one source of this absence of embedded software research in universi-ties is the disciplinary specialization of European computer science and informatics departments, which appear to lack the application experi-ence and interdisciplinarity required for advances in knowledge in this area (Steinmueller, chapter 6 in this book).

### 3.4.4    Summing-up

In Europe the packaged software industry suffers primarily from first-mover effects stemming from the PC revolution and the effects of network externalities in software. Government, military and social security system investments have also played an important role in stimulating research in universities, creating infrastructures and enhancing the supply of skilled personnel. In Europe fragmented markets were a significant constraint. In addition, the industrial, university and public research systems provided feeble support for the development of PC applications.

Those segments that are markedly less affected by these factors are the ones with closer ties to local content or business practice (integrated sys-tem software and multimedia software, as well as the large "hidden" sec-tor represented by in-house development and related systems integration and consulting businesses). Open-source software is an emergent area of European participation and expertise, which offers considerable promise in revitalizing European systems integration and consulting activities.

### 3.5    Machine tools

In the nineteenth century the machine tool industry had a British leader-ship. Then mass production had a big impact on the American indus-try, which became the leader for most of the twentieth century and performed the early R&D activity that transformed machine tools from mechanical devices to numerical and computer-controlled systems. In the United States machine tool producers have been highly dependent on the defense and automotive sectors. Demand from high-end users led American machine tool makers to develop machine tools for manufacturing operations with high stringency requirements. After World War II they produced NC machines. Later on Japanese firms became leaders through licenses from the United States, stimulated by the Ministry of International Trade and Industry and protected by trade tariffs. Differences in domestic demand were a crucial determinant here. The protected Japanese home market was characterized by small, general-purpose machine tools for flexible and labor-saving processes (automobiles and general machinery industry). As a result, there was a rapid application of NC machines. Large volumes of standardized machine tools were adopted. FANUC became a world leader. Standardization and concentration on the supplier side helped users and builders. In turn, FANUC invested in the development of modular design, which was easier to customize. Conversely, US firms thought that the control choice was a prerogative of the customer, and that they could maintain high market shares because buyers had sunk specific investments about particular control systems. However, this provided the basis for the success of Japanese firms in the United States: with the help of the downturn in 1975, US firms that were restructuring started buying low-cost, general-purpose NC machine tools from Japanese firms (Mazzoleni, 1999).

In the European Union NC machine tools arrived later, because German and Italian firms had specialized in market niches where the NC design was more difficult to apply. In Germany machine tool producers developed highly reliable and high-quality machines benefiting from the strong public research infrastructure (the Fraunhofer-Gesellschaft and technical institutes). The role of industrial associations (such as the VDMA and VDW), which had been very strong in earlier times, has declined more recently. User-producer relationships have always been intense, but they have recently changed. Beforehand, engineers and technicians on the user side were close partners in the design process. Now the relationship has moved toward a more market-based interaction, with major consequences on system responsibility in the maintenance and in the repair business (Wengel and Shapira, chapter 7 in this book).

In Italy firms are of small size and produce highly customized products. They are localized in clusters, with local training and local financial institutions. The role of the public research infrastructure is less relevant than in Germany. In a recent survey carried out by the Ente per le Nuove tecnologie, l'Energia e l'Ambiente (ENEA – the Italian National Agency for New Technologies, Energy and the Environment), CESPRI (Università Bocconi) and Politecnico-Milan on 100 Italian machinery producers

(Ferrari et al., 2001), internal resources and the intelligent use of innovative components have been recognized as the driving force of innovation. These two factors are much more common with respect to another group of innovation channels: namely collaboration (either through the acquisition of external proprietary technology patents or licenses, or through collaboration with other firms or external consultancies).

In the United Kingdom the machine tool sector has been characterized by formal and informal institutional linkages weaker than elsewhere in Europe, and by different sectoral demand structures. For example, while well-developed "industrial districts" of textile machine producers existed in Yorkshire in the period after World War II, it has been suggested that they subsequently fell behind Italian districts because the concentrated British retail clothing sector demanded high-volume standardized products that constrained innovation in the textile equipment sector (Owen, 2001). The more fragmented structure of the Italian clothing sector opened up opportunities for the new textile machines, which were flexible and adaptable and which subsequently found greater success on world markets. Similar arguments can be made about sectoral linkages between the long decline of the domestic automotive sector in the United Kingdom and its effects on UK automotive machine tool producers, although the relatively strong role of aerospace in the United Kingdom continues to provide opportunities for highly specialized (but not necessarily high-volume) tool producers.

For all machine tool producers, innovation through internal resources and through the integration of innovative components increased in importance during the 1990s. Research and design were kept in-house and relations with customers were strategic. Component inputs were often outsourced. Traditionally, collaboration with competitors and with university and research centers was limited, although partnerships with suppliers (of innovative components) and users have been more common. However, in recent years there has been greater participation by machine tool producers in public-private consortia that involve technology centers. Examples of such consortia include the National Center for Manufacturing Sciences in the United States and VDW/WGP collaboration and several bilateral consortia between single companies and technical institutes at universities in Germany. At the international level the intelligent manufacturing systems (IMS) program involves companies and researchers in intelligent machining systems from the United States, Europe, Japan and other countries (Wengel and Shapira, chapter 7 in this book).

In the 1980s EU firms started to suffer from Japanese competition that had earlier been focused mainly on the bigger markets in the United States. British firms lost significant market share to Japanese and other European firms (although the United Kingdom did gain some Japanese machine tool transplants). German companies were concerned about excessively fragmented markets and the lack of a market leader (Mazzoleni, 1999). However, at present in Europe the changing SSI seems to be more open, more international in scope and more information-intensive. After some restructuring, German firms have overcome the problems of the 1980s and early 1990s and continue to be successful in exporting high-value tools. Italian producers have also gained ground, emerging as Europe's second largest exporter of machine tools (after Germany). The British industry has stabilized, although at a much reduced level.

Overall, linkages with research centers, producers and users, and codified knowledge are increasingly important, and the role of strategic partnership is even more important. Faced with the transformation of the knowledge bases and the increased level of international competition, a critical factor in Europe is the continuous upgrading of labor and engineering skills. Germany faces shortages of qualified labor (both of engineers and on the shop floor). A strength of the industry is the integration of theory and practice, manufacturing and design. Italian firms have greatly upgraded their human capital in terms of external formal training. The greater focus on human capital has been associated with a larger number of employees dedicated to technological innovation (Wengel and Shapira, chapter 7 in this book). In Europe and the United States the effect of niche user-supplier interaction has been twofold. On the one hand it has helped prevent strong competition from standardized, low-cost, general-purpose technologies. On the other hand it has prevented the growth of a market leader. This is recognized as one of the major causes of the US decline (Mazzoleni, 1999).

As a final remark, it can be noted that a well-established and in some respects efficient sectoral system may be overcome by developments elsewhere. The US post-war experience and the Italian case are interesting examples. In the United States firms managed to invent the R&D-based NC machines, but the Japanese had a better environment for applications. In Italy, despite a stable, hard-working and dedicated labor force, the machine tool industry may be jeopardized by increased standardization based upon different knowledge bases and international competition. The rise of new producer locations (such as China, Taiwan and South Korea) adds new global complications to the mix, particularly since these emerging producers are developing stronger capabilities in research and innovation and augmenting their human capital capabilities. Strong regional sectoral linkages and a close coupling of regional production complexes with users are likely to continue to be key elements of competitive advantage in machine tools, as in the past. However, increased investments in system integration, innovation and emerging technologies, public-private collaboration, formal training systems, technology and market intelligence, and international partnerships and linkages are also likely to characterize the most successful elements of the sector in future years.

### 3.6    *Three service activities: airports, a remedy for cataracts, and retailing*

There is a great amount of empirical literature emphasizing that services include a heterogeneous set of activities, from banking and finance (with big firms and a higher focus on process innovations) to hotels, catering and retailing (with smaller firms) to R&D (with small firms and a focus on product innovations – Evangelista, 2000). Accordingly, it is misleading to presume homogeneity across these different fields in the systemic nature of innovative activity and its impact on economic performance.

At the same time, within this heterogeneity, the literature has also pointed at some common features. It has been claimed that service activities – relative to manufacturing – are more associated with skills that require the supply and transformation of information and knowledge. As a result, in order to study the relationship between innovation and performance in services, there is the necessity to be as explicit as possible about the mechanisms behind the creation and use of different types of knowledge. Moreover, in services the high degree of institutional specificity and the often fragmented character of demand imply that sectoral systems also define the trajectory to be pursued and the set of bottlenecks to be solved. These constraints are, in many cases, contingent and heavily affected by the regulatory and institutional settings.

These circumstances bring about two connected considerations. First, the concept of economic performance has to be evaluated with respect to this context-specific set of problems. Performance in services may be evaluated according to different perspectives: efficiency of provision, firm growth, profits, consumer satisfaction or welfare. Thus, relative to manufacturing, it is more difficult to take a leadership approach. Second, institutional specificities and fragmented demand often imply the lack of an appropriate common basis for international comparison.

Tether and Metcalfe (chapter 8 in this book) emphasize the need to understand some innovations at a very micro-level in their work, constructed around specific problem sequences. In the case of *airports*, different resource constraints set different problems in terms of runway capacity. For example, at airports such as Frankfurt and London Heathrow the problem of inadequate runway capacity would not exist (or, at least, would be very different) if, like Paris Charles de Gaulle, they were permitted to build new runways. In fact, at Frankfurt, Heathrow and Gatwick airports there has been a significant increase in runway capacity without new investment in new runways. At Heathrow, for example, this has been done in many ways: improvements in airport layout and pilot performance, reordering arrivals and bunching departures. Improvements depend upon the ability to solve the problems of institutions, such as ATC and airlines and their cooperation. This brings to the fore the importance of learning by cooperating and negotiating procedural changes. Decision processes are distributed, and innovations are based upon new ideas (e.g. how to optimize arrival or departure sequences) and, at the same time, upon the procedures and the institutional arrangements required to achieve them (e.g. negotiation or cooperation). At Charles de Gaulle Paris and many US airports runway capacity is less constrained, and therefore innovation activity has followed different sets of problems (Tether and Metcalfe, 2003).

In the case of seeking a remedy to failing eyesight due to *cataracts*, the technological problem is created around a new treatment based on the use of IOLs. Nevertheless, the main opportunities and constraints are found again in what are called "distributed capabilities" across individuals (in particular surgeons, clinicians and scientists) and organizations (healthcare organizations and complementary firms). However, it seems that in this case the link with manufacturers (of medical instruments and devices) is closer than in the case of airports. Market structures and competition in the supply of these goods seem to have played an important role (Metcalfe and James, 2002).

In the case of *retailing*, different national markets (the United Kingdom and Sweden) resulted in widely differing patterns of change. The main technological problem is to gain and maintain primary access to consumers. In the last forty years food retailing in the United Kingdom has changed, thanks to new forms of organization and IT in packaging, display, transport, logistics and food manufacture. This has been achieved by the development of firms able to create, for example, centralized buying power, centrally controlled distribution systems via regional distribution systems and retailer-owned supply and manufacture.

Even though market concentration is very high in both countries, Sweden is different from the United Kingdom because there is a lower level of vertical integration. In the tradition of a cooperative movement, Swedish groups have more fragmented ownership and are centralized at the wholesale level. At the same time, retail shops are often privately owned and managed. The adoption of hypermarkets was slower because this would have created competition for existing member stores. This slow adoption does not seem to have penalized the major Swedish groups against other federative groups that also embarked upon a higher level of centralization in retailing. These business models are different from the branded manufacturers, which tend to achieve, through concentration, economies of scale in the production of a commodity (Nestlé, Kellogg, Danone, etc.) for standard consumers (Harvey, Nyberg and Metcalfe, 2002).

## 4    The diverse determinants of industrial leadership

This book has shown that each sectoral system has its specific features, structure and dynamics. What, then, are the specific determinants of industrial leadership? We can identify the following.

### 4.1    *The specific coevolution between firms' capabilities and the knowledge base, actors and networks, and institutions of a sector*

First of all, industrial leadership is determined by the specific coevolution of knowledge bases, actors and networks, and institutions of a sector. This emerges quite clearly from all the sectoral studies of this book.

### 4.2    *Technological and scientific research capabilities*

In some sectoral systems, technological and scientific research capabilities and education were major sources of industrial leadership. Success stories are a combination of the ability to create new products, to open up new disciplines and markets and, at the same time, to integrate research, teaching and industrial needs. The construction of a solid knowledge and scientific base in specific fields has often benefited from different forms and levels of public investments in their early stages (i.e. pharmaceuticals, biotechnology and software), above all in the United States.

Moreover, the integration between in-house research and advancements in the relative transfer sciences (chemical engineering, automation and robotics, computer sciences, biotechnology, microbiology and pharmaceutical chemistry) helped firms to be ahead of their competitors' product and process technologies. The quality of the research systems and the ability to change and transform the technological knowledge bases has also provided firms with exploitable technological opportunities (Dosi, Nelson and Winter, 2000).

### 4.3  Demand and interactions with sophisticated users

Close and continuous interactions with sophisticated users has been particularly important for machine tools and chemicals (and in some segments of software and biotechnology). In machine tools and chemicals, co-location also supported the innovative performance of firms. However, the mechanisms connecting demand to economic success are different according to the sector. Demand can be important in terms of level (size of the market: chemicals, pharmaceuticals and packaged software), quality (machine tools in Europe and chemical engineering in the United States), composition (software and machine tools in Europe), specific requirements (machine tools in the United States and Japan, chemical engineering and telecommunications) and government share.

### 4.4  The size of the market

The size of the market and its degree of integration were factors conducive to US success in many sectors. The European Union seems to have been penalized by fragmentation in some sectors with low marginal costs (packaged software and pharmaceuticals) and increasing returns to user adoption (packaged software). In these cases, the fragmentation of markets often leads to different monopolies or separate vertically integrated structures, which constrained the development of technologies (see software, biotechnology and chemical engineering). At the same time, different markets and heterogeneous users helped European firms to be ahead of their competitors due to the possibility of creating customized product and process technologies (machine tools and integrated software solutions).

### 4.5  Technology and innovation policies

Technology and innovation policies played an important role in affecting the industrial, institutional and organizational settings and the rate of innovative activities. In most of the sectors examined in this book, agents have drawn incentives and opportunities from different types of institutional packages: IPR systems, specific regulations and laws, types of standards, product approvals, government support and corporate governance. Patent policies have been particularly important in support of the activities of smaller technology-based firms and university licensing (particularly in biotechnology and chemicals). In the United States this has created the basis for a division of labor between technology suppliers and users, and allowed the development of markets for technology.

Finally, standardization has affected the mobile telephone industry. In particular, European firms have benefited widely from the European decision to adopt GSM technology.

## 5    Enlarging the discussion on European sectoral performance: the roles of product differentiation, industrial life cycles and science

The main factors discussed in section 4 point to some weaknesses and strengths of the European sectors examined in this book. In this section we want to enlarge the discussion by bringing in other results and studies. Our main point here is that European firms seem to face a somewhat more difficult challenge in "new sectors" and activities, where emerging disciplines are an opening door to new products and services (biotechnology, the Internet and some sub-segments of ICT). Conversely, Europe has enjoyed a better performance in sectors where the products derive from established disciplines (chemicals and aerospace), where user-supplier interaction is important (as in the cases of embedded software and machine tools) and where the "non-price" elements of competitiveness are important (as in the case of top-of-the-range and luxury cars, for example, but also in many other domains – see Dosi, Coriat and Pavitt, 2000). In discussing this point, we focus on product differentiation, range and life cycles and on the role of science.

### 5.1    *Product range, product differentiation and non-price competitiveness*

A qualitative investigation[4] of subsectors in which European products are recognized in the world for their quality and image provides the following list:[5]

i) *A group of diversified industrial products covered by strong "brand names."*

This is the case for products and sectors such as top-of-the-range luxury cars (e.g. Rolls-Royce, Bentley, BMW, Mercedes, Ferrari and Saab) and machine tools (German, Italian or Swiss), not to mention top-of-the-range products in diversified traditional sub-segments such as "haute

---

[4]  See the works and the report published by the European Organization for Quality (2000), in which one of the authors of this chapter (Benjamin Coriat) was involved.

[5]  This does not mention a fourth group, based on agricultural products characterized by the *franchising of brand goods associated with a specific traditional knowledge*, often covered by "labels" and "appellations contrôlées." Included here are wines and spirits (from Irish whiskies through French and Italian wines to Portuguese port) and high-quality foods (from Parma ham to Nordic salmon, for example). Overall, some two thousand European products benefit from well-known "labels," which serve to provide a guarantee of brand image and quality to exports.

couture," select jewellery, the watch making industry, fashionable clothing, shoes or cosmetics (see, for example, the case of machine tools discussed by Wengel and Shapira in chapter 7 of this book).

ii) *Another domain of European excellence covers a number of sub-segments of short production runs of customized products, integrated complex systems and prototypes.*

For these types of products, competitiveness depends less on price than on quality (see Fontagné, Freudenberg and Ünal-Kesenci, 2000). These activities are dependent upon advanced technology and a highly skilled labor force. They include aerospace (Arianespace, Airbus Industrie, etc.), key segments of telecommunications (for example, digital exchange equipment), and the delivery of different types of complex product systems – high-speed trains (French, German or Italian), nuclear power stations, services of water management, etc. (for examples, see the cases discussed by Dalum and Villumsen, 2002; Coriat, 2000a; and Dosi, Coriat and Pavitt 2000);

iii) More recently (and, perhaps, more unexpectedly), Europe has demonstrated a proven ability to assert itself *in some markets of mass-produced products in highly R&D-intensive industries*. This is the case with mobile telephony. As has been argued above, during the last few years Ericsson and Nokia have demonstrated a European capacity to achieve a dominant share of the world market in small high-tech products. Also, in the semiconductor industry SGS Microelectronics has gained a significant presence in world markets for some customized products (for examples, see the cases discussed by Edquist, in chapter 5 of this book, and by Hommen and Manninen, 2003).

Notwithstanding the variety of sectors that they incorporate, the activities listed above do share some common denominators. A common characteristic is the relative advantage gained by products and services that are *vertically differentiated* and which involve a number of different partners and competencies. Whether it is a seemingly "simple" product (e.g. a luxury perfume) or a more complex one (e.g. an airplane), European competitiveness results from a capacity to combine different types of expertise along the chain, converging in the delivery of the final product. The latter results from complex arrangements that combine institutional dimensions with large and composite organizational networks (between firms and different organizations and regulatory agencies – e.g. high-speed train systems, the management of utility networks, etc.). In most of these domains, coordination between complementary activities is a key condition underlying the production of quality. Thus, specific networks of agents based on a highly skilled, diversified labor force and competencies seem to be a crucial dimension of Europe's distinctive capabilities.

*5.2    Stages in industry life cycle and the role of science*

If we look at the European performance from the perspective of industry life cycle and the role of science, the picture (as suggested above) looks somewhat different. Whilst European performance appears to be good in "mature" sectors and products, even (as argued in the previous paragraph) for the most sophisticated parts of these sectors, in emerging industries and fields of activity – biotechnology, the Internet and important segments of IT (see McKelvey, Orsenigo and Pammolli, chapter 3 in this book; Casper and Kettler, 2002; and Corrocher, 2003a, 2003b) – Europe is clearly facing difficulties.

Many factors can be evoked here to explain this situation. Each one by itself does not provide a full and satisfactory explanation. However, the combined effects of a series of elements seem to provide some convincing ways to understand the situation. The main issues at stake here seem to be the following:

i) *There is a lack on investment in R&D in the new emerging fields of science and basic research.* This is obvious for life sciences, if the levels of European investment are compared with those of the United States (see Muldur, 2000; and Pavitt, 2001, 2000). Casper and Kettler (2002) recall that, in the case of the UK biotechnology sector, the main problem was not the lack of venture capitalists ready to embark on new biotechnology start-ups but *the lack of good scientists able to promote this type of firm.* When the scientific capacities exist, they seem to be too highly dispersed throughout European universities and regions. Thus, no network effect can emerge and structure the right division of labor and efforts able to ensure the promotion of these new activities. One has to remember here that, in the United States, some 80 percent of venture capitalists' investments are concentrated in two regions: California, around Silicon Valley, and Route 128. No "regional advantages" (Saxenian, 1994) have yet emerged in Europe in these fields.

ii) Close to this point, another argument has to do with *the type of educational systems and labor markets prevailing in Europe, especially in the field of highly skilled engineers, researchers and the like.* Here the relative advantage of European systems (largely based on internal labor markets) seems to turn into a series of relative disadvantages. Insufficient mobility and flexibility in these specialized labor markets make it difficult for firms engaged in the new emerging fields to find the right skills and to be able to gather the necessary assets to launch new products or services. This is the case with multimedia and the Internet, where innovative firms face shortages in the supply side of the labor markets (see Corrocher, 2003b). This, in a way, can be analyzed as an institutional failure (or, at least, an institutional limitation) of most of the European educational systems. These systems were unable to react with sufficient speed and flexibility to the reorganization of the knowledge base and the recombination of disciplines and research fields driven by the scientific and technological revolution opened in IT and life sciences some twenty-five years ago.

To conclude this section, it can be said that, for European firms, there is *not* a general weakness in science-based sectors. The European difficulties are much more focused. The European problem is: new disciplines, new and emerging fields of knowledge, and new firms' capabilities for the industrial and commercial exploitation of this knowledge.

## 6        Conclusions, with a controversial point

This chapter provides an attempt to assess how differences in sectoral systems affect the international performance of countries and to point at the specific characteristics of sectoral systems that have been comparatively key factors for industrial leadership in each sector. We have found that in the sectoral systems examined in this book (pharmaceuticals and biotechnology, chemicals, telecommunications, software, machine tools and some segments of services) major differences exist across sectors, and that these differences have greatly affected the determinants of countries' international performance. We have also identified some common factors affecting the international performance of European firms.

A major policy implication, derived from these studies and also supported by the study of automobiles (Coriat, 2000b), relates to latecomers, and could be summarized in the phrase "innovate, don't replicate." In automobiles, for example, the Japanese car makers, even though they were latecomers (most of the companies – including Toyota – started their business in the 1950s), were very successful in "catching" up with Western companies. But these companies were able to "catch up" because they were able to innovate and to follow their own paths toward the "state of the art" in the sector (in this case, mass production of standardized products marketed at lower and lower prices). Basically, through a series of organizational innovations, they were able to build their own competitive advantages and find their access to world markets. This was achieved through the systematic implementation of the "just in time" protocols and routines. "Just in time" allowed the Japanese car makers to catch up with the state of the art (mass production) whilst offering clients a greater range of options in terms of variety and product differentiation. Thus they introduced a new "dominant architectural design" as regards the organization of the sector envisaged as a whole.

Finally, a provocative and maybe controversial interpretation based on these studies can be advanced by way of conclusion, and related to chapter 9 by Coriat and Weinstein in this book. It can be claimed that European firms performed less well in those sectors characterized by a complementarity between a strong IPR regime, an efficient external labor market and corporate systems dominated by outsiders. This type of institutional setting creates favorable environments for activities based on the commercial exploitation of science discoveries and, more generally, for activities related to the exploration of the state of the art. The existence of a property rights regime protecting scientific discoveries through patents provides firms specialized in R&D with intangible assets (patents on discoveries). These intangible assets, and the perspective to capture innovation rents, are used in financial markets designed to finance risky, but potentially highly profitable, firms. Some specific devices of the corporate governance mechanisms are also required to give sufficient confidence and control to financial investors. Thus, the existence of an outsider corporate model is very favorable to this type of activity. Finally, since the activity itself (research and development in very specialized and fast-moving fields) calls for the ability to recruit at short notice the right highly skilled people required at different stages of the R&D process, the existence of an efficient external labor market is the final condition that guarantees the success of these activities. This typology can represent the case of *biotechnology*, some segments of *software* and *telecommunications equipment*, where new start-ups built on intellectual property rights are put on NASDAQ and recruit staffs of researchers on the external market.

Conversely, European firms have been somewhat stronger in sectoral systems where internal markets are more important and corporate governance systems are dominated by insiders. In these cases the institutional setting exhibits the following features. There is relatively "open technology," which allows (at zero or low cost) the benefits of the discoveries, and many of the technological advances made in the field, to be captured freely. Each new entrant (follower) can benefit at very low cost[6] from the innovations of previous innovators, adding its own contribution – which, in turn, is made available for its followers. This sectoral typology can be sustainable because appropriability is based on the specific capabilities and internal learning of the firms. Strong internal markets are needed and firms' core capabilities are built mainly on organizational learning. Finally, such a model does not require strong and specialized financial markets, as in the previous case. Even if the companies operating in these

---

[6] For example, in some segments of software each designer (or firm) can reuse the algorithms created by its rivals.

sectors are publicly owned, there is no need to give any strong control and power to outsiders. On the other hand, insider models are more convenient for monitoring and guiding the strategy of the firms. This is the case for "scale-intensive" and "specialized suppliers" sectors (e.g. *automobiles, machine tools* and some segments of *software*).

REFERENCES

Amable, B., and B. Verspagen (1995), The role of technology in market share dynamics, *Applied Economics*, 27, 197–204

Amendola, G., G. Dosi and E. Papagni (1993), The dynamics of international competitiveness, *Weltwirtshaftliches Archiv*, 129, 451–471

Arora, A., R. Landau and N. Rosenberg (1999), Dynamics of comparative advantage in the chemical industry, in D. C. Mowery and R. R. Nelson (eds.), *Sources of Industrial Leadership: Studies of Seven Industries*, Cambridge University Press, Cambridge, 217–266

Casper, S., and H. Kettler (2000), *National Institutional Frameworks and the Hybridization of Entrepreneurial Business Models: The German and UK Biotechnology Sectors*, ESSY working paper http://www.cespri.it/ricerca/es_wp.htm

Coriat, B. (2000a), *Compétences, Structures de Gouvernance et Rente Relationnelle, Le Cas de la Conception des Grands Projets Complexes*, Dynacom working paper, http://lem.sssup.it/Dynacom/D25.html

(2000b), The "abominable Ohno production system": competencies, monitoring and routines in the Japanese production system in G. Dosi, R. R. Nelson and S. G. Winter (eds.), *The Nature and Dynamics of Organizational Capabilities*, Oxford University Press, Oxford, 117–138

Coriat, B., and O. Weinstein (2002), Organizations and institutions in the generation of innovations, *Research Policy*, 31, 2, 273–290

Corrocher, N. (2003a), The Internet services industry: sectoral dynamics of innovation and production, in C. Edquist (ed.), *The Internet and Mobile Telecommunications System of Innovation: Development in Equipment, Access and Content*, Edward Elgar Publishing, Cheltenham, 177–209

(2003b), The Internet services industry: country-specific trends in the UK, Italy and Sweden, in C. Edquist (ed.), *The Internet and Mobile Telecommunications System of Innovation: Developments in Equipment, Access and Content*, Edward Elgar Publishing, Cheltenham

D'Adderio, L. (2002), *The Diffusion of Integrated Software Solutions: Trends and Challenges*, ESSY working paper, Science Policy Research Unit, University of Sussex, Brighton [http://www.cespri.it/ricerca/es_wp.htm]

Dalum, B., C. Freeman, R. Simonetti, N. von Tunzelmann and B. Verspagen (1999), Europe and the information and communication technologies revolution, in J. Fagerberg, P. Guerrieri and B. Verspagen (eds.)., *The Economic Challenge for Europe*. Edward Elgar Publishing, Cheltenham

Dalum, B., and G. Villumsen (2002), *Fixed Data Communications – Challenges For Europe*, ESSY working paper, http://www.cespri.it/ricerca/es_wp.htm

Dasgupta, P., and P. A. David (1994), Toward a new economics of science, *Research Policy*, 23, 4, 487–521

David, P. A. (2001), *From Keeping "Nature's Secrets" to the Institutionalization of "Open Science,"* Discussion Paper no. 23 in Economic and Social History, University of Oxford

Dosi, G., B. Coriat and K. Pavitt (2000), *Competencies, Capabilities and Corporate Performances,* Dynacom final report, http://lem.sssup.it/Dynacom/DFR.html

Dosi, G., K. Pavitt and L. Soete (1990), *The Economics of Technical Change and International Trade,* Harvester Wheatsheaf, Hemel Hempstead

Dosi, G., R. R. Nelson and S. G. Winter (2000), *The Nature and Dynamics of Organizational Capabilities,* Oxford University Press

European Organization for Quality (2000), *Towards a European Vision of Quality: The Way Forward,* www.eoq.org

Evangelista, R. (2000), Innovation and employment in services, in M. Pianta and M. Vivarelli (eds.), *The Employment Impact of Innovation: Evidence and Policy,* Routledge, London

Fagerberg, J. (1988), International competitiveness, *Economic Journal,* 98, 355–374

Ferrari, S., P. Guerrieri, F. Malerba, S. Mariotti and D. Palma (2001), *L'Italia nella Competizione Tecnologica Internazionale: La Meccanica Strumentale,* Franco Angeli, Milan

Fontagné, M., M. Freudenberg and D. Ünal-Kesenci (2000), La spécialisation technologique des pays Européens, in M. Delapierre, P. Moati and M. El Mouhoud (eds.), *Connaissance et Mondialisation,* Economica, Paris, 17–29

Gompers, P., and J. Lerner (1999), *What Drives Venture Capital Fundraising?* Working Paper no. 6,906, National Bureau of Economic Research, Cambridge, MA

Greenhalg, C. (1990), Innovation and trade performance in the United Kingdom, *Economic Journal,* 100, 105–118

Grossman, G., (1991), A model of quality competition and dynamic comparative advantage, in G. Grossman (ed.), *Imperfect Competition and International Trade,* MIT Press, Cambridge, MA, 367–383

Grossman, G., and E. Helpman (1991), *Innovation and Growth in the Global Economy,* MIT Press, Cambridge, MA

Harvey, M., A. Nyberg and J. S. Metcalfe (2002), *Deep Transformation in the Service Economy: Innovation and Organisational Change in Food Retailing in Sweden and the UK,* ESSY working paper, Centre for Research on Innovation and Competition, University of Manchester and University of Manchester Institute of Science and Technology [http://www.cespri.it/ricerca/es_wp.htm]

Henderson, R., L. Orsenigo and G. P. Pisano (1999), The pharmaceutical industry and the revolution in molecular biology: interactions among scientific, institutional, and organisational change, in D. C.Mowery and R. R. Nelson (eds.), *Sources of Industrial Leadership: Studies of Seven Industries,* Cambridge University Press, Cambridge, 267–311

Hommen, L., and E. Manninen (2003), The global system for mobile telecommunications (GSM): second generation, in C. Edquist (ed.), *The Internet and Mobile Telecommunications System of Innovation: Developments in Equipment, Access and Content,* Edward Elgar Publishing, Cheltenham

Jaffe, A. B. (2000), The US patent system in transition: policy innovation and the innovation process, *Research Policy,* 29, 4/5, 531–557

Krugman, P. (1979), A model of innovation, technology transfer, and the world distribution of income, *Journal of Political Economy*, 89, 253–266

(1994), A technology gap model of international trade, in P. Krugman (ed.), *Rethinking International Trade*, MIT Press, Cambridge, MA

Landes, D. (1966), Technological change and development in Western Europe, 1750–1914, in H. Habbakuk and M. Postan (eds.), *The Cambridge Economic History of Europe*, vol. VI, Cambridge University Press, Cambridge

Lehrer, M. (2002), *From Factor of Production to Autonomous Industry: The Transformation of Germany's Software Sector*, ESSY working paper, http://www.cespri.it/ricerca/es_wp.htm

Magnier, A., and J. Toujas-Bernate (1994), Technology and trade: empirical evidences for the major five industrialized countries, *Weltwirtschaftliches Archiv*, 130, 494–520

Malerba, F., and S. Torrisi (1996), The dynamics of market structure and innovation in the Western European software industry, in D. C. Mowery (ed.), *The International Computer Software Industry: A Comparative Study of Industry Evolution and Structure*, Oxford University Press, Oxford

Mazzoleni, R. (1999), Innovation in the machine tools industry: a historical perspective on the dynamics of comparative advantage in D. C. Mowery and R. R. Nelson (eds.), *Sources of Industrial Leadership: Studies of Seven Industries*, Cambridge University Press, Cambridge, 169–216

Metcalfe, J. S., and A. James (2002), *Emergent Innovation Systems and the Delivery of Clinical Services: The Case of Intra-Ocular Lenses*, ESSY working paper, Centre for Research on Innovation and Competition, University of Manchester and University of Manchester Institute of Science and Technology [http://www.cespri.it/ricerca/es_wp.htm]

Montobbio, F. (2003), Sectoral patterns of technological activity and export market share dynamics, *Cambridge Journal of Economics*, 27, 4, 523–545

Mowery, D. C. (1999), The computer software industry, in D. C. Mowery and R. R. Nelson (eds.), *Sources of Industrial Leadership: Studies of Seven Industries*, Cambridge University Press, Cambridge

Mowery, D. C., and R. R. Nelson (eds.) (1999), *Sources of Industrial Leadership: Studies of Seven Industries*, Cambridge University Press, Cambridge

Mowery, D. C., and B. N. Sampat (2001), University patents and patent policy debates in the USA, 1925–1980, *Industrial and Corporate Change*, 10, 3, 781–814

Muldur, U. (2000), L'allocation des capitaux dans le processus global d'innovation: est-elle optimale en Europe? in E. Cohen and J. H. Lorenzi (eds.), *Politiques Industrielles pour l'Europe*, Cahiers du Conseil d'Analyse Economique, Premier Ministre, La Documentation Française, Paris, 34–67

Orsi, F. (2001), *Marchés Financiers et Droits de Propriété Intellectuelle dans les Nouvelles Relations Science/Industrie: Le Cas de la Recherche sur le Génome*, Ph.D. dissertation, Université de la Méditerranée, Aix-Marseille II

Orsi, F., and J. P Moatti (2001), D'un droit de propriété intellectuelle sur le vivant aux firmes de génomique: vers une marchandisation de la connaissance scientifique sur le génome humain, *Economie et Prévisions*, 150/151, 123–138

Owen, G. (2001), A perfect climate for industrial success, *Financial Times*, November 6

Owen-Smith, J., M. Riccaboni, F. Pammolli and W. W. Powell (2002), *A Comparison of US and European University-Industry Relations in the Life Sciences*, ESSY working paper, http://www.cespri.it/ricerca/es_wp.htm

Pavitt, K. (2000), *Academic Research in Europe*, paper prepared for EU-funded Europolis Project, Workshop II, Lisbon, June 5–6

  (2001), Public policies to support basic research: what can the rest of the world learn from US theory and practice? (And what they should not learn), *Industrial and Corporate Change*, 10, 3, 761–779

Posner, M. V. (1961), International trade and technical change, *Oxford Economic Papers*, 13, 3, 323–342

Saxenian, A. (1994), *Regional Advantage: Culture and Competition in Silicon Valley and Route 128*, Harvard University Press, Cambridge, MA

Steinmueller, W. E. (2002), *The European Software Sectoral System of Innovation*, ESSY working paper, Science Policy Research Unit, University of Sussex, Brighton [http://www.cespri.it/ricerca/es_wp.htm]

Tether, B. S., and J. S. Metcalfe (2003), Horndal at Heathrow? Capacity expansion through co-operation and system evolution, *Industrial and Corporate Change*, 12, 3, 437–476

Thomas, L. G. (1994), Implicit industrial policy: the triumph of Britain and the failure of France in global pharmaceuticals, *Industrial and Corporate Change*, 3, 2, 451–490

Vernon, R. (1966), International investment and international trade in the product cycle, *Quarterly Journal of Economics*, 80, 2, 190–207

Zucker, L. G., and M. R. Darby (1996), Star: scientists and institutional transformation patterns of invention and innovation in the formation of the biotechnology industry, *Proceedings of the National Academy of Sciences*, 93, 23, 12,709–12,716

# 12    Sectoral systems: implications for European innovation policy

*Charles Edquist, Franco Malerba, J. Stan Metcalfe,
Fabio Montobbio and W. Edward Steinmueller*

## 1    Introduction

It is generally accepted that governments have an important role to play
in fostering the conditions supporting innovation and competitiveness.
The economic and political discourse on these issues reflects existing
political debates about the capacities of firms and the market mechanisms
to deliver desired outcomes.

For about forty years, academic research, in the tradition of innovation
studies and the economics of technological change, has attempted to sort
out what has been learned from experience throughout the world. The
record of experience that they have studied includes the ambit of current
political discourse as well as the more extreme examples of state socialism
and autocratic regimes.

From a policy viewpoint, the results of these investigations are somewhat disappointing. No simple and obvious formula for reliably achieving
success in promoting or fostering innovation has emerged. Instances can
be cited of both failure and success for the prescriptions suggested by
each of the poles of the current political discourse. The results of academic discourse on innovation policy have been a series of frameworks for
analysis and evaluation rather than success in formulating a universally
applicable policy. The value of these frameworks is that they provide a
tool kit for a structured analysis of policy objectives and instruments in
relation to industrial conditions and behaviors.

The results of this book promise to lead to new insights into the conduct of innovation policy by national governments and by the European
Commission.

In recent years innovation policy research has followed a long progres-
sion of themes, which are identified, on the one hand, with the market
failure approach and the economics of the R&D grants and, on the other,
with the national and sub-national systems of innovation. The market failure approach to R&D is applicable only in certain contexts and situations,
while the approach at the level of the national system has run its course.

How does the research in this book add to and modify these approaches? A useful starting point is that innovation can be considered as the result of systemic interactions among organizations and institutions, and that the SIs are assembled around sequences of innovation problems and their conjectured solutions. All systems depend on patterns of interconnections, and the connections that make an innovation system have to be articulated. The questions are: "By whom?" and "Who does the assembly?" and "What determines the organizational and institutional components that are available?" It has long been recognized that many kinds of organizations contribute to the division of labor in innovation. However, a principal role is played by for-profit firms. Firms are unique in having the requirement to combine and articulate the multiple kinds of knowledge required to innovate and build the capabilities to develop a commitment to a particular mode of solution. Each firm has its internal innovation capability, but what matters today is the ability to connect this with organizations that are external to the firm, which, collectively, comprise the innovation system that is relevant for innovative performance in a specific context.

The notion of a "*sectoral system*" is one way to pull all this together. This book has focused on the sectoral system as the appropriate unit of analysis for examining industrial conditions and the behavior shaping innovation performance. A sectoral system is the collection of economic activities organized around a common technological or knowledge base in which individual enterprises are likely to be either actual or potential competitors with one another. A sector encompasses many individual markets and enterprises that are interrelated with one another. Any system is defined in terms of boundaries, components and connections together with a set of principles that define the purpose and modus operandi of the system. In this book we focus, as specified in chapter 1 by Franco Malerba, on the three broad dimensions of sectoral systems that affect the generation and adoption of new technologies and the organization of innovation at the sectoral level: knowledge and the related boundaries; actors and networks; and institutions. Thus, sectoral systems include the supply chain and non-firm organizations such as universities as well as public and private research organizations. These organizations may be located in different national domains; and they are instituted, as a system, by virtue of the connections and interactions between the different organizations. SIs also include institutions, in the sense of the rules of the game, that influence organizations in their pursuit of innovations. Sectors can have within them several different innovation systems, focused around different problems or centered around different groups of firms. Therefore, where to draw the boundary is not always clear. Moreover, boundaries in SIs are not static; they must be expected to evolve as the underlying problems of innovation evolve.

This sectoral system perspective, and the insight that innovation systems are not naturally given, lead us to what we consider to be a new and important insight into innovation policy. This is, namely, that the principal role of the policy maker is to facilitate the *self-organization of innovation systems* within the relevant policy domain. This approach is fully consistent with the idea that capitalism is a system that facilitates and encourages *new business experiments* as its primary process of change and development.

The structure of this chapter is as follows. Section 2 examines the reasons for public policy intervention in an innovation system perspective, while section 3 moves to a sectoral system approach and analyzes general public policy considerations. Then, in sections 4 and 5, we discuss some specific policy conclusions derived from this book in general and from the sectoral studies.

## 2     Reasons for public policy intervention in an innovation system perspective[1]

### 2.1     *The rationale*

In a modern society, the market mechanism and capitalist firms best fulfill many economic functions. The market mechanism evaluates and coordinates the behavior and resources of private and public actors – often in a smooth and flexible manner; this concerns the production of most goods, and a large proportion of service production. It is also true for many innovations, in particular incremental ones. Most of them occur through the actions of firms and in collaboration projects between firms. This is, however, less true for radical innovations, especially in the early stages of the development of new technologies.

Sometimes there are reasons to complement the market and capitalist firms through public intervention. This is true in the areas of law, education, the environment, infrastructure, social security, income distribution, research, radical innovations, etc. In some of these fields there is no market mechanism operating at all and the functions are fulfilled through other mechanisms, such as regulation. In other fields the market mechanism has, for decades, been complemented by public intervention in most industrial countries.

---

[1] This section is based upon Edquist, 1997, 2001a, 2001b.

What is at issue here is what should be performed by the state or public sector and what should not. This is an issue that is not only subject to ideological judgments but could – and should – be discussed in an analytical way.

What, then, are the reasons for public policy intervention in a market economy? As regards, for example, technical change and other kinds of innovations, two conditions must be fulfilled for there to be reasons for public intervention in a market economy:

(1) The market mechanism and capitalist firms must fail to achieve the objectives formulated. A *problem* of imperfect self-organization must exist (see below).

(2) The state (national, regional or local) and its public agencies must also have or be able to build the *ability* to solve or mitigate the problem.

There are no reasons for public intervention if the market and capitalist actors (including the government) fulfill the objectives.[2] Innovation policy – or other kinds of public intervention – should be a complement to the market, not intended to replace or duplicate it. In other words, there must be a "problem" – which is not automatically solved by market forces and capitalist actors – for public intervention to be "considered." Such problems can be identified through analysis.

When we talk about a "problem," we do so on an empirical basis and in a pragmatic way, not within the framework of a formal model. This is conscious and intentional. The reason is that this approach is more useful as a basis for policy design in the fields of innovation and technical change.

One difficulty in this context is, of course, that it is not possible to know for sure – *ex ante* – if public intervention can solve the problem or not.[3] The decision to intervene or not must thus be based upon whether it is likely or not that intervention will mitigate the problem. Hence, the decision must be taken in a situation of uncertainty. Then one can afterwards – *ex post* – determine through evaluations whether the problem was solved or mitigated. If this was not the case, we might be talking about a political failure. In other words, political failures can never be avoided

---

[2] We assume that the objectives – whatever they are – have already been determined in a political process. It should be mentioned that they do not necessarily have to be of an economic kind. They can also be of a social, environmental, ethical or military kind. They must be specific and unambiguously formulated in relation to the current situation in the country and/or in comparison to other countries. With regard to innovation policy, the most common objectives are formulated in terms of economic growth, productivity growth or employment.

[3] This is especially the case with innovation. Here, by definition, it is highly unlikely that there will be any clear-cut precedents for the problem to be solved.

completely because of the uncertainty mentioned. We must accept some mistakes in public activity – as we do in private activities. However, they should be exceptions and not the rule. Moreover, in order to determine the success or failure of a given policy intervention through an evaluation, it is necessary that the objectives of the policy were clearly formulated – *ex ante*.

There may be two reasons why public intervention cannot solve or mitigate a problem. One is that it may not be possible at all to solve the problem from a political level. Then all types of intervention will be in vain.[4] The other reason is that the state may first need to develop its ability to solve the problem. A detailed analysis of the problems and their causes may be a necessary means of acquiring this ability.[5] The creation of new organizations and institutions to carry out the intervention may also be necessary. A particular body of knowledge may not be represented in the national portfolio, requiring the establishment of a new research organization or the creation of a new policy instrument – eg. an R&D tax break. A patent office is another example of such an organization, and a patent law of such an institution.

There are two main categories of policies to solve or mitigate "problems":

(a) The state may use *non-market mechanisms*. This is mainly a matter of using regulation instead of the mechanisms of supply and demand. One example is a subsidy to poor regions. The state may also provide educational services free of charge or at a subsidized cost. Other kinds of regulation – particularly related to innovation activities – are the creation of technical standards, public subsidies for firms' R&D, or tax incentives for R&D and innovation activities.

(b) Through various public actions, the functioning of markets can be improved or the state may create markets. The *improvement* of the functioning of markets is the objective of competition law and competition (antitrust) policies. It is often a matter of increasing the degree of competition in a market. This might sometimes be achieved through "deregulation" – i.e. getting rid of old or obsolete regulations. An example is the liberalization or deregulation of the telecommunications sector in the 1980s and 1990s. One example of market *creation* is in the area of inventions. The creation of intellectual property rights through the institution of a patent law gives a temporary

---

[4] Hence, the problem is solvable neither by the market mechanism and private actors nor by public intervention.

[5] Hence, it may be necessary to carry out a detailed comparative empirical analysis.

monopoly to the patent owner. This makes the selling and buying of technical knowledge easier.[6] Public policy makers can also enhance the creation of markets by supporting legal security or the formation of trust. Another example is public technology procurement.[7]

In both cases, public policy is very much a matter of formulating the "rules of the game" that will facilitate the formation of operational SIs. These rules might have nothing to do with markets, or they might be intended to create markets or make the functioning of markets more efficient. In other words, policy is very much a matter of creating, changing or getting rid of institutions in the form of rules, laws, etc.

The example of market creation through the institution of patent law mentioned above indicates that a "problem" that motivates public intervention may concern the future. A "problem" may be something that has not yet emerged. A *problem-solving* policy of this kind could alternatively be called an *opportunity-creating* or anticipatory policy.[8] One of the problems to be solved could be that uncertainty prevents new technologies from emerging. One example of such a problem would be the case where public funding of basic R&D may be necessary because capitalist actors do not have the incentive to fund it. Another example could be that training people and stimulating research in public organizations in a certain field – e.g. multimedia – could create new opportunities that would not be realized without such a policy. This has been present in most of the sectors analyzed in this book. We will come back to these opportunity-creating kinds of innovation policies when discussing lock-in situations below.[9]

Another example pointing in this direction is the public creation of standards, which decreases the uncertainty for firms. For example, the creation of the NMT 450 standard by the Nordic PTTs in the 1970s and 1980s was crucial for the development of mobile telephony in the Nordic countries. This made it possible for the private firms to develop mobile systems. Ericsson and Nokia would not have assumed global leadership in this field without the NMT 450 (which later developed into

---

[6] Paradoxically, then, a monopoly is created by law, in order to create a market for knowledge – i.e. to make it possible to trade in knowledge. This has to do with the peculiar characteristics of knowledge as a product or commodity. It is hard to know the price of knowledge as a buyer, since you do not know what it is before the transaction. And if you know what it is you do not want to pay for it. In addition, knowledge is not worn out when used – unlike other products.

[7] Public technology procurement is addressed in detail in Edquist, Hommen and Tsipouri, 2000.

[8] There may even be reasons to treat the solving of existing problems and the creation of future opportunities as two different situations calling for public intervention.

[9] Obviously, the degree of uncertainty increases when the problems concern the future. Sometimes the problems may be very difficult to identify.

the NMT 900 and the digital GSM standard) (discussed in Edquist, 2003).[10]

A further example of a policy leading to market creation is public technology procurement – i.e. the public buying of technologies and systems that did not exist at the time. Public technology procurement was used in combination with NMT 450 in Finland and Sweden to provoke Nokia and Ericsson to enter the new field – which they were reluctant to do in the beginning (discussed by Fridlund, 2000, and Palmberg, 2000, in more detail). In this way, public innovation policy may take the role of a "midwife" in the emergence of new technology fields and whole production sectors. It could even be argued that most innovation policies should take this proactive approach – an issue that will be further discussed below.

## 2.2    *Selectivity in innovation policy*

When state intervention is intended to improve the functioning of markets, it is often a matter of increasing the degree of competition – rather than increasing the rate of innovation. This kind of policy can be argued to be "general" or "horizontal," in the sense that it tries to achieve the same thing everywhere. At other times policies are "specific" to certain sectors – or even products – of the economy in certain countries or regions. In these cases the degree of competition has to be estimated, and if ways to increase it are needed they must be appropriately designed and implemented.

When markets are created by public action, the policy is also "specific" to various functional areas, whether they concern inventions or the right to pollute. The creation of standards or public technology procurement is always technology-specific.

In most other kinds of public policy the state does not use the market mechanism. Instead, it complements the market or influences the consequences of its operation. Most public policy of this kind is allocative and "selective," rather than "general." It is selective in the sense that its consequences are not uniformly distributed among different activities and actors. This actually follows from the first of the two conditions that constitute reasons for public intervention: if a certain "problem" is to be solved, it has to be targeted in a selective manner. Public policy for basic research is selective. Politicians and policy makers, for example, allocate public research funds among competing fields of research. Someone must decide which fields of research are to be given priority. Should the

---

[10] The NMT story is told in Fridlund (2000) and Palmberg (2000).

funds be used for nuclear physics or biotechnology?[11] Regional policies are selective in a similar manner. Someone has to decide which regions to favor, why and how.

### 2.3    Policy implications of the systems of innovation approach

.We can identify two main kinds of policy implications of the SI approach:
(1) The SI approach contains *general* policy implications (just like standard economic theory) that can be extracted from the characteristics of the approach. They are "general" in the sense that they are of a "signpost" character.
(2) The SI approach provides a framework of analysis for identifying *specific* policy issues. It is helpful in identifying "problems" that should be the object of policy and for specifying how innovation policies to solve or mitigate these problems can be designed. Since this cannot be based on comparisons between existing SIs and an optimal one, it will have to be based upon comparisons between different existing ones – geographically and/or historically.

### 2.4    General policy issues in the systems of innovation approach

Two general policy issues that emanate directly from the SI approach are:
*(1) Organizational actors might need to be created, redesigned or abolished.*
*(2) Institutional rules might need to be created, redesigned or abolished.*

In any SI it is important, from a policy point of view, to study whether the existing organizations and institutions are appropriate for promoting innovation. How should institutions and organizations be changed or "engineered" to induce innovation? This dynamic perspective on institutions and organizations is crucial in the SI approach, in both theory and practice. Not only organizational change but also the evolution and design of new institutions were very important in the development strategies of the successful Asian economies, as well as in the ongoing transformation of Eastern Europe. Hence, organizational and institutional changes are particularly important in situations of rapid structural change.

A general policy implication of the fact that much learning and innovation is interactive is also that this interaction should be targeted much more directly than is normally the case in innovation policy today. Thus, another general policy issue is:
*(3) Innovation policy should focus not only on the elements of the systems but also – and perhaps primarily – on the relations among them.*

---

[11] Such allocations are made every year, but are seldom discussed explicitly and publicly.

This includes the relations among various kinds of organizations and also those between organizations and institutions. For example, the long-term innovation performance of firms in science-based industries is strongly dependent upon the interactions of these firms with universities and research organizations. These interactions should be facilitated by means of policy – if they are not spontaneously functioning smoothly enough. This can partly be done by changing the laws and rules that govern the relations between universities and firms. Incubators, technology parks and public venture capital organizations may also be important in similar ways. This means that the public sector may create organizations to facilitate innovation. At the same time, however, it may create the rules and laws that govern these organizations and their relations to private ones.

From the evolutionary approach, a new indication can be derived. Because innovation processes are evolutionary and path-dependent, there is the danger of negative "lock-in" situations; that is, patterns or trajectories of innovation that lead to low growth and decreasing employment. This may apply to patterns of learning and the production specialization of firms, industries, regions and countries. The next general policy issue is, therefore:

*(4) Innovation policy should ensure that negative lock-in situations are avoided.*

This point is strongly emphasized by *evolutionary theory*. As Arthur (1989) and David (1987, 1985) have shown, the working of path-dependency, global or local positive feedbacks and network externalities may lead a system to be locked into an inferior technology. Potentially superior technologies may not take off and the generation of diversity may be reduced or blocked.

What are the policy options here? Three can be identified.

*(4a) Keeping technological rivalry alive by supporting alternatives.*

A first policy option is to keep technological rivalry open. This is not an easy task, however. David (1987) identifies a "narrow policy window paradox." Path-dependency, increasing returns and positive network feedbacks may lock an industry into a given technology or standard rather early in an industry life cycle. In order to keep options open the government has a very short period for intervention, which usually comes rather early in the competition among technologies or standards. The government may do that by using public technology procurement and R&D subsidies supporting possible alternatives to the winning technologies and by favoring experimentation. A related issue is: how can a government choose which technologies to support? This is the "blind giant quandary," discussed by David (1987). It concerns the lack of knowledge by public agencies as to the real features and potentialities of alternatives very early in the technological competition and industry life cycle. In this respect, the government may do two things. First, it may support organizations that have the specific task of exploration and experimentation, such as universities. Second, it may indirectly keep technology rivalry open by supporting "an" alternative (it may be the second most relevant at the moment of government intervention) to the winning technology. The US procurement policy on semiconductors and computers in the 1950s and 1960s did exactly that. It kept various alternatives open by supporting the competitive approaches of several firms early on in the history of the industry. High levels of exploratory activity then generated an environment in which American firms developed the winning technologies for the later stages of industry evolution (Bresnahan and Malerba, 1999).

In this respect, innovation policy may develop "anticipatory policies" or provide the domestic industry with a "vision" regarding potentially new, interesting technological alternatives, in order that domestic firms can start carrying out research in these new directions. Here, the example of the concerted "vision" of Japanese government policy with respect to new electronics technologies comes to the fore (Fransman, 1995). This "vision" by the government, however, is not easy to develop. Government policy is quite effective if it is able *ex ante* to pick the winning technology or trajectory, but it fails otherwise. In a changing, uncertain and complex world choosing the winning technologies is not an easy task to accomplish, all the more so because the government may not have the necessary competencies, the appropriate information filters or the institutional network.

*(4b) Introducing diversity into the industry through the provision of support for firm entry and the survival of new firms*

In addition, economic variety may be increased by the provision of support for the entry and survival of new firms. Compared to incumbents, entrants may well be characterized by different capabilities, cognitive frames and approaches. As has clearly been shown by several empirical studies, entry is not an equilibrating force. Rather, innovators bring new ideas, products and technologies with respect to incumbents. As a consequence, the government may create an environment favorable to the entry of new firms – in particular small and medium-sized enterprises – and to the growth of successful ones. As the empirical studies have demonstrated, it is the survival and growth, and not just the entry into an industry, that are the crucial processes for the long-term survival of innovative firms, because they require continuous innovation as well as major managerial and organizational changes. One of the reasons for the continuous US leadership in minicomputers and PCs and computer networks has been the high entry rates of new actors into the industrial scene. These new actors had different products, competencies and strategies, and introduced a high rate of exploratory activities and high variety into American industry. This was not the case with European industry, which remained characterized for a long time by a few established oligopolistic actors.

*(4c) Supporting the generation of variety through a common infrastructure (standards and gateway technologies).*

Public policy may create the conditions for the generation of diversity by reducing the incompatibility among competing approaches and by providing a common base upon which new varieties of products may be introduced. This is the role of norms and standards. Norms and standards create a platform upon which new products and technologies may be developed, while reducing the risk of introducing incompatible innovations (Cohendet and Llerena, 1997). However, when competing approaches have progressed significantly, and have established a sufficiently large user base, the government may push for gateway technologies, which connect these previously incompatible technologies (David, 1987). In both cases, variety is reduced at the level of basic technologies, but it is potentially increased in terms of ranges of product and process innovations. Another way to support a common infrastructure upon which a variety of products and processes may be developed is the diffusion of codified information about various competing technologies, so that firms themselves may try to develop gateway technologies. This can be done through the widespread and intensive use of IT. Examples of the increasing role of standards in the innovation process are the establishment of ETSI, the creation of standards within the ESPRIT (Engineering, Science, Preparation and Introductory Training) program and the role played by the National Institute of Standards and Technology in the United States in the initial development of the semiconductor and computer industries (Mowery, 1996; and Edquist, 2003).

The final general policy issue is:

*(5) Governments can facilitate changes in the production structure and the ability of firms to create new products.*

There are three mechanisms through which the production structure can change through the addition of new products: existing firms may diversify into new products (examples are Japan and South Korea); new firms in new product areas may grow rapidly (the United States is an example); and foreign firms may invest in new product areas in the country (the case of Ireland is an example). In the last thirty years some countries, and regions, dominated by process innovations have experienced high and persistent unemployment rates. At the same time, product innovations have displayed the opposite tendency to generate new employment. If the objective of innovation policy is to secure job creation, governments can therefore support structural changes in the direction of production sectors, dominated by product innovations. The demand for new products often grows more rapidly than for old ones. Moreover, new products are often intermediate goods or process technologies for other sectors, and this would create productivity increases and cost reductions, as in the chemical engineering, software and machine tools sectors. The implications of these arguments are that firms, regions and countries producing new products tend to do so for markets that are growing rapidly. Growing markets mean an increase in demand and output, which reinforces the intrinsic employment creation effect of product innovations. Governments should therefore create opportunities and incentives for changes in the production structure. They should promote sectors characterized by high knowledge intensity and a high proportion of product innovations. Policy issues in this context concern how policy makers can help develop alternative patterns of learning and innovation and nurture emerging SSIs.

In sum, the general policy implications of the SI approach are different from those of standard economic theory. This has to do with the fact that the characteristics of the two frameworks are very different. The SI approach shifts the focus away from actions at the level of individual and isolated units within the economy (firms, consumers) towards that of the collective underpinnings of innovation. It addresses the overall system that creates and distributes knowledge rather than its individual components, and innovations are seen as the outcome of evolutionary processes within these systems.

These general policy issues derived from the SI approach can serve as signposts and suggest where to look for problems and possible solutions in innovation policy making. However, this is not a sufficient basis for designing specific innovation policies. The general policy issues do not tell a policy maker exactly what to do in order to improve the functioning of the system. The SI approach cannot provide this; neither can any other approach or theory. Take, again, standard economic theory as an example. The market failure analysis of this theory argues that a completely competitive, decentralized market economy would provide suboptimal investment in knowledge creation and innovation. Firms under-invest in R&D because of uncertainty and appropriation problems. This leads, for example, to a case for public subsidies for knowledge creation, or for the creation of intellectual property rights. This nicely links up with the "linear model" approaches, and economists and policy makers often consider this as a justification – or theoretical foundation – for governments to subsidize R&D.

However, the policy implications that emerge from the market failure theory are, in fact, not very helpful for policy makers from a practical and specific point of view. They are too blunt to provide much guidance: they assume that the policy maker has at least the same information at his disposal as is available to the private decision maker – and more. They do not indicate how large the subsidies or other interventions should be or within which specific area one should intervene. They say almost nothing about how to intervene – i.e. which policy instruments should be used and the process through which they should be implemented. Standard economic theory is not of much help when it comes to formulating and implementing specific R&D and innovation policies. It provides only general policy implications – e.g. that basic research should sometimes be subsidized (Metcalfe, 1995).

## 3      From systems of innovation to sectoral systems: general public policy considerations

The SSI approach can be used as a framework for designing specific innovation policies. We now outline, very briefly, how this can be done. It has been mentioned that a necessary condition for public intervention in processes of innovation is that a "problem" – which is not automatically solved by markets and firms – must exist.[12] Substantial analytical and methodological capabilities are needed to identify these "problems."[13]

The important insight in the sectoral systems approach is that innovation systems are constructed and operate at multiple levels in an economy and that, to various degrees, they interact within and across national economies and technologies. The sector becomes the focusing device to identify the intersection of these different levels and scales of analysis. The idea of SIs, which can be traced back to List and Babbage in the nineteenth century, began by privileging national-level institutions and organizations that frame science, technology and innovative activities within a national political system. Here the role of universities in conducting research and training minds, and the role of public research laboratories, are often cited as examples of the components of a national system. Connections also matter in defining these systems and particular emphasis has been given to the mode of interaction between firms and public organizations in promoting innovation nationally. The idea of a national system has subsequently been generalized by recognizing that innovation processes increasingly spill across national boundaries (in the European Union this is built explicitly into the Programs of Community R&D subsequent to the Single European Act of 1987) and by

---

[12] This means that neutral or general policies are normally irrelevant; selectivity is necessary if specific problems are to be solved or mitigated.

[13] Such capabilities are also needed to design policies that can mitigate the problems.

recognizing that innovation processes have to be articulated at the sectoral level.

In this view, sectoral production systems and their related markets are important because it is within these systems that sequences of innovation problems are defined and "solved" by firms. The problems are specific to the sector but the solutions typically draw on a more extended division of labor that goes beyond narrowly defined production/market systems. Thus, nations and sectors support what can be called "bundles" of innovative capabilities and resources of a general kind. Firms in the pursuit of competitive advantage stimulate the application of these resources to specific innovation problems, and the context in which firms interact with the wider innovation milieu depends on the nature of the sector. Notice here the important role of the firm to act as the combinatorial locus for the many different kinds of knowledge typically required to innovate. Innovation requires more than knowledge of science and technology: it also requires knowledge of organization and market, and the latter are exclusively the province of firms, or – more precisely – business activities in sectoral contexts.

The importance of the sectoral system is that it forms the locus of intersection of numerous networks generating particular kinds of knowledge. A typical "technologist" in a firm may interact with other technologists in the community of the relevant discipline, with industry and government groups establishing standards and regulations, with technologists in rival firms and with academic researchers in supporting fields. Each of these networks has different members and different purposes, but they all contribute to innovation. Indeed, innovative ability may depend on the ability to participate in and manage these network relations. Thus, the wider significance of the sectoral perspective is to identify the complex of networks and the dynamics of their birth, growth and – even – decline in relation to innovation performance.

Of course, SSIs are quite *different* from each other, for example with regard to knowledge base, resources spent on R&D, firms' characteristics, etc. In addition, organizations and institutions constituting elements of the sectoral systems may have different roles in different countries. For example, research institutes and company-based research departments may be important organizations in one country (e.g. Japan) while research universities may perform a similar function in another (e.g. the United States). Institutions such as laws, norms, and values also vary considerably across countries.

In this book, we emphasize that sectoral systems are different and that, within each sector, there are important regional and country specificities that affect the different trajectories of industrial development. We would like to bring to the fore the importance of a sound, empirically driven comparison between sectoral systems and across countries within a sectoral system. Without such comparisons, it is difficult (as mentioned earlier) to single out "problems," missing functions, organizations and institutions. Comparisons are, therefore, the most important means for understanding the relationships within sectoral systems and their impact on the performance of firms.

Genuinely empirical and very detailed comparisons can be performed between existing systems (geographically or historically). They are similar to what is often called "benchmarking" at the firm level. Such comparisons are crucial for policy purposes. They can identify the "problems" that should be subject to policy intervention, and are necessary also to identify the causes behind the problems – at least the most important ones[14] – in order to be able to design appropriate innovation policy instruments.

Within an SI framework, an identification of the causes behind the problems is the same as identifying deficiencies in the functioning of the system. It is a question of identifying those systemic dimensions that are missing or inappropriate and that lead to the "problem" in terms of comparative performance. Let us call these deficient functions *system failures*. When we know the causes behind a certain "problem" – for example, weak technological transfer between university and industry – we have identified a "system failure."

Not until they know the character of the system failure can policy makers know whether to influence or change organizations or institutions or the interactions between them – or something else. Therefore, an identification of a problem should be supplemented with an analysis of its causes as a part of the analytical basis for the design of an innovation policy. Benchmarking is not enough.

*3.1    A sectoral system approach provides a new methodology for the study of sectors and, therefore, for the identification of the variables that should be the policy targets*

While, up to now, industrial economics and industrial organizations have focused on dimensions such as structure-conduct-performance, strategy in a game-theoretic way, transaction costs, sunk cost and the "bounds" approach, the view suggested here is that sectoral analyses should focus on systemic features in relation to knowledge and boundaries, the

[14] A causal analysis may also reveal that public intervention may be unlikely to solve the problem identified, due to a lack of ability from the government's side.

heterogeneity of actors and networks, institutions, and transformation through coevolutionary processes. As a consequence, the understanding of these dimensions becomes a prerequisite for any policy addressed to a specific sector.

In fact, one of the problems that governments may face is the inability to understand the specificity of the sector, the technology or the institutional setting in which policy has to take place. For example, in very general terms, policies that try to correct for lock-ins and variety failures (discussed in section 3.4) by promoting firms' entry should pay considerable attention to the type of sectoral system. In an entrepreneurial (Schumpeter Mark I) regime, characterized by high entry rates, policies promoting entry would be very much in tune with the organization of innovative activity in a sector characterized by high turbulence. In a routinized regime (Schumpeter Mark II), characterized by strong rivalry among a core group of innovators exploiting economies of scale and scope in R&D, policies favoring small firm entry would risk the disruption of the inner innovative dynamics of the industry. In this case, rather than entry promotion, a policy of basic research or "technology vision" addressed to the oligopolistic core of the industry could be more appropriate.

### 3.2    The impact of general or horizontal policies may differ drastically across sectors

A second point relates to the major differences that exist among sectors in the variables identifying a sectoral system. As a consequence, the impact of horizontal policies may differ greatly from sector to sector, as well as the channels and ways that policies have their effects. It is clear that, for these purposes, biotechnology and pharmaceuticals is a different sectoral system from machine tools or telecommunications, and that the differences vary with the maturity of the sector.

For example, two of the major policy statements derived from the SI approach could be further qualified by looking at the different relevance of the following phenomena across sectors.

- *Cooperation and networks (as primary policy targets in an innovation system approach) may have different relevance and characteristics among sectors.* As mentioned above, simple economic models of competition poorly represent the extent of enterprise interdependence within modern sectors. In a sector, the generation and commercialization of innovation is likely to involve extensive cooperation and division of labor, much of which is negotiated in networks rather than governed by ordinary market-clearing mechanisms. Here, the important shift in policy emphasis toward strengthening SIs, organizations and institutions (rather than seeking to influence specific innovation events) has to be supplemented by an understanding of the relevance of the role of cooperation and networks in the specific SI.

- *Non-firm organizations and institutions (as major targets of policy in an innovation system approach) may have different relevance in different sectors.* Thus, the institutional setting is very important in a sectoral system, and should be monitored and evaluated by the public authorities. For example, the legal and institutional rules governing cooperative exchange are evolving within existing legal frameworks – such as, for example, those governing intellectual property rights – that were devised for other purposes. It is very likely that there will be major unintended consequences stemming from changes in these rules. An SSI is composed of for-profit firms but its performance in any particular sectoral setting is likely to be affected by not-for-profit organizations such as public research organizations and universities. The interactions between all the organizations contribute to the sustainability and success of commercial activities within the sector. When the role of public organizations is well understood in the context of the innovation needs of a particular sector, policy can have a major impact in reshaping the missions of existing, or in creating new, public organizations.

3.3     *The analysis of the rationale and the effects of policies requires a deep and careful comparative evaluation over time, across countries and across sectoral systems*

As previously mentioned, each sector has different features, organization and dynamics, and the actual outcome is the result of the interplay of the various basic variables affecting a sectoral system and of their interaction over time. Thus, establishing a basis for the comparative analysis of the configuration of the active institutions and organizations in any particular sector is a necessary step in policy formulation. These configurations can differ across national or regional contexts, but the effectiveness of variant configurations must be analyzed rather than presumed to be sustainable. Finally, different contexts may limit the transferability across borders of sectoral policies and require different interventions.

3.4     *For fostering innovation and diffusion in a sector, not just technology and innovation policies but a wide range of other policies may be relevant*

A sectoral system approach emphasizes that innovation and technology policy are linked with and affect other types of policies, such as science policy, industrial policy and policies related to standards, intellectual property rights and competition policy. In sectors such as pharmaceuticals and biotechnology, science policies, technology policies and IPR policies all play a major and interrelated role (see McKelvey, Orsenigo and Pammolli, chapter 3 in this book). In telecommunications, standards, competition policies and IPR policies have major effects (see Edquist, chapter 5 in this book; Hommen and Manninen, 2003; and Corrocher, 2003a, 2003b).

In addition, a sectoral system approach highlights the interdependencies, links and feedbacks among all these policies, and their effects on the dynamics and transformation of sectors. In fact, the problems that shape innovation arise within the context of the sector, and neither the trajectory of the technology nor the trajectory of the market are independent of one another.

### 3.5    *The policy maker is an active internal part of sectoral systems at different levels*

The public actor has to be aware that it is inside a sectoral system at various levels. In the sectors examined in this book, the policy maker intervenes actively in the creation of knowledge, IPR regimes, corporate governance rules, technology transfer, financial institutions, skill formation and public procurement. As a consequence, it has to develop competencies and an institutional setting in order to be effective and consistent at the various different levels.

### 3.6    *Policy should consider the different geographical dimensions of sectoral systems*

The sectoral approach takes into account developments in the local, national, regional and global dimensions of markets and institutions. For example, in the chemical industry policies at the national level have been highly relevant (Cesaroni et al., chapter 4 in this book), while in telecommunications both national and transnational policies – such as the European ones – have been important (Edquist, chapter 5 in this book). On the contrary, in machine tools the local dimension has always been key (Wengel and Shapira, chapter 7 in this book).

Each of these levels influence the development and articulation of technological capabilities. While political boundaries and local proximity are influential in the generation and diffusion of innovation, modern enterprises in a liberalized global economy must take a global perspective on actual and potential competition. Policies that focus on only one level of aggregation are likely to miss constraints or opportunities that are influential in the innovative behavior of individual organizations. While technology policies can, and sometimes should, be addressed at one level of aggregation, the rationale for these policies and their implementation must reflect a global perspective.

## 4    Some specific policy conclusions

This book provides a basis for making further distinctions that are relevant to policy analysis. These distinctions derive from a programme of research that was "deep" in its penetration of the workings of particular sectors while not "extensive" in its coverage of the many different sectors. The evidentiary basis for these distinctions is, therefore, provisional, and relies upon a more extensive body of research than that presented in this book. A further qualification in the generality of these distinctions is that in the sectors examined in this book innovation plays a critically important role to competitive success.

A key issue here is, therefore, the choice between supporting existing systems – with their historically accumulated knowledge bases – and supporting the development of radically new products and sectoral systems. Radical innovations and the emergence of new SSIs, especially in Europe, seem to be more of a "problem" for markets and private firms than reproduction and incremental innovation in established sectors (see Coriat, Malerba and Montobbio, chapter 11 in this book). We also know that large-scale and radical technological shifts – i.e. shifts to new trajectories – have rarely taken place without public intervention in the OECD countries. This is true for most of electronics as well as for aircraft and biotechnology – in the United States as well.

### 4.1    Policies in periods of radical technological change

In cases where technological change within a sector breaks from the past accumulation of knowledge, and current expertise and capability:
- SSIs will experience substantial stress because of the difficulties of aligning the incentives and the capabilities of the actors to the new problem sequence. For example, incumbent actors may underestimate the scope of change and focus on reactive rather than adaptive strategies. Adaptation in other parts of the sectoral system may, therefore, be delayed, increasing the long-term risks to the sector.
- Sectoral systems are neither naturally given nor static. They are constructed for a changing purpose and their boundaries, components and connections change significantly with the growth of knowledge and the evolution of problem sequences. A system can become outmoded and constrain innovation performance.

Examples of sectoral systems that constrained the innovative activity of firms can be found in the history of machine tools in the United States and pharmaceuticals in Europe. The innovation of the IOL provides an interesting example of the dynamics of the emergence of an innovation system within the broader ophthalmological sector. From its tentative origins of interaction between the innovating clinician, a lens supplier and a materials supplier, an international innovation system has been constructed by a small group of multinational medical companies. Each company articulates its own network of clinicians, suppliers and customers for IOLs, and to a degree these networks intersect within the wider, relatively autonomous networks of, for example, practitioner communities and healthcare systems (see Metcalfe and James, 2002, and Tether and Metcalfe, chapter 8 in this book).

• Radical technological change often involves an especially active role for public organizations in recognizing and promoting, or even creating, the initial conditions for market success. Governments can play important roles as lead users of radical new technologies and in supporting the early use of these technologies in public organizations. This is very clear in the case of public procurement with regard to defense capabilities and public health.

Three examples from this book can be proposed. First, the innovation of the IOL and the considerable changes over time in the related innovation systems in the United Kingdom and United States, in particular, depended greatly on the take-up of the procedure in public and private healthcare systems and on the different norms for translating clinical need into "market demand" in the two national medical systems (Metcalfe and James, 2002). Second, the US government has played a very active and decisive role in the launching of the fixed Internet (Edquist, 2003; and Corrocher, 2003a). Finally, the BioRegio program in Germany is another interesting example.

• In this respect, government capacities for monitoring the emergence of radical technological change differ substantially across countries.

• It is also particularly important to encourage transparent and open debates about the significance of emerging technologies, in order to support the formation of consensus as well as to identify possibilities for experimentation and trial.

This book has shown clearly how, in a dynamic setting, new sectoral or subsectoral systems of innovation may rapidly emerge from existing ones, such as biotechnology (McKelvey, Orsenigo and Pammolli, chapter 3 in this book) or the Internet and multimedia (Edquist, chapter 5 in this book).

- If governments do intervene, they should do so early in the development of new subsystems and new SSIs. Such intervention at an early stage in the product/industry cycle may have a tremendous impact.

In the case of the public creation of the NMT 450 mobile telecommunications technical standard in the Nordic countries about twenty years ago, this proved to be important. It was crucial for the emergence of the mobile telephone industry and for the rise of both Ericsson and Nokia to global leadership in this field.[15] On the other hand, there are many examples showing that massive government support to old and dying industries has had limited effect. Often it has only marginally delayed the death of these industries. One example is the Swedish shipyard industry in the late 1970s and early 1980s. The cost of the support to the shipyard industry was several hundred times larger than the cost of developing NMT 450.

- On a methodological level, this book indicates that existing approaches in industrial economics and standard measurement methods are not adequate for the task of identifying the changing configurations of sectoral systems and subsystems of innovation, particularly the processes of knowledge exchange between different types of organizations.
- The costs of constructing new sectoral subsystems of innovation are substantial, but this activity is not explicitly recognized in the existing literature of policy or management.
- There are major strategic opportunities available in discovering better ways to monitor, promote and reduce the costs of reconfiguration or expansion for sectoral systems and subsystems of innovation.

### 4.2    Sector-specific policy conclusions

Additional specific recommendations in relation to the various sectors examined in this book may be found in the individual chapters. These policy implications and conclusions are closely related to the problems faced by the various actors operating in the sectoral context and its specificity in terms of knowledge and boundaries, actors and networks, and institutions.

### 4.2.1    Policies in services

The application of the sectoral system concept to services creates many challenges, not least in relation to the economic importance of services

---

[15] In addition to the creation of standards, incubators, technology parks and the financing of new technology-based firms are examples of policy instruments relevant for the early stages of technological developments.

and the immense diversity of activities that can be grouped under this label (Tether and Metcalfe, chapter 8 in this book). Many services are premised on high degrees of interaction with manufacturing activities and many services contribute to the production of manufactures. Services can be defined in many ways but they all involve the articulation of specific transformation processes, and these are the basis for innovation.

The three cases in this book examine different aspects of the self-organization of innovation systems, the way in which they are transformed over time, the process of business experimentation and the (often complex) ways in which the relations between different actors are instituted. In relation to airport services, it is shown that the specific service features of the co-production of runway operations by airlines and airport operators have been key factors in the innovation of new operation procedures – procedures that have had a considerable impact in increasing productivity (Tether and Metcalfe, 2003). In the case of the innovation of the IOL, it is shown how the interaction between clinical practice and medical companies, and thus between clinical norms and commercial norms, has transformed this medical procedure from a craft to a virtual assembly line procedure, with great benefits to patients and the productivity of service delivery. In the process, new divisions of medical labor have emerged and the relation between need and demand has been transformed. In this case, medical companies have played a key role in assembling innovation systems at a micro-level in pursuit of competitive advantage. In the third case study (see Harvey, Nyberg and Metcalfe, 2002), the development of innovation in retailing is examined through the lens of the growth of new models of retailing business in the supermarket revolution. Even such a traditional sector as retailing has a well-defined edge of modernity, with supermarkets articulating an SI that has produced a range of important innovations in relation to the logistics of supply chains, the organization of demand and the market, and the packaging and display of foods. The different ways in which the Swedish and UK systems of retailing are organized has had a deep effect on the SIs that the two countries articulate. Thus, service activities are far from passive producers of innovations. The three sectors studied have embedded within them SIs in which the firms in question play a key role in generating their systemic properties.

Some interesting remarks can be advanced for sector-specific policies in *services*. Service innovations are often unusual in the number and type of connections that are required to assemble the components of a commercially successful innovation. This makes the problems of coordination in services particularly acute. In terms of policy, it suggests the need for identifying actual innovation requirements and for critically assessing existing approaches. In some cases, the commercialization of service innovations relies upon the development of a relatively "standardized" package of components in which either inter-firm cooperation or a single coordinator may play a particularly important role. Such standardized packages often require changes that at least parallel (if they do not replace) existing regulatory practices and rules. For example, the issues of "interoperability" have been a central concern in European telecommunications and information services policy. In some cases, such as telecommunications interconnection, these concerns have been incorporated into regulatory practice and have reshaped the commercial environment in which firms operate. In other areas, such as standards for interfaces between software, policies have been "enabling" rather than directive, and it is important to monitor whether they are having the desired effect of increasing data transferability and mitigating the problems of "orphaned" users. Early notification of the intent to promote "standardization" is likely to lead to specific industrial proposals that can be enacted and provide an important instrument for supporting innovation, despite the inconvenience and complexity of enacting multiple rules. Correspondingly, existing rules and regulatory practices may serve as a constraint on service industry innovation, just as in manufacturing. It may be particularly important to examine these rules and practices with a view to identifying the constraints that they create for innovative behaviors.

### 4.2.2    Policies in software

The SSI in software is broadly distributed among private and public organizations throughout the world. In considering European interests in the software industry, the single most important issue is in developing effective means of supporting complex software systems that are specific to particular applications. These range from ERP software systems to the embedded software incorporated in consumer white goods and producer goods. The effective design of such systems requires the advantages of technical progress to be weighed against the costs of coordination. Increasingly, the design issues that underlie the construction of such application-specific software involves coordination across the boundaries of organizations, with the risk that coordination failures may occur. These failures constitute the type of "problem" for which specific sectoral policies are the solution.

The challenges of formulating such policies are, however, daunting. No directive policy is likely to be effective given both the uncertainties about the course of technical change and the difficulties of assessing the relative merits of different paths that might be followed in constructing new generations of complex software or building infrastructures for the "information society." It is possible, however, to conclude that policy has a role in bringing about industrial dialogue, particularly interactions between producers and users that are aimed at mitigating the costs of coordination. Procurement and regulatory policies that favor interoperability and that ease the costs of interconnection are a principal instrument for improving innovative performance and entry in the software industry. The publication of interface standards between software components is, arguably, as important as the establishment of reference standards for components in the manufacturing industries. While these activities are best organized and carried out by industrial associations, particularly those that include representation by user communities, they can be encouraged and promoted by policy action.

In this book, the study of the software sector has specifically illustrated that the problems of moving from intra-firm to inter-firm organization in the production of some forms of software create new demands on other actors in the SI, such as universities and public research laboratories. In embedded software, for example, the tradition of major firms assuming almost complete responsibility for the design of software tools and the implementation of systems may be replaced in the near future by specialized companies. From a European viewpoint, this appears to be a case of a larger sectoral system failure in which neither public research laboratories nor universities (with a few conspicuous exceptions) have been sufficiently active to provide the basis for European participation in emerging specialized segments. The example serves to highlight the importance of identifying potential changes in the division of labor that rely upon external research capabilities. Funding research and encouraging dialogue about such changes is likely to have positive impacts on the innovative capabilities of European software companies.

In the last few years the "open-source" or "free software" movement has grown very rapidly, creating major new challenges for policy. Some have claimed that this movement endangers the current "business model," which is responsible for generating the revenues for funding research and innovation in the industry. Others claim that this movement represents a viable alternative to the current system of using copyright to generate this revenue. It appears highly unlikely that this movement will be able to match the performance of commercial software development, either in innovation or in serving the needs of the average user. Nonetheless, free and open-source software provides two important advantages from a European perspective. First, this software provides a means of constructing components of the information society infrastructure, such as WWW servers, that support the active participation of those seeking to develop new service innovations and platforms. To the extent that such systems provide a way to support entry and innovation in the industry, it is relevant to support their development through complementary research, education and procurement policies. Second, open-source or free software appears to provide an excellent means for supporting the acquisition of practical programming skills and knowledge. Skills shortages in software design and development have been identified as a major impediment to future European employment and growth. An assessment of the potential of open-source and free software for mitigating these problems is of considerable policy relevance.

### 4.2.3    Innovation policy in the Internet and mobile telecommunications

The US state was extremely important in the *very early stages* of the development of fixed data communications – i.e. in the period when the SSI of fixed data communication was fragile and not well established. Government agencies were very important as financiers of the research developing fixed data communications: they were initiating public technology procurement of elements of the system. Other agencies placed demands on organizations receiving public economic support that they had to use a certain data communications protocol. The government also injected increased dynamism into the telecommunications sector by pursuing deregulation.

State agencies were, however, not strong leaders in the creation of standards for the Internet in the United States. This was, instead, a rather spontaneous process, where private firms had a large influence. The idea of "open standards," or "compatibility of standards," appears to have been the characteristic US response.

The relations among various organizations were crucial for the development of innovations in the SSI. These included the relations between public and private organizations – as in public research funding and in public technology procurement. Relations among different private organizations were also important, both in terms of competition and in terms of collaboration.

The fact that the early development and diffusion of the Internet took place in the United States – with government support – gave a head start to US Internet equipment producers. This is an important explanatory factor behind the fact that US Internet equipment-producing firms, such as Cisco, are still very dominant globally. It is obviously very important for firm competitiveness in high-tech areas to be early, and to be close to customers in these early stages.

State-controlled organizations were very important in creating the first successful mobile telephony standard in Europe. Public telecommunications monopolies in the Nordic countries created the NMT 450 mobile telephony standard in collaboration with firms. The PTOs pushed the technical development of the standard and pulled national equipment-producing firms along their trajectory. They placed orders with firms and, up to a point, used the instrument of public technology procurement to create incentives for firms to develop equipment appropriate for NMT 450. NMT 450 provided the cradle for the development of mobile telephony in Europe. Deregulation of the telecommunications sector was also of some importance in some European countries, such as Sweden and the United Kingdom.[16] However, liberalization was not a key factor in Sweden's success with NMT and GSM. At most, it aided the diffusion process that was already under way at the time of deregulation (1993).

The relationships among organizations were obviously important in the process just described. So, were the relations between various kinds of institutions – such as NMT 450 – and the firms and other organizations involved also important? The relations between the operators – who were the main standard creators – and the equipment producers were very important for the fact that European equipment producers became leading ones, globally speaking. For firms such as Nokia and Ericsson it was also important that mobile telephony got a head start in the Nordic countries and that it grew rapidly.

Most second-generation standards were developed with the potential to become de facto world standards through international adoption. The European GSM standard – which developed out of the NMT standard – more than fulfilled the expectation of wide international diffusion. Initially conceived as a pan-European standard, it became a world standard, in practical terms. No other 2G standard achieved this. Deregulated operators (such as the Swedish Televerket/Telia) as well as firms (such as Ericsson and Nokia) were very active in the consortium that supported the development of the GSM standard. Hence, the close relations between users and producers continued. Over the longer term, however, these close relations gradually became looser. The GSM success could not be ascribed only to the strategies of a few innovative organizations but to the collaborations of a variety of different organizations: PTOs, standard-setting organizations and research organizations, plus equipment producers.

The European Commission also had a leading role in the development of GSM. The European Union was pushing one standard. This was also a standard that was technologically advanced, operated well and,

---

[16] Considering that state support was so important both for fixed data communications and for mobile telephony, it is tempting to think that the failure of satellite communications in the latter half of the 1990s was due to the lack of support from the state in the early stage of its development.

therefore, diffused rapidly outside Europe. In contrast, the US digital standards diffused internationally only to a limited extent, and the single Japanese standard not at all. The European Commission pushed liberalization and competition in the (mobile) telecommunications sector.[17] It did so within one single standard, and it did not care about letting standards compete, as with the US standards policy. The standard pushed by the European Union was secured to serve all member states, while the US digital standards were not completely compatible with each other. What the European Union did over – originally – thirteen European countries the United States did not manage to do over one – albeit large – country. It proved to be a major policy mistake to have several standards in the United States. This can be considered a serious policy failure for the United States as well as a great success for the European Union. The reasons for this are that it led to a slower diffusion of mobile telecommunications in the United States than in Europe, and the strongest equipment producers emerged in the GSM area.

It was of great importance for the European dominance in the production of equipment for the mobile telecommunications industry that one single standard was promoted; for example, economies of scale could be exploited. That the relations between users and producers were close also proved very important, primarily for the producers. The way GSM developed strengthened the leadership position of Nokia and Ericsson. This is all the more notable in the light of the lack of European success – and US/Asian dominance – in other ICT sectors.

Europe has emerged as a clear leader in mobile telephony due to its success in defining good standards in mobile communications. Ericsson's and Nokia's dominance among equipment producers in mobile telephony is often traced to the early success of the NMT standard, and GSM is similarly regarded as the means by which early Nordic success was generalized to other European Union countries in the second generation of mobile communications.

One reason for the relatively poor international performance of US-based 2G mobile standards was the "division" of the market between standards, none of which could match the subscriber base of GSM. These developments are considered to account for the subsequent loss of market share by US equipment manufacturers to European rivals during the second generation of mobile telephony. The slower transfer from first- to second-generation standards in the United States was due to regulatory decisions that stressed the necessity of achieving "backward

---

[17] In 1996 the European Commission decided that mobile services had to be competitive, with multiple GSM licenses in each member state.

compatibility" with the existing analog standards, rather than compatible digital standards. Decisions with regard to charging were another factor contributing to the low subscriber penetration rates: often the receiver has to pay for all or part of a mobile phone call.

The crisis at Ericsson during 2001–03 was mainly caused by a drastic decrease in demand because of the slowdown in the international business cycle, and thereby in telecommunications system investments. It serves to conceal the fact that Ericsson is still dominant in base stations and switches, while Nokia strongly dominates global handset production.

In the 1990s a convergence took place between traditional telecommunications, the Internet and mobile telecommunications. This was also accompanied by a wave of mergers and acquisitions (and strategic alliances), both among equipment producers and among operators. A strategic question for the equipment producers is whether they should select voice as their main business area and thus go for the growing mobile markets, or, alternatively, whether they should concentrate on the rapidly growing Internet equipment market or focus on the mobile Internet.

It is clear that Europe has had the initiative so far in mobile voice telephony. Whether this will continue during the third-generation UMTS standard is unclear. NTT DoCoMo's i-mode had 31 million subscribers in late 2001, and DoCoMo was also the first operator to enter 3G in October 2001. This means that the locus of the center of experimentation may have moved from Europe to Japan. This may spur equipment producers, since user/producer interaction proved to be important earlier. In the United States some operators have transferred to GSM, and they will be more standardized in 3G than they were in 2G. However, the United States seems to be a slow starter in third-generation mobile telephony. Although Europe will probably enter 3G earlier than the United States, it is doing so at a slower pace than Japan. This might to some extent be because of the very high prices European operators had to pay in some countries for a 3G license – i.e. it might partly be a consequence of public policy.

In 2001–03 3G was developing quite slowly. However, telecommunications operator revenue was growing by 10 percent per year in 2001 and the immediately preceding years. This indicates that telecommunications operators were not subject to a structural crisis, but that they had been hit by the business cycle downturn during 2000–03.

The most important obstacles to the diffusion of 3G are, in the short run, the availability of handsets and, in the longer run, the existence of attractive content suited for the mobile Internet. This points to the crucial role of demand in the emergence of new sectoral systems. With regard to equipment, the policy instrument of public technology procurement was used both with regard to the Internet (the United States) and with regard to mobile telephony (Scandinavia). When it comes to content in the 3G mobile Internet, the demand has to be provided by final consumers – firms and individuals – outside the public sphere to the largest extent. The success of i-mode in Japan seems to indicate that this will happen[18] but access providers and content providers will have to be innovative, not only with regard to access and content proper but also with regard to charging systems and other innovations in the field of management and administration. It is also a matter of developing niche strategies adapted to the new medium; movies will never best be watched on a mobile phone!

With regard to the fixed Internet, diffusion is proceeding; by 2001 about 70 percent of households in the United States had access. In other countries the degree of diffusion varied considerably. The dominance of US equipment producers, which was established early in the history of the fixed Internet, seems set to remain, at least for some years. At the same time, this sector may be entering a more mature stage of development, with slower growth and smaller profits.

Here follows a summary of the three most important policy issues with regard to the fixed Internet and mobile telecommunications. They are presented in telegraphic form, and in no particular order.

- *The role of institutions has been crucial for policy*. Standards have played a major role in innovation and the success of European mobile telecommunications, both in terms of the diffusion of use and with regard to the success of equipment-producing companies. Deregulation has also played a role for the diffusion of the Internet and mobile telecommunications. Other important institutions are the structure and level of tariffs. Some institutions are national, some are sectoral and others are firm-specific. An important firm strategy objective may be to influence institutions to the firm's benefit.
- *The relations between different organizations and between institutions and organizations are crucial for the functioning and performance of the sectoral systems of innovation*. Examples are the relations between private and public organizations, in the form of research funding, standard setting or public technology procurement. Relations between different kinds of firms and other private organizations are also important – e.g. collaboration between users and producers. Organizations provoke institutional changes, and, when the new institutions come into effect, they may greatly influence the same or other organizations.

---

[18] The slow diffusion of WAP and GPRS in Europe and the United States points in the opposite direction, however.

- *It is of crucial importance that public policy intervention occurs early in the development of the sectoral system.* This is the stage in the development of an SSI when private actors and markets function least efficiently and dynamically. Therefore, policy intervention in these very early stages often means the difference between success and failure, between life and death. Hence, limited policy resources should mainly be allocated to the early stages of the development of new SSIs or new product areas. This has proved to be very important for equipment producers in the fields of the Internet and mobile telephony.

### 4.2.4    Technology policy in chemicals

The study conducted using the sectoral system approach revealed that the chemical industry is characterized by the leading role played by the large firms, both for their capability to promote innovation and technology development and for their contribution to regional performance and competitiveness. At the same time, the study highlighted that, at the industry level, a division of labor can be observed between large companies and technology-based small companies, with the latter mainly engaged in licensing (process) technologies to other chemical firms. Hence, policy intervention should be focused on these two actors, and the related markets for technologies. In so doing, other elements of the chemical sectoral system will have to be considered, such as universities and other research organizations, financial organizations and IPR regimes.

**4.2.4.1 Innovation policies and the large chemical firms**    The analysis of the process of knowledge generation and the exploration of new technologies has shown that the European chemical companies perform most of their research in their home country, and that patenting activity clusters in a few regions. This confirms that the globalization of R&D by MNEs is, at best, a quite incomplete process. Compared to the geographical cluster, the multinational company is a better mechanism for creating larger networks, for enhancing collaborations amongst delocalized inventors and for producing interdisciplinary patents. In short, this confirms that the firms, and particularly the large companies, typically promote larger research networks, and that they produce a rather general type of research, at least in the chemical business.

However, this also suggests that, as far as the large European chemical firms are concerned, there is no urgent policy intervention required for promoting the generation of R&D and related activities. The large European chemical firms do engage in these activities, they do indeed give rise to large networks of inventors and they do produce patents with wide potential applicability.

Furthermore, the analysis of the globalization process of the chemical industry has revealed that European companies have proven to be particularly active in this process, as they have typically increased their share of plants abroad. This has happened both in advanced markets, such as the United States and Japan, and in the open market of developing countries, particularly in Asia. Thus, the chemical industry has become more global, with a lower share of plants of companies from one region located in the same region, and a higher share of plants from one region in the other regions.

In sum, large (European) chemical companies have been able to invest in R&D and to compete internationally, and so they need limited policy support.

**4.2.4.2 Innovation policies and the small firms**   In contrast to large companies, smaller firms need greater policy support, at least in terms of the creation of suitable conditions for their growth, and for enhancing the potential that their growth may have for the evolution of the industry (especially the new high-tech segments) and its effects on competitiveness and employment. The role of the smaller companies is linked to the opportunities for the development of a full-fledged market for technology in Europe, and – more generally – for the participation of the European firms in the global market for chemical technologies.

Policy interventions should be focused on removing the barriers to the creation of this market. Indeed, European markets for technology are far from being developed, and this requires policy support for their formation. However, these markets have two important features: a) they allow a significant diffusion of technology, which increases the investments of the companies operating in the final markets; and b) they enable the formation of companies that specialize in the development of the technology even if the same companies lack downstream complementary assets.

Among others, the specialized engineering firms are key in such markets. The SEFs imply efficiency gains, greater investments and greater entry by chemical producers in downstream markets, especially by producers that would not have been able to enter if they had to develop their technology in-house. Similarly, the SEFs can be quite important in diffusing new environmental technologies. This calls for policy actions to encourage the rise and growth of smaller firms specialized in the development of such technologies.

Specifically, the following policy actions could be promoted for enhancing the markets for technology in the European chemical industry, and particularly in its engineering and technological subsectors:

- *The development of proper forms of intellectual property rights to support the activities of smaller technology-based companies.* Compared to larger firms, small firms have little access to other means for appropriating the returns on their internal R&D activity, and property rights often represent the only form they can employ.
- *The development of adequate forms of financing for new technology-based companies.* These companies face a high technological risk, which can be faced only by using appropriate forms of financing (e.g. venture capital). By allowing small technology-based firms to arise and grow, markets for technology will grow as well, which implies reduced barriers to entry, greater technological diffusion and new patterns and opportunities for economic growth.
- *The development of new forms of technology diffusion by universities, and the scientific organizations more generally.* Organizations without downstream complementary assets in production and marketing have the highest incentives to license, because they have nothing to lose in the downstream markets if new competitors arise. This is the case with universities and other research organizations. As a result, by encouraging the diffusion of technology by universities (either directly through patent licensing or through spin-offs), established producers in that technological domain will also be encouraged to license, hence increasing the diffusion of these technologies.

The rise of markets for technology also has implications for the vertical structure of the chemical industry, and implies a division of innovative labor, which in turn benefits the downstream producers. The classical advantages of a division of labor are, indeed, that the downstream producers can take advantage of the input at lower costs than if such input had to be produced in-house. Apart from efficiency gains in the downstream industries, this implies greater diffusion of the technology downstream, greater entry of new competitors in final markets, etc. In turn, these advantages of vertical specialization suggest some further policy actions, focused particularly on the reduction of search costs for new technologies, the reduction of the effects of the so-called "not invented here" syndrome and, in general terms, the reduction of transaction costs emerging from technology exchange.

## 5    Conclusions

This chapter has presented some additions to the existing body of knowledge supporting evidence-based policy. They reflect a shift of emphasis in the formulation of innovation policies, which are, of course, much broader than policies for science and technology. Traditional innovation policies have been formulated in providing public resources for R&D and changing the incentives for firms to innovate. Tax breaks for R&D, innovation subsidies and patents are typical examples of these policies. The sectoral system perspective does not deny the significance of this approach but recognizes that in practice it may run rapidly into diminishing returns. To offset this it is necessary that innovation opportunities be enhanced, and for this to be achieved by connecting firms within a wider division of innovative labor within and across economies. Improving the organization of an innovation system is an almost certain route to improving the complementary pay-offs from public and private R&D in any sector.

The sectoral perspective provides a tool for policy makers to comprehend the relevant innovation systems and for identifying the actors that should be influenced by policy. The quid pro quo, however, is that policy makers need to invest much more effort in understanding the idiosyncrasies of the sectors. An approach to innovation policy that is not sensitive to the important sectoral distinctions of the kind identified by this book will not yield much pay-off to the policy maker.

REFERENCES

Arthur, B. (1989), Competing technologies, increasing returns and lock-in by historical events, *Economic Journal*, 99, 1,116–1,146

Bresnahan, T., and F. Malerba (1999), Industrial dynamics and the evolution of firms' and nations' competitive capabilities in the world computer industry, in D. C. Mowery and R. R. Nelson (eds.), *Sources of Industrial Leadership: Studies of Seven Industries*, Cambridge University Press, Cambridge

Cohendet, P., and P. Llerena (1997), Learning, technical change and public policy: how to create and exploit diversity, in C. Edquist (ed.), *Systems of Innovation: Technologies, Institutions and Organizations*, Frances Pinter, London, 223–241

Corrocher, N. (2003a), The Internet services industry: sectoral dynamics of innovation and production, in C. Edquist (ed.), *The Internet and Mobile Telecommunications System of Innovation: Developments in Equipment, Access and Content*, Edward Elgar Publishing, Cheltenham, 177–209

(2003b), The Internet services industry: country-specific trends in the UK, Italy and Sweden, in C. Edquist (ed.), *The Internet and Mobile Telecommunications System of Innovation: Developments in Equipment, Access and Content*, Edward Elgar Publishing, Cheltenham, 210–235

David, P. (1985), Clio and the economics of QWERTY, *American Economic Review*, 75, 2, 332–337

(1987), Some new standards for the economics of standardisation in the information age, in P. Dasgupta and P. Stoneman (eds.), *Economic Policy and Technological Performance*, Cambridge University Press, Cambridge

Edquist, C. (1997), Systems of innovation approaches – their emergence and characteristics, in C. Edquist (ed.), *Systems of Innovation – Technologies, Institutions and Organizations*, Frances Pinter, London, 1–35

——— (2001a), Innovation policy – a systemic approach, in B.-Å. Lundvall and D. Archibugi (eds.), *Major Socio-Economic Trends and European Innovation Policy*, Oxford University Press, Oxford, 212–237

——— (2001b), Innovation policy in the systems of innovation approach: some basic principles, in M. N. Fischer and J. Fröhlich (eds.), *Knowledge Complexity and Innovation Systems*, Springer-Verlag, Berlin, 46–57

——— (2003), The fixed Internet and mobile telecommunications sectoral system of innovation: equipment, access and content, in C. Edquist (ed.), *The Internet and Mobile Telecommunications System of Innovation: Developments in Equipment, Access and Content*, Edward Elgar Publishing, Cheltenham, 1–39

Edquist, C., L. Hommen and L. Tsipouri (eds.) (2000), *Public Technology Procurement: Theory, Evidence and Policy*, Kluwer Academic, Dordrecht

Fransman, M. (1995), Is national technology policy obsolete in a globalised world? The Japanese response, *Cambridge Journal of Economics*, 19, 1, 95–119

Fridlund, M. (2000), Switching relations and trajectories: the development procurement of the AXE Swedish switching technology, in C. Edquist, L. Hommen and L. Tsipouri (eds.), *Public Technology Procurement: Theory, Evidence and Policy*, Kluwer Academic, Dordrecht, 143–165

Harvey, M., A. Nyberg and J. S. Metcalfe (2002), *Deep Transformation in the Service Economy: Innovation and Organisational Change in Food Retailing in Sweden and the UK*, ESSY working paper, Centre for Research on Innovation and Competition, University of Manchester and University of Manchester Institute of Science and Technology [http://www.cespri.it/ricerca/es_wp.htm]

Hommen, L., and E. Manninen (2003), The global system for mobile telecommunications (GSM): second generation, in C. Edquist (ed.) *The Internet and Mobile Telecommunications System of Innovation: Developments in Equipment, Access and Content*, Edward Elgar Publishing, Cheltenham, 71–128

Metcalfe, J. S., (1995), Equilibrium and evolutionary perspectives on technology policy, in P. Stoneman (ed.), *Handbooks of the Economics of Innovation and Technology Change*, Basil Blackwell, Oxford

Metcalfe, J. S., and A. James (2002), *Emergent Innovation Systems and the Delivery of Clinical Services: The Case of Intra-Ocular Lenses*, ESSY working paper, Centre for Research on Innovation and Competition, University of Manchester and University of Manchester Institute of Science and Technology [http://www.cespri.it/ricerca/es_wp.htm]

Mowery, D. C. (ed.) (1996), *The International Computer Software Industry: A Comparative Study of Industry Evolution and Structure*, Oxford University Press, Oxford

Palmberg, C. (2000), Industrial transformation through public technology procurement? The case of Nokia and the Finnish telecommunications industry, in C. Edquist, L. Hommen, and L. Tsipouri (2000) (eds.), *Public*

*Technology Procurement: Theory, Evidence and Policy*, Kluwer Academic, Dordrecht, 167–196

Tether B. S., and J. S. Metcalfe (2001), *Services and Systems of Innovations*, Discussion Paper no. 58, Centre for Research on Innovation and Competition, University of Manchester and University of Manchester Institute of Science and Technology

(2003), Horndal at Heathrow? Capacity expansion through co-operation and system evolution, *Industrial and Corporate Change*, 12, 3, 437–476

*Part IV*

# Conclusions

# 13    Summing-up and conclusions

*Franco Malerba*

## 1    Introduction

This chapter aims to sum up and draw some conclusions about the sectoral systems studied in the book. The concept of the sectoral system has proven a useful tool in various respects:
- for a descriptive analysis of the differences and similarities in the structure, organization and boundaries of sectors;
- for a full understanding of the differences and similarities in the working, dynamics and transformation of sectors;
- for the identification of the factors affecting innovation and the commercial performance and international competitiveness of firms and countries in the different sectors;
- for the development of new public policy indications.

The chapter presents a brief characterization of the sectors examined in this book (section 1), followed by a discussion of the results concerning the role of the three building blocks – knowledge and technologies, actors and networks, and institutions (section 2) – and of the actual geographical boundaries (section 3) of sectoral systems in Europe. Then the main coevolutionary processes (section 4) are examined. Sectoral systems in services are different from those in manufacturing, and their differences are discussed in section 5. Finally, the international performance of Europe in the six sectors and the factors affecting it (section 6), the policy implications of a sectoral system approach (section 7) and the challenges ahead (section 8) are discussed.

As mentioned in the introduction, in the chapters of this book concerning specific SSIs sectors have been defined broadly: pharmaceuticals, chemicals, telecommunications, software and machine tools. This definition has allowed our emphasis on interdependencies, linkages and transformations spanning a large set of products, actors and functions. However, in some chapters a more disaggregated level has also been used in order to show that, within the broadly defined sectors, different SIs may coexist. In these cases it has also been possible to discuss SIs, but at a much higher level of disaggregation. In these conclusions (as in the book), the term "sector" is used for the broad sector aggregations and the terms "sub sector," "product group" and "product segment" for more narrowly defined aggregations within broad sectors.

## 2     A characterization of the various sectoral systems

How can the five major sectoral systems examined in this book be characterized? The analysis carried out in this book provides a first approach.

- In *biotechnology and pharmaceuticals*, science and universities, the division of innovative labor and networks, venture capital and national health systems play a major role in the innovative process. There are several relevant actors: large firms, small firms and NBFs. NBFs have entered the sector competing as well as cooperating with (or being bought up by) the large, established pharmaceutical firms. In this sector, demand and institutions (such as regulation, intellectual property rights and national health systems) affect the innovation process. A wide variety of science and engineering fields are playing important roles in renewing the search space. At the same time, recent changes in regulation and demand are opening up new opportunities in generic drugs.

- In *telecommunications equipment and services*, a convergence of different technologies, demand and industries with processes of knowledge integration, combination and production specialization has taken place. This convergence has been associated with the presence of a wide variety of different specialized and integrated actors, ranging from large equipment producers to new service firms. In this broad sector, innovation is very much affected by standards, the institutional setting and the processes of privatization and liberalization.

- Conversely, *chemicals* are characterized by continuous innovation by large multinational firms through R&D, economies of scale and scope and the cumulativeness of progress, as well as by research and commercialization capabilities. Firms' internal R&D has been complemented by external links and by the capability of absorbing external scientific and technological knowledge.

- *Software* has a highly differentiated knowledge base (in which the context of application is relevant) and several different and distinctive product groups in which specialized firms are active. User-producer interaction, global and local networks of innovation and production, and the high mobility of highly skilled human capital are all present. Since the early 1980s, with the spread of networked computing, the Internet, the development of open-system architectures and the growth of

Web-based network computing, the role of large computer suppliers in developing integrated hardware and software systems has been displaced by a large number of specialized software companies innovating either in packaged software or in customized software. The role of the university has become important in the open-source domain. IPR regimes, standards and standard-setting alliances play a major role in innovation, diffusion and competition.

• Finally, in *machine tools*, an application-specific knowledge base has been associated with firms' specialization. Here, user-producer interaction, local networks of innovators and in-house experienced human capital are key factors for innovation. However, products are increasingly being modularized, and standardized, and suppliers of components are increasingly becoming involved in innovation.

## 3     Sectoral systems in Europe: a summing-up

In this section, for each of the three broad dimensions of sectoral systems – knowledge and technologies, actors and networks, and institutions – the main results deriving from the studies in this book are discussed.

### 3.1     *The knowledge at the base of innovative activities has changed over time and has affected the boundaries and structure of sectoral systems*

In terms of knowledge and learning processes, some key relevant features have been highlighted by the studies.

• First, the features and sources of knowledge are very different from sector to sector.
• Second, they are very important for an understanding of the workings of a sector and for an explanation of the rate and direction of technological change, the organization of innovative and production activities and the identification of the factors at the base of successful performance.
• Third, in most sectors knowledge has shown major changes, with a consequent change in the organization of innovative activities.
• Fourth, both science and development activities have gained in importance in all sectors.
• Fifth, the boundaries of several sectoral systems have changed greatly over time, as a consequence of the transformation of knowledge, firms' acquisition of knowledge and the changes in demand and competition.

In the *pharmaceutical sectoral system*, the knowledge base and learning processes have greatly affected innovation and the organization of innovative activities. In the early stages (1850 to 1945) the industry was close to chemicals, with little formal research until the 1930s and the widespread use of licenses. The following period (1945 to the early 1980s) was characterized by the introduction of the random screening of natural and chemically derived compounds. This led to an explosion of R&D. A few blockbuster products were discovered in every decade: each one experienced high growth. The advent of molecular biology in the 1980s led to a new learning regime based on molecular genetics and DNA technology, with two basic search processes – one concerning co-specialized technologies, the other generic technologies. Nowadays no individual firm can gain control of more than a subset of the search space. Innovation increasingly depends on strong scientific capabilities and on the ability to interact with science and scientific institutions in order to explore the search space (McKelvey, Orsenigo and Pammolli, chapter 3 in this book; and Henderson, Orsenigo and Pisano, 1999).

In *chemicals*, learning processes based on formal search processes have been present since the beginning of the history of the industry, with the diffusion of the "synthetic dyestuff model" (which introduced a scientific base to innovation) and, later on, with the development of organic chemistry (related to the understanding of the chemical structure of new molecules and the possibility of exploiting economies of scope in knowledge for the development of different organic products). This has led to the presence of firms with large R&D departments (some of which have been active since the beginning of the industry) and to a greater role for universities and other scientific organizations. Second, changes in knowledge and learning processes have been accompanied by the development of new products that were radically different from previous ones, and by the emergence of different actors and organizations. Let us take the second major change in the industry, polymer chemistry (in the 1920s), based on the idea that materials consist of long chains of molecules – polymers – linked together by chemical bonds. This change led to the development of materials by design, in which the scientific understanding of chemical composites is the basis for different product applications. Polymer chemistry provided a common technological base for developing applications and product differentiation in five distinct markets: plastics, fibers, rubbers, surface coatings and adhesives. The other major change in the industry, the development of chemical engineering and the concept of unit operation (1915 – introduced by Arthur D. Little at MIT), broke down chemical processes into a limited number of basic components, common to many product lines. This development became the general-purpose technology of the chemical sector. It allowed the separation of process innovation from product innovation: process innovation became a commodity that could be traded. In general, one can claim that these changes led to a transformation of firms' learning processes away from trial and error procedures to a science-based approach to industrial research.

Third, advances in chemical disciplines such as polymer chemistry and chemical engineering have created the base for the greater codificability of knowledge. At the same time, firms' behavior has enhanced the transferability of chemical technologies. Separability and transferability made possible the transaction of technology in the chemical industry and the emergence of new markets for engineering and process design services for chemical plants. Fourth, this type of knowledge base has implied that internal R&D has been complemented by external links and knowledge. Nowadays in chemicals, innovation requires interaction between R&D capabilities and external sources of scientific and technological knowledge (Cesaroni, et al. chapter 4 in this book; Arora and Gambardella, 1998; Freeman, 1968; and Rosenberg, 1998). Fifth, technological knowledge in chemicals is related to strict links between chemical companies and university research. This was certainly true in the past, but university-industry relationships are important even today, especially in some specific and emerging fields.

In *telecommunications equipment and services*, the knowledge base has been quite diversified because the sectoral system examined in this book is rather large, expanding rapidly and encompassing fixed communications (Dalum and Villumsen, 2003), satellite communications (Dalum, 2003), mobile phones (Hommen and Maninen, 2003) and Internet services (Corrocher, 2003). All these product groups present different features, but they are related in some way or another technologically. Moreover, this broad sectoral system has recently been affected by the processes of convergence between information and communication technologies and between ICT and broadcasting/audio-visual technologies. Until the advent of the Internet, the telecommunications service industry did not experience major technological and market discontinuities (Dalum and Villumsen, 2003). With the Internet and its open-network architecture, modular components and distributed intelligence, both the knowledge base and the types of actors and competencies have changed significantly (Corrocher, 2003).

The *software* sectoral system has a quite differentiated knowledge base, with extended complementarities. Here knowledge refers both to the control of the operations of the computer system providing the platform for the different functionalities and to the software employing these functionalities. However, the boundaries between operating systems and application software are becoming blurred because of the dynamics of the inward and the outward integration of software functions: upward (from system-level software to the user interface), and inward (from software designers closer to the definition of system resources – Steinmueller, chapter 6 in this book). The strength of the forces favoring the creation of generic platforms (and, therefore, favoring internationally dominant platform suppliers) is moderated by the continuing need for variety generation in the organizations producing the subsystems that allow these platforms to be customized, the potential for new methods of "platform" creation (based on the use of the Internet as a tool for collaborative innovation and the distribution of software products), the identification of emerging segments where dominance in "platform" creation remains contestable (such as embedded software) and the identification of areas of software that do not follow the "platform" model and remain in a predominant design state of variety generation (such as multimedia software). Much of the innovative challenge of the software industry therefore involves design innovation, not only of the basic operations of the information processing "machine" defined by software but of the very conceptualization of the information that needs to be processed. Nowadays the three broad product groups in which software can be examined (global package, situated software and middleware software) require different types of knowledge and learning processes. Global package software products are characterized by the search for generic solutions, and experience as a major input for innovation, with process innovation playing a key role. Situated and embedded software, on the other hand, have knowledge related to specific contexts and specialized purposes. Middleware software and integrated software solutions – such as product data managers and enterprise resource planning – aim to reach many users but focus on situated specific applications (Steinmueller, chapter 6 in this book; Mowery, 1996; and Torrisi, 1998).

In *machine tools*, innovation has been mainly incremental, and it is now becoming increasingly systemic. Knowledge about applications is very important: therefore, user-producer relationships as well as partnerships with customers are common. The knowledge base is embodied in skilled personnel on the shop floor with applied technical qualifications and in design engineers with long-term employment in the company. Internal training (particularly apprenticeships) is quite relevant. In small firms R&D is not done extensively and R&D cooperation is not common. In summary, the sector is characterized by local skills and user-producer interaction, with national differences in the structure of demand (which has, in turn, led to international differences in the rate and direction of technical change). Recently, however, the knowledge base has shifted from being purely mechanical to being mechanical, microelectronic and information-intensive, with increasing codification and the use of formal R&D. Products have increasingly been modularized and standardized. A key role is also played by information flows about components among producers of different inputs and technologies, such as lasers, materials or measurement and control devices (Wengel and Shapira, chapter 7 in this book; and Mazzoleni, 1999).

*3.2    Actors and networks are highly affected by the characteristics*
*of and changes in the knowledge base and differ greatly*
*across sectoral systems*

In the sectors examined the features and sources of knowledge have affected the types of actors and networks. We can identify the following points.

• The changes in knowledge and learning processes discussed above have implied major changes in the organization and characteristics of R&D. In most sectors R&D has been increasingly decentralized, externalized and internationalized (Coriat and Weinstein, chapter 9 in this book). This has happened in conjunction with an increasing focus on market-oriented R&D, the growth of external sources of knowledge and the need to obtain access to knowledge about markets or to key technological or scientific resources. The organization and the features of R&D have differed greatly across groups of sectors. While in chemicals and pharmaceuticals large-scale internal R&D plays a major role, with key links with universities, the emergence of biotechnology has led to an increased role for science and for R&D projects among large pharmaceutical firms, NBFs and universities. In other sectors, such as telecommunications and software, R&D requires the integration of different competencies and sources. Finally, in machine tools little formal R&D is done in most small and medium-sized machinery producers, while intense informal innovative activity is carried out on the shop floor because knowledge is embodied in experienced human capital.

• The combination of a rich, multidisciplinary and multi-source knowledge base and rapid technological change has implied a great heterogeneity of actors in most sectors.

• In addition to firms within a sector, some actors have proven particularly important for innovation. In particular, suppliers (and co-invention involving suppliers or users) have become a key aspect of the organization of innovative activities.

• Suppliers and users have also affected the boundaries of sectoral systems, by greatly affecting sectoral linkages and interdependencies.

- Demand, as composed by users and by consumers, has often proven important in several respects: a major source of the redefinition of the boundaries of a sectoral system; a stimulus for innovation; and a factor shaping the organization of innovative and production activity. In addition, the emergence of new demand or the transformation of existing demand has been one of the major elements of the change in sectoral systems over time.
- In all sectors universities have played a key role in basic research and human capital formation, and in some sectors (such as biotechnology and software) they have also been a source of start-ups, and even innovation.
- In sectoral systems such as software and biotechnology and pharmaceuticals new actors, including venture capital, have emerged over time.
- Financial organizations have played a different role according to the stage of the industry life cycle. When industry matures or large firms are relevant, capital constraints become lighter and much investment is self-financed. Conversely, for start-ups in emerging or new high-tech sectors (e.g. biotechnology and software), capital constraints are very high and specific financial intermediaries, such as venture capital, are important. In this respect, observed differences across sectors and countries do not matter significantly except for the well-known distinction between capital-market-based economies and bank-based economies (Rivaud-Danset, 2002; and Dubocage, 2002).
- Sectoral specificities in actors and networks have been relevant.

A brief discussion of the relevant actors and networks in each sectoral system is provided below.

### 3.2.1 *Pharmaceuticals and biotechnology: the division of innovative labor and networks among firms and non-firm organizations*

The change in the knowledge base discussed above has led to a different organization of innovative activity within and across firms. A division of labor has taken place between NBFs that lacked experience in clinical testing and established companies that (over time) adopted molecular biology. Networks of collaborative relations (facilitated by the science base and by the abstract and codified nature of knowledge generated by the NBFs) emerged in the sector. Further, mergers and acquisitions allowed established firms to obtain complementary knowledge for the development of innovative products. As of now, the pharmaceutical/biotechnology sectoral system has a structure of innovative actors that includes large firms, NBFs, small firms and individuals (such as scientists or NBF entrepreneurs). In addition, a very rich set of non-firm organizations and institutions affect innovation greatly, ranging from universities to the public and private research organizations, the financial system and venture capital, the legal system and IPR regimes. Demand channeled through agencies, physicians and the health system, and institutions (such as regulation) played a significant role in the diffusion of new drugs. Nowadays the innovativeness and competitiveness of the largest pharmaceutical firms depends on strong scientific capabilities and on the ability to produce and interact, on the one hand, with science and scientific organizations (in order to explore such a complex space) and, on the other, with specialized innovative firms (in order to develop new products) (McKelvey, Orsenigo and Pammolli, chapter 3 in this book).

### 3.2.2 Chemicals: large multinational firms and a vertical division of labor

In chemicals, the structure of the sectoral system has been centered around large firms, which have been the major source of innovation over a long period of time. Large R&D expenditures, economies of scale and scope (Chandler, 1990), the cumulativeness of technical advance and commercialization capabilities have given these firms major innovative and commercial advantages (Arora, Gambardella and Garcia-Fontes, 1998). The changes in the knowledge base discussed above have affected the types of actors and networks. As mentioned previously, with the diffusion of the synthetic dyestuff model firms scaled up their R&D departments and the role of universities increased. The introduction of polymer chemistry in the 1920s affected the structure of the industry, as knowledge about the characteristics of different market segments became important, with the result that firms had to develop extensive linkages with downstream markets. The other major change related to the development of chemical engineering, and the concept of a unit of operation led to an increasing division of labor between chemical companies and technology suppliers with the rise of the specialized engineering firms, which developed vertical links with chemical companies. In this period university research continued to be important for the development of innovations, and links between university and industry increased. In addition, advances in chemical disciplines and the separability and transferability of knowledge increased the transfer of chemical technologies. Thus, there has also been a greater role for licensing by large firms, which, in turn, increased knowledge diffusion. It must be noted that large firms also licensed process technology and that the SEFs did not develop radically new processes. Rather, they acted as independent licensors on behalf of other firms' technology. The increasing reliance on external links for complementary scientific and technological knowledge has led to the emergence of networks of three types: inter-firm, university-industry, and user-producer in specialty segments. However, the relevant networks have changed in relation to the type of knowledge base. In the synthetic dyestuff model, firms developed links with universities and with users. In polymer chemistry and with the diffusion of chemical engineering, networks between producers and users, industry-university networks and vertical networks between chemical companies and engineering contractors have been common, with the use of mergers and acquisitions to related and unrelated sectors in order to acquire capabilities (Cesaroni et al., chapter 4 in this book). In general, however, the inventive capability of a country depends heavily upon the strength of the underlying universities and public research organizations. In this sense, the innovation process of firms relies to a great extent upon research carried out by the universities and by the public research centers of their own countries.

### 3.2.3  *Telecommunications equipment and services: the coexistence of large integrated actors and of small actors specialized in segments or niches*

The process of convergence has generated the entry of several new actors from various previously separated industries, each one emphasizing different sets of competencies. For example, in telecommunications equipment and networks, firms may range from incumbent telecommunications equipment suppliers and incumbent network operators to new entrant telecommunications operators, cable TV operators and alternative network providers (Dalum and Villumsen, 2003). In Internet services, firms may range from Internet service providers to Internet content providers, e-commerce companies and software- and Internet-specialized consulting companies. Specialized competencies and specific knowledge have increasingly become a key asset for firms' survival and growth. Even more important in the new telecommunications environment is the combination of existing and new competencies – e.g. software programming, network management and content provision – that traditionally belonged to different companies (Corrocher, 2003). Also in this sector, networks among a variety of actors (not only firms, but also standard-setting organizations and research organizations) are relevant. Demand plays a key role in innovation, not just in terms of user-producer interaction but also in terms of emerging characteristics. This is particularly true in the Internet services sector, where the changing requirements of the final users – from standardized services, such as Internet access and e-mails, to more complex applications such as Intranets, Extranets and platforms for electronic commerce – have stimulated firms to upgrade the quality of their services.[1]

### 3.2.4 Software: the specialization of global players and local producers alike

In software, the changing knowledge base and the blurring boundaries between operation system and application software have created an evolving division of labor among users, "platform" developers and specialized software vendors, and a further tension between horizontal integration and specialization. The historical role of computer producers has largely been displaced by a division of labor between software and hardware "platform" producers, which is governed by the needs of the other as well as by the aim to preserve market position. In the case of the PC this is characterized by the existence of a large installed base with specialized applications and operating system software with high switching costs (Bresnahan and Greenstein, 1998). The SSI in software, however, is incomplete without the addition of companies that utilize these platforms to deliver enterprise-critical applications. Many of these applications continue to be self-produced by organizations that use the tools either provided as part of the platform or available from the development tools markets. The specialized generic platforms, however, are creating a market for specialized software producers the outputs of which are aimed at the customization of the needs of a particular class of users. In some software product groups, such as embedded software, this division of

---

[1] Networks, for example, played a role in the case of GSM. GSM's success could, in fact, be ascribed not only to the strategies of a few innovative producers but also to the role played by a variety of quite different actors: PTOs and PTTs, standard-setting organizations and research organizations. GSM was introduced by a Nordic consortium formed by national PTOs/PTTs with the major involvement of key producers such as Ericsson and Nokia. These firms were combined in a regional consortium that was based on a close historical collaboration between Nordic producers and the Nordic PTOs/PTTs. These public sector actors had already been key to the development of the 1G standard NMT. These PTOs/PTTs cooperated within a formal organizational framework provided by CEPT. This regional Nordic consortium then became a pan-European standard, ratified by ETSI. The membership of ETSI consisted of PTOs/PTTs telecommunications equipment manufacturers, public research organizations and telecommunications service providers (there were 300 members).

The shift from CEPT to ETSI was also marked by a shift from a closed to an open approach to standard development. Public research organizations had a major role in the development of GSM, whereas they did not have a role in the development of NMT. For example, in Sweden Ericsson cooperated with universities. In addition, COST (European cooperation in the domain of technological and scientific research – a European intergovernmental agreement for promoting research by supporting public research organizations) heavily funded the development of GSM and made the results available to ETSI (Hommen and Manninen, 2003).

labor is particularly high, but it appears to be threatened by the need for more consistent and reliable approaches, which can be achieved only by concentrating development resources in the production of software platforms (Steinmueller, chapter 6 in this book). By contrast, in the ERP and open-source software product groups, variety generation is being accompanied by a growing diversification of the actors and ever more complex network relationships among them, with universities and public research organizations increasingly involved in supporting the knowledge infrastructure for such developments. In enterprise software a transformation in demand from large industrial users is emerging. However, as the competencies required by enterprise systems are so extended that no one supplier can master the entire range required to satisfy demand in all sectors, scope is created for the growth of specialized niche software producers and systems integrators (D'Adderio, 2001b).

### 3.2.5    *Machine tools: specialized firms and local networks*
In machine tools, firms are highly specialized and often focused on specific vertical segments. Networks here differ from country to country, because the types of products and the different users and demand structures have led to different sectoral systems, each of which has been innovative in its own way. In any case, local financial organizations and vertical links with users play a major role. In addition, any nation with a significant machine tool industry sought in the past to strengthen these "providers of productivity" by public (partly indirect) measures – for example, the German Manufacturing Technology Programs or the US Manufacturing Extension Partnership. Thus, organizations and networks engaged in technology transfer in a broad sense developed. While "old" actors (industrial and professional associations, specialized research organizations, user firms, producers, traditional suppliers, etc.) still dominate, "new" actors are appearing on the horizon (such as the "communities" related to specific technological shifts – e.g. fuel cells or nanotechnology). Market mechanisms increasingly show up in previously "non-market" relationships, such as cooperation within industrial/professional associations, or special customer-supplier interactions. And public-private industry consortia increasingly complement the latter (Wengel and Shapira, chapter 7 in this book).

### 3.3    *The role of national as well as sectoral institutions is relevant for innovation*

The main points on institutions developed in this book can be summarized as follows.

- In all the sectors examined, institutions have played a major role in affecting the rate of technological change, the organization of innovative activity and the performance of sectoral systems.
- As is shown below, each sector is characterized by the presence of a different set of relevant institutions.
- Some of these institutions are national and are present in all the sectors (and in all European countries), although with different effects on innovation and performance according to the sector or the country.
- Other institutions are sector-specific (i.e. they are present only in one sector).
- In some cases the relevant institutions in a sector have been the outcome of the interplay between sectoral and national variables (Casper and Soskice, chapter 10 in this book; and Coriat and Weinstein, chapter 9 in this book). In broad terms, one can identify in Europe an Anglo-Saxon (liberal market economy) model and a German/Scandinavian (coordinated market economy) model. In the first model (exemplified by the United Kingdom) the national institutional framework is characterized by liberal labor markets, a shareholder system, R&D links between university and industry, and a capital market system with a market for corporate control. In the second model (exemplified by Germany) the national institutional framework is characterized by long-term employee careers within companies, a stakeholder system, apprenticeship systems, close links between industry and technical universities in skill formation and, finally, a bank-based financial system (Casper and Soskice, chapter 10 in this book). In biotechnology, software and telecommunications, the trend is toward the outsider/shareholder model with an external labor market. Conversely, in machine tools (as in automobiles), the forms of corporate governance are more internal. The same holds for the labor market (Coriat and Weinstein, chapter 9 in this book; and Geoffron and Rubinstein, 2002).

Here a brief discussion of the relevant institutions in each sectoral system is advanced.

In *pharmaceuticals*, national health systems and regulation have played a major role in affecting the direction of technical change, in some cases even blocking or retarding innovation. In addition, the form of corporate governance is closely related to the country of origin: the outsider system in the United Kingdom and insider system in Germany, with France in between (Geoffron and Rubinstein, 2002). Patents have played a major role in the appropriability of the returns from innovations.

In *chemicals*, institutions have played a critical role concerning two different situations: the restructuring processes and patent policy.

Concerning the restructuring processes, in the past (during and after World War I) national governments allowed or promoted the creations of cartels and national giants. Germany and the United Kingdom are clear example in this respect. While in Germany the presence of chemical trade associations made it easier to create a link between the government and the individual firms, in the United Kingdom the absence of such associations necessitated a deeper intervention by the authorities. The British state reorganized the chemical industry (traditionally independent of the government) in order to supply chemicals for war needs. As a consequence of this "forced" coordination, the leaders of the largest chemical firms came to know one another. Both in the United Kingdom and in Germany different trade associations and alliances among firms emerged. In the United Kingdom the chemical industry organized itself into the Association of Chemical Manufacturers. In Germany the eight largest dye producers formed a "quasi-cartel." The interesting aspect of this situation is that, apart from their role in wartime, the stronger interaction between chemical firms was influential in defining the structure of the chemical industry in the inter-war period. Since the 1980s the chemical industry has entered a new phase of restructuring, in which public policy has played a role as well. In this period governments have managed the restructuring process to a large extent, especially in France and Italy.

The second important role of institutions in chemicals is related to patent policies. These are especially relevant to small firms. Indeed, proper forms of intellectual property rights and sufficiently strong patent protection supported the activity of smaller technology-based firms. In turn, this created the bases for a division of labor between technology suppliers and users, and allowed the development of markets for technology. This pattern is particularly evident in the United States, where patent protection has been properly defined. By contrast, European markets for technology are far from being developed. This requires policy support for intellectual property rights.

In *software*, intellectual property rights play a major role in strengthening appropriability, but they have been greatly affected by the emerging open-source movement. In addition, standards play a major role (Steinmueller, chapter 6 in this book). Standard development organizations, country and industry consortia (such as PDES and ProSTEP) and standard-setting alliances (such as the Object Management Group) are very important. Networks of users also play an increasingly important function, as the involvement of the Manufacturing Domain Task Force in the development of standards for PDM software illustrates. Users also often gather around user mailing lists (e.g. the International PDM Users Group for PDM software): these are used as vehicles to test and compare the performance and capabilities of competing software products (D'Adderio, 2002).

In *machine tools*, internal and regional labor markets and local institutions and organizations (e.g. local banks) have played a major role in influencing the international advantages of specific areas. In the United Kingdom and the United States, formal and informal institutional support for machine tool companies has typically been "thinner" than in Japanese, German and Italian regions. Trust-based, close relationships at the regional level have, over a long time, ensured sufficient financing of the innovation and expansion plans of family businesses in Germany and Italy. The consequence has been that other riskier or more expensive ways were rarely used and more radical changes seldom took place. In Germany, vocational training has greatly fostered the development of skills in the machine tools industry. The "Maschinenbau-Ingenieur" (mechanical engineer) in the German higher education system went along with the predominance of mechanical innovations. Fairly stable employment conditions and company employment strategies (internal labor markets) formed the background for cumulative knowledge building and incremental innovations (Soskice, 1997). Standards have a long tradition, not only with respect to health and safety but also with respect to economies of scale. They built a basis for the share of development tasks between the machine tool makers and the suppliers of components and peripheral equipment. This adds again to a predominantly incremental innovation regime. The European Union's machine directive was fundamental for the realization of the Common Market, particularly in the machine tool industry. And the way it was shaped probably influenced the development of the industry and the respective success of certain companies (and member states). The "self-certification" or relatively open definition in the directive turned out to favor the companies that were already more competitive internationally rather than opening up competition (Wengel and Shapira, chapter 7 in this book).

Finally, in *telecommunications*, the roles of regulation, liberalization, privatization and standards have been key in the organization and performance of the sector. As discussed in Dalum and Villumsen (2003), liberalization and privatization have had major effects on the behavior and performance of incumbents and have transformed the structure of the industry.

## 4 The coexistence of the local, national and global dimensions

Another major result coming out of this book is that, in the sectors studied, the global, national and local dimensions coexist.

In the *pharmaceutical and biotechnology* sectoral system, European countries exhibit differences in terms of national institutions, demand, networks of knowledge acquisitions, etc., and such national differences have appeared historically to affect the national firms (McKelvey, Orsenigo and Pammolli, chapter 3 in this book). Over time, the markets for knowledge as well as the markets for products are becoming increasingly international, as are regulations and scientific and technological knowledge flows. Nevertheless, national institutional arrangements appear to influence not only the number and types of new biotechnology firms but also their specialization into different areas, as evidenced by the differences between Germany and the United Kingdom (Casper and Soskice, chapter 10 in this book). In Sweden, firms tend to engage in collaborations in knowledge areas at the intersection of biotechnology and pharmaceuticals with international partners – especially American and British ones. Moreover, local interaction among firms in order to collaborate to develop new knowledge has been uncommon in Sweden, while interaction among small firms and local universities has been more likely (McKelvey, Alm and Riccaboni, 2002).

The *chemical* sectoral system has always been global. For many years the industry has shown considerable flows of international investments and engineering and process licenses. While, up to the 1980s, foreign investments were to a large extent confined to advanced countries, in recent decades there has been an increase toward the developing countries as well. Indeed, chemical investments in these countries have become a critical strategy for the major multinational chemical firms from the developed world, and to some extent the ability to invest in these countries has become a major factor in enhancing their competitiveness, and – more generally – an important element for competition in the industry. Moreover, apart from FDI in plants, developing countries have become important areas for inflows of process licenses and engineering services. Again, the competitiveness of the chemical firms in developed countries is often related to the ability to operate and invest in these markets, as well as to the ability to complement these investments with related technology flows through licenses or engineering services. Analyses of investment flows (Arora, Gambardella and Garcia-Fontes, 1998) show that the European chemical industry has moved its investments abroad. However, the same can be said for the US and Japanese chemical industries. This means that there has been an increasing globalization process for this industry, with a significant increase in the number of chemical plants built in Asia, coupled with a decrease in the domestic share of Japanese firms in Japan, American firms in the United States and European firms in the European Union. In general, there is a trend toward the location of plants near customers and fast-growing regions, where demand and consumption are stronger. This trend is also related to an increase in product differentiation and the customization of plants, together with a growing concern for reducing transport costs.

In *enterprise software*, while centralizing their R&D activities, global players have been forced to address the needs of customers at the local level. A focus on local knowledge has become increasingly mandatory for software development, to the point that a popular strategy by large producers is to locate near key customers in order to acquire sector- and firm-specific (user) knowledge (D'Adderio, 2002). An increasing trend sees the configuration of new individual software modules according to the geographical determinants of a leading market. For example, the creation of SAP's "campus management" module for universities according to the characteristics of the dominant US market (a local module) is then used as a global standard and implemented across all other universities worldwide that are adopting SAP. This suggests a cycle of adaptation and a continuing tension between the local and global levels and vice versa, corresponding to the tension between greater generality and greater customization of the software product (D'Adderio, 2002).

*Machine tools* are often local in the organization of supply although they are global in terms of demand and outputs. Data from the Fraunhofer ISI *Manufacturing Innovation Survey* 1999 in Germany show that almost one-third of inputs comes from suppliers within fifty kilometers. Only around 10 percent of the output is delivered to customers within the region. Similar figures are observed when the border is set at the national level. The same variability holds for knowledge flows, which can range from very local to very global (see Breschi and Lissoni, 2001). The recruitment of skilled shop-floor personnel is usually a local activity. For higher education workers the strategies are increasingly international, and the VDMA lobbies for an extension of the German "green card." At the same time, the relocation of production or the acquisition of firms abroad in order to fulfill local content expectations, to reach customers or to round up the product range is now common. Many institutions relevant to the sector are national (such as the education system), while others are mainly European (Wengel and Shapira, chapter 7 in this book).

## 5    Coevolutionary processes in sectoral systems

In sectoral systems, changes in the knowledge base or in demand affect the characteristics of the actors, the organization of R&D and of the innovative process, the type of networks and the structure of the market and the relevant institutions. All these variables, in turn, lead to further modifications in the technology, the knowledge base, demand and so on.

In *pharmaceuticals*, the interactions between knowledge, actors and institutions have shaped the evolution of the SI. Changes in the knowledge base and in the relevant learning processes of firms have induced deep transformations in the behavior and structure of the agents and in their relationships with each other. However, the specific ways these transformations have occurred across countries have been profoundly different, due to the details of the institutional structure of each country. Thus, in addition to supply and demand, institutions and incentives have also influenced the development of knowledge. For example, the nature of the process of drug discovery and drug development had an important impact on the patterns of competition and on market structure. Overall market competition and market structure were dependent on the strategies and fortunes of individual companies, which were linked to different national contexts and/or international settings. Firms had diverse reactions in order to try to increase their "fit" and survive in their particular environment. These environments kept changing, not least due to innovations and choices made by all the constituent competitors. However, while these environments could previously be said to be national, now the defining characteristics are increasingly international (McKelvey, Orsenigo and Pammolli, chapter 3 in this book). Product approval regulations provided an incentive for more innovative strategies, at least for those firms and countries that had the capabilities to invest in the new technologies. Similarly, weak patent protection induced imitative strategies, but this effect was much less important for firms and countries that had developed strong technological and scientific capabilities (as, for example, Germany until the advent of the molecular biology revolution). Conversely, the introduction of stronger patent protection might have contributed to the practical disappearance of the Italian industry, which was, until the mid-1970s, one of the most successful producers of generics. As a final example, consider how the molecular biology revolution, by creating new competencies and a new technological regime, induced deep changes in the incentive structures within firms, universities, etc. (McKelvey, Orsenigo and Pammolli, chapter 3 in this book). In this process of adaptation and change, different dynamic processes lead to differential patterns of competition and performance.

Also, in *chemicals*, processes of coevolution have been present for technology, demand, markets, agents and institutions. One interesting example of a coevolutionary process in chemicals is related to the environmental issue. The chemical industry has often been accused of having considerable responsibility for pollution, and chemical firms have been ahead of others in becoming highly committed to solving environmental problems. Some significant accidents (e.g. Seveso and Bhopal) have contributed to the generation of widespread suspicion against chemical firms and the industry as a whole. This greater attention on the part of consumers to pollution and environmental problems has resulted in three different, but related, consequences. First, all developed countries have observed the rise of new markets for environmentally safe products that generate less pollution. Second, governments have paid greater attention to pollution, and have subsequently tried to impose regulations and define appropriate control measures in order to reduce waste production and pollution. Third, as a consequence of both trends, chemical firms have had to develop and adopt new production technologies (environmental technologies and "green" processes) and new products (e.g. less polluting solvents and paints). Moreover, rigid environmental standards and strong public pressure have had a positive influence on the environmental innovations of chemical firms. Indeed, another consequence of the growing attention to environmental issues has been the birth of an intermediate market for environmental technologies and engineering services related to environmental technologies. In a manner similar to the birth of the SEFs, providing process technologies in chemicals, new environmentally related SEFs have started to operate (especially in the United States), and a new market for environmental technologies and engineering services is about to emerge (Arduini and Cesaroni, 2001).

In *telecommunications equipment and services*, the early separation of the radio spectrum for use in one-way broadcasting and two-way telephony gave rise to an oligopolistic structure in the industry, which persisted for an extended period (Dalum and Villumsen, 2003). The convergence first between information and communication technologies and then between ICT and broadcasting/audio-visual technologies, together with the emergence of the Internet, inaugurated a more fluid market structure, with many different actors with different specialization and capabilities, and new types of users. This, in turn, has greatly expanded the boundaries of the sector by creating new segments and new opportunities – as well as national differences in the organization of innovation. Moreover, the emergence of the Internet has generated more pressure in favor of open standards, and has led to the rise of new actors such as ISPs and ICPs.

In *software*, since the early 1980s the spread of networked computing, embedded software and the Internet, the development of open-system architectures and open-source software, and the growth of Web-based network computing have led to the decline of large computer producers as developers of integrated hardware and software systems. This has led to the emergence of numerous specialized software companies, which innovate either in package software or in customized software, and to an increasing role for the university as the open source approach is adopted. This, in turn, has contributed to the expansion and growth of several software product groups, each of which has different types of products, firms and capabilities. Moreover, software distribution has also changed greatly in line with these developments, from licensing agreements in the early days to the rise of ISVs, to price discounts for package software, and (with the diffusion of the CD-ROM and the Internet) to shareware and freeware (the latter is particularly relevant with Linux – see Steinmueller, chapter 6 in this book). In *enterprise software*, higher demand for integration by user organizations has reinforced the role of existing actors (i.e. large producers of standardized integrated software solutions) as well as creating scope for new actors (i.e. systems integrators, specialized niche applications producers and software implementation consultants – D'Adderio, 2001a). The increasingly generic nature of large systems has also introduced a greater need for customization, whereby customer knowledge and requirements (expressed by global or industry-specific user group associations, such as SAP's higher education user group, or individual firms) have become an important source of input into the development of new or revised modules, with user groups attempting to influence the shaping of a system directly. In response to the increasing need for customization, large software producers are pursuing a higher level of internal specialization by creating subunits that address specific market segments and compete for resources with other units.

In *machine tools*, a major driving force for coevolutionary processes has been the demand from advanced customer sectors – namely automotive, aerospace and defense. In recent decades there has been an engagement in new production concepts ("lean production," teamwork, total quality management, etc.), growing environmental concern and a continuous incremental innovation in the products. As a consequence, in the machine tool sector incremental innovation has remained dominant, some internationalization of production has taken place and user relationships have become more market-driven. A coevolutionary process can be observed in the context of technological developments, chiefly in electronics but also with respect to new materials and micro- or nanotechnologies. Electronic devices constitute an increasing share of the value of machine tools, and IT systems (e.g. PCs, operating systems, the Internet) often determine technical solutions on how to control machine tools and on how to integrate them into company production systems. As a consequence, besides electrical engineers, computer scientists have partly replaced mechanical engineers in the design departments of machine tool manufacturers and brought with them other ways of working. Some firms have followed strategies of outsourcing or of separating such units. At the shop-floor level, a related change in the qualifications that are required has taken place. New apprenticeships have developed (e.g. "Mechatroniker"); others are disappearing. However, the institution of the "Facharbeiter" in Germany does not seem at risk. Links to basic research are now looked for and patenting has been growing strongly in recent years.

## 6      A note on sectoral systems in services

As there are several sectoral systems of innovation and production in manufacturing, so there are several sectoral systems in services. The taxonomies by Miozzo and Soete (2001) and Sundbo and Gallouj (2000) show how different services are, and how rich and differentiated a taxonomy of sectoral systems in services can be. Although it is difficult to generalize, it is possible to identify, as in the papers by Tether and Metcalfe (2003) and Tether, Metcalfe and Miles (2002), some general features of sectoral systems in services. These features and dimensions are also present in manufacturing, but in services they often have a prominent place. The first point is that, in services, products are closely related to processes. Often innovation has restructured the SSI by creating markets for specialized equipment and suppliers, such as the one related to the clinic-based delivery of surgical service in the case of IOLs. In this case the removal of cataracts, combined with the implantation of an artificial lens, was achieved by the change in procedure from that requiring one surgeon with craft techniques within capital-intensive contexts to a routinized procedure that can be carried out in a local medical centre (Metcalfe and James, 2002).

Second, great relevance is given to knowledge embodied in equipment and in people, and to changes in the domain of this knowledge. This is the result of the diffusion of ICT, as well as instrumentation and other devices. Thus, the link with manufacturing (and the related transformation of the knowledge domain that has taken place recently) is quite relevant in most services. In airports, the case of runway capacity extensions shows a move away from direct operating experience and observations toward the use of sophisticated IT support tools (such as the final approach separation tool that regulates the spacing between arriving aircraft). This is also associated with the use of new types of knowledge (such as mathematical modeling, computer science and so on) and with the pressure to change the use of integers as units of distance in order to measure minimum-distance separations better. R&D, on the other hand, is less relevant for services than for high-tech manufacturing, except in sectors such as software or telecommunications services.

Third, actors such as suppliers (of equipment) and users play a major role. Interaction is particularly important in services. As the cases of air traffic services in airports and the creation of runway capacity show, the innovation process is usually the outcome of the interaction of the service provider and the service user. Indeed, this co-production is much more relational than in manufacturing, in which the manufacturer may change unilaterally the organization of production. It may involve both joint operations and the search for mutually acceptable solutions (Tether and Metcalfe, 2003). In retailing, the actors involved include food suppliers, logistics companies, retailers and consumers (Harvey, Nyberg and Metcalfe, 2002). Universities and research centers, on the other hand, have less relevance in services than in manufacturing. Thus, as in manufacturing, demand is particularly important for innovation, and the process of construction of demand is central to the emergence and growth of specific SSIs. The close interaction with users is quite relevant in the creation of new services (and, consequently, new sectoral systems).

Fourth, institutions play a significant role, both in terms of procedures and mechanisms (as in the mechanisms of airport slots discussed by Tether and Metcalfe, 2003) and in terms of formal regulations, standards and privatization. Procedural change plays a major role in services. In the air traffic service case, procedural change related to the bunching of aircraft away from the "first come first served" basis, and the use of dual glideslopes for aircraft landing, is negotiated between the service provider (ATC) and the users (airlines). In the case of medical services – IOLs – innovation results from the interaction between clinicians and the different national ophthalmic health systems, connected by international networks of clinicians and transnational health companies. Various practices and theories within ophthalmology played a major role (Metcalfe and James, 2002). In the case of embedded software, efforts to ensure safety involve considerable potential for displacing own-production in favor of specialized embedded software "system" producers that can invest the resources necessary for "robust" systems by serving many different clients (Steinmueller, chapter 6 in this book).

Fifth, services are less international than manufacturing, and are usually produced locally. However, new technologies are allowing a more extensive division of labor that also has a geographical dimension, such as the decentralization of back office functions (routine operations) and the centralization of control functions and of value-added services (core control functions). Thus, the internationalization of services in terms of the spatial division of labor has taken place, with certain functions being internationalized with the diffusion of ICT. These tendencies are observable in ERP software markets, where the generic systems produced by SAP and the American competitors Oracle and Microsoft rely upon international markets for achieving the necessary investments in platform development and an international supplier network for accommodating user needs for specialized "modules" to customize the platform for specific applications (D'Adderio, 2002).

Sixth, services show continuous change and transformation over time. Services have all been affected by ICT, which has triggered major changes at all levels. They have also become more and more characterized by the presence of professional management. In addition, as stated above, a major geographical division of labor has taken place. In retailing, Harvey, Nyberg and Metcalfe (2002) show the major transformation of grocery distribution in terms of leading actors from global food manufacturers to retailers and supermarkets, and from the production of generic products with the exploitation of economies of scale to the differentiation of areas and stores and a major attention to consumer interface. Here, however, national differences due to historical starting conditions and contexts have affected the specific path of transformation. In the United Kingdom, for example, retailing is an integrated business and the retailer orchestrates the business. In Sweden, too, retailers have a leading role, but the cooperative movement tradition led to a federation of end-retailers and to a more decentralized pattern of local and small-scale production.

The previous example indicates that country differences in organization and performance raise relevant issues for services. First (as shown in the case of retailing), differences in the organization of sectoral systems may be due to the local content of services. The case of IOLs also emphasizes the fact that differences in ophthalmic health systems played a major role in affecting the international competitiveness of countries. However, the internationalization of services, the spread of professionalization and the role of multinational companies may introduce both local and international dimensions in the innovation process. Again, the case of IOLs has shown that differences in ophthalmic health systems and the role of major ophthalmic multinationals have greatly shaped the system in various countries. Second (and relatedly), the interaction of these elements has major consequences for performance. Again, in the case of IOLs, the interaction of national health systems and multinational ophthalmic corporations resulted in the leadership of the United States after an early predominance of Europe (and, particularly, of the United Kingdom). However, the international performance of various countries in services may be difficult to assess in a clear and uniform way, because the value of services may be difficult to measure and because services may be organized in different ways in different countries. In general, however, as Tether, Metcalfe and Miles (2002) mention, the United States has adopted new technologies more rapidly and more widely and has applied scientific management and commercial logic to processes in services more consistently than Europe has.

Finally, public policy considerations stress different aspects for services from those for manufacturing: skilled labor training (a key element for services); advanced regulations; standards for professionalization; responsiveness to change (see, for example, the case of GSM); the diffusion of IT in the provision of high-quality services; and, eventually, the support of small and medium-size enterprises in some advanced services (such as knowledge-intensive business services – see Tether, Metcalfe and Miles, 2002).

## 7   International performance seen through the lens of sectoral systems

What about the relationship between specific dimensions of sectoral systems and the international innovative performance of firms and countries? Some remarks may be advanced in this respect.

- In several sectoral systems, differences between Europe, the United States and Japan in the sources of knowledge, and types and competencies of actors, networks and institutions, have greatly affected the international performance of countries.
- The lack of success of some European countries in some sectors has been due to problems and deficiencies in their sectoral systems.
- Even within the sectors in which Europe does not generally fare well, those European countries that specialize in product groups with knowledge, actors and institutional requirements that match their specific institutional framework are successful.

For a more in-depth discussion of the international performance of sectoral systems, see Coriat, Malerba and Montobbio, chapter 11 in this book. These points are discussed only briefly below.

### 7.1   *Pharmaceuticals and biotechnology: major inter-country differences and the dominance of the US model*

Sectoral systems of innovation differ drastically between those of the United States and those of the various European countries. These differences have affected the innovative performance of firms in the different countries.

### 7.1.1    The United States: a case of success in biotechnology

The random screening period and, even more, the molecular biology revolution has seen the United States moving into a position of leadership. The United States had a first-mover advantage, but also developed an SSI capable of generating a high rate of innovation. A transformation in the vertical structure of the industry, new patterns of the division of labor in the innovative process, the development of a market for technology and new forms of interaction among firms and other institutions all took place very rapidly. The United States evolved into a highly decentralized but also integrated structure, successful in combining exploration and exploitation. Large pharmaceutical firms as well as new biotechnology firms have both been major innovators. Large pharmaceutical companies were very fast in adopting biotechnology: these large, innovative and more experienced firms had an advantage in the exploitation of these techniques (Owen-Smith et al. 2002). Similarly, a wave of NBFs entered the industry and innovated by introducing new biotechnology products.

In addition, non-firm organizations and institutions in the United States played a major role as facilitators of innovation. The university system and the NIH have provided advanced basic research and trained scientists and researchers in medicinal chemistry, pharmacology, biochemistry, enzymology and molecular genetics. The rapid adaptation of academic norms permitted a fast translation of academic results into industrial applications, with easy access to capital. Stronger IPR regimes also favored the early days of biotechnology. The US government strongly supported patent protection for intellectual property rights in pharmaceuticals, and provided effective regulation of the safety and efficacy of products and processes in this industry. This regulatory climate did not restrict generic experimentation. Rather, it positively affected the formation of new firms. Finally, the interfaces between the various components of the US pharmaceutical sectoral system have allowed intense interaction between different actors, giving the American industry a major advantage over its European rival (Henderson, Orsenigo and Pisano, 1999).

### 7.1.2    Biotechnology in Europe: the emergence of specialization in product groups

Compared to the United States, the large European pharmaceutical companies did not benefit from the set of non-firm organizations and institutions that characterized the American sectoral system. First of all, basic research has not been funded so extensively as in the United States, and has had fewer incentives and less support to encourage change and redirection into new areas. A few pockets of research at European universities were at the frontier, and in general advanced scientific competencies were not widespread. Moreover, some European countries remained attached to the more academic focus of their national research organizations, with research separated from universities and confined to specialized research laboratories. In these organizations, research tended to have little interaction with teaching, medical practice or industrial research (except in the cases where biomedical research was conducted in medical schools). Also, university-industry links were less developed than in the United States (McKelvey, Orsenigo and Pammolli, chapter 3 in this book).

In biotechnology, European funding has been administered at the national level, with strongly contrasting approaches, and has either been dispersed across a very large number of small laboratories (thus being unable to reach a critical mass) or concentrated in too few centers of excellence. In addition, compared to the United States, in Europe (with the exception of the United Kingdom) there were less stringent approval procedures. This created less competitive pressure and negatively affected potentially innovative firms. Moreover, the consolidation of national health systems in Europe led to various forms of price regulation based on equity considerations. In most cases, price regulation (particularly in France and Italy) was organized in such a way as to protect the domestic industry, offering little incentive to radical innovations: they favored incremental innovation and "me too" products. Thus, invasive regulation in prices coexisted with softer attitudes in product approval procedures. Finally, in Europe, the organization of labor and company laws constrained the possibility of achieving a high mobility of people, both across firms and from university to industry. In the past, venture capital was not abundant as in the United States, although many other sources of funds (mainly through government programs) have been available (McKelvey, Orsenigo and Pammolli, chapter 3 in this book).

However, in Europe, as Casper and Kettler (2002) and Casper and Soskice (chapter 10 in this book) show, countries may end up specializing in segments of biotechnology that are less in tune with their national institutional frameworks. German biotechnology firms have specialized in platform technologies that are then sold to other research laboratories (for example, consumable kits to rationalize common molecular biology laboratory processes). These technologies are more generic and more cumulative than the standard therapeutic products, are often related to the development of equipment for pharmaceutical firms, and have a library of core technologies that are then customized for specific market niches. These features fit the German institutional framework (characterized by "insider" corporate governance, long-term internal relationships between firms and employees, and investments in firm-specific knowledge) better than the standard therapeutic products. On the other hand, firms in the United Kingdom specialized in standard therapeutic products that were related to the ones developed by the dominant American industry. Here the UK institutional framework has been characterized by features some-what similar to the American system. However, over the years UK ven-ture capital has moved away from high-risk biotechnology projects. In addition, managers of UK venture funds are relatively unsophisticated. Finally, British biotechnology firms have a lower scientific intensity than those in the United States, and basic research does not have the scale of the American one (Casper and Kettler, 2002; and Casper and Soskice, chapter 10 in this book).[2]

### 7.2    Telecommunications: international performance in global as well as local systems

In telecommunications equipment hardware, European countries have a market structure similar to that of the United States: large global players coexisting with specialized firms (Dalum and Villumsen, 2003). Con-versely, in Internet services, national features strongly influence innova-tion and the rate and the direction of technological change. In the various European countries the characteristics of local markets differ greatly, as the cases of the United Kingdom and Italy show (Corrocher, 2003). Major differences also exist between Europe, the United States and Japan.

In Internet services, the advent of free service in Europe has seriously undermined the position of ISPs while strengthening the position of con-tent and network providers. In markets with a well-developed network and with a high level of competition – the United States and Japan, but also the United Kingdom and the Scandinavian countries – incumbents and new entrants compete both in traditional communications services and in more advanced services over the Internet. In these countries, the devel-opment of new access technologies and of increasingly efficient trans-mission protocols stimulates the introduction of value-added services, which can be customized to the specific requirements of users. On the other hand, countries such as Italy, Spain and France have a less devel-oped Internet market, not only in terms of the diffusion of services among potential users but also in terms of infrastructure and competition among

---

[2] As to Sweden, McKelvey, Alm and Riccaboni (2002) show that European firms are increasingly carrying out joint research with Swedish firms. This indicates that Swedish firms have research projects that are highly valuable on the international market, probably linked to the traditionally high standard of Swedish research in medical fields and to a specialization in some bioengineering fields.

providers. These countries generally do not have a wide installed base of cable TV infrastructure. In terms of institutional framework, the Internet sector greatly benefited from the process of liberalization. However, technological and market developments may anticipate and thus constrain regulators' decisions. This process is heavily dependent upon country-specific characteristics. As we have seen, the United Kingdom and Italy have had two different experiences: in the first case technological progress has been anticipated by changes in the regulatory framework, while in the second case the liberalization of the market has followed the process of technological convergence, without stimulating the development of innovations.

### 7.2.1    A case of European success and the role of institutions

In telecommunications, Europe has had a major success: GSM. As mentioned before, GSM was the result of the interplay of several factors: the presence of large, capable and innovative firms; an increase in external cooperative links; a regionally based consortium with close collaboration among actors; and the move to a pan-European standard ratified by European standard organizations (Hommen and Manninen, 2003). GSM success can not be ascribed solely to the strategies of a few innovative producers but to the collaboration of a variety of quite different actors: PTOs/PTTs, standard-setting organizations and research organizations.

### 7.2.2    The modification of the features of the Scandinavian model in telecommunications

As Casper and Soskice (chapter 10 in this book) note, recently in the telecommunications sectoral system some of the institutional features that characterize the Swedish national framework (such as long-term relationships between firms and employees) have been modified in order to take into account the new characteristics of the innovation process in mobile phones. Ericsson recognized that wireless technologies require open standards and the full exploitation of network effects. Thus, in the late 1990s Ericsson decided to make its latest system integration language open rather than proprietary, and sponsored the formation of new start-ups that were spin-offs from Ericsson and that aimed to develop products compatible with Ericsson's new generation of wireless technologies. While introducing this new policy of supporting open standards and new firm formation, Ericsson maintained some of the features of the Swedish system by allowing engineers leaving Ericsson to return if their start-up failed.

### 7.3    Chemicals: large multinational firms in global markets

For a long time the United States and Europe have had sectoral systems dominated by large multinational firms. The internal R&D of large chemical firms has been complemented by external links with other firms, universities, users and the SEFs. International leadership has always been associated with the same set of large US and European multinationals. However, over time international leadership has expanded from German firms, which strongly benefited from German university strengths (1870 to 1920), to American firms as well, which profited from the emergence of chemical engineering in American universities. The rise of the SEFs has reinforced this balanced leadership. In most countries, public policy directly aimed at innovation in the industry has not played a major role in innovation (except during World War II). Indirect policies through environmental regulation, strong IPR protection and university support, on the other hand, has (Cesaroni et al., chapter 4 in this book).

In analyzing international performances one cannot forget that the chemical industry is becoming more and more "global." This means not only that the national dimension might not be relevant in the analysis of competitiveness but that the multinational dimension might not be enough either. The case of specialty chemicals is representative in this respect. In specialty chemicals, national companies competing as oligopolists in predominantly national or regional (e.g. European) markets have become international companies competing against each other in the global market place. This has important implications. The process of specialization via mergers and acquisitions (consider the demerger of Zeneca from ICI, or the mergers of Zeneca with Astra, Ciba Geigy with Sandoz, ICI with Unilever and Hoechst with Rhône-Poulenc) has essentially meant that what was a national or regional oligopoly has been transformed into a global oligopoly. Within the sector competition is taking place between the six to twelve large firms that dominate the market. New entrants need to compete in terms of both scale and marketing. It is often at the level of marketing that new entrants find it most difficult to penetrate. This means that, in spite of the intense global competition, it is still possible for one or two firms to dominate each national market, because they effectively control access to consumers.

Hence, in general terms, it seems that the international performance of countries and regions is strictly linked to the presence of large multinational companies, which – in turn – is related to the presence of substantial and innovative local demand, strong research capabilities and an advanced scientific and technological knowledge base. Large firms locate their production plants and their R&D facilities according to the presence of these factors. However, the comparison between the US and the European chemical industries can also be conducted in terms of the respective capabilities of translating public research into commercial innovations. Inevitably, differences also emerge in product groups. In agrochemicals, the current discovery process requires the integration of various distinct scientific disciplines. Europe shows a high publication level in fields relevant to agrochemicals. However, the number of patents and products is low, indicating that Europe has difficulty in bringing its research to market. Contrary to scientifically more dynamic segments, in paints, coatings and printing inks European firms seem in a better position. In new materials the research effort is mainly public, as the private sector seems to wait for commercial opportunities. However, these large firms have been the main source of incremental innovation, with an important cumulative impact. In summary, in all these product groups the laboratories of large firms, frequently working in conjunction with users and/or outside specialists from academia or specialist firms, are the sources of incremental innovations. The scientific and technological base plays a key role in defining the competitive positions of different countries and regions in different product groups.

## 7.4    Software: American domination through specialization in standard global products and European success in custom products

### 7.4.1    Packaged software
In software, the competitive situation differs among product groups. A major distinction is between packaged and custom software. The United States dominates most markets for *packaged software*. The reasons for this dominance include several interconnected elements. US firms achieved first-mover advantages due to specific demand conditions: the US industry was ahead in the production and adoption of computers. The origins of this first-mover advantage and its consequences for the development of system and application software predated the advent of PCs, but this advantage was increased by the rapid diffusion of PCs during the 1980s. In the United States federal government investments also played an important role in stimulating research in universities, creating infrastructures and enhancing the supply of skilled personnel. The development of US software capabilities was also assisted by large-scale projects undertaken for the American military and social security systems. US computer hardware companies internationalized their production operations at a relatively early stage and supported a liberal trade policy toward hardware imports (often of components and subsystems that were integrated domestically). This further

accelerated the diffusion of PCs, creating a mass market for software (Mowery, 1999).

IPR systems have been one way of providing the incentives for innovation and market development. In the use of packaged software, positive "network externalities" may serve to strengthen the market position of leading firms by ensuring that, if usage is sufficiently widespread, the resulting pool of skills and knowledge reduces the incentives to develop and use alternative software products. Packaged software producers have devised a further means for reinforcing the effects of positive network externalities by creating proprietary standards. The first-mover advantages of US producers have proven to be persistent and powerful in this part of the software market.

Many of the factors that explain US success are also able to explain Europe's lagging behind in packaged software. In Europe markets are fragmented, and languages, laws and regulations differ. Historically, "national champion" computer firms have been vertically integrated, which has hindered market development for an independent software industry and thus obstructed competition. For example, European mainframe and minicomputer producers were not able to decide upon a common operating system or application software standards despite their relatively small size in global markets. By choosing to remain strong in domestic markets and shelter themselves from competition these companies did maintain their market shares for some time. By the 1990s, however, these companies had largely exited the market, taking with them the proprietary software platforms that were the basis of their business applications (Malerba and Torrisi, 1996).

### 7.4.2   Custom, open-source and embedded software

Most European firms are specialized in *custom software*, where local markets and the interaction with local customers play a key role in affecting the performance of firms (Malerba and Torrisi, 1996). Here software development involves the creation of applications that are localized and situated to specific users. While these software applications are also protected by IPR systems (principally the rules governing trade secrets), their value in other situated contexts is limited. The economic features of this type of software favor the growth of independent companies that are able to "reuse" software codes or development experience in producing value for their clients or customers. They also provide the basis for the creation of specific types of software products.

European firms retain a foothold in product groups such as *open-source*, *multimedia* and *embedded software*. The European version of open-source software activity, like similar and earlier US activities associated with

GNU and public domain software distribution (such as USENET), grew out of university student efforts. Historically, university environments have provided relatively open access to computer system resources and a research context that tolerates experimentation and invention. Open-source software has important implications for the European software industry because it represents a body of emerging competencies and specialization that can provide the basis for further software development efforts. A very important policy facilitating the sustainability of these positive European developments is continuing activity in promoting open standards for the exchange of information. Without such open standards, the processes favoring the mass adoption of products that store information in proprietary formats are likely to prevail.

European firms are also quite active in multimedia software. The United States appears to have an advantage in this market due to the large size of its internal market, which permits larger budgets for product engineering and promotion. A share of multimedia content will, however, remain culturally specific. In embedded software, Europe is strong but is currently losing ground. Europe has created a much weaker infrastructure for the support of embedded software than the United States. Moreover, fewer independent companies in Europe were able to emerge because large companies tend to be vertically integrated and to produce in-house embedded software. In addition, in Europe very few universities or public research organizations are active in this area. Perhaps one source of the absence of embedded software research in universities is the academic specialization of European computer science and informatics departments, which appears to lack the application experience and interdisciplinarity required for advances in knowledge in this area (Steinmueller, chapter 6 in this book).

### 7.4.3  *German specialization in specific product groups, such as enterprise resource planning*

German firms are specialized in specific product groups (such as ERP, CRM, sector-specific enterprise tools, groupware and system integration – see D'Adderio, 2002; Lehrer, 2002; Steinmueller, 2002; and Casper and Soskice, chapter 10 in this book). In integrated software solutions the success of European players has also been the result of a strategy based on developing a product built upon the accumulated experience regarding user needs, setting standards and becoming more open about applications developed outside by specialized application suppliers. European firms, however, are not alone in developing this type of strategy; US firms such as Microsoft and Oracle have adopted similar strategies in organizing specialized suppliers. In these product groups customization and interaction with users are important features of success (D'Adderio, 2002) and German firms have indeed benefited from demanding users. Germany has also been the European country where the shortage of programmers was least constraining and the links between university and industry were most developed (Lehrer, 2002). As Casper and Soskice (chapter 10 in this book) and Lehrer (2002) claim, this is more in tune with the German national institutional framework, which is characterized by the development of in-house competencies, long-term relationships with employees and "diversified quality production."

## 7.5 Machine tools: the international performance of different systems with different specialization

International performance is related to countries' different specialization and different organization of production. Let us take the cases of the United States and Japan. In the United States machine tool producers have been highly dependent on sectors such as defense, aerospace, and automobiles. Demand from high-end users led American machine tool producers to develop machine tools for manufacturing operations with high stringency requirements. Japan, on the other hand, emerged as a major producer of low-cost CNC machine tools, benefiting from the establishment of a standard for electronic controllers by FANUC. FANUC's innovative effort was focused on low-cost uses of NC technology, and general-purpose machine tools (Mazzoleni, 1999).

European countries that are highly competitive, such as Germany and Italy, are characterized by a sectoral system different from the Japanese one. However, in Germany formal, strong national and regional institutional linkages characterize the sectoral system. German machine tool producers have developed highly reliable and high-quality machines, benefiting from strong public research and advanced infrastructure (Fraunhofer-Gesellschaft and technical institutes). Industrial associations (such as the VDMA and VDW), previously very strong, have reoriented themselves recently toward a service provider role, operating partly on a commercial basis. User-producer relationships have always been close, but they too have recently changed. Beforehand, engineers on the producer side and technicians on the user side were close partners in the design process. Now the relationship has moved toward a more market-based interaction, with major consequences on system responsibility in the maintenance and in the repair business. Consequently, product-accompanying services ranging from traditional training to teleservice play a growing role in competition.

In Italy the sectoral system is characterized by strong and frequently informal regional institutional linkages. Italian machine tool firms are typically of small size and produce highly customized products. They form clusters with local training and local financial institutions. The role of the public research infrastructure is less relevant than in Germany. In a recent survey carried out by ENEA, CESPRI (Università Bocconi) and Politecnico-Milan on 100 Italian machinery producers (Ferrari et al., 2001), internal resources and the intelligent use of innovative components have been recognized as the driving force of innovation. These two factors are much more common with respect to other innovation channels – namely through the acquisition of external proprietary technologies (such as patents or licenses) or through collaboration with other firms or external consultancies. Innovation through internal resources and through the integration of innovative components increased in importance during the 1990s. Research, design and relations with customers are strategic and are kept in-house by machinery firms. Production and, to a lesser extent, distribution are often outsourced. While collaboration with competitors and with university and research centers is very limited, partnerships with suppliers (of innovative components) and users is more common. Recently, a few Italian firms have grown in size, while many firms have greatly upgraded their human capital in terms of external formal training. The greater focus on human capital has been associated with having a larger number of employees dedicated to technological innovations.

## 7.6    *Some common factors affecting international performance*

Are there common determinants of industrial leadership in the various sectors? From the analysis in this book, the following four would appear to be the major ones.

### 7.6.1    *Technological and scientific research capabilities*
In some sectors, technological and scientific research capabilities and education are a major source of industrial leadership. Success stories are a combination of the ability to create new products, to create new disciplines, to open up new markets and, at the same time, to integrate research, training and industrial needs. Importantly, the construction of a solid knowledge and scientific base in specific fields has often benefited from different forms and levels of public investments in their early stages (e.g. pharmaceuticals, biotechnology and software), particularly in the United States. Moreover, the integration between in-house research and advancements in transfer sciences (chemical engineering, automation and robotics, computer sciences, biotechnology, microbiology and

pharmaceutical chemistry) has helped firms to stay ahead of their competitors' products and process technologies.

### 7.6.2   Demand and interaction with sophisticated users

Close and continuous interactions with sophisticated users have been particularly important for machine tools and chemicals (and for some segments of software and biotechnology). In these sectors, co-location supported the innovative performance of firms. However, the mechanisms connecting demand to economic success are different according to the sector. Demand has been important in terms of level (the size of the market: e.g. chemicals, pharmaceuticals or packaged software), quality (machine tools in Europe, chemical engineering in the United States), composition (software and machine tools in Europe), specific requirements (machine tools in the United States and Japan, chemical engineering and telecommunications) and public sector share.

The size of the market and its degree of integration have been significant factors behind US success in many sectors. The European Union instead seems to be penalized by fragmentation in some sectors, with low marginal costs and increasing returns to users' adoption in another packaged software, for example. At the same time, according to the characteristics of the industry, different markets and heterogeneous users help European firms to stay ahead of their competitors on account of their ability to create customized product and process technologies (as in machine tools and ISS).

### 7.6.3   Technology and innovation policies

Technology and innovation policies have played an important role in affecting the industrial, institutional and organizational settings and the rate of innovative activities. In most of the sectors, agents have had incentives and opportunities from different types of institutional packages: IPR systems, specific norms and laws, types of standards, product approvals, government support and corporate governance. Patent policies are particularly important in supporting the activity of smaller technology-based firms and university licensing (particularly in biotechnology and chemicals). In the United States this has created the bases for a division of labor between technology suppliers and users, and allowed the development of markets for technology. In addition, standardization has affected the mobile phone industry. In particular, European firms have benefited widely from the European decision to adopt GSM technology.

### 7.6.4   The stage in the industry life cycle and the role of science

Whilst European performance appears to be good or relatively good in "mature" industries and products, even for the most sophisticated parts of these industries, in emerging industries and fields of activities – biotechnology, the Internet and segments of IT (see McKelvey, Orsenigo and Pammolli, chapter 3 in this book; Casper and Kettler, 2002; and Corrocher, 2003) – Europe is clearly facing difficulties. First, there is a lack of investment in R&D in science and basic research in the new, emerging fields. This is obvious for life sciences, for example, if European investment is compared with that of the United States (Muldur, 2000; and Pavitt, 2000a and 2000b). Casper and Kettler (2002) recall that, in the case of UK biotechnology sector, the main problem was not the lack of venture capitalists ready to embark on new biotechnology start-ups but the lack of good scientists able to promote this type of firm. The conclusion is that, even when the scientific capacities exist, they seem to be too highly dispersed throughout European universities and locations. Thus, no network effect can emerge, create an effective division of labor and generate enough effort to ensure the promotion of these new activities. In this respect, in the United States about 80 percent of venture capitalists' investments are concentrated in just two regions: California around Silicon Valley and Route 128. No "regional advantages" (Saxenian, 1994) have yet emerged in Europe in biotechnology or in advanced ICT segments. Close to this point, another argument has to do with the type of educational systems and labor markets prevailing in Europe, especially for highly skilled engineers and researchers. Here the relative advantage of European systems (often based on internal labor markets) seems to turn into a series of relative disadvantages. There is insufficient mobility and flexibility in these specialized labor markets, making it difficult for firms engaged in the new emerging fields to find the right skills and to be able to gather the necessary assets to launch new products or services. This is the case with multimedia and the Internet, where innovative firms face shortages in the supply side of the labor market (see Corrocher, 2003). This is also related to an institutional limitation of most of the European educational systems: they are unable to react with sufficient speed and flexibility to the transformation of the knowledge base and the recombination of disciplines and research fields driven by the scientific and technological changes opened up by IT and life sciences.

To conclude, the European difficulties are much more focused. The European problems are in: new disciplines, new emerging fields of knowledge and new firms' capabilities for the industrial and commercial exploitation of this knowledge.

## 8    Policy implications

From a sectoral system perspective, the principal role of the policy maker is to facilitate the self-organization of the SSIs within the relevant policy domain. An important consequence of this is that the policy-making process is itself the reflection of bounded rationality and learning in the presence of high heterogeneity in techical change and the innovation process. The sectoral system approach is an alternative to the concept of the optimizing policy maker, which characterizes the market failure approach to innovation policy (for a more detailed discussion see Edquist et al., chapter 12 in this book). The reasons for public policy intervention in a market economy are related to two conditions. First, the market mechanism and the actors must fail to achieve the objectives formulated. A problem of inadequate self-organization must exist. Second, the state (national, regional or local) and its public agencies must also have the ability to solve or mitigate the problem.

SSI approach can be used as a framework for designing specific innovation policies. As mentioned above, a necessary condition for public intervention in the innovation process is that a "problem" – which is not automatically solved by markets and firms – must exist. Substantial analytical and methodological capabilities are needed to identify these "problems." The important insight in the sectoral systems approach is that, in an economy, innovation systems operate at multiple levels, and that, to various degrees, they operate within and across national economies and technologies. The sectoral system forms the locus of intersection of numerous networks generating particular kinds of knowledge. Each of these networks has different members and different purposes, but they all contribute to innovation. Indeed, innovative ability may depend on the ability to participate in and manage these network relations.

Within an SI framework, an identification of the causes behind the problems is the same as identifying deficiencies in the functioning of the system (i.e. identifying those systemic dimensions that are missing or inappropriate, and which lead to the "problem" in terms of comparative performance). These deficient functions are "system failures." When we know the causes behind a certain "problem" – for example, weak technological transfer between university and industry – we have identified a "system failure." Not until they know the character of the system failure can policy makers know whether to influence or change organizations or institutions or the links between them. Therefore, the identification of a problem should be supplemented with an analysis of its causes as an integral part of the analytical basis for the design of an innovation policy. Benchmarking is not enough.

In terms of policy, it is possible to state the principal contributions of the sectoral system approach. First, a sectoral system approach provides a new methodology for the study of sectors, the new challenges facing sectoral systems and, therefore, the identification of the variables that should be the policy targets. As we have seen in this book, sectoral analyses should focus on the systemic features of innovation in relation to knowledge and boundaries, the heterogeneity of actors and networks, institutions, and transformation through coevolutionary processes. As a consequence, the understanding of these dimensions becomes a prerequisite for any policy addressed to a specific sector. A second and related point is that the impact of horizontal policies may greatly differ from sector to sector. Third, the analysis of the rationale and the effects of policies also requires a deep and careful comparative analysis of sectoral systems over time and across countries. Fourth, a sectoral system approach emphasizes that innovation and technology policies affect and are linked with other types of policies, such as science policy, industrial policy, policies related to standards and intellectual property rights, and competition policy. A sectoral system approach highlights the interdependencies, links and feedbacks among all these policies, and their effects on the dynamics and transformation of sectors. Fifth, the public actor has to be aware of being inside a sectoral system at various levels, because it intervenes actively in the creation of knowledge, IPR regimes, corporate governance rules, technology transfer, financial institutions, skill formation and public procurement. Sixth, policies should take into account the different geographical boundaries of a sectoral system. Policies that focus on only one spatial dimension are likely to miss constraints or opportunities that are influential in the innovative behavior of organizations. While technology policies should be addressed at the local, national or European level, the rationale for these policies and their implementation must also reflect a global perspective.

In addition, the emphasis on the diversity of sectoral systems highlights different policy measures for different sectors. These policy implications are closely related to the problems faced by the various actors operating in the sectoral context, and to the sectoral specificity of knowledge, boundaries, actors and networks. For a more detailed discussion see Edquist et al., chapter 12 in this book.

Finally, the new challenges related to the development of new sectoral systems or new clusters may involve an active role for public organizations in recognizing and promoting, or even creating, the conditions for market success. Three examples from research can be put forward. First, the innovation of the IOL. The considerable changes over time in the related innovation systems in the United Kingdom and the United States depended greatly on the take-up of this procedure in the public and private healthcare systems, and on the different norms for translating clinical needs into "market demand" in the two national medical systems (Metcalfe and James, 2003). Second, the US government played a very active and decisive role in the launching of the fixed Internet

(Corrocher, 2003). Finally, the BioRegio program in Germany is another interesting example. In general, if governments should intervene, they should do so at an early stage in the development of new subsystems and new SSIs. Such intervention at an early stage may have a tremendous impact. In the case of the public creation of the NMT 450 mobile telecommunications technical standard in the Nordic countries some twenty years ago, this proved to be important for the emergence of mobile telephony and for Ericsson and Nokia becoming global leaders in this field.

On a methodological level, research indicates that the existing approaches in industrial economics and standard statistics may not be adequate to the task of identifying the changing configurations of sectoral systems and the processes of knowledge creation and exchange between different types of organizations. The costs of constructing new SSIs are substantial, but this activity is not explicitly recognized in the existing literature on policy or management. These are major strategic opportunities available in discovering better ways to monitor, promote and reduce the costs of the reconfiguration or expansion of sectoral systems of innovation.

## 9 The challenges ahead

This book has proposed an integrated and comparative way to look at sectors and has conducted an analysis of several sectors in Europe along these same dimensions. The results point implicitly to research directions that can be undertaken in future studies. These can be summarized in the following points.

First, future research on sectoral systems should examine in detail some key variables and aspects of sectoral systems that are still relatively unexplored: demand, boundaries, networks, coevolution and the interplay between sectoral variables and national institutional frameworks.

Second, taxonomies of sectoral systems have to be constructed. Here, comparative work is particularly relevant. These taxonomies should group sectoral systems in terms of elements, structure and dynamics, so that common features among sectors can be identified and a general description of their characteristics can be proposed. Pavitt's taxonomy (1984) is a useful starting point as far as the sources of innovation, the appropriability means and the industrial structure are concerned. The same holds for the Schumpeter Mark I and Schumpeter Mark II distinction, with its related technological regimes (Malerba and Orsenigo, 1996). The work by Marsili (2001) in extending Pavitt's taxonomy goes in this direction.

Third, conceptual and theoretical work has to be carried out on the basic relationships among the elements of a sectoral system, the emergence and persistence of firms' heterogeneity, the basic processes of variety creation and selection, and coevolution. Here, theoretical models of industry dynamics and history-friendly models can both be useful. In the best evolutionary (and innovation system) tradition, this work should go hand in hand with, and be continuously confronted by, empirical work.

Fourth, analyses of international performance should be carried out by taking into full account the role played by the various elements of a sectoral system, as discussed in Coriat, Malerba and Montobbio (chapter 11 in this book). Similarly, public policy indicators should be developed, along the lines suggested by Edquist et al. (chapter 12 in this book).

REFERENCES

Arduini, R., and F. Cesaroni (2001), *Environmental Technologies in the European Chemical Industry*, Working Paper no. 2001/09, Laboratory of Economics and Management, Scuola Superiore Sant'Anna, Pisa

Arora, A., and A. Gambardella (1998), Evolution of industry structure in the chemical industry, in A. Arora, R. Landau and N. Rosenberg (eds.), *Chemicals and Long-term Economic Growth: Insights from the Chemical Industry*, John Wiley, New York, 379–413

Arora, A., A. Gambardella and W. Garcia-Fontes (1998), *Investment Flows of Large Chemical Companies*, Universitat Pompeu Fabra, Barcelona, mimeograph

Breschi, S., and F. Lissoni (2001), *Knowledge Spillovers and Local Innovation Systems: A Critical Survey*, Paper in Economics no. 84, Università Carlo Cattaneo, Castellanza, Italy

Bresnahan, T., and S. Greenstein (1998), Technical progress in computing and in the uses of computers, *Brookings Papers on Economic Activity: Microeconomics*, 1, 1–78

Casper, S., and H. Kettler (2002), *National Institutional Frameworks and the Hybridization of Entrepreneurial Business Models: The German and UK Biotechnology Sectors*, ESSY working paper, http://www.cespri.it/ricerca/es_wp.htm

Chandler, A. (1990), *Scale and Scope: The Dynamics of Industrial Capitalism*, Harvard University Press, Cambridge, MA

Corrocher, N. (2003), The Internet services industry: country-specific trends in the UK, Italy and Sweden, in C. Edquist (ed.), *The Internet and Mobile Telecommunications System of Innovation: Developments in Equipment, Access and Content*, Edward Elgar Publishing, Cheltenham, 210–235

D'Adderio, L. (2001a), *Inside the Virtual Product: The Influence of Integrated Software Systems on Organisational Knowledge Dynamics*, working paper, Science Policy Research Unit, University of Sussex, Brighton

(2001b), Crafting the virtual prototype: how firms integrate knowledge and capabilities across organizational boundaries, *Research Policy*, 30, 9, 1,409–1,424

(2002), *The Diffusion of Integrated Software Solutions: Trends and Challenges*, ESSY working paper, Science Policy Research Unit, University of Sussex, Brighton [http://www.cespri.it/ricerca/es_wp.htm]

Dalum, B. (2003), Data communication: satellite and TV subsystems, in C. Edquist (ed.), *The Internet and Mobile Telecommunications System of Innovation: Development in Equipment, Access and Content*, Edward Elgar Publishing, Cheltenham, 162–176

Dalum, B., and G. Villumsen (2003), Fixed data communications: challenges for Europe, in C. Edquist (ed.), *The Internet and Mobile Telecommunications System of Innovation: Developments in Equipment, Access and Content*, Edward Elgar Publishing, Cheltenham, 40–70

Dubocage, E. (2002), *The Financing of Innovation by Venture Capital in Europe and in the USA: A Comparative and Sectoral Approach*, ESSY working paper, http://www.cespri.it/ricerca/es_wp.htm

Ferrari, S., P. Guerrieri, F. Malerba, S. Mariotti and D. Palma (2001), *L'Italia nella Competizione Tecnologica Internazionale: La Meccanica Strumentale*, Franco Angeli, Milan

Freeman, C. (1968), Chemical process plant: innovation and the world market, *National Institute Economic Review*, 45, 3, 29–51

Geoffron, P., and M. Rubinstein (2002), *Sectoral Systems of Innovation and Production*, ESSY working paper, http://www.cespri.it/ricerca/es_wp.htm

Harvey, M., A. Nyberg and J. S. Metcalfe (2002), *Deep Transformation in the Service Economy: Innovation and Organisational Change in Food Retailing in Sweden and the UK*, ESSY working paper, Centre for Research on Innovation and Competition, University of Manchester and University of Manchester Institute of Science and Technology [http://www.cespri.it/ricerca/es_wp.htm]

Henderson, R., L. Orsenigo and G. P. Pisano (1999), The pharmaceutical industry and the revolution in molecular biology: exploring the Interaction between scientific, institutional and organizational change, in D. C. Mowery and R. R. Nelson (eds.), *Sources of Industrial Leadership*: Studies of Seven Industries, Cambridge University Press, Cambridge, 267–312

Hommen, L., and E. Manninen (2003), The global system for mobile telecommunications (GSM): second generation, in C. Edquist (ed.), *The Internet and Mobile Telecommunications System of Innovation: Developments in Equipment, Access and Content*, Edward Elgar Publishing, Cheltenham, 71–128

Lehrer, M. (2002), *From Factor of Production to Autonomous Industry: The Transformation of Germany's Software Sector*, ESSY working paper, http://www.cespri.it/ricerca/es_wp.htm

Malerba, F., and L. Orsenigo (1996), Schumpeterian patterns of innovation, *Cambridge Journal of Economics*, 19, 1, 47–65

Malerba, F., and S. Torrisi (1996), The dynamics of market structure and innovation in the Western European software industry, in D. C. Mowery (ed.), *The International Computer Software Industry: A Comparative Study of Industry Evolution and Structure*, Oxford University Press, Oxford, 165–196

Marsili, O. (2001), *The Anatomy and Evolution of Industries: Technological Change and Industrial Dynamics*, Edward Elgar Publishing, Cheltenham

Mazzoleni, R. (1999), Innovation in the machine tools industry: a historical perspective or the dynamics of comparative advantage, in D. C. Mowery and R. R. Nelson (eds.), *Sources of Industrial Leadership: Studies of Seven Industries,* Cambridge University Press, Cambridge, 169–216

McKelvey, M., H. Alm and M. Riccaboni (2002), *Does Co-location matter? Knowledge Collaboration in the Swedish Biotechnology-Pharmaceutical Sector,* ESSY working paper, http://www.cespri.it/ricerca/es_wp.htm

Metcalfe, J. S., and A. James (2002), *Emergent Innovation Systems and the Delivery of Clinical Services: The Case of Intra-Ocular Lenses,* ESSY working paper, Centre for Research on Innovation and Competition, University of Manchester and University of Manchester Institute of Science and Technology [http://www.cespri.it/ricerca/es_wp.htm]

Miozzo, M., and L. Soete (2001), Internationalization of services: a technology perspective, *Technological Forecasting and Social Change,* 67, 2/3, 159–185

Mowery, D. C. (ed.) (1996), *The International Computer Software Industry: A Comparative Study Of Industry Evolution and Structure,* Oxford University Press, Oxford

(1999), The global computer software industry, in D. C. Mowery and R. R. Nelson (eds.), *Sources of Industrial leadership: Studies of Seven Industries,* Cambridge University Press, Cambridge

Muldur, U. (2000), L'allocation des capitaux dans le processus global d'innovation: est-elle optimale en Europe? in E. Cohen and J. H. Lorenzi (eds.), *Politiques Industrielles pour l'Europe,* Cahiers du Conseil d'Analyse Economique, Premier Ministre, La Documentation Française, Paris, 34–67

Owen-Smith, J., M. Riccaboni, F. Pammolli and W. W. Powell (2002), *A Comparison of US and European University-Industry Relations in the Life Sciences,* ESSY working paper, http://www.cespri.it/ricerca/es_wp.htm

Pavitt, K. (1984), Sectoral patterns of technical change: towards a taxonomy and a theory, *Research Policy,* 13, 6, 343–373

(2000a), Costing innovation: vain search for benchmarks, *Research Technology Management,* 44, 1, 16–17

(2000b), *Academic Research in Europe,* paper prepared for EU-funded Europolis Project, Workshop II, Lisbon, June 5–6

Rivaud-Danset, D. (2002), *The Financing of Innovation and Venture Capital: The National Financial and Sectoral Systems,* ESSY working paper, http://www.cespri.it/ricerca/es_wp.htm

Rosenberg, N. (1998), Technological change in the chemicals: the role of university-industry relationships, in A. Arora, R. Landau and N. Rosenberg (eds.), *Chemicals and Long-term Economic Growth: Insights from the Chemical Industry,* John Wiley, New York, 193–230

Saxenian, A. (1994), *Regional Advantage: Culture and Competition in Silicon Valley and Route 128,* Harvard University Press, Cambridge, MA

Soskice, D. (1997), German technology policy, innovation and national institutional frameworks, *Industry and Innovation,* 4, 1, 75–96

Steinmueller, W. E. (2002), *The European Software Sectoral System of Innovation System,* ESSY working paper, Science Policy Research Unit, University of Sussex, Brighton [http://www.cespri.it/ricerca/es_wp.htm]

Sunabo, J., and F. Gallouj (2000), Innovation as a loosely coupled system in services, in J. S. Metcalfe and I. D. Miles (eds.), *Innovation Systems in the Service Economy: Measurement and Case Study Analysis*, Kluwer Academic, Borton

Tether, B. S., and J. S. Metcalfe (2003), Horndal at Heathrow? Capacity expansion through co-operation and system evolution, *Industrial and Corporate Change*, 12, 3, 437–476

Tether, B. S., J. S. Metcalfe and I. D. Miles (2002), *Innovation Systems and Services: investigating "Systems of Innovation" in the Services Sectors – an Overview*, ESSY working paper, Centre for Research on Innovation and Competition, University of Manchester and University of Manchester Institute of Science and Technology [http://www.cespri.it/ricerca/es_wp.htm]

Torrisi, S. (1998), *Industrial Organisation and Innovation: An International Study of the Software Industry*, Edward Elgar Publishing, Cheltenham

# Index

Printed in the United States
By Bookmasters